CONTEMPORARY MARKETING

FOURTH EDITION

THE DRYDEN PRESS

Chicago   New York   Philadelphia
San Francisco   Montreal   Toronto
London   Sydney   Tokyo
Mexico City   Rio de Janeiro   Madrid

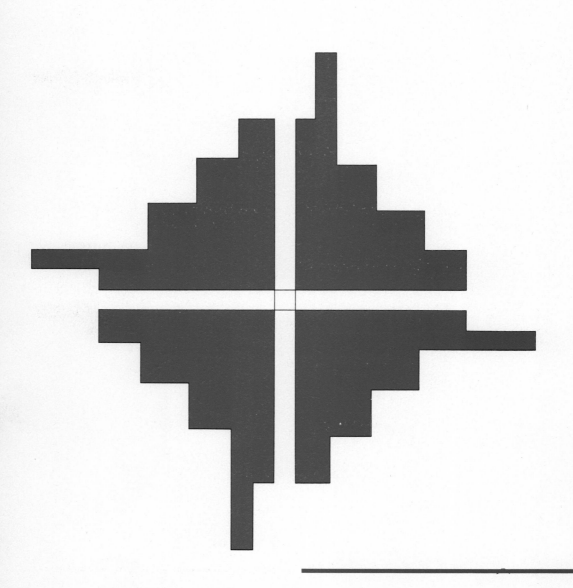

CONTEMPORARY MARKETING

Fourth Edition

Louis E. Boone
University of Central Florida

David L. Kurtz
Seattle University

Library of Congress Catalog Card Number: 82-72170
ISBN: 0-03-062638-2
Printed in the United States of America
345-032-987654321

Address orders to:
383 Madison Avenue
New York, New York   10017

Address editorial correspondence to:
One Salt Creek Lane
Hinsdale, Illinois   60521

CBS COLLEGE PUBLISHING
The Dryden Press
Holt, Rinehart and Winston
Saunders College Publishing

Acquisitions Editor:	Karen Emilson
Developmental Editor:	Paul Psilos
Project Editor:	Brian Link Weber
Managing Editor:	Jane Perkins
Production Manager:	Mary Jarvis
Design Director:	Alan Wendt

Cover design by **William Seabright**

Copy editing and indexing by **Kathryn Jandeska**

Compositor:	The Clarinda Company
Text type:	Univers 55

To Pat, Barry, and Christopher Boone;
Reed, Catherine, and Jennifer Kurtz

THE DRYDEN PRESS SERIES IN MARKETING Stephen W. Brown, Consulting Editor

CONTENTS

PART   TWO

IDENTIFYING CONSUMER NEEDS   48

CHAPTER   3

MARKETING PLANNING AND FORECASTING   50

CHAPTER 4

MARKETING RESEARCH: INFORMATION FOR DECISION MAKING   **76**

CHAPTER   7

UNDERSTANDING CONSUMER BEHAVIOR   **166**

CHAPTER   13

MANAGEMENT OF PHYSICAL DISTRIBUTION   346

PART   SIX

PROMOTIONAL STRATEGY   370

CHAPTER   14

INTRODUCTION TO PROMOTION   372

CHAPTER   15

**ELEMENTS OF PROMOTIONAL STRATEGY: ADVERTISING,
SALES PROMOTION, PUBLIC RELATIONS, AND PUBLICITY   392**

CHAPTER   18

ELEMENTS OF PRICING STRATEGY   464

PREFACE

The publication of the first edition of *Contemporary Marketing* in 1974 was a milestone in the evolution of textbooks developed for the first marketing course. At that time the market was dominated by two texts. In the foreword to *Contemporary Marketing,* Professors Paul Green and Philip Kotler summarized the challenges facing a marketing author and their evaluation of the new book:

Those who undertake to write a quality marketing textbook face a double challenge. First, they must present the latest concepts, tools, and findings that will prepare the reader to cope effectively with the complex and changing marketing scene. Second, they must present these ideas in a lively, engaging way that makes learning exciting as well as rewarding. Professors Boone and Kurtz have faced and admirably surmounted this double challenge. Their readers will learn from and enjoy the pages of this book as they journey through the ceaselessly interesting world of marketing.

Contemporary Marketing established a model for marketing texts written during the past decade. It was decidedly shorter than other texts. Although it provided a thorough, conceptually sound treatment of marketing subjects, its concepts were reinforced by hundreds of real-life examples, up-to-date illustrations, and problem-solving approaches. The writing style and emphasis on applications of marketing concepts, while retaining the necessary rigor and integrity, relieved students of the tedious, boring reading that traditionally characterized the study of marketing.

Contemporary Marketing introduced a number of firsts to marketing textbooks. It stressed pedagogical soundness by identifying specific learning objectives for each chapter. Each chapter began with an example of an actual individual or firm attempting to apply the concepts discussed in the chapter. Boxed items were used to show additional applications—often in novel settings. Summaries and end-of-chapter discussion questions reinforced student retention of concepts developed in the chapter.

Worldwide acceptance of the new text demonstrated the correctness of its underlying philosophy: both students and instructors want a teaching/learning package that makes the study of marketing interesting, realistic, and practical. In their foreword to the second edition, Professors Green and Kotler stated:

Perhaps the greatest compliment directed toward this book is the fact that students uniformly like *Contemporary Marketing.* They find it current, sufficiently rigorous, and interesting! The authors have demonstrated that a book can be highly readable and conceptually sound. The first step in learning a subject is to develop a genuine interest in it. *Contemporary Marketing* provides the mechanism for accomplishing this objective. . . . We think this edition will establish itself as a classic introductory text on the subject of marketing.

Like its predecessors, the fourth edition has been based upon numerous comments by both users and nonusers, as well as extensive marketing research by the publisher. The result is a text designed to provide instructors and students with the following:

EMPHASIS ON UNDERSTANDING BUYER BEHAVIOR AND ELEMENTS OF THE MARKETING MIX

Contemporary Marketing is designed to meet instructor requests to provide thorough treatment of such topics as market segmentation, consumer behavior, and elements of the marketing mix. Part Three devotes two chapters to analyzing market segmentation in both consumer and industrial markets. Understanding consumer behavior is the subject of Chapter 7. At least two chapters focus on each of the elements of the marketing mix. Unlike some recent texts, *Contemporary Marketing* does not neglect the vital role of marketing institutions. Separate chapters are devoted to the subjects of retailing and wholesaling.

NEW CHAPTERS FOCUS ON IMPORTANT MARKETING CONCEPTS

A number of marketing instructors requested specific coverage of subjects typically neglected in most marketing texts. As a result, the following chapters have been added to the new edition:

- Chapter 3: Marketing Planning and Forecasting
- Chapter 5: Market Segmentation: Consumer Markets
- Chapter 6: Market Segmentation: Industrial Markets
- Chapter 20: Marketing in the 1980s: Societal Issues and Nonprofit Applications

NEW EMPHASIS ON SERVICES AND INTERNATIONAL MARKETING

Like industrial marketing, service strategy is a vital and often neglected area. Part Four in the new edition was expanded to Product/Service Strategy in order to thoroughly treat both tangible and intangible products. In addition, unique aspects of the marketing of services are discussed at appropriate locations throughout the text. For instance, Chapter 10 contains a section entitled "Marketing Channels for Services."

A separate chapter on international marketing has been included. The added coverage is indicative of the growing importance of world marketing and is a response to AACSB requirements.

LONGER, MORE COMPREHENSIVE MARKETING CASES

In response to instructor requests, the cases in *Contemporary Marketing* are decidedly longer and more comprehensive than those in previous editions and in most competing texts. A careful blending of actual cases focusing on nonprofit and profit-seeking firms, consumer goods, industrial products, and services provide considerable flexibility for the instructor. The cases involve such well-known firms and products as Xerox Corporation, Morton Salt, and the San Francisco Giants.

EMPHASIS ON NONPROFIT APPLICATIONS, MARKETING CAREERS, AND MARKETING ARITHMETIC

During the 1980s, much of the increased awareness of the impact of marketing upon society has come from its implementation by a number of nonprofit organizations. Increasingly, marketing concepts and techniques are being employed by hospitals, financial institutions, state tourism offices, politicians, accountants, the local symphony orchestra, and the federal government.

This broadened view of marketing is incorporated throughout the text, beginning in Chapter 1. Several cases—such as the Milwaukee Blood Center and Undercroft Montessori School—are devoted to nonprofit applications. In addition, Chapter 20 discusses the subject.

Appendix A provides a thorough treatment of careers in marketing; a new appendix deals with marketing arithmetic.

REAL-WORLD EXAMPLES DEMONSTRATE APPLICATIONS OF MARKETING CONCEPTS

Contemporary Marketing provides a comprehensive, systematic, and rigorous treatment of marketing. In order to avoid the uninteresting prose found in many textbooks, it includes hundreds of real-world examples to illustrate *applications*—both correct and incorrect—of fundamental marketing concepts discussed in the text. Students will immediately identify with such examples as:

Hanes Hosiery

Trademark Infringement Quiz

Applying Psychological Concepts to Increase Perception

A Touch of Class at K mart?

Need Hardware? Homeowner's Insurance? A Home? Go to Sears

The Kevlar Story

Turning the University into a Lab

Why the Miracle Medicine Failed

How Wholesaling Helped Make Perrier a Success

Quotas for Japanese Autos

Setting Customer Service Standards at American Airlines

Each chapter begins with an opening vignette designed to provide the reader with a flavor of the marketing concepts to be treated in the chapter. Examples follow the explanation of each concept to reinforce student learning. Comprehensive cases then require application of this knowledge.

THE MOST COMPREHENSIVE TEACHING/ LEARNING PACKAGE

Since both authors of *Contemporary Marketing* teach introductory marketing courses, we are very much aware of the challenges facing the instructor. While it can be argued that this is the most important course in the marketing curriculum, it is often taught by professors with large classes and heavy teaching loads. We have attempted to assist the instructor in meeting this challenge by providing the most comprehensive teaching/learning package available in marketing. In addition to the textbook, the instructional package includes the following:

- *Instructor's Guide to Contemporary Marketing*—containing full lecture outlines for each chapter with new examples not found in the text

- *Film Guide*—listing and detailed description of numerous films for classroom use. The *Guide* is the most thorough and up-to-date listing of marketing films available anywhere.

- *Four-Color Transparency Acetates*—60 examples and color illustrations with text descriptions relating them to lecture materials

- *Test Bank*—a 2,200-item test bank keyed to specific text pages and available in printed form and on floppy disc for maximum instructor flexibility

- *Contemporary Marketing Slide/Lecture Series*—a first for the basic marketing course. Three lectures accompanied by about 50 slides per lecture provide self-contained modules for the following topics:

- Marketing Planning and Segmentation

- International Marketing

- Marketing for Small Business

    These one-hour lectures present fundamental marketing concepts, applications, and examples keyed to material in *Contemporary Marketing,* but with new materials, examples, and illustrations.

- *Study Guide for Contemporary Marketing*—co-authored by Professors Stephen K. Keiser (University of Delaware), Robert E. Stevens (Oral Roberts University), and Lynn J. Loudenback (Iowa State University)

ACKNOWL- EDGMENTS

Most successful textbooks are the product of many people's work. *Contemporary Marketing* is no exception. First, we would like to acknowledge the many individuals whose works are cited here for their contributions to the marketing discipline. Textbooks are, after all, merely a reflection of contemporary thought in a discipline. In this respect, marketing is blessed with a strong cadre of academicians and practitioners who are constantly seeking to improve and advance the discipline.

The authors gratefully acknowledge the contributions of a large number of persons—colleagues, students, and professional marketers in businesses and nonprofit organizations—for their contributions in making the fourth edition of *Contemporary Marketing* a reality. For their reviews of all or part of one or more of the editions, we would like to express our appreciation to Professors Keith Absher (University of Northern Alabama), Dub Ashton (University of Arkansas), Wayne Bascom (Northern Essex Community College), Richard C. Becherer (Wayne State University), Benjamin Cutler (Bronx Community College), Howard B. Cox (Youngstown State University), Gordon Di Paolo (College of Staten Island), Jeffrey T. Doutt (Sonoma State University), Sid Dudley (Delta State University), John W. Ernest (Los Angeles City College), Jack E. Forrest, Gary T. Ford (University of Maryland), Ralph M. Gaedeke (California State University), James Gould (St. John's University), Donald Granbois (Indiana University), Paul E. Green (University of Pennsylvania), Blaine Greenfield (Bucks County Community College), Matthew Gross (Moraine Valley Community College), John H. Hallaq (University of Idaho), Cary Hawthorn (Central Piedmont College), Sanford B. Helman (Middlesex County College), Nathan Himelstein (Essex County College), Ray S. House (Loyola College), Don L. James (Fort Lewis College), David Johnson (Northern Essex Community College), Eugene M. Johnson (University of Rhode Island), James C. Johnson (St. Cloud State University), Bernard Katz (Oakton Community College), Harold Kellar (Bernard Baruch College), Stephen K. Keiser (University of Delaware), Charles Keuthan (Florida Institute of Technology), Donald L. Knight (Lansing Community College), Philip Kotler (Northwestern University), Francis J. Leary (Northern Essex Community College), Paul I. Londrigan (Charles S. Mott Community College), Lynn J. Loudenback (Iowa State University), Dorothy Maass (Delaware County Community College), James McCormick (Monroe Community College), James McHugh (St. Louis Community College, Forest Park), Robert D. Miller (Hillsborough Community College), J. Dale Molander (University of Wisconsin, Oshkosh), John F. Monoky (University of Toledo), James R. Moore (Southern Illinois University, Carbondale), Carl McDaniel (University of Texas, Arlington), Colin Neuhaus (Eastern Michigan University), Robert T. Newcomb (Broome Community College), Constantine Petrides (Manhattan Community College), Barbara Piasta (Somerset Community College), Barbara A. Pletcher, Arthur E. Prell (Southern Illinois University, Edwardsville), Gary Edward Reiman (City College of San Francisco), Arnold M. Rieger (Staten Island Community College), C. Richard Roberts (University of Tulsa), Patrick J. Robinson (Robinson Associates), William C. Rodgers (St. Cloud State

University), William H. Ronald (Miami-Dade College), Carol Rowey (Rhode Island Junior College), Jack Seitz (Oakton Community College), Bruce Seaton (Florida International University), Howard Seigelman (Brookdale Community College), Steven L. Shapiro (Queensborough Community College), A. Edward Spitz (Eastern Michigan University), William Staples (University of Houston at Clear Lake City), Robert E. Stevens (Oral Roberts University), Howard A. Thompson (Eastern Kentucky University), Dennis H. Tootelian (California State University, Sacramento), Dinoo T. Vanier (San Diego State University), Robert J. Williams (Eastern Michigan University), and Julian Yudelson (Rochester Institute of Technology).

We are especially indebted to the following academicians and marketing practitioners for permitting us to include their cases in the text: Richard F. Beltramini (Arizona State University), Thomas J. Cosse (University of Richmond), Ron Franzmeier (Zigman-Joseph-Skeen), Thomas D. Giese (University of Richmond), Robert D. Hay (University of Arkansas), Michael D. Hutt (Arizona State University), John Knox McGill (University of North Carolina at Chapel Hill), Robert W. Mondy (Northeast Louisiana University), Patrick E. Murphy (Marquette University), C. Richard Roberts (University of Tulsa), Steven J. Shaw (University of South Carolina), Thomas W. Speh (Miami University), Clifford H. Springer (General Electric), Nancy Stephens (Arizona State University), Ian Stewart (A. H. Robins, Inc.), Eddie Sutton (University of Arkansas), W. Wayne Talarzyk (The Ohio State University), James R. Young (East Texas State University), William G. Zikmund (Oklahoma State University).

Finally, we would like to express our thanks to the editorial staff of The Dryden Press. Their many contributions are sincerely appreciated.

Louis E. Boone
David L. Kurtz
January 1983

PART   ONE

THE CONTEMPORARY MARKETING ENVIRONMENT

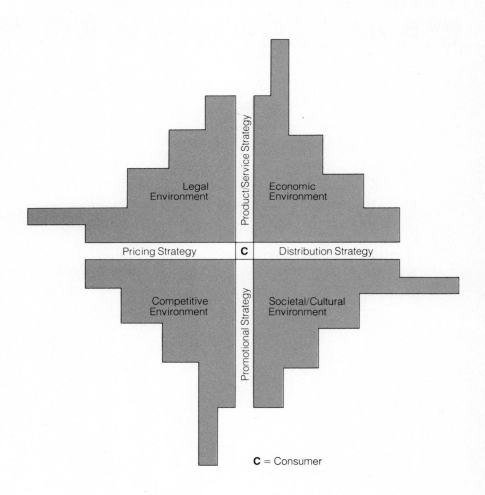

Legal Environment

Economic Environment

Product/Service Strategy

Pricing Strategy

C

Distribution Strategy

Competitive Environment

Societal/Cultural Environment

Promotional Strategy

C = Consumer

CHAPTER 1

THE MARKETING PROCESS: AN OVERVIEW

KEY TERMS

utility
marketing
seller's market
buyer's market
marketing concept
marketing myopia
broadening concept
product strategy
distribution strategy
marketing channels
promotional strategy
pricing strategy
marketing mix

LEARNING GOALS

1. To examine the evolution of the marketing process

2. To recognize how the marketing concept has been widely accepted in business

3. To analyze the four strategic elements of marketing—product, distribution, promotion, and pricing; and the environmental factors that impact on the market

4. To understand the broadening concept

5. To identify the three basic reasons for students to study marketing

6. To explain the alternative approaches to studying marketing

What do Willie Nelson and a Doobie Brothers band member have in common? Both have been known to wear Moosehead T-shirts, a sign that the new beer craze is nearing cult standing in the United States.

Moosehead Breweries of New Brunswick, Canada, provides an excellent illustration of the effective integration of the two basic operating functions of any organization. All businesses and nonprofit organizations must produce and market goods and services. Production and marketing are the essence of all organizations, and of the economy itself.

Moosehead Breweries is a family-owned firm founded in the 1860s by Susannah Oland. The firm ranked a distant fourth in the Canadian market behind Molson's, Labatt's, and Carling O'Keefe. But until recently, little Canadian beer was exported into the United States. In fact, all imports amounted to only 0.6 percent of the U.S. beer market in 1970. Transportation and tariff costs made imports expensive. But things changed during the past decade. Many Americans acquired a taste for imported beer, which tends to be heavier than U.S. brands. Today, over 225 imports are sold in the United States. The 25 million American import beer drinkers have created a $1.5 billion market.

Moosehead was a late entrant into the U.S. import market. But the

Source: Courtesy of Moosehead and All Brands Importers, Inc.

brand caught on fast, quickly moving into seventh place among the imports. Texas bumper stickers claim "The Moose Is Loose." One million Moosehead T-shirts have been distributed in the United States. And the beer has become a rage in such diverse localities as Memphis, Boston, Atlanta, and Detroit. Moosehead is available in every state except Utah, where it is prohibited because its alcoholic content exceeds 3.2 percent.

The Canadian firm was successful in the U.S. market because it was able to integrate effective production and marketing strategies. Consider the decision made with respect to production. The brewing formula was modified to give it longer shelf life. The short, brown bottles used in Canada were replaced by taller, green ones similar to those used by the Netherlands' Heineken, the leading U.S. import. New bottling and labeling equipment was installed in the brewery. Later, when Moosehead sales soared, the firm expanded capacity and went to double work shifts.

The marketing decisions were even more critical. Moosehead reached an importing agreement with All Brand Importers, Inc., of Roslyn Heights, New York (now part of Nabisco Brands, Inc.). A promotional strategy stressing the Canadian outdoors and wilderness was chosen. A new label was created, featuring a moosehead against a green background. The distribution system was based on 600 wholesalers selected for their experience with imported beer. The success of Moosehead is legend. The company's plants are operating at capacity, while allocating 25 percent of its output to export. Moosehead's production and marketing functions did create what consumers sought.[1]

PRODUCTION AND MARKETING CREATE UTILITY FOR THE CONSUMER

Society allows businesses to operate only so long as they make a contribution to the members of society. By producing and marketing desired goods and services, businesses satisfy this societal commitment. They create what economists call **utility**—*the want-satisfying power of a product or service.* There are four basic kinds of utility—form, time, place, and ownership.

Form utility is created when the business firm converts raw materials into finished products. Glass, steel, fabrics, rubber, and other components are combined to form a new Aries or Escort. Cotton, thread, and buttons are converted into Van Heusen shirts. The creation of form utility is one of the production functions of the firm.

The three other kinds of utility—*time, place,* and *ownership*—are created by marketing. They appear when products are made available to consumers at convenient locations and at times when the consumers want to purchase them and when facilities are available for transferring title to the products at the time of purchase.

**HANES
HOSIERY**

The miniskirt of the late 1960s and early 1970s was largely responsible for the growth of the panty hose industry. The product offered a leg covering that improved appearance. Hanes Hosiery of Winston-Salem, North Carolina, became a market leader with its L'eggs brand. The rapid acceptance of the brand in supermarkets and other nontraditional outlets suggested that Hanes was creating utility for its customers.

Styles changed in the mid-1970s. The miniskirt disappeared. Many women began to wear slacks. Knee-high socks or no hosiery became standard for these consumers. Most panty hose manufacturers ignored the pants wearers, preferring to concentrate on a reduced market.

Hanes was an exception. The firm decided to position panty hose as an accessory item—not just a leg covering—that improved appearance. Consumer research helped Hanes develop a new product—Underalls—that combined a panty and panty hose into one garment. Further research was conducted including user tests in order to refine the product and its major feature: improved comfort because of less clothing, economy, and no panty line under dresses and slacks.

Women were most impressed with the improved appearance factor. So Hanes decided to use the "No Lines" theme in its promotional strategy. The new product was an immediate success; it provided significant advantages over competitive items.

When other companies followed the Hanes lead, the North Carolina firm expanded the product line to include Slenderalls, a control-top version, and Winteralls, a heavier-weight product. It is apparent that Hanes Hosiery is determined to keep offering utility to its marketplace.

Source: "Underalls' Success Due to 'Flanking Strategy', Product Idea, Positioning," *Marketing News,* November 14, 1980, p. 11. Used by permission of the American Marketing Association. Photo reprinted by permission of Hanes Corporation.

WHAT IS MARKETING?

All organizations must create utility if they are to survive: Hanes Hosiery is an example of a firm that has been quite successful in providing utility to its marketplace.

Marketers do not always achieve the immediate success that characterized Hanes' introduction of Underalls. Stephanie Kwolek, a Du Pont scientist, discovered a truly remarkable product in 1965, and the company is still trying to turn it into a commercial success in the 1980s.

THE KEVLAR STORY

Source: Courtesy of Du Pont Corporation.

Du Pont has invested more in Kevlar—about $500 million—than any other product in the company's history. Kevlar is a fiber with amazing strength. A Kevlar cable can anchor an oil rig in the North Sea. Kevlar vests—with a mere 3/8 of an inch of fiber—can stop a .357 magnum bullet. But despite its significant advantages, Kevlar has not yet become a major success. In fact, Du Pont estimates that it has lost millions of dollars on Kevlar.

The chemical company is betting that its marketing effort can overcome a variety of problems that have plagued Kevlar. First, initial production was delayed because the solvent that was used became a suspected carcinogen. When this situation was resolved, the first major Kevlar user—higher-priced auto tires—experienced a substantial drop because of a recession.

Du Pont also experienced a rapid escalation of Kevlar's production costs that put the fiber at a significant price disadvantage. Kevlar requires hydrocarbons that are also used in gasoline additives, so the Du Pont product suffered when gasoline prices went up. To add to Du Pont's woes, the company overestimated the size of the market for oil rig anchor lines. But there are a few bright spots for Kevlar. The fiber's light weight makes it attractive to aircraft manufacturers. Several planes use Kevlar in their construction. Du Pont estimates that each pound of Kevlar can save $300 in fuel costs over the airplane's life.

Du Pont thinks that Kevlar is an eventual winner. Management apparently believes that its marketing strategy will be as effective as its production efforts. But as one Du Pont executive commented: ". . .it takes a long time to convince people they can tie down rigs in the North Sea with Kevlar."

Source: Lee Smith, "A Miracle in Search of a Market," *FORTUNE,* December 1, 1980, pp. 92–94, 96, 98. © 1980 Time, Inc. All rights reserved.

MARKETING DEFINED

In order to standardize terminology in the field of marketing, an American Marketing Association committee developed a list of definitions for the major terms. First on the list was *marketing,* defined as "the performance of business activities that direct the flow of goods and services from producer to consumer or user."[2]

This definition is somewhat narrow because it emphasizes the flow of products that already have been produced. A broader and more descriptive view is that of the firm or other entity as an organized behavior system designed to generate outputs of value to consumers. Under this view, **marketing** is *the development and efficient distribution of goods and services for chosen consumer segments.* Profitability is achieved through creating customer satisfaction. Marketing activities begin with new product concepts and designs analyzed and developed to meet specific unfilled consumer needs—not with finished goods ready for shipment. In this way, the marketing system reflects consumer and societal needs.

The expanded conception of marketing activities permeates all organizational activities. Marketing is applicable to both profit-oriented and nonprofit organizations. The definition assumes that marketing effort will be in accordance with ethical business practices and that it will be effective from the standpoint of both society and the individual firm. It also emphasizes the need for efficiency in distribution, although the nature and degree of efficiency depend on the kind of business environment within which the firm operates. Finally, it assumes that the consumer segments that will be satisfied through the organization's production and marketing activities have been selected and analyzed prior to production.

PRODUCTION ORIENTATION IN BUSINESS

Fifty years ago, most firms were production oriented. Manufacturers stressed production of quality products and then looked for people to purchase them. The Pillsbury Company of this period is an excellent example of a production-oriented company. Here is how the company's board chairman, the late Robert J. Keith, described the Pillsbury of the early years:

We are professional flour millers. Blessed with a supply of the finest North American wheat, plenty of water power, and excellent milling machinery, we produce flour of the highest quality. Our basic function is to mill high-quality flour, and, of course (and almost incidentally), we must hire salesmen to sell it, just as we hire accountants to keep our books.[3]

The general attitude of this era was that a good product (defined in terms of physical quality) would sell itself. This production orientation dominated business philosophy for decades.

One explanation for the late emergence of the study of marketing is that time, place, and ownership utilities were not widely recognized until recent years. This is not to say, however, that marketing activities were nonexistent. Since people first created surpluses, they have wanted to exchange them for other needed items. One writer points out that "historical accounts of trade lead one to conclude that marketing has always existed. More than six thousand years of recorded history show the roots of both Western and Eastern civilizations to have included various forms of trade."[4]

SHIFT IN EMPHASIS TO MARKETING AND CONSUMER ORIENTATION

Experience has shown that a firm's ability to produce a quality product is simply not enough for it to achieve success in a dynamic business environment; marketing effort is also required. Sharp Electronics is known for its effective marketing as well as for its innovative products. One Sharp executive summed up the company philosophy this way: "Many companies develop a product in the lab and then try to find a market for it. We find the void in the market first."[5]

More than 100 years ago, Ralph Waldo Emerson remarked, "If a man writes a better book, preaches a better sermon or makes a better mousetrap than his neighbor, though he builds his house in the woods, the world will make a beaten path to his door."[6] The implications of this statement are that a quality product will sell itself and that an effective production function is the key to high profits. But this is not always the case.

In 1956, the Pioneer Tool and Die Company produced a perfect mousetrap from an engineering/production viewpoint. It was automatic, baitless, and odorless—a complex product about the size of an attaché case. The mouse was enticed to enter a hole, then proceed to a trap door. The rodents would follow a corridor onto a plank that would drop them into a water compartment, where they would drown. The product was truly innovative compared to the familiar wooden trap.

Pioneer produced 5,600 of these traps, but management abandoned the project after selling only 400. Its loss was $63,000. Apparently, consumers did not think the better mousetrap was worth its $29.95 price tag![7]

Pioneer failed in its new product venture because it forgot consumer constraints on purchase decisions. Consumers may view a new product as unique, well designed, and possessing favorable features. But if the price is too high relative to the need satisfaction it provides, they will reject the item in the marketplace.

A marketing orientation can sometimes conflict with a production orientation.

"Just keep your marketing smarts to yourself. You grow it and I'll push it."

Source: Drawing by Donald Reilly; © 1980 The New Yorker Magazine, Inc.

The moral of the mousetrap story is obvious. A quality product will not be successful until it is effectively marketed, and marketing requires a thorough understanding of consumer needs. Paul Zinkann, Pioneer's president, explained this point well when he said, "Our big mistake was that nobody ever found out whether anyone wanted to buy a mousetrap as elaborate as ours for the original high retail price."[8]

Of course, Zinkann is not alone in his mistake. Inadequate consumer research is a leading cause of marketing failure. One company, however, avoided this error in an interesting way. The company had developed a dog shampoo with the unique advantage of using very little water, thereby saving the pet owner from an unplanned soaking. From a production and design viewpoint, the product was a major advance in dog shampoos. But, according to marketing research, dog owners did not trust the drier shampoo. They doubted whether it would actually clean their dogs as effectively as their previous brand. So the company included a tick-killing ingredient in order to convince consumers that the new shampoo was capable of doing a special job.[9]

To be successful, products require effective marketing based on a thorough understanding of what consumers want and need. Therefore, marketing is a primary function of any organization.

AND NOW AN ELECTRIC MOUSETRAP

A Pennsylvania mail-order firm has offered an electric mousetrap that relies on a scent to lure mice to their doom. The eight-inch tubular device can be plugged in anywhere, and does not require bait that can also attract insects. The device is safe to use around children and pets, and comes equipped with disposal bags. The price. . .$14.88!

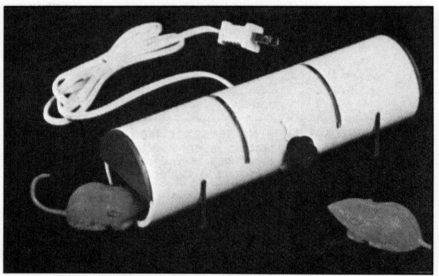

Source: Courtesy of Hanover House Industries.

How, then, does marketing activity develop? The marketing function does not exist in subsistence-level economies (those having an absolute minimum standard of living). It needs a production surplus in order to appear.

For example, assume the populace of a primitive society consists solely of Person A and Person B. Assume also that the only elements of their standard of living are food, clothing, and shelter. The two live in adjoining caves on a mountainside. They weave their own clothes and tend their own fields independently of each other. They are able to subsist even though their standard of living is minimal.

However, Person A is an excellent weaver but a poor farmer, while Person B is an excellent farmer but a poor weaver. In this situation, it will be wise for each to specialize in the line of work that each does best. The net result will be a greater total production of both clothing and food. In other words, specialization and division of labor will lead to a production surplus. But neither A nor B will be any better off until each trades the products of individual labor, thereby creating the exchange process.

Exchange is the origin of marketing activity. In fact, marketing has been described as "the process of creating and resolving exchange relationships."[10] When there is a need to exchange goods, the natural result is marketing effort on the part of the people involved.

Wroe Alderson, a leading marketing theorist, once said, "It seems altogether reasonable to describe the development of exchange as a great invention which helped to start primitive man on the road to civilization."[11]

While the cave-dweller example is simplistic, it does point up the essence of the marketing function. Complex industrial society may have a more complicated exchange process, but the basic concept is the same. Production is not meaningful until a system of marketing has been established. Perhaps publisher Red Motley's adage sums it up best: "Nothing happens until somebody sells something."[12]

MARKETING MOVES INTO THE TWENTIETH CENTURY

Although marketing had emerged as a functional activity within the business organization prior to the twentieth century, management's orientation remained with production for quite some time. In fact, what might be called industry's production era did not reach its peak until the early part of this century. The apostle of this approach to business operations was Frederick Taylor, whose *Principles of Scientific Management* was widely read and accepted at that time. Taylor's approach reflected his engineering background by emphasizing efficiency in the production process. Later writers, such as Frank and Lillian Gilbreth, the originators of motion analysis, expanded on Taylor's basic concepts.[13]

On the practitioner's side, Henry Ford's mass-production line was certainly an example of this orientation. Ford's slogan "they [customers] can have any color they want, as long as it is black" reflected a prevalent attitude toward marketing. Production shortages and intense consumer demand were the rule of the day. It is no wonder that production activities took precedence.

As personal income and consumer demand for goods and services dropped rapidly during the Great Depression of the 1930s, marketing was thrust into a more important role. Organizational survival dictated that managers pay closer attention to the markets for their products. This trend was halted by the outbreak of World War II, when

The exchange process is the origin of marketing activity.

"Psssst, I can get it for you wholesale!"

Source: Drawing by Clem Scalzitti from *AG World* (January 1977). Reprinted by permission of Clem Scalzitti.

rationing and shortages of consumer goods became commonplace. The war years, however, were only a pause in a trend that was resumed almost immediately after the hostilities ceased. The marketing concept was about to be born.

NEW WAY OF DOING BUSINESS

What was the setting for the crucial change in management philosophy? Perhaps it can best be explained by the shift from a **seller's market**—*one with a shortage of goods and services*—to a **buyer's market**—*one with an abundance of goods and services.* When World War II ended, factories stopped making tanks and jeeps and started turning out consumer goods again—an activity that had for all practical purposes stopped in early 1942.

The advent of a strong buyer's market occasioned the need for a consumer orientation on the part of U.S. business. Goods had to be sold, not just produced. This is the basis of the marketing concept. The recognition of this concept and its dominating role in business can be dated from 1952, when General Electric's annual report heralded a new management philosophy:

[The concept] introduces the marketing man at the beginning rather than at the end of the production cycle and integrates marketing into each phase of the business. Thus, marketing, through its studies and research, will establish for the engineer, the design and manufacturing man, what the customer wants in a given product, what price he is willing to pay, and where and when it will be wanted. Marketing will have authority in product planning, production scheduling, and inventory control, as well as in sales distribution and servicing of the product.[14]

Marketing would no longer be regarded as an activity to be performed after the production process had been accomplished. For instance, the marketer would now play the lead role in product planning. Marketing and selling would no longer be synonymous. Business persons would first begin to realize that "marketing is as different from selling as chemistry is from alchemy, astronomy from astrology, chess from checkers."[15] Selling would be recognized as only one aspect of marketing.

Formally, the **marketing concept** is *a company-wide consumer orientation with the objective of achieving long-run profits.*[16] The key words are *company-wide consumer orientation.* All facets of the business must be involved with assessing and then satisfying customer wants and needs. The effort is not something to be left only to the marketers. Accountants working in the credit office and engineers employed in product design also play important roles.

The words *with the objective of achieving long-run profits* are used in order to differentiate the concept from policies of short-run profit maximization. The marketing concept is a modern philosophy for dynamic business growth. Since the continuity of the firm is an assumed part of it, company-wide consumer orientation will lead to greater long-run profits than will managerial philosophies geared to reaching short-run goals.

THE MARKETING MYOPIA PROBLEM

The emergence of the marketing concept has not been devoid of setbacks. One troublesome situation has been what Theodore Levitt called "marketing myopia."[17] According to Levitt, **marketing myopia** is *the failure of management to recognize the scope of its business.* Future growth is endangered because management is product oriented rather than customer oriented. Levitt cited many service industries—dry cleaning, electric utilities, movies, and railroads—as examples.

For years, the Chicago White Sox had been known as the city's South Side baseball team. But new management considered the White Sox to be in the entertainment business. A pay-TV plan was adopted. And the White Sox implemented an aggressive marketing strategy to expand their franchise in the Chicago market. Special promotional nights were set up for the suburbs and other areas. A vice-president of marketing was hired to direct the strategy that included extensive radio and TV advertising, an expanded ticket sales system, new uniforms and symbols, improved security at the ball park, and the acquisition of name players.[18] Clearly, the Chicago White Sox have gone a long way toward overcoming marketing myopia.

THE BROADENING CONCEPT

Industry has been responsive to the marketing concept as an improved method of doing business.[19] Since consideration of the consumer is now well accepted in most organizations, the relevant question has become: What should be the nature and extent of the concept's parameters?[20]

Some marketers argue for the **broadening concept**—*the idea that the marketing concept should be substantially broadened to include many areas formerly not concerned with marketing efforts.*[21] Others contend that the marketing concept has been extended too far.[22] Recent experience has shown that many nonprofit organizations have accepted the marketing concept.

Consider the area of health care. The U.S. Department of Agriculture conducted a major consumer research study dealing with children's eating habits and food preferences. A promotional campaign to improve this aspect of child life is a result of this marketing research. The American Hospital Association conducts marketing seminars for hospital administrators in an attempt to boost preventive health programs. The National Institute of Health developed a "Help Smokers Quit" kit and an extensive educational and follow-up package for physicians to use in counseling patients about smoking dangers.[23]

Many other nonprofit organizations are now pursuing marketing strategies. Well-known examples of the broadening concept in practice include political campaigns, charitable solicitations, armed-forces recruiting, library outreach programs, a community college's continuing education offerings, and the like. Marketing is now a vital activity of most nonprofit organizations.

It would be difficult to envision business returning to an era when engineering genius prevailed at the expense of consumer needs. It would be equally difficult to envision nonprofit organizations returning to a time when they lacked the marketing skills necessary to present their messages to the public. Marketing is a dynamic function, and in one form or another it is playing a more important role in all organizations and in people's daily lives.

INTRODUCTION TO THE MARKETING VARIABLES

The starting place for effective marketing is the consumer. (Consumer behavior is treated in detail in Chapter 7.) Once a particular consumer group has been identified and analyzed, the marketing manager can direct company activities to profitably satisfy that segment.

American Motors, Southwest Airlines, and United Parcel Service are among the firms that have successfully analyzed the markets they seek to serve. As a result:

- American Motors' marketing strategy emphasizes Jeeps rather than a full line offering competitive with General Motors and Ford.

- Southwest Airlines concentrates on business commuters instead of competing head-on with American Airlines for all air travelers.

- United Parcel Service seeks to serve business customers, as opposed to the wider market of the U.S. Postal Service.[24]

Although thousands of variables are involved, marketing decision making can be conveniently classified into four strategies: product, distribution, promotional, and pricing.

Product strategy comprises *decisions about package design, branding, trademarks, warranties, guarantees, product life cycles, and new product development.* The marketer's concept of product strategy involves more than the physical product; it considers also the satisfaction of all consumer needs in relation to the good or service. **Distribution strategy** deals with *the physical distribution of goods and the selection of marketing channels.* **Marketing channels** are the *steps a good or service follows from producer to user or consumer.* Channel decision making means establishing and maintaining the institutional structure in marketing channels. It involves retailers, wholesalers, and other institutional middlemen. **Promotional strategy** comprises *personal selling, advertising, and sales promotion tools.* The various aspects of promotional strategy must be blended together in order for the company to communicate effectively with the marketplace. **Pricing strategy,** one of the most difficult areas of marketing decision making, deals with *the methods of setting profitable and justified prices.* It is closely regulated and subjected to considerable public scrutiny.

The total package forms the **marketing mix**—*the blending of the four strategy elements of marketing decision making to satisfy chosen consumer segments.* Each of the strategies is a variable in the mix (see Figure 1.1).

RIUNITE: DEVELOPING AN EFFECTIVE MARKETING MIX

Riunite provides an excellent example of an effective marketing mix.[25] The popular brand is the nation's leading imported table wine, with a 25 percent share of the market. Riunite outsells the second place import by a 3-1 margin. Villa Banfi, Riunite's importer and marketer, developed the following marketing mix:

Consumer target *(covered in Chapters 3–7)*

- The mass market consisted of many first-time wine consumers.

**FIGURE 1.1
Elements of the
Marketing Mix**

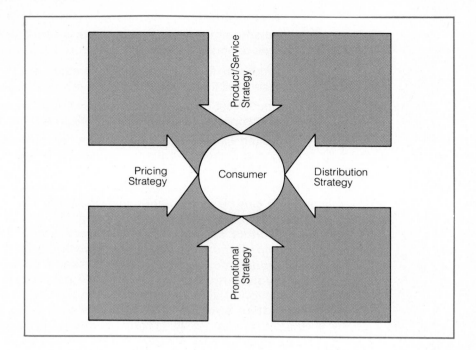

Product strategy (covered in Chapters 8 and 9)

- Riunite is a Lambrusco wine; sweeter, fruitier, fizzier, and with a lower alcohol content than its competitors. It also does not require aging.
- The Villa Banfi product strategy is based on the premise that Americans prefer sweeter and colder drinks.
- The company has also produced a 6.3-ounce bottle in an attempt to reach markets like airlines, fast-food franchises, and sporting events.
- Villa Banfi is also marketing other brands. Bell 'Agio is similar to Riunite and carries a comparable price. A higher-priced vintage label is also being introduced.

Distribution strategy (covered in Chapters 10–13)

- The marketing channel for Riunite leads from an Italian grape co-operative to Villa Banfi to wine dealers to the consumer.
- Villa Banfi is soliciting other sales outlets such as airlines, fast-food franchises, sports events, and restaurant salad bars via the 6.3-ounce bottle.
- The 6.3-ounce bottle is also being promoted through supermarkets, a traditional outlet.

Promotional strategy *(covered in Chapters 14–16)*

- Villa Banfi's promotional strategy is based primarily on an extensive advertising budget equal to more than 6 percent of annual sales.
- Approximately two-thirds of the advertising budget is allocated to television.
- Riunite is now being promoted as a competitor for all drinks, not just wine. Villa Banfi has targeted some of its promotional efforts at soft drinks, beer, and other beverages, in addition to competitive brands of wine.

Pricing strategy *(covered in Chapters 17 and 18)*

- Because Riunite does not require aging, Villa Banfi was able to introduce the wine at $1.99 per bottle. It now sells for $3.00—still low by wine industry standards.
- Villa Banfi's Bell 'Agio brand is priced close to Riunite. The importer's vintage wines are priced higher than Riunite.

ENVIRONMENTAL FACTORS IMPACTING MARKETING

Marketing decisions are not made in a vacuum. Marketers cannot experiment with single variables while holding other factors constant. Instead, marketing decisions are made on the basis of the constant changes in the mix variables and the dynamic nature of environmental forces. To be successful, these decisions must take into account the four environments—competitive, legal, economic, and societal and cultural—in which they operate.

Consider the case of Riunite. Villa Banfi's competition originally came from Cella and Giacobazzi. Later, Coca-Cola's acquisition of Taylor Wines added a new dimension to Riunite's competitive environment. Villa Banfi's legal environment is characterized by import regulations as well as by state and local laws dealing with alcoholic beverages. All of these factors impact marketing decisions.

The economic environment affects all marketers. So Villa Banfi diversified into two other Italian and one California wine venture. The societal environment has also played a major role in the marketing of Riunite. For instance, many of the brand's customers were first-time wine buyers. And the American preference for sweeter, colder drinks is another societal factor that figured in Riunite's marketing strategy.[26] Environmental influences are the topic of Chapter 2. Consideration of these factors is crucial to effective marketing.

THE STUDY OF MARKETING

In an era when relevance and practicality are often viewed as important criteria in evaluating any educational effort, this introductory chapter would be remiss if it did not address the following question: Why study marketing?

The response is that marketing is as relevant to modern life as any discipline currently existing. In one form or another, it is close to every person. Three of its most important concerns for students are the following:

1. Marketing costs may be the largest item in the personal budget. Numerous attempts have been made to determine these costs, and most estimates have ranged between 40 and 60 percent (with an approximate average of 50 percent). Regardless of the exact cost, however, marketing is obviously a key item in any consumer's budget.

    However, the cost alone does not indicate the value of marketing. If someone says that marketing costs are too high, that person should be asked, "Relative to what?" The standard of living in the United States is in large part a function of the country's efficient marketing system. Looked at that way, the costs of the system seem reasonable. Marketing expands sales, thereby spreading fixed production costs over more units of output and reducing total output costs. Reduced production costs offset many marketing costs.

2. There is a good chance that individual students will become marketers. Marketing-related occupations account for a significant portion of the nation's jobs. Indeed, marketing opportunities remained strong even during recent periods when one out of four college graduates could not find jobs. History has shown that the demand for good marketers is not affected by cyclical economic fluctuations.

3. Marketing provides an opportunity to contribute to society as well as to an individual company. Marketing decisions affect everyone's welfare. Furthermore, opportunities to advance to decision-making positions come sooner in marketing than in most occupations. (Societal aspects of marketing will be covered in detail in later chapters.)

Approaches to the Study of Marketing

Table 1.1 outlines six approaches to the formal study of marketing. Commodity, functional, and institutional approaches are usually considered the traditional methods of study, while managerial, systems, and societal approaches are the most popular methods today.[27]

All the approaches to studying marketing have their merits, and all have been popular at one time or another. This textbook takes an integrated approach to studying the field. It considers the key concepts of each method at the practitioner's level.

SUMMARY

The two primary functions of any business organization are production and marketing. Traditionally, industry has emphasized production effi-

TABLE 1.1
Six Approaches to the Formal Study of Marketing

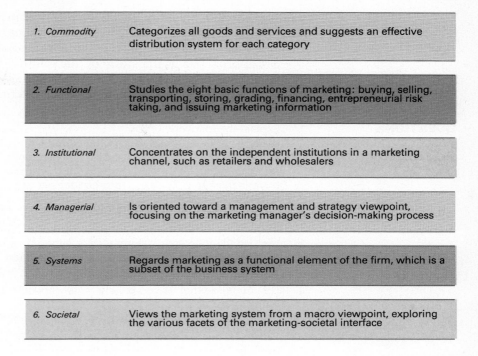

1. Commodity	Categorizes all goods and services and suggests an effective distribution system for each category
2. Functional	Studies the eight basic functions of marketing: buying, selling, transporting, storing, grading, financing, entrepreneurial risk taking, and issuing marketing information
3. Institutional	Concentrates on the independent institutions in a marketing channel, such as retailers and wholesalers
4. Managerial	Is oriented toward a management and strategy viewpoint, focusing on the marketing manager's decision-making process
5. Systems	Regards marketing as a functional element of the firm, which is a subset of the business system
6. Societal	Views the marketing system from a macro viewpoint, exploring the various facets of the marketing-societal interface

ciency, often at the expense of marketing. Sometime after World War II, however, the marketing concept became the accepted business philosophy. The change was caused by the economy shifting from a seller's market to a buyer's market.

Marketers must be careful to avoid marketing myopia, the tendency to define one's market too narrowly. The term was coined by Theodore Levitt, who argued that too many executives were product oriented rather than consumer oriented.

Marketing is the development and efficient distribution of goods and services for chosen consumer segments. First, a consumer target is determined. Then, a marketing mix is developed. Marketing decision making can be classified into four strategies: (1) product, (2) distribution, (3) promotional, and (4) pricing. These four variables together form the total marketing mix. Marketing decisions must be made in a dynamic environment determined by competitive, legal, economic, and societal functions.

Marketing is now a major determinant of success for nonprofit, as well as profit-oriented, organizations. Enlarging the scope of marketing to include nonprofit entities is known as the broadening concept.

Three basic reasons for studying marketing are these: (1) marketing costs may be the largest item in the personal budget; (2) there is a good chance individual students may become marketers; and (3) marketing provides an opportunity to contribute to society as well as to a company.

Six approaches to the study of marketing are commodity, functional, institutional, managerial, systems, and societal. This textbook follows an integrated approach in studying the field.

QUESTIONS FOR DISCUSSION

1. Explain the following terms:

utility	product strategy
marketing	distribution strategy
seller's market	marketing channels
buyer's market	promotional strategy
marketing concept	pricing strategy
marketing myopia	marketing mix
broadening concept	

2. Discuss the following statement: For a long time, most business people acknowledged only one line function—production.

3. What are the four types of utility? With which is marketing concerned?

4. Do you agree that "if you build a better mousetrap, the world will beat a path to your door"?

5. Contrast the production era with the emergence of the marketing concept.

6. What did the General Electric annual report mean when it said it was introducing "the marketing man at the beginning rather than at the end of the production cycle"?

7. How would you explain marketing to someone not familiar with the subject?

8. Discuss the relationship between the major strategy elements in the marketing mix and the factors involved in the decision-making environment.

9. Discuss the following statement: Marketing costs are too high.

10. Describe the various approaches to the study of marketing. Illustrate how each approach can be used with a specific product.

11. What should be the parameters of the marketing concept?

12. How would you explain Moosehead beer's success in the U.S. market?

13. What can be learned from Du Pont's difficulties in marketing Kevlar?

14. Evaluate the marketing strategy devised for Riunite.

15. Why did Pioneer Tool and Die Company try to sell its new mousetrap at $29.95?

16. What are some other products that have failed because of poor marketing?

17. Jennifer Shannon is a recreation major at Center City College. She hopes eventually to direct a community recreation program involving sports leagues, youth camps, adult education classes, cultural programs, and other leisure-time activities. What does she need to know about marketing?

18. Prepare a brief report on a recent marketing success. What can be learned from this story?

19. Assume that a recent series of traffic tragedies involving drunk drivers

has led to a public protest in your community. You have been asked to explain how marketing can help a group crusading against drinking drivers. What will you say?

20.   Write a one-page report on the views you held about marketing prior to enrolling in your marketing class. Discuss it with other class members; then, file it away until the end of the term. At that time, check to see if your thinking has changed.

NOTES

1.   Stephen Probyn, "The Moose that Roared," *Canadian Business,* February 1981, pp. 42, 44, 46. Reprinted by permission of the author.

2.   Committee on Definitions, *Marketing Definitions: A Glossary of Marketing Terms* (Chicago: American Marketing Association, 1960), p. 15.

3.   Robert J. Keith, "The Marketing Revolution," *Journal of Marketing,* January 1980, p. 36.

4.   Robert Bartels, *The Development of Marketing Thought* (Homewood, Ill.: Richard D. Irwin, 1962), p. 4.

5.   "Marketing, Technical Research Lead Sharp from Pencil Pushing to $2 Billion in Electronic Sales," *Marketing News,* March 6, 1980, p. 1. Used by permission of the American Marketing Association.

6.   Quoted in Robert Suro, "In Iowa: the Mice Aren't Telling," *Time,* March 17, 1980, p. 8.

7.   The Pioneer Tool and Die Company story is from Lee Berton, "Firms Strive to Avoid Introducing Products that Nobody Will Buy," *Wall Street Journal,* March 6, 1967.

8.   *Ibid.*

9.   Roger Ricklefs, "Success Comes Hard in the Tricky Business of Creating Products," *Wall Street Journal,* August 23, 1978.

10. Richard P. Bagozzi, "Marketing as an Organized Behavioral System of Exchange," *Journal of Marketing,* October 1974, p. 77. Further work by Bagozzi on this subject appears in "Marketing as Exchange," *Journal of Marketing,* October 1975, pp. 32–39, and "Marketing as Exchange: A Theory of Transactions in the Marketplace," *American Behavioral Scientist,* March–April 1978, pp. 535–36.

11. Wroe Alderson, *Marketing Behavior and Executive Action* (Homewood, Ill.: Richard D. Irwin, 1962), p. 292.

12. T. G. Povey, "Spotting the Salesman Who Has What it Takes," *Nation's Business,* July 1972, p. 70.

13. For a discussion on scientific management, see Louis E. Boone and David L. Kurtz, *Principles of Management* (New York: Random House, 1981), pp. 35–38.

14. *1952 Annual Report* (New York: General Electric, 1952), p. 21.

15. Theodore Levitt, *Innovations in Marketing* (New York: McGraw-Hill, 1962), p. 7.

16. This definition is offered in Lawrence A. Klatt, *Small Business Management* (Belmont, Calif.: Wadsworth Publishing, 1973), p. 157.

17. Theodore Levitt, "Marketing Myopia," *Harvard Business Review,* July–August 1960, pp. 45–56.

18. Bernard F. Whalen, "Pro Sports Teams Must Enter Pay TV Market to Survive," *Marketing News,* May 1, 1981, pp. 1, 3.

19. The current status of the marketing concept is explored in such articles as Charles W. Lamb, Jr. and John L. Crompton, "The Status of the Marketing Concept in Public Recreation and Park Agencies," *Journal of the Academy of Marketing Science* Winter 1980, pp. 1–14; Stuart U. Rich, "The Marketing Concept Revisited," *Alabama Business,* August 1980, pp. 2–3, 5, 11; Leigh Lawton and A. Parasuraman, "The Impact of the Marketing Concept on New Product Planning," *Journal of Marketing,* Winter 1980, pp. 19–25; and Peter C. Riesz, "Revenge of the Marketing Concept," *Business Horizons,* June 1980, pp. 49–53.

20. An interesting discussion appears in Shelby D. Hunt, "The Nature and Scope of Marketing," *Journal of Marketing,* July 1976, pp. 17–28.

21. Pioneering articles related to the subject include Philip Kotler and Sidney J. Levy, "Broadening the Concept of Marketing," *Journal of Marketing,* January 1969, pp. 10–15; Leslie M. Dawson, "The Human Concept: New Philosophy for Business," *Business Horizons,* December 1969, pp. 29–38; and Sidney J. Levy and Philip Kotler, "Beyond Marketing: The Furthering Concept," *California Management Review,* Winter 1969, pp. 67–73.

22. This viewpoint is expressed in David J. Luck, "Broadening the Concept of Marketing—Too Far," *Journal of Marketing,* July 1969, pp. 53–55.

23. These examples are noted in Karen F. A. Fox and Philip Kotler, "The Marketing of Social Causes: The First 10 Years," *Journal of Marketing,* Fall 1980, p. 29. Other excellent articles related to the broadening concept are Philip D. Cooper and William J. Kehoe, "Marketing's Status, Dimensions, and Directions," *Business,* July–August 1979, pp. 14–20; and Philip Kotler, "Strategies for Introducing Marketing into Nonprofit Organizations," *Journal of Marketing,* January 1979, pp. 37–44.

24. Keith K. Cox, "Marketing in the 1980's—Back to Basics," *Business,* May–June 1980, p. 22. Copyright © 1980 by the College of Business Administration, Georgia State University, Atlanta. Reprinted by permission from *Business* Magazine.

25. Bill Abrams, "Selling Wine Like Soda Pop, Riunite Uncorks Huge Market," *Wall Street Journal,* July 2, 1981. Reprinted by permission of *The Wall Street Journal,* © Dow Jones & Company, Inc. 1981. All rights reserved.

26. *Ibid.*

27. A good review of the traditional methods is contained in Harry L. Hansen, *Marketing: Text, Cases and Readings,* 4th ed. (Homewood, Ill.: Richard D. Irwin, 1977), pp. 5–6.

CHAPTER 2

THE ENVIRONMENT FOR MARKETING DECISIONS

KEY TERMS

competitive environment
legal environment
corrective advertising
economic environment
inflation
stagflation
energy crisis
demarketing
societal/cultural environment

LEARNING GOALS

1. To explain how marketing decisions must be made within an environmental framework

2. To determine how competitive strategies influence the marketplace and are in turn influenced by competitors' strategies

3. To examine the legal environment for marketing

4. To illustrate how the economic environment affects marketing decisions

5. To recognize the importance of the societal/cultural environment for marketing

Source: Courtesy of
Pel-Freez, Inc.

Pel-Freez of Rogers, Arkansas, understands the role of environmental factors in marketing its product. The company produces up to 3 million pounds of rabbit meat a year, the largest output in the nation. Rabbit meat has many pluses. First, rabbit meat retails at about $1.99 to $2.29 per pound. Rabbit is also lower in calories, fat, cholesterol, and sodium, and higher in protein than chicken, beef, or pork. Rabbits can be ready for market in only eight weeks. They use less grain per pound of meat than does other livestock.

Despite all of these advantages, rabbit-meat consumption per capita in the United States is only .005 pounds per year, as compared with that of Spain (6.5 pounds), France (4 pounds), and Germany (3 pounds). The U.S. market tends to be concentrated in ethnic areas. What is the explanation for Americans' low consumption of this excellent meat value?

Source: Photo courtesy of Albertina Museum. Reprinted by permission. Engraving by Albrecht Dürer, 1520.

**FIGURE 2.1
Elements of the
Marketing Mix as
They Operate within
an Environmental
Framework**

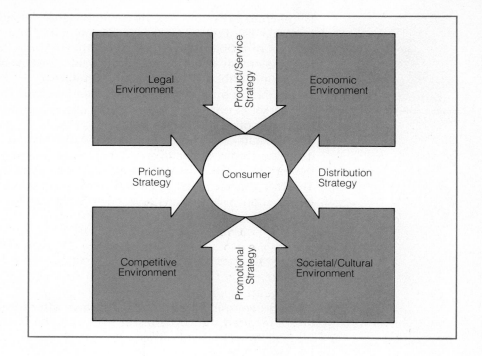

Peter Cheeke of Oregon State University calls it the "Easter-Bunny syndrome." Cheeke has expressed it this way: "Americans are not used to thinking of a rabbit as food, but rather as a cute, cuddly pet."[1]

The situation faced by Pel-Frez and other rabbit producers suggests how important environmental factors are to marketing decisions. The marketer's product, distribution, promotion, and pricing strategies must filter through various environmental factors before they reach their goal: the consumers who represent the firm's market target.

The environment for marketing decisions is actually four interacting environments: competitive, legal, economic, and societal/cultural. These factors are important because they provide the frame of reference within which marketing decisions are made.[2] However, they are not decision variables in the marketing process; instead, they are outside factors that influence marketing strategy.

Even though marketing managers cannot direct them, they must take them into account when making marketing decisions. The strategy elements that can be directed—product planning, distribution, promotion, and pricing—are modified through pressures exerted by the uncontrollable environmental factors. Figure 2.1 illustrates these elements' influence on the consumer.

The dynamic nature of the environmental factors puts additional pressure on all levels of management to continually reevaluate marketing decisions in light of the contemporary business environment. Even modest environmental shifts can alter the results of marketing decisions. Ford Motor Company's failure to properly monitor environmental conditions contributed to the Edsel's demise—one of the most publicized product failures of all times.

COMPETITIVE ENVIRONMENT

The interactive process that occurs in the marketplace is referred to as the **competitive environment.** One firm's marketing decisions influence its market and are in turn affected by competitors' decisions. Miller Brewing's phenomenal success with its "Lite" beer led to a rush of competitors attempting to get part of a growing market segment—diet-conscious beer drinkers.

The competitive environment often determines the success or failure of a product. Consider the case of Corfam, a leather substitute introduced by Du Pont during the 1960s. The product introduction was backed by a sizable advertising budget, which was cut back when management concluded that Corfam was a can't-miss product. But Corfam eventually had to be withdrawn after foreign shoe manufacturers invaded the U.S. market with genuine leather shoes that sold for less than Du Pont's substitute.[3]

Ford Motor Company provides another illustration of the competitive environment. At the beginning of the 1970s, Ford was competing with General Motors for control of the U.S. auto market. Although General Motors' 40 percent market share (the percentage of a market that a firm controls) outdistanced Ford's 27 percent, Ford was better positioned in the more profitable full-sized segment of the market. But the shift to smaller, more fuel-efficient vehicles caused a tremendous increase in the sale of imported models. Ford was hurt badly. By 1980 its market share had dropped to 17 percent. In one 18-month period (1980 to mid-1981), Ford lost $2 billion.

But Ford fought back. It shifted its product mix to smaller cars. By 1982, the subcompact Escort line comprised about half of the company's passenger-car volume. The company also cut costs with layoffs and plant closings. Many components were purchased from overseas, particularly from Tozo Kogyo Company of Japan—the makers of Mazda, and 25 percent owned by Ford. Ford realized that there were profitable opportunities in small cars, and it shifted its orientation to meet a changed competitive environment.[4]

The competitive environment has also affected Scott Paper. The company has lost market share to competitors like Procter & Gamble. Aging technology made it difficult for Scott to produce competitive products for the upper end of the sanitary paper (such as tissues) market.

Scott decided to adjust its competitive strategy. The firm increased its promotional expenditures. It modified products like Family Scott, Waldorf, and Scott Towels, and cut their prices accordingly. Scott also expanded its position in private-label products, the type that carries the label of a dealer, not a manufacturer. The company also chose certain higher-priced markets in which it would compete on a selective basis. Scott Paper had adjusted its product mix and marketing strategy in order to better deal with the competitive environment of the 1980s.[5]

Expanded Role of Competition

Through the years, the marketing system has become increasingly competitive. Traditional economic analysis views competition as a struggle among companies in the same industry or among substitutable products. Marketers, however, tend to accept the argument that all firms are competing for a limited amount of discretionary buying power. Toyota competes with a vacation in Aspen. A General Cinema theater competes with the Detroit Tigers for the entertainment dollar. And plastics manufacturers compete with U.S. Steel in some markets.

Industry has also found numerous new uses for existing products, thereby expanding the arena of competition. While this trend forces business to reassess long-established marketing practices, it also opens new avenues of business opportunity. The demand for "running flats" caused by millions of health-conscious joggers has created vast new business opportunities, as well as restructured the recreational shoe industry.

Marketing: A Visible Business Activity

While it is sometimes difficult to define the relationship between the competitive environment and the marketplace, it is easily recognized that marketing is the most visible of all business functions. No other one is exposed to public evaluation as continuously. The marketer is the company to most consumers. A Republic Airlines passenger's opinion of the airline is determined largely by his or her impression of the passenger agent and the flight service crew. A shopper's assessment of a store is significantly affected by its sales personnel.

Other functional activities, such as accounting, quality control, credit management, production, and engineering, are performed within the organization. Contact between the public and the people doing these jobs is minimal. Marketing, by contrast, performs the bulk of its duties within full view of an often critical public. It is understandable, therefore, that marketing usually receives the brunt of the public's displeasure. Marketers realize that public acceptance of their activities sets the type of competitive environment in which they operate.

DEVELOPING A COMPETITIVE STRATEGY

All marketers must develop an effective strategy for dealing with the competitive environment. Some compete in a broad range of product markets in many areas of the world. Others prefer to specialize in particular market segments such as those determined by geographical, age, or income factors. Essentially, the determination of a competitive strategy involves three questions:

1.   Should the firm compete?
2.   If so, in what markets?
3.   How should it compete?

The first question should be answered on the basis of expected profit potential. If the expected profits are insufficient to pay an adequate return on the investment, the firm should consider moving into other lines of business. This decision should, of course, be continually reevaluated so as to avoid becoming tied to a market with declining profit margins. Texas Instruments, for instance, abandoned its digital watch business recently to concentrate in other businesses like semiconductors and distributed computers.[6]

In answer to the second question, the markets in which to compete should be those offering the greatest opportunity. Marketers have limited resources (sales personnel, advertising budgets, product development capability, and so on); they must therefore select only those markets in which they can do an effective job. Scott Paper has chosen to concentrate in lower-priced and private-label markets.

The third question requires marketers to make tactical decisions in setting up their comprehensive marketing strategies. Product, distribution, promotion, and pricing decisions are the major elements of these strategies. Texas Instruments, for example, has adopted an aggressive pricing strategy featuring rebates in its electronic calculator business.[7]

LEGAL ENVIRONMENT

In the late 1970s, Schlitz attorneys concluded that the Food and Drug Administration was about to prepare regulations mandating that beer labels list all ingredients. The Schlitz legal staff asked that all ingredients that might trouble consumers be removed from the product.

Schlitz immediately substituted Chill-garde for an enzyme stabilizer that gave beer a longer shelf life. Chill-garde was filtered out in the brewing process, so it would not have to be listed on the label. But the firm did not know that Chill-garde, when mixed with Kelcoloid (a foam stabilizer), created flakes that gave the beer a hazy appearance. Although the beer was completely safe to drink, its odd appearance turned off Schlitz buyers.

At first management refused to do anything about the hazy beer, blaming it on a high-protein-content barley crop. When action did come, it was the wrong decision: Schlitz removed Kelcoloid instead of Chill-garde, and the beer went flat. It was only sometime later that the company corrected the problem, and wrote off $1.4 million worth of beer. Perhaps it was then that Schlitz learned that the Food and

Drug Administration had never instituted the regulations its legal staff feared.[8] But the legal environment had certainly had a major impact on the brewer.

The **legal environment** for marketing decisions in the United States *is characterized by numerous, often vague, laws passed by a multitude of authorities.* These laws have been enacted at the federal, state, and local levels as well as by independent regulatory agencies. Their provisions often are confusing and poorly written and sometimes conflict with each other. The legal framework was constructed on a piecemeal basis, often in response to some popular issue.

The country has tended to follow a public policy of promoting a competitive marketing system. To maintain the system, competitive practices within it have been heavily regulated. Pricing and promotion are the most highly regulated areas of marketing.[9]

Table 2.1 indicates whether a particular law was primarily intended to promote a competitive environment or regulate a specific marketing practice. The table also lists the elements of marketing strategy affected by the legislation.

Antitrust Legislation

The *Sherman Antitrust Act* (1890) prohibits restraint of trade and monopolization. It subjects violators to civil suits as well as to criminal prosecution.[10] Although the practices covered by the act were unlawful under common law and under several state acts passed in the previous decade, the Sherman Act was the first piece of federal legislation to clearly set out the maintenance of a competitive marketing system as national policy.

The Reagan Administration has indicated it will ease some antitrust restraints, particularly as they apply to mergers of large companies. Attorney General William French Smith has commented: "Bigness doesn't necessarily mean badness. . . . Efficient firms shouldn't be hobbled under the guise of antitrust enforcement." The impact of this policy is less certain, since the government files only a small percentage of all antitrust cases. In fact, 95 percent of this litigation is brought by private parties.[11]

The economic philosophy of the Sherman Act stands in marked contrast to that of many foreign countries, where monopolies are openly encouraged by the government. In such cases, the government is usually attempting to foster productive efficiency that might be injured by excessive competition. Few nations have antitrust legislation comparable to that of the United States. As a result, foreign cartels (monopolies) once had a distinct advantage over U.S. companies operating independently in international markets.

Because of this situation, the *Webb-Pomerene Export Trade Act* (1918) exempted voluntary export trade associations from the Sherman Act restrictions—but only in their foreign trade dealings. (See Chapter 19 for more details.) Exemptions of a similar nature have

TABLE 2.1
Relating Marketing Legislation to Marketing Strategy

Legislation	Date Enacted	Assists in Maintaining a Competitive Environment	Regulates Specific Marketing Activities	Impact on the Marketing Mix			
				Product Strategy	Distribution Strategy	Promotion Strategy	Pricing Strategy
Sherman Antitrust Act	1890	X		X	X	X	X
Clayton Act	1914	X		X	X	X	X
Federal Trade Commission Act	1914	X	X	X	X	X	X
Webb-Pomerene Export Trade Act	1918	X		X	X	X	X
Unfair Trade Laws	1930	X	X	X			X
Fair Trade Laws	1931	X	X				X
Celler-Kefauver Antimerger Act	1950	X		X	X	X	X
Consumer Goods Pricing Act	1975	X	X				X
Pure Food and Drug Act	1906		X	X			
Robinson-Patman Act	1936		X				X
Miller-Tydings Resale Price Maintenance Act	1937		X				X
Wheeler-Lea Act	1938		X			X	
Food, Drug, and Cosmetic Act	1938		X	X			
Wool Products Labeling Act	1939		X	X			
Fur Products Labeling Act	1951		X	X			
Flammable Fabrics Act	1953		X	X			
Kefauver-Harris Drug Amendments	1962		X	X			
Fair Packaging and Labeling Act	1967		X	X			
Consumer Credit Protection Act	1968		X	X		X	X
Fair Credit Reporting Act	1970		X	X	X	X	X
National Environment Protection Act	1970		X	X	X	X	X
Public Health Cigarette Smoking Act	1971		X			X	
Consumer Product Safety Act	1972		X	X			
Equal Credit Opportunity Act	1975–77		X	X	X	X	X
Fair Debt Collection Practices Act	1978		X	X	X	X	X

since been granted on the domestic front for the merger of the National and American football leagues and for pollution control research carried on by automobile manufacturers.

The *Clayton Act* (1914) strengthened antitrust legislation by restricting practices such as price discrimination, exclusive dealing, tying contracts, and interlocking boards of directors where the effect "may be to substantially lessen competition or tend to create a monopoly." Later, the *Celler-Kefauver Antimerger Act* (1950) amended the Clayton Act to include the "purchase of assets" where the purchase would reduce competition.

Role of the Federal Trade Commission

Another important aspect of the regulation of competition is the *Federal Trade Commission Act,* which also became law in 1914. This act prohibited "unfair methods of competition" and established the Federal Trade Commission (FTC) as an administrative agency to oversee the various laws dealing with business. The agency's powers have since been strengthened by the passage of additional laws.

Since its early days, the FTC has assumed a large workload that continues to grow each year. Under the original act, it had to demonstrate injury to competition before a court would declare a marketing practice unfair. The *Wheeler-Lea Act* (1938), however, amended the Federal Trade Commission Act so as to ban deceptive or unfair business practices per se. At that point, the FTC no longer had to show injury to competition. The Wheeler-Lea Act was designed primarily to protect the consumer by preventing deceptive advertising and sales practices.

Corrective Advertising and Other FTC Remedies

Armed with the Wheeler-Lea requirements, the FTC has assumed an activist role in protecting consumers. For example, it has adopted the concept of **corrective advertising,** under which *companies found to have used deceptive advertising are required to correct their earlier claims with new promotional messages.*[12]

In one case, STP Corporation was fined $500,000 and was required to spend another $200,000 on corrective advertising. The advertisements carried the headline "FTC Notice" and went on to tell about the "$700,000 settlement" and the FTC investigation into "certain allegedly inaccurate advertisements." The ad ran in a variety of publications, among them the *Wall Street Journal,* the *New York Times,* the *Washington Post, Business Week, U.S. News & World Report, Esquire, Guns & Ammo,* and *People.*[13]

The FTC's position in this case was that STP had advertised that its oil treatment would cut oil consumption by 20 percent, but that the company's tests of this feat had been unreliable. The STP board chairman noted that the firm has a policy of backing all advertising

Environmental factors affect consumer expectations of products.

"When it gets in the middle of the tub, this little valve opens, and, presto, you have an oil spill."

Source: Cartoon Features Syndicate.

with valid information and that the tests in question had been conducted some time before.

The FTC has traditionally employed three procedures in carrying out its duties:

1. Conferences with the individuals or industries involved to secure voluntary compliance with its rules

2. The consent method, under which the FTC secures the agreement of the firm or industry to abandon a practice the FTC deems unfair

3. Formal legal action (All FTC decisions can be appealed through the courts.)[14]

Robinson-Patman Act

The *Robinson-Patman Act* (1936) was typical of depression-era legislation. Known in some circles as the Anti-A&P Act, it was inspired by price competition from the developing grocery store chains. In fact, the law was originally prepared by the United States Wholesale Grocers Association. The country was in the midst of the Great Depression, and legislative interest was directed toward saving jobs. The developing chain stores were seen as a threat to traditional retailers and to employment. The Robinson-Patman Act was a government effort to reduce this threat.[15]

Technically an amendment to the Clayton Act, the act prohibited price discrimination that was not based on a cost differential. It also disallowed selling at an unreasonably low price in order to eliminate competition. The Clayton Act had applied only to price discrimination by geographic areas that injured local sellers.[16] The supporting rationale for the Robinson-Patman legislation was that the chain stores might be able to secure discounts from suppliers that were not available to the smaller, independent stores. As one writer expressed it: "The designers of the law, aiming to strengthen the precautionary element in antitrust and to afford greater equality of opportunities, thus gave consideration to the individual competitor as well as to competition in general."[17] The major defenses against charges of price discrimination are that it has been used in an attempt to meet competitors' prices and that it is justified by cost differences.

When a firm asserts that price differentials are used to meet competition in good faith, the logical question is: What constitutes good faith pricing behavior? The answer depends on the circumstances of each situation.

When cost differentials are claimed as a defense, the price differences must not exceed the cost differences resulting from selling to different classes of buyers.[18] A major difficulty of the defense is justifying the differences. Many authorities consider this area one of the most confusing in the Robinson-Patman Act.

The varying interpretations of the act certainly qualify it as one of the vaguest of marketing laws. For the most part, charges brought under the act are handled on a case-by-case basis. Marketers must therefore continually evaluate their pricing actions to avoid potential Robinson-Patman violations.

Unfair Trade Laws

Unfair trade laws are state laws requiring sellers to maintain minimum prices for comparable merchandise. Enacted in the 1930s, these laws were intended to protect small specialty shops, such as dairy stores, from the loss-leader pricing of like products by chain stores. Typically, the retail price floor was set at cost plus some modest markup. While most of these laws remain on the books, they have become less important in the more prosperous years since the 1930s and are seldom enforced.

Removing Barriers to Competition

Fair trade is a concept that affected regulation of competitive activity for decades. In 1931, California became the first state to enact fair trade legislation. Most other states soon followed suit. Only Missouri, the District of Columbia, Vermont, and Texas failed to adopt such laws. *Fair trade laws* permitted manufacturers to stipulate a minimum retail price for a product and to require their retail dealers to sign contracts stating that they would abide by such prices.[19]

The basic argument behind the legislation was that a product's image, implied by its price, was a property right of the manufacturer, who should have the authority to protect the asset by requiring retailers to maintain a minimum price. Fair trade legislation can be traced to lobbying by organizations of independent retailers who feared chain store growth. The economic mania of the Depression years was clearly evident in these statutes.

A U.S. Supreme Court decision holding fair trade contracts illegal in interstate commerce led to passage of the *Miller-Tydings Resale Price Maintenance Act* (1937). This law exempted interstate fair trade contracts from compliance with antitrust requirements. The states were thus authorized to keep these laws on their books if they so desired.

Over the years, fair trade declined in importance as price competition became a more important marketing strategy. The end of these laws occurred on March 11, 1976, when the *Consumer Goods Pricing Act* (1975) went into effect. This act halted all interstate usage of resale price maintenance, an objective long sought by consumer groups.

Regulating Specific Marketing Practices

The first legislation dealing with a specific marketing practice was the *Pure Food and Drug Act* (1906), which prohibited the adulteration and misbranding of foods and drugs in interstate commerce. The bill was enacted because of the unsanitary meat-packing practices of Chicago stockyards. It was strengthened in 1938 by the *Food, Drug, and Cosmetic Act* and in 1962 by the *Kefauver-Harris Drug Amendments* (the latter instigated in response to the thalidomide tragedies).[20] Since that time, the Food and Drug Administration (FDA) has held increased regulatory authority in such matters as product development, branding, and advertising.

Another sphere of marketing's legal environment is the whole gamut of rules governing advertising and labeling. The *Wool Products Labeling Act* of 1939 (requiring that the kind and percentage of each type of wool be identified), the *Fur Products Labeling Act* of 1951 (requiring that the name of the animal from which the fur was derived be identified), and the *Flammable Fabrics Act* of 1953 (prohibiting the interstate sale of flammable fabrics) formed the original legislation in this area.[21] A more recent law—the *Fair Packaging and*

Labeling Act, passed in 1967—requires the disclosure of product identity, the name and address of the manufacturer or distributor, and information concerning the quality of the contents.[22] In 1971, the *Public Health Cigarette Smoking Act* restricted tobacco advertising on radio and television.

The *Truth-in-Lending* law deserves special attention. Formally known as *Title I of the Consumer Credit Protection Act* (1968), the statute requires disclosure of the annual interest rates on loans and credit purchases. The basic premise is that this information will make it easier for consumers to compare sources of credit. Various assessments of the law, however, suggest that many consumers pay relatively little attention to interest rates; furthermore, they often have limited alternative credit sources.

Other laws that may influence marketing practices are the *Fair Credit Reporting Act* and the *National Environmental Policy Act,* both of which became law in 1970. The Fair Credit Reporting Act gives individuals access to credit reports prepared about them and permits them to change information that is incorrect. The National Environmental Policy Act established the Environmental Protection Agency (EPA) and gave it the power to deal with major types of pollution. EPA actions, of course, have a considerable impact on the marketing system.

The *Consumer Product Safety Act* (1972) may have far-reaching effects on marketing strategy and on the environment in which marketers act. This legislation set up the Consumer Product Safety Commission, which has the authority to specify safety standards for most consumer products.

The *Equal Credit Opportunity Act* (1975–1977) banned discrimination in lending practices based on sex, marital status, race, national origin, religion, age, or receipt of payments from a public assistance program. The sex and marital status portions of the act went into effect in 1975, and the remaining portions of the act became effective in 1977.

The *Fair Debt Collection Practices Act* (1978) outlawed harassing, deceptive, or unfair collection practices by debt-collecting agencies. In-house debt collectors such as banks, retailers, and attorneys are exempt, however. Misrepresentation of consumers' legal rights is an example of a specific practice that was banned by the act.[23]

The legal framework for marketing decisions is basically a positive environment in that it attempts to encourage a competitive marketing system employing fair business practices. What marketing's legalistic future will be, of course, is open to debate. It appears, however, that future marketing legislation will be more directly concerned with protecting consumer interests and will probably come from three sources: (1) state and local governments, (2) court decisions, and (3) regulations by administrative agencies such as the FTC and FDA.[24]

PUBLIC NOTICE: DO NOT DRINK THE WATER

Government regulations are often designed to protect the public. One recent example was the Consumer Product Safety Commission's proposal that warning labels be attached to automobile batteries warning consumers not to drink the battery water. The cost of the program was estimated to be $5 million![a]

[a]Source: Al Hooper, "Editor's Notes," *Seattle Business Journal,* December 29, 1980, p. 3.

Some product labeling is unnecessary.

Source: Cartoon Features Syndicate.

ECONOMIC ENVIRONMENT

The **economic environment** is made up of *dynamic business fluctuations that generally follow a four-stage pattern: prosperity, recession, depression, and recovery; as well as other economic conditions such as inflation.* The cosmetics industry provides a good example of how the economic environment affects a firm, and how marketing strategies must be adapted accordingly. Cosmetic sales and profit increases are down as inflation-weary consumers have adopted a more practical attitude toward such purchases. But the industry has had to face an even tougher economic problem. The industry's prime market—15 to 24-year-old women—is expected to decline 1.4 percent annually through the mid-1980s. Cosmetic industry firms have adapted by introducing new, "pragmatic" products, often in the skin care and fragrance categories. These new products are being supported by large advertising budgets. And, in a break with tradition, Gillette has begun mailing samples to promote a new facial scrub. Pricing strategies have also changed. Chesebrough-Pond's has offered refunds in connection with its Prince Matchabelli and Aziza lines. Revlon has used discount coupons for Natural Wonder.[25]

No marketer can disregard the economic climate, since the type, direction, and intensity of a firm's marketing strategy depend on it. In addition, marketers must be aware of the economy's relative position in the business cycle and how it will affect the position of the particular firm.

The type of marketing activity differs with each stage of the business cycle. Consumers are usually more willing to buy during prosperous times than when they feel economically threatened. Marketers must pay close attention to this relative willingness to buy. The aggressiveness of the marketing strategy and tactics often must depend on current buying intentions. For example, more aggressive marketing may be called for in periods of lessened buying interest.

While sales figures show cyclical variations, the successful firm has a rising sales trend line. The line depends on management's ability to foresee, correctly interpret, and reach new market opportunities. Effective forecasting and research are only partial solutions. Equally important is the intuitive awareness of potential markets that requires the ability to correctly delineate opportunities. The life-style concept is an example of where environmental forecasting is critical.

Life-style Concept

Life-style is simply the way people decide to live their lives. It concerns family, job, social activities, and consumer decisions. Changing life-styles are a variable that influences marketing. The increased number of single-person households is an excellent example. This trend has created a demand for single-serving food products, leisure time offerings, and entertainment opportunities. At the same time, it has had a negative impact on life insurance companies and other firms that cater to married households. Life-style decisions have a significant effect on the economic environment for the competitive marketing system.

Inflation

Another economic factor that influences marketing strategy is inflation, which can occur during any stage in the business cycle. **Inflation** is a *rising price level that results in reduced purchasing power for the con-*

sumer. That is, a person's money is devalued in terms of what it can buy. Traditionally, inflation has been more prevalent in foreign countries than in the United States. However, the United States has been experiencing double-digit inflation in recent years. This has led to widespread concern over public policy to stabilize price levels and over ways of adjusting personally to the reduced spending power.

Stagflation describes a peculiar kind of inflation that characterized some of the recent U.S. economic experience. Stagflation occurs when *an economy has high unemployment and a rising price level at the same time.* Marketing strategy is particularly difficult under this circumstance.[26]

Inflation affects marketing by modifying consumer behavior.[27] Modest increases in the general price level (often called creeping inflation) go largely unnoticed—except when current prices are well publicized. People have boycotted meat because of high prices even though food costs have increased far less than many other costs. But as purchasing power continues to decline, consumers become more conscious of inflation. The result is that they also become more price conscious. This consciousness can lead to three possibilities, all of them important to marketers. Consumers can (1) elect to buy now in the belief that prices will be higher later, (2) decide to reallocate their purchasing patterns, or (3) postpone a certain purchase.

The Energy Crisis

The term **energy crisis** refers to *the general realization that energy resources are not limitless.* This realization was first brought on by the 1973–1974 Arab oil embargo. The energy crisis has had a tremendous impact on marketers. Consider the U.S. tire industry, which has had to deal with three energy-related setbacks:

1. Reduced driving, causing a reduction in tire sales
2. Lower new-car sales, reducing the original equipment market (OEM) for tires
3. Increased cost of raw materials, which are petroleum-based[28]

Other markets have faced similar problems. The toy industry, for example, depends on a petroleum derivative, plastic. And the price of some plastics has risen 100 percent over one year.[29]

Certain facts have become evident about the energy crisis. First, this is not the first U.S. energy crisis and probably not the last. In 1872, for instance, a virus hit New England's horse population. About a quarter of the country's 15 million horses—the primary energy source of the day—were afflicted. Transportation lines ceased to operate. Homes were cold, and factories were shut down because there was no way to deliver coal. Trash was not collected. Mail delivery stopped. When the crisis subsided, the nation began to shift to other energy sources.[30]

Second, the energy crisis has forced business and society to rethink their current allocation of energy resources. Existing sources are being expanded, traditional sources (such as coal) are being rediscovered, and new sources are being sought. Perhaps most importantly, attempts are being made to cut waste in energy usage.

Third, the energy crisis has also affected marketing. It has led to a whole assortment of other shortages, including even a once-heralded toilet paper shortage. As various shortages began to appear in crucial industrial areas, marketers were faced with an unusual question: How should limited supplies be allocated to customers whose demands exceeded the quantities available for distribution? At first, many marketers were not prepared to cope with such a situation. But the energy crisis and related shortages have forced marketers to come up with a range of strategy alternatives.[31]

Demarketing: Dealing with Shortages

Shortages—whether temporary or permanent—can be caused by a number of factors. A brisk demand may exceed manufacturing capacity. A lack of raw materials, energy, or labor can bring them on. Regardless of the cause, shortages require marketers to reorient their thinking.[32]

Demarketing is *the process of cutting back consumer demand for a product to a level that can reasonably be supplied by the firm.* Some oil companies, for example, have publicized tips on how to cut gasoline consumption. Many cities have discouraged central business district traffic by raising parking fees and violation penalties.

Shortages also can force marketers to be allocators of limited supplies—a situation that is in sharp contrast to marketing's traditional objective of expanding sales volume. Shortages may require marketers to spread a limited supply over all customers or to back order for some customers when the supply is depleted.

SOCIETAL/ CULTURAL ENVIRONMENT

In 1911, while the Reynolds Tobacco Company was preparing to introduce the country's first mass-marketed cigarette, President Theodore Roosevelt returned from a widely reported trip to Berlin. In honor of the occasion, young Richard S. Reynolds commissioned an artist to design a package for the new product. Reynolds wanted a picture of Germany's Kaiser Wilhelm in full regalia mounted on a white charger. The senior R. J. Reynolds rejected the proposal for Kaiser Wilhelm cigarettes, saying: "I don't think we should name a product after a living man. You can never tell what the damn fool might do." Instead, he chose the name Camels. Introduced in 1913, Camels captured 50 percent of the national market by 1921.[33]

What would have happened to Kaiser Wilhelm cigarettes during the U.S. involvement in World War I is a matter for speculation only. This near disaster illustrates how important a nation's societal/cultural environment can be to marketing decisions.

The **societal/cultural environment** refers to *the marketer's relationship with society and/or its culture.* The societal environment for marketing decisions has both expanded in scope and increased in importance. Today, no marketer can initiate a strategy without taking the societal environment into account—without developing an awareness of the manner in which it affects decisions. PPG Industries, for example, has created a new position of Manager of Public Policy Research to study the changing societal environment's future impact on the corporation.[34]

The cultural environment also has a sizable impact on marketers. The United States is a mixed society composed of varied submarkets. These market segments can be classified by age, race, place of residence, sex, and numerous other determinants. All can influence marketing strategy. Consider the following examples:

- Black consumers are now recognized as a distinct market. This market is particularly important in urban centers, where the bulk of the black population and its buying power is concentrated.

- The feminist movement has had a decided effect on marketing, particularly on promotion. Television commercials, for example, now feature women in career-oriented as well as traditional roles.

- Hispanics are the nation's second largest minority. The Spanish-speaking population of the United States is now the fifth greatest in the world. Recently, Donnelly Marketing's "Carol Wright" discount coupon program was used to reach the market: one in which media selection has always been a problem because of its diversity.[35]

The societal/cultural environment is constantly changing. What is taboo today may be tomorrow's greatest market opportunity. Consider the case of Kleenex. At one time, the Puritan ethic ingrained in U.S. society prohibited wastefulness. But Kimberly-Clark was able to show consumers the value of disposability, and Kleenex was launched.[36] Marketers must be ever alert to changing environmental conditions that can provide the markets of tomorrow.

SUMMARY

The four specific environments for marketing decisions are competitive, legal, economic, and societal/cultural. These four are important to the study of marketing because they provide a framework within which marketing strategies are formulated. They are among the most dynamic aspects of contemporary business.

The competitive environment is the interactive process that occurs in the marketplace. A firm's marketing decisions influence the market and are in turn affected by competitors' strategies. The legal environment attempts to maintain competition as well as regulate specific marketing practices. The economic environment often influences the manner in which consumers will behave toward marketing appeals. Inflation, stagflation, the energy crisis, and the business cycle are some of the economic factors impacting marketing. The societal/cultural environment may become the most important to marketers as the matter of adapting to a changing society or cultural environment advances to the forefront of marketing thought.

QUESTIONS FOR DISCUSSION

1. Explain the following terms:
   competitive environment   stagflation
   legal environment   energy crisis
   corrective advertising   demarketing
   economic environment   societal/cultural environment
   inflation

2. List and briefly describe the four segments of the environment for marketing decisions.

3. Comment on the following statement: The dynamic nature of the contemporary business environment puts pressure on all levels of management to continually reevaluate marketing decisions.

4. Explain the relationship between the general public and the competitive marketing system.

5. Discuss the competitive environment for an industry in your area.

6. Trace the FTC's evolution into a watchdog of marketing practices. Evaluate its success.

7. How did the Great Depression influence marketing legislation?

8. Identify and evaluate the major defenses to the Robinson-Patman Act.

9. Some people argue that inflation can be moderated only by mandatory wage and price controls. Comment on this issue. Defend your position with specific arguments for or against wage and price controls.

10. The Federal Trade Commission now requires more appliances to carry labels about their energy efficiency. Do you support this action? What are the advantages and disadvantages of such an effort?

11. Comment on the following statement: The legal framework for marketing decisions is basically a positive one.

12. How does inflation affect marketing activity?

13. Discuss the following statement: Marketing is becoming an activist business function since it is influencing the societal environment by contributing its tremendous ability to reach its potential markets.

14. Assess how the recent federal budget and tax cuts have affected marketing.

15. Research the most important state and local consumer protection regulations in your area. Discuss whether this legislation is accomplishing its original objectives.

16. In your opinion, are the benefits of government regulation of marketing activities worth the cost? Are there any factors that would cause you to change your opinion?

17. Would a gas station that sold gasoline to a city's police department for two cents per gallon less than to its customers be in violation of the Robinson-Patman Act? Explain.

18. In post–World War I Germany, the exchange rate was 4.2 trillion marks to a U.S. dollar. While recent U.S. double-digit inflation did not come close to Germany's earlier experience, many people in the United States did adjust their consumer behavior. Identify some of the steps they took to cope with inflation. Explain the role of the marketer during periods of rapid inflation.

19. How does one shop for credit? What role does the Truth-in-Lending Act play in the search?

20. Comment on the viewpoint expressed by former Procter & Gamble's board chairman, Edward G. Harness: "I have no quarrel with the citizenry, the bureaucrats, the legislators or the educators who say that corporations have a responsibility to society beyond the obligation to generate a fair return or profit for the investor. . . .

    However, I take real issue with the critics when they propose that corporations must put their other citizenship responsibilities ahead of their responsibility to earn a fair return for the owners. The only way in which corporations can carry their huge and increasing burden of obligations to society is for them to earn satisfactory profits. If we cannot earn a return on equity investment which is more attractive than other forms of investment, we die. I am not aware of any bankrupt corporations which are making important social contributions."[37]

NOTES

1. Nicole Mindt, "Rabbit Fanciers Jump in with High Nutritional Facts," *Seattle Times,* June 17, 1981. Reprinted with permission.

2. The importance of environmental factors is noted in a variety of articles. See, for example, R. F. Magill, "A Prescription for Survival in a Regulated World," *Business Horizons,* February 1980, pp. 75–81; and Michael E. Porter, "How Competitive Forces Shape Strategy," *Harvard Business Review,* March–April 1979, pp. 137–45.

3. The Corfam story is told in Lee Smith, "A Miracle in Search of a Market," *FORTUNE,* December 1, 1980, p. 92; and Fred Danzig, "Du Pont's Corfam: What Went Wrong," *Advertising Age,* April 5, 1971, pp. 6–7.

4. Peter Behr, "Ford Struggling up from Auto Industry's Collapse," *Washington Post,* June 6, 1981. © 1981 The Washington Post.

5. "Scott Paper Fights Back, at Last," *Business Week,* February 16, 1981, pp. 104, 108.

6. "When Marketing Failed at Texas Instruments," *Business Week,* June 22, 1981, p. 91.

7. *Ibid.,* p. 92.

8. Jacques Neher, "Lost at Sea," *Advertising Age,* April 20, 1981, p. 49. Copyright 1981 by Crain Communications, Inc. Reprinted with permission.

9. An excellent reference source on the legal environment of marketing is Joe L. Welch, *Marketing Law* (Tulsa, Okla.: PPC Books, 1980). See also "Interventionist Government Came to Stay," *Business Week,* September 3, 1979, pp. 39–41, 43.

10. Antitrust legislation is reviewed in Welch, *Marketing Law,* pp. 3–6.

11. Robert E. Taylor and Stan Crock, "Reagan Team Believes Antitrust Legislation Hurts Big Business," *Wall Street Journal,* July 8, 1981. Reprinted by permission of *The Wall Street Journal,* © Dow Jones & Company, Inc. All Rights Reserved.

12. Corrective advertising is examined in Richard W. Mizerski, Neil K. Allison, and Stephen Calvert, "A Controlled Field Study of Corrective Advertising Using Multiple Exposure and a Commercial Medium," *Journal of Marketing Research,* August 1980, pp. 341–48; Thomas C. Kinnear and James R. Taylor, "Corrective Advertising: An Empirical Tracking of Residual Effects," Richard P. Bagozzi, Kenneth L. Bernhardt, Paul S. Busch, David W. Cravens, Joseph F. Hair, Jr., and

Carol A. Scott, *Marketing in the 1980s: Changes and Challenges* (Chicago: American Marketing Association, 1980), pp. 416–19; and Gary M. Armstrong and Metin N. Gurol, "The Effects of Corrective Advertising on Company and FTC Images," Venkatakrishna V. Bellur, ed., *Developments in Marketing Science* vol. 4 (Marquette, Mich.: Academy of Marketing Science, 1981).

13. "Corrective Ads for STP Publicize Settlement Costs to Business Execs," *Advertising Age,* February 13, 1978, p. 1, 106

14. These methods are discussed in Vernon A. Mund, *Government and Business* (New York: Harper & Row, 1960), pp. 294–99.

15. The Robinson-Patman Act provisions have been the subject of considerable discussion in the marketing literature. A recent example is Joseph F. Moffatt, "The Legal Barrier in the Development of Distribution, Marketing, and Business Science," in *Proceedings of the Southwestern Marketing Association,* eds. Robert H. Ross, Frederic B. Kraft, and Charles H. Davis, Wichita, Kans., 1981, pp. 55–57.

16. See Lawrence X. Tarpey, "Buyer Liability under the Robinson-Patman Act: A Current Appraisal," *Journal of Marketing,* January 1972, pp. 38–42.

17. Marshall C. Howard, *Legal Aspects of Marketing* (New York: McGraw-Hill, 1962), p. 8.

18. Robert A. Lynn, "Is the Cost Defense Workable," *Journal of Marketing,* January 1965, pp. 37–42. It has been pointed out that logistics cost evidence is the best justification under the Robinson-Patman Act. See J. L. Heskett, Robert M. Ivie, and Nicholas A. Glaskowsky, Jr., *Business Logistics* (New York: Ronald Press, 1964), p. 235.

19. The fair trade concept is reviewed in L. Louise Luchsinger and Patrick M. Dunne, "Fair Trade Laws—How Fair?" *Journal of Marketing,* January 1978, pp. 50–54.

20. The Kefauver-Harris legislation is discussed in Paul Hugajab and George Tesar, "Some Issues in the Federal Regulation of Advertising," in *Proceedings of the Southwestern Marketing Association,* eds. John Swan and Robert C. Haring, Dallas, Texas, March 1978, p. 56.

21. Marshall C. Howard, "Textile and Fur Labeling Legislation: Names, Competition, and the Consumer," *California Management Review,* Winter 1971, pp. 69–80.

22. Dik Warren Twedt, "What Effect Will the 'Fair Packaging and Labeling Act' Have on Marketing Practices?" *Journal of Marketing,* April 1977, pp. 58–59. See also David M. Gardner, "The Package, Legislation, and the Shopper," *Business Horizons,* October 1968, pp. 53–58; and Warren A. French and Leila O. Shroeder, "Package Information Legislation: Trends and Viewpoints," *MSU Business Topics,* Summer 1972, pp. 39–44.

23. For information about the Equal Credit Opportunity Act, see John R. Nevin and Gilbert A. Churchill, Jr., "The Equal Credit Opportunity Act: An Evaluation," *Journal of Marketing,* Spring 1979, pp. 95–104; for information about the Fair Debt Collection Practices Act, see Richard A. Ryan, "Limits Put on Debt Collection," *Detroit News,* September 21, 1977.

24. An interesting discussion appears in Bernard A. Morin and Thomas L. Wheelan, "Status Report on Consumer Protection at the State Level," in *Contemporary Marketing Thought: 1977 Educators' Proceedings,* eds. Barnett A. Greenberg and Danny W. Bellenger (Chicago: American Marketing Association, 1977), p. 534.

25. Gail Bronson, "Cosmetic Firms, Beset by Stagnation, Put on New Face to Lift Sales," *Wall Street Journal,* June 23, 1981. Reprinted by permission of *The Wall Street Journal,* © Dow Jones & Company, Inc., 1981. All Rights Reserved.

26. Avraham Shama's research on the impact of stagflation on consumers is discussed in "Middle Class Suffers the Most from 'Stagflation'," *Marketing News,* October 5, 1979, pp. 1, 16.

27. This issue is explored in Zoher E. Shipchandler, "Inflation and Life Styles: The Marketing Impact," *Business Horizons,* February 1976, pp. 90–96.

28. Ralph E. Winter, "Tire Industry Drops into Deep Recession; Gasoline Shortage, Rising Costs Take Toll," *Wall Street Journal,* October 10, 1979.

29. Ruth Youngblood, "Oil Crunch Spells Trouble—Even in Toyland," *Detroit News,* November 23, 1979.

30. The 1872 energy crisis is described in Jan Scherer, "Energy Crunch—1872," *PEN,* June 1974, pp. 21–22.

31. Interesting discussions appear in Keith K. Cox, "Marketing in the 1980s—Back to Basics," *Business,* May-June 1980, pp. 19–23; and James R. Stock and Douglas M. Lambert, "Business, Make Room for the Energy Executive," *Business,* November-December 1980, pp. 27–30.

32. Classical articles on this subject include Philip Kotler and Sidney J. Levy, "Demarketing, Yes, Demarketing," *Harvard Business Review,* November-December 1971, pp. 74–80; and Philip Kotler, "Marketing during Periods of Shortages," *Journal of Marketing,* July 1974, pp. 20–29.

33. See "The Reynolds Saga: The Sweet with the Bitter," *Forbes,* December 1, 1971, p. 32.

34. "Capitalizing on Social Change," *Business Week,* October 29, 1979, pp. 105–6.
35. "Donnelly to Mail Spanish-Language Coupons to Two Million Upscale Hispanic Households," *Marketing News,* February 20, 1981, pp. 1, 10.
36. The Kleenex story is told in Ronald D. Michman, "Culture as a Marketing Tool," *Marquette Business Review,* Winter 1975, pp. 177–84.
37. "Views on Corporate Responsibility," excerpts from a talk to Procter & Gamble management on December 8, 1977, by Edward G. Harness, Chairman of the Board, p. 6. Reprinted by permission.

PART TWO

IDENTIFYING CONSUMER NEEDS

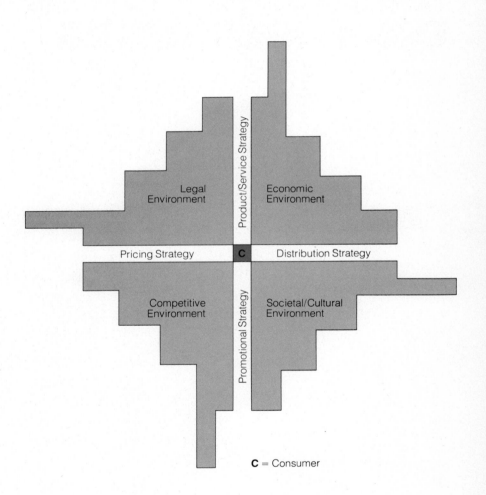

Legal Environment

Economic Environment

Product/Service Strategy

Pricing Strategy

C

Distribution Strategy

Competitive Environment

Societal/Cultural Environment

Promotional Strategy

C = Consumer

CHAPTER 3

MARKETING PLANNING AND FORECASTING

KEY TERMS

planning
marketing planning
strategic planning
tactical planning
conglomerate
concentric diversification
strategic business unit (SBU)
BCG growth-share matrix
market share
experience curve
PERT
undifferentiated marketing
differentiated marketing
concentrated marketing
sales forecasting
gross national product
marketing audit

LEARNING GOALS

1. To differentiate the various types of planning
2. To outline the steps in the planning process
3. To explain the portfolio approach and the BCG matrix approach to marketing planning
4. To compare the three basic strategies for matching markets with product offerings
5. To list the steps involved in sales forecasting
6. To discuss how the marketing audit can assist marketing planning

Pepsi-Cola hits the spot.
Twelve full ounces, that's a lot.
Twice as much for a nickel too,
Pepsi-Cola is the drink for you.

That was the jingle Pepsi-Cola used to promote the reduction of its per-bottle price from 10 cents to 5 cents. It was Pepsi's first major attack on Coca-Cola. The year? 1940! Although the advertisement proved to be very popular, the Atlanta-based Coca-Cola Company still outsold its rival 5 to 1 seventeen years later. Today, Coca-Cola continues to command a huge margin over Pepsi in vending machine sales, and a 3 to 1 sales lead at soda fountains. But Pepsi-Cola has moved slightly ahead in the crucial food store trade.

The competitive strategies of these two firms depend on a substantial planning effort. Much of Pepsi's recent growth can be attributed to the "Pepsi Challenge," an advertising campaign that uses taste tests of the two products. The campaign was first used in Dallas-Fort Worth in 1975, and has been used in selected regional markets ever since. Pepsi-Cola limits the "challenge" to markets in which it trails Coca-Cola by a substantial margin. In some of these markets, the campaign was credited with doubling Pepsi sales.

The Coca-Cola Company's planners faced several problems. First, the growth of soft-drink sales had slowed in recent years owing to higher retail prices and an aging population. So Coca-Cola and Pepsi were fighting for a share of a relatively stable market. Second, there was considerable conflict in the distribution channel. The firm's bottlers complained of neglect from the Atlanta headquarters. And third, there was the Pepsi Challenge.

Coca-Cola Company management took decisive action to remedy these problems. The firm has diversified in recent years in both soft drinks and other product lines. Bottler complaints were resolved by decentralizing the company's executive hierarchy. Field sales personnel were authorized to make more decisions on the spot. Only the Pepsi Challenge remained. Coca-Cola Company's initial response was to flood the advertising media with commercials criticizing Pepsi taste tests. Then the "Have a Coke and a Smile" theme was used. One commercial featuring Mean Joe Greene of the Pittsburgh Steelers getting a Coke from a young admirer was particularly well received.[1] The Pepsi and Coke strategies are excellent examples of how firms can use planning to deal with the competitive marketplace of the 1980s.

A DEFINITION OF PLANNING

"Should we grant a license for our new liquid-crystal watch display to a Japanese firm or simply export our models to Japan?"

"Will changing the performance time and date affect concert attendance?"

History of Pepsi-Cola Trademark

Source: Courtesy of PepsiCo, Inc.

"Should we utilize company sales personnel or independent agents in the new territory?"

"Should discounts be offered to cash customers? What impact would such a policy have on our credit customers?"

These questions are examples of thousands of both major and minor decisions that regularly face marketing managers. Continual changes in the marketplace—resulting from changing consumer expectations, competitive actions, economic trends, and political and legal changes, as well as such developments as product innovations or pressures from distribution channel members—are likely to have substantial impact on the operations of any organization. Although changes are often beyond the control of the marketing manager, effective planning can anticipate change and redirect the action. Effective planning often makes the difference between success or failure.

Planning is *the process of anticipating the future and determining the courses of action to achieve organizational objectives.* A continuous process, planning includes the specification of objectives and the actions required to achieve them. The planning process results in the creation of a blueprint that not only specifies the means of achieving organizational objectives, but also includes checkpoints where actual performance can be compared with expectations to determine whether the organizational activities are moving the organization in the direction of its objectives.

Marketing planning, *the implementation of planning activities as they relate to the achievement of marketing objectives,* is the basis for all marketing strategies. Product line, pricing decisions, selection of distribution channels, and decisions on promotional campaigns all depend on the plans formulated in the marketing organization.[2]

THE MARKETING PLANS OF CADILLAC, K MART, AND WOLVERINE WORLD WIDE

Marketing plans are often lengthy and very detailed. Still others can be relatively brief and to the point. Capsule summaries of some marketing plans follow:

Cadillac Division of General Motors

- Maintain the existing customer with traditional Cadillac models.
- Target the smaller Cimarron at the wealthy 35-year-old group who has been buying the BMW 320 and the Audi 5000.

K mart

- Use low prices on commodity-type items to attract customers who may also buy merchandise with higher margins.
- Reach a larger proportion of the urban market by locating stores within 3 miles of each other, rather than the former strategy of 10 miles.

Wolverine World Wide

▪ Update and expand both women's and men's lines of Hush Puppies so as to appeal to a younger age group.

▪ Sell about 60 percent of its pigskin tanning output to other shoe companies.

Sources: Leonard M. Apcar, "Cadillac Marketers Hope Usual Buyers Won't Like New Car," *Wall Street Journal,* April 30, 1980, Reprinted by permission of *The Wall Street Journal,* © Dow Jones & Company, Inc. 1980. All Rights Reserved; "Where K mart Goes Next Now That It's No. 2," *Business Week,* June 2, 1980, pp. 109–10, 114; and Linda Snyder Hayes, "Hush Puppies Roar Again," *FORTUNE,* July 14, 1980, pp. 143–44. © 1980 Time, Inc. All Rights Reserved.

STRATEGIC PLANNING VERSUS TACTICAL PLANNING

Planning is often classified on the basis of scope or breadth. Some plans are quite broad and long-range, focusing on major organizational objectives significant over a period of five or more years. Such plans are typically called strategic plans. **Strategic planning** can be defined as *the process of determining the primary objectives of an organization and the adoption of courses of action and the allocation of resources necessary to achieve those objectives.*[3] Coca-Cola's efforts at diversification would represent strategic planning.

W. R. Grace provides an excellent example of strategic planning. Few companies have experienced the changes in their business mix that W. R. Grace and Company has been through since 1950. At that time Grace was essentially a steamship line operating in Latin America. Today it is a diversified multinational corporation with substantial investments in natural resource industries and consumer products and services; it also ranks fifth among U.S. chemical companies. The repositioning of W. R. Grace is shown in Table 3.1.[4]

The word *strategy* is derived from a Greek term meaning "the general's art." Strategic planning has a critical impact on the destiny of the organization since it provides long-run direction for decision makers. By contrast, **tactical planning** focuses on *the implementation of those activities specified by the strategic plans.* Tactical plans are typically more short-term than strategic plans, focusing more on current and near-term activities needed to implement overall strategies. Resource allocation is a common decision area for tactical planning.

TABLE 3.1
W. R. Grace & Company's Composition of Operating Capital (in Millions)

Industry	1950	1979
Chemicals	$ 5	$1,245
Oil, gas, and coal	—	446
Consumer products and services	—	1,095
Steamship (Grace Line) and other businesses	121	22

Source: Adapted by permission from W. R. Grace & Company, *A Management Perspective* (New York: W. R. Grace & Company, 1976), p. 4.

TABLE 3.2
Types of Plans
Prepared by
Different Levels of
Management

Management Level	Type of Plan	General Content
Top board of directors, president, operating division vice presidents including marketing	strategic planning	objectives of organization fundamental strategies total budget
Middle general sales manager, marketing research director, head of advertising department	tactical planning	quarterly and semiannual plans; subdivision of budgets; policies and procedures for each individual's department
Supervisory district sales manager, supervisors	tactical planning derived from planning at higher organizational levels	daily and weekly plans unit budgets

Source: Adapted from William F. Glueck, *Management,* 2nd ed. (Hinsdale, Ill.: The Dryden Press, 1980), p. 246. Copyright © 1980 by The Dryden Press, A division of Holt, Rinehart and Winston, Publishers. Reprinted by permission of Holt, Rinehart and Winston, CBS College Publishing.

Coke's efforts to counter the Pepsi Challenge were the result of tactical planning.

PLANNING AT DIFFERENT LEVELS IN THE ORGANIZATION

Planning is a major managerial responsibility. Although all managers devote some of their workday to planning, the relative proportion of time spent in planning activities and the type of planning vary at different levels within an organization.

Top management of a corporation—the board of directors, president, and functional vice presidents such as the chief marketing officer—spends greater proportions of their time engaged in planning than do middle- and supervisory-level managers. For example, J. Thomas Schanck, president of Signode Corporation, feels that 30 to 50 percent of a chief executive's time should be spent on strategic planning.[5] Also, top management is more likely to devote more of its planning activities to longer-range strategic planning, while middle-level managers (such as the director of the advertising department, regional sales managers, or the physical distribution manager) tend to focus on narrower, tactical plans for their departments, and supervisory management is more likely to engage in developing specific programs designed to meet goals for their responsibility areas. Table 3.2 indicates the types of planning engaged in at the various organizational levels.

Although organizational structures vary, many firms attempt to integrate strategic planning throughout the organization. Honey-

**FIGURE 3.1
Steps in the Planning
Sequence**

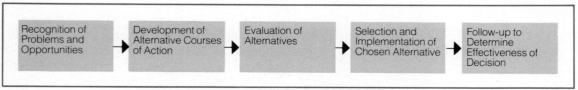

well's structure illustrates such an attempt. At Honeywell, all levels
of the organization play a prescribed role in the strategic planning
process. Top management specifies the restraints to be applied in
meeting overall corporate objectives. Lower levels of management
are then responsible for identifying suitable options within these constraints.[6]

STEPS IN THE PLANNING PROCESS

All planning, including marketing planning, follows the same general
sequence. The steps in the planning process are shown in Figure 3.1.

Planning initially involves recognition of the problems and opportunities in any situation. An analysis of sales data, for example,
may indicate that a certain market segment is not being served by
the company. Next, alternative courses of action must be developed.
Perhaps an existing product can be adapted to the needs of an unful-
filled consumer segment, or a new product can be developed. Once
an alternative has been selected, a plan must be chosen to implement
it. Finally, the planning should include some evaluation and feedback
mechanism to assess the effectiveness of the decisions. All planning
involves these basic steps in some fashion.[7]

THE EVOLUTION OF STRATEGIC PLANNING

Strategic planning has gone through several eras: conglomerates (1960s),
internal growth (1970s), and concentric diversification (1980s). During
the 1960s strategic planning meant essentially investment or acquisitions planning. **Conglomerates,** or *firms with unrelated multiple businesses,* dominated the private sector. Diversification into unrelated
businesses was viewed as a hedge against setbacks in the marketplace.
One conglomerate acquired over 350 separate businesses in a single
year.[8]

When many of these conglomerates failed to live up to expectations, the strategic planning emphasis switched. The 1970s were characterized by concentration in internal business opportunities. Acquisitions were considered only if they provided necessary resources as related economies to the proposed parent.

The 1980s are characterized by strategic planning designed to obtain integrated growth. Acquisitions are again popular, but the emphasis is on firms that can be easily integrated into the existing organization. Philip Kotler calls this strategy **concentric diversification,** *". . .the company's seeking to add new products that have technological and/or marketing synergies with the existing product line; these products normally will appeal to new classes of customers."* [9] Philip Morris's acquisition of Miller Brewing Company fits the definition of concentric diversification. Cigarettes and beer are sold through the same type of distribution structure and to a very similar marketplace. Philip Morris was able to utilize its experience in consumer marketing and move Miller from a distant seventh-place ranking to a strong second place behind Busch within a six-year period.

THE PORTFOLIO APPROACH TO MARKETING PLANNING

General Electric has made a number of major contributions to the concept of strategic planning. GE, often labeled the world's most diversified company, decided in 1971 to reorganize its nine product groups and 48 divisions into a *"portfolio"* of businesses labeled **strategic business units** (SBUs). Various GE applicances used in food preparation previously had been scattered throughout three separate divisions; now they are merged into a housewares SBU.

The GE reorganization forced the firm's personnel to focus on customer needs rather than on internal divisions. The SBU concept was quickly adopted by such major firms as Union Carbide, Boise Cascade, and International Paper. Although such early experimenters as General Foods have already returned to traditional organizational structures, the SBU concept is estimated to be utilized currently in 20 percent of the largest manufacturing corporations in the United States.[10]

In 1970, General Electric underwent a major reorganization by separating planning- and policy-oriented activity from administration. GE is regarded as having one of the best long-range planning functions in the United States.[11]

THE BCG MATRIX

The work of the Boston Consulting Group (BCG) is widely known in industry. BCG has developed a four-quadrant matrix that is also useful in understanding the strategic planning-marketing strategy interface.[12] BCG states that all of a firm's various businesses can be placed in one

FIGURE 3.2
The Growth-Share
Matrix

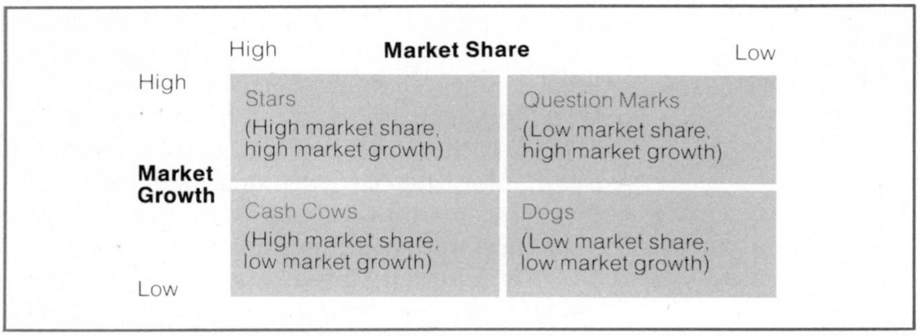

	High	Market Share	Low
High	Stars (High market share, high market growth)		Question Marks (Low market share, high market growth)
Market Growth			
	Cash Cows (High market share, low market growth)		Dogs (Low market share, low market growth)
Low			

Source: "The Product Portfolio," Perspectives No. 66, The Boston Consulting Group, Inc., 1970. Reprinted by permission.

of four quadrants, each with a unique marketing strategy. The BCG matrix is shown in Figure 3.2.

The **BCG growth–share matrix** plots *market share, the percentage of a market controlled by a firm against market growth potential.* The resulting quadrants are labeled "cash cows," "stars," "dogs," and "question marks." Marketers employ varying strategies for each category of business.

Cash Cows (high market share, low market growth): Marketers would want to maintain this status for as long as possible since these businesses are producing a strong cash flow, which BCG considers to be the basic objective of the firm.

Stars (high market share, high market growth): These businesses show potential for high sales and profits, but marketers must invest heavily in stars to maintain them. Stars often produce a negative cash flow.

Dogs (low market share, low market growth): Marketers minimize their positions in these businesses, withdrawing if possible. Cash should be pulled out of these enterprises as quickly as possible.

Question Marks (low market share, high market growth): These situations require that marketers make a basic go/no go decision. Question marks should be converted to stars, or the firm should pull out of these markets.

The BCG matrix highlights the importance of creating a mix that positions the firm to its best advantage. This matrix is largely the result of the firm's pioneering work with the experience curve.[13] BCG says that the highest market-share competitor will have a cost advantage over others because of the experience curve. First identified in 1966, the **experience curve** indicates that *higher market shares reduce costs because of factors like learning advantages, increased specialization, higher investment, and economies of scale.* BCG says that doubling the experience factor will cut product costs by 25 to 30 percent. The consultants suggest that market share is a better measure of performance than is profitability.[14]

FIGURE 3.3
PERT Network of the
Porta-Vac Project

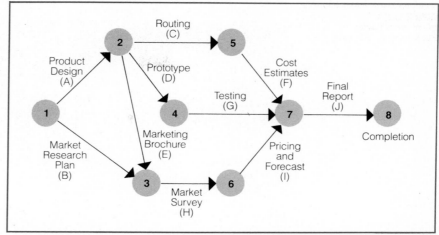

PERT: A SPECIAL TECHNIQUE IN PLANNING

PERT (*P*rogram *E*valuation and *R*eview *T*echnique) is *a commonly used planning technique for creating a marketing strategy.* Originally developed for defense projects, PERT is now applied to a variety of industries to minimize project completion time. The objective is to establish the most efficient sequence for work to be performed.

Consider the following illustration. The H. S. Daugherty Company is considering the introduction of Porta-Vac, a cordless vacuum cleaner powered by a rechargeable battery.[15] Daugherty management has initiated a feasibility study to evaluate Porta-Vac: it wants the study to indicate the action that should be taken with respect to the product. Figure 3.3 offers a PERT diagram for the project. The diagram shows the activities that must be accomplished in order to complete the overall project. For instance, the market research plan (B) and the marketing brochure (E) must precede the market survey (H).

ALTERNATIVE MARKETING STRATEGIES

Much of the strategic planning effort is dedicated to the development of marketing strategies that best match product offerings to customer needs. A successful match is vital to the market success of the firm.

Three basic strategies for achieving consumer satisfaction are available. *Firms that produce only one product and market it to all customers with a single marketing mix* practice **undifferentiated marketing.**[16] *Those that produce numerous products with different marketing mixes designed to satisfy smaller market segments* practice **differentiated marketing.** *Firms that concentrate all marketing re-*

FIGURE 3.4
Three Alternative
Marketing Strategies

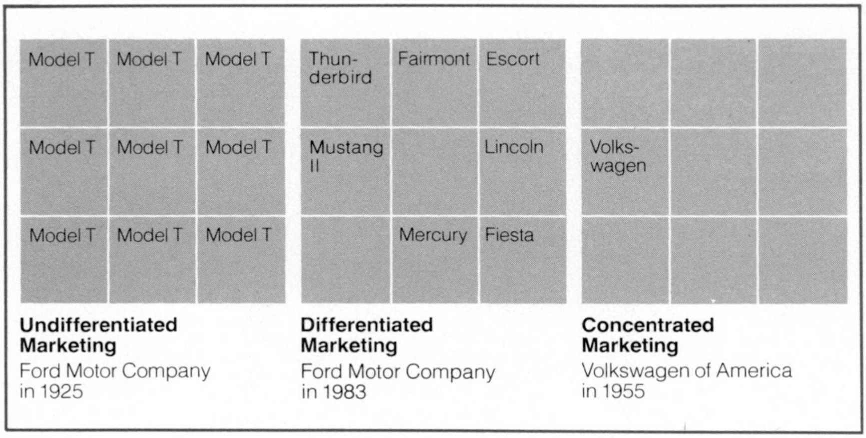

Model T	Model T	Model T	Thun- derbird	Fairmont	Escort			
Model T	Model T	Model T	Mustang II		Lincoln	Volks- wagen		
Model T	Model T	Model T		Mercury	Fiesta			

Undifferentiated Marketing	**Differentiated Marketing**	**Concentrated Marketing**
Ford Motor Company in 1925	Ford Motor Company in 1983	Volkswagen of America in 1955

sources on a small segment of the total market practice **concentrated marketing.** These product marketing strategies are illustrated in Figure 3.4.

UNDIFFERENTIATED MARKETING

The policy of undifferentiated marketing was much more common in the past than it is today. Henry Ford built the Model T and sold it for one price to everyone. He agreed to paint the car "any color they want, as long as it is black."

Although marketing managers recognize the existence of numerous segments in the total market, they tend to ignore minor differences and focus on the broad market using mass advertising, mass distribution, and broad themes. One benefit of undifferentiated marketing is the efficiency involved in longer production runs. Undifferentiated marketing enabled Ford to mass-produce and market a simple, well-designed product. It also minimized inventories, since neither Ford nor its dealers had to contend with optional equipment and numerous color combinations.

However, undifferentiated marketing has inherent dangers. A firm that attempts to satisfy *everyone* in the market faces the threat of competitors who sell specialized products to smaller market segments and can better satisfy each of those segments. Firms using a strategy of differentiated marketing or concentrated marketing may enter the market and capture sufficient small segments to make the strategy of undifferentiated marketing unworkable.

A firm using undifferentiated marketing may also encounter problems in foreign markets. Campbell Soup Company suffered heavy losses when it attempted to market tomato soup in the United Kingdom before discovering that the British prefer a more bitter taste. Another U.S. firm, Corn Products Company, discovered real differences in American and European soup preferences when it failed in an attempt to market Knorr dry soups in the United States. Although Europeans regularly purchase dry soups, American homemakers prefer liquid soup because of the shorter cooking time required.

DIFFERENTIATED MARKETING

When a company employs **differentiated marketing,** it *attempts to satisfy a large part of the total market by marketing a number of products designed to appeal to individual parts of the total market.* As Figure 3.5 indicates, Ford now offers Fairmonts, Mustangs, Lincolns, Fiestas, and Escorts to various segments of the new-car market. The firm's objective is to produce higher total sales and to develop more product loyalty in each of the submarkets. Firms use a marketing mix designed to serve the needs of each market target, rather than attempt to sell just one product to everyone.

Most firms practice differentiated marketing. Procter & Gamble markets Bold, Bonus, Cheer, Dash, Duz, Gain, Oxydol, Tide, and other detergents to meet the desires of detergent buyers. Lever Brothers offers two brands of complexion soap, Dove and Lux, and two brands of deodorant soap, Lifebuoy and Phase III.

By increasing satisfaction in each of numerous market targets, the company with a differentiated marketing strategy can achieve higher sales than are possible with undifferentiated marketing. But the costs of differentiated marketing strategy are also greater, because additional products mean shorter production runs and increased setup time. Inventory costs rise due to added space needs for the products and increases in necessary recordkeeping. Promotional costs also increase as unique promotional mixes are developed for each market segment.

Even though differentiated marketing strategy is more costly, consumers are usually better served. Also, a firm wishing to employ a single marketing strategy for an entire market may be forced to choose a strategy of differentiated marketing instead. If competitors appeal to each market in the total market, the firm must also use this approach to remain competitive.

CONCENTRATED MARKETING

A firm may also choose **concentrated marketing**—*focusing its marketing efforts on profitably satisfying a smaller market target.* Concentrated marketing is particularly appealing to new, small firms that lack the financial resources of their competitors.

The most famous example of a firm practicing the concentrated marketing strategy is Volkswagen of America. For twenty years, the Volkswagen beetle was symbolic of a product specifically designed and marketed to buyers wanting economy and practical performance. Similarly, Rolls-Royce is famous throughout the world for producing and marketing the ultimate in expensive, luxury automobiles.

Concentration on a limited market segment often allows a firm to maintain a profitable operation. Fisher-Price has developed an enviable image in the toy industry because of its reputation as a high-quality manufacturer and marketer of children's toys.

Concentrated marketing also poses some dangers. Since the firm's growth is tied to a particular market segment, changes in the size of the segment or in customers' buying patterns may hurt sales volume. Sales may also drop if new competitors appeal to the same segment.

CHOOSING A STRATEGY

Although most business firms adopt the strategy of differentiated marketing, there is no single best strategy. Any of the three alternatives may prove to be best in a particular situation. The basic determinants in the decision are company resources, product homogeneity, stage in the product life cycle, and competitors' strategies.

A concentrated marketing strategy may be a necessity for a firm with limited resources. Small firms, for example, may be forced to choose small market targets because of limitations in financing, size of sales force, and promotional budgets.

On the other hand, an undifferentiated marketing strategy should be used for products perceived by consumers as relatively homogeneous. Marketers of grain sell their products on the basis of standardized grades rather than individual brand names. Some petroleum companies use a strategy of undifferentiated marketing in distributing their gasoline to the mass market.

The firm's strategy may also change as the product progresses through the various stages of its life cycle. During the introduction and growth stages, an undifferentiated marketing strategy may be useful as the firm attempts to develop initial demand for the product. In the later stages, competitive pressures may result in modified products and marketing strategies aimed at smaller segments of the total market.

A final factor affecting the choice of a product marketing strategy is the strategies used by competitors. A firm may find it difficult to use an undifferentiated marketing strategy if its competitors are actively cultivating smaller segments. Competition usually forces each firm to adopt the differentiated marketing strategy.[17]

SALES FORECASTING

A vital aspect of marketing planning is **sales forecasting,** *the estimate of company sales for a specified future period.* In addition to its use in marketing planning, the sales forecast also plays an instrumental role in production scheduling, financial planning, inventory planning and procurement, and in determining personnel needs. An inaccurate forecast may result in poor decisions in these areas. The sales forecast is also an important tool for marketing control because it produces standards against which actual performance can be measured. Without such standards, no comparisons can be made.

Sales forecasts are either short-run or long-run. Short-run forecasts usually involve a period of one year or less, while long-run forecasts typically cover a longer period. Since both forecasts are devel-

The computer plays a vital role in forecasting.

"I get depressed thinking of all the data out there, much of it yearning to be processed."

Source: *Playboy,* September 1977. Reproduced by special permission of PLAYBOY Magazine; copyright © 1977 by Playboy.

oped in basically the same manner, and since more firms forecast sales for the coming year, short-run forecasting will be discussed here.

TYPES OF FORECASTING METHODS

Although forecasters utilize dozens of techniques of divining the future (ranging from complex computer simulations to crystal-ball gazing by professional futurists), two broad categories exist.[18] *Quantitative* forecasting methods utilize such statistical techniques as trend extensions based upon past data; computer simulation; and econometrics. *Qualitative* forecasting techniques are more subjective in nature. They include surveys of consumer attitudes and intentions; estimates by the field sales force; and predictions of key executives in the firm and in the industry. Since each method has advantages, most organizations utilize both in their attempts to predict future events.

STEPS IN SALES FORECASTING

Although sales forecasting methods vary, the most typical method begins with a forecast of general economic conditions and uses it to forecast industry sales and then to develop a forecast of company and product sales. This approach can be termed the *top-down method.*[19]

Forecasting General Economic Conditions

The most common measure of economic output is **gross national product** (GNP), *the market value of all final products produced in a country in a given year.* Trend extension is the most frequently used method of forecasting increases in GNP. As Figure 3.5 shows, past data are plotted on a scatter diagram, and a trend line is drawn through the scattered points to produce the point at which next year's expected GNP will be located. The trend line is usually developed by a statistical technique

**FIGURE 3.5
Sales Forecast for the Next Year, Using the Least Squares Method of Trend Extension**

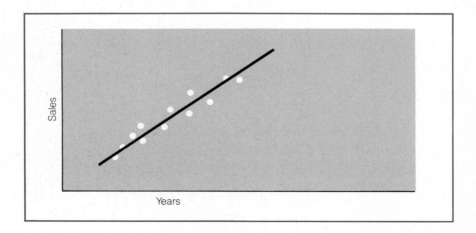

called the *least squares method.* This method utilizes a mathematical formula to plot a line in such a manner that the sum of the squared distances from each of the points on the diagram to the line is at a minimum.

Input-Output Models as Aids in Economic Forecasting

During periods of steady growth, the trend extension method of forecasting produces satisfactory results. But it implicitly assumes that the factors contributing to the attainment of a certain level of output in the past will operate in the same manner in the future. When conditions change, the trend extension method often produces incorrect results. For this reason, forecasters are increasingly using more sophisticated techniques and more complex mathematical models.

Input-output models, which depict the interactions of various industries in producing goods, are being developed by the U.S. Department of Commerce and by private agencies. Since outputs (sales) of one industry are the inputs (purchases) of another, a change of outputs in one industry affects the inputs of other industries. Input-output models show the impact on supplier industries of increased production in a given industry and can be used to measure the impact of increased demand in any industry throughout the economy.

Since many federal agencies and other organizations develop regular forecasts of the GNP, a firm may choose to use their estimates. These forecasts are regularly reported in such publications as the *Wall Street Journal* and *Business Week.*

Developing the Industry Sales Forecast

Once the economic forecast has been produced, the next step is developing an industry sales forecast. Since industry sales may be related to GNP or some other measure of the national economy, a forecast may begin by measuring the degree of this relationship and then applying the trend extension method to forecast industry sales. More sophisticated techniques, such as input-output analysis or multiple regression analysis, may also be used.

Forecasting Company and Product Sales

Once the industry forecast has been done, the company and product forecasts are developed. They begin with a detailed analysis of previous years. The firm's past and present market shares are reviewed, and product managers and regional and district sales managers are consulted about expected sales. Since an accelerated promotional budget or the introduction of new products may stimulate additional demand, the marketing plan for the coming year is also considered.

The product and company forecast must evaluate many aspects of company sales: sales of each product, future trends, sales by customer, territory, salesperson, and order size; financial arrangements; and other aspects. Once a preliminary sales forecast has been devel-

New product sales forecasting can be hazardous.

Source: Reprinted by permission of Phil Frank.

oped, it is reviewed by the sales force and by district, regional, and national sales managers.

New Product Sales Forecasting

Forecasting sales for new products is an especially hazardous undertaking, since no historical data is available. Companies typically employ consumer panels to obtain reactions to the products and probable purchase behavior. Test market data is also utilized.

Since few products are totally new, forecasters carefully analyze the sales of competing products that may be displaced by the new entry. A new type of fishing reel, for example, will compete in an established market with other reels. This substitute method provides the forecaster with an estimate of market size and potential demand.

THE MARKETING AUDIT

William S. Woodside, the president of American Can Company, has been quoted as saying, "The roughest thing to get rid of is the Persian Messenger Syndrome, where the bearer of bad tidings is beheaded by the king. You should lean over backward to reward the guy who is first with the bad news. Most companies have all kinds of abilities to handle problems, if they only learn about them soon enough."[20]

If the marketing organization is to avoid the Persian Messenger Syndrome, as Woodside calls it, it must not only institute periodic reviews of marketing plans, but must also be willing to accept the objective results of such evaluations. For most organizations, this means the use of a **marketing audit**—*a thorough, objective evaluation of an organization's marketing philosophy, goals, policies, tactics, practices, and results.*[21]

A comprehensive marketing audit can provide a valuable—and sometimes disquieting—perspective on the performance of the firm's marketing plans. The need to assess performance was noted earlier. An excellent example of this need is the pharmaceutical firm that was delighted with an 83 percent awareness rating for an advertising campaign, but was shocked upon learning that this amounted to only a 28 percent intent-to-buy figure.[22]

All marketing organizations need to evaluate the success of their marketing plans periodically. Such a review is invaluable not only in identifying the tasks that the organization does well but also in high-lighting its failures. Periodic review, criticism, and self-analysis are crucial to the vitality of any organization. They are particularly critical to a function that is as diverse and dynamic as marketing.

Marketing audits are especially valuable in pointing out areas in which managerial perceptions differ sharply from reality. Table 3.3 reports some of the things that were learned in marketing audits at various pharmaceutical enterprises.

The marketing audit goes beyond the normal control system. The control process for marketing essentially asks: Are we doing things right? The marketing audit extends this question to: Are we also doing the right thing?[23]

Marketing audits are applicable to all organizations—large or small, profitable or profitless, and nonprofit or profit-oriented. Audits are particularly valuable when they are performed for the first time or when they are conducted after a long absence from the managerial process. Not all organizations have implemented marketing audits, but the number of firms using them is expected to grow. One study found that 28 percent of the firms surveyed had used a marketing audit. Table 3.4 reflects the use of audits in different industries.

Selecting the Marketing Auditors

Selecting the auditors is a critical aspect of conducting a marketing audit. Three potential sources of auditors are regular corporate executives, special marketing audit staffs, and outside marketing consultants.[24]

Some firms prefer to assign executives to perform marketing audits on a periodic basis. The difficulties in such an arrangement include the time pressure of the executives' regular duties and the problem of maintaining impartiality. Other organizations set up a separate auditing staff if company size permits such a structure. This arrangement can provide an excellent balance between impartiality and extensive in-house knowledge. Marketing consultants are often recommended for marketing audits because they enter the evaluation with an independent viewpoint that is valuable. Consultants also may be able to offer the most up-to-date evaluation methodology.

Conducting a Marketing Audit

Marketing audits are probably as diverse as the people who conduct them. Some auditors follow only informal procedures. Others have formulated elaborate checklists, questionnaires, profiles, tests, and related

**TABLE 3.3
Findings of
Marketing Audits in
Pharmaceutical
Firms**

Focus	Comparison of staff assumptions and audit findings	
	Marketing Staff Assumptions	Audit Findings
Personal selling		
1. Scale of efforts	6.5 calls daily	4.0 calls daily
2. Quality of effort	Full presentation, 100 percent of calls	Full presentation, 70 percent of calls
3. Message integrity	100 percent accuracy	65 percent accuracy
4. Communication with sales force	100 percent readership	82 percent readership 81 percent accuracy 2.7 retail calls daily
Advertising		
1. Ad agency interface	Harmonious	Disharmonious
2. Message integrity	100 percent accuracy	62 percent accuracy
3. Message impact		83 percent awareness; 28 percent acceptance; percent intention to buy
Product		
1. Manufacturing cost	No change	11 percent increase
2. Market growth	7 percent growth	2 percent growth
3. Penetration	45 percent accepting; 25 percent neutral; 10 percent rejecting	28 percent accepting; 57 percent neutral; 15 percent rejecting
Intra-company		
1. Interface processing	No problems	Communication and cooperation problems
2. Marketing intelligence system		Unsatisfactory
3. Approval processing		3-14 working days; average, 9 working days

Source: Ed Roseman, "An Audit Can Make the 'Accurate' Difference," *Product Marketing,* August 1979, p. 24. Reprinted with permission of *Product Marketing Magazine.*

**TABLE 3.4
Marketing Audit
Usage by Industry**

Type of Company	Percentage Conducting Marketing Audits
Industrial goods manufacturers	36
Consumer goods manufacturers	19
Manufacturers of both consumer and industrial goods	22
Service related firms	28
Total of all firms	28

Source: Adapted from Louis R. Capella and William S. Sekely, "The Marketing Audit: Usage and Applications," in *Proceedings of the Southern Marketing Association,* eds. Robert S. Franz, Robert M. Hopkins, and Alfred G. Toma, New Orleans, La., November 1978, p. 412. Used by permission of the Southern Marketing Association. Copyright © 1978 by the Southern Marketing Association. All rights reserved.

research instruments. Regardless of the tools employed, all marketing audits follow four major steps:

1. Securing agreement between the auditor and the organization on the audit's objectives and scope

2. Developing a framework for the audit
   Studying the company's external environment
   Profiling the major elements of the marketing system
   Examining the key marketing activities

3. Preparing an audit report with findings and recommendations

4. Presenting the report in a manner that will lead to action[25]

These steps can be implemented in a variety of ways. Often, some basic issues are raised during the process. For instance, during the initial stage, the auditor and the organization should agree on the audit's goals, its coverage and depth, and the provision of data sources for the audit. Similar questions can be raised during the other stages of the audit as well. The marketing audit can provide invaluable assistance to future marketing planning.

THE KOTLER AUDIT OF MARKETING EFFECTIVENESS

Philip Kotler has devised a checklist to measure marketing effectiveness. The Kotler audit is based on five variables: consumer philosophy, integrated marketing organization, adequate marketing information, strategic orientation, and operational efficiency. These activities are defined as follows:[26]

1. *Customer philosophy*—Does management acknowledge the primacy of the marketplace and of customer needs and wants in shaping company plans and operations?

2. *Integrated marketing organization*—Is the organization staffed so that it will be able to carry out marketing analysis, planning, and implementation and control?

3. *Adequate marketing information*—Does management receive the kind and quality of information needed to conduct effective marketing?

4. *Strategic orientation*—Does marketing management generate innovative strategies and plans for long-run growth and profitability?

5. *Operational efficiency*—Are marketing plans implemented in a cost-effective manner, and are the results monitered for rapid corrective action?

Table 3.5 presents the Kotler marketing effectiveness audit and his scoring system for assessing overall effectiveness.

TABLE 3.5
Kotler's Marketing
Effectiveness Audit

Outline for marketing effectiveness (check one answer to each question)

Customer philosophy

A. Does management recognize the importance of designing the company to serve the needs and wants of chosen markets?

Score	
0 ☐	Management primarily thinks in terms of selling current and new products to whoever will buy them.
1 ☐	Management thinks in terms of serving a wide range of markets and needs with equal effectiveness.
2 ☐	Management thinks in terms of serving the needs and wants of well-defined markets chosen for their long-run growth and profit potential for the company.

B. Does management develop different offerings and marketing plans for different segments of the market?

0 ☐	No.
1 ☐	Somewhat.
2 ☐	To a good extent.

C. Does management take a whole marketing system view (suppliers, channels, competitors, customers, environment) in planning its business?

0 ☐	No. Management concentrates on selling and servicing its immediate customers.
1 ☐	Somewhat. Management takes a long view of its channels although the bulk of its effort goes to selling and servicing the immediate customers.
2 ☐	Yes. Management takes a whole marketing systems view, recognizing the threats and opportunities created for the company by changes in any part of the system.

Integrated marketing organization

D. Is there high-level marketing integration and control of the major marketing functions?

0 ☐	No. Sales and other marketing functions are not integrated at the top and there is some unproductive conflict.
1 ☐	Somewhat. There is formal integration and control of the major marketing functions but less than satisfactory coordination and cooperation.
2 ☐	Yes. The major marketing functions are effectively integrated.

E. Does marketing management work well with management in research, manufacturing, purchasing, physical distribution, and finance?

0 ☐	No. There are complaints that marketing is unreasonable in the demands and costs it places on other departments.
1 ☐	Somewhat. The relations are amicable although each department pretty much acts to serve its own power interests.
2 ☐	Yes. The departments cooperate effectively and resolve issues in the best interest of the company as a whole.

TABLE 3.5 continued

F. How well-organized is the new product development process?

0 ☐ The system is ill-defined and poorly handled.

1 ☐ The system formally exists but lacks sophistication.

2 ☐ The system is well-structured and professionally staffed.

Adequate marketing information

G. When were the latest marketing research studies of customers, buying influences, channels, and competitors conducted?

0 ☐ Several years ago.

1 ☐ A few years ago.

2 ☐ Recently.

H. How well does management know the sales potential and profitability of different market segments, customers, territories, products, channels, and order sizes?

0 ☐ Not at all.

1 ☐ Somewhat.

2 ☐ Very well.

I. What effort is expended to measure the cost-effectiveness of different marketing expenditures?

0 ☐ Little or no effort.

1 ☐ Some effort.

2 ☐ Substantial effort.

Strategic orientation

J. What is the extent of formal marketing planning?

0 ☐ Management does little or no formal marketing planning.

1 ☐ Management develops an annual marketing plan.

2 ☐ Management develops a detailed annual marketing plan and a careful long-range plan that is updated annually.

K. What is the quality of the current marketing strategy?

0 ☐ The current strategy is not clear.

1 ☐ The current strategy is clear and represents a continuation of traditional strategy.

2 ☐ The current strategy is clear, innovative, data-based, and well-reasoned.

L. What is the extent of contingency thinking and planning?

0 ☐ Management does little or no contingency thinking.

1 ☐ Management does some contingency thinking, although little formal contingency planning.

2 ☐ Management formally identifies the most important contingencies and develops contingency plans.

Operational efficiency

M. How well is the marketing thinking at the top communicated and implemented down the line?

0 ☐ Poorly.

1 ☐ Fairly well.

2 ☐ Successfully.

N. Is management doing an effective job with the marketing resources?

0 ☐ No. The marketing resources are inadequate for the job to be done.

1 ☐ Somewhat. The marketing resources are adequate, but they are not employed optimally.

2 ☐ Yes. The marketing resources are adequate and are deployed efficiently.

O. Does management show a good capacity to react quickly and effectively to on-the-spot developments?

0 ☐ No. Sales and market information is not very current and management reaction time is slow.

1 ☐ Somewhat. Management receives fairly up-to-date sales and market information; management reaction time varies.

2 ☐ Yes. Management has installed systems yielding highly current information and fast reaction time.

Total score

Rating marketing effectiveness

The auditing outline can be used in this way. The auditor collects information as it bears on the 15 questions. The appropriate answer is checked for each question. The scores are added—the total will be somewhere between 0 and 30. The following scale shows the equivalent in marketing effectiveness:

TABLE 3.5 continued

0-5	None
6-10	Poor
11-15	Fair
16-20	Good
21-25	Very good
26-30	Superior

To illustrate, 15 senior managers in a large building materials company were recently invited to rate their company using the auditing instrument in this exhibit. The resulting overall marketing effectiveness scores ranged from a low of 6 to a high of 15. The median score was 11, with three-fourths of the scores between 9 and 13. Therefore, most of the managers thought their company was at best "fair" at marketing.

Several divisions were also rated. Their median scores ranged from a low of 3 to a high of 19. The higher scoring divisions tended to have higher profitability. However, some of the lower scoring divisions were also profitable. An examination of the latter showed that these divisions were in industries where their competition also operated at a low level of marketing effectiveness. The managers feared that these divisions would be vulnerable as soon as competition began to learn to market more successfully.

An interesting question to speculate on is the distribution of median marketing effectiveness scores for *FORTUNE* "500" companies. My suspicion is that very few companies in that roster would score above 20 ("very good" or "superior") in marketing effectiveness. Although marketing theory and practice have received their fullest expression in the United States, the great majority of U.S. companies probably fail to meet the highest standards.

Source: Reprinted by permission of the *Harvard Business Review.* Exhibit from "From Sales Obsession to Marketing Effectiveness," by Philip Kotler (November/December 1977). Copyright © 1977 by the President and Fellows of Harvard College; all rights reserved.

SUMMARY

Planning is the basis for all strategy decisions. Planning is the process of anticipating the future and determining the courses of action to achieve company objectives. Strategic planning refers to strategy-oriented planning. Marketing planning is the implementation of planning activity as it relates to the achievement of marketing objectives. The planning process begins with a recognition of problems and opportunities. Subsequent steps are the development of alternative courses of action, the evaluation, selection, and implementation of alternatives, and the follow-up to determine the effectiveness of the decisions.

Chapter 3 describes the evaluation of the strategic planning process as well as General Electric's special contribution to the development of this activity. The portfolio approach to marketing planning and strategic business units are highlighted. Effective strategic planning is now regarded as a prerequisite to survival. It should be viewed as an organization-wide responsibility involving chief executive officers, heads of operating units, and corporate strategic planning personnel. The BCG matrix plots relative status of market share and market growth, dividing the market into "cash cows," "dogs," "questions marks," and "stars." Much of the BCG work is based on the experience curve concept, which states that higher market share results in lower product costs. PERT is a commonly used planning technique.

Considerable strategic planning effort goes into the development of alternative marketing strategies: undifferentiated, differentiated, and concentrated marketing.

Sales forecasting is also an important component of marketing planning. Forecasting techniques may be categorized as quantitative or qualitative. The most common approach to sales forecasting is to begin with a forecast of the national economy and use it to develop an industry sales forecast. That forecast is then used to develop a company and product forecast.

The marketing audit is a comprehensive review of the firm's marketing effort. Marketing audits are important because they assess the performance of the firm's marketing plans.

QUESTIONS FOR DISCUSSION

1. Explain the following terms:

planning	market share
marketing planning	experience curve
strategic planning	PERT
tactical planning	undifferentiated marketing
conglomerate	differentiated marketing
concentric diversification	concentrated marketing
strategic business unit (SBU)	sales forecasting
GE business screen	gross national product
BCG growth-share matrix	marketing audit

2. Compare and contrast planning, strategic planning, and marketing planning.
3. Outline the steps in the planning process.
4. Discuss the evolution of strategic planning.
5. Comment on General Electric's contributions to strategic planning.
6. How is the BCG growth-share matrix useful to planners?
7. Describe the organization for strategic planning.
8. Explain these terms: "cash cow," "dogs," "stars," and "question marks."
9. How can PERT be useful in planning?
10. Develop a hypothetical PERT chart for the introduction of a new product familiar to you. Specify any necessary assumptions.
11. Evaluate the marketing plans of Cadillac, K mart, and Wolverine World Wide.
12. Describe BCG's work with the experience curve.
13. Explain the strategies of undifferentiated, differentiated, and concentrated marketing.
14. On what basis would a marketer select one of the strategies listed in Question 13?
15. Describe the top-down method of sales forecasting.
16. Discuss the advantages and disadvantages of basing sales forecasts exclusively on estimates developed by the company's sales force.
17. Assume that growth in industry sales will remain constant for the coming

year. Forecast company sales for the coming year based upon the following data:

Year	Sales
1	$1,600,000
2	$1,750,000
3	$1,700,000
4	$1,900,000
5	$2,900,000

What assumptions have you made in developing your forecast?

18. What is industry's current usage of marketing audits?

19. Who should conduct a marketing audit?

20. Discuss the actual implementation of a marketing audit.

NOTES

1. John Koten, "Coca-Cola Executives Believe 1980 Is Critical in Battle with Pepsi," *Wall Street Journal,* March 6, 1980. Reprinted by permission of *The Wall Street Journal,* © Dow Jones & Company, Inc. 1980. All Rights Reserved. Lyrics © Pepsico, Inc. 1940. Reprinted by permission.

2. An interesting discussion appears in Barbara Coe, "Strategic Planning and Marketing: A Constructive Partnership in Industrial Firms," in *Proceedings of the Southwestern Marketing Association,* eds. Robert H. Ross, Frederic B. Kraft, and Charles H. Davis, Wichita, Kans., 1981, pp. 17–20.

3. Alfred D. Chandler, Jr., *Strategy and Structure* (Cambridge, Mass.: MIT Press, 1962), p. 13.

4. An interesting discussion of W. R. Grace's repositioning is in Maurice Barnfather, "The House that Peter Built," *Forbes,* October 13, 1980, p. 188.

5. "Strategic Planning Should Occupy 30–50% of C.E.O.'s Time: Schanck," *Marketing News,* June 1, 1979, p. 1.

6. " 'Key Issue': It's Key Issue in Strategic Planning: Johnson," *Marketing News,* June 1, 1979, p. 1.

7. Excellent discussions of planning appear in Wesley J. Johnston, "Real-World Strategic Planning Isn't as Neat as Its Theory," *Marketing News,* June 26, 1981; Milton Leontiades, "Perspective on Planners and Planning," *Business,* September–October 1980, pp. 20–24; and Stanley F. Stasch and Patricia Lanktice, "Can Your Marketing Planning Procedure Be Improved?" *Journal of Marketing,* Summer 1980, pp. 79–90.

8. This section is based on William L. Shanklin, "Strategic Business Planning: Yesterday, Today, and Tomorrow," *Business Horizons,* October 1979, pp. 7–14.

9. Philip Kotler, *Marketing Management, Analysis, Planning, and Control,* 4th ed. (Englewood Cliffs, N.J.: Prentice-Hall, 1980), p. 75. Copyright © 1980. Adapted by permission of Prentice-Hall, Inc., Englewood Cliffs, N.J.

10. "GF Splits Marketing and Sales," *Sales & Marketing Management,* May 19, 1980, p. 10.

11. "Does GE Really Plan Better?" *MBA,* November 1975, p. 42.

12. The discussion of the BCG Matrix is based on "Managing High Technology Portfolio Milks Cows, Kills Dogs," *Marketing News,* July 13, 1979, p. 6. Used by permission of the American Marketing Association.

13. This is pointed out in Gilbert D. Harrell and Richard O. Keefer, "Multinational Strategies," *MSU Business Topics* (Winter, 1981), pp. 5–15.

14. This description of the experience curve is based on "BCG'S Market-Share Experience 'Law'," *Marketing News,* December 15, 1978, p. 6. Used by permission of the American Marketing Association.

15. The Porta-Vac example is taken from David R. Anderson, Dennis J. Sweeney, and Thomas A. Williams, *An Introduction to Management Science* (St. Paul, Minn.: West Publishing Co., 1976), pp. 295–310.

16. This strategy has also been called *product differentiation.* See Wendell R. Smith, "Product Differentiation and Market Segmentation as Alternative Marketing Strategies," *Journal of Marketing,* July 1956, pp. 3–8. The terms *undifferentiated marketing, differentiated marketing,* and

concentrated marketing were suggested by Philip Kotler. See his *Marketing Management,* 4th ed. (Englewood Cliffs, N.J.: Prentice-Hall, 1980), pp. 206–9.

17. A similar list is suggested in Kotler, *Marketing Management,* pp. 209–10. Also see R. William Kotrba, "The Strategy Selection Chart," *Journal of Marketing,* July 1966, pp. 22–25.

18. Two recent papers of interest are Anthony C. Petto, "Guidelines for Selecting Sales Forecasting Methods," Ross et al, *Proceedings,* pp. 243–46; and Arthur J. Adams, "Modeling and Forecasting Sales after a Major Market Change," in Venkatakrishna V. Bellur, Editor; Thomas R. Baird, Paul T. Hertz, Roger L. Jenkins, Jay D. Lindquist, and Stephen W. Miller, Co-Editors, *Developments in Marketing Science,* vol. 4 (Marquette, Mich.: Academy of Marketing Science, 1981), pp. 291–93.

19. A similar approach is discussed in Charles Futrell, *Sales Management: Behavior, Practice and Cases* (Hinsdale, Ill.: The Dryden Press, 1981), pp. 100–101.

20. Quoted in Arthur R. Roolman, "Why Corporations Hate the Future," *MBA,* November 1975, p. 37.

21. The basis of this section and the next was taken from an excellent discussion of marketing audits appearing in David T. Kollat, Roger D. Blackwell, and James F. Robeson, *Strategic Marketing* (New York: Holt, Rinehart and Winston, 1972), pp. 498–500.

22. Ed Roseman, "An Audit Can Make the 'Accurate' Difference," *Product Marketing,* August 1979, pp. 24–25.

23. Kollat, Blackwell, and Robeson, *Strategic Marketing,* p. 500.

24. *Ibid.,* pp. 499–500.

25. This section is adapted from an address by Philip Kotler to the Chicago chapter of the American Marketing Association. Reported in "Kotler Presents Whys, Hows of Marketing Audits for Firms, Nonprofit Organizations," *Marketing News,* March 26, 1976, p. 21. Used by permission of the American Marketing Association.

26. Philip Kotler, "From Sales Obsession to Marketing Effectiveness," *Harvard Business Review*, November–December 1977, pp. 67–75. The list of definitions is reprinted with permission from p. 72. Copyright (c) 1977 by the President and Fellows of Harvard College; all rights reserved.

CHAPTER 4

MARKETING RESEARCH: INFORMATION FOR DECISION MAKING

KEY TERMS

marketing research
exploratory research
sales analysis
sales quota
marketing cost analysis
hypothesis
research design
primary data
secondary data
focus group interview
marketing information system (MIS)

LEARNING GOALS

1. To identify the different forms of marketing information

2. To list the steps in the marketing research process

3. To explain the types of primary data

4. To identify the methods of collecting survey data

5. To distinguish between marketing research and marketing information systems

"**T**he most successful new product introduction in the history of Johnson Wax" was how marketing executives described the introduction of Agree Creme Rinse and Agree Shampoo. Marketing research was utilized at every step in the process. Specific information was collected to assist in identifying the opportunity, specifying the target user, defining the appropriate marketing strategy, and identifying the physical features and performance attributes of the new products.

The success of their Edge shaving cream convinced the Johnson Wax managers of their ability to successfully market superior personal care products. They were equally convinced that a "me-too" product would not be successful. Preliminary studies of market size and potential resulted in a more specific focus on women's hair care products. Management agreed that the market was big, growing, and represented a good match with the firm's research and development abilities and marketing skills. During the next three years, several hair care products were considered and ultimately rejected: hair dressings (the category was not growing); hair coloring (management felt the company lacked the technological base); and hair sprays (management felt that changes in style and grooming practices were trending away from hair sprays). The major categories that still remained were shampoos and creme rinse/conditioners.

In the early stages, marketing data was collected to establish market sizes and trends, and to assess general attitudes of users and nonusers. Once the firm began to concentrate on shampoo and creme rinse, a representative group of consumers was used to provide feedback over a period of time to provide background knowledge, to ascertain characteristics of women's hair, and to collect specific user and nonuser data. The data revealed that women were shampooing more frequently, and were more likely to use creme rinses and conditioners. It also revealed that the respondents considered oily hair their major hair care problem, especially after using current creme rinse and conditioner brands.

In-depth interviews were conducted on potential products that emerged from research and development activities. A new formula conditioner with virtually no oil was blind-tested (by removing identifying marks and packages) against a target competitor's product and was significantly preferred over the competition. During the research, the slogan "Helps stop the greasies" was suggested. Agree was test-marketed in Fresno, California, and South Bend, Indiana. Sales performance exceeded expectations and the product was launched on a nationwide basis. Within six months, Agree Creme Rinse was selling more bottles of conditioner than any other brand. Agree Shampoo, launched later, achieved considerable success as well. Johnson Wax executives clearly understand the importance of information in marketing decision making.[1]

When Eastman Kodak executives recognized the need for specialized marketing information, they hired Perception Research Service, independent reseachers, to conduct a series of "eye tracking" tests. These tests recorded the patterns of viewer eye movements when looking at advertisements featuring television personality Michael Landon. When the tests showed that most viewer eye movements flowed to the top, Eastman Kodak moved the headline, "Kodak introduces the Ektra pocket camera," from the bottom to the top of the ad.[2]

**FIGURE 4.1
Marketing Research
Activities of 798
Companies**

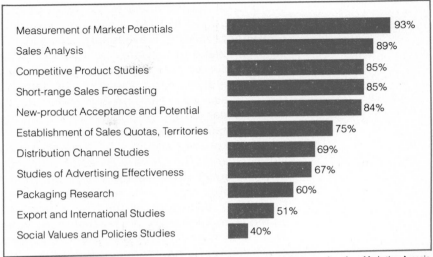

Measurement of Market Potentials — 93%
Sales Analysis — 89%
Competitive Product Studies — 85%
Short-range Sales Forecasting — 85%
New-product Acceptance and Potential — 84%
Establishment of Sales Quotas, Territories — 75%
Distribution Channel Studies — 69%
Studies of Advertising Effectiveness — 67%
Packaging Research — 60%
Export and International Studies — 51%
Social Values and Policies Studies — 40%

Source: Data from Dik Warren Twedt, ed., *1978 Survey of Marketing Research* (Chicago: American Marketing Association, 1978), p. 41. Used with permission.

MARKETING RESEARCH: MAJOR SOURCE OF MARKETING INFORMATION

There exists a variety of sources for decision-oriented marketing information. Some, such as the physiological study sponsored by Eastman Kodak and the research that led to the introduction of Agree Shampoo, are well-planned investigations designed to elicit specific information. Other valuable information may be obtained from sales force reports, accounting data, or published reports. Still other information may be obtained from controlled experiments or computer simulations.

A major source of information takes the form of marketing research. The American Marketing Association defines **marketing research** as *"the systematic gathering, recording, and analyzing of data about problems relating to the marketing of goods and services."*[3] The critical task of the marketing manager is decision making. Managers must make effective decisions that enable their firms to solve problems as they arise, and must anticipate and prevent future problems. Many times, though, managers are forced to make decisions without sufficient information. Marketing research aids the decision maker by presenting pertinent facts, analyzing them, and suggesting possible action.

All marketing decision areas are candidates for marketing research investigations. As Figure 4.1 indicates, marketing research efforts are commonly centered around determining market and sales potential, developing sales forecasts for the firm's products and services, determining appropriate channel strategies, evaluating the effectiveness of the firm's advertising and packaging decisions, and studying export and international marketing potential.

Marketing research is a relatively new field. Just over a hundred years have passed since N. W. Ayer conducted the first organized research project in 1879. A second important milestone in the development of marketing research occurred in 1911, when Charles C. Parlin organized and became manager of the nation's first commercial research department at the Curtis Publishing Company.

Much of the early research represented little more than written testimonials received from purchasers of the firm's products. Research became more sophisticated during the 1930s as the development of statistical techniques led to refinements in sampling procedures and greater accuracy in research findings.[4] However, mistakes still occurred. The *Literary Digest* conducted a major national study of U.S. households selected at random from lists of telephone numbers and auto registration records and reported that Alf Landon—not Franklin D. Roosevelt—would be elected president. The fiasco resulted from a failure to realize that many voters (most of whom were apparently Democrats) did not have telephones in 1936. The difficulty of predicting human behavior was all too apparent a few years ago when political research organizations called the Carter-Reagan presidential campaign of 1980 "too close to call" just days before the Reagan landslide.

Marketing research is frequently used in marketing mix decisions.

"Well, among the names we researched, that was the most favored choice."

Source: Reprinted with permission from page 14 of the June 5, 1978, issue of *Advertising Age.* Copyright © 1978 by Crain Communications, Inc.

In its most recent survey, the American Marketing Association reported that 87 percent of the nation's leading manufacturing firms had established their own formal marketing research departments. Although such operations are found mostly in companies manufacturing consumer products, a substantial increase in marketing research departments has occurred in recent years in financial service firms, such as banks, savings and loan associations, and other lending institutions; insurance companies; and major nonprofit organizations.[5] Total expenditures for marketing research in 1983 are estimated at more than $1 billion.

THE ROLE OF INFORMATION IN THE DECISION PROCESS

It has been said that the recipe for effective decisions is 90 percent information and 10 percent inspiration. Figure 4.2 separates the management decision process into a series of stages and indicates the type of information required at each stage. Specific types of information are needed to assist management at each stage of the decision-making process. The following description of the marketing research inputs that resulted in the introduction of the Scripto erasable pen illustrates how various types of information are used by management at each step in the decision-making process.

FIGURE 4.2
Information Needs at Each Stage of the Management Decision Process

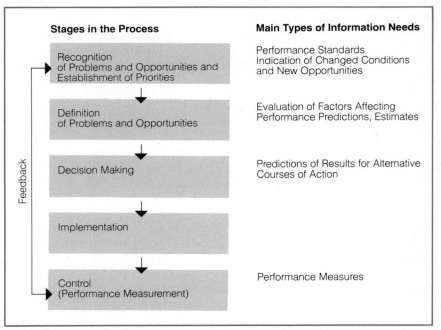

Source: Robert D. Buzzell, Donald F. Cox, and Rex F. Brown, *Marketing Research and Information Systems* (New York: McGraw-Hill, 1969), p. 5. Copyright © 1969 by McGraw-Hill Book Company. Used with the permission of McGraw-Hill Book Company.

SCRIPTO PRODUCES A MARKETING WINNER

"Putting the right products in the right markets at the right time" is the motto of Scripto, Inc., a small Doraville, Georgia-based firm. But years had passed since management applied its motto and the firm's line of mechanical pencils was being marketed to a shrinking segment of the $1 billion writing instrument market. In addition, the once-dominant firm recognized that its customers had aged. As president K. Douglas Martin pointed out, "We showed particular weakness among teenagers and young adults who obviously represent the key to current and future markets."

The answer proved to be a new erasable, disposable pen. But nearly two years passed between the initial new-product consideration and its eventual market entry, and marketing research was used at every stage of the decision process. Information was obtained to more precisely define the opportunity, estimate consumer reactions, and design a viable marketing mix.

One of Martin's first activities following his acceptance of the Scripto presidency in 1978 was to critically evaluate the new product ideas under consideration. Martin and his marketing colleagues knew that the right product must satisfy a number of objectives: move the firm toward the ball-point pen mainstream, appeal to a young audience, and satisfy the high margin requirements of channel members. At about the same time, Scripto's research department developed an erasable pen with ink 150 times thicker than a conventional ball-point pen and a gas charge to force the ink out of the cartridge and onto the paper. The new product, which had been in research since 1964, was a major technological breakthrough. Only one other firm in the entire world was capable of making such a pen, and its research and development efforts rivaled those of Scripto. The competitor, Gillette, launched its version under the name Eraser Mate in early 1979.

Since Scripto was beaten to the market by its giant competitor, it decided to monitor the marketing decisions of Gillette and to analyze consumer response. Scripto purchased syndicated marketing research data on product sales and learned that Eraser Mate sales exceeded those of Flair markers and were second only to Bic stick pens, even though its $1.69 retail price was more than six times that of Bic.

MARKETING RESEARCH PROCEDURE

Most marketing research investigations begin with recognizing a problem or opportunity. The first important task of the researcher is to define precisely this problem or opportunity.

Defining the Problem

Someone once remarked that "Well-defined problems are half solved." Problems are barriers that prevent the accomplishment of organizational goals. A clearly defined problem permits the researcher to focus the research process on securing the necessary data to solve the problem.

SCRIPTO PRODUCES A MARKETING WINNER (continued)

A few months later Scripto marketing researchers decided to utilize a telephone survey to determine whether Eraser Mate was a fad. One household in nine surveyed reported ownership of an Eraser Mate pen and 86 percent of those consumers stated that they would buy the product again. Of equal interest to Scripto executives was the discovery that two-thirds of the users were under age 18 and over 40 percent were in the 11—14 age category. This was astounding news considering the price of the pen.

President Martin made the decision to enter the market, but he insisted that Scripto's product must not be a "me-too" market follower. Groups of students were invited to Scripto's headquarters for a plant tour and for a series of group interviews. Scripto's question, "What writing instruments do teenagers use most often?" was answered in this way: "Disposable, ball-point pens." So management began to focus upon development of the world's first disposable, erasable pen.

Additional interviews with students centered upon such marketing mix elements as price. The disposability feature appeared to dictate a less-than-one dollar retail price and 98 cents was ultimately chosen. Marketing analysts compared the price with production and marketing costs and needed distributor margins and agreed that a 98-cent retail price was adequate. During the research, the slogan "Erases the ink, not the paper" was suggested. It became an important part of the marketing mix for the Scripto Erasable Pen. Advertising tests of the slogan revealed an extremely high recognition rate for the product and its distinguishing features.

The disposable Scripto Erasable Pen proved a huge marketing success. As President Martin states, "The Scripto Erasable Pen is testimony to the fact that a small corporation, with limited resources, can hope to compete with the giants; that marketing research can be an invaluable marketing tool; and that the right product, in the right market, at the right time, is a concept just as important today as it ever was."

Source: "Success of Scripto Erasable Pen Due to Marketing Research: CEO," *Marketing News,* January 23, 1981, p. 8. Used by permission of the American Marketing Association.

It is often difficult to determine the specific problem, however, since the researcher may be confronted with *symptoms* of an underlying problem. In the late 1970s, Ciba-Geigy was stunned when its newly acquired Airwick Industries suffered a $2 million loss on sales of such products as liquid room fresheners. But the parent firm recognized the losses as symptoms of a bitter price war in this market and of the need for a more systematic method of developing and introducing product innovations to keep pace with competition. In order to solve the problems facing the firm, management had to look beyond the symptoms and search for causes.

**TABLE 4.1
Topics for the
Exploratory Analysis**

The Company and Industry	Sales Organization
1. Company objectives 2. The companies comprising the industry (size, financial power) and industry trends 3. Geographic locations of the industry 4. The company's market share as compared with competitors' 5. Marketing policies of competitors	1. Market coverage 2. Sales analysis by number of accounts per salesperson, size of account, type of account, and so on 3. Expense ratios for various territories, product types, account sizes, and so on 4. Control procedures 5. Compensation methods
The Market	**Pricing**
1. Geographic location 2. Demographic characteristics 3. Purchase motivations 4. Product use patterns 5. Nature of demand	1. Elasticity 2. Seasonal or special promotional price cuts 3. Profit margins of resellers 4. Legal restrictions 5. Price lines
Products	**Advertising and Sales Promotion**
1. Physical characteristics 2. Consumer acceptance—strengths and weaknesses 3. Package as a container and as a promotional weapon 4. Manufacturing processes, production capacity 5. Closeness and availability of substitute products	1. Media employed 2. Dollar expenditures as compared with competitors' 3. Timing of advertising 4. Sales promotional materials provided for resellers 5. Results from previous advertising and sales promotional campaigns
Marketing Channels	
1. Channels employed and recent trends 2. Channel policy 3. Margins for resellers	

Searching for the cause of a problem allows the researcher to learn about the problem area and to focus on specific areas for study in seeking solutions. This search, often called **exploratory research,** consists of *discussing the problem with informed sources within the firm and with wholesalers, retailers, customers, and others outside the firm and examining secondary sources of information.* Marketing researchers often refer to internal data collection as the *situation analysis* and to exploratory interviews with informed persons outside the firm as the *informal investigation.* Exploratory research also involves evaluating company records, such as sales and profit analyses of the company's and its competitors' products. Table 4.1 lists major topics for any exploratory research.

TABLE 4.2
Income Statement
for ABC
Manufacturing
Company

ABC Manufacturing Company
Income Statement
for the Year Ended December 31, 198X

Sales		$5,783,000
Cost of Goods Sold		3,291,000
Gross Margin		$2,492,000
Expenses:		
Selling Expenses	$753,000	
Other Expenses	301,000	1,054,000
Profit before Taxes		$1,438,000
Income Taxes		719,000
Profit after Taxes		$ 719,000

Using Internal Data

An organization's sales records contain valuable sources of information. Analysis of these records should provide a basis for obtaining an overall view of company efficiency and a clue to the problem under investigation.

The basis for analysis of internal data is traditional accounting data, provided by the accounting department and usually summarized on the firm's financial statements. Table 4.2 shows a simplified income statement.

Basic financial statements are often too broad to be very useful in marketing analysis. Where nondetailed accounts are used, their main contribution is that they assist the analyst in raising more specific questions. The income statement in Table 4.2 shows that the company earned a profit for the period involved and that selling expenses represent approximately 13 percent of sales.

$$\text{Cost/sales ratio} = \frac{\$753,000}{\$5,783,000} = 13\%$$

Comparison of the 13-percent selling expense to sales ratio with previous years may hint at possible problems, but it will not specifically reveal the cause of the variation. To discover the cause, a more detailed breakdown is necessary.

Sales Analysis Table 4.3 shows a typical breakdown of sales by territories. This kind of breakdown becomes part of an overall sales analysis. The purpose of the **sales analysis**—*the in-depth evaluation of a firm's sales*—is to obtain meaningful information from the accounting data.[6]

Easily prepared from company invoices stored on computer tapes, the sales analysis can be quite revealing for the marketing executive. As Table 4.3 shows, the sales force in District 4 has a much higher cost/sales ratio than the sales force in other districts.

**TABLE 4.3
Sales and Expense
Analysis by Territory**

District	Average Salary	Average Expenses	Total Sales Costs	Total Sales	Cost/ Sales Ratio
1	$23,600	$10,400	$34,000	$654,000	5.2%
2	21,900	12,800	34,700	534,000	6.5
3	27,200	13,100	40,300	790,000	5.1
4	25,700	12,300	38,000	180,000	21.1
5	24,200	11,700	35,900	580,000	6.2

**TABLE 4.4
Sales Breakdown by
Sales
Representatives in
District 4**

Salesperson	Quota	Actual	Performance to Quota
Holtzman	$136,000	$128,000	94%
Thompson	228,000	253,000	111
Shapiro	118,000	125,000	106
Chandler	246,000	160,000	65
Total	$728,000	$666,000	91%

In order to evaluate the performance of the salespeople in the five districts, the marketing executive must have a standard of comparison. District 4, for example, may be a large territory but with relatively few industrial centers. Consequently, the costs involved in obtaining sales will be higher than for other districts.

The standard by which actual and expected sales are compared typically results from a detailed sales forecast by territories, products, customers, and salespersons. Once the **sales quota**—*the level of expected sales by which actual results are compared*—has been established, it is a simple process to compare the actual results with the expected performance. Table 4.4 compares actual sales with the quota established for each person in District 4.

Even though Shapiro had the smallest amount of sales for the period, her performance was better than expected. However, the district sales manager should investigate Chandler's performance since it resulted in the district's failure to meet its quota for the period.

The performance of the salespersons in District 4 provides a good illustration of the *iceberg principle,* which suggests that important evaluative information is often hidden by aggregate data. The tip of the iceberg represents only one-tenth of its total size. The remaining nine-tenths lies hidden beneath the surface of the water. Summaries of data are useful, but the marketing researcher must be careful that they do not actually conceal more than they reveal. If the sales breakdown by salesperson for the district had not been available, Chandler's poor performance would have concealed the unexpectedly high sales performances by Thompson and Shapiro.

**TABLE 4.5
Allocation of
Marketing Costs**

Marketing Costs	By Customer		By District		
	Large	Small	A	B	C
Advertising	$14,000	$ 30,000	$20,000	$10,000	$14,000
Selling	52,000	62,000	38,000	38,000	38,000
Physical Distribution	33,000	26,000	28,000	14,000	17,000
Credit	400	2,600	1,600	600	800
Total	$99,400	$120,600	$87,600	$62,600	$69,800

Other possible breakdowns for sales analysis include customer type, product, method of sale (mail, telephone, or personal contact), type of order (cash or credit), and size of order. Sales analysis is one of the least expensive and most important sources of marketing information, and any firm with data processing facilities should include it as part of its information system.

Marketing Cost Analysis A second source of internal information is **marketing cost analysis**—*the evaluation of such items as selling costs, billing, warehousing, advertising, and delivery expenses in order to determine the profitability of particular customers, territories, or product lines.*

Marketing cost analysis required a new way of classifying accounting data. *Functional accounts* must be established to replace the traditional natural accounts used in financial statements. These traditional accounts—such as salary—must be reallocated to the purpose for which the expenditure was made. A portion of the original salary account, for example, will be allocated to selling, inventory control, storage, billing, advertising, and other marketing costs. In the same manner, an account such as supply expenses will be allocated to the functions that utilize supplies.

The costs allocated to the functional accounts will equal those in the natural accounts. But instead of showing only total profitability, they can show the profitability of, say, particular territories, products, customers, salespersons, and order sizes. The most common reallocations are to products, customers, and territories or districts. Table 4.5 shows how they can be made.

The marketing decision maker can then evaluate the profitability of particular customers and districts on the basis of the sales produced and the costs incurred in producing them.

Table 4.6 indicates that District B is the most profitable region and District A is unprofitable. Attention can now be given to plans for increasing sales or reducing expenses in this problem district to make market coverage of the area a profitable undertaking. Marketing cost analysis is similar to sales analysis in that both provide warning sig-

TABLE 4.6
Income Statement
for Districts A, B,
and C

	District			
	A	B	C	Total
Sales	$260,000	$200,000	$191,000	$651,000
Cost of Sales	175,000	135,000	120,000	430,000
Gross Margin	$ 85,000	$ 65,000	$ 71,000	$221,000
Marketing Expenses	87,000	62,600	69,800	220,000
Contribution of each Territory	($ 2,000)	$ 2,400	$ 1,200	$ 1,000

nals of deviations from plans and allow the marketing executive the opportunity to explain and possibly correct the deviations.[7]

Formulating the Hypothesis

After the problem has been carefully investigated, using all the techniques described earlier, the decision maker should be able to formulate a **hypothesis,** *a tentative explanation about some specific event.* A hypothesis is a statement about the relationship between variables, and carries clear implications for testing this relationship.

A marketer of industrial products might formulate the following hypothesis:

Failure to provide 36-hour delivery service will reduce our sales by 20 percent.

Such a statement may prove correct or incorrect. The formulation of this hypothesis does, however, provide a basis for investigation and an eventual determination of its accuracy. Also, it allows the researcher to move to the next step: formulation of the research design.

PLANNING THE MARKETING RESEARCH PROCESS: THE RESEARCH DESIGN

The research design represents a comprehensive plan for testing the hypotheses formulated about the problem. **Research design** refers to *a series of advanced decisions that, taken together, comprise a master plan or model for the conduct of the investigation.* Developing such a plan allows the researcher to control each step of the research process. Table 4.7 lists the steps involved in the research design.

COLLECTING DATA

A major step in the research design is determining what data is needed to test the hypotheses. Two types of data are typically used: primary data and secondary data. **Primary data** refers to *data being collected*

TABLE 4.7
Sixteen Steps in the
Research Design

Questions Faced	Steps to Take or Choices
1. What is needed to measure the outcome of the alternative solutions?	1. Decide the subjects on which data are needed. 2. Examine the time and cost considerations.
2. What specific data are needed for that approach?	3. Write exact statements of data to be sought.
3. From whom are such data available?	4. Search and examine relevant secondary data. 5. Determine remaining data gaps.
4. How should primary data be obtained?	6. Define the population from which primary data may be sought.
a. What are the types of data?	7. Determine the various needed facts, opinions, and motives.
b. What general collection methods shall be used?	8. Plan for obtaining data by survey, observational, or experimental methods.
c. How shall the sources be contacted?	9. If using a survey, decide whether to contact respondents by telephone, by mail, or in person.
d. How may the data be secured from the sources?	10. Consider the questions and forms needed to elicit and record the data.
e. Shall there be a complete count of the population or a sample drawn from it? How chosen?	11. Decide on the coverage of the population: a. Choose between a complete enumeration or sampling. b. If sampling, decide whether to select from the whole population or restricted portions of it. c. Decide how to select sample members.
f. How will the fieldwork be conducted?	12. Map and schedule the fieldwork. 13. Plan the personnel requirements of the field study.
5. How will the data be interpreted and presented?	14. Consider editing and tabulating requirements. 15. Anticipate possible interpretation of the data. 16. Consider the way the findings may be presented.

Source: David J. Luck, Hugh G. Wales, and Donald Taylor, *Marketing Research*, 3rd ed., Copyright © 1970, p. 87. Adapted by permission of Prentice-Hall, Inc., Englewood Cliffs, N.J.

for the first time during a marketing research study. This topic will be discussed at length later in the chapter.

Secondary data is *previously published matter.* It serves as an extremely important source of information for the marketing researcher.

Collecting Secondary Data

Not only is secondary data important to the marketing researcher, it is also very abundant. The overwhelming quantity of secondary data available at little or no cost challenges the researcher to select only pertinent secondary data.

Secondary data consists of two types: internal and external. *Internal secondary data* includes records of sales, product performances, sales force activities, and marketing costs. These important sources of valuable marketing information are described on pages *93–96.*

External data is obtained from a variety of sources. Governments—local, state, and federal—provide a wide variety of secondary data. Private sources also supply secondary data for the marketing decision maker.

Government Sources The federal government is the nation's most important source of marketing data, and the most frequently used government statistics are census data. Although the U.S. government spent more then $1 billion conducting the 1980 Census of Population, census information is available for use at no charge at local libraries, or it can be purchased on computer tapes for instantaneous access at a nominal charge. In addition to the Census of Population, the Bureau of the Census also conducts a Census of Housing (which is combined with the Census of Population), a Census of Business, a Census of Manufactures, a Census of Agriculture, a Census of Minerals, and a Census of Governments.

The 1980 census is so detailed for large cities that breakdowns of population characteristics are available by city block. Thus, local retailers and shopping center developers can easily gather specific information about customers in the immediate neighborhood without spending the time or money to conduct a comprehensive survey.

So much information is produced by the federal government that marketing researchers often purchase summaries such as the *Monthly Catalog of United States Government Publications,* the *Statistical Abstract of the United States,* the *Survey of Current Business,* and the *County and City Data Book.* Published annually, the *Statistical Abstract* contains a wealth of current data. The *Survey of Current Business,* updated monthly, focuses on a variety of industrial data. The *County and City Data Book,* typically published every three years, provides a variety of data for each county and each city of over 25,000 residents.

State and city governments serve as other important sources of information on employment, production, and sales activities. In addition, university bureaus of business and economic research often collect and disseminate such information.

Private Sources Many private organizations provide information for the marketing executive. For data on activities in a particular industry, trade associations are excellent sources. Advertising agencies continually collect information on the audience reached by various media. A wide range of valuable data is found in the annual *Survey of Buying Power* published by *Sales and Marketing Management* magazine. Figure 4.3 illus-

FIGURE 4.3
The Survey of
Buying Power
Provides Detailed
Information for the
Marketing
Researcher

CAL. (cont.) $$ EFFECTIVE BUYING INCOME 1980							
S&MM ESTIMATES							
METRO AREA / County / City	Total EBI ($000)	Median Hsld. EBI	% of Hslds. by EBI Group: (A) $8,000–$9,999 (B) $10,000–$14,999 (C) $15,000–$24,999 (D) $25,000 & Over				Buying Power Index
			A	B	C	D	
LOS ANGELES - LONG BEACH	68,250,824	21,231	4.4	11.8	25.8	40.5	3.5761
Los Angeles	68,250,824	21,231	4.4	11.8	25.8	40.5	3.5761
Alhambra	602,498	20,136	4.9	12.0	27.6	37.0	.0333
Arcadia	604,308	26,674	3.0	9.6	21.5	53.8	.0327
Baldwin Park	287,150	18,820	4.4	13.6	34.9	29.6	.0160
Bellflower	456,834	20,378	4.0	12.5	31.6	34.9	.0260
Burbank	848,080	21,900	4.0	13.0	27.9	41.1	.0422
Carson	584,650	25,686	2.6	8.9	28.2	52.2	.0374
Compton	389,455	16,840	5.8	16.0	33.6	22.6	.0239
Downey	874,392	25,616	2.6	9.0	26.5	51.8	.0509
El Monte	465,838	17,090	5.7	16.5	32.4	25.0	.0311
Gardena	418,012	23,716	4.0	9.9	27.2	46.0	.0228
Glendale	1,511,824	21,019	4.5	12.2	25.1	40.6	.0798
Hawthorne	516,481	22,185	3.6	12.6	31.6	40.5	.0287
Inglewood	800,296	19,579	4.4	14.2	30.5	34.3	.0421
Lakewood	694,541	26,512	2.0	6.9	28.4	55.7	.0340
● Long Beach	3,427,841	18,426	5.4	12.2	24.9	34.0	.1731
● Los Angeles	27,419,425	19,067	5.1	13.3	24.8	36.0	1.4223
Lynwood	288,306	18,488	5.0	13.2	33.8	28.5	.0164
Montebello	466,533	22,583	3.7	11.1	27.9	43.3	.0245
Monterey Park	522,790	24,979	2.8	9.8	26.3	49.9	.0248
Norwalk	604,056	23,535	2.4	8.4	35.8	44.1	.0339
Pasadena	1,247,004	19,248	5.6	12.5	23.5	37.5	.0691
Pico Rivera	363,061	22,970	3.1	9.9	33.6	42.9	.0178
Pomona	664,754	19,374	5.3	13.3	29.0	33.5	.0411
Redondo Beach	576,442	24,272	3.4	8.8	27.3	47.7	.0306
Rosemead	266,537	18,696	5.0	13.0	31.5	30.5	.0155
Santa Monica	988,090	18,802	5.0	13.8	25.1	35.3	.0533
South Gate	443,294	17,544	5.1	16.0	32.1	26.7	.0240
Torrance	1,384,252	28,393	2.2	7.3	22.6	60.0	.0878
West Covina	765,402	28,803	1.9	5.8	23.5	62.4	.0436
Whittier	748,962	24,544	3.9	9.8	23.3	48.8	.0416
SUBURBAN TOTAL	37,403,558	23,111	3.8	10.6	26.4	44.8	1.9807

Source: Survey of Buying Power, *Sales & Marketing Management,* July 27, 1981. Reprinted by permission from *Sales & Marketing Management* magazine. © 1981. S&MM Survey of Buying Power.

trates the detailed information it collects for each state of the United States and the provinces of Canada.[8]

Several national firms also offer information to businesses on a subscription basis. The largest of these, A. C. Nielsen Company, collects data every two months on product sales, retail prices, display space, inventories, and promotional activities of competing brands of food and drug products. Its data sample consists of about 1,600 supermarkets, 750 drugstores, and 150 mass merchandisers.

Market Research Corporation of America (MRCA) gathers information on consumer purchases of food and other household items from a panel of over 7,000 U.S. households. The panel periodically gives MRCA a detailed list of all food and other household products

**TABLE 4.8
Estimated Time
Involved in
Conducting a
Marketing Research
Study Utilizing
Primary Data**

Step	Estimated Time Required for Completion
Problem Definition	Several Days
Development of Methodology and Sample Design	One Week
Questionnaire Design	One Week
Questionnaire Pre-test and Evaluation of Pre-test Results	Two Weeks
Field Interviews	One to Six Weeks
Coding of Returned Questionnaires	One Week
Data Transfer to Computer Tape	One Week
Data Processing and Statistical Analysis	Seven to Ten Days
Interpretation of Output	One Week
Written Report and Presentation of Findings	Two Weeks
TOTAL ELAPSED TIME	12 to 17 WEEKS

Source: Estimates by Alfred S. Boote, Corporate Director of Market Research, The Singer Company. Quoted in "Everyone Benefits from Closer Planning, Research Ties," *Marketing News,* January 9, 1981, p. 30. Used by permission of the American Marketing Association.

purchased during a particular time. This information can be extremely useful in determining brand preferences, the effects of various promotional activities on retail sales in a particular region or among an age group, and the degree of brand switching that occurs with different products.

Advantages and Limitations of Secondary Data

The use of secondary data offers two important advantages: (1) the assembly of secondary data is almost always less expensive than the collection of primary data; and (2) less time is involved in locating and using secondary data. Table 4.8 shows the estimated time involved in completing a research study requiring primary data. Although the time involved in a marketing research study will vary considerably, depending on such factors as the research subject and the scope of the study, an additional time and cost investment is required when primary data are needed.

The researcher, however, must be aware of two potential limitations: the data may be obsolete, or its classifications may not be usable in the proposed research study.

Published information can quickly become obsolete. A marketing researcher analyzing the population of the Orlando, Florida, metropolitan market in early 1983 discovers that most of the 1980 census data is obsolete due to the influx of residents to the area. Also, data may have been collected previously on the basis of county or city boundaries, but the marketing manager may require data broken down by city blocks or census tracts. In such cases, the marketing researcher may not be able to rearrange the secondary data in usable form and may have to begin collecting primary data.

Collecting Primary Data

The marketing researcher has three alternatives in the collection of primary data: observation, survey, or controlled experiment. No single method is best in all circumstances, and any of these methods may prove the most efficient in a particular situation.

The Observation Method Observational studies are conducted by actually viewing the overt actions of the person being studied. They may take the form of a traffic count at a potential location for a fast-food franchise, the use of supermarket scanners to record sales of certain products, or a check of license plates at a shopping center to determine where shoppers live.

A. C. Nielsen's audimeter records the times television sets are turned on and which channels are viewed. And in a famous study reported by Vance Packard, a special camera equipped with a telephoto lens recorded the number of consumer eye blinks per minute and, in some instances, allegedly indicated the mild hypnotic trance of a person "overcome" by the complexity of colors and packages on a supermarket shelf.[9]

The Survey Method Some information cannot be obtained through observation. The researcher must ask questions in order to obtain information on attitudes, motives, and opinions. The most widely used approach to collecting primary data is the survey method. Three kinds of surveys exist: telephone, mail, and personal interviews.

Telephone interviews are inexpensive and fast for obtaining small quantities of relatively impersonal information. Since many firms have leased WATS services (telephone company services that allow businesses to make unlimited long-distance calls for a fixed rate per state or region), a call to the most distant state costs no more than an across-town interview.[10]

Telephone interviews account for an estimated 55 to 60 percent of all primary marketing research. A national survey revealed that one woman in five had been interviewed by telephone in 1980, as compared with one in seven only two years earlier. The percentage of men who had participated in telephone interviews had grown from one in ten in 1978 to one in seven in 1980.[11] Telephone interviews are, however, limited to simple, clearly worded questions. Also it is extremely difficult to obtain information on respondents' personal characteristics, and the survey may be prejudiced by the omission of households without phones or with unlisted numbers.

One survey reported that alphabetical listings in telephone directories excluded one-third of blacks with telephones and one-fourth of large-city dwellers and that they underrepresented service workers and separated and divorced persons. In addition, the mobility of the population creates problems in choosing names from telephone directories. As a result, a number of telephone interviewers have resorted to using digits selected at random and matched to telephone prefixes in the geographic area to be sampled. This technique is designed to correct the problem of sampling those with new telephone listings and those with unlisted numbers.[12]

Mail interviews allow the marketing researcher to conduct national studies at a reasonable cost. Whereas personal interviews with a national sample may be prohibitive in cost, the researcher can contact each potential respondent for the price of a postage stamp. Costs can be misleading, however. For example, returned questionnaires for such studies may average only 40 to 50 percent, depending on the length of the questionnaire and respondent interest. Also, some mail surveys include a coin to gain the reader's attention (such as the illustration in Figure 4.4), which further increases costs.[13] Unless additional information is obtained from nonrespondents, the results of mail interviews are likely to be biased, since there may be important differences in the characteristics of respondents and nonrespondents. For this reason, follow-up questionnaires are sometimes mailed to nonrespondents, or telephone interviews are used to gather additional information.[14]

In 1980, the U.S. Bureau of the Census conducted the largest mail survey in history when it mailed census questionnaires to 80 million households. A number of questions were raised, including the difficulties of developing an accurate population count utilizing mail questionnaires. Another sensitive subject concerned confidentiality of answers. The 85 percent response rate was a pleasant surprise to Census Bureau officials and to researchers throughout the world who rely upon mail surveys to obtain research data.

Personal interviews are typically the best means of obtaining detailed information, since the interviewer has the opportunity to establish rapport with each respondent and can explain confusing or vague questions. Although mail questionnaires are carefully worded and often pretested to eliminate potential misunderstandings, such misunderstandings can occur anyway. When an employee of the U.S. Department of Agriculture accidentally ran into and killed a cow with his truck, an official of the department sent the farmer an apology and a form to be filled out. The form included a space for "disposition of the dead cow." The farmer responded, "Kind and gentle."[15]

Personal interviews are slow and are the most expensive method of collecting survey data. However, their flexibility coupled with the detailed information that can be collected often offset these limita-

FIGURE 4.4
Use of a Coin to
Attract Attention and
Increase Mail Survey
Response Rates

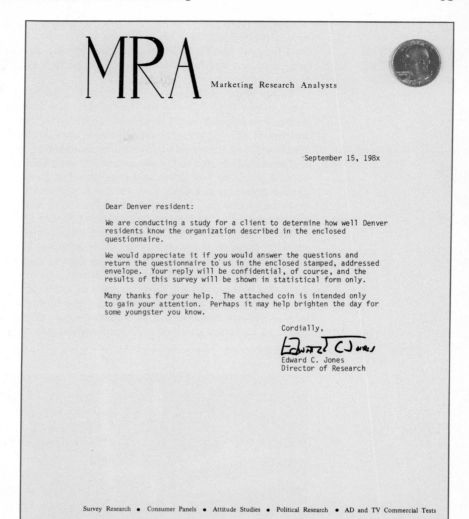

MRA   Marketing Research Analysts

September 15, 198x

Dear Denver resident:

We are conducting a study for a client to determine how well Denver residents know the organization described in the enclosed questionnaire.

We would appreciate it if you would answer the questions and return the questionnaire to us in the enclosed stamped, addressed envelope. Your reply will be confidential, of course, and the results of this survey will be shown in statistical form only.

Many thanks for your help. The attached coin is intended only to gain your attention. Perhaps it may help brighten the day for some youngster you know.

Cordially,

Edward C. Jones
Director of Research

Survey Research   •   Consumer Panels   •   Attitude Studies   •   Political Research   •   AD and TV Commercial Tests

tions. The refusal to be interviewed and the increasing difficulty of hiring interviewers to call on respondents at night present additional problems in utilizing this technique.

Focus group interviews have been widely used in recent years as a means of gathering research information. In a **focus group interview,** *eight to twelve individuals are brought together in one location to discuss a subject of interest.* Although the moderator typically explains the purpose of the meeting and suggests an opening discussion topic, he or she is interested in stimulating interaction among group members in order to develop the discussion of numerous points about the subject. Focus group sessions, which are often one to two hours long, are usually taped so the moderator can devote full attention to the discussion.[16]

TURNING THE UNIVERSITY INTO A LAB

Clad in gym shoes, T-shirts, and faded blue jeans, the students wait two, three, even four deep in line to participate in a research project at the University of Illinois.

The project—begun in 1977—tests the latest amusement games of every major U.S. manufacturer of pinball and video games. Dozens of the games are packed into a basement corridor in the student union building and the U of I ice arena in one of those rare, mutually profitable collaborations between business and academia.

The students get to try the latest in electronic game technology at 25 cents a game or half-price and they play the games months before the games show up in trendy bars on the Near North Side of Chicago. The manufacturers can get a reading on how well their games are accepted by a representative sample of their precise target group.

Says a pleased Cliff Strain, assistant sales manager for games manufacturer D. Gottlieb and Co. of Northlake, Illinois, "The university is one of the top five spots in the country that I depend on."

What Mr. Strain—and dozens of others like him—bases his faith on is a weekly printout of the performance of each game and manufacturer that provides the information in terms the manufacturers understand best—"dollars and cents." Says Jerry Fuqua, director of Campus Vending, the U of I agency charged with running the game room: "Ninety-five

Photos courtesy of Dean Meador.

percent of the time, the money in the coin box determines a game's success."

The printout includes information on the amount of money each game made for the past week, the amount it made for the past five weeks, the number of times it was beaten, the number of times it broke down, the date it arrived on campus, and its location. Because all the manufacturers receive the same printout, they can compare their games with their competitors' . . . . The university also benefits from the game room, netting $250,000 last year . . . .

And the intelligence from here seems to indicate that Atari's Missile Command is destined for greatness. It is racking up a whopping $400-a-week gross in the Illini Union, four times the $100 a week a game needs to survive in the hotly competitive game corridor. Asteroids, also from Atari, and Exidy's Targ are in the same $400 league and can expect national promotion, thanks to the support from U of I students . . . .

But when it comes to longevity in a business where product life is measured in weeks, none can top Space Invaders from Midway. The game of the marching aliens continues to pull in a respectable $100 a week some three years after it first bowed in the union . . . .

Source: Mary McNicholas, "Students Score as the Professors while Testing Video Games at U of I," *Crain's Chicago Business*, January 5, 1981, pp. 1, 23. Reprinted by permission of *Crain's Chicago Business*. Copyright 1981 by Crain Communications Inc.

The Experimental Method The final and least-used method of collecting marketing information is that of controlled experiments. An experiment is a scientific investigation in which a researcher controls or manipulates a test group or groups and compares the results with that of a control group that did not receive the controls or manipulations. Although such experiments can be conducted in the field or in a laboratory setting, most have been conducted in the field. To date, the most common use of this method by marketers has been in test marketing.

Marketers face great risk in their efforts to gain acceptance for new products. They often attempt to reduce this risk by *test marketing*—introducing the product into a particular metropolitan area and then observing its degree of success. Frequently used cities include Toledo, Ohio; Peoria, Illinois; Des Moines, Iowa; and Phoenix, Arizona. Consumers in the test market city view the product as any other new product since it is available in retail outlets and advertised in the local media. The test market city becomes a microcosm of the total market.

The marketing manager compares actual sales with expected sales and projects the figures on a nationwide basis. If the test results are favorable, the risk of a large-scale failure is reduced. Many products fail at the test market stage; thus consumers who live in these cities may have purchased products that no one else will ever buy.

The major problem with controlled experiments is controlling all variables in a real-life situation. The laboratory scientist can rigidly control temperature and humidity. But how can the marketing manager determine the effect of, say, reducing the retail price through refundable coupons when the competition simultaneously issues such coupons?

Experimentation in this area will become more common as firms develop sophisticated competitive models for computer analysis. Simulation of market activities promises to be one of the great new developments in marketing.[17]

Sampling

Information is rarely gathered from all sources during a survey. If all sources are contacted, the results are known as a census. But unless the number of sources is small, the costs will be so great that only the federal government will be able to afford them—and it uses this method only once every ten years. Instead, researchers select a representative group called a sample. If this sample is chosen in such a way that every member has an equal chance of being selected, then the sample is a probability sample. A probability sample of students at Florida International University in Miami, for example, can be drawn by obtaining a list of names from the college registrar and assigning each a number, then selecting numbers on the list from a table of random numbers and questioning those selected.

A method of obtaining a probability sample where population lists are unavailable is area sampling. Here, blocks instead of individuals are selected at random for the survey. Then, either everyone on the se-

**TABLE 4.9
Management and
Researcher
Complaints**

A. Management complaints about marketing researchers:

1. Research is not problem-oriented. It tends to provide a plethora of facts, not actionable results or direction.
2. Researchers are too involved with techniques. They tend to do research for research's sake and they appear to be reluctant to get involved in management "problems."
3. Research is slow, vague, and of questionable validity. It depends too much on clinical evidence.
4. Researchers can't communicate; they don't understand; and they don't talk the language of management. In many cases, researchers are inexperienced and not well rounded.

B. Marketing researcher complaints about management:

1. Management doesn't include research in discussions of basic fundamental problems. Management tends to ask only for specific information about parts of problems.
2. Management pays no more than lip service to research and doesn't really understand or appreciate its value. Research isn't given enough corporate status.
3. Management has a propensity to jump the gun—not allowing enough time for research. Management draws preliminary conclusions based on early or incomplete results.
4. Management relies more on intuition and judgment than on research. Research is used as a crutch, not a tool. Management tends to "typecast" the marketing researcher.

Source: Reprinted by permission from "Communication Gap Hinders Proper Use of Market Research," *Marketing Insights,* February 19, 1968, p. 7. Copyright 1968 by Crain Communications, Inc.

lected blocks is interviewed or respondents are randomly chosen from each designated block.

**Interpreting
Research
Findings**

A number of marketing research books contain solutions to the many problems involved in surveying the public.[18] Among these problems are designing the questionnaires; selecting, training, and controlling the field interviewers; editing, coding, tabulating, and interpreting the data; presenting the results; and following up on the survey.

It is imperative that marketing researchers and research users cooperate at every stage in the research design. Too many studies go unused because marketing management views the results as too restricted due to the lengthy discussion of research limitations or the use of unfamiliar terminology such as "levels of confidence" and "Type 1 errors."[19]

Occasional misunderstandings between marketing researchers and the manager-user may lead to friction between the parties and failure to make effective utilization of the research findings. Table 4.9 lists several complaints that each party may express about the other.

These complaints reflect lack of understanding of the needs and capabilities of both parties. Such complaints can often be settled by involving both managers and researchers in specifying needed information, developing research designs, and evaluating the findings of the research. The research report should include recommendations and, whenever possible, an oral report should explain, expand upon, or clarify the written summary. These efforts also serve to increase the likelihood of management's utilizing the research findings.

Using Outside Research Agencies

Although most large companies have their own marketing research departments, many smaller ones depend on independent marketing research firms to conduct their research studies. Even large firms typically rely on outside agencies to provide interviewers, and they often farm out some research studies to independent agencies as well. The decision of whether to conduct a study through an outside organization or internally is usually based on cost. Another consideration is the reliability and accuracy of the information collected by the agency.

Research is likely to be contracted to outside groups when the following requirements are met:

1. Problem areas can be defined in terms of specific research projects.
2. There is a need for specialized know-how or equipment.
3. Intellectual detachment is a requirement.[20]

An outside group is often able to provide technical assistance and expertise not available within the firm. Also, the use of outside groups helps ensure that the researcher is not conducting the study only to validate the wisdom of a favorite theory or package design. The most recent survey of marketing research by the American Marketing Association revealed that almost half the total marketing research budget of the responding firms was spent on outside research.[21]

MARKETING INFORMATION SYSTEMS

Many marketing managers discover that their information problems result from an overabundance—not a paucity—of marketing data. What they need is a systematic way to obtain relevant information. One can achieve this goal by installing a planned marketing information system (MIS). The ideal **marketing information system** should be *a designed set of procedures and methods for generating an orderly flow of pertinent information for use in making decisions, providing management with the current and future states of the market, and indicating market responses to company and competitor actions.*[22]

A properly constructed MIS can serve as the nerve center for the company, providing instantaneous information suitable for each level of management. It can act as a thermostat, monitoring the marketplace continuously so that management can adjust its actions as conditions change.

The role of marketing information in a firm's marketing system can be illustrated with the analogy of how an automatic heating system works (see Figure 4.5). Once the objective of a particular temper-

**FIGURE 4.5
A Heating System
Decision: Turn the
Furnace On or Off**

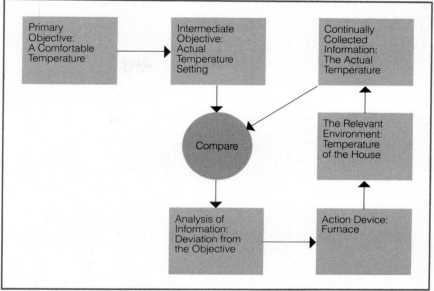

Source: Reprinted by permission from Bertram Schoner and Kenneth P. Uhl, *Marketing Research: Information Systems and Decision Making* (New York: John Wiley & Sons, Inc., 1975), p. 10.

ature setting (for example, 68 degrees Fahrenheit) has been established, information about the actual temperature is collected and compared with the objective, and a decision based on this comparison is made. If the temperature drops below the established figure, the decision is to activate the furnace until the temperature reaches the established level. If the temperature is too high, the decision is to turn off the furnace.

Any change the firm experiences may necessitate changes in price structures, promotional expenditures, package design, or other marketing alternatives. The firm's MIS should be capable of revealing such deviations and of suggesting new plans for attaining the established goals. Creating an effective MIS, however, is more easily said than done. Several firms' attempts have succeeded only in further complicating their data-retrieval systems.

**Marketing
Research and
the Marketing
Information
System**

Many marketing executives feel that their organizations are too small to make use of a marketing information system. Others contend that their marketing research department provides adequate research data for decision making. Such contentions often result from a misconception of the services and functions performed by the marketing research department. Marketing research has already been described as typically focusing on a specific problem or project; its investigations have a definite beginning, middle, and end.

Marketing information systems, on the other hand, are much wider in scope, involving the continual collection and analysis of

**FIGURE 4.6
Information
Components of the
Firm's Marketing
Information System**

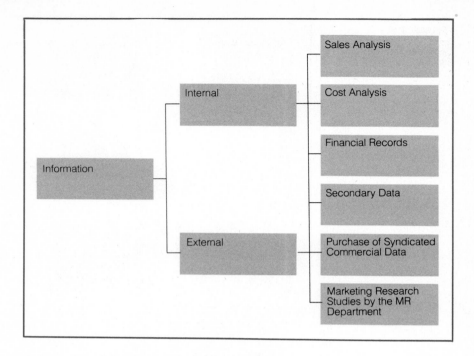

marketing information. Figure 4.6 indicates the various information inputs—including marketing research studies—that serve as components of a firm's MIS.

Robert J. Williams, creator of the first marketing information system, explains the difference:

The difference between marketing research and marketing intelligence is like the difference between a flash bulb and a candle. Let's say you are dancing in the dark. Every 90 seconds you're allowed to set off a flash bulb. You can use those brief intervals of intense light to chart a course, but remember everybody is moving, too. Hopefully, they'll accommodate themselves roughly to your predictions. You may get bumped and you may stumble every so often, but you can dance along.

On the other hand, you can light a candle. It doesn't yield as much light, but it's a steady light. You are continually aware of the movements of other bodies. You can adjust your own course to the courses of the others. The intelligence system is a kind of candle. It's no great flash on the immediate state of things, but it provides continuous light as situations shift and change.[23]

By focusing daily on the marketplace, the MIS provides a continuous systematic and comprehensive study of areas that indicate deviations from established goals. The up-to-the-minute information allows problems to be corrected before they adversely affect operations.

FIGURE 4.7
Current and Future Allocation of MIS Resources

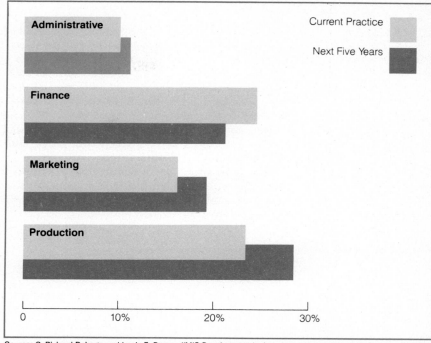

Source: C. Richard Roberts and Louis E. Boone, "MIS Development in American Industry: The Apex," *Journal of Business Strategy,* Winter 1983. Reprinted by permission of the authors.

Current Status of Marketing Information Systems

Marketing information systems have progressed a long way from the days when they were primarily responsible for clerical activities—and usually at an increased cost over the old method. Today, managers have available special computer programs, remote access consoles, better data banks, direct communication with the computer, and assignment of authority to the computer for review and referral. In some instances, the computer simulates market conditions and makes decisions based on the results of the model. But how does the marketer's information system relate to similar systems for decision makers in other functional areas?

Marketing information systems are major components of the firm's overall management information system—the information base for decision making in all functional areas. A recent survey of the 500 largest firms in the United States focused on the allocation of overall management information resources to each of the functional areas. A total of 202 responding companies indicated the approximate percentage of their total information system resources—including hardware, software, facilities, and personnel—allocated to four organizational functions: administration, finance, marketing, and production. Figure 4.7 shows their responses and their predictions of relative allocations for the next five years. Although production and finance currently receive most of the management information system's re-

MONSANTO

Monsanto, a diversified international industrial company headquartered in St. Louis, has designed one of the most advanced marketing information systems in operation. The system provides detailed sales analyses by product, sales district, type of mill, and end use. Consumer analyses for the ultimate use of some Monsanto products (tires, fabrics, and synthetic fibers for carpets, for instance) are obtained from a continuing panel of 7,500 households who represent a cross-section of the national market. Information is collected on purchase patterns by socioeconomic group and is then analyzed to determine current buying trends.

Monsanto also collects survey data to record the actions of competitors. In addition, the system generates short-, medium-, and long-range forecasts for the company and industry. Short-term forecasts are developed for each of 400 individual products.

sources, additional resources are expected to be devoted to marketing during the next five years.

Successful Marketing Information Systems

Although only a few large companies currently have sophisticated computer-based marketing information systems, considerable attention is being focused on their contributions. By the end of the decade, most medium-sized companies will have established their own information systems. Monsanto and General Mills are two firms with a successful MIS in operation.

Developing an MIS

Constructing an MIS requires the full support of top management. Management not only must be truly enthusiastic about the potential of the system, but also must believe that it is top management's place to oversee its development. Too often, technical staffs are left to build the system. The next step involves a review and appraisal of the entire marketing organization and of the policies that direct it. The marketing managers' responsibilities must be clearly defined if the system is to measure their performance against company plans.

Next, the organization's level of sophistication must be determined. Relating to this, the company's needs and the costs of meeting those needs must be carefully considered. The ability of managers to develop and effectively use a sophisticated system must also be considered. A questionnaire such as the one illustrated in Table 4.10 can be used to pinpoint managers' specific information requirements.

Management must also be able to state explicitly its planning, decision-making, and control processes and procedures. An auto-

GENERAL MILLS

The General Mills computer supplies each zone, regional, and district manager with a daily teletype report on (1) the previous day's orders by brand and (2) current projections of monthly sales compared with the monthly total projected the week before. Each of 1,700 products is analyzed in terms of current profitability and projected annual profitability as compared with target projections made at the beginning of the year. "Problem" products requiring management attention are also listed in the daily report. A similar report looks for problem areas in each region and breaks down each problem by cause.

Source: Information from "Marketing Management and the Computer," *Sales Management,* August 20, 1965, pp. 49–60. See also Leon Winer, "Effective Computer Use in Marketing Information Systems and Model Building," *Marketing: 1776–1976 and Beyond,* ed. Kenneth L. Bernhardt (Chicago: American Marketing Association, 1976), pp. 626–29.

mated exception reporting system can be developed for the manager who states: "I always like to know about all situations in which sales, profits, or market shares are running 4% or more behind plan. Furthermore, in any exceptional cases I also require the following diagnostic information: prices, distribution levels, advertising, and consumer attitudes."[24]

MIS in the Future

As marketing research becomes increasingly scientific and is combined by a growing number of organizations into fully functional information systems, decision makers benefit by making *informed* decisions about problems and opportunities. Sophisticated computer simulations make it possible to consider alternative courses of action by posing a number of "what if?" situations. These developments may convert the imaginary scenario described below into reality in a few years.

TABLE 4.10 Sample Questionnaire for Determining Marketing Information Needs

1. What types of decisions are you regularly called upon to make?
2. What types of information do you need to make the decision?
3. What types of information do you regularly get?
4. What types of special studies do you periodically request?
5. What types of information would you like to get but are not currently receiving?
6. What information would you like to receive daily? weekly? monthly? yearly?
7. What magazines and trade journals would you like to receive regularly?
8. What types of data analysis programs would you like to receive?
9. What are four improvements you would like to see made in the present marketing information system?

Source: Philip Kotler, "A Design for the Firm's Marketing Nerve Center," *Business Horizons,* Fall 1966, p. 70. Copyright © 1966 by the Foundation for the School of Business at Indiana University. Reprinted by permission.

A PEEK AT THE FUTURE OF INFORMATION SYSTEMS

The year is 1988. The place is the office of the marketing manager of a medium-sized consumer products manufacturer. The participants in the following discussion are John, the marketing manager; Anne, the director of marketing science; Rod, Anne's assistant, who specializes in marketing research; and Scott, the sales manager for the company. The scene opens as Anne, Rod, and Scott enter John's office.

John: *Good morning. What's on the agenda for this morning?*

Anne: *We want to take a look at the prospects for our new beef substitute.*

John: *What do we have on that new product?*

Rod: *We test-marketed it late in 1987 in four cities; so we have those data from last quarter.*

John: *Let's see how it did.*

(All four gather around the remote console video display unit. John activates the console and requests it to display the sales results from the most recent test market. The systems retrieves the data and displays the information on the video device.)

John: *That looks good! How does it compare to the first test?*

(The console retrieves and displays the data from the first test on command from John.)

Rod: *Let me check the significance of the sales increase of the most recent test over last year's test.*

(Rod requests that the system test and display the likelihood that the sales increase could be a chance occurrence.)

Rod: *Looks like a solid sales increase.*

Anne: *Good! How did the market respond to our change in price?*

(Anne commands the system to display the graph of the price-quantity response based on the most recent test data.)

John: *Is that about what our other meat substitute products show?*

(John calls up past price-quantity response graphs for similar products.)

John: *Just as I suspected. This new product is a bit more responsive to price. What's the profit estimate?*

(John calls for a profit estimate from the product-planning model within the system.)

John: *Hmm . . . $5,500,000. Looks good. Is that based on the growth model I supplied to the model bank last week?*

Anne: *No. This is based on the market-share progress other food substitutes have shown in the past as well as the information we have on the beef substitute from our test markets.*

John: *Let's see what mine would do.*

(He reactivates the product-planning model, this time using his growth model. The profit implications are displayed on the console.)

John: *Well, my model predicts $5 million. That's close. Looks like my feelings are close to the statistical results.*

Anne: *Let's see if there's a better marketing strategy for this product.*

We must remember that these profit estimates are based on the preliminary plan we developed two weeks ago.

(Anne calls for the marketing mix generator to recommend a marketing program based upon the data and judgmental inputs on file for this product.)

John: *I'm a little worried about our advertising appeals. Can we improve in this area?*

Anne: *Let's see what the response to advertising is.*

(The video unit shows a graph of the predicted sales-advertising response function.)

Anne: *If we changed from a taste appeal to a convenience appeal, what would the results be, John?*

John: *I think it would look like this.*

(John takes a light pen and describes a new relationship on the video unit based upon his judgment of the effectiveness of the new appeal.)

Rod: *Let me check something.*

(Rod calls for a sample of past sales-advertising response curves of similar products using the convenience appeal.)

Rod: *I think you are underestimating the response on the basis of past data.*

John: *Well, this product is different. How much would it cost for a test of this appeal?*

(Rod calls a marketing research evaluation model from the console.)

Rod: *It looks like a meaningful test would cost about $5,000.*

John: *I wonder what risk we'd run if we made a decision to go national with the product right now. What are the chances of a failure with this product as it stands if we include this morning's revisions to the marketing mix?*

(A risk-analysis model is called up on the system.)

John: *Looks like a 35 percent chance of failure. Maybe we'd best run further tests in order to reduce the risk of failure. What's next on the agenda this morning?*

Source: David B. Montgomery and Glen L. Urban, *Management Science in Marketing* (Englewood Cliffs, N.J.: Prentice-Hall, 1969), pp. 1–3. Adapted by permission of Prentice-Hall, Inc., Englewood Cliffs, N.J.

SUMMARY

Information is vital for marketing decision making. No firm can operate without detailed information of its market. Information may take several forms: one-time marketing research studies, secondary data, internal sales and marketing cost analyses, and subscriptions to commercial information sources.

Marketing research, an important source of decision information, includes the systematic gathering, recording, and analyzing of data about marketing problems and opportunities. It involves the specific delineation of problems, research design, collection of secondary and primary data, interpretation of research findings, and presentation of results for management decision making.

The scope of marketing information has broadened as an increasing number of firms have installed planned marketing information systems. Properly designed, the MIS will generate an orderly flow of decision-oriented information as the marketing executive needs it. The number of firms with planned information systems will grow during the 1980s as more managers recognize their contribution to dealing with the information explosion.

QUESTIONS FOR DISCUSSION

1. Explain the following terms:

   marketing research   research design
   exploratory research   primary data
   sales analysis   secondary data
   sales quota   focus group interview
   marketing cost analysis   marketing information system (MIS)

2. You have been asked to determine the effect on Gillette of Schick's introduction of a revolutionary new blade that is guaranteed to give a hundred nick-free shaves. Outline your approach to the study.

3. Describe how Scripto, Inc., used marketing research to successfully market their erasable, disposable pen.

4. Identify the steps in the management decision process. Give an example of a type of information that may be used at each step.

5. Distinguish between primary and secondary data.

6. What advantages does the use of secondary data offer the marketing researcher? What potential limitations exist in using such data?

7. What type of marketing information can be obtained from the metropolitan chamber of commerce in your city (or a nearby city)?

8. Collect from secondary sources the following information:
   a. retail sales in Akron, Ohio, for last year
   b. number of persons over sixty-five in Springfield, Massachusetts
   c. earnings per share for Chrysler last year
   d. bituminous coal production in the United States in a recent year
   e. consumer price index for a given month
   f. number of households earning more than $15,000 in Miami, Florida

9. Distinguish among surveys, experiments, and observational methods of data collection.

10. Suggest several instances in which an area sample rather than a simple random sample might be used in gathering primary data.

11. Illustrate each of the three methods for gathering survey data. Under what circumstances should each be used?

12. Under what circumstances would nonrandom sampling techniques be used?

13. What are the chief problems in using telephone interviews?

14. Why do marketing researchers sometimes resort to secretly coding mail questionnaires? What ethical issues are involved?

15. Under what circumstances should a firm use an outside marketing research firm to conduct research studies?

16. Frank Antonelli, the marketing vice-president of the Digital Time Company, refuses to involve himself with the activities of his marketing research staff. He explains that he has hired competent professionals for the research department, and he does not plan to meddle in their operation. Critically evaluate Antonelli's position.

17. Distinguish between marketing research and marketing information systems.

18. Explain the similarities between marketing information and the thermostat of a heating system.

19. Identify the major information components of a marketing information system.

20. A business executive has asked your assistance in developing a new MIS for her firm. Describe how you would proceed with this task.

NOTES

1. Adapted with permission from "Key Role of Research in Agree's Success Is Told," *Marketing News,* January 12, 1979, pp. 14–15. Used by permission of the American Marketing Association.

2. Reported in John E. Cooney, "In Their Quest for Sure Fire Ads, Marketers Use Physiological Tests to Find Out What Grabs You," *Wall Street Journal,* April 12, 1979, p. 40. Reprinted by permission of *The Wall Street Journal,* © Dow Jones Company, Inc. 1979. All rights reserved.

3. Committee on Definitions, *Marketing Definitions: A Glossary of Marketing Terms* (Chicago: American Marketing Association, 1960), p. 17.

4. For a detailed treatment of the historical development of marketing research, see Robert Bartels, *The Development of Marketing Thought* (Homewood, Ill.: Richard D. Irwin, 1962), pp. 106–24.

5. Dik Warren Twedt, ed., *1978 Survey of Marketing Research* (Chicago: American Marketing Association, 1978), pp. 10–13. Used with permission. See also Rohit Deshpande, "The Usefulness of Marketing Information in Decision Making: An Empirical Study of Marketing Research Projects," in *Evolving Marketing Thought for 1980,* eds. John H. Summey and Ronald D. Taylor (New Orleans: Southern Marketing Association, 1980), pp. 482–85.

6. For a discussion of sales analysis, see Donald W. Jackson, Jr., and Lonnie L. Ostrom, "Grouping Segments for Profitability Analysis," *MSU Business Topics,* Spring 1980, pp. 33–44.

7. Patrick M. Dunne and Harry I. Wolk, "Marketing Cost Analysis: A Modularized Contribution Approach," *Journal of Marketing,* July 1977, pp. 83–94.

8. Charles Waldo and Dennis Fuller, "Just How Good Is the 'Survey of Buying Power'?" *Journal of Marketing,* October 1977, pp. 64–66.

9. Vance Packard, *The Hidden Persuaders* (New York: David McKay, 1957).

10. William Lyons and Robert F. Durant, "Interviewer Costs Associated with the Use of Random Digit Dialing in Large Area Samples," *Journal of Marketing,* Summer 1980, pp. 65–69.

11. "Marketing Research Industry Survey Finds Increase in Phone Interviewing," *Marketing News,* January 9, 1981, p. 20.

12. Reported in A. B. Blankenship, "Listed versus Unlisted Numbers in Telephone-Survey Samples," *Journal of Advertising Research,* February 1977, pp. 39–42. See also Roger Gates, Bob Brobst, and Paul Solomon, "Random Digit Dialing: A Review of Methods," in *Proceedings of the Southern Marketing Association,* New Orleans, La., November 1978, pp. 163–65; and Donald S. Tull and Gerald S. Albaum, "Bias in Random Digit-Dialed Surveys," *Public Opinion Quarterly,* Fall 1977, pp. 389–95.

13. Stephen W. McDaniel and C. P. Rao, "The Effect of Monetary Inducement on Mailed Questionnaire Response Quality," *Journal of Marketing Research,* May 1980, pp. 265–68; and Robert A. Hansen, "A Self-Perception Interpretation of the Effect of Monetary and Nonmonetary Incentives on Mail Survey Respondent Behavior," *Journal of Marketing Research,* February 1980, pp. 77–83.

14. Kevin F. McCrohan and Larry S. Lowe, "A Cost/Benefit Approach to Postage Used on Mail Questionnaires," *Journal of Marketing,* Winter 1981, pp. 130–33; and Jacob Hornik, "Time Cue

and Time Perception Effect on Response to Mail Surveys," *Journal of Marketing Research,* May 1981, pp. 243–48.

15.   "About That Cow," *Wall Street Journal,* June 28, 1972.

16.   Fred D. Reynolds and Deborah K. Johnson, "Validity of Focus-Group Findings," *Journal of Advertising Research,* June 1978, pp. 21–24; and Bobby J. Calder, "Focus Groups and the Nature of Qualitative Marketing Research," *Journal of Marketing Research,* August 1977, pp. 353–64.

17.   John R. Nevin, "Using Experimental Data to Suggest and Evaluate Alternative Marketing Strategies," in *Research Frontiers in Marketing,* ed. Subhash C. Jain (Chicago: American Marketing Association, 1978), pp. 207–11; Chem L. Narayana and James F. Horrell, "Evaluation of Quality Factors in Marketing Experiments," *Journal of the Academy of Marketing Science,* Summer 1976, pp. 599–607; and Alan G. Sawyer, Parker M. Worthing, and Paul E. Sendak, "The Role of Laboratory Experiments to Test Marketing Strategies," *Journal of Marketing,* Summer 1979, pp. 60–67.

18.   Two excellent marketing research texts are Gilbert A. Churchill, Jr., *Marketing Research* (Hinsdale, Ill.: The Dryden Press, 1983); and Paul E. Green and Donald S. Tull, *Research for Marketing Decisions* (Englewood Cliffs, N.J.: Prentice-Hall, 1978).

19.   Kenneth Gary McCain, "Business Decision Researchers Can't Afford to be 'Pure'," *Business and Economic Perspectives,* Spring 1979, pp. 41–46; Jeffrey Gandz and Thomas W. Whipple, "Making Marketing Research Accountable," *Journal of Marketing Research,* May 1977, pp. 202–8; and Dwight L. Gentry and John Hoftyzer, "The Misuse of Statistical Techniques in Evaluating Sample Data," *Journal of the Academy of Marketing Science,* Spring 1977, pp. 106–12.

20.   Bertram Schoner and Kenneth P. Uhl, *Marketing Research: Information Systems and Decision Making* (New York: John Wiley & Sons, Inc., 1975), p. 199.

21.   Twedt, *1978 Survey of Marketing Research,* p. 38.

22.   Donald F. Cox and Robert E. Good, "How to Build a Marketing Information System," *Harvard Business Review,* May–June 1967, p. 147. See also Charles D. Schewe and William R. Dillon, "Marketing Information Systems Utilization: An Application of Self-concept Theory," *Journal of Business Research,* January 1978, pp. 67–79.

23.   "Marketing Intelligence Systems: A DEW Line for Marketing Men," *Business Management,* January 1966, p. 32.

24.   Cox and Good, "How to Build a Marketing Information System," p. 152.

PART THREE

MARKET SEGMENTATION AND CONSUMER BEHAVIOR

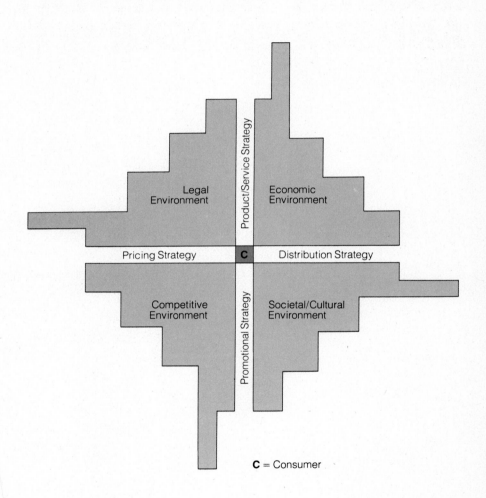

Legal Environment

Economic Environment

Product/Service Strategy

Pricing Strategy   C   Distribution Strategy

Competitive Environment

Societal/Cultural Environment

Promotional Strategy

C = Consumer

CHAPTER 5

MARKET SEGMENTATION: CONSUMER MARKETS

KEY TERMS

market
consumer goods
industrial goods
market segmentation
geographic segmentation
demographic segmentation
psychographic segmentation
benefit segmentation
Standard Metropolitan Statistical Area
    (SMSA)
Standard Consolidated Statistical Area
    (SCSA)
megalopolis
family life cycle
Engel's laws
life-style
psychographics
AIO statements
market target decision analysis

LEARNING GOALS

1. To enumerate the four requirements that must be present for a market to exist

2. To distinguish between consumer goods and industrial goods

3. To list the bases for market segmentation

4. To identify the major recent population shifts and the age groups that will grow fastest during the 1980s

5. To explain the use of the family life cycle in analyzing markets

6. To explain the use of market target decision analysis in segmenting markets

At the beginning of the twentieth century, only one woman in five worked outside the home. By 1985, more than 51 percent of the nation's adult female population will be part of the work force. Three of five married women work.

For most women, the primary motivation for working is economic. William Lazer and John E. Smallwood report that 90 percent of working mothers in sales, clerical, and blue-collar occupations and 71 percent of women employed in the professions worked for economic reasons.[1] Although unprecedented increases in the cost of living have forced the emergence of many two-income households, equal employment legislation has also played a role in stimulating increased female employment by opening job opportunities in traditionally male-dominated occupations.

Source: Reprinted with permission from *Working Woman.* Copyright © 1982 by HAL Publications, inc.

A third factor in stimulating female employment is the social acceptability of women with careers. Women are increasingly represented in the college classroom, and account for almost half the students receiving college degrees each year. Approximately one-third of all students in the nation's Master of Business Administration (MBA) degree programs are women. Such academic preparation helps to move well-qualified women into middle- and top-management positions.

Astute marketers recognize the working woman as an increasingly important market target. Marketing researchers have determined that working women play a greater role in household decision making than do their counterparts who are full-time homemakers.[2] As a result, a growing number of organizations have focused their marketing efforts on this consumer segment.

A number of magazines have been launched in recent years seeking to challenge such long-established women's magazines as the mass-circulation *Family Circle, Woman's Day,* and *Ladies' Home Journal.* The pioneer was *Ms.,* founded in 1972. It was followed by such magazines as *Self* and *New Woman.*

Other newly founded magazines focused more specifically on the working woman. In 1977, *Working Woman* became the first magazine to respond to the working female market. By 1982 it had attracted a monthly readership of 2¼ million with its articles ranging from female success stories to fashion. Monthly issues contain sections on such subjects as law, money, jobs, style, leisure, ethics, and MBA (management/business advice).

Working Woman's success has attracted a number of competitors, including *Enterprising Woman, Savvy, Working Mother,* and *Women Who Work.*

The success rate for new magazines is only about one in ten, and magazines focusing on working women face special hurdles.

Like any publication that tries to be both women-minded and business-minded, they must compete with traditional business publications that provide more business information and with traditional women's magazines that offer more fashion and lifestyle material. In effect, they are gambling on the possibility that women achievers want different business and lifestyle information than is available in old-line publications or, at least, want it in magazines they can regard as their own.[3]

The growth in the number of such magazines reflects both the size and rate of growth in their chosen market target. Such magazines are more than products being offered to this segment; of equal importance is their ability to provide advertisers with a means of communicating with this important segment of the consumer marketplace.

WHAT IS A MARKET?

Although marketers may face hundreds of decisions in developing an effective plan for achieving organizational objectives, these decisions may be summarized in two fundamental tasks:

1. They must identify, evaluate, and ultimately select a *market target.*
2. Once the market target has been selected, they must develop and implement a *marketing mix* designed to satisfy the chosen target group.

These two tasks reflect the philosophy of consumer orientation in action.

A market is people—but people alone do not make a market. A real estate salesperson would be unimpressed by news that 50 percent of a marketing class raised their hands in response to the question: "Who wants to buy a condominium in Daytona Beach?" More pertinent would be the answer to this question: "How many of them have $10,000 for the down payment and can qualify for the mortgage loan?" A **market** *requires not only people and willingness to buy, but also purchasing power and authority to buy.*

A successful salesperson quickly learns how to pinpoint which individual in an organization or household has the authority to make particular purchasing decisions. Without this knowledge, too much time can be spent convincing the wrong person that the product or service should be bought.

Consumer Markets versus Industrial Markets

Products are often classified as either consumer goods or industrial goods. **Consumer goods** are *products purchased by the ultimate consumer for personal use.* **Industrial goods** are *products purchased for use either directly or indirectly in the production of other goods for resale.* Most products purchased by individual consumers—books, records, and clothes, for example—are consumer goods. Rubber and raw cotton, however, are generally purchased by manufacturers and are therefore classified as industrial goods. Rubber will be used in many products by a producer such as Goodyear Tire and Rubber Company; a manufacturer such as Burlington Industries will convert raw cotton into cloth.

Sometimes the same product is destined for different uses. The spark plugs purchased for the family car constitute a consumer good. But spark plugs purchased by American Motors for use on its American Eagle "four-wheel-drive" line is an industrial good, since it becomes part of another good destined for resale.* The key to proper

---

*Some marketers use the term *commercial goods* to refer to industrial goods not directly used in producing other goods.

classification of goods is the determination of the purchaser and the reasons for the purchase. This chapter will discuss the consumer goods market. The industrial goods market is examined in Chapter 6.

The Rationale for Market Segmentation

The world is too large and filled with too many diverse people and firms for any single marketing mix to satisfy everyone. Unless the product or service is an item such as an unbranded, descriptive-label detergent aimed at the mass market, an attempt to satisfy everyone may doom the marketer to failure. Even a seemingly functional product like toothpaste is aimed at a specific market segment. Crest focused on tooth-decay prevention; Stripe was developed for children; Close-Up hints at enhanced sex appeal; and Aim promises both protection and a taste children like.

The auto manufacturer who decides to produce and market a single model to satisfy everyone will encounter seemingly endless decisions about such variables as the number of doors, type of transmission, color, styling, and engine size. In its attempt to satisfy everyone, the firm may be forced to compromise in each of these areas and, as a result, may discover that it *does not satisfy anyone very well.* Other firms appealing to particular segments—the youth market, the high-fuel-economy market, the larger family market, and so on—may capture most of the total market by satisfying the specific needs of these smaller, more homogeneous market targets. This *process of dividing the total market into several homogeneous groups* is called **market segmentation.**

One marketing authority defines market segmentation as follows:

Market segmentation is the subdividing of a market into homogeneous subsets of customers, where any subset may conceivably be selected as a market target to be reached with a distinct marketing mix.[4]

BASES FOR MARKET SEGMENTATION

Market segmentation results from a determination of factors that will serve to distinguish a certain group of consumers from the overall market. These characteristics—such as age, sex, geographic location, income and expenditure patterns, and population size and mobility, among others—are vital factors in the success of the overall marketing strategy. Toy manufacturers such as Ideal, Hasbro, Mattel, and Kenner study not only birthrate trends, but also shifts in income and expenditure patterns. Colleges and universities are affected by such factors as the number of high school graduates, changing attitudes toward the value of a college education, and the increased enrollment of older adults. Figure

FIGURE 5.1
Bases for Market
Segmentation

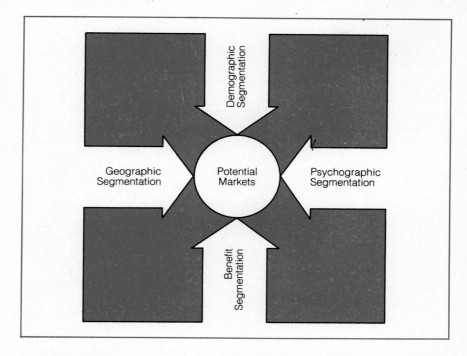

5.1 identifies four commonly used bases for segmenting consumer markets.

Geographic segmentation, *the dividing of an overall market into homogeneous groups on the basis of population location,* has been used for hundreds of years. The second basis for segmenting markets is **demographic segmentation**—*dividing an overall market into homogeneous groups based upon characteristics such as age, sex, and income level.* Demographic segmentation is the most commonly used method of subdividing total markets.

The third and fourth bases represent relatively recent developments in market segmentation. **Psychographic segmentation** utilizes *behavioral profiles developed from analyses of the activities, opinions, interests, and life-styles of consumers in identifying market segments.* The final basis, **benefit segmentation,** focuses on *benefits the consumer expects to derive from a product or service.*

GEOGRAPHIC SEGMENTATION

A logical starting point in market segmentation is to examine population characteristics. It is not surprising, therefore, that one of the earliest bases for segmentation was geographic.

Although the U.S. population had reached 225 million by 1983, it is not distributed evenly. Instead, it is concentrated in large metro-

**FIGURE 5.2
The United States in
Proportion to
Population**

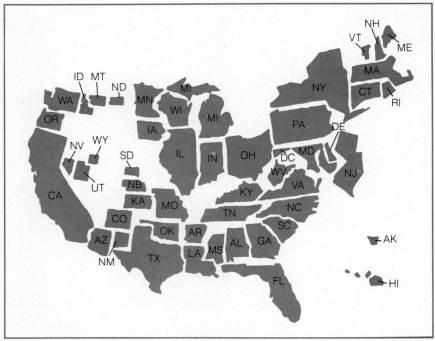

Source: State population data from U.S. Department of Commerce, Bureau of the Census, *U.S. Summary: Final Population and Housing Unit Counts* (Washington, D.C.: U.S. Government Printing Office, 1981.)

politan states, such as California, Illinois, Michigan, New York, Ohio, Pennsylvania, and Texas. Figure 5.2 illustrates this point by reducing Alaska, the largest state in land area, to diminutive size on the basis of its population.

Not only do states vary widely in population density, but pronounced shifts are also evident. Recent population data reveal that Alaska, Arizona, Florida, Nevada, Utah, and Wyoming have experienced the most rapid growth during the last decade, while the populations of the District of Columbia, New York, and Rhode Island actually declined. The figures indicate three major population shifts: (1) shifts to the Sunbelt states of the Southeast and Southwest; (2) continuing shifts from interior states to seacoast states; and (3) shifts to the West. While the 11.8 percent population growth rate was the slowest in the United States since the 1930s, the Southeast, Southwest, Rocky Mountain, and Far West regions all experienced population growth of more than 20 percent.

Such shifts have also occurred *within* states. The migration of farmers to urban areas has occurred steadily since 1800 and the per-

TABLE 5.1
The 25 Largest
Metropolitan Areas
in the United States

		1980 Population	Percent Change since 1970
1	New York	9,080,777	− 9.0%
2	Los Angeles-Long Beach	7,444,521	5.7
3	Chicago	7,057,853	1.2
4	Philadelphia	4,700,996	− 2.6
5	Detroit	4,339,768	− 2.1
6	San Francisco-Oakland	3,225,981	3.8
7	Washington, D.C.	3,041,909	4.5
8	Dallas-Fort Worth	2,964,342	24.7
9	Houston	2,891,146	44.6
10	Boston	2,759,800	− 4.8
11	St. Louis	2,341,351	− 2.9
12	Pittsburgh	2,260,336	− 5.9
13	Baltimore	2,164,853	4.5
14	Minneapolis-St. Paul	2,108,950	7.3
15	Seattle-Everett-Tacoma	2,083,636	−13.4
16	Atlanta	2,010,368	26.0
17	Cleveland	1,895,391	− 8.2
18	San Diego	1,857,492	36.8
19	Denver-Boulder	1,613,965	30.2
20	Miami	1,572,842	24.1
21	Tampa-St. Petersburg	1,550,035	42.4
22	Phoenix	1,511,552	55.6
23	Milwaukee	1,392,872	0.8
24	Cincinnati	1,355,455	− 1.7
25	Kansas City	1,322,156	3.9

Source: U.S. Census Bureau

centage of farm dwellers has now dropped below 4 percent. The 25 largest metropolitan areas listed in Table 5.1 represent one-third of the U.S. population. Each of these metropolitan areas contains more inhabitants than the entire population of such states as Alaska, Delaware, Hawaii, Idaho, Maine, Montana, Nevada, New Hampshire, New Mexico, North Dakota, Rhode Island, South Dakota, Vermont, and Wyoming.

The U.S. population ranks with those of Australia and Canada as the most mobile in the world. In an average year, approximately 40 million people in the United States change their home address at least once. The average person moves twelve times in a lifetime, as compared with eight times for the average English citizen and five times for the average Japanese citizen. Mobile home parks are ap-

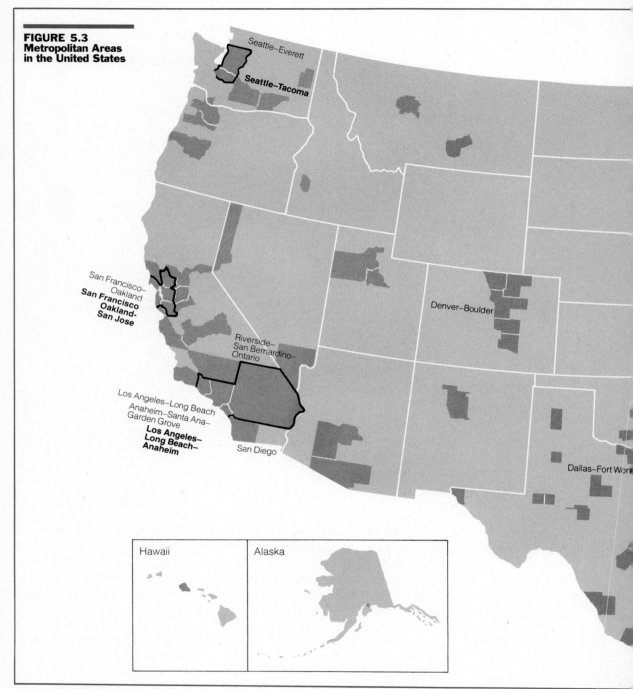

**FIGURE 5.3
Metropolitan Areas
in the United States**

Seattle–Everett

Seattle–Tacoma

San Francisco–
Oakland
**San Francisco
Oakland-
San Jose**

Denver–Boulder

Riverside–
San Bernardino–
Ontario

Los Angeles–Long Beach
Anaheim–Santa Ana–
Garden Grove
**Los Angeles–
Long Beach–
Anaheim**

San Diego

Dallas–Fort Wor

Hawaii

Alaska

Source: U.S. Department of Commerce, Bureau of the Census, *County and City Data Book, 1981: A Statistical Abstract Supplement* (Washington, D.C.: Government Printing Office, 1981).

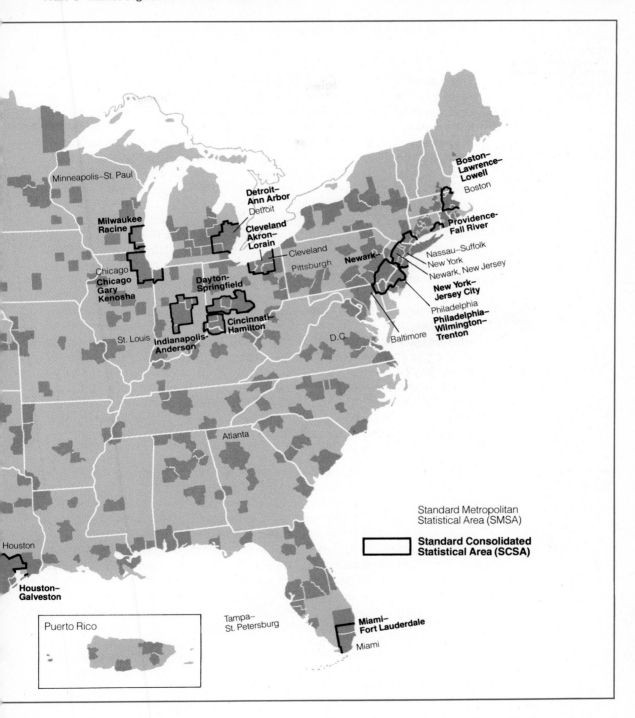

Minneapolis–St. Paul

**Boston–
Lawrence–
Lowell**
Boston

**Detroit–
Ann Arbor**
Detroit

**Milwaukee
Racine**

**Cleveland
Akron–
Lorain**

**Providence–
Fall River**

Cleveland

Pittsburgh

Nassau–Suffolk
New York
Newark, New Jersey

Newark

Chicago
**Chicago
Gary
Kenosha**

**Dayton–
Springfield**

**New York–
Jersey City**

St. Louis

**Cincinnati–
Hamilton**

Philadelphia
**Philadelphia–
Wilmington–
Trenton**

**Indianapolis–
Anderson**

D.C.

Baltimore

Atlanta

Standard Metropolitan
Statistical Area (SMSA)

**Standard Consolidated
Statistical Area (SCSA)**

Houston

**Houston–
Galveston**

Tampa–
St. Petersburg

**Miami–
Fort Lauderdale**

Puerto Rico

Miami

pearing in every U.S. city, and more than 6 million people inhabit them.[5]

New Definition of the City

The movement of the U.S. population from the farm to the city has been accompanied during recent years by a shift to the suburbs and small towns in nearby areas. Recent population statistics report 102 million suburban residents, 34 million more than in central cities and 44 million more than in nonmetropolitan areas. The population of such suburban areas as Fort Myers-Cape Coral, Florida; Bryan-College Station, Texas; McAllen-Pharr-Edinburg, Texas; West Palm Beach-Hollywood, Florida; and Richland-Kennewick-Pasco, Washington, all grew more than 50 percent during the past decade.

Primarily middle-class families have made the shift to the suburbs. The move has resulted in radical changes in the cities' traditional patterns of retailing and has led to a disintegration of the downtown shopping areas of many U.S. cities. It has also rendered traditional city boundaries almost meaningless. To accommodate the needs of urban—and marketing—planners, the U.S. Bureau of the Census has developed an improved classification system for compiling urban data. In urban areas, this data is now collected on the basis of a **Standard Metropolitan Statistical Area (SMSA)**—*an integrated economic and social unit containing one city of at least 50,000 inhabitants or "twin cities" with a combined population of at least 50,000.* The boundaries of an SMSA can cross state lines (as they do for the Duluth-Superior SMSA), but they must represent an integrated unit. The 305 SMSAs shown in Figure 5.3 account for almost three of every four residents in the United States.

Emerging "Supercities"

Figure 5.3 also reveals a concentration of population along the eastern seaboard, stretching from Boston to Washington, D.C. This region of connecting SMSAs, which has been given the nickname *Boswash,* is home for one of every five U.S. residents. Other concentrations of SMSAs are found along the shores of the Great Lakes and on the California coastline. In recent years, these supercities have become known as Standard Consolidated Statistical Areas. A **Standard Consolidated Statistical Area (SCSA)** *contains an SMSA with a population of at least 1 million and one or more adjoining SMSAs that are related to it by high-density population centers and intermetropolitan commuting of workers.* More than a third of the U.S. population resides in the fifteen SCSAs shown in Figure 5.3.

As the exodus to the suburbs continues, and as more industries follow their employees away from the central business districts, the growth of SCSAs will undoubtedly continue. The term **megalopolis** describes these *extensive urban-suburban strip cities.* Currently, 26 major strip cities in the United States house two out of every three Americans.

**FIGURE 5.4
Residence Location
of the U.S.
Population: 1970–
1980**

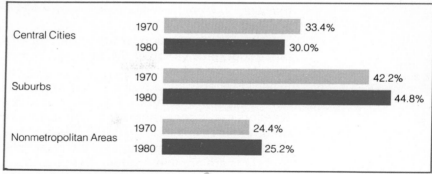

Central Cities
1970 33.4%
1980 30.0%

Suburbs
1970 42.2%
1980 44.8%

Nonmetropolitan Areas
1970 24.4%
1980 25.2%

Source: U.S. Department of Commerce, Bureau of the Census.

Population Growth in Nonmetropolitan Areas

Although the number of farmers in the United States has been declining for more than a century, in recent years the rural areas have been repopulated by people moving from central cities and suburban areas. During the past decade, the nonmetropolitan growth rate outpaced that of the urban and suburban areas. Figure 5.4 indicates the changes in the location of the U.S. population between 1970 and 1980.

A number of factors contribute to the population growth in small towns and rural areas. In some instances, energy and other mining developments have created job opportunities. Growth in such areas as the Rocky Mountains, the Ozark-Ouachita regions of Arkansas and Missouri, and in other resort-retirement developments has been stimulated considerably by the creation and expansion of retirement and recreation communities. Another component of the nonmetropolitan growth rate is "urban flight," as some big-city residents seek to escape the overcrowding, crime, pollution, and noise associated with cities. Nearly half of the U.S. cities with populations of 100,000 or more experienced population declines during the 1970s. Finally, for still another group, rural living is simply an extension of the suburbs made possible by improved roads to the city.

The growth of the nonmetropolitan population produces more challenges for marketers who attempt to serve this market than for those marketers who choose market targets in the more densely settled cities and suburban areas. Increased marketing costs may result when marketers focus upon nonmetropolitan consumers who, by definition, are less concentrated geographically. On the other hand, this may stimulate development of such communication innovations as cable television and direct-broadcast satellites as a means of serving these growing markets.[6]

When Should Geographic Segmentation Be Used?

There are many instances where markets for products and services may be segmented on a geographic basis. Regional variations in consumer tastes often exist. Per-capita consumption of Mexican food, for example, is higher in the Southwest than in New England. Basements, a mainstay in many homes in the North, are relatively rare in the South and Southwest.

Residence location within a geographic area is another important geographic variable. Urban dwellers may have less need for automobiles than their suburban and rural counterparts do, while suburban dwellers spend proportionally more on lawn and garden care than do people in rural or urban areas. Both rural and suburban dwellers may spend more of their household income on gasoline and automobile needs than do urban households.

Climate is another important factor. Snow blowers, snowmobiles, and sleds are popular products in the northern sections of the United States. Residents of the Sunbelt states may spend proportionally less of their total income on heating and heating equipment and more on air conditioning. Climate also affects patterns of clothing purchases.

Geographic segmentation is useful only when differences in preference and purchase patterns for a product emerge along regional lines. Moreover, geographic subdivisions of the overall market tend to be rather large and often too heterogeneous for effective segmentation without careful consideration of additional factors. In such cases, several segmentation variables may need to be utilized.

DEMOGRAPHIC SEGMENTATION

The most common approach to market segmentation is to divide consumer groups according to demographic variables. These variables—age, sex, income, occupation, education, household size, and stage in the family life cycle, among others—are typically used to identify market segments and to develop appropriate marketing mixes. Demographic variables are often used in market segmentation for three reasons:

1. They are easy to identify and measure.
2. They are associated with the sale of many products and services.
3. They are typically referred to in describing the audiences of advertising media, so that media buyers and others can easily pinpoint the desired market target.[7]

Vast quantities of data are available to assist the marketing planner in segmenting potential markets on a demographic basis. Sex is an obvious variable for segmenting many markets, since many products are sex-specific. Cigarette manufacturers have utilized sex as a variable in the successful marketing of such brands as Eve, More Light 100s, and Virginia Slims. The development of low-calorie light beer and of smaller packaging has led to increased beer consumption among women.[8]

Age, household size, family life cycle stage, and income and expenditure patterns are important factors in determining purchase patterns. The often distinct differences based upon such demographic factors justifies their frequent use as a basis for segmentation.

Identifying Market Targets by Age

The population of the United States is expected to increase by 7 percent between 1983 and 1990, but this growth will be concentrated in two age groups—young to middle-aged adults between thirty and forty-five and persons aged sixty-five and older. Both markets represent potentially profitable market targets.

The young to middle-aged adult segment includes family households with demands for such goods as homes, furniture, recreation, clothes, toys, and food. Although this segment currently represents only about one-fifth of the U.S. population, it will account for two-thirds of population growth during the 1980s.

Not so many years ago, there was no such thing as a senior adult market, since few people reached old age. At present, however, one out of nine people is sixty-five or older. It is comforting for this year's retiree to learn that at age sixty-five his or her average life expectancy is at least another sixteen years. This increase also presents the marketing manager with a unique and potentially profitable market segment.[9]

Each age group in Figure 5.5 represents different consumption patterns, and each serves as the market target for several firms. For instance, Gerber traditionally has been extremely successful in aiming at the infants' and children's market. Table 5.2 lists some of the types of merchandise most often purchased by the various age groups.

Family Life Cycle as a Segmentation Variable

The **family life cycle** is *the process of family formation and dissolution.* Using this concept, the marketing planner combines the family characteristics of age, marital status, presence or absence of children, and ages of children in developing a marketing strategy.

Patrick E. Murphy and William A. Staples have proposed a five-stage family life cycle with several subcategories. The stages of the family life cycle are shown in Table 5.3.

The behavioral characteristics and buying patterns of persons in each life cycle stage often vary considerably. Young singles have relatively few financial burdens; tend to be early purchasers of new fashion items; are recreation oriented; and make purchases of basic kitchen equipment, cars, and vacations. By contrast, young marrieds with young children tend to be heavy purchasers of baby products, homes, television sets, toys, and washers and dryers. Their liquid assets tend to be relatively low and they are more likely to watch television than do young singles or young marrieds without children. The "empty nest" households in the middle-aged and older categories with no dependent children are more likely to have more disposable income; more time for recreation, self-education, and travel; and

FIGURE 5.5
Population
Projections to 1990,
by Age Groups

Population (in millions)		Change, 1980–1990
1980	1990	
Children and Teenagers		The absolute decline in the number of teenagers more than offset by the slight increase in the number of babies and children under ten
70.5	72.0	Up 2%
Young Adults, 20–29		Decline in the 20–29 age category in which people take their first jobs, marry, look for homes, start families, spend and borrow freely
39.8	38.1	Down 4%
Younger Middle-Aged Group, 30–44		Huge surge in the number of people in the younger middle-aged group, where families climb the income ladder, spend money on clothing and education for their children, move into larger homes, purchase larger autos
43.0	57.5	Up 34%
Older Middle-Aged Group, 45–64		Slight growth for the older middle-aged group, where incomes tend to be highest and spending per person heaviest for such items as children's college education, travel, leisure, luxury goods, and services
43.9	46.1	Up 5%
Persons 65 and Over		Sizable growth for 65 and older age category, which means increased demand for medical care, apartments, retirement homes, and luxuries such as travel, fashionable clothing, recreation, and books
24.9	29.4	Up 18%

Source: U.S. Department of Commerce, Bureau of the Census, *Current Population Reports,* Series P-25, No. 704 (Washington, D.C.: U.S. Government Printing Office, July 1977), pp. 40, 50.

more than one member in the labor force than their "full nest" counterparts with young children. Similar differences in behavioral and buying patterns are evident in the other stages of the family life cycle as well.[10]

Analysis of life cycle stages often gives better results than does reliance on single variables such as age. The buying patterns of a 25-year-old bachelor are much different from those of a father of the same age. The family of five headed by parents in their forties is a more likely prospect for *The World Book Encyclopedia* than is the childless forty-year-old divorced person.

Marketing planners can use published data such as census reports and divide their markets into more homogeneous segments

**TABLE 5.2
Merchandise
Purchased, by
Consumer Age
Groups**

Age	Name of Age Group	Merchandise Purchased
0–5	Young children	Baby food, toys, nursery furniture, children's wear
6–19	Schoolchildren (including teenagers)	Clothing, sports equipment, records, school supplies, food, cosmetics, used cars
20–34	Young adult	Cars, furniture, houses, clothing, recreational equipment, purchases for younger age segments
35–49	Younger middle-aged	Larger homes, better cars, second cars, new furniture, recreational equipment
50–64	Older middle-aged	Recreational items, purchases for young marrieds and infants
65 and over	Senior adult	Medical services, travel, drugs, purchases for younger age groups

than would be possible if they were analyzing single variables. Such data is available for each classification of the family life cycle.

Diminishing Household Size: Its Impact on Consumer Behavior

Slightly more than half the households in the United States are comprised of only one or two persons. This development is in marked contrast to households that averaged 5.8 persons when the first census was taken in 1790.

The U.S. Department of Commerce cites several reasons for the trend toward smaller households. Among them are lower fertility rates; the tendency of young people to postpone marriage; the increasing desire among younger couples to limit the number of children; the ease and frequency of divorce; and the ability and desire of many young single adults and the elderly to live alone.

More than 15 million people live alone today—more than one household in five. The single-person household has emerged as an important market segment with a special title: SSWD (Single, Separated, Widowed, and Divorced). SSWDs buy 26 percent of all passenger cars, but 50 percent of the Ford Mustangs and other specialty cars. They are also customers for single-serving food products, such as Campbell's Soup-for-One and Green Giant's single-serving casseroles.

Today, the average household size is 2.7 persons. And while married-couple households continue to dominate, they will probably account for only 55 percent of all 1990 households, as compared to 70 percent in 1970.[11]

TABLE 5.3
Stages of the Family
Life Cycle

Stage	Number of Individuals or Families (in thousands)[1]	% Total U.S. Population[2]	Approximate Ages
1. *Young Single*	16,626	8.2	Under 35
2. *Young Married without Children*	2,958	2.9	Under 35
3. *Other Young*			Under 35
a. Young divorced without children	277	0.1	
b. Young married with children	8,082	17.1	
c. Young divorced with children	1,144	1.9	
4. *Middle-aged*			35–64
a. Middle-aged married without children	4,815	4.7	
b. Middle-aged divorced without children	593	0.3	
c. Middle-aged married with children	15,574	33.0	
d. Middle-aged divorced with children	1,080	1.8	
e. Middle-aged married without dependent children	5,627	5.5	
f. Middle-aged divorced without dependent children	284	0.1	
5. *Older*			65 and older
a. Older married	5,318	5.2	
b. Older unmarried (divorced, widowed)	3,510	2.0	
6. *Other*[3]	34,952	17.2	

Notes:
1. Figures for the table were taken or derived from U.S. Bureau of the Census 1973, Tables 2 and 9.
2. As there are single and divorced individuals in some of the stages, the numbers were calculated as a percentage of the entire population, not just the number of families. Also, the percentages of the total for families were determined by multiplying the number of families by 2.3 (average number of children per family in 1970) and adding the parents (or parent, in divorced instances) to the number. For example, the 17.1 percent in the young married with children was computed as follows:

$$\frac{8,082 \ (2.3 \ children) \ + \ 16,164 \ (parents)}{203,210 \ (U.S. \ Population)} = 17.1\%.$$

3. Includes all adults and children not accounted for by the family life cycle stages.

Source: Reprinted with permission from Patrick E. Murphy and William A. Staples, "A Modernized Family Life Cycle," *Journal of Consumer Research*, June 1979, p. 16.

Using Income and Expenditure Patterns as Segmentation Variables

Markets were defined earlier as people and purchasing power. A common method of segmenting consumer markets is on the basis of income. Fashionable specialty shops stocking designer clothing make most of their sales to high-income shoppers. Other retailers aim their appeals at middle-income groups. Still others focus almost exclusively on low-income shoppers.

Income distribution in most countries is shaped like a pyramid, with a small percentage of households having high incomes and the majority of families earning very low incomes. As Figure 5.6 shows, this pattern was also true of the United States only a few decades ago. In 1955, more than half of all families earned less than $10,000. In recent years, however, the income pyramid has been overturned. By 1975, two-thirds of the U.S. households earned $10,000 or more.

The average American household contains 2.7 members.

"At these prices you should be glad I'm not eating."

Source: Reprinted by permission from Cartoon Features Syndicate.

An estimated 30 percent of all U.S. families will have incomes of $25,000 or more by 1985, while only 22 percent will earn less than $10,000. Higher incomes for the typical household should mean more discretionary spending power.

Household expenditures can be divided into two categories: basic purchases of essential household needs and other purchases

**FIGURE 5.6
Redistribution of Family Income, 1955–1985**

	1955	1975	1985
$25,000 and Over	3	14	30
$15,000–$24,999	13	30	32
$10,000–$14,999	26	22	16
Under $10,000	58	33	22

Percent of Families in Income Class, 1975 Dollars

Source: Data used by permission from Helen Axel, ed., *A Guide to Consumer Markets, 1977/1978* (New York: Conference Board, 1977), p. 127.

TABLE 5.4
Annual Family
Expenditures by
Income Groups

Category	Family Income			
	Under $10,000	$10,000-$19,999	$20,000-$24,999	$25,000 and Over
	Percent of Total Expenditures			
Food, Beverages, and Tobacco	24	22	20	18
Housing, House Furnishings, and Equipment	34	30	28	29
Clothing and Accessories	7	8	9	10
Other Goods and Accessories[a]	35	40	43	43

[a]Includes transportation, medical and personal care, recreation and equipment, reading and education, and other goods and services.

Source: Adapted with permission from Helen Axel, ed., *A Guide to Consumer Markets 1977/1978* (New York: Conference Board, 1977), p. 173.

made at the discretion of household members once the necessities have been purchased. Total discretionary purchasing power is estimated to have tripled since 1950.

Engel's Laws

How do expenditure patterns vary with increased income? More than a hundred years ago Ernst Engel, a German statistician, published what became known as **Engel's laws,** *three general statements based on his studies of the impact of household income changes on consumer spending behavior.* According to Engel, as family income increases:

1. A smaller percentage of expenditures goes for food.
2. The percentage spent on housing and household operations and clothing remains constant.
3. The percentage spent on other items (such as recreation and education) increases.

Are Engel's laws still valid? Table 5.4 supplies the answers. A steady decline in the percentage of total income spent for food, beverages, and tobacco occurs from low to high incomes. Although high-income families spend a greater absolute amount on food purchases, their purchases represent a smaller percentage of their total expenditures than is true of low-income families. The second law is partly correct, since percentage expenditures for housing and household operations remain relatively unchanged in all but the very lowest income group. The percentage spent on clothing, however, increases with increased income. As Table 5.4 indicates, households earning less

Engel's laws predict increases in relative spending on non-necessities as income increases.

Source: Reprinted by permission of Sydney Harris.

than $10,000 annually spend a smaller percentage of their income on clothing than do those earning more than $10,000. The third law is also true, with the exception of medical and personal care, which appear to decline with the increased income.

Engel's laws provide the marketing manager with useful generalizations about the types of consumer demand that will evolve with increased income. They can also be useful for the marketer evaluating a foreign country as a potential market target.

PSYCHOGRAPHIC SEGMENTATION

Although geographic and demographic segmentation traditionally have been the primary bases for dividing consumer and industrial markets into homogeneous segments to serve as market targets, marketers have long recognized the need for fuller, more lifelike portraits of consumers for use in developing marketing programs. Even though traditionally used variables such as age, sex, family life cycle, income, and population size and location are important in segmentation, life-styles of potential consumers may prove equally important.

Life-style refers to *the mode of living of consumers.* It is how an individual lives. Consumers' life-styles are regarded as a composite of their individual psychological makeups—their needs, motives, perceptions, and attitudes. A life-style also bears the mark of many other influences—those of reference groups, culture, social class, and

TABLE 5.5
Life-style Dimensions

Activities	Interests	Opinions	Demographics
Work	Family	Themselves	Age
Hobbies	Home	Social issues	Education
Social events	Job	Politics	Income
Vacation	Community	Business	Occupation
Entertainment	Recreation	Economics	Family size
Club membership	Fashion	Education	Dwelling
Community	Food	Products	Geography
Shopping	Media	Future	City size
Sports	Achievements	Culture	Stage in life cycle

Source: Joseph T. Plummer, "The Concept and Application of Life Style Segmentation," *Journal of Marketing,* vol. 38, January 1974, p. 34. Used by permission of the American Marketing Association.

family members. A frequently used classification system for life-style variables is shown in Table 5.5.

Psychographics: Developing Consumer Profiles

In recent years, a new technique has been developed which promises to elicit more meaningful bases for segmentation. Although definitions vary among researchers, **psychographics** generally means *the psychological profiles of different consumers developed from quantitative research.* These profiles are usually developed as a result of asking consumers their agreement or disagreement with **AIO statements**—*several hundred statements dealing with the activities, interests, and opinions* listed in Table 5.5.

Hundreds of psychographic studies have been conducted on products and services ranging from beer to air travel. A national study of household food buying identified four distinct segments based on psychographic research. Of the 1,800 adults interviewed, 98 percent could be categorized into one of the following groupings:

- *Hedonists,* who represent 20 percent of the population, want the good life—foods that taste good, are convenient, and are not expensive. They aren't worried about sugar, fat, cholesterol, salt, calories, additives, or preservatives. They are most likely young, male, and childfree. Hedonists are above-average consumers of regular soft drinks, beer, margarine, presweetened cereal, candy, and gum.

- *Don't Wants,* another 20 percent of the population, are the mirror image of the Hedonists. They avoid all the "no-no" ingredients in some processed foods. They will sacrifice taste and convenience, and will pay more to obtain foods without sugar, artificial ingredients, cholesterol, and fat. They are concerned about calories and nutrition. In effect, their avoidance behavior is more health oriented than diet conscious. This segment is older; more than half are over age 50. They tend to be better educated, live in large urban areas, and don't have children at home. The Don't Wants are major consumers of decaffeinated coffee, fruit juices, wine, unsalted butter, corn-oil margarine, nutritionally fortified cereal, yogurt, and sugar-free foods and beverages.

- The *Weight Conscious,* who comprise about one-third of the population, are primarily concerned about calories and fat. They like convenience foods, but try to avoid cholesterol, sugar, and salt. They're not particularly nutrition- or taste-conscious, and don't avoid foods simply because they have artificial ingredients or preservatives. Members of this segment tend to have higher incomes and many are women employed full-time. Given their concern for calories, the Weight Conscious are above-average consumers of iced tea, diet soft drinks, diet margarine, and sugar-free candy and gum.

- The *Moderates,* the final 25 percent of the population, are average in everything. They balance the trade-offs they make in food selection and don't exhibit strong concerns about the avoidance factors. They closely profile the population in demographics, and their consumption levels were average for the foods and beverages listed in the study.[12]

Table 5.6 excerpts a psychographic study of heavy users of eye makeup and shortening.

Combining Segmentation Bases

As Table 5.6 reveals, the marketing implications of psychographic segmentation are considerable. Psychographic profiles produce a much richer description of a potential market target, and should assist promotional decisions in attempting to match the image of the company and its product offerings with the type of consumer using the product.

Psychographic segmentation often serves as a component of an overall segmentation strategy in which markets are also segmented on the basis of such demographic/geographic variables as age, city size, education, family life cycle stage, and geographic location. These more traditional bases provide the marketer with accessibility to consumer segments through orthodox communication channels such as newspapers, radio and television advertising, and other promotional outlets. Psychographic studies may then be implemented to develop lifelike, three-dimensional profiles of the life-styles of the firm's market target. When combined with demographic/geographic characteristics, psychographics emerges as an important tool in understanding the behavior of present and potential market targets.[13]

BENEFIT SEGMENTATION

A fourth approach to market segmentation is to focus on such attributes as product usage rates and the benefits derived from the product. These factors may reveal important bases for pinpointing prospective market targets.

TABLE 5.6
Profile of Heavy Users: Eye Makeup and Shortening

Heavy User of Eye Makeup	Heavy User of Shortening
Demographic Characteristics	
Young, well-educated, lives in metropolitan areas	Middle-aged, medium to large family, lives outside metropolitan areas
Product Use	
Also a heavy user of liquid face makeup, lipstick, hair spray, perfume, cigarettes, gasoline	Also a heavy user of flour, sugar, canned lunch meat, cooked pudding, catsup
Media Preferences	
Fashion magazines, *The Tonight Show*, adventure programs	*Reader's Digest*, daytime TV serials, family-situation TV comedies
Activities, Interests, and Opinions *Agrees more than average with*	
"I often try the latest hairdo styles when they change."	"I love to bake and frequently do."
"An important part of my life and activities is dressing smartly."	"I save recipes from newspapers and magazines."
"I like to feel attractive to all men."	"I love to eat."
"I want to look a little different from others."	"I enjoy most forms of housework."
"I like what I see when I look in the mirror."	"Usually I have regular days for washing, cleaning, etc., around the house."
"I take good care of my skin."	"I am uncomfortable when my house is not completely clean."
"I would like to spend a year in London or Paris."	"I try to arrange my home for my children's convenience."
"I like ballet."	"Our family is a close-knit group."
"I like to serve unusual dinners."	"Clothes should be dried in the fresh air and out-of-doors."
"I really do believe that blondes have more fun."	"I would rather spend a quiet evening at home than go out to a party."
Disagrees more than average with	
"I enjoy most forms of housework."	"My idea of housekeeping is once over lightly."
"I furnish my home for comfort, not for style."	"Classical music is more interesting than popular music."
"If it was good enough for my mother, it's good enough for me."	"I like ballet."
	"I'd like to spend a year in London or Paris."

Source: William D. Wells and Arthur D. Beard, "Personality and Consumer Behavior," in Scott Ward and Thomas S. Robertson, eds., *Consumer Behavior: Theoretical Sources,* © 1973, pp. 195–96. Adapted by permission of Prentice-Hall, Inc., Englewood Cliffs, N.J.

Usage Rates

Marketing managers may divide potential segments into two categories: users and nonusers. Users may be further divided into heavy, moderate, and light users.

In some product categories, such as air travel, car rentals, dog food, and hair coloring, less than 20 percent of the population accounts for more than 80 percent of the total purchases. Even for such widely used products as coffee and soft drinks, half of all U.S. households account for almost 90 percent of the total usage.[14]

An early study of usage patterns by Dik Warren Twedt divided users into two categories: light and heavy. Twedt's analysis of consumer-panel data revealed that 29 percent of the sample households could be characterized as heavy users of lemon-lime soft drinks. This group represented 91 percent of sales in the product category.[15] It is, therefore, not surprising that usage rates are important segmentation variables for Coca-Cola, Pepsi-Cola, and 7-Up.

Heavy users often can be identified through analysis of internal records. Retail stores and financial institutions have records of charge-card purchases and other transactions. Warranty records may also be used.[16]

Product Benefits

Market segments may also be identified by the benefits the buyer expects to derive from a product or brand. In a pioneering investigation, Daniel Yankelovich revealed that much of the watch industry operated with little understanding of the benefits watch buyers expect in their purchases. At the time of the study, most watch companies were marketing relatively expensive models through jewelry stores and using prestige appeals. However, Yankelovich's research revealed that less than one-third of the market purchased a watch as a symbol. In fact, 23 percent of his respondents reported they purchased the lowest-price watch and another 46 percent focused on durability and overall product quality. The U.S. Time Company decided to focus its product benefits on those two categories and market its Timex watches in drugstores, variety stores, and discount houses. Within a few years of adopting the new segmentation approach, U.S. Time Company became the largest watch company in the world.[17]

Table 5.7 illustrates how benefit segmentation might be applied to the toothpaste market. The table reveals that some consumers are primarily concerned with price, some with tooth decay, some with taste, and others with brightness. Also included in Table 5.7 are the demographic and other characteristics utilized in focusing on each subgrouping.[18]

IDENTIFYING MARKET TARGETS

Market target decision analysis is *a useful tool in the market segmentation process.* Targets are chosen by segmenting the total market on the basis of any given characteristic (as discussed earlier in the chapter). The following example shows how market target decision analysis can be applied.[19]

Consider the decisions of a small firm wishing to analyze the market potential for a proposed line of typewriters. Because of limited financial resources, the company must operate on a regional ba-

To attract media buyers journals often advertise their ability to reach narrowly defined demographic groups.

BEYOND MACHO.

Today, millions of husbands actively participate in running the home. In fact, nearly one-fourth of all principal supermarket shoppers are men.

With yesterday's stereotypes crumbling as new lifestyles emerge, men have become a significant target for many family-oriented products.

How to influence influential males.

In today's complex marketplace, advertisers must look beyond traditional demographic targeting aimed only at women. If your media emphasis overlooks husbands or men living alone, you miss a huge audience that buys—or influences the purchase of—most products and services.

By limiting your target, you limit your sales.

The solution is intermarketing: reaching all the various, narrowly-defined demographic groups that make up your total target audience.

TV Guide makes intermarketing work. Because it reaches more women and more men than any other magazine, TV Guide lets you build big reach in any key marketing base, and it goes on to help you cover your secondary market, your tertiary market, etc. With TV Guide, you hit the full dimensions of your prospects, reap the benefits of purchase influence relationships, and cover the intermarket with every ad.

That's because the people who interest you are interested in television and the way TV Guide writes about it—from men attracted to such timely articles as how tv manipulates the news to young couples comparing their views of new programs with those of critic Robert MacKenzie. All in all, we deliver nearly 38 million involved adult readers. With the largest in-home readership of any magazine. And the speed to market that you once expected only from broadcast.

Get all your sales with the marketing concept of the '80s. Sell to today's intermarket in TV Guide.

INTERMARKETING TV GUIDE

TV Guide® and the TV Guide logo are registered trademarks of Triangle Publications, Inc.   TRIANGLE PUBLICATIONS, INC.

Source: Courtesy of Triangle Publications, Inc.

sis. The grid in Figure 5.7 illustrates the first two decisions for the firm: choosing a geographic area and marketing the typewriters to the ultimate consumers. The typewriter company also could have chosen the industrial market. But to have done so would have required a separate marketing strategy, since each of the cells in Figure 5.7 represents unique markets with distinguishing characteristics.

**TABLE 5.7
Benefit
Segmentation of the
Toothpaste Market**

	Segment Name			
	The Sensory Segment	The Sociables	The Worriers	The Independent Segment
Principal Benefit Sought	Flavor, Product Appearance	Brightness of Teeth	Decay Prevention	Price
Demographic Strengths	Children	Teens, Young People	Large Families	Men
Special Behavioral Characteristics	Users of Spearmint-flavored Toothpaste	Smokers	Heavy Users	Heavy Users
Brands Disproportionately Favored	Colgate, Stripe	MacLean's, Plus White, Ultra Brite	Crest	Brands on Sale
Personality Characteristics	High Self-involvement	High Sociability	High Hypochondriasis	High Autonomy
Life-style Characteristics	Hedonistic	Active	Conservative	Value Oriented

Source: Russell I. Haley, "Benefit Segmentation: A Decision-Oriented Research Tool," *Journal of Marketing,* vol. 32, July 1968, p. 33. Used by permission of the American Marketing Association.

**FIGURE 5.7
Market Target for
Typewriters**

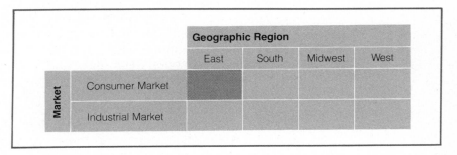

The next steps involve the decision to market the typewriters to high-income households in the young and middle-aged stages of the family life cycle, which in turn involves evaluating the market for typewriters as gifts for school-age children. These decisions are shown in Figure 5.8. Data can be gathered about the size of the market target in the eastern United States and the firm's predicted market share.

The cross-classifications in Figure 5.8 can be further subdivided to gather more specific data about the characteristics of the proposed market target. The potential bases for segmenting markets is virtually limitless. Such divisions are sometimes made intuitively, but usually the decisions are supported by concrete data.[20]

FIGURE 5.8
Market Target for
Typewriters to
Consumers in the
Eastern United
States

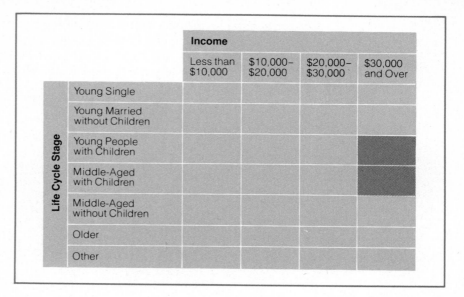

FIGURE 5.8
Market Target for
Typewriters to
Consumers in the
Eastern United
States

Life Cycle Stage	Income			
	Less than $10,000	$10,000– $20,000	$20,000– $30,000	$30,000 and Over
Young Single				
Young Married without Children				
Young People with Children				▓
Middle-Aged with Children				▓
Middle-Aged without Children				
Older				
Other				

SUMMARY

Markets are people with purchasing power and the authority to make purchase decisions. The total market can be divided into consumer and industrial markets. The ultimate consumer makes purchases for his or her own use, while the industrial purchaser buys products for use in making other products for resale.

Marketing managers must isolate and evaluate potential market targets that can be profitably served by their firms. This step permits managers to gather pertinent information about a market target for a second task: developing and implementing an effective marketing mix to satisfy the market target.

Markets may be segmented on a number of bases. Geographic segmentation uses such variables as city size, climatic variations, population density, region, and urban/suburban/rural locations. Demographic segmentation, the most widely used basis of segmentation, employs such variables as age, sex, marital status, race/ethnic group, income, education, home ownership, religion, and family life cycle stage. Demographic characteristics typically are easily matched with the audiences of advertising media in reaching market targets.

Psychographic segmentation, the third approach in market segmentation, uses life-style analysis to develop profiles of different consumers. Such an approach focuses on the activities, interests, and opinions of product users.

A fourth possible basis for market segmentation is the evaluation of such consumer attributes as varying usage rates and the benefits derived by purchasers. Heavy users of the product often represent a sizable share of the overall market.

Market target decision analysis allows marketing managers to isolate and evaluate potential market targets. This technique employs grids of overall markets, divided on the basis of geography, demographics, life-styles, usage rates, product benefits, or some combination of two or more variables. Such an approach provides the decision maker with a systematic, step-by-step delineation of homogeneous consumer segments within an overall market.

QUESTIONS FOR DISCUSSION

1. Explain the following terms:

   market
   consumer goods
   industrial goods
   market segmentation
   geographic segmentation
   demographic segmentation
   psychographic segmentation
   benefit segmentation
   Standard Metropolitan
     Statistical Area (SMSA)

   Standard Consolidated
     Statistical Area
     (SCSA)
   megalopolis
   family life cycle
   Engel's laws
   life-style
   psychographics
   AIO statements
   market target decision analysis

2. Identify the two-step process of developing a marketing strategy. Why is it essential that the steps be conducted in the proper sequence?

3. Explain why each of the four components of a market is needed for a market to exist.

4. Bicycles are consumer goods; iron ore is an industrial good. But what about trucks—are they consumer goods or industrial goods? Defend your answer.

5. Identify and briefly explain the bases for market segmentation.

6. What effect will a low birthrate have on future buying patterns? Which kinds of companies will benefit in the next ten years from a declining birthrate? Which will suffer?

7. Identify the major population shifts that have occurred in recent years. How do you account for these shifts?

8. What types of markets have been created in the past because of population mobility? What new markets are likely to develop in the final decades of the twentieth century because of this mobility?

9. Why is demographic segmentation the most commonly used approach to market segmentation?

10. Identify five demographic variables and illustrate the importance of each by citing an appropriate product or service whose market is affected by each of the variables you list.

11. Distinguish between a SMSA and a SCSA.

12. List two products most likely to be purchased by persons in each stage of the family life cycle.

13. Why is family life cycle analysis an improvement over market segmentation by variables such as age or marital status?

14. Discuss the following statement: Based on Engel's laws, we should expect family expenditures for food to decline as income increases.

15. Are Engel's laws valid today?

16.   Describe the distribution of household income in the United States.

17.   How can life-styles be used in market segmentation?

18.   Explain the use of product usage rates as a segmentation variable.

19.   What market segmentation basis would you recommend for the following:
   a. professional soccer team
   b. Porsche 924 sports car
   c. Columbia Records
   d. Scope mouthwash

20.   Develop a market target decision analysis for home video recorders.

NOTES

1.   William Lazer and John E. Smallwood, "The Changing Demographics of Women," *Journal of Marketing,* July 1977, p. 19. See also Mary Joyce, "The Professional Woman: A Potential Market Segment for Retailers," *Journal of Retailing,* Summer 1978, pp. 59–70; and Suzanne H. McCall, "Meet the 'Workwife'," *Journal of Marketing,* July 1977, pp. 55–65.

2.   Dorothy Cohen, *Consumer Behavior* (New York: Random House, 1981), pp. 122–26. See also Henry Assael, *Consumer Behavior and Marketing Action* (Boston: Kent Publishing Co., 1981), pp. 354–56.

3.   "Magazines Targeted at the Working Woman," *Business Week,* February 18, 1980, p. 150.

4.   Philip Kotler, *Marketing Management* (Englewood Cliffs, N.J.: Prentice-Hall, 1980), p. 195.

5.   Fabian Linden, "America on the Move—and Marketers Too," *Across the Board,* October 1980, pp. 34–41.

6.   The growth of nonmetropolitan areas is discussed in Thayer C. Taylor, "Targeting Sales in a Changing Marketplace," *Sales & Marketing Management,* July 27, 1981, pp. A-6 to A-11.

7.   Kenneth Runyon, *Consumer Behavior* (Columbus, Ohio: Charles E. Merrill, 1980), p. 35.

8.   George W. Wynn, "'Rosebud' or 'Lone Starlet': Is There a Market for 'Female' Beer?" in *Proceedings of the Southwestern Marketing Association,* eds. Robert H. Ross, Frederic B. Kraft, and Charles H. Davis, Wichita, Kansas, 1981, pp. 9–12.

9.   Rena Bartos, "Over 49: The Invisible Consumer Market," *Harvard Business Review,* January–February 1980, pp. 140–49; Betsy D. Gelb, "Exploring the Gray Market Segment," *MSU Business Topics,* Spring 1978, pp. 41–46; and Lynn W. Phillips and Brian Sternthal, "Age Differences in Information Processing: A Perspective on the Aged Consumer," *Journal of Marketing Research,* November 1977, pp. 444–57.

10.   These examples are from an earlier life cycle study. See William D. Wells and George Gubar, "Life Cycle Concept in Marketing Research," *Journal of Marketing Research,* November 1966, p. 362. See also Frederick W. Derrick and Alane K. Lehfeld, "The Family Life Cycle: An Alternative Approach," *Journal of Consumer Research,* September 1980, pp. 214–17.

11.   "A Peek at a Changing America," *U.S. News & World Report,* December 10, 1979, p. 8.

12.   Reported in "Research on Food Consumption Values Identifies Four Market Segments; Finds 'Good Taste' Still Tops," *Marketing News,* May 15, 1981, p. 17. Used by permission of the American Marketing Association.

13.   For a thorough survey of previous psychographic studies and some case histories of the uses of psychographic research, see William D. Wells, "Psychographics: A Critical Review," *Journal of Marketing Research,* May 1975, pp. 196–213. See also John J. Burnett, "Psychographic and Demographic Characteristics of Blood Donors," *Journal of Consumer Research,* June 1981, pp. 62–86; Mary Ann Lederhaus and Ronald J. Adams, "A Psychographic Profile of the Cosmopolitan Consumer," *Proceedings of the Southwestern Marketing Association,* eds. Robert H. Ross, Frederic B. Kraft, and Charles H. Davis, Wichita, Kansas, 1981, pp. 142–45; and J. Paul Merenski, "Psychographics: Valid by Definition and Reliable by Technique," Venkatakrishna V. Bellur, ed. *Developments in Marketing Science* (Miami Beach: Academy of Marketing Science, 1981), pp. 161–66.

14.   Reported in David T. Kollat, Roger D. Blackwell, and James F. Robeson, *Strategic Marketing* (New York: Holt, Rinehart and Winston, 1972), p. 192.

15.   Dik Warren Twedt, "How Important to Marketing Strategy is the 'Heavy User'?" *Journal of Marketing,* January 1964, pp. 71–72.

16.   These methods are suggested in Martin L. Bell, *Marketing: Concepts and Strategy* (Boston: Houghton Mifflin, 1979), p. 129.

17.   Daniel Yankelovich, "New Criteria for Market Segmentation," *Harvard Business Review,* March–April 1964, pp. 83–90.

18.   See Russell I. Haley, "Benefit Segmentation: A Decision-Oriented Research Tool," *Journal of Marketing,* July 1968, pp. 30–35.

19.   A similar analysis is suggested in Robert M. Fulmer, *The New Marketing* (New York: Macmillan, 1976), pp. 34–37; Philip Kotler, *Marketing Management* (Englewood Cliffs, N.J.: Prentice-Hall, 1976), pp. 141–51; and E. Jerome McCarthy, *Basic Marketing* (Homewood, Ill.: Richard D. Irwin, 1975), pp. 111–26.

20.   A good example of this systematic approach to identifying a precise market target appears in Richard P. Carr, Jr., "Developing a New Residential Market for Carpeting: Some Mistakes and Successes," *Journal of Marketing,* July 1977, pp. 101–2.

CHAPTER 6

MARKET SEGMENTATION: INDUSTRIAL MARKETS

KEY TERMS

industrial market
producers
trade industries
value added by manufacturing
reciprocity
derived demand
joint demand
Standard Industrial Classification (SIC)
bids
specifications
life-cycle costing

LEARNING GOALS

1. To list the three components of the industrial market

2. To describe the nature and importance of the industrial market

3. To identify the major characteristics of industrial market demand

4. To compare government markets with other industrial markets

Although David Hannah, Jr., estimated the total start-up costs of his business to amount to between $20 million to $30 million, he was convinced that he could succeed in a growing market monopolized by a single organization. The current monopolist is the National Aeronautics and Space Administration (NASA) and the monopoly service is the launching of private communications satellites.

Source: Photo by Michael Alexander. *People Weekly* © 1981 Time Inc.

Taking on NASA, the famed space agency responsible for launching the space shuttle *Columbia* and placing more than a dozen astronauts on the moon's surface, would be too risky an assignment for most marketers. However, Hannah was aware of the $28 million cost of placing satellites into stationary orbit; his engineers have convinced him that he can perform the same services for an estimated $15 million and make a tidy profit. He was also aware that NASA rockets are booked solid until 1987 and that reservations have been made for the first 68 flights of the space shuttle, another means of launching satellites.

Hannah has employed 17 engineers, many of them former NASA employees, to build a series of 55-foot-long, kerosene-fueled Percheron rockets. The Percheron, named after a rugged breed of French workhorses, costs about $1 million and is built with off-the-shelf hardware developed by NASA and others.

Hannah's firm, Space Services, Inc., assembles the rockets in a Sunnyvale, California, factory, then hauls them aboard a flatbed truck to its own version of Cape Kennedy: a launch pad at Matagorda Island in the Gulf of Mexico, about 150 miles south of Houston. The site was once considered by NASA for its own launches.

Hannah expects to win customers through a series of test flights and by spending up to $30 million during the firm's first four years of operation. Potential clients include RCA, Comsat, Western Union, and numerous cable television systems. If the venture is successful, Hannah should quadruple his investment by 1985.[1]

THE INDUSTRIAL MARKET

Space Services, Inc., represents just one of the nearly 15 million organizations involved in the industrial market. In Chapter 5, the consumer market was defined as those individuals who purchase goods and services for personal use. The **industrial market** consists of *those individuals and organizations who acquire goods and services to be used, directly or indirectly, in the production of other goods and services or to be resold to governments, retailers and wholesalers, and producers.* Although industrial marketers face decisions very similar to those of their consumer-market counterparts, important differences also exist—both in the characteristics of market targets and in the development of appropriate marketing mixes. Professor James D. Hlavacek recognized the differences between the two markets when he noted, "Overall, the strategic and tactical emphasis and elements in the industrial and consumer marketing mixes are as different as silicon chips and potato chips."[2]

Components of the Industrial Market

The industrial market can be divided into three categories: producers, trade industries (wholesalers and retailers), and governments. **Producers** are *industrial customers who purchase goods and services for the* *production of other goods and services.* An American Airlines purchase of the new fuel-efficient Boeing 757 plane, a wheat purchase by General Mills for its cereals, and the purchase of light bulbs and cleaning materials for an Owens-Illinois manufacturing facility all represent industrial purchases by producers. Some products aid in producing another product or service (the new plane); others are physically used up in the production of a product (the wheat); and still others are routinely used in the day-to-day operations of the firm (the maintenance items). Producers include manufacturing firms; farmers and other resource industries; construction contractors; providers of such services as transportation, public utilities, and banks; and nonprofit organizations.

Trade industries are *organizations such as retailers and wholesalers who purchase for resale to others.* In most instances, such resale products as clothing, appliances, sports equipment, and automobile parts are finished goods that are marketed to customers in the selling firm's market area. In other instances, some processing or repackaging may take place. For instance, retail meat markets may make bulk purchases of sides of beef and convert them into individual cuts for their customers. Lumber dealers and carpet retailers may purchase in bulk, then provide quantities and sizes to meet customers' specifications. In addition to resale products, trade industries also buy cash registers, computers, display equipment, and other products required to operate their business. These products (as well as maintenance items and the purchase of such specialized services as marketing research studies, accounting services, and consulting) all represent industrial purchases.

Governments at the federal, state, and local level represent the final category of industrial purchasers. This important component of the industrial market purchases a wide variety of products, ranging from highways to education to F-16 fighter aircraft. The primary motivation of government purchasing is to provide some form of public benefit such as national defense, education, or public welfare.

Size of the Industrial Market

The industrial market accounts for about half of all the manufactured goods in the United States. The **value added by manufacturing**—*the difference between the price charged by manufacturers and the cost of their inputs*—totals about $600 million.[3]

The size of the industrial market is shown in Table 6.1. The nearly 15 million organizations employ more than 100 million workers. Producers account for approximately 80 percent of the total number of industrial organizations and two-thirds of total employment. However, differences may occur among the three categories. As expected, governmental employees per unit are significantly larger than producers and trade industries. Also, there are five times as many retail establishments as manufacturers. However, manufacturing units av-

COMPARING INDUSTRIAL AND CONSUMER MARKETING: THE CASE OF SMUCKER'S

"With a name like Smucker's, it has to be good!" This amusing slogan, coupled with a sound marketing program for its jellies and preserves has made the J. M. Smucker Company a successful, well-known firm to its customers. Yet the firm has been equally successful in the industrial market. Smucker's produces filling bases that are used by other manufacturers in such products as yogurt and bakery items. The tasks involved in marketing strawberry preserves to ultimate consumers is significantly different from the tasks of marketing a related strawberry filling to a manufacturer of yogurt.

Smucker's: A Consumer Goods Marketer. In marketing its jellies and preserves to the consumer market, the J. M. Smucker Company engages in the classic marketing tasks of identifying market targets and developing an appropriate marketing mix. Each new product to be sold in retail food outlets is carefully developed, tested, and targeted for specifically chosen consumer segments. A company sales force calls on larger accounts, while independent middlemen also make calls on retail and wholesale channel members. Promotional programs are designed to stimulate consumer demand and to provide incentives for retailers to handle Smucker's products. Pricing decisions reflect cost, prices of competitors, and consumer demand. All areas of marketing strategy are included in the Smucker's plan.

Smucker's: An Industrial Marketer. A radically different marketing program is used in the industrial segment. The market consists of manufacturers who might use Smucker products in the goods they produce. Smucker's products will lose their identity in the manufacturing process as they are blended into forms such as cakes, cookies, or yogurt.

Once a potential industrial customer is identified, a Smucker's sales representative will call on the account. In some instances, the initial contact is with top management. More typically, the early contacts are with the individual in charge of research and development. Early discussions typically center on specifications for the texture and composition of the required goods.

These specifications are provided to the research and development division at Smucker's and samples are developed. The samples are then supplied to the potential customer who may request further modifications. It is not uncommon for a period of months to pass and a series of modifications to occur before a mixture is finally approved. Next, attention turns to price, and the salesperson's contact point shifts to the purchasing department. Since large quantities are involved (truckloads or drums rather than jars), a few cents per pound can be significant to both parties. Quality and service are also major criteria in the decision.

Once a contract has been signed, the product will be shipped directly from the Smucker's warehouse to the manufacturer's plant. The salesperson will follow up frequently with the purchasing agent and the plant manager. The ultimate sales for Smucker's will depend upon both the manufacturer's satisfaction with Smucker's products and on the performance of the manufacturer's product in the marketplace.

Source: Michael D. Hutt and Thomas W. Speh, *Industrial Marketing Management* (Hinsdale, Ill.: The Dryden Press, 1981), pp. 7–8. Copyright © 1981 CBS College Publishing. Adapted by permission of The Dryden Press, CBS College Publishing.

**TABLE 6.1
The Industrial
Market: Size and
Scope**

Category	Number of Organizations	Number of Employees	Employees per Unit
A. Producers			
1. Agriculture, Forestry, Fisheries	3,365,000	3,383,000	1
2. Mining	112,000	814,000	7
3. Construction	1,279,000	5,504,000	4
4. Manufacturing	482,000	20,637,000	43
5. Transportation, Public Utilities	486,000	5,833,000	12
6. Finance, Insurance, Real Estate	1,805,000	5,038,000	3
7. Services	4,043,000	25,658,000	6
Total	11,572,000	66,867,000	6
B. Trade Industries			
1. Wholesaling Establishments	575,000	3,597,000	6
2. Retailers	2,459,000	15,109,000	6
Total	3,034,000	18,706,000	6
C. Governments			
1. Federal Government	1	2,848,000	
2. State Governments	50	3,491,000	
3. Local Governments	79,862	9,274,000	
Total	79,913	15,613,000	195
Overall Totals	14,685,913	101,186,000	

Source: *Statistical Abstract of the United States* (Washington, D.C.: U.S. Government Printing Office, 1981), pp. 318, 406, 557.

erage 43 employees, as compared with six employees in the average retail establishment.

CHARACTERISTICS OF THE INDUSTRIAL MARKET

The industrial market has three distinctive characteristics: geographic market concentration, a relatively small number of buyers, and systematic buying procedures.

Market Concentration

The industrial goods market in the United States is much more concentrated geographically than is the consumer goods market. Figure 6.1 shows the concentration in eastern states like New Jersey, New York, and Pennsylvania; Sunbelt states like California, North Carolina, and Texas; and the Great Lakes states of Illinois, Indiana, Michigan, and Ohio. These ten states accounted for 57 percent of the $1.7 billion in manufacturing shipments during 1980.[4]

FIGURE 6.1
The United States in Proportion to Value of Manufactured Products

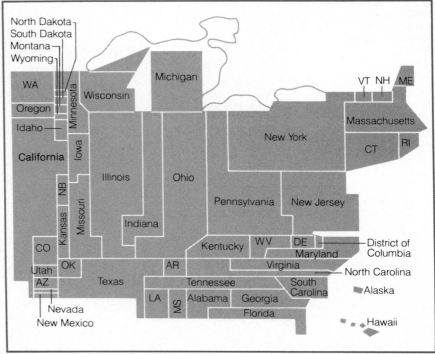

Source: U. S. Department of Commerce, Bureau of the Census, *Census of Manufactures Area Statistics* (Washington, D.C.: U.S. Government Printing Office, 1971), p. 39.

Limited Number of Buyers

In addition to geographic concentration, the industrial market has a limited number of buyers. Even though factories with 20 or more employees represent less than one-third of the total number of U.S. manufacturing establishments, they produce 95 percent of total industry output. Figure 6.2 shows the number of production facilities in each region according to the most recent *Census of Manufactures.* The industrial growth of the Sunbelt region is reflected in the fact that the Southeast, with 69,558 industrial prospects (plants), leads the Great Lakes region. Only the Mideast region contains a greater number of manufacturing facilities than this emerging industrial market. The Rocky Mountain and Far West regions experienced the largest increases in new plants during the five-period since the last census, with gains of 32.4 percent and 26.6 percent, respectively. The Mideast region posted a slight decline in the number of production facilities.

Individual industries also have a limited number of buyers. Four companies produce over two-thirds of the U.S. automobile tire output. The aircraft industry is concentrated in Seattle; Wichita, Kansas; Burbank, California; and Marietta, Georgia, and is comprised of only 99 manufacturing facilities. All U.S. production of aluminum sheet, plate, and foil takes place in 62 plants.

The industrial market tends to be concentrated in such states as New York.

"Sell the house, cars, stove, refrigerator, lawn mower, hedge cutter, power saw, fertilizer spreader, snow blower, and playroom furniture. The corporate headquarters is moving back to New York City."

Source: Reprinted by permission of Joseph Farris and *Sales & Marketing Management*. Copyright © 1979.

The concentration of the industrial market greatly influences the marketing strategy used in serving it. Industrial marketers usually can make profitable use of a sales force to provide regular personal contacts with a small, geographically concentrated market. Wholesalers are less frequently used, and the marketing channel for industrial goods is typically much shorter than for consumer goods. Advertising also

FIGURE 6.2
The Geographical
Location of Industrial
Buyers

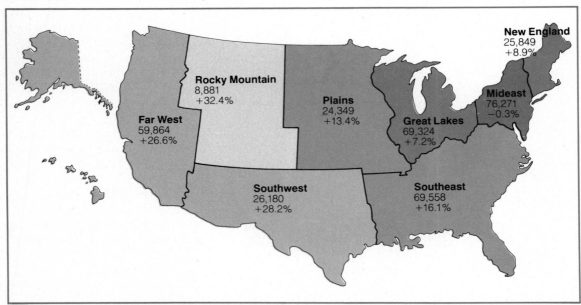

Note: figures indicate the number of plants in each region and the percentage change in total number of plants for the five-year period between the 1972 and the 1977 Census of Manufactures.

Source: *Sales & Marketing Management* calculations; Census Bureau, 1977 *Census of Manufactures: Selected Statistics for States: MC77-S-2 (P),* and individual state reports in the geographic area series. Used by permission of *Sales & Marketing Management.*

plays a much smaller role in the industrial goods market. It is used primarily as an aid to personal selling and to enhance the reputation of the firm and its products and services.

INDUSTRIAL PURCHASING BEHAVIOR

Industrial purchase behavior tends to be more complex than the consumer decision process described in Chapter 5. There are several reasons for this increased complexity:

1.   Many persons may exert influence in industrial purchases, and considerable time may be spent in obtaining the input and approval of various organizational members.

2.   Organizational purchasing may be handled by committees, with greater time requirements for majority or unanimous approval.

3.   Many organizations attempt to utilize several sources of supply as a type of "insurance" against shortages.

Most industrial firms have attempted to systematize their purchases by employing a professional consumer—the industrial purchasing manager. These technically qualified professional buyers are responsible for handling much of the organization's purchases and for securing needed products at the best possible price. Unlike the ultimate consumer who makes periodic purchase decisions, a firm's purchasing department devotes all its time and effort to determining needs, locating and evaluating alternative sources of supply, and making purchase decisions.

Where major purchases are involved, negotiations may take several weeks or even months, and the buying decision may rest with a number of persons in the organization. The choice of a supplier for industrial drill presses, for example, may be made jointly by the purchasing agent and the company's production, engineering, and maintenance departments. Each of these principals may have a different point of view to be taken into account in making a purchase decision. As a result, representatives of the selling firm must be well versed in the technical aspects of the product or service and capable of interacting socially and professionally with managers of the various departments involved in the purchase decision. In the transportation equipment industry, for instance, it takes an average of 4.9 face-to-face presentations to make a sale. The average cost of

The industrial purchase decision is often characterized by numerous decision makers and extensive negotiations.

"Mr. Edelman? Mr. Clavershorn and his buckaroos—er, associates—are here to see you."

Source: Drawing by Miller; © 1981 by *The New Yorker* Magazine.

Industry	Average Number of Calls to Close a Sale	Average Cost to Close a Sale[1]
Food and Kindred Products	2.6	$ 229.16
Furniture & Fixtures	3.8	388.20
Paper & Allied Products	4.7	597.22
Petroleum/Refining & Related Industries	4.0	360.56
Primary Metal Industries	3.9	465.89
Transportation Equipment	4.9	1,121.02
Transportation by Air	4.1	265.68
Business Services	5.6	800.01
Automotive Repair, Services & Garages	5.0	488.00

[1]Determined by multiplying the average number of calls to close a sale by the average cost per sales call for each industry
Source: "Industrial Sales Call Tops $137, but New 'Cost to Close' Hits $589," *Marketing News,* May 1, 1981, p. 1. Used by permission of the American Marketing Association.

closing the sale—including salesperson compensation and travel and entertainment expenses—is $1,121.02. Table 6.2 shows the average number of sales calls required to complete a sale in several industries, and the average cost of each sale.

The manufacturer of a reinforced fiberglass utility lighting pole faced a complicated decision process that involved the members of several departments and months of negotiations before a sale could be made. The new pole had several advantages over the traditional steel, wood, or aluminum pole: lightweight; nonelectrical conducting and noncorrosive properties; and the fact that it never needs painting while meeting strength requirements. Its major disadvantage, other than purchaser unfamiliarity, is its high initial purchase price compared to the metal alternatives. The decision process began with the manager of the utility company. Next, the utility's purchasing department manager was contacted who, in turn, contacted the engineering head. After a list of alternative suppliers and materials was prepared by purchasing and approved by engineering, the agent then discussed the organization's needs with salespeople representing three suppliers. The salespeople met with the heads of the stores department and the marketing department, and with the engineering department manager. After a series of meetings with the salespeople and numerous discussions among the utility's various department heads, a decision was made to submit the new fiberglass pole to a test conducted by the engineering department. The results of the test were reported to the various department heads. Bids were then requested from Suppliers A, B, and C. These bids were reviewed by the department heads, who ultimately decided to select the new fiberglass pole offered by Supplier B. This complex decision process is diagrammed in Figure 6.3.[5]

Many industrial products are purchased for long periods of time

FIGURE 6.3
The Decision to
Purchase a New
Type of Utility Pole

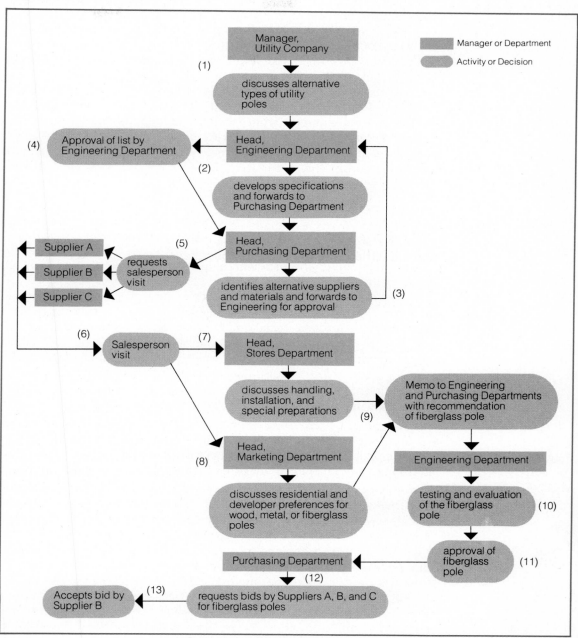

Source: Adapted from Arch G. Woodside, "Marketing Anatomy of Buying Process Can Help Improve Industrial Strategy," *Marketing News,* May 1, 1981, sec. 2, p. 11. Used by permission of the American Marketing Association.

on a contractual basis. Manufacturing operations require a continuous supply of materials, and one- or two-year contracts with suppliers ensure this steady supply. Other industrial goods, such as conveyors, forklifts, and typewriters, generally last several years before replacement is necessary.[6]

Purchase decisions frequently are made on the basis of service, certainty of supply, and efficiency of the supplied products. These factors must be considered along with the prices quoted for the products.

Automobile manufacturers purchase batteries, glass windows, spark plugs, and steel as ingredients for their output. Since demand for these items is derived from the demand for consumer goods, most price changes do not substantially affect their sale. For example, price increases for paint have little effect on auto sales at Ford because paint represents only a minute portion of an automobile's total cost of manufacture.

Reciprocity

A highly controversial practice in a number of industries is **reciprocity,** *the extension of purchasing preference to suppliers who are also customers.* Reciprocal agreements formerly were used in industries involving homogeneous products with similar prices, such as the chemical, paint, petroleum, rubber, and steel industries.

Reverse reciprocity is the practice of extending supply privileges to firms who provide needed supplies. In times of shortages, a form of reverse reciprocity occasionally emerges as firms attempt to obtain crucial raw materials and parts to continue operations. Although some reciprocal agreements still exist, both the Justice Department and the Federal Trade Commission view them as attempts to reduce competition. Federal intervention is common in cases where agreements are used systematically.[7]

CHARACTERISTICS OF INDUSTRIAL MARKET DEMAND

Considerable differences exist in the marketing of consumer and industrial products. Gillette's Paper Mate division had long been a successful provider of medium-priced ballpoint pens to consumer markets. But this market is becoming increasingly divided into low- and premium-priced segments. So Paper Mate decided to come out with new offerings at both ends of the price spectrum.

The firm also decided to enter the office supplies field—an industrial market. It established a special commercial salesforce to promote its pens to industrial buyers. Paper Mate also acquired Liquid Paper, an established name in the office supplies field. Liquid Paper's industrial marketing strengths are seen as complementing the consumer marketing in which Paper Mate has specialized.[8] The Gillette division clearly recognized that the industrial marketplace was different from the consumer markets in which they had traditionally competed. The unique characteristics of industrial settings require that marketing strategies be tailored to the special requirements of this marketplace.

What are the primary characteristics of industrial market demand? Most lists would include the following:[9]

Derived Demand The term **derived demand** refers to *the linkage between desires to make industrial purchases and the desires of customers for the firm's output.* For example, the demand for cash registers (an industrial good) is partially derived from demand at the retail level (consumer products). Increased retail sales may ultimately result in greater demand for cash registers.

On the other hand, the "downsizing" of automobile engines by auto manufacturers in an attempt to develop smaller, fuel-efficient cars adversely affects such spark plug manufacturers as Champion. Since the four-cylinder engines use half as many plugs as V-8s, Champion's total sales may decline drastically unless total auto sales increase dramatically, or unless Champion can increase its share of the total market.

Joint Demand *The demand for some industrial products is related to the demand for other industrial goods to be used jointly with the first item,* a concept known as **joint demand.** Coke and iron ore are required to make pig iron. If the coke supply is reduced, there will be an immediate effect on the demand for iron ore.

Inventory Adjustments Changes in inventory policy can have an impact on industrial demand. A two-month supply of raw materials is often considered the optimal inventory in some manufacturing industries.[10] But suppose economic conditions or other factors dictates that this level be increased to a 90-day supply. The raw materials supplier would then be bombarded with a tremendous increase in new orders. Thus, inventory adjustments can be a major determinant of industrial demand.

Demand Variability Derived demand in the industrial market is linked to immense variability in industrial demand. Assume the demand for industrial product A is derived from the demand for consumer product B—an item whose sales volume has been growing at an annual rate of 10 percent. Now suppose that the demand for product B slowed to a 5 percent annual increase. Management might decide to delay further purchases of product A, using existing inventory until market conditions were clarified. Therefore, even modest shifts in the demand for product B greatly affect product A's demand.

SEGMENTING THE INDUSTRIAL MARKET

Chapter 5 discussed the segmentation of the consumer market. A similar process can be applied to the industrial market. For instance, *geographic* segmentation can be used in such instances as the automobile industry, concentrated in the Detroit area, or the tire industry, which continues to be centered in Akron, Ohio. Segmentation by *product* is often practiced, since industrial users tend to have much more precise product specifications than ultimate consumers do. A third segmentation base is *end-use applications,* or precisely how the industrial purchaser will use the product. A manufacturer of, say, printing equipment may serve markets ranging from the Bell System to a bicycle manufacturer to the U.S. Department of Defense. Each end-use of the equipment may dictate unique specifications of performance, design, and price.

Information for the Industrial Segmentation Process

The industrial segmentation process is aided by a wealth of published information. The federal government is the largest single source of information. Every five years it conducts a Census of Manufactures as well as a Census of Retailing and Wholesaling, providing detailed information on industrial establishments, output, and employment. Specific industry studies are summarized in the annual *U.S. Industrial Outlook,* a government publication providing statistical data and discussing industry trends.

Trade associations and business publications provide additional information on the industrial market. Private firms such as Dun & Bradstreet publish detailed reports on individual firms. These data serve as useful starting points for analyzing industrial markets.

Standard Industrial Classification (SIC) Codes

The federal government's **Standard Industrial Classification (SIC)** system greatly simplifies the process of focusing on an industrial market target. This numerical system *subdivides the industrial marketplace into more detailed product/service industries or market segments.* The SIC codes are divided into ten broad industry groups, into which all types of organization can be classified:

- 01–09 Agriculture, Forestry, Fishing
- 10–14 Mining
- 15–17 Contract Construction
- 20–39 Manufacturing
- 40–49 Transportation and Other Public Utilities
- 50–59 Wholesale and Retail Trade
- 60–67 Finance, Insurance, and Real Estate
- 70–89 Services
- 91–97 Government—Federal, State, Local, and International
- 99   Others

Each major industry within these classifications is assigned its own two-digit number; three- and four-digit numbers subdivide the industry into smaller segments. For example, a *major group* such as the food industry is assigned SIC 20. A specific three-digit *industry group*

FIGURE 6.4
The Standard
Industrial
Classification System

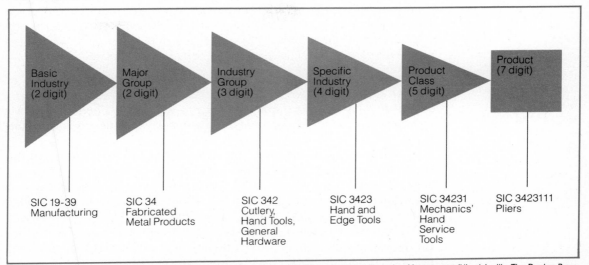

Basic Industry (2 digit)	Major Group (2 digit)	Industry Group (3 digit)	Specific Industry (4 digit)	Product Class (5 digit)	Product (7 digit)
SIC 19-39 Manufacturing	SIC 34 Fabricated Metal Products	SIC 342 Cutlery, Hand Tools, General Hardware	SIC 3423 Hand and Edge Tools	SIC 34231 Mechanics' Hand Service Tools	SIC 3423111 Pliers

Source: Michael D. Hutt and Thomas W. Speh, *Industrial Marketing Management* (Hinsdale, Ill.: The Dryden Press, 1981), p. 105. Copyright © 1981 CBS College Publishing. Reprinted by permission of The Dryden Press, CBS College Publishing.

such as dairy products is SIC 202. The next category, *specific industries,* would use the fourth digit. Creamery butter, for example, is SIC 2021 and fluid milk is SIC 2026.[11]

In the most recent Census of Manufactures, the Census Bureau assembled industrial data at two additional levels: five-digit *product classes* and seven-digit *product* or *commodity categories.* Figure 6.4 illustrates the classification system and the detail in which data is available.

Since most published data on industrial markets utilize the SIC system, the SIC codes are invaluable tools in analyzing the industrial marketplace. The detailed information for each market segment provides the marketer with a comprehensive description of the activities of his or her potential customers on both a geographical and a specific industry basis.

GOVERNMENT MARKETS

Government markets can be considered another aspect in the marketing of industrial products. There are many similarities between other industrial markets and the government market. Both seek to purchase many similar goods and services. However, there are differences in the way items are procured—primarily due to the numerous regulations that impact government markets.

Size of the Government Market

The government—at all levels—is a sizable segment of the industrial market. Total spending for goods and services by all three levels of government—federal, state, and local—amounted to about $650 billion in 1982, an increase of 10 percent over the previous year. Although total federal expenditures rose modestly from previous years, defense expenditures and overall purchases by state and local governments experienced sharp increases.[12]

How Government Markets Are Organized

Most government purchases, by law, must be made on the basis of **bids,** or *written sales proposals,* from vendors. As a result, government buyers develop **specifications**: *specific descriptions of needed items for prospective bidders.* An example of government specifications is shown in Figure 6.5.

The federal government buys most branded items through the General Services Administration (GSA), specifically the organization's Federal Supply Service. But about 500 other federal offices also maintain procurement functions, including military purchases.[13] Most states have offices comparable to the GSA.

Prospective government suppliers can learn of opportunities for sales by contacting the various government agencies. Most contracts are advertised by each agency, and information on bidding procedures can be obtained directly from the agency. Directories explaining procedures involved in selling to the federal government are available from the Government Printing Office, and most states provide similar information.[14]

Selling to Government Markets

The GSA was recently unable to find three bidders for some $50,000 in purchases of facial tissue, filing cabinets, garbage cans, and table napkins. Despite its immense size, the government market is often viewed as unprofitable by many suppliers. A survey conducted by *Sales & Marketing Management* reported that industrial marketers registered a variety of complaints about government purchasing procedures. These included excessive paperwork; bureaucracy; needless regulations; emphasis on low bid prices; decision-making delays; frequent shifts in procurement personnel; and excessive policy changes.[15]

On the other hand, marketers generally credit the government with being a relatively stable market. Once an item is purchased by the government, the probability of additional sales is good. Other marketers cite such advantages as the instant credibility established by sales to the federal government; timely payment; excise tax and sales tax exemptions; acceptance of new ideas; and reduced competition.

One survey reported that 68 percent of its industrial respondents did not maintain a separate government sales manager or sales force. But many firms report success with specialized government marketing efforts. J. I. Case, Goodyear, Eastman Kodak, and Sony are

FIGURE 6.5
An Example of a
Government
Specification

GG–P–115
OCTOBER 20, 1954

FEDERAL SPECIFICATION

PARACHUTE, METEOROLOGICAL

This specification was approved by the Commissioner, Federal Supply Service, General Services Administration, for the use of all Federal agencies.

1. SCOPE AND CLASSIFICATION

1.1 Scope.—This specification covers a paper parachute used to regulate the descent of the radiosonde after the ballon has burst.

1.2 Classification.—The meteorological parachute covered by this specification shall be of one type and grade only.

3.4 Hoop.—The reed used in the loop shall be $\frac{3}{16}$ inch, plus or minus $\frac{1}{16}$ inch, in diameter. The reed shall be twisted, one complete twist in from 6 inches to 10 inches of length and formed into a circular hoop 18 inches, plus or minus 1 inch, in diameter. The ends of the reeds shall be lapped 5 inches, plus or minus 1 inch, and securely taped to the hoop. The ends of the reeds and any other sharp projections from the reeds shall be covered with tape. The hoop shall not break or collapse under applicable pull test of 4.8.1 or 4.9.

3.5 Shroud lines.—A 25-pound-test hard-twist cord shall be used for the shroud lines. Each shroud line shall be tied with a tight nonslip knot to the canopy reinforcement tape in such a manner that from 1 inch to 1½ inches of the shroud line and tape remain. Each shroud line shall be tied to the hoop in a secure and nonslip manner. These tie points shall be equally spaced around the hoop at each 45 degree of arc. The shroud line shall be tied below the hoop in a hard nonslip knot in such a manner that 8 inches plus or minus 1 inch of tassel remains. Each shroud line shall be carefully measured and tied so that the total effective lengths of the cords plus tapes between the centers of the knots in the upper and lower tassels will be approximately equal. The length of the shroud lines from the canopy to the hoop, and from the hoop to the knot forming the lower tassel, shall be as shown in figure I.

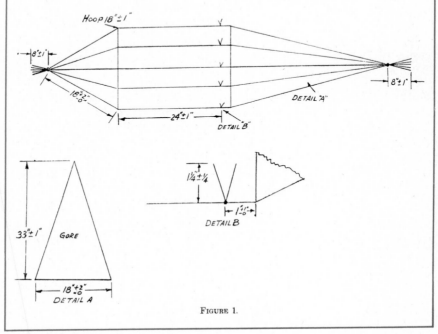

FIGURE 1.

Source: Courtesy of the GSA.

examples. There are also specialist distributors—such as Government Marketing Services of Rockville, Maryland—that sell small orders of branded, off-the-shelf-type items to government buyers for manufacturers like Texas Instruments and General Electric.

Recent Developments for Government Markets

Four recent actions have impacted the federal government market. Similar developments have influenced some state and local governments.[16] The Washington developments are as follows:

1. The Office of Federal Procurement Policy (OFPP)—part of the Office of Management and Budget—requires that government agencies use a single set of procurement regulations, the so-called *Federal Acquisition Regulation (FAR)*. The intent is to reduce the red tape and excessive regulation that currently characterize the federal government market.

2. The Pentagon, GSA, and other government buyers, in an attempt to reduce spending, are turning to more off-the-shelf goods rather than issuing special-order contracts.

3. **Life-cycle costing**—*the cost of using a product over its lifetime, not just the initial bid price*—is now accepted by the GSA. Potential energy savings are part of this new policy in granting government contracts.[17]

4. A variety of reforms are being implemented in the GSA itself. Most of these involve streamlining its organization, increasing procurement efficiency, and improving its counseling of would-be suppliers.

SUMMARY

The industrial goods market consists of all entities that buy goods and services for use in producing other products for resale. The market has three distinctive characteristics: 1) geographical market concentration, 2) a relatively small number of buyers, and 3) systematic buying procedures.

The market concentration is verified by the fact that ten states—California, Illinois, Indiana, Michigan, New Jersey, New York, North Carolina, Ohio, Pennsylvania, and Texas—account for about 60 percent of the value added by manufacturing in the United States. The limited number of buyers in the marketplace is illustrated by the fact that while less than a third of all U.S. plants employ over 20 people, these larger facilities account for 95 percent of total industrial output.

The systematic nature of industrial purchasing is reflected by the use of purchasing managers who direct such efforts. Major industrial purchases may require an elaborate and lengthy decision-making process that involves many people. Purchase decisions typically depend on price, service, certainty of supply, and the efficiency of item being purchased.

Industrial market demand is characterized by derived demand, joint demand, inventory adjustments, and demand variability, all of these factors influencing the nature and extent of industrial market demand.

The industrial market may be segmented using a number of bases. *Geographic* segmentation is often used, since many firms and entire industries are concentrated geographically. A second possibility is segmentation by *product,* since many different firms can be categorized on the basis of precise product specifications. *End-use* segmentation locates homogeneous industrial market targets by focusing on the precise use the purchaser will make of the product. The Standard Industrial Classification (SIC) system is a useful tool in analyzing the market.

The government market—federal, state, and local—provides a sizable market for industrial marketers.

QUESTIONS FOR DISCUSSION

1. Explain the following terms:
   industrial market
   producers
   trade industries
   value added by manufacturing
   reciprocity
   derived demand

   joint demand
   Standard Industrial Classification (SIC)
   bids
   specifications
   life-cycle costing

2. Contrast the purchasing practices of producers, trade industries, and governments. Which types of products are most frequently purchased by each?

3. Identify the types of organizations that comprise the industrial market.

4. Why is the industrial market important?

5. Outline the three distinctive features of the industrial market.

6. Describe the concentration that exists in the industrial marketplace.

7. Discuss the number and location of industrial buying prospects.

8. How are SIC codes useful to industrial marketers?

9. Comment on industrial purchasing behavior as compared to consumer purchasing behavior.

10. Discuss the issue of reciprocity.

11. Identify the major characteristics of industrial market demand.

12. Contrast derived demand with joint demand.

13. How do inventory adjustments impact industrial market sales?

14. Describe the demand variability that exists in industrial markets.

15. Identify the major bases for industrial market segmentation. Illustrate each segmentation base with an appropriate product or service example. Defend your choice.

16. Explain how end-use segmentation might be used by a manufacturer of gauges.

17. Compare the government market to other industrial markets.

18. Discuss the organization of the government market.

19. Why do some firms ignore sales opportunities in the government marketplace?

20. Describe the recent developments that have affected government markets.

NOTES

1. David Hannah's private space venture is described in "Free Enterprise Space Shot," *Time,* June 29, 1981, p. 63; and abridged from Kent Demaret, "Shooting for the Stars, Texan David Hannah Fires up His Own Private Space Program," *People,* July 6, 1981, pp. 37–38. © 1981, Time, Inc.

2. Quoted in James D. Hlavacek, "Business Schools Need More Industrial Marketing," *Marketing News,* April 4, 1980, p. 1.

3. "Up Goes the Factory Count," *Sales & Marketing Management,* March 17, 1980, p. 37.

4. Thayer C. Taylor, "The 1981 Survey of Industrial Purchasing Power," *Sales & Marketing Management,* April 27, 1981, p. 6.

5. The development of the new type of pole and the problems involved in its adoption are described in Arch G. Woodside, "Marketing Anatomy of Buying Process Can Help Improve Industrial Strategy," *Marketing News,* May 1, 1981, sec. 2, p. 11.

6. Alvin J. Williams, "Fast Complaint Response Should Help Develop Long-Term Marketing Success," *Marketing News,* May 1, 1981, sec. 2, p. 8.

7. The history and current status of reciprocal agreements is summarized in E. Robert Finney, "Reciprocity: Gone but Not Forgotten," *Journal of Marketing,* January 1978, pp. 54–59. See also William J. Kehoe and Byron D. Hewett, "Reciprocity and Reverse Reciprocity: A Literature Review and Research Design," in *Proceedings of the Southern Marketing Association,* eds. Robert S. Franz, Robert M. Hopkins, and Al Toma, New Orleans, La., November 1978, pp. 481–83; and Monroe M. Bird, "Reverse Reciprocity: A New Twist to Industrial Buyers," *Atlanta Economic Review,* January-February 1976, pp. 11–13.

8. "Paper Mate's Broader Outlook," *Business Week,* January 28, 1980, p. 69.

9. These characteristics are suggested in Robert W. Haas, *Industrial Marketing Management* (New York: Petrocelli/Charter, 1976), pp. 21–26; and Richard M. Hill, Ralph S. Alexander, and James S. Cross, *Industrial Marketing,* Fourth Edition (Homewood, Illinois: Richard D. Irwin, Inc., 1975), pp. 46–47.

10. The 60-day figure is suggested in Bob Luke, "Purchasing Agents: Supply Sergeants to the Business World," *Detroit News,* May 20, 1979, p. 2-E.

11. "What Is This Thing Called SIC?" *Sales & Marketing Management,* April 27, 1981, pp. 26–27.

12. "Business at Midyear: Turn for Better Ahead," *U.S. News & World Report,* July 6, 1981, pp. 26–27.

13. "Out of the Maze," *Sales & Marketing Management,* April 9, 1979, p. 45.

14. An excellent discussion appears in John M. Rathmell, "Marketing by the Federal Government," *MSU Business Topics,* Summer 1973, pp. 21–28.

15. This section is based on "Out of the Maze," pp. 44–46, 48, 50, 52. Used by permission.

16. *Ibid.,* pp. 46, 48, 50, 52. Used by permission.

17. For a discussion of the application of life-cycle costing to energy-related products, see R. Bruce Hutton and William L. Wilkie, "Life Cycle Cost: A New Form of Consumer Information," *Journal of Consumer Research,* March 1980, pp. 349–60.

CHAPTER 7

UNDERSTANDING CONSUMER BEHAVIOR

KEY TERMS

self-concept
consumer behavior
need
motive
perception
subliminal perception
attitude
semantic differential
learning
status
role
reference groups
opinion leaders
culture
subcultures
evoked set
evaluative criteria
cognitive dissonance

LEARNING GOALS

1. To explain the self-concept and its components

2. To identify the individual factors influencing consumer behavior

3. To list the levels of the needs hierarchy

4. To identify the components of the learning process

5. To identify the environmental influences on consumer behavior

6. To explain the determinants of reference-group influence on the individual

7. To evaluate the two-step flow of communications concept

8. To outline the model of the consumer decision process

Study the photograph carefully, paying particular attention to the reflections and shadows. Rotate the book in a clockwise manner, but stop every few degrees to restudy the drink. Now repeat the procedure by rotating the book in a counterclockwise manner. Did you see them—the hidden messages, the sexual symbols, the four-letter words?

Is this a flagrant example of unethical marketing? Are hidden messages being secretly transmitted to unwary consumers, or should the secret message theory be added to a mythological category, along with Big Foot and those secret recorded messages of rock stars discernable only when records are played backwards at 16 rpm?

Author Wilson Bryan Key feels that such hidden messages do exist in print advertising. He categorizes them as attempts by unscrupulous marketers to seduce consumers into buying. In this book *Subliminal Seduction: Secret Ways Ad Men Arouse Your Desires to Sell Their Product,* Key includes several illustrations of such "hidden persuaders" to support his theory.[1]

But marketing authorities Harold W. Berkman and Christopher Gilson offer a much simpler explanation:

Much photography for advertising art is sent to professional retouching studios, where artists set to work correcting photographic imperfections and adding visual effects not captured by the camera. Ice cubes in ads, for example, are usually plastic ice cubes with highlights painted by retouching artists directly on the photos, since real ice cubes would melt under the hot lights of the photographer's studio. Retouchers, like most artistic people in commercial fields, want to add something of their own creativity to their work. Some find it humorous to introduce carefully disguised sexual elements to an ad that must be puritanically straitlaced for the mass market. (One such artist, according to the advertising industry grapevine, has been fired from several retouching studios for that nasty habit, but always manages to find another shop where he can continue his diabolical work.)[2]

To some, the hidden-message controversy illustrates the steps that cunning, unethical marketers will take to understand and manipulate consumer behavior. To others, the mere mention of this bizarre scheme is even stronger evidence of the difficulty any marketer experiences in attempting to predict consumer reactions to product and service offerings.

The marketing concept, briefly stated, is: Find a need and fill it. The key to marketing success lies in locating unsatisfied consumers. These people may not be purchasing goods due to current unavailability, or they may be buying products that provide them with only limited satisfaction. In the latter case, they are likely to switch to new products that provide more satisfaction. Unsatisfied consumers should comprise the market targets for consumer-oriented firms.

WHY THE MIRACLE MEDICINE FAILED

Extensive consumer research on the burgeoning headache-remedy and antacid market led one major U.S. pharmaceutical firm to develop a new pill with the virtues of aspirin, Alka-Seltzer, Tylenol, Excedrin, and similar tablets gulped down daily by tension-ridden people. The firm's product development department created a product with the one advantage no other competitor had. It could be taken without water.

The product, a cherry-flavored combination painkiller and stomach sweetener called Analoze, was tested for consumer acceptance. Samples were given to a panel of potential buyers, who compared it with competing products. They chose Analoze overwhelmingly.

Ads were then developed around the theme "works without water." The price was competitive, and the package design was eye-catching. Confident of success, the marketing vice-president gave Analoze its first real market test in four cities—Denver, Memphis, Omaha, and Phoenix— and sat back to await the positive results . . . and waited . . . and waited. Sales were virtually nil, and a few months later Analoze was withdrawn from the market.

What went wrong? In-depth research with headache sufferers revealed a ritual associated with pain relief. They swallowed (or dissolved) a pill and drank a glass of water. These people somehow associated water consumption with obtaining relief, and they were unwilling to spend money on a remedy that dissolved in the mouth. In their minds, the glass of water acquired medicinal qualities that a waterless remedy could never provide.

Source: Burt Schorr, "The Mistakes: Many New Products Fail despite Careful Planning, Publicity," *Wall Street Journal*, April 5, 1961, pp. 1, 22.

Marketing research studies can provide data to answer the following questions about consumer buying habits:

1.   *Who* are the buyers?
2.   *When* do they buy (time of day, seasonality of product sales)?
3.   *Where* do they buy?
4.   *What* do they buy?
5.   *How* do they buy (how much and what type of sales—cash or credit)?

But answers to the question "*Why* do they buy (or not buy)?" are much more difficult to ascertain.

SELF-CONCEPT THEORY

Individuals are physical and mental entities possessing multifaceted pictures of themselves. One man, for example, may view himself as

**FIGURE 7.1
Components of
Self-image**

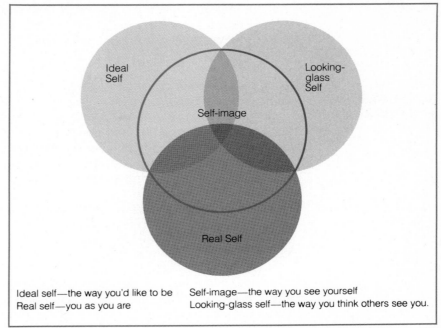

Ideal Self

Looking-glass Self

Self-image

Real Self

Ideal self—the way you'd like to be   Self-image—the way you see yourself
Real self—you as you are   Looking-glass self—the way you think others see you.

Source: John Douglas, George A. Field, and Lawrence X. Tarpey, *Human Behavior in Marketing* (Columbus, Ohio: Charles E. Merrill Publishing Co., 1967), p. 65. Reprinted by permission.

intellectual, self-assured, moderately talented, and a rising young business executive. People's actions, including their purchase decisions, are related to their *mental conception of self*—their **self-concept**. And the response to direct questions like "Why do you buy Jovan cologne?" is likely to reflect this desired self-image.[3]

As Figure 7.1 indicates, the self has four components: real self, self-image, looking-glass self, and ideal self. The real self is an objective view of the total person. The self-image, the way individuals view themselves, may distort the objective view. The looking-glass self, the way individuals think others see them, may also be quite different from self-image, since people often choose to project a different image to others. The ideal self serves as a personal set of objectives, since it is the image to which the individual aspires.

In purchasing goods and services, people are likely to choose products that will move them closer to their ideal self. Those who see themselves as scholars are more likely than others to join literary book clubs. The young woman who views herself as a budding tennis star may become engrossed in evaluating the merits of graphite versus steel rackets and may view with disdain any cheaply made imports. The college graduate on the way up the organization ladder at a bank may hide a love for bowling and instead take up golf—having determined that golf is the sport for bankers. One writer used the self-concept idea to explain the failure of the Edsel. He claimed that potential Edsel purchasers were unsure of the car's image and faced the risk of moving away from their self-concept.[4]

WHAT IS CONSUMER BEHAVIOR?

Consumer behavior consists of *the acts of individuals in obtaining and using economic goods and services, including the decision processes that precede and determine these acts.*[5] This definition includes both the ultimate consumer and the purchaser of industrial products. A major difference between the purchasing behavior of industrial consumers and ultimate consumers is the additional influence that may be exerted on the industrial purchasing agent from within the organization.

Consumer Behavior as a Decision Process

As indicated by the definition, consumer behavior is a decision process and the act of purchasing is merely one step in the process. To understand consumer behavior, the events that precede and follow the purchase act must be examined.

Consumers make decisions—including purchase decisions—as a result of the need to solve problems and to take advantage of opportunities that arise. Such decisions permit consumers to correct differences between their actual and desired states. Feedback from each decision serves as additional experience to rely upon in subsequent decisions.

Consumer behavior results from individual and environmental influences. Consumers often purchase goods and services to achieve their ideal self and to project the self-image they want others to accept. Behavior is therefore determined by the individual's psycholog-

**FIGURE 7.2
Basic Determinants
of Consumer
Behavior**

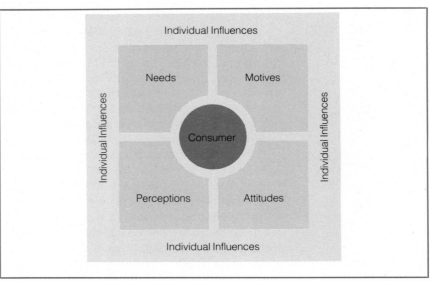

Source: Adapted with permission from C. Glenn Walters and Gordon W. Paul, *Consumer Behavior: An Integrated Framework* (Homewood, Ill.: Richard D. Irwin, 1970), p. 14. © 1970 by Richard D. Irwin, Inc.

ical makeup and the influences of others. This dual influence can be summarized as

$$B = f(P, E)$$

Consumer behavior *(B)* is a function *(f)* of the interaction of consumers' personal influences *(P)* and the pressures exerted upon them by outside forces in the environment *(E)*.[6] Understanding consumer behavior requires an understanding of the nature of these influences.

INDIVIDUAL INFLUENCES ON CONSUMER BEHAVIOR

The basic determinants of consumer behavior include the individual's needs, motives, perceptions, and attitudes. The interaction of these factors with influences from the environment causes the consumer to act. Figure 7.2 illustrates these interactions.

Needs and Motives

The starting point in the purchase decision process is the recognition of a felt need. A **need** is simply *the lack of something useful.* The consumer is typically confronted with numerous unsatisfied needs, but a need must be sufficiently aroused before it can serve as a motive to buy something.

A **motive** is an *inner state that directs people toward the goal of satisfying a felt need.* The individual is moved to take action to reduce a state of tension and to return to a condition of equilibrium.

Although psychologists disagree on specific classifications, a useful theory of the hierarchy of needs has been developed by A. H. Maslow. Maslow's hierarchy is shown in Figure 7.3. His list is based on two important assumptions:

1. People are wanting animals, whose needs depend on what they already possess. A satisfied need is not a motivator; only those needs that have not been satisfied can influence behavior.

**FIGURE 7.3
Hierarchy of Needs**

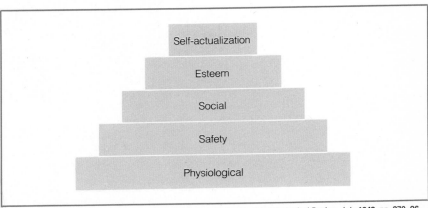

Source: Adapted from A. H. Maslow, "A Theory of Human Motivation," *Psychological Review*, July 1943, pp. 370–96.

2. People's needs are arranged in a hierarchy of importance. Once one need has been at least partially satisfied, another emerges and demands satisfaction.[7]

Physiological Needs The primary needs for food, shelter, and clothing that are present in all humans and must be satisfied before the individual can consider higher-order needs are physiological needs. A hungry person, possessed by the need to obtain food, ignores other needs. Once the physiological needs are at least partially satisfied, other needs enter the picture.

Safety Needs The second-level safety needs include security, protection from physical harm, and avoidance of the unexpected. Gratification of these needs may take the form of a savings account, life insurance, the purchase of radial tires, or membership in a local health club.

The family satisfies many of the individual's social needs.

Source: Drawing by Opie. © 1978 *The New Yorker* Magazine, Inc.

Social Needs Satisfaction of physiological and safety needs leads to the third level—the desire to be accepted by members of the family and other individuals and groups—the social needs. The individual may be motivated to join various groups, to conform to their standards of dress and behavior, and to become interested in obtaining status as means of fulfilling these needs.

Esteem Needs The higher-order needs are more prevalent in developed countries, where a sufficiently high per-capita income has allowed most consumers to satisfy the basic needs and to concentrate on the desire for status, esteem, and self-actualization. These needs, which are near the top of the ladder, are more difficult to satisfy. At the esteem level is the need to feel a sense of accomplishment, achievement, and respect from others. The competitive need to excel—to better the performance of others—is almost a universal human trait.

  The esteem need is closely related to social needs. At this level, however, the individual desires not just acceptance but also recognition and respect. The person has a desire to stand out from the crowd in some way.

Self-actualization Needs The highest level of human needs is self-actualization—the need for fulfillment, for realizing one's own potential, for using one's talents and capabilities totally. Maslow defines self-actualization this way: "The healthy man is primarily motivated by his needs to develop and actualize his fullest potentialities and capacities. What man can be, he must be."[8]

Perception

Individual behavior resulting from motivation is affected by how stimuli are perceived. **Perception** is *the meaning that each person attributes to incoming stimuli received through the five senses.*

$$
\text{To perceive is}\begin{cases} \text{to see} \\ \text{to hear} \\ \text{to touch} \\ \text{to taste} \\ \text{to smell} \end{cases} \text{some}\begin{cases} \text{thing} \\ \text{event} \\ \text{idea}^{9} \end{cases}
$$

  Psychologists once assumed that perception was an objective phenomenon, that the individual perceived only what was there to be perceived. Only recently have researchers come to recognize that what people perceive is as much a result of what they want to perceive as of what is actually there. This does not mean that dogs may be viewed as pigeons or shopping centers as churches. But a retail store stocked with well-known brand names and staffed with helpful, knowledgeable sales personnel is perceived differently from a largely self-service discount store. The Renault Le Car and the Mazda RX-7 are both automobile imports, but they carry quite different images.

USING PSYCHOLOGICAL CONCEPTS TO INCREASE THE LIKELIHOOD OF PERCEPTION

The church billboard and the Sherwin-Williams trademark are just two examples of the application of a psychological concept called *closure.* Closure is the tendency of individuals to develop a complete figure when perceptual gaps exist. Supplying the missing letters on the church billboard completes the word, answers the question, and rewards the viewer through awareness of the underlying intent of the message. Similar rewards result from viewing the trademark. This active involvement in organizing the stimulus may increase the likelihood of perception taking place, although this has not been verified by researchers.

One company that has frequently used this concept in requiring the consumer to make the connection between the actual printed or spoken message and the illustration is the Kellogg Company. During one advertising campaign promoting the incorporation of fresh fruit into a bowl of Kellogg cereal, the company's advertising simply substituted two bananas for the two *l*'s in "Kellogg." During a twenty-five cents coupon redemption program, a quarter was inserted in the Kellogg name to replace the letter *o.* A classic advertising jingle by the makers of Salem cigarettes repeated the line "You can take Salem out of the country, but you can't take the country out of Salem." At the end of the commercial, the jingle ended abruptly at: "You can take Salem out of the country, but . . . ." Listeners had to go to great lengths to prevent themselves from filling in the rest of the sentence.

Photograph courtesy of C. S. Boone. Trademark reproduced by permission of the Sherwin-Williams Company, Cleveland, Ohio.

The perception of an object or event is the result of the interaction of two types of factors:

1. *Stimulus factors*—characteristics of the physical object, such as size, color, weight, or shape.

2. *Individual factors*—characteristics of the individual, including not only sensory processes but also past experiences with similar items and basic motivations and expectations.

The individual is continually bombarded with many stimuli, but most are ignored. In order to have time to function, people must respond selectively. Determining which stimuli they do respond to is the problem of all marketers. How can the consumer's attention be gained so he or she will read the advertisement, listen to the sales representative, react to the point-of-purchase display?

Even though studies have shown that the average consumer is exposed to more than a thousand ads daily, most of these ads never break through people's perceptual screens. Sometimes breakthroughs are accomplished in the printed media through large-sized ads. Doubling the size of an ad increases its attention value by about 50 percent. Using color in newspaper ads—in contrast to the usual black and white ads—is another effective way of breaking through the reader's perceptual screen. However, the color ad must reach enough additional readers to justify the extra cost. Other methods using contrast include large amounts of white space around the printed area or white type on a black background.

Selective Perception Considerable light is shed by selective perception on the problem of getting consumers to try a product for the first time. The manufacturer bombards people with television and magazine advertising, sales promotion discounts and premiums, and point-of-purchase displays—often with little change in sales. Follow-up research shows that many consumers have no knowledge of the product or promotion. Why? Because this information simply never penetrated their perceptual filters. Consumers perceive incoming stimuli on a selective basis. To a large extent they are consciously aware of only those incoming stimuli they wish to perceive.

In general, the marketer seeks to make the message distinctive, to make it sufficiently different from other messages that it will gain the attention of the prospective customer. Menley & James Laboratories followed the practice of running hay-fever radio commercials for their Contac capsules only on days when the pollen count was above certain minimum levels. Each commercial was preceded by a live announcement of the local pollen count.

Analysis of audience reaction to television commercials shows either a sharp drop or rise in interest during the first five seconds. After that point, the audience will become only less interested, never more. The attention-grabbing opening of commercials for American Express Travelers Cheques is, "You are about to witness a crime!" Viewers then

USING HUMOR TO OVERCOME PERCEPTUAL BARRIERS

The use of humor has escalated in recent years as marketers attempt to overcome the perceptual screening that occurs as consumers are exposed to hundreds of advertising messages. One study of advertising content revealed that approximately one of every six advertisements made use of humor. The following phrases quickly identify the brands involved:

"Butter . . . Parkay . . . "
"You can call me . . . or you can call me . . ."
"With a name like Smucker's . . ."
"The Noisiest Potato Chip in the World . . ."

During the 1950s and 1960s many advertisers avoided the use of humor on the theory that it would detract from the product message. Potential consumers might appreciate the humor, but they would be less likely to perceive the advertising message than in cases where more orthodox advertising themes were used.

More recently, research has indicated that humorous messages may prove effective in attracting attention and changing brand preference if the following steps are taken:

1 The brand must be identified in the opening ten seconds in a radio or television commercial, or humor may inhibit recall of important selling points.
2 The type of humor makes a difference. Subtlety is more effective than the bizarre.
3 The humor must be relevant to the brand or key idea. Recall and persuasion both are diminished where this linkage is not present.

Source: Adapted from James F. Engel and Roger D. Blackwell, *Consumer Behavior,* 4th ed. (Hinsdale, Ill.: The Dryden Press, 1982), pp. 474–75. The three steps are suggested in Harold L. Ross, Jr., "How to Create Effective Humorous Commercials Yielding Above Average Brand Preference Changes," *Marketing News,* March 26, 1976, p. 4.

---

watch a pickpocket at work. The campaign showing the dangers of carrying cash reportedly helped American Express increase sales 28 percent.[10]

With such selectivity at work it is easy to see the importance of the marketer's efforts to obtain a "consumer franchise" in the form of brand loyalty to a product. Satisfied customers are less likely to seek information about competing products. And even when it is forced on them, they are not as likely as others to allow it to pass through their perceptual filters. They simply tune out information that is not in accord with their existing beliefs and expectations.

Subliminal Perception Is it possible to communicate with persons without their being aware of the communication? In 1957, the words "Eat popcorn" and "Drink Coca-Cola" were flashed on the screen of a New Jersey movie theater every five seconds for 1/3000th of a second. Researchers reported that these messages, though too short to be recognizable at the conscious level, resulted in a 58 percent increase in popcorn sales and an 18 percent increase in Coca-Cola sales. After the findings were published, advertising agencies and consumer protection groups became intensely interested in **subliminal perception**—*the receipt of incoming information at a subconscious level.*

Subliminal advertising is aimed at the subconscious level of awareness to avoid viewers' perceptual screens. The goal of the original research was to induce consumer purchasing while keeping consumers unaware of the source of their motivation to buy. Further attempts to duplicate the test findings, however, have invariably been unsuccessful.

Although subliminal advertising has been universally condemned (and declared illegal in California and Canada), it is exceedingly unlikely that it can induce purchasing except in those instances where the person is already inclined to buy. The reasons for this are:

1. Strong stimulus factors are required to even gain attention.

2. Only a very short message can be transmitted.

3. Individuals vary greatly in their thresholds of consciousness.[11] Messages transmitted at one person's threshold of consciousness will not be perceived at all by some people and will be all too apparent to others. The subliminally exposed message "Drink Coca-Cola" may go unseen by some viewers, while others may read it as "Drink Pepsi-Cola," "Drink Cocoa," or even "Drive Slowly."

Despite early fears, research has shown that subliminal messages cannot force the receiver to purchase goods that he or she would not consciously want.

Attitudes

Perception of incoming stimuli is greatly affected by attitudes about them. In fact, the decision to purchase a product is based on currently held attitudes about the product, the store, or the salesperson.

An **attitude** is *a person's enduring favorable or unfavorable evaluation, emotional feelings, or pro or con action tendency in regard to some object or idea.* Attitudes are formed over a period of time through individual experiences and group contacts and are highly resistant to change.

Components of an Attitude Attitudes consist of three related components: cognitive, affective, and behavioral. The *cognitive* component refers to the individual's information and knowledge about an object or concept. The *affective* component deals with feelings or emotional reactions. The *behavioral* component has to do with tendencies to act or to behave in a certain manner. In considering the decision to shop at a warehouse-type food store, the individual would obtain information from advertising, trial visits, and input from family, friends, and associates (cognitive). The consumer would also receive inputs from others about their acceptance of shopping at this new type of store, as well as information about the type of people who shop there (affective). The shop-

FIGURE 7.4
Three Components
of an Attitude

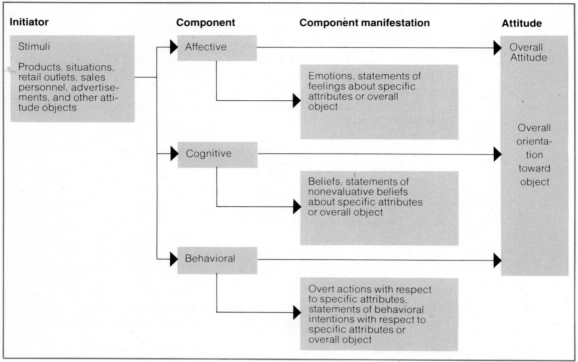

Initiator	Component	Component manifestation	Attitude
Stimuli Products, situations, retail outlets, sales personnel, advertisements, and other attitude objects	Affective	Emotions, statements of feelings about specific attributes or overall object	Overall Attitude
	Cognitive	Beliefs, statements of nonevaluative beliefs about specific attributes or overall object	Overall orientation toward object
	Behavioral	Overt actions with respect to specific attributes, statements of behavioral intentions with respect to specific attributes or overall object	

Source: Adapted from M. J. Rosenberg and C. I. Hovland, *Attitude Organization and Change* (New Haven, Conn.: Yale University Press, 1960), p. 3. Reprinted by permission.

per may ultimately decide to make some purchases of canned goods, cereal, and bakery products there, but continue to rely on a regular supermarket for major food purchases (behavioral).

All three components exist in a relatively stable and balanced relationship to one another and combine to form an overall attitude about an object or idea. Figure 7.4 illustrates the three components.

Measuring Consumer Attitudes Since favorable attitudes are likely to be conducive to brand preferences, marketers are interested in determining consumer attitudes toward their products. Numerous attitude scaling devices have been developed, but the semantic differential is probably the most commonly used technique.

The **semantic differential** is *a test using pairs of bipolar adjectives—such as new-old, reliable-unreliable, sharp-bland—to measure consumer attitude.* The respondent evaluates the product by checking a point on the seven-point scale between the two extremes. The average rankings of all respondents then become a profile of the product.

FIGURE 7.5
Product Images of
Brands X, Y, and Z

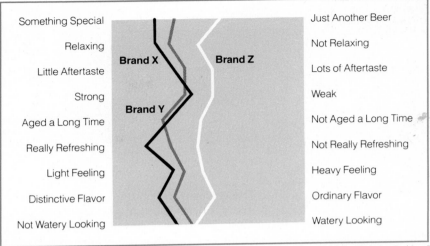

Source: Adapted with permission from William A. Mindak, "Fitting the Semantic Differential to the Marketing Problem," *Journal of Marketing,* April 1961, pp. 28–33, published by the American Marketing Association.

A test comparing three unidentified brands of beer produced the profiles illustrated in Figure 7.5. Brands X and Y dominated the local market and enjoyed generally favorable ratings. Brand Z, a newly introduced beer, was less well known and was reacted to neutrally.

Using the information provided by the profiles, weak areas in the image of any of the brands can be noted for remedial action. The semantic differential scale thus provides management with a more detailed picture of both the direction and the intensity of opinions and attitudes about a product than can be obtained through a typical research questionnaire. It supplies a comprehensive multidimensional portrait of brand images.

How Attitudes Change Given that a favorable consumer attitude is a prerequisite to marketing success, how can a firm lead prospective buyers to adopt this kind of attitude toward its products? The marketer has two choices: to attempt to change consumer attitudes, making them consonant with the product; or to first determine consumer attitudes and then change the product to match them.

If consumers view the product unfavorably, the firm may choose to redesign it to better conform to their desires. It may make styling changes, vary ingredients, change package size, or switch retail stores.

The other course of action—changing consumer attitudes—is much more difficult. A famous study of coffee drinkers revealed surprisingly negative attitudes toward those who serve instant coffee. Two imaginary shopping lists, shown in Table 7.1, were shown to a sample of one hundred homemakers. Half were shown List 1 and half List 2. Each respondent was then asked to describe the hypothetical shopper who purchased the groceries. The only difference in the lists was the instant versus the regular coffee.

**TABLE 7.1
Shopping Lists Used
in the Haire Study**

Shopping List 1	Shopping List 2
1½ lbs. of hamburger	1½ lbs. of hamburger
2 loaves of Wonder Bread	2 loaves of Wonder Bread
Bunch of carrots	Bunch of carrots
1 can Rumford's Baking Powder	1 can Rumford's Baking Powder
Nescafé Instant Coffee	1 lb. Maxwell House coffee (drip grind)
2 cans Del Monte peaches	2 cans Del Monte peaches
5 lbs. potatoes	5 lbs. potatoes

Source: Reprinted with permission from Mason Haire, "Projective Techniques in Marketing Research," *Journal of Marketing,* April 1950, pp. 649–56, published by the American Marketing Association.

The woman who bought instant coffee was described as lazy by 48 percent of the women evaluating List 1; but only 24 percent of those evaluating List 2 described the woman who bought regular coffee as lazy. Forty-eight percent described the instant coffee purchaser as failing to plan household purchases and schedules well; only 12 percent described the purchaser of regular coffee this way.

But consumer attitudes often change with time. The shopping list study was repeated twenty years later, and the new study revealed that much of the stigma attached to buying instant coffee had disappeared. Instead of describing the instant coffee purchaser as lazy and a poor planner, most respondents felt she was a working wife.[12] Nonetheless, General Foods took no chances when it introduced its new freeze-dried Maxim as a coffee that "tastes like *regular* and has the convenience of *instant.*"

Producing Attitude Change Attitude change frequently occurs when inconsistencies among the three attitudinal components are introduced. The most common example of such inconsistencies are changes to the cognitive component of an attitude as a result of new information. The Pepsi Challenge was launched in an attempt to convince consumers that they preferred the taste of Pepsi, giving them new information that might lead to increased sales. The recent Life Savers advertising campaign built around the theme that a Life Saver contains only ten calories was designed to correct misconceptions in the minds of many consumers about the candy's high caloric content.

The affective component may be altered by relating the use of the new product or service to desirable consequences for the user. The attractive, healthy appearance of a deep suntan and the convenience of acquiring it are primary appeals of the thousands of tanning salons that have diffused rapidly throughout North America.

The third alternative in attempting to change attitudes is to focus upon the behavioral component by inducing the person to engage in behavior that contradicts currently held attitudes. Attitude-discrepant behavior may occur if the consumer is given a free sample of a product. Trying the product may lead to attitude change.

Consumers often respond to certain cues due to previous experience with them.

Source: Reprinted by permission of Newspaper Enterprise Association.

Learning

Marketing is as concerned with the process by which consumer decisions change over time as with describing those decisions at any one point. Thus, the study of how learning takes place is important. **Learning** refers to *changes in behavior, immediate or expected, as a result of experience.*

The learning process includes several components. The first component, *drive,* is any strong stimulus that impels action. Examples of drives are fear, pride, desire for money, thirst, pain avoidance, and rivalry.

The *cue,* the second component of the learning process, is any object existing in the environment that determines the nature of the response to a drive. Examples of cues are a newspaper advertisement for a new French restaurant, an in-store display, and an Exxon sign on an interstate highway. For the hungry person, the shopper seeking a particular item, or the motorist needing gasoline, these cues may result in a specific response to satisfy a drive.

A *response* is the individual's reactions to the cues and drive. Responses might include such reactions as purchasing a package of Gillette Trac II blades, dining at Burger King, or deciding to enroll at a particular college or university.

Reinforcement is the reduction in drive that results from a proper response. The more rewarding the response, the stronger the bond between the drive and the purchase of that particular product becomes. Should the purchase of Trac II blades result in closer shaves through repeated use, the likelihood of their purchase in the future is increased.

ENVIRONMENTAL INFLUENCES ON CONSUMER BEHAVIOR

Thus far Chapter 7 has concentrated on *individual* factors that affect consumer decisions. But people's lives are not dictated solely by their individual makeup. Both their behavior and their purchase actions are influenced to varying degrees by others. People are social animals, and often they buy goods and services that will enable them to project a favorable self-image to others. These influences may result from the family, reference groups, or the individual's cultural environment. These interrelationships are shown in Figure 7.6.

**FIGURE 7.6
Determinants of
Consumer Behavior:
Individual and
Environmental**

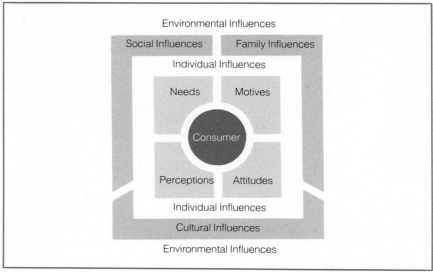

Source: Adapted with permission from C. Glenn Walters and Gordon W. Paul, *Consumer Behavior: An Integrated Framework* (Homewood, Ill.: Richard D. Irwin, 1970), p. 16. © 1970 by Richard D. Irwin, Inc.

Social Influences

Children's earliest awareness is of their membership in a very important group—the family. From this group they seek total satisfaction of their physiological and societal needs. As they grow older, they join other groups—neighborhood play groups, school groups, Scouts, Little League, and groups of friends, among others—from which they acquire both status and roles.

Status is *the relative position in the group of any individual member;* a **role** is *what the other members of the group expect of the individual who is in any particular position within the group.* Some groups (like the Scouts) are formal, and others (like friendship groups) are informal. Groups of either sort supply each member with both status and roles; in doing so, they influence the member's activities. Figure 7.6 shows how the social environment interacts with all other influences on the individual consumer.

Group Influence Although most persons view themselves as individuals, groups are often highly influential in purchase decisions. In situations where individuals feel that a particular group (or groups) is important, they tend to adhere in varying degrees to the general expectations of that group.

The surprising impact that groups and group norms can exhibit on individual behavior has been called the *Asch phenomenon.* The phenomenon was first documented in the following study conducted by the psychologist S. E. Asch:

Eight subjects are brought into a room and asked to determine which of a set of three unequal lines is closest to the length of a fourth line shown some distance from the other three. The subjects are to announce their judgments publicly. Seven of the subjects are working for the experimenter and they announce incorrect matches. The order of announcement is arranged such that the naive subject responds last. In a control situation, 37 naive subjects performed the task 18 times each without any information about others' choices. Two of the 37 subjects made a total of 3 mistakes. However, when another group of 50 naive subjects responded *after* hearing the unanimous but *incorrect* judgment of the other group members, 37 made a total of 194 errors, all of which were in agreement with the mistake made by the group.[13]

This widely replicated study illustrates the role of groups upon individual choice-making. Marketing applications range from the choice of automobile models and residential locations to the decision to purchase at least one item at a Tupperware party.

Reference Groups In order for groups to exert such influence on individuals, they must be categorized as reference groups. **Reference groups** *are those with which an individual identifies to the point where the group becomes a standard, a norm, a point of reference for him. In effect, the individual "refers" to such groups for his standards of behavior and even for his goals and personal values.*[14]

Although a reference group can also be a membership group, it is not essential that the individual be a member in order for the group to serve as a point of reference. This concept helps explain the use of athletes in advertisements. Even though few racing fans possess the skills necessary to power a racing car, all can identify with the Indianapolis winner by injecting their engines with STP.

The extent of reference group influence varies widely. For the influence to be great, two factors must be present:

1. The item must be one that can be seen and identified by others.
2. The item must also be conspicuous; it must stand out, be unusual, and be a brand or product that not everyone owns.

Reference group influence for a variety of products and brands is shown in Figure 7.7. In the case of cars, a most conspicuous purchase, reference group influence is quite strong. Groups also exert strong influence on the purchase of air conditioners but not on the choice of particular brands. At the other extreme, there is negligible group influence on the purchase of canned peaches and soap, since these are typically products whose purchase is unknown to others.

Social Classes Although people prefer to think of the United States as the land of equality, a well-structured class system does exist. Research conducted a number of years ago by W. Lloyd Warner revealed a six-class system within the social structure of both small and large cities. A

FIGURE 7.7
Classification of Products and Brands on the Basis of Reference Group Influence

	PRODUCT		
Strong +	Clothing Furniture Magazines Refrigerator (type) Toilet Soap	Cars Cigarettes Beer (premium vs. regular) Drugs	+
Reference- Group Influence Relatively: Weak −	Soap Canned peaches Laundry soap Refrigerator (brand) Radios	Air conditioners Instant coffee TV (black and white)	Brand or Type −
	Weak −	Strong +	

Source: Francis S. Bourne, *Group Influence in Marketing and Public Relations,* Foundation for Research on Human Behavior, copyright © 1956, p. 8. Reprinted by permission.

description of the members of each class and an estimate of its population percentage is shown in Table 7.2.

Warner's class rankings are determined by occupation, source of income (not amount), education, family background, and dwelling area. Income is not a primary determinant; a pipefitter paid at union scale earns more than many college professors, but his or her purchase behavior may be quite different. Thus the adage "A rich man is a poor man with more money" is wrong.

Richard Coleman illustrates the behavior of three families, all earning less than $35,000 a year but all in decidedly different social classes. The upper-middle-class family in this income bracket—a young lawyer or college professor and family—is likely to spend its money in a prestige neighborhood, buy expensive furniture from high-quality stores, and join social clubs.

At the same time, the lower-middle-class family—headed by a grocery store owner or a sales representative—will probably purchase a good house in a less expensive neighborhood. It buys furniture from less expensive stores and typically has a savings account at the local bank.

The lower-class family—headed by a truck driver or welder—spends less money on the house but buys one of the first new cars sold each year and owns one of the largest color television sets in town. It stocks its kitchen with appliances—symbols of security.[15]

Usage of the same product or service often varies among social classes. A study of commercial bank credit card holders, for example, uncovered class variations in how the cards were used. Lower-class families were more likely to use their credit cards for installment purchases, while upper-class families used them mainly for their convenience as a cash substitute.[16]

TABLE 7.2
The Warner Social
Class Hierarchy

Social Class	Membership	Percentage[a]
Upper-upper	Locally prominent families, third- or fourth-generation wealth. Merchants, financiers, or higher-level professionals. Wealth inherited. A great amount of traveling.	1.5
Lower-upper	Newly arrived in upper class—*"nouveau riche."* Not accepted by upper class. Executive elite, founders of large businesses, doctors, lawyers.	1.5
Upper-middle	Moderately successful professionals, owners of medium-sized businesses, and middle management. Status conscious. Child- and home-centered.	10.0
Lower-middle	Top of the average world. Nonmanagerial office workers, small business owners, and blue-collar families. "Striving and respectable." Conservative.	33.0
Upper-lower	Ordinary working class. Semiskilled workers. Income often as high as the next two classes above. Enjoy life. Live from day to day.	38.0
Lower-lower	Unskilled, unemployed, and unassimilated ethnic groups. Fatalistic. Apathetic.	16.0
	Total	100.0

[a]Estimates are based on Warner and Hollings's distributions in rather small communities. However, an estimate of social class structure for the United States approximates these percentages.
Source: Adapted with permission from Charles B. McCann, *Women and Department Store Advertising* (Chicago: Social Research, 1957).

Role of the Opinion Leader Each group usually contains a few members who can be considered **opinion leaders**—*trend setters.* These individuals are likely to purchase new products before others do and to serve as information sources for others in the group. Their opinions are respected, and they are often sought out for advice.

Generalized opinion leaders are rare; instead, individuals tend to be opinion leaders for specific products and services. Their interest in the product motivates them to seek out information from mass media, manufacturers, and other supply sources; and, in turn, to transmit this knowledge to their non-opinion leader associates through interpersonal communication. Opinion leaders are found within all segments of the population.

Communication Flows Information about products, retail outlets, and ideas flows through a number of channels. In some cases, the flows are from radio, television, and other mass media to opinion leaders, and then from opinion leaders to the masses of the population. Elihu Katz and Paul Lazarsfeld referred to this channel as the *two-step process* of communication.[17]

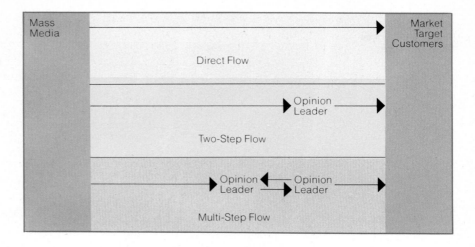

**FIGURE 7.8
Alternative Channels
for Communication
Flows**

In some instances, the information flow is direct. Continuing access to communications channels allows much information to be transmitted directly to individuals who represent the organization's market target with no intermediaries. Preliminary findings indicating some success in the use of the experimental drug Interferon, in treating certain types of cancer, was quickly disseminated to the general public by the mass media. Researchers were forced to utilize the same channels in an attempt to dispel the general public's belief that the new drug was a miracle cure.

Another possible channel for information flows is a multi-step flow. In this case, the flows are from mass media to opinion leaders and then on to other opinion leaders before being disseminated to the general public. Figure 7.8 illustrates the types of communication flows.

Applying the Opinion Leadership Concept Because of the importance of opinion leaders in distributing information and advice, a number of firms have focused on likely opinion leaders as information outlets for new product introductions. When Ford introduced the Mustang, probable opinion leaders such as college newspaper editors, disc jockeys, and airline flight attendants were loaned Mustangs. In a similar attempt, Chrysler tried to generate conversation about its new Plymouth by offering 5,000 taxi drivers in 67 cities $5 if they would ask Chrysler "mystery riders" if they had seen the new Plymouth. Some restaurants and bars offer taxi drivers and bellhops meals and drinks at cost if they refer traveling executives and other out-of-towners to their establishments.[18]

Family Influence

The second major environmental variable is the family. The influence of household members is often significant in the purchase decision process. Because of the close, continuing interactions among family members, the family often represents the strongest source of group influence on the individual.

Most people are members of two families during their lifetime—the family into which they are born and the one they eventually form as they marry and have children.

The establishment of a new household upon marriage results in new marketing opportunities. A new household means a new house or apartment and accompanying furniture. The need for refrigerators, vacuum cleaners, and an original oil painting for the living room is dependent not on the number of persons comprising the household but on the number of households themselves.

Since the average household size is less than four persons, most milk is sold in half-gallons, most automobiles seat four or five, and most washing machines hold nine pounds of laundry. Nissan Motors has been able to greatly expand the market for its Datsun Z cars by adding a four-seat "2 + 2" series to meet the needs of family purchasers who are sports car enthusiasts.

A second market is established for parents who are left alone when children move away from home. These parents may find themselves with a four-bedroom "empty nest" and a half-acre of lawn to maintain. Lacking maintenance assistance from their children and no longer needing the large-sized house, they become customers for town houses, condominiums, and high-rise luxury apartments in the larger cities. Some become residents of St. Petersburg, Sun City, or other centers for retired persons. Others become market targets for medical insurance, travel, and hearing aids. Designing houses specifically for senior citizens is one effort to reach that market.

Traditional Household Roles Historically, the wife made the majority of the family purchases, and the husband worked at a paying job most of the day. Even though the preferences of the children or the husband may have influenced her decisions, the wife usually was responsible for food buying and for most of the clothing purchases.

Although an infinite variety of roles can be played in household decision making, four role categories are often used: (1) *autonomic*—an equal number of decisions is made by each partner, but each decision is individually made by one partner or the other; (2) *male dominant;* (3) *female dominant;* and (4) *syncratic*—most decisions are jointly made by male and female.[19] Figure 7.9 shows the roles played by household members in the purchase of a number of products.

Changing Family Roles Two forces have changed the female's role as sole purchasing agent for most household items. First, a shorter workweek provides each wage-earning household member with more time for shopping. Second, there are a large number of women in the work force. In 1950, only one-fourth of married women were also employed; by 1981, almost 50 percent were working wives. Currently, over half of all married women with school-age children hold jobs outside the home.[20] Studies of family decision making have shown that working wives tend to exert more influence in decision making than do nonworking wives.

**FIGURE 7.9
Marital Roles in 25
Decisions**

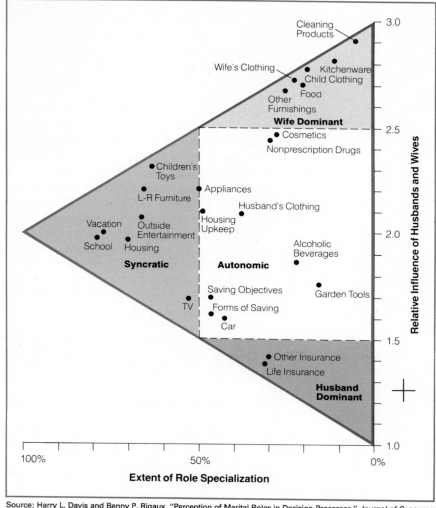

Source: Harry L. Davis and Benny P. Rigaux, "Perception of Marital Roles in Decision Processes," *Journal of Consumer Research,* June 1974, p. 57. Reprinted by permission from the *Journal of Consumer Research* published by the Journal of Consumer Research, Inc.

Households with two wage earners also exhibit a large number of joint decisions and an increase in night and weekend shopping.

These changing roles of household members have led many marketers to adjust their marketing programs to match the changes. Saint Laurie, Ltd., which has specialized in the manufacture of men's suits since 1915, now offers suits for the career woman. Although nationwide demand for men's suits has been sluggish in recent years, sales of women's suits increased 70 percent in 1980. A survey of 1,000 married men revealed that 77 percent participate in shopping and 70 percent cook. Del Monte's current promotional campaign recognizes these changes and deemphasizes women as the sole meal preparer. Its theme,

FACTS ABOUT WOMEN AS MARKET TARGETS

1. Women annually spend an estimated $30 billion for new cars.
2. They buy or have a major influence on at least half of all car purchases.
3. Women account for 39 percent of new car purchases annually.
4. In 1980, 55 percent of the buyers of Buick Regal were women.
5. Driving to and from work is the principal use for cars bought by 67 percent of female car buyers.
6. A *Woman's Day* survey showed 85 percent of new car purchases involve women, either shopping alone or with men, according to purchasers.
7. More than half of all women—52 percent—work outside the home.
8. Three-fifths of husband-wife households have two paychecks. In 1950, the figure was 36 percent.
9. Between 1960 and 1980, the number of working women increased from 23 million to 40 million.
10. Warranty and service-related benefits, operating cost, ride, handling and safety are of greater concern to women than to men.
11. Women tend to be more concerned with the functional, practical aspects, while many men look more for a swinging image and self-expression in a car, according to a Ford official.
12. About 75 percent of all women car buyers work, and the typical career female is surprisingly young.
13. Young, single and working women have a much stronger preference than men for smaller cars. This trend, according to Ford, may be related to economics rather than preference.

Source: Reprinted with permission from Julie Chandler, "A Long Drive for Recognition," *Advertising Age,* (June 22, 1981, p. S-24. Copyright 1981 by Crain Communications, Inc.

"Good things happen when you bring Del Monte home," is applicable to both male and female food shoppers.[21]

Children's Roles in Household Purchasing The role of the children in purchasing evolves as they grow older. Children's early influence is generally centered around toys to be recommended to Santa Claus and the choice of cereal brands. Younger children are also important to marketers of fast-food restaurants. Even though the parents may decide when to eat out, the children usually select the restaurant.

As children gain maturity, they increasingly influence their clothing purchases. One study revealed that teenagers in the thirteen to fifteen age group spend an average of $12 per week. At sixteen to nineteen, their average weekly expenditures increase to $45. Teenage boys spend most of their funds on food, soft drinks, candy, gum, recreation, hobbies, movies, records, gasoline, and car accessories. Teenage girls spend most of their money on clothes and gifts.[22]

TABLE 7.3
American Core
Values

Value	General Features	Relevance to Consumer Behavior
Achievement and success	Hard work is good; success flows from hard work	Acts as a justification for acquisition of goods ("You deserve it")
Activity	Keeping busy is healthy and natural	Stimulates interest in products that save time and enhance leisure-time activities
Efficiency and practicality	Admiration of things that solve problems (e.g., save time and effort)	Stimulates purchase of products that function well and save time
Progress	People can improve themselves; tomorrow should be better	Stimulates desire for new products that fulfill unsatisfied needs; acceptance of products that claim to be "new" or "improved"
Material comfort	"The good life"	Fosters acceptance of convenience and luxury products that make life more enjoyable
Individualism	Being one's self (e.g., self-reliance, self-interest, and self-esteem)	Stimulates acceptance of customized or unique products that enable a person to "express his own personality"
Freedom	Freedom of choice	Fosters interest in wide product lines and differentiated products
External conformity	Uniformity of observable behavior; desire to be accepted	Stimulates interest in products that are used or owned by others in the same social group
Humanitarianism	Caring for others, particularly the underdog	Stimulates patronage of firms that compete with market leaders
Youthfulness	A state of mind that stresses being young at heart or appearing young	Stimulates acceptance of products that provide the illusion of maintaining or fostering youth

Source: From *Consumer Behavior,* by Leon G. Schiffman and Leslie Lazar Kanuk, © 1978, p. 359. Reprinted by permission of Prentice-Hall, Inc., Englewood Cliffs, New Jersey 07632.

Cultural
Influences

Culture, the third environmental variable in the consumer decision process, is a more elusive concept than social class or reference groups. It can be defined as *the complex of values, ideas, attitudes, and other meaningful symbols created by people to shape human behavior and the artifacts of that behavior as they are transmitted from one generation to the next.*[23] It is the completely learned and handed-down way of life that gives each society its own peculiar flavor.

The U.S. culture historically has been materialistic, an attitude derived from the Protestant ethic of hard work and the accumulation of material wealth. However, cultural values do change over time, and a number of Western core values are currently undergoing major shifts. Table 7.3 provides a useful summary of trends in U.S. cultural values.

As Joe Kent Kerby points out, language is an interesting cultural trait that changes within the space of a very few years. The word *rip-off* meant nothing in 1950, but it is widely used today to mean cheating, price-gouging, and other negative things. The meaning of the same word can also vary from one section of the country to another. The word *dude* elicits quite different responses in New York and Montana.[24]

Many U.S. citizens have an unfortunate habit of stereotyping citizens of other countries or of using their own cultural backgrounds in relating to foreigners. But cultural differences do result in different attitudes, mores, and folkways. Consider how the examples below might influence marketing strategy:

A Goodyear advertisement demonstrated the strength of its "3T" tire cord by showing a steel chain breaking. When the commercial was shown in West Germany, however, it was perceived as an insult to steel chain manufacturers.

Because of inept translation, Schweppes Tonic Water was advertised in Italy as "bathroom water." In South America, Parker Pen Company unwittingly indicated that its product would prevent unwanted pregnancies.[25]

Deodorant usage among men ranges from 80 percent in the United States to 55 percent in Sweden, 28 percent in Italy, and 8 percent in the Philippines.[26]

White is the color of mourning in Japan, and purple is associated with death in many Latin American countries.

Feet are regarded as despicable in Thailand. Athlete's-foot remedies with packages featuring a picture of feet will not be well received.

Most U.S. hotels have eliminated the thirteenth floor.

In Ethiopia, the time required to make a decision is directly proportional to its importance. This is so much the case that low-level bureaucrats attempt to elevate the prestige of their work by taking a long time to make decisions. U.S. citizens working in Ethiopia are innocently prone to downgrading their work in the local people's eyes by trying to speed things up.[27]

A marketing program that has proven successful in the United States often cannot be applied directly in international markets because of cultural differences. Real differences do exist among different countries, and they must be known and evaluated by the international firm. When Helene Curtis introduced its Every Night shampoo line in Sweden, it renamed the product Every Day because Swedes usually wash their hair in the morning.[28]

Denture makers are aware of the impact of cultural differences on sales of false teeth. The people of Thailand are extremely fond of betel nuts, which stain their teeth black. For many years, once their

CONSUMPTION PATTERNS OF BLACK SHOPPERS

Blacks represent the largest racial/ethnic subculture in the United States. They account for 11 percent of the total population, twice as many as the nation's second largest minority, the Spanish-speaking Americans. Several striking differences between the black and white populations are present. Almost 30 percent of blacks are below the poverty level, as defined by the U.S. Department of Commerce, compared to 10 percent of whites. Also, the black population is very young. The median age of the white population is 30 years; for blacks the median age is 24 years.

While marketers recognize that no group of 27 million people can be considered a homogeneous market segment for all products, a number of marketing studies have compared consumption patterns of blacks and nonblacks. The major findings are these:

1. Blacks save more out of a given income than do whites with the same income.
2. Blacks spend more than whites at comparable levels for clothing and nonautomobile transportation; less for food, housing, medical care, and automobile transportation; and similar amounts for recreation and leisure, home furnishings, and equipment.
3. Blacks tend to own more higher-priced automobiles than comparable income white families.
4. Blacks appear to be more brand loyal than equivalent whites.
5. Black families purchase more milk and soft drinks, less tea and coffee, and more liquor than white families.
6. Black consumers react more favorably to advertisements with all black models or to integrated models than to advertisements with all white models. Whites appear to react to black models as favorably as to white models (or more so), although this varies by type of product and amount of prejudice. Black consumers under the age of 30 appear to react unfavorably to advertisements with integrated settings.
7. Black grocery consumers tend to make frequent trips to neighborhood stores. This may be due to inadequate refrigeration and storage units and lack of transportation that would allow them to carry large amounts of groceries.
8. Black consumers tend to shop at discount stores as compared to department stores more than do comparable white consumers.

Source: James F. Engel and Roger D. Blackwell, *Consumer Behavior,* 4th ed. (Hinsdale, Ill.: The Dryden Press, 1982), pp. 89–93. Copyright © 1982 by The Dryden Press, A division of Holt, Rinehart and Winston, Publishers. Reprinted by permission of Holt, Rinehart and Winston, CBS College Publishing.

original teeth wore out, they were replaced with black dentures. After World War II, however, fashions changed, and the Thais began using abrasives to scrub off the black stains. Abrasives are now popular items in Thailand. Scandinavians like greyish false teeth, mostly because the teeth of Scandinavians tend to be naturally grey. The Japanese select false teeth noticeably longer than their natural ones.[29]

World marketers face competition from firms in Germany, France, the Soviet Union, Japan, and several other countries, as well as firms in the host nation. Therefore, they must become familiar with all aspects of the local population—including its cultural heritage. This can be accomplished by treating each country as having additional market segments that must be thoroughly analyzed prior to the development of a marketing plan for use there.

Subcultures Within each culture are numerous **subcultures**—*subgroups with their own distinguishing modes of behavior.* Any culture as heterogeneous as that of the United States is composed of significant subcultures based on factors such as race, nationality, age, rural-urban location, religion, and geographic distribution.

Inhabitants of the Southwest display a life-style that emphasizes casual dress, outdoor entertaining, and water recreation. Mormons refrain from using tobacco and liquor. Orthodox Jews purchase kosher or other traditional foods. Blacks may exhibit interest in products and symbols of their African heritage.

Hispanics—Growing Market Targets The alert marketing manager should recognize that subcultures may represent distinct market segments and should seek to increase the understanding of their motivations, needs, and attitudes. The U.S. Spanish-speaking population is increasing by more than one-half million a year and is becoming an increasingly important market segment. This is particularly true in metropolitan Miami, whose Cuban population of 430,000 is exceeded only by Havana's; Greater Los Angeles, whose 1.6 million Hispanic population is second only to Mexico City's; and New York, whose Puerto Rican population of 1.3 million is greater than San Juan's. Other concentrations of Spanish-speaking persons are found in the border states from Texas to California.

Marketers focus on these markets in several ways. In many communities, the sign *"Aqui se habla español"* (Spanish is spoken here) is displayed in store windows. Over 300 television and radio stations now broadcast all or a large portion of the time in Spanish. Procter & Gamble has hired Spanish-speaking salespeople to call on the 5,000 Spanish grocery stores *(bodegas)* and 750 drugstores *(farmacias)* in New York that cater to families of Puerto Rican origin.

THE CONSUMER DECISION PROCESS

Consumer behavior research traditionally has focused on such specific areas as attitudes, personality, and the influence of reference groups on the individual. To see these fragments in their proper perspective, a conceptual model of the entire consumer decision process is needed. Such a model makes possible the integration of the various components of consumer behavior and assists in understanding the complex relationships among them. It also provides a means of integrating new research findings in the search for a more complete explanation of why consumers behave as they do.

FIGURE 7.10
The Consumer
Decision Process

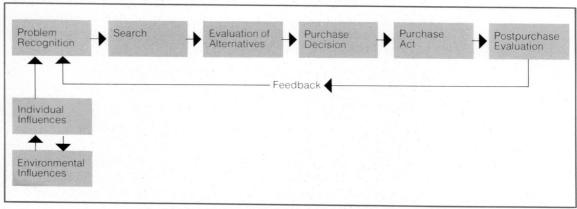

Source: Adapted with permission from C. Glenn Walters and Gordon W. Paul, *Consumer Behavior: An Integrated Framework* (Homewood, Ill.: Richard D. Irwin, 1970), p. 18. © 1970 by Richard D. Irwin, Inc.

The total model approach can be used in major buying situations such as a first-time purchase of a new product or the purchase of a high-priced, long-lived article. By contrast, it can also be applied to cases of routine purchases handled by the individual in a largely habitual manner, such as the purchase of a newspaper or a particular brand of chewing gum. Figure 7.10 is a schematic model of consumer decision making. The model contains six stages: problem recognition, search, evaluation of alternatives, the purchase decision, the purchase act, and postpurchase evaluation.

Problem Recognition

The first stage in the decision process occurs when the consumer becomes aware of a discrepancy of sufficient magnitude between the existing state of affairs and a desired state of affairs. Once the problem has been recognized, it must be defined.

Problem recognition may occur for a number of reasons. Perhaps the most common one is the routine depletion of an individual's stock of supplies. A large number of consumer purchases involves the replenishment of items ranging from gasoline to groceries. In other instances, the consumer may possess an inadequate assortment of products. The individual whose hobby is gardening, for example, may make regular purchases of different fertilizers, seeds, or gardening tools as the size of the garden grows.

A third cause of problem recognition is dissatisfaction with the consumer's present brand or product type. This situation is common in the purchase of a new automobile, furniture, or a fall wardrobe. In many instances, the consumer's boredom with current products and a desire for novelty may be the reason for purchasing a new product.

Another important factor in problem recognition is changed financial status. The infusion of added financial resources (for example, a salary increase, a second job, or an inheritance) may permit the consumer to make purchases that previously had been postponed.

Search

Search, the second stage in the decision process, is the gathering of information related to attaining a desired state of affairs. This stage permits the identification of alternative means of problem solution.

Search may be internal or external. Internal search is a mental review of stored information relevant to the problem. This includes actual experiences, observations, and memories of personal communication and exposures to persuasive marketing efforts.

External search is the gathering of information from outside sources by the consumer who is involved in the search process. Outside information sources may include family members, friends and associates, store displays, sales representatives, brochures, and such product-testing publications as *Consumer Reports.*

In many instances, the consumer solves problems through internal search. The individual merely relies upon stored information in making a purchase decision. Achieving favorable results using DuPont's Rain Dance car polish may sufficiently motivate a consumer to repurchase this brand rather than to consider possible alternatives. Since external search involves both time and effort, the consumer will rely upon it only in instances in which adequate information is unavailable in memory.

Alternative brands are identified during the search process. *The number of brands that a consumer actually considers in making a purchase decision* is known as the **evoked set**. In some instances, the consumer will be aware of the brands worthy of further consideration; in other situations, the external search process will involve the consumer learning about those brands that will comprise the evoked set. Not all brands will be included in the evoked set. In some instances, the consumer will be unaware of certain brands. Other brands will be rejected as too costly. Still others will have been tried previously and considered unsatisfactory. In other instances, unfavorable word-of-mouth communication or negative reactions to advertising or other marketing efforts will eliminate some brands from the evoked set. While the number of brands in the evoked set will vary by product categories, research indicates that the number is likely to be as few as four or five.[30]

Evaluation of Alternatives

The third step in the consumer decision process involves the evaluation of alternatives identified during the search process. Actually, it is difficult to completely separate the second and third steps since some evaluation takes place simultaneously with the search process as consumers accept, discount, distort, or reject some incoming information as they receive it.

Since the outcome of the evaluation stage is the choice of a brand or product (or, possibly, the search for additional alternatives should all alternatives identified during the search process prove unsatisfactory), the consumer must develop a set of evaluative criteria for use in making the selection. **Evaluative critera** may be defined as *those features the consumer considers in making a choice among alternatives.* These criteria can be objective (federal government automobile engine tests of miles per gallon, or comparison of retail prices) or subjective (favorable image of Jordache sportswear). Commonly used evaluative criteria include price, reputation of the brand, perceived quality, packaging, size, performance, durability, and color. Most research studies indicate that consumers utilize six or fewer criteria in the evaluation process. Evaluative criteria for the cleaning power of detergents include suds level and smell. High quality and potential for long wear were the underlying criteria in the choice of nylon stockings, according to one research study.[31]

The Purchase Decision and the Purchase Act

The purchase decision and the act of making the purchase constitute the end result of the search and alternative evaluation stages of the decision process. The consumer has evaluated each alternative in the evoked set utilizing his or her personal set of evaluative criteria and narrowed the alternatives to one.

Another decision facing the consumer is the purchase location. Consumers tend to make store choices by considering such factors as location, prices, assortment, store personnel, store image, physical design, and services provided. In addition, the store selected will be influenced by the product category. In other instances, some consumers will choose the convenience of in-home shopping via telephone or mail order rather than complete the transaction in a retail store.

Postpurchase Evaluation

The purchase act results in satisfaction to the buyer—and removal of the discrepancy between the existing state and the desired state—or dissatisfaction with the purchase. It is also common for consumers to experience some postpurchase anxieties. Leon Festinger refers to this postpurchase doubt as **cognitive dissonance.**[32]

Dissonance is *a psychologically unpleasant state that occurs when there exists an imbalance among a person's cognitions (knowledge, beliefs, and attitudes).* Consumers may, for example, experience dissonance after choosing a particular automobile over several alternative models, when one or more of the rejected models have some desired features not available with the chosen one.

Dissonance is likely to increase (1) as the dollar value of the purchase increases; (2) when the rejected alternatives have desirable features not present in the chosen alternative; and (3) when the decision is a major one. The consumer may attempt to reduce dissonance in a variety of ways. He or she may seek out advertisements and other information supporting the chosen alternative or seek reassurance from acquaintances who are satisfied purchasers of the product. The individual will also avoid information favoring the unchosen alternative. The Toyota purchaser is likely to read Toyota advertisements and to avoid Nissan and Volkswagen ads. The cigarette smoker may ignore the magazine articles reporting links between smoking and cancer.

Marketers can assist in reducing cognitive dissonance by providing informational support for the chosen alternative. Automobile dealers recognize "buyer's remorse" and often follow up purchases with a warm letter from the president of the dealership, who offers personal handling of any customer problems and includes a description of the product's quality and the availability of convenient service. General Motors provides Corvette purchasers with a subscription to a magazine filled with articles depicting the desirable life-style of Corvette owners.

A final method of dealing with cognitive dissonance is opinion change. In this instance, the consumer may ultimately decide that one of the rejected alternatives would have been the best choice and may decide to purchase it in the future.[33]

Should the purchase prove unsatisfactory, the consumer's purchase strategy must be revised to allow need satisfaction to be obtained. Whether satisfactory or not, feedback on the results of the decision process will serve as experience to be called upon in similar buying situations in the future.

SUMMARY

Consumer behavior is defined as the acts of individuals in obtaining and using goods and services, including the decision processes that precede and determine these acts. Understanding the behavior of consumers is the first step in formulating a marketing strategy. Consumer behavior is viewed as a problem-solving approach by which the individual makes decisions and takes actions in order to satisfy needs.

Consumer behavior results from both individual and environmental influences. Individual influences include needs, motives, perceptions, and attitudes—the basic determinants in shaping the consumer's behavior. Another vital factor in the study of consumer behavior is learning—the changes in behavior that result from experience. The components of the learning process are drive, cues, response, and reinforcement.

Environmental influences include such outside forces as the influences of social class, reference group, family, and an individual's particular culture or subculture. The simplified model of the consumer decision process shows the interaction of the basic determinants and the influences of forces from the individual's environment in shaping consumer behavior.

The consumer decision process consists of problem recognition, search, evaluation of alternatives, the purchase decision, the purchase act, and postpurchase evaluation. Consumers who suffer postpurchase anxiety over their decision experience cognitive dissonance.

QUESTIONS FOR DISCUSSION

1. Explain the following terms:

   consumer behavior   role
   self-concept   reference group
   need   social class
   motive   opinion leader
   perception   culture
   subliminal perception   subculture
   attitude   evoked set
   learning   evaluative criteria
   status   cognitive dissonance

2. Identify and briefly explain each component of the self-concept.

3. Relate each of the following to the appropriate component of the self-concept:
   a. "Three more semesters until I finish the degree, get a good job, and move into my own apartment."
   b. "I'm outgoing, fun to be with, own a complete Rolling Stones collection. My friends see me as a terrific mixer and extremely witty."
   c. "It's true that I'm outgoing and fun to be with, but I'm also much too hesitant when meeting people, especially older people."
   d. "Debby is a C–student, has average athletic abilities, and is quite involved in the ecology movement."

4. What are the individual determinants of consumer behavior?

5. Identify and briefly explain each of the levels in Maslow's hierarchy of needs.

6. Based on Maslow's hierarchy, which needs are being referred to in the following advertisements?
   a. "Never pick up a stranger!" (Prestone)
   b. "Diamonds are forever." (De Beers)
   c. "Gatorade reaches the bloodstream fast!"
   d. "Country Club malt liquor is a step up from beer."

7. Due to the changing roles of men and women, various marketers have found themselves with "new" market segments to target. Give some examples of such products and market segments.

8. Why are techniques such as the semantic differential useful in measuring consumer attitudes?

9. Identify the components of an attitude. Give an example of how attitude change may occur as a result of focusing on each component.

10. Explain and illustrate each of the components of the learning process.

11. Identify and briefly explain the primary environmental influences on consumer decision making.

12. Under what conditions are reference-group influences likely to be strongest?

13. For which of the following products is reference-group influence likely to be strong?
    - a. digital watch
    - b. skis
    - c. shaving cream
    - d. 10-speed bicycle
    - e. portable radio
    - f. cigarettes
    - g. electric blanket
    - h. contact lenses

14. List two products for which the following family members might be most influential:
    - a. mother
    - b. six-year-old child
    - c. father
    - d. teen-age son
    - e. teen-age daughter
    - f. two-year-old child

15. Which two social classes contain the largest membership? The smallest?

16. What role does the opinion leader play in consumer behavior?

17. Distinguish between culture and subcultures. Give several examples of subcultures, and specify your reasons for including each example as a subculture.

18. Use the model of the consumer decision process in Figure 7.10 to explain what happened during and after the following decision. Make any assumptions that are necessary.

    Greg Montgomery, a senior at Lincoln High School, faces the dilemma of choosing a college. He is a good student and an All-State defensive end. His father is a graduate of a well-known midwestern school and wants Greg to go there. Two major football powers have offered him scholarships. One of these is located in his hometown, where his best female friend has decided to go. After visiting both campuses, he decides to sign with the university located 1,800 miles away.

19. Relate the model of the consumer decision process to an industrial purchasing agent for General Mills who is buying pecans to serve as a basic ingredient for the company's new cake mix.

20. Under what circumstances is cognitive dissonance most likely to occur? What steps may be taken to reduce it?

NOTES

1. Wilson Bryan Key, *Subliminal Seduction: Secret Ways Ad Men Arouse Your Desires to Sell Their Product* (New York: Signet Books, 1975).

2. Harold W. Berkman and Christopher Gilson, *Consumer Behavior: Concepts and Strategies* (Boston: Kent Publishing Co., 1981), p. 249.

3. Naresh K. Malhotra, "A Scale to Measure Self-Concepts, Person Concepts, and Product Concepts," *Journal of Marketing Research,* November 1981, pp. 456–64.

4. Richard H. Buskirk, *Principles of Marketing,* 3rd ed. (Hinsdale, Ill.: The Dryden Press, 1970), pp. 139–40.

5. James F. Engel and Roger D. Blackwell, *Consumer Behavior,* 4th ed. (Hinsdale, Ill.: The Dryden Press, 1982), p. 9.

6. Kurt Lewin, *Field Theory in Social Science* (New York: Harper & Row, 1951), p. 62. See also C. Glenn Walters, "Consumer Behavior: An Appraisal," *Journal of the Academy of Marketing Science,* Fall 1979, pp. 273–84.

7. A. H. Maslow, *Motivation and Personality* (New York: Harper & Row, 1954).

8. *Ibid.,* p. 382. See also George Brooker, "The Self-actualizing Socially Conscious Consumer," *Journal of Consumer Research,* September 1976, pp. 107–12.

9. Adapted from Paul T. Young, *Motivation and Emotion* (New York: Wiley, 1961), pp. 280–99.

10. Kenneth Roman and Jane Maas, *How to Advertise* (New York: St. Martin's Press, 1976), pp. 15–16.

11. James H. Myers and William H. Reynolds, *Consumer Behavior and Marketing Management*

(Boston: Houghton Mifflin, 1967), p. 14; J. Steven Kelly and Barbara M. Kessler, "Subliminal Seduction: Fact or Fantasy?" in *Proceedings of the Southern Marketing Association,* November 1978, pp. 112–14; and Joel Saegert, "Another Look at Subliminal Perception," *Journal of Advertising Research,* February 1979, pp. 55–57.

12.   Frederick E. Webster, Jr., and Frederick Von Pechmann, "A Replication of the 'Shopping List' Study," *Journal of Marketing,* April 1970, pp. 61–63. See also George S. Lane and Gayne L. Watson, "A Canadian Replication of Mason Haire's 'Shopping List' Study," *Journal of the Academy of Marketing Science,* Winter 1975, pp. 48–59.

13.   Del I. Hawkins, Kenneth A. Coney, and Roger J. Best, *Consumer Behavior: Implications for Marketing Strategy* (Dallas: Business Publications, 1980), pp. 181–82. The quotation is adapted from S. E. Asch, "Effects of Group Pressure upon the Modification and Distortion of Judgments," in *Readings in Social Psychology,* eds. E. E. MacCoby et al. (New York: Holt, Rinehart and Winston, 1958), pp. 174–83.

14.   James H. Myers and William H. Reynolds, *Consumer Behavior and Marketing Management* (Boston: Houghton Mifflin, 1967), pp. 173–74. See also Jeffrey D. Ford and Elwood A. Ellis, "A Reexamination of Group Influence on Member Brand Preference," *Journal of Marketing Research,* February 1980, pp. 125–32.

15.   See Richard P. Coleman, "The Significance of Social Stratification in Selling" and "Retrospective Comment," in *Classics in Consumer Behavior,* ed. Louis E. Boone (Tulsa, Okla.: PPC Books, 1977), pp. 288–302; and Richard P. Coleman and Lee Rainwater, *Social Standing in America: New Dimensions of Class* (New York: Basic Books, 1978).

16.   John W. Slocum, Jr., and H. Lee Mathews, "Social Class and Income as Indicators of Consumer Credit Behavior," *Journal of Marketing,* April 1970, pp. 69–74. See also Gillian Garcia, "Credit Cards: An Interdisciplinary Survey," *Journal of Consumer Research,* March 1980, pp. 327–37; Charles M. Schaninger, "Social Class versus Income Revisited: An Empirical Investigation," *Journal of Marketing Research,* May 1981, pp. 192–208; and Luis V. Dominguez and Albert L. Page, "Use and Misuse of Social Stratification in Consumer Behavior Research," *Journal of Business Research,* June 1981, pp. 151–73.

17.   Elihu Katz and Paul F. Lazarsfeld, *Personal Influence* (New York: Free Press, 1957), p. 32.

18.   Quoted in Engel and Blackwell, *Consumer Behavior,* p. 373.

19.   *Ibid.,* p. 176. See also Wilson Brown, "The Family and Consumer Decision Making," *Journal of the Academy of Marketing Science,* Fall 1979, pp. 335–45.

20.   Charles M. Schaninger and Chris T. Allen, "Wife's Occupational Status as a Consumer Behavior Construct," *Journal of Consumer Research,* September 1981, pp. 189–96; Pierre Filiatrault and J. R. Brent Ritchie, "Joint Purchasing Decisions: A Comparison of Influence Structure in Family and Couple Decision-Making Units," *Journal of Consumer Research,* September 1980, pp. 131–40; and Robert M. Cosenza and Duane L. Davis, "The Effect of the Wife's Working Status on Familial Dominance Structure," *Journal of the Academy of Marketing Science,* Spring 1980, pp. 73–82.

21.   "Business Shifts Its Sales Pitch for Women," *U.S. News & World Report,* July 9, 1981, p. 46; and Margaret LeRoux, "Exec Claims Most Ads to Women Miss the Mark," *Advertising Age,* May 21, 1979, p. 24.

22.   "Keeping Up . . . with Youth," *Parade,* December 11, 1977, p. 20. See also James U. McNeal, "Children as Consumers: A Review," *Journal of the Academy of Marketing Science,* Fall 1979, pp. 346–59; George P. Moschis and Roy L. Moore, "Decision Making among the Young: A Socialization Perspective," *Journal of Consumer Research,* September 1979, pp. 101–12; and George P. Moschis and Gilbert A. Churchill, Jr., "An Analysis of the Adolescent Consumer," *Journal of Marketing,* Summer 1979, pp. 40–48.

23.   Engel and Blackwell, *Consumer Behavior,* p. 65.

24.   Joe Kent Kerby, *Consumer Behavior* (New York: Dun-Donnelley Publishing, 1975), p. 569.

25.   Robert Linn, "Americans Turn Deaf Ear to Foreign Tongues," *Orlando Sentinel Star,* November 1, 1981.

26.   "Personal Care Items' Global Outlook Good," *Advertising Age,* April 1, 1974, p. 28.

27.   Edward T. Hall, "The Silent Language of Overseas Business," *Harvard Business Review,* May–June 1960, p. 89.

28.   Patricia L. Layman, "In Any Language, the Beauty Business Spells Success," *Chemical Week,* September 17, 1975, p. 26.

29.   N. R. Kleinsfield, "This Is One Story with Teeth in It—False Ones, That Is," *Wall Street Journal,* August 18, 1975, p. 1.

30.   B. M. Campbell, "The Existence of Evoked Set and Determinants of Its Magnitude in Brand Choice Behavior," in *Buyer Behavior: Theoretical and Empirical Foundations,* eds. John A. Howard and Lonnie Ostrom (New York: Alfred A. Knopf, Inc., 1973), pp. 243–44.

31.   Donald H. Cox, "The Measurement of Information Values: A Study in Consumer Decision Making," in W. S. Decker, ed., *Emerging Concepts in Marketing* (Chicago: American Marketing Association, 1962), pp. 414–15.

32.   Leon Festinger, *A Theory of Cognitive Dissonance* (Stanford, Calif.: Stanford University Press, 1958), p. 3.

33.   Robert J. Connole, James D. Benson, and Inder P. Khera, "Cognitive Dissonance among Innovators," *Journal of the Academy of Marketing Science,* Winter 1977, pp. 9–20; David R. Lambert, Ronald J. Dornoff, and Jerome B. Kernan, "The Industrial Buyer and the Postchoice Evaluation Process," *Journal of Marketing Research,* May 1977, pp. 246–51; and William H. Cummings and M. Venkatesan, "Cognitive Dissonance and Consumer Behavior: A Review of the Evidence," *Journal of Marketing Research,* August 1976, pp. 303–8.

PART FOUR

PRODUCT/SERVICE STRATEGY

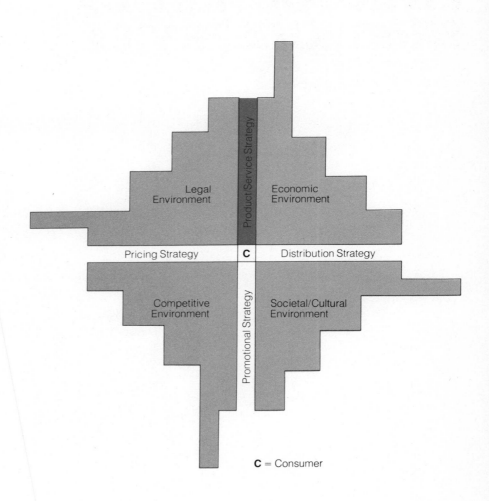

Product/Service Strategy

Legal
Environment

Economic
Environment

Pricing Strategy   **C**   Distribution Strategy

Competitive
Environment

Societal/Cultural
Environment

Promotional Strategy

C = Consumer

CHAPTER 8

INTRODUCTION TO PRODUCT/SERVICE STRATEGY

KEY TERMS

product
warranty
product life cycle
adoption process
consumer innovators
diffusion process
convenience goods
impulse goods
shopping goods
specialty goods
installations
accessory equipment
industrial distributor
fabricated parts and materials
raw materials
supplies
MRO items
goods-service continuum
services

LEARNING GOALS

1. To explain the concept of the product life cycle

2. To identify the determinants of the speed of the adoption process

3. To explain the methods for accelerating the speed of adoption.

4. To identify the classifications for consumer goods and to briefly describe each category

5. To identify the types of industrial goods

6. To explain the key distinguishing features of services

By the millions, they trek through the streets, parks, and sidewalks of cities and suburbia. The jogger, once a rarity, has become a familiar component of the landscape. An estimated 25 million Americans engage in running as a sport or exercise.

A variety of jogger types abound. Some joggers are health-oriented; they recognize the superiority of running to virtually every other exercise in developing and maintaining physical fitness. Many joggers stress the physical and intellectual satisfaction that accompanies running. Others are attracted to the sport because of its popularity. Still others view jogging as a necessary evil: a quick, painful, and boring means of exercise.

A variety of marketers have recognized the growth of this sport and have offered its followers a variety of products and services. Specialized magazines such as *Runner*; clothing ranging from sweat pants to designer ("dry clean only") warm-up suits; and shoes with names like Nike, Puma, and Adidas all compete for the runner's dollar. By 1980, running shoes had reached annual sales of $750 million.

Bored runners with $200 to spend can cure their boredom with Walkman: a lightweight, paperback-book-sized portable stereo tape player with mini-headphones. The product, developed and marketed by Sony Corporation board chairman Akio Morita over the protests of his marketing experts, has been an immediate sales success. King Juan Carlos of Spain is just one of nearly four million Walkman owners.

Sony marketers (who at first felt that Walkman was a poor name) have succeeded in broadening the sales of the new product by focusing on different uses. Since the product enables the consumer to listen to tapes without disturbing others, Walkman is often used in college libraries. It is also effective in drowning out noise. In addition, Walkman frequently settles potential arguments among household members concerning choice of television channel or radio station. The new product provides mobile entertainment not only for joggers, but also for skaters, bicyclists, and skiers.

The lightweight stereo earphones produce markedly increased quality sounds over its predecessor, the earplug, with its distorted monophonic sound. Some safety concerns have been expressed for joggers and cyclists who may not hear outside sounds, and Sony engineers have modified the Walkman to allow outside sounds to enter the ear. The Walkman III model includes a "hot-line"—a button-activated microphone that allows two people to converse without having to remove the headphones.

Evidence of the Walkman success story abounds. The most typical account follows:

". . .the straight-ahead stare; the Mona Lisa smile crossing faintly moving lips; the rhythmic gait usually reserved for dance floors; and a voracious appetite for fresh batteries."[1]

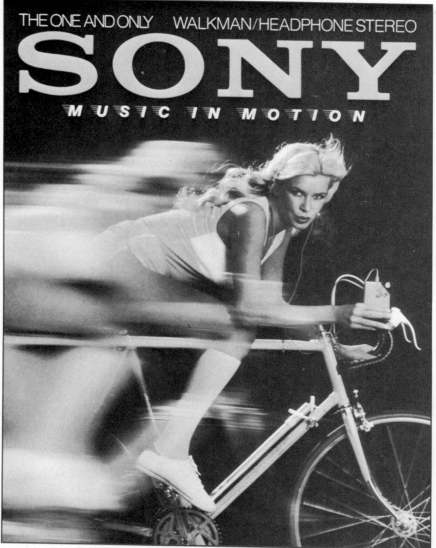

Source: Courtesy of Sony Corporation of America.

These "symptoms" also reflect the success of an astute marketer who was convinced of a consumer need and who was willing to risk his reputation to design a product offering to fill it.

WHAT IS A PRODUCT?

The chapters in Part 4 analyze the decisions and problems involved with the first element of the marketing mix—the product or products to be offered to the firm's market target. Planning efforts begin with the choice of products to offer the market target. The other variables of the marketing mix—pricing structures, marketing channels, and promotional plans—must be based on product planning.

A narrow definition of the word *product* would focus on the physical or functional characteristics of a good or service offered to consumers. For example, a videocassette recorder is a rectangular container of metal and plastic with wires connecting it to a television set, accompanied by a series of special tapes for recording and viewing. But the purchaser has a much broader view of the recorder. He bought the convenience of viewing television programs at his leisure; the warranty and service facilities of Sony; the prestige of owning this relatively new product innovation; and the ability to rent or purchase recently released movies for home viewing.

Marketing decision makers must have this broader conception of product in mind and realize that people are buying *want satisfaction.* For example, most consumers know little about the gasoline they buy. In fact, many view it not as a product at all, but rather as a premium they must pay for the privilege of driving their car.

The shopper's conception of a product may be altered by such features as packaging, labeling, or even the retail outlet at which the product is purchased. An image of high quality has been created for Maytag appliances by virtue of the advertising campaign featuring the Maytag repairer as the "loneliest person in town." Maytag's standard of high product quality is responsible for its continued sales growth record—even though a Maytag washer retails at about $70 higher than the nearest competitor.

Some products have few or no physical attributes. A haircut and blow-dry by the local hairdresser produces only well-groomed hair. A tax counselor produces only advice. Therefore, a broader view of products must include services. Consequently, a **product** is *a bundle of physical, service, and symbolic attributes designed to produce consumer want satisfaction.* Figure 8.1 reflects this broader definition by identifying the various components of the total product.

The Warranty: An Important Product Component

An important feature of many products is the product **warranty**—*the guarantee to the buyer that the manufacturer will replace the product or refund its purchase price if it proves defective during a specified period of time.* Warranties increase consumer purchase confidence and often represent an important means by which demand is stimulated. The manufacturer of Zippo lighters offers a lifetime guarantee, promising to repair or replace any damaged or defective Zippo lighter regardless of age. This warranty is one of the most important features of the firm's marketing strategy.

In 1981, Chrysler Corporation chairman Lee A. Iacocca shocked the automobile industry by initiating an unprecedented warranty program in an attempt to stimulate demand for Chrysler products. The

**FIGURE 8.1
The Total Product
Concept**

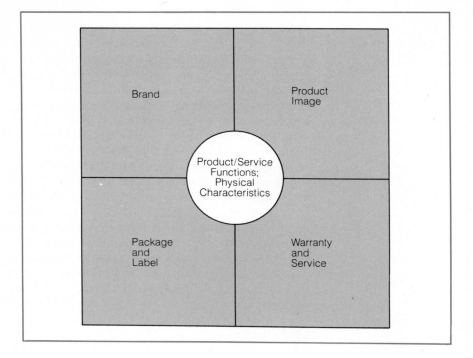

new warranty included a 30-day, 1000-mile money-back guarantee and an offer of a $50 rebate for customers who agreed to test-drive a Chrysler and who subsequently purchased a Chrysler—or a competitor's—automobile or truck.

The *Magnuson-Moss Warranty Act* (1975) gives the Federal Trade Commission the power to develop regulations affecting warranty practices for any product costing more than $15 that is covered by a written warranty. While the act does not require firms to give warranties, it is designed to assist the consumer in comparison shopping. Warranties must be easy to read and understand, and firms offering them must also establish informal mechanisms for processing consumer complaints.[2]

Figure 8.2 shows the ultimate product warranty. Hammacher Schlemmer, a 132-year-old retailer of consumer products, will make full refunds to any purchaser for any reason. This money-back guarantee produces risk-free purchase decisions and enhances the image of the firm and its products.

THE PRODUCT LIFE CYCLE

Products—like individuals—pass through a series of stages. While humans progress from infancy to childhood to adulthood to retirement to death, *successful products progress through four stages—introduction,*

FIGURE 8.2
The Hammacher
Schlemmer
Warranty: A Money-
back Guarantee for
Any Reason

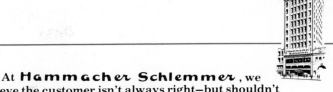

At **Hammacher Schlemmer**, we
believe the customer isn't always right—but shouldn't
have to suffer for it.

So, if you send for something from us, and then decide it wasn't
exactly what you wanted or expected, we'll simply take it back.

Maybe the color wasn't quite right; maybe you decided you might
not use it very often after all. It won't matter. We won't ask you a lot
of questions. We won't have you fill out a complicated form and we won't
restrict your return privilege to a certain number of days.

This is what Hammacher Schlemmer has been doing for 132 years,
and we suspect it is unique. Just as we've been at it longer than
anybody else, so we've learned to do it better. Our guarantee doesn't
simply mean your commercial grade Cuisinart or baseball computer
or champagne recorker must reach you intact. It means you must like
it...and keep on liking it.

There's a reason for this. People shop Hammacher Schlemmer for
the unusual—singular items for singular tastes. And for our many
customers who shop through the catalogue rather than at the store,
we know that the best picture and description of an item often may
not do it justice. Perhaps on inspection it won't be to your taste.

Frankly, this is to our advantage. After all, Hammacher Schlemmer
has spent these 132 years building a unique reputation, and we
prosper by capitalizing on it.

So feel free to indulge your curiosity. Send for that egg
peeler or desk top copier or whatever else strikes your fancy.
Chances are it will turn out to be exactly what you're looking for.
But if not, remember: WE WILL GLADLY TAKE IT BACK.

Dominic Tampone, President

CALL TOLL FREE 800-228-5656

Source: Reprinted by permission of Hammacher Schlemmer.

growth, maturity, and decline—before their death; this progression is
known as the **product life cycle.** The cycle is depicted in Figure 8.3.

Introduction The firm's objective in the early stages of the product life
cycle is to stimulate demand for the new market entry. Since the product is not known to the public, promotional campaigns stress information about its features. They also may be directed toward middlemen in
the channel to induce them to carry the product. In this phase, the public becomes acquainted with the merits of the product and begins to
accept it.

**FIGURE 8.3
Stages in the
Product Life Cycle**

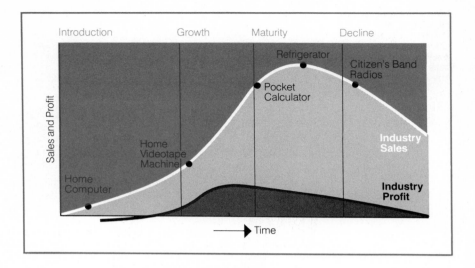

As Figure 8.3 indicates, losses are common during the introductory stage due to heavy promotion and extensive research and development expenditures. But the groundwork is being laid for future profits. Firms expect to recover their costs and to begin earning profits when the new product moves into the second phase of its life cycle—the growth stage.

Growth Sales volume rises rapidly during the growth stage as new customers make initial purchases and early ones repurchase the product. Word-of-mouth and mass advertising induce hesitant buyers to make trial purchases. Eight hundred thousand videotape machines were sold in the United States in 1980, six times the number sold in 1977. These machines, a product that is currently in the growth stage, are in 10 percent of all U.S. homes.

As the firm begins to realize substantial profits from its investment during the growth stage, it attracts competitors. Success breeds imitation, and other firms inevitably rush into the market with competitive products in search of profit.

Maturity Industry sales continue to grow during the early part of the maturity stage, but eventually they reach a plateau as the backlog of potential customers is exhausted. By this time, a large number of competitors have entered the market, and profits decline as competition intensifies.

In the maturity stage, differences among competing products diminish as competitors discover the product characteristics and promotional characteristics most desired by the market. Heavy promotional outlays emphasize subtle differences among competing products, and brand competition intensifies.

For the first time, available products exceed industry demand.

**FIGURE 8.4
Overlap of Life
Cycles for Products
A and B**

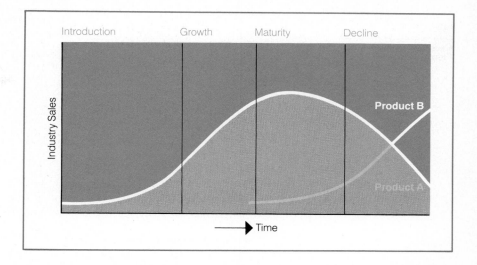

Companies attempting to increase their sales and market share must do so at the expense of competitors. As competition intensifies, the competitors tend to cut prices in an attempt to attract new buyers. Even though a price reduction may be the easiest method of inducing additional purchases, it is also one of the simplest moves for competitors to duplicate. Reduced prices result in decreased revenues for all firms in the industry unless the price cuts produce enough increased purchases to offset the loss in revenue on each item sold.[3]

Decline In the final stage of the product's life, innovations or shifting consumer preferences bring about an absolute decline in industry sales. The safety razor and electric shaver replace the straight razor, Pac-Man replaces Rubik's Cube as the latest fad, and the black and white television is exchanged for a color set. As Figure 8.4 indicates, the decline stage of the old product doubles as the growth stage for a new market entry.

Industry profits decline and in some cases actually become negative as sales fall and firms cut prices in a bid for the dwindling market. Manufacturers gradually begin to leave the industry in search of more profitable products.

**Utilizing the
Concept**

The product life cycle concept provides important insights about developments at the various stages of the product's life. Knowledge that profits assume a predictable pattern through the stages and that promotional emphasis must shift from product information in the early stages to brand promotion in the later ones should allow the marketing decision maker to improve planning.

The length of the life cycle and of each of its stages varies considerably. A new shoe fashion may have a total life span of one calendar year, with an introductory stage of two months. But the auto-

FIGURE 8.5
Hypothetical Life
Cycle for Denim
Fabric

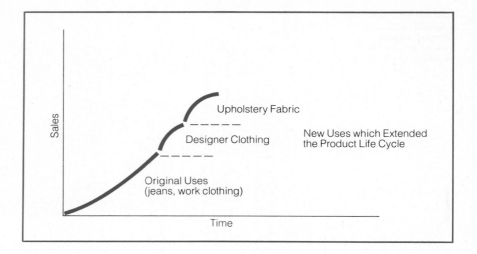

mobile has been in the maturity stage for more than twenty years. Marketing managers may be able to extend the product life cycle indefinitely if they take action early in the maturity stage. Products such as Jell-O, nylon, and Scotch tape have been given extended lives through marketing moves designed (1) to increase the frequency of use by present customers, (2) to add new users, (3) to find new uses for the products, and (4) to change package sizes, labels, or product quality.[4] Nylon was originally used by the military in the production of parachutes, thread, and rope. Next, it revolutionized the women's hosiery industry and has since been used in producing stretch socks, sweaters, panty hose, body stockings, tires, carpets, and ball bearings, to name only a few products.

Denim is another product whose life was extended through the development of new uses (see Figure 8.5). Denim was pioneered in the 1850s by Levi Strauss and Company in the form of durable jeans and work shirts. Later work jackets were added, but for more than 100 years the products had been aimed at a market consisting of children, teenagers, and blue-collar adults.

The fashion changes of the 1970s and 1980s converted the Levi name into a status symbol as the denim fabric—and the Levi label—began to appear on premium-priced clothing. Dress suits were made from denim. Other markets for denim included automobile seat covers, backpacks, and hats.

Church & Dwight had been marketing Arm & Hammer baking soda for more than 125 years when a decision to emphasize new uses for the product revitalized its sales. Six months after its promotion as a refrigerator deodorant, an estimated 70 percent of the nation's refrigerators contained a box of Arm & Hammer baking soda! The changes in both organizational and environmental conditions and the adjustments in marketing efforts at each stage in the product life cycle are summarized in Table 8.1.

**TABLE 8.1
Organizational
Conditions,
Marketing Efforts,
and Environmental
Conditions at Each
Stage of the Product
Life Cycle**

	Introduction	Growth	Maturity		Decline
			Early Maturity	Late Maturity	
Organizational Conditions	High costs Inefficient production levels Cash demands	Smoothing production Lowering costs Operation efficiencies Product improvement work	Efficient scale of operation Product modification work Decreasing profits	Low profits Standardized production	
Environmental Conditions	Few or no competitors Limited product awareness and knowledge Limited demand	Expanding markets Expanded distribution Competition strengthens Prices soften a bit	Slowing growth Strong competition Expanded market Heightened competition	Faltering demand Fierce competition Shrinking number of competitors Established distribution patterns	Permanently declining demand Reduction of competitors Limited product offerings Price stabilization
Marketing Efforts	Stimulate demand Establish high price Offer limited product variety Increase distribution	Cultivate selective demand Product improvement Strengthen distribution Price flexibility	Emphasize market segmentation Improve service and warranty Reduce prices	Ultimate in market segmentation Competitive pricing Retain distribution	Increase primary demand Profit opportunity pricing Prune and strengthen distribution

Source: Adapted from Burton H. Marcus and Edward M. Tauber, *Marketing Analysis and Decision Making* (Boston: Little, Brown, 1979), pp. 115–16.
Copyright © 1979 by Burton H. Marcus and Edward M. Tauber. Reprinted by permission of Little, Brown and Company.

CONSUMER ADOPTION PROCESS

Consumers also make decisions about the new product offering. In the **adoption process,** potential consumers go through *a series of stages from learning of the new product to trying it and deciding to purchase it regularly or to reject it.* These stages in the consumer adoption process can be classified as:

1. *Awareness.* Individuals first learn of the new product but lack information about it.

2. *Interest.* They begin to seek out information about it.

3. *Evaluation.* They consider whether the product is beneficial.

4. *Trial.* They make a trial purchase in order to determine its usefulness.

5.   *Adoption/Rejection.* If the trial purchase is satisfactory, they decide to make regular use of the product.[5]

The marketing manager needs to understand the adoption process so that he or she can move potential consumers to the adoption stage. Once the manager is aware of a large number of consumers at the interest stage, steps can be taken to stimulate sales. For example, Gillette introduced Aapri Apricot Facial Scrub by mailing 15 million samples to households in the United States and Canada. Total sampling costs for the new skin product designed to compete with Noxzema, Pond's, and Oil of Olay were $4.1 million.[6] Sampling is a technique that reduces the risk of evaluation and trial, moving the consumer quickly to the adoption stage.

Adopter Categories

Some people purchase a new product almost as soon as it is placed on the market. Others wait for additional information and rely on the experiences of the first purchasers before making trial purchases. **Consumer innovators**—*first purchasers*—are likely to be present in each product area. Some families are first in the community to buy color television sets. Some doctors are first to prescribe new drugs, and some farmers plant new hybrid seeds much earlier than their neighbors. Some people are quick to adopt new fashions, and some drivers make early use of automobile diagnostic centers.

A number of investigations analyzing the adoption of new products has resulted in the identification of five categories of purchasers based on relative time of adoption. These categories, shown in Figure 8.6, are innovators, early adopters, early majority, late majority, and laggards.

**FIGURE 8.6
Categories of
Adopters on the
Basis of Relative
Time of Adoption**

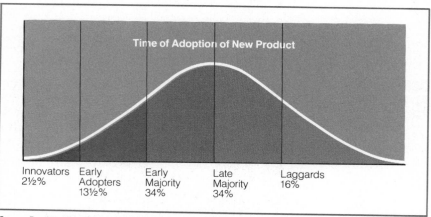

Source: Reprinted by permission of Macmillan Publishing Company, Inc., from *Communication of Innovations: A Cross Cultural Approach* by Everett M. Rogers and F. Floyd Shoemaker. Copyright © 1971 by The Free Press, a Division of Macmillan Publishing Company, Inc.

The **diffusion process** is *the acceptance of new products and services by the members of a community or social system.* Figure 8.6 shows this process as following a normal distribution. A few people adopt at first; then the number of adopters increases rapidly as the value of the innovation is apparent. The rate finally diminishes as fewer potential consumers remain in the nonadopter category.

Since the categories are based on the normal distribution, standard deviations are used to partition them. Innovators are the first 2.5 percent to adopt the new product; laggards are the last 16 percent to do so. Excluded from Figure 8.6 are the nonadopters (those who never adopt the innovation).

Identifying the First Adopters

Locating first buyers of new products represents a challenge for the marketing manager. If first buyers can be reached early in the product's development or introduction, they can serve as a test market, evaluating the products and making suggestions for modifications. Since early purchasers are often opinion leaders from whom others seek advice, their attitudes toward new products are quickly communicated to others. Acceptance or rejection of the innovation by these purchasers can help forecast the expected success of the new product.

Unfortunately, first adopters of one new product are not necessarily first adopters of other products or services. A large number of research studies has, however, established some general characteristics of most first adopters.

First adopters tend to be younger, to have a higher social status, to be better educated, and to enjoy a higher income than others. They are more mobile than later adopters and change both their jobs and home addresses more often. They are also more likely to rely on impersonal information sources than are later adopters, who depend more on promotional information from the company and word-of-mouth communication.[7]

Rate of Adoption Determinants

Frisbees progressed from the product introduction stage to the market maturity stage in a period of six months. But it took the U.S. Department of Agriculture thirteen years to convince corn farmers to use hybrid seed corn—an innovation capable of doubling corn yields. The adoption rate is influenced by five characteristics of the innovation:

1. *Relative advantage*—the degree to which the innovation appears superior to previous ideas. The greater the relative advantage—manifested in terms of lower price, physical improvements, or ease of use—the faster the adoption rate.

2. *Compatibility*—the degree to which the innovation is consistent with the values and experiences of potential adopters. The failure of Analoze, the waterless pain remedy discussed in Chapter 7, resulted largely from consumers' unwillingness to accept a product

whose directions for use conflicted drastically with consumer custom.

3. *Complexity*—the relative difficulty of understanding the innovation. The more difficult the new product is to understand or to use, the longer it will take to be generally accepted in most cases.

4. *Divisibility*—the degree to which the innovation can be used on a limited basis. First adopters face two types of risk, financial losses and ridicule by others, if the new product proves unsatisfactory. The option of sampling the innovation on a limited basis allows these risks to be reduced and generally accelerates the rate of adoption.

5. *Communicability*—the degree to which the results of using the product are observable or communicable to others. If the superiority of the innovation can be displayed in a tangible form, the adoption rate will be increased.[8]

These five characteristics can be implemented to some extent by the marketing manager in accelerating the rate of adoption. Product complexity must be overcome by informative promotional messages. Products should be designed to emphasize their relative advantages and, whenever possible, should be divisible for sample purchases. If divisibility is physically impossible, in-home demonstrations or trial placements in the home can be used. Positive attempts must also be made to ensure compatibility of the innovation with the adopters' value systems.

These actions are based on extensive research studies of innovators in agriculture, medicine, and consumer goods. They should pay off in increased sales by accelerating the rate of adoption in each of the adopter categories.

CONSUMER GOODS AND INDUSTRIAL GOODS: A DEFINITION

How a firm markets its product depends largely on the product itself. For example, Chanel stresses subtle promotions in prestige media such as *The New Yorker* and *Vogue* magazines and markets its perfumes through department stores and specialty shops. Hershey markets its candy products through candy wholesalers to thousands of supermarkets, variety stores, discount houses, and vending machine companies. A firm manufacturing and marketing forklifts may use sales representatives to call on industrial buyers and ship its product either directly from the factory or from regional warehouses.

Product strategy differs for consumer goods and industrial goods. As explained in Chapter 5, *consumer goods* are products destined for use by the ultimate consumer, and *industrial goods* are products used directly or indirectly in producing other goods for resale. These two major categories can be broken down further.

Consumer Goods: Characteristics

Although a number of classification systems have been suggested, the system most often used is based on consumer buying habits. The three categories of consumer goods are convenience goods, shopping goods, and specialty goods.[9]

Convenience Goods *The products that the consumer wants to purchase frequently, immediately, and with a minimum of effort* are called **convenience goods.** Milk, bread, butter, eggs, and beer (the staples of most twenty-four-hour convenience food stores) are all convenience goods. So are newspapers, chewing gum, magazines, M&M's, and the items found in most vending machines.

Convenience goods are usually sold by brand name and are low priced. Many of them—such as bread, milk, and gasoline—are staple items, and the consumer's supply must be constantly replenished. In most cases, the buyer has already decided to purchase a particular brand of gasoline or candy or to buy at a particular store, and spends little time deliberating about the purchase decision. *Products purchased on the spur of the moment and out of habit when the supply is low* are referred to as **impulse goods.**

The consumer rarely visits competing stores or compares price and quality in purchasing convenience goods. The possible gains to be made from such comparisons are outweighed by the costs of acquiring the additional information. This does not mean, however, that the consumer is destined to remain permanently loyal to one brand of beer, candy, or cigarettes. People continually receive new information from radio and television advertisements, billboards, and word-of-mouth communication. Since the price of most convenience goods is low, trial purchases of competing brands or products are made with little financial risk, and often new habits are developed.

Since the consumer is unwilling to spend much effort in purchasing convenience goods, the manufacturer must strive to make them as convenient as possible. Candy, cigarettes, and newspapers are sold in almost every supermarket, variety store, service station, and restaurant. Where retail outlets are physically separated from a large number of consumers, the manufacturer constructs small "stores" in the form of vending machines and places them in spots that are convenient for its customers (such as office buildings and factories). Even though Coca-Cola distributors believe that most people prefer their soft drink over Pepsi-Cola, they also know that consumers will not leave the building in search of a Coke if the vending machine is completely stocked with Pepsi. Coca-Cola distributors must protect this fragile loyalty by ensuring that their product is equally available.

Retailers usually carry several competing brands of convenience products and are unlikely to promote any particular one. The promotional burden, therefore, falls on the *manufacturer,* who must advertise extensively to develop consumer acceptance of the product. The Coca-Cola promotional program consists of radio and television commercials, magazine ads, billboards, and point-of-purchase displays in stores. These efforts to motivate the consumer to choose Coke over competing brands are a good example of a manufacturer's promotion designed to stimulate consumer demand.

Shopping Goods In contrast with convenience goods, **shopping goods** are *purchased only after the consumer has made comparisons of competing goods in competing stores on bases such as price, quality, style, and color.* The purchaser of shopping goods lacks complete information prior to the shopping trip and gathers information during it.

A woman intent on adding a new dress to her wardrobe may visit many stores, try on a number of dresses, and spend days making the final choice. She may follow a regular route from store to store in surveying competing offerings and ultimately will select the dress that most appeals to her. New stores carrying assortments of shopping goods must ensure that they are located near other shopping goods stores so that they will be included in shopping expeditions.

Shopping goods are typically more expensive than convenience goods and are most often purchased by women. In addition to women's apparel, shopping goods include such items as appliances, furniture, jewelry, shoes, and used automobiles.

Some shopping goods, such as children's shoes, are considered *homogeneous*; that is, the consumer views them as essentially the same. Others, such as furniture and clothing, are considered *heterogeneous*—essentially different. Price is an important factor in the purchase of homogeneous shopping goods, while quality and styling are relatively more important in the purchase of heterogeneous goods.[10]

Important features of shopping goods are the physical attributes of the product, its price and styling, and even the retail store that handles it. The brand is often of lesser importance, in spite of the large amounts of money manufacturers often spend promoting their brands.

Since buyers of shopping goods expend some effort in making their purchases, manufacturers of shopping goods utilize fewer retail stores than for convenience goods. Retailers and manufacturers work closely in promoting shopping goods, and retail purchases are often made directly from the manufacturer or its representative rather than the wholesaler. Fashion merchandise buyers for department stores and specialty shops make regular buying trips to regional and national markets in New York, Dallas, and Los Angeles. Buyers for furniture retailers often go directly to the factories of furniture manufacturers or visit furniture trade shows.

Specialty Goods The specialty goods purchaser is well aware of what he or she wants and is willing to make a special effort to obtain it. The nearest Cartier dealer may be 100 miles away, for example, but the watch purchaser willing to spend several thousand dollars will go there to buy this prestigious watch.

TABLE 8.2
Marketing Impact of the Consumer Goods Classification System

Factor	Convenience Goods	Shopping Goods	Specialty Goods
Consumer Factors			
Planning time involved in purchase	Very little	Considerable	Extensive
Purchase frequency	Frequent	Less frequent	Infrequent
Importance of convenient location	Critical importance	Important	Unimportant
Comparison of price and quality	Very little	Considerable	Very little
Marketing Mix Factors			
Price	Low	Relatively high	High
Advertising	By manufacturer	Both	Both
Channel length	Long	Relatively short	Very short
Number of retail outlets	Many	Few	Very small number; often one per market area
Store image	Unimportant	Very important	Important

Specialty goods *possess some unique characteristics that cause the buyer to prize that particular brand.* For these products, the buyer has complete information prior to the shopping trip and is unwilling to accept substitutes.

Specialty goods are typically high priced and are frequently branded. Since consumers are willing to exert considerable effort to obtain them, fewer retail outlets are required. Mercury outboard motors and Porsche sports cars may be handled by only one or two retailers for each 100,000 people.

Table 8.2 summarizes the impact of the consumer goods classification system on the development of an effective marketing mix.

Applying the Consumer Goods Classification System

The three-way classification system allows the marketing manager to gain additional information for use in developing a marketing strategy. Once the new food product has been classified as a convenience good, insights are gained about marketing needs in branding, promotion, pricing, and distribution methods.

But the classification system also poses problems. The major problem is that it suggests a circumscribed, three-way series of demarcations into which all products can easily be fitted. Some products do fit neatly into one of the classifications, but others fall into the grey areas between each category.

How, for example, should a new automobile be classified? It is expensive, sold by brand, and handled by a few exclusive dealers in

**FIGURE 8.7
Product
Classification
Continuum**

each city. But before classifying it as a specialty good, other characteristics must be considered. Most new-car buyers shop extensively among competing models and auto dealers before deciding on the best deal. A more effective way to utilize the classification is to consider it a continuum representing degrees of effort expended by the consumer (as in Figure 8.7).[11] If this is done, the new-car purchase can be located between the categories of shopping and specialty goods but nearer the specialty-goods end of the continuum.

A second problem with the classification system is that consumers differ in their buying patterns. One person will make an unplanned purchase of a new Chevy Citation, while others will shop extensively before purchasing a car. But one buyer's impulse purchase does not make the Citation a convenience good. Goods are classified by the purchase patterns of the majority of buyers.

CLASSIFICATION OF INDUSTRIAL GOODS

Industrial goods can be subdivided into five categories: installations, accessory equipment, fabricated parts and materials, raw materials, and industrial supplies. Industrial buyers are professional consumers; their job is to make effective purchase decisions. The purchase decision process involved in buying supplies of flour for General Mills, for example, is much the same as that used in buying the same commodity for Pillsbury. Thus the classification system for industrial goods must be based on product uses rather than on consumer buying patterns.

Installations

Specialty goods of the industrial market are called **installations.** Included in this classification are such major capital assets as factories and heavy machinery, new planes for Republic Airlines, or locomotives for the Burlington Northern.

Since installations are relatively long-lived and involve large sums of money, their purchase represents a major decision for an organization. Negotiations often extend over a period of several months and involve the participation of numerous decision makers. In many cases, the selling company must provide technical expertise. When custom-made equipment is involved, representatives of the selling firm work closely with the buyer's engineers and production personnel to design the most feasible product for the buying firm.

Price is almost never the deciding factor in the purchase of installations. The purchasing firm is interested in the product's efficiency and performance over its useful life. The firm also wants a minimum of breakdowns. "Down time" is expensive because employees are nonproductive (but still are paid) while the machine is being repaired.

Since most of the factories of firms purchasing installations are geographically concentrated, the selling firm places its promotional emphasis on well-trained salespeople who often have a technical background. Most installations are marketed directly on a manufacturer-to-user basis. Even though a sale may be a one-time transaction, contracts often call for regular product servicing. In the case of extremely expensive installations, such as computer and electronic equipment, some firms lease the installations rather than sell them outright, and assign personnel directly to the lessee to operate or to maintain the equipment.

Accessory Equipment

Fewer decision makers are usually involved in purchasing **accessory equipment**—*capital items that are usually less expensive and shorter-lived than installations.* Although quality and service still remain important criteria in purchasing accessory equipment, the firm is likely to be much more price-conscious. Accessory equipment includes such products as desk calculators, hand tools, portable drills, small lathes, and typewriters. Although these goods are considered capital items and are depreciated over several years, their useful life is generally much shorter than that of an installation.

Because of the need for continuous representation and the more widespread geographic dispersion of accessory equipment purchasers, a wholesaler—often called an **industrial distributor**—contacts potential customers in each geographic area. Technical assistance is usually not necessary, and the manufacturer of accessory equipment often can effectively utilize wholesalers in marketing the firm's products. Manufacturers also use advertising more than installation producers do.

Fabricated Parts and Materials

While installations and accessory equipment are used in producing the final product, **fabricated parts and materials** are *the finished industrial goods that actually become part of the final product.* Champion spark plugs make a new Chevrolet complete; batteries are often added to Mattel toys; tires are included with Checker taxis. Some fabricated materials, such as flour, undergo further processing before producing a finished product.

Purchasers of fabricated parts and materials need a regular, continuous supply of uniform quality goods. These goods are generally purchased on contract for a period of one year or more. Direct sale is common, and satisfied customers often become permanent buyers. Wholesalers sometimes are used for fill-in purchases and in handling sales to smaller purchasers.

Raw Materials

Farm products—such as cattle, cotton, eggs, milk, pigs, and soybeans—*and natural products*—such as coal, copper, iron ore, and lumber—constitute **raw materials.** They are similar to fabricated parts and materials in that they are used in producing the final products.

Since most raw materials are graded, the purchaser is assured of standardized products with uniform quality. As with fabricated parts and materials, direct sale of raw materials is common, and sales are typically made on a contractual basis. Wholesalers are increasingly involved in the purchase of raw materials from foreign suppliers.

Price is seldom a deciding factor in the purchase of raw materials, since it is often quoted at a central market and is virtually identical among competing sellers. Purchasers buy raw materials from the firms they consider most able to deliver in the quantity and the quality required.

Supplies

If installations represent the "specialty goods" of the industrial market, then operating supplies are the "convenience goods." **Supplies** are *regular expense items necessary in the daily operation of the firm, but not part of the final product.*

Supplies are sometimes called **MRO items** because they *can be divided into three categories:* 1) *maintenance items,* such as brooms, floor-cleaning compounds, and light bulbs; 2) *repair items,* such as nuts and bolts used in repairing equipment; *and* 3) *operating supplies,* such as heating fuel, lubricating oil, and office stationery.

The regular purchase of operating supplies is a routine aspect of the purchasing agent's job. Wholesalers are very often used in the sale of supplies due to the items' low unit prices, small sales, and large number of potential buyers. Since supplies are relatively standardized, price competition is frequently heavy. However, the purchasing agent spends little time in making purchase decisions. He or she frequently places telephone orders or mail orders, or makes regular purchases from the sales representative of the local office supply wholesaler.

SERVICES: INTANGIBLE PRODUCTS

Both industrial buyers and ultimate consumers are frequent purchasers of services as well as goods.[12] Services—ranging from necessities such as electric power and medical care to luxuries such as foreign travel, backpacking guides, ski resorts, and tennis schools—now account for almost half of the average consumer's total expenditures. While *product* was defined to include both tangible and intangible items earlier in the chapter, differences do exist between tangible products and intangible services. In addition, services account for two-thirds of the private (nongovernment) labor force; they are therefore important enough to require careful analysis.

Some services are difficult to define.

"It'll bring in a lot of business until everyone learns the metric system."

Source: *"Grin and Bear It"* by George Lichty. © Field Enterprises, Inc., 1977. Courtesy of Field Newspaper Syndicate.

The Difficulty of Defining Services

Services are difficult to define. Marketers have traditionally considered them simply another form of goods, so little attention has been given them until recently. It is also difficult to distinguish between certain kinds of goods and services. Personal services, such as hair styling and dry cleaning, are easily recognized as services; but they represent only a small part of the total service industry.

Some firms provide a combination of goods and services to their customers. Wackenhut Corporation, a protection specialist, markets alarms and closed-circuit TVs (goods) in addition to uniformed guards and trained dogs (services). An optometrist may give eye examinations (a service) and sell contact lenses and eyeglasses (goods). Some services are an integral part of the marketing of physical goods. For example, a Burroughs computer sales representative may emphasize the firm's service capabilities at minimizing down time. These illustrations suggest that some method of alleviating definitional problems in the marketing of services is needed.

One useful method is the utilization of a product spectrum, which shows that most products have both goods and services components. Figure 8.8 presents a **goods-services continuum**—*a method for visualizing the differences and similarities of goods and services.*[13] A tire is a pure good, although the service of balancing may be sold along with it or included in the total price. Hair styling is a pure service. In the middle ranges of the continuum are products with both goods and services components. The satisfaction that results from dining in an exclusive restaurant is derived not only from the food and drink but also from the services rendered by the establishment's personnel. **Services,** then, can be defined as *intangible tasks that satisfy consumer and industrial user needs when efficiently developed and distributed to chosen market segments.*

**FIGURE 8.8
The Goods-Services
Continuum**

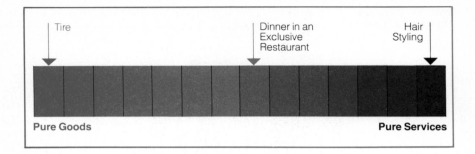

**Classifying
Consumer and
Industrial
Services**

Literally thousands of services are offered to consumers and industrial users. In some instances, they are provided by specialized machinery with almost no personal assistance (such as an automated car wash). In other cases, they are provided by skilled professionals with little reliance on specialized equipment (such as accountants and management consultants). Figure 8.9 provides a means of classifying services based on the degree of reliance on equipment in providing the service and the degree of skill possessed by the people who provide the service.

**FIGURE 8.9
Types of Service
Businesses**

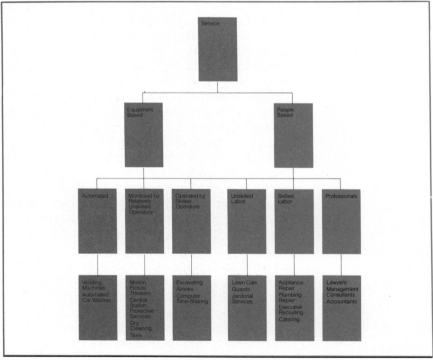

Source: Dan E. Thomas, "Strategy Is Different in Service Businesses," *Harvard Business Review,* July–August 1978, p. 161. Copyright © 1978 by the President and Fellows of Harvard College; all rights reserved. Reprinted by permission.

FEATURES OF SERVICES

Services have four key features with major marketing implications:

1. Services are intangible.
2. They are perishable.
3. Their standardization is difficult.
4. Buyers are often involved in their development and distribution.

Intangibility Services do not have tangible features that appeal to consumers' sense of sight, hearing, smell, taste, or touch. They are therefore difficult to demonstrate at trade fairs, to display in retail stores, and to illustrate in magazine advertisements. They are nearly impossible to sample, and they cannot make use of many other forms of sales pro-

The difficulty of standardizing service offerings often complicates the selection process.

Source: Cartoon by Ziegler. © 1978 The New Yorker Magazine, Inc.

MAKING TANGIBLE THE INTANGIBLE

Professors Theodore Levitt and Leonard L. Berry have recommended that successful service marketers attempt to create surrogates of tangibility for their intangible offerings. Hotel marketers create the impression of individual service and concern for the traveler when they deliver the morning newspaper to the guest's door, wrap each drinking glass in fresh bags or film, and prepare the bed by turning down the cover and placing a packaged mint on the pillow. Berry cites examples from the insurance industry of methods for associating the intangible of insurance with relevant tangible objects:

- "You're in good *hands* with Allstate."
- "I've got a piece of the *rock*."
- "Under the Traveler's *umbrella*."
- "The Nationwide *blanket* of protection."

Levitt illustrates the importance of this "tangibilizing" process by describing the sale of home insulation by two different firms.

Take the instructive case of purchasing house insulation, which most home owners approach with understandable apprehension. Suppose you call two companies to bid on installing insulation in your house. The first insulation installer arrives in a car. After pacing once around the house with measured self-assurance and after quick calculations on the back of an envelope, there comes a confident quote of $2,400 for six-inch fiberglass—total satisfaction guaranteed.

Another drives up in a clean white truck with a clipboard in hand and proceeds to scrupulously measure the house dimensions, count the windows, crawl the attic, and consult records from a source book on the area's seasonal temperature ranges and wind velocities. The installer then asks a host of questions, meanwhile recording everything with obvious diligence. There follows a promise to return in three days, which happens at the appointed hour, with a typed proposal for six-inch fiberglass insulation at $2,800—total satisfaction guaranteed. From which company will you buy?

The latter has tangibilized the intangible, made a promise into a credible expectation. Even more persuasive tangible evidence is provided by an insulation supplier whose representative types the relevant information into a portable intelligent printing terminal. The analysis and response are almost instant, causing one user to call it "the most powerful tool ever developed in the insulation industry."

Source: The insurance examples are cited in Leonard L. Berry, "Services Marketing Is Different," *Business,* May-June 1980, p. 28. The quotation is reprinted by permission from Theodore Levitt, "Marketing Intangible Products and Product Intangibles," *Harvard Business Review,* May-June 1981, p. 101. Reprinted by permission of the *Harvard Business Review.* Copyright © 1981 by the President and Fellows of Harvard College; all rights reserved.

motion. Consequently, imaginative personal selling is usually essential in marketing services.

Furthermore, buyers are often unable to judge the quality of a service prior to purchase. Because of this, the reputation of the service's vendor is often a key factor in a buyer's decision.

Perishability The utility of most services is short-lived; therefore, they cannot be produced ahead of time and stored for periods of peak demand. Vacant seats on an airplane, idle dance instructors, and unused electrical generating capacity represent economic losses that can never be recovered. Sometimes, however, idle facilities during slack periods must be tolerated so the firm will have sufficient capacity for peak periods. Electric and gas utilities, resort hotels, telephone companies, and airlines all face the problem of perishability.

Difficulty of Standardization It is often impossible to standardize offerings among sellers of the same service or even to assure consistency in the services provided by one seller. No two paint jobs from the same house painter are identical. Although standardization is often desirable, it occurs only in the case of equipment-based firms such as those offering automated banking services, automated car washes, and computer time sharing. Creative marketing is needed to adapt nonstandardized services to the unique needs of individual customers.

Involvement of Buyers Buyers often play major roles in the marketing and production of services. The house painter's customer may provide samples of the desired colors for the house and the trim, and may offer suggestions at several stages during the painting process. Different firms often want unique blends of insurance coverage, and the final policy may be developed after several meetings between the purchaser and the insurance agent. Although purchaser specifications also play a role in the creation of major products such as installations, the interaction of buyer and seller at both the production and distribution stages is a common feature of services.

Personal contact between salespeople and customers occurs in the marketing of goods as well as services; however, service representatives play an even more important role. One writer described it this way:

With service retailing there is a change in the sequence of events that occur—the sale must be made before production and consumption take place. Thus the truism that all customer contact employees are engaged in personal selling is much more real for the service firm than for the goods firm. With goods, the physical object can carry some of the selling burden. With services, contact personnel *are* the service. Customers, in effect, perceive them to be "the product." They become the physical representation of the offering. The service firm employees are both factory workers *and* salespersons because of the simultaneous production and consumption of most services.[14]

SUMMARY

A critical variable in the firm's marketing mix is the product it plans to offer its market target. The best price, most efficient distribution channel, and most effective promotional program cannot gain continuing purchases of an inferior product.

Consumers view products not only in physical terms but more often in terms of expected want satisfaction. The broad marketing conception of a product encompasses a bundle of physical, service, and symbolic attributes designed to produce this want satisfaction.

All successful products pass through the four stages of the product life cycle: introduction, growth, maturity, and decline. Consumers also go through a series of stages in adopting new product offerings: initial product awareness, interest, evaluation, trial purchase, and adoption or rejection of the product.

Although first adopters of new products vary among product classes, several common characteristics have been isolated. First adopters are often younger, better educated, and more mobile, and they have higher incomes and higher social status than later adopters.

The rate of adoption for new products depends on five characteristics: (1) relative advantage, the degree of superiority of the innovation over the previous product; (2) compatibility, the degree to which the new product or idea is consistent with the value system of potential purchasers; (3) complexity of the new product; (4) divisibility, the degree to which trial purchases on a small scale are possible; and (5) communicability, the degree to which the superiority of the innovation can be transmitted to other potential buyers.

Products are classified as either consumer or industrial goods. Consumer goods are used by the ultimate consumer and are not intended for resale or further use in producing other products. Industrial goods are used either directly or indirectly in producing other products for resale.

Differences in consumer buying habits can be used to further classify consumer goods into three categories: convenience goods, shopping goods, and specialty goods. Industrial goods are classified on the basis of product uses. The five categories in the industrial goods classification are installations, accessory equipment, fabricated parts and materials, raw materials, and industrial supplies.

Almost half of all personal consumption expenditures go to the purchase of services—intangible tasks that satisfy consumer and industrial user needs when efficiently developed and distributed to chosen market segments. The marketing of services has many similarities to the marketing of goods, but there are also significant differences. The key features of services are their intangibility and perishability, the difficulty of standardizing them, and the involvement of buyers in their development and distribution.

Once the firm's products have been classified, the marketing manager is provided with a number of insights in making decisions about distribution channels, price, and promotion—the three other variables of the marketing mix.

QUESTIONS FOR DISCUSSION

1. Explain the following terms:

product	shopping goods	raw materials
warranty	specialty goods	supplies
product life cycle	installations	MRO items
adoption process	accessory equip-	goods-services
consumer innovator	ment	continuum
diffusion process	industrial distributor	services
convenience goods	fabricated parts and	
impulse goods	materials	

2. Justify the inclusion of services in the definition of *product.*

3. Select a specific product in each stage of the product life cycle (other than those shown in Figure 8.3). Explain how the marketing strategies vary by life cycle stage for each product.

4. Suggest several means by which the life cycle of a product (such as Scotch tape) can be extended.

5. Identify and briefly explain the stages in the consumer adoption process.

6. Discribe each of the determinants of the rate of adoption.

7. Choose a newly introduced product with which you are familiar and make some positive suggestions to accelerate its adoption rate.

8. Suggest some practical uses for currently known facts about the consumer innovator.

9. Home burglar alarm systems using microwaves are the fastest-growing product in the home security market. Such systems operate by filling rooms with microwave beams, which set off alarms when an intruder intercepts one of them. What suggestions can you make to accelerate the rate of adoption for this product?

10. Why is the basis used for categorizing industrial goods different from that used for categorizing consumer goods?

11. Of what possible value is a classification scheme that allows an automobile tire to be both a consumer and an industrial good?

12. What determines whether a product is a consumer good or an industrial good?

13. Compare a typical marketing mix for convenience goods with a mix for specialty goods.

14. Give two illustrations from your own experience of each of the following kinds of goods: convenience goods, shopping goods, and specialty goods. Justify your classifications.

15. Explain how a suit can be a convenience good for one person, a shopping good for a second, and a specialty good for a third. Does this fact of life

destroy the validity of the consumer goods classification? Support your answer.

16. Classify the following consumer goods:
    a. furniture
    b. Puma running shoes
    c. felt-tip pen
    d. swimsuit
    e. Datsun sports car
    f. Binaca breath freshener
    g. *Sports Illustrated* magazine
    h. original oil painting

17. Outline the typical marketing mix for a shopping good.

18. Classify the following products into the appropriate industrial goods category. Briefly explain your choice for each product.
    a. calculators
    b. land
    c. light bulbs
    d. wool
    e. paper towels
    f. nylon
    g. airplanes
    h. tires

19. How will the marketing mix for installations differ from the mix for raw materials? Support your answer with specific illustrations.

20. Identify and explain the key features of services.

NOTES

1. Bill Paige, "Tuned in, Turned off, Personal Stereo Runs into a Little Static," *Orlando Sentinel Star,* November 16, 1981. Reprinted by permission of United Press International.

2. Janet Marr, "The Magnuson-Moss Warranty Act," *Family Economics Review,* Summer 1978, pp. 3–7.

3. Students of economics will recognize this situation as exemplifying price elasticity of demand. For a discussion of the concept of elasticity, see Edwin G. Dolan, *Basic Economics* (Hinsdale, Ill.: The Dryden Press, 1983).

4. See David R. Rink and John E. Swan, "Product Life Cycle Research: A Literature Review," *Journal of Business Research,* September 1979, pp. 219–42.

5. Everett M. Rogers and F. Floyd Shoemaker, *Communication of Innovation* (New York: The Free Press, 1971), pp. 135–57.

6. "Gillette Spends $17.4 Million to Introduce Aapri, Gain Foothold in Skin Care Market," *Marketing News,* May 29, 1981, p. 6. For a discussion of the use of marketing techniques to facilitate trial purchases, see James W. Taylor and Paul S. Hugstad, " 'Add-on' Purchasing: Consumer Behavior in the Trial of New Products," *Journal of the Academy of Marketing Science,* Winter 1980, pp. 294–99.

7. Ronald Marks and Eugene Hughes, "Profiling the Consumer Innovator," John H. Summey and Ronald D. Taylor, eds. *Evolving Marketing Thought for 1980* (New Orleans: Southern Marketing Association, 1980), pp. 115–18; Elizabeth Hirschman, "Innovativeness, Novelty Seeking and Consumer Creativity," *Journal of Consumer Research,* December 1980, pp. 283–95; and Richard W. Olshavsky, "Time and the Rate of Adoption of Innovations," *Journal of Consumer Research,* March 1980, pp. 425–28.

8. For a more thorough discussion of the speed of the adoption process, see Rogers and Shoemaker, *Communication of Innovations,* pp. 135–57.

9. This three-way classification of consumer goods was first proposed by Melvin T. Copeland. See his *Principles of Merchandising* (New York: McGraw-Hill, 1924), chapters 2–4. For a more recent discussion of this classification scheme, see Marvin A. Jolson and Stephen L. Proia, "Classification of Consumer Goods—A Subjective Measure?" in *Marketing: 1776–1976 and Beyond* (Chicago: American Marketing Association, 1976), pp. 71–75.

10. For an early discussion of the distinctions between homogeneous and heterogeneous shopping goods, see E. J. McCarthy, *Basic Marketing* (Homewood, Ill.: Richard D. Irwin, 1964), pp. 398–400. See also Harry A. Lipson and John R. Darling, *Marketing Fundamentals* (New York: Wiley, 1974), p. 244.

11. A similar classification scheme has been proposed by Leo Aspinwall, who considers five product characteristics in classifying consumer goods—*replacement rate, gross margin* (the difference between cost and selling price), *adjustment* (the necessary changes made in a goal to satisfy precisely the consumer's needs), *time of consumption* (the time interval during which the product

provides satisfaction), and length of consumer *searching time*. See Leo V. Aspinwall, "The Characteristics of Goods Theory," in *Four Marketing Theories* (Boulder: Bureau of Business Research, University of Colorado, 1961).

12.   Some of the information in this section is from Eugene M. Johnson, "The Selling of Services," in *Handbook of Modern Marketing,* ed. Victor P. Buell (New York: McGraw-Hill, 1970), pp. 12–110 to 12–120.

13.   A goods-services continuum is suggested in G. Lynn Shostack, "Breaking Free from Product Marketing," *Journal of Marketing,* April 1977, p. 77. See also John M. Rathmell, "What Is Meant by Services?" *Journal of Marketing,* October 1966, pp. 32–36.

14.   William R. George, "The Retailing of Services—A Challenging Future," *Journal of Retailing*, Fall 1977, pp. 89–90. Reprinted with permission.

CHAPTER 9

ELEMENTS OF PRODUCT/ SERVICE STRATEGY

KEY TERMS

product line
product manager
venture team
test marketing
brand
brand name
trademark
generic name
brand recognition
brand preference
brand insistence
family brand
individual brands
national brands
private brands
generic products
label

LEARNING GOALS

1. To explain the reasons most firms develop a line of related products rather than a single product

2. To identify and explain the four organizational arrangements for new-product development

3. To list the stages in the product development process

4. To identify the characteristics of a good brand name

5. To describe the major functions of the package

6. To explain the functions of the Consumer Product Safety Commission

By 1978, Robert Taylor was convinced that he could develop a superior alternative to bar soap, which fouls soap dishes, gets dirty and slippery, and shrinks or crumbles to a messy, barely usable sliver. Taylor's tiny company, Minnetonka, Inc., offered consumers a choice in the form of Softsoap, a liquid soap in a pump dispenser.

The mere idea of taking on such international giants as Procter & Gamble, Armour-Dial, Lever Brothers, and Colgate-Palmolive would have convinced most would-be marketers to seek out less risky avenues to success, but Taylor was convinced that his better idea could mean sales and profits in the $1-billion soap business. He tested his new product in a dozen cities prior to its national distribution in 1980 and sales exceeded his 5 percent market share goal. Guaranteed advertising expenditures of $6 million in 1980 was enough to convince 99 out of the top 100 grocery chains and all of the large nonfood retailers (K mart, Woolco, T.G.& Y., and Eckerd Drugs, among others) to stock the product, and first-year Softsoap sales reached $35 million.

By the end of 1981, the 10.5-ounce Softsoap had captured 6 percent of the total dollar volume of all soaps; Dial, the market leader, had about 14 percent. Although this market share represented outstanding growth, Softsoap marketers recognized that the total market potential was limited. Research studies revealed that consumers typically used liquid soaps at sinks rather than in tubs and showers—the places that account for about three-fourths of all soap use.

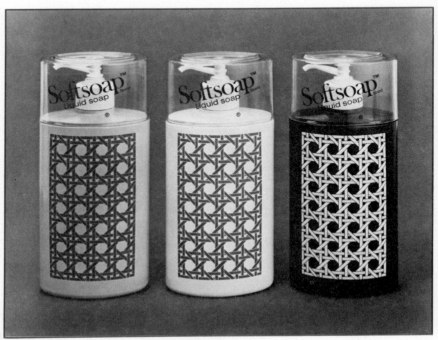

Source: Courtesy of Minnetonka, Inc., Minnetonka, Minnesota.

Another factor for Softsoap marketers to contend with was the growing number of competitors. If imitation is the sincerest form of flattery, Softsoap had every reason to feel flattered, for a total of 42 competitors had entered the market by 1981. Some imitators appeared to be carbon copies and the company was successful in eliminating some "me-too" products through legal action. Minnetonka Vice-President Wallace A. Marx compared the flurry of imitators with the introduction of Hamburger Helper in the early 1970s: "They [the competitors] all perished and only Hamburger Helper is left. The reason is that Hamburger Helper was the first with the most. It concentrated on building a consumer franchise with a product positioned for the mainstream of the consumer market. Softsoap is doing precisely the same."

Minnetonka marketers are already at work in an attempt to fashion a complete line of related products based on the liquid soap concept. Possibilities include a heavy-duty version called Worksoap; liquid baby soap for infants and people with sensitive skins; liquid soaps containing skin moisturizers; and even toothpaste in a pump dispenser.[1]

DEVELOPING A PRODUCT/ SERVICE STRATEGY

Developing a marketing strategy for a product or service involves several major elements. These include product line planning, the introduction of new products, the deletion of products from the product line, product identification, packaging, labeling, product safety, and product liability. Each of these decision variables represents an important area of responsibility for the marketing manager.

Athletes market their services to teams and to marketers.

"I can't get rid of the feeling they're going to trade me."

Source: Courtesy of Wall Street Journal and Cartoon Features Syndicate.

Product Line Planning

Firms who market only one product are rare today. Most offer their customers a **product line**—*a series of related products.* Polaroid Corporation, for example, began operations with a single product—a polarized screen for sunglasses and other products. Then, in 1948, it introduced the world's first instant camera. For the next thirty years, these products proved to be sufficient for annual sales and profit growth. By 1983, however, instant cameras accounted for only about two-thirds of Polaroid's sales. The company had added hundreds of products in both industrial and consumer markets, ranging from nearly 40 different types of instant films for various industrial, medical, and other technical operations, to batteries, sonar devices, and machine tools.[2] Several factors account for the inclination of firms such as Polaroid to develop a complete line rather than concentrate on a single product.

Desire to Grow A company places definite limitations on its growth potential when it concentrates on a single product. In a single 12-month period, Lever Brothers introduced 21 new products in its search for market growth and increased profits. A survey by Booz, Allen & Hamilton management consultants revealed that consumer-goods firms expect 25 to 35 percent of 1985 sales to be generated by newly developed products.[3]

Firms often introduce new products to offset seasonal variations in the sales of their current products. Since the majority of soup purchases are made during the winter months, Campbell Soup Company has made attempts to tap the warm-weather soup market. A line of fruit soups (to be served chilled) was test-marketed, but results showed that U.S. consumers were not yet ready for fruit soups. The firm continued to search for warm-weather soups, however, and in the 1980s it added gazpacho and other soups to be served chilled, to its product line.

Optimal Use of Company Resources By spreading the costs of company operations over a series of products, it may be possible to reduce the average costs of all products. The Texize Company started with a single household cleaner—and learned painful lessons about marketing costs when a firm has only one major product. Management rapidly added the products K2r and Fantastik to the line. The company's sales representatives can now call on middlemen with a series of products at little more than the cost of a single product. In addition, Texize's advertising produces benefits for all products in the line. Similarly, production facilities can be used economically in producing related products. Finally, the expertise of all the firm's personnel can be applied more widely to a line of products than to a single one.

Increasing Company Importance in the Market Consumers and middlemen often expect a firm that manufactures and markets small appliances to also offer related products under its brand name. The Maytag Company offers not only washing machines but also dryers, since con-

PRODUCT LINES MEAN GROWTH FOR THE ULTIMATE MARKETER

A survey to identify the world's best marketing company would probably reveal a single name: Procter & Gamble. The Cincinnati-based giant rings up over $11 billion in annual sales of consumer products ranging from its 104-year-old Ivory Soap to Jif peanut butter. In addition to marketing six of the top ten household products shown below, Procter & Gamble also has the leading dishwasher detergent (Cascade), dishwashing liquid (Ivory), and scouring cleanser (Comet). Its products also include two of the top ten shelf food products (Folger's regular coffee and 72-year-old Crisco shortening) and three of the ten leading health and beauty aids (Crest toothpaste, Head & Shoulders Shampoo, and Scope mouthwash). Its Duncan Hines baking mixes rank eleventh in food products.

This success record is not totally unblemished, however. Pringle's, the firm's uniformly shaped, canned potato chips, designed to solve the

Charts by Bob Alcorn. Data compiled by Selling Areas-Marketing, Inc.

traditional potato chip problems of shipping and limited shelf life, was a product failure. Rely tampons, which had quickly attracted 25 percent of the market, were withdrawn from the market in 1980 after being tentatively linked with a disease called toxic-shock syndrome.

What's next for Procter & Gamble? Rumors flourished that the firm would take on Coca-Cola and Pepsi-Cola when it acquired Crush International, makers of the concentrate for such products as Orange Crush and Hires Root Beer, in 1980. Analysis of P & G's patent applications reveal such amazing possibilities as a margarine that could reduce blood cholesterol; a dental product to eliminate plaque; and a possible cure for male baldness. Just imagine the markets for those products!

sumers often demand matching appliances. Gillette markets not only razors and blades but also a full range of grooming aids, including Foamy shave cream, Right Guard deodorant, Gillette Dry Look hair spray, and Super Max hair dryers.

The company with a line of products is often more important to both the consumer and the retailer than is the company with only one product. Shoppers who purchase a tent often buy related items such as tent heaters, sleeping bags and air mattresses, camping stoves, and special cookware. Recognizing this tendency, the Coleman Company now includes in its product line dozens of items associated with camping. The firm would be little-known if its only product were lanterns.

Exploiting the Product Life Cycle As its output enters the maturity and decline stages of the product life cycle, the firm must add new products if it is to prosper. The regular addition of new products to the firm's line helps ensure that it will not become a victim of product obsolescence. The development of stereophonic sound in the 1950s shifted high-fidelity phonographs from the maturity stage to the decline stage. And companies such as RCA, Magnavox, and Zenith began to develop new products utilizing stereo.[4]

INTRODUCING NEW PRODUCTS

Business has been compared to bicycling: In both, you either keep moving or you fall down. New and profitable products are the lifeblood of the business firm. But new-product introductions are also probably the most risky of the decision maker's responsibilities. A Conference Board study of 148 medium- and large-sized American manufacturing

FIGURE 9.1
Decay Curve of
New-Product Ideas

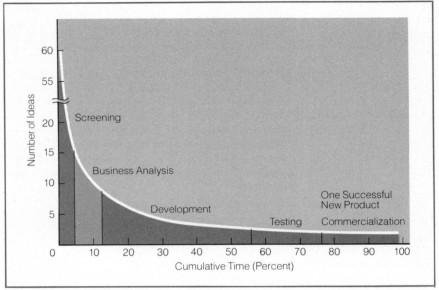

Source: Adapted by permission from *Management of New Products* (New York: Booz, Allen & Hamilton, 1968), p. 9.

companies revealed that one out of three new industrial and consumer products introduced within the past five years has failed. The leading cause of new-product failure was insufficient and poor marketing research.[5]

Dozens of new-product ideas are required to produce even one successful product. Booz, Allen & Hamilton surveyed fifty-one companies and reported its findings in the form of the product decay curve depicted in Figure 9.1. Of every fifty-eight ideas produced in these firms, only twelve passed the preliminary screening test designed to determine whether they were compatible with company resources and objectives. Of these twelve, only seven showed sufficient profit potential in the business analysis phase. Three survived the development phase, two made it through the test marketing stage, and only one, on the average, was commercially successful. Thus, of fifty-eight ideas, less than 2 percent resulted in a successful product.

What Is a New Product?

New products are not always major innovations such as digital watches or the Polaroid camera. They may merely involve a packaging innovation, such as pump dispensers, with the same ingredients as in the previous product. Or they may be an imitation of competitive products. In other words, a new product is simply a product new to either the company or its customers.

**Organizing for
New-Product
Introduction**

A prerequisite for efficient product innovations is an organizational arrangement designed to stimulate and coordinate new-product development. New-product development is a specialized task and requires the expertise of many departments.[6] A company that delegates new-product development responsibility to the engineering department often discovers that engineers sometimes design good products from a design standpoint but bad ones in terms of consumer needs. The major criticism of many new products is that they contain more quality than the consumer really wants to buy. Most successful medium- and large-sized companies assign new-product development to one or more of the following alternatives: new-product committees, new-product departments, product managers, or venture teams.

New-Product Committees The most common organizational arrangement for new-product development is the new-product committee. It is typically composed of representatives of top management in such areas as marketing, finance, manufacturing, engineering, research, and accounting. Committee members are less concerned with the conception and development of new-product ideas than with reviewing and approving new-product plans.

Since the committee members are key executives in the functional areas, their support for any new-product plan is likely to result in its approval for further development. However, new-product committees tend to be slow in making decisions and conservative in their views, and sometimes they compromise so members can get back to their regular company responsibilities.

New-Product Departments Many companies establish a separate, formally organized new-product department. The organization of a department overcomes the limitations of the new-product committee system and makes new-product development a permanent, full-time activity. The department is responsible for all phases of the product's development within the firm, including screening decisions, development of product specifications, and coordinating product testing. The head of the department has substantial authority and typically reports to the president or to the top marketing officer.

Product Managers For decades, product managers have been used in department stores, where they have complete responsibility for marketing a limited line of goods. However, except in a few firms—such as Johnson & Johnson and Procter & Gamble, where they are called brand managers—the product manager concept is a relatively new one for many manufacturing firms.

The typical **product manager** *is assigned one product or product line and is given complete responsibility for determining objectives and establishing marketing strategies for it.* The manager sets prices, devel-

THE GENERAL MILLS PRODUCT MANAGERS' FAMILY PORTRAIT

The concept of assigning one person responsibility for a single brand has been in existence since 1927, when Procter & Gamble made the first assignment for Camay soap. General Mills adopted the practice in the early 1960s. In the consumer food product categories, some 33 product managers collect relevant internal and external information, set goals, and plot strategies and tactics for such brands as Yoplait yogurt, Potato Buds, Betty Crocker cake mixes, Honey Nut Cheerios, Hamburger Helper, and Nature Valley Granola Bars. The young, ambitious men and women shown in the photo are responsible for the sales, market share, and profits of the brand they hold. The product managers presenting the "question" brands are involved in thinking up new products, naming them, and testing them in the marketplace.

It takes an average of three years for a newly hired graduate to work up to product manager at General Mills. Base salaries average $30,000 to $40,000 and the product manager is eligible for annual bonuses averaging 15 percent to 25 percent of base salary.

Source: The General Mills product management system is described in Ann M. Morrison, "The General Mills Brand of Managers," *FORTUNE,* January 12, 1981, pp. 99–107. © 1981 Time, Inc. All rights reserved. Photo courtesy of John Marmaras/Woodfin Camp and Associates.

ops advertising and sales promotion programs, and works with sales representatives in the field. Although the product manager has no line authority over the field sales force, the objective of increasing sales for the brand is the same, and the manager attempts to help the salespeople accomplish their task.

In multiproduct companies, product managers are key people in the marketing department. They provide individual attention to each product, while the firm as a whole has a single sales force, marketing research department, and advertising department that all product managers can utilize.

In addition to having primary responsibility for marketing a particular product or product line, the product manager is often responsible for new-product development, the creation of new-product ideas, and recommendations for improving existing products. These suggestions become the basis for proposals submitted to top management.

The product manager system is open to one of the same criticisms as the new-product committee: new-product development may get secondary treatment because of the manager's time commitments on existing products. Although a number of extremely successful new products have resulted from ideas submitted by product managers, it cannot be assumed that the skills required for marketing an existing product line are the same as those required for successfully developing new products.[7]

Venture Teams An increasingly common technique for organizing new-product development is the use of venture teams. One-third of the hundred largest U.S. industrial firms utilize venture teams, and at least twenty of these teams have been established within the last fifteen years.

The **venture-team** concept is *an organizational strategy for developing new-product areas by combining the management resources of technological innovations, capital, management, and marketing expertise.* Like new-product committees, venture teams are composed of specialists from different areas of the organization: engineering representatives for expertise in product design and the development of prototypes; marketing staff members for development of product concept tests, test marketing, sales forecasts, pricing, and promotion; and financial accounting representatives for detailed cost analyses and decisions concerning the concept's probable return on investment.

Unlike committees, venture teams do not disband after every meeting. Team members are assigned the project as a major responsibility, and teams possess the necessary authority to both plan and carry out a course of action.

As a means of stimulating product innovation, the team is typically separated from the permanent organization and linked directly with top management. The Cudahy Packing Company moved its three-member venture team from the Phoenix headquarters to a suite of offices in New York City. Since the venture team manager reports to the division head or the chief administrative officer, communication problems are minimized and high-level support is assured.

The venture team usually begins as a loosely organized group of members with a common interest in a new-product idea. The members often are given time during the workday to devote to the venture. If the team comes up with viable proposals, it is formally organized as a task force within a "venture department" for reporting to a vice-president or the chief executive officer.

The venture team must meet such criteria as prospective return on investment, uniqueness of the product, existence of a well-defined need, degree of the product's compatibility with existing technology, and strength of patent protection. Although the organization is considered temporary, the actual life span of venture teams is flexible, often extending over a number of years. When the commercial potential of new products has been demonstrated, the products may be assigned to an existing division, become a division within the company, or serve as the nucleus of a new company.

The flexibility and authority of the venture team allows large firms to develop the maneuverability of smaller companies. Venture teams established by Colgate-Palmolive have already broadened the base of the toiletries and detergents manufacturer into such products as freeze-dried flowers. Such teams also serve as an outlet for innovative marketing by providing a mechanism for translating research and development ideas into viable products:

> The venture team with its single mission, unstructured relationships, insulation from the daily routine, and entrepreneurial thrust is an organizational concept uniquely suited to the task of product innovation. For many companies whose future depends as much on the successful launching of new products as the successful marketing of existing ones, the venture-team concept offers a promising mechanism for more innovative marketing and the growth which it makes possible.[8]

Developing New Products

Once the firm has organized for new-product development, it can establish procedures for evaluating new-product ideas. The new-product development process involves six stages: (1) idea generation, (2) screening, (3) business analysis, (4) product development, (5) test marketing, and (6) commercialization. At each stage, management faces the decision to abandon the project, continue to the next stage, or seek additional information before proceeding further.[9]

Idea Generation New-product development begins with ideas that emanate from many sources: the sales force, customers who write letters asking "Why don't you . . .," marketing employees, research and development specialists, competitive products, retailers, and inventors outside the company. It is important for the firm to develop a system for stimulating new ideas and for rewarding persons who develop them.[10]

Screening This critical stage involves separating ideas with potential from those incapable of meeting company objectives. Some organizations use checklists to determine whether product ideas should be eliminated or subjected to further consideration. These checklists typically include such factors as product uniqueness; availability of raw materials; and compatibility of the proposed product with current product offerings, existing facilities, and capabilities. In other instances the screening stage consists of open discussions of new-product ideas among representatives of different functional areas in the organization. Screening is an important stage in the development process, since any product ideas that proceed beyond this stage will cost the firm time and money.[11]

Business Analysis Product ideas surviving the intitial screening are subjected to a thorough business analysis. The analysis involves an assessment of the potential market, its growth rate, and the likely competitive strength of the new product. Decisions must be made about the compatibility of the proposed product with such company resources as financial support for necessary promotion, production capabilities, and distribution facilities. The consideration of the product idea prior to its actual development is often referred to as *concept testing.*

Product Development Those product ideas with profit potential are converted into a physical product. The conversion process is the joint responsibility of the development engineering department, which turns the original concept into a product, and the marketing department, which provides feedback on consumer reactions to product designs, packages, colors, and other physical features. Numerous changes may be necessary before the original mock-up is converted into the final product.

The series of tests, revisions, and refinements should result ultimately in the introduction of a product with great likelihood of success. Some firms obtain the reactions of their own employees to proposed new-product offerings. Employees at Levi Strauss test new styles by wearing them and reporting on the various features. Thom McAn asks its workers to report regularly over an eight-week testing period on shoe wear and fit.

But occasional attempts to be the first with a new product result in the product's premature introduction. Kellogg and several other cereal makers experienced this problem several years ago when they all failed in their attempts to introduce freeze-dried fruit cereal. In the rush to be first on the market with the new offering, they did not perfect the product. The small, hard pellets of real fruit took too long to reconstitute in the bowl, and millions of bowls of cereal went into garbage cans.[12]

Test Marketing To determine consumer reactions to its product under normal conditions, many firms test market their new-product offerings. Up to this point, consumer information has been obtained by submitting free products to consumers, who then give their reactions. Other information may come from shoppers asked to evaluate competitive products. But test marketing is the first stage at which the product or service must perform in a real-life environment.

Test marketing is *the process of selecting a specific city or television-coverage area considered reasonably typical of the total market and introducing the product or service with a total marketing campaign in this area.* A carefully designed and controlled test allows management to estimate what sales will be on a full-scale introduction. Figure 9.2 indicates U.S. test-market cities frequently used by marketers.

Some firms omit the test marketing stage and move directly from product development to full-scale production. They cite four problems with test marketing:

1. Test marketing is expensive. As one marketing executive at Ralston Purina pointed out:

It's very difficult to run a little [test market] for six months or a year in three or four markets across the United States and then project what

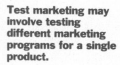

Test marketing may involve testing different marketing programs for a single product.

"Four years of research, and now you tell me you forgot which is the control group."

Source: Drawing by Gil Spitzer from *APA Monitor*, August 1971. Reprinted by permission of Gil Spitzer.

**FIGURE 9.2
Recommended Test
Markets**

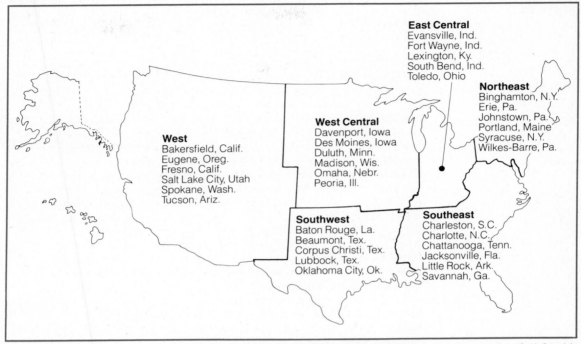

East Central
Evansville, Ind.
Fort Wayne, Ind.
Lexington, Ky.
South Bend, Ind.
Toledo, Ohio

Northeast
Binghamton, N.Y.
Erie, Pa.
Johnstown, Pa.
Portland, Maine
Syracuse, N.Y.
Wilkes-Barre, Pa.

West Central
Davenport, Iowa
Des Moines, Iowa
Duluth, Minn.
Madison, Wis.
Omaha, Nebr.
Peoria, Ill.

West
Bakersfield, Calif.
Eugene, Oreg.
Fresno, Calif.
Salt Lake City, Utah
Spokane, Wash.
Tucson, Ariz.

Southwest
Baton Rouge, La.
Beaumont, Tex.
Corpus Christi, Tex.
Lubbock, Tex.
Oklahoma City, Ok.

Southeast
Charleston, S.C.
Charlotte, N.C.
Chattanooga, Tenn.
Jacksonville, Fla.
Little Rock, Ark.
Savannah, Ga.

Source: Reported in Janet Neiman, "Grocers Look Beyond Data," *Advertising Age,* February 9, 1981, p. S–12. Copyright 1981 by Crain Communications, Inc. Reprinted with permission.

your sales volume is going to be two or three years in the future, mainly because you're testing in such small localities, generally to keep your costs down.

You simply can't afford to test your product in markets like New York, Philadelphia, Los Angeles. So you run your test in Tucson, Arizona; Fort Wayne, Indiana; Fresno, California. And your test costs are over $1 million even in places like that.[13]

2. Competitors who learn about the test market often disrupt the findings by reducing the price of their products in the test area, distributing cents-off coupons, installing attractive in-store displays, or giving additional discounts to retailers to induce them to display more of their products. In a recent court settlement Hartz Mountain agreed not to engage in advertising designed to disrupt the test of a new pet product by a subsidiary of A. H. Robins.

3. Long-lived durable goods such as dishwashers, hair dryers, and videodisc players are seldom test-marketed due to the major fi-

WRECKING TEST MARKET RESULTS

Many competitors have been known to disrupt test market results through price cuts, free sample offers, use of coupon offers, and special dealer allowances. But Edward Buxton lists several other steps sometimes used by unethical competitors to discourage new product tests:

> They'll take other steps, too, that are not so open. For example, sending in salesmen who, while supposedly checking stock, will rearrange the new brand into bottom-shelf positions. Rearranging gambits are varied. Someone will see that his competitor has moved in a handsome new stand-up rack neatly stacked with his stack products. The wily competitor will, if unobserved, remove the top few rows of merchandise and put in his own. Or maybe it's a jumble display, a full bin of his competitor's products at a choice end-of-the-aisle location. The alert competitive salesman will sprinkle his own wares over the top of this bin. Another trick often used in the dairy cabinets is to rearrange a competitive milk brand so that the fresh milk is always up front. Customarily, when a driver salesman leaves off new milk in the morning, he will put yesterday's leftovers up front so that they will move out before turning bad. By pushing these to the back again, the competitor may succeed in getting some customers to buy sour milk under his rival's label. Another dairy-case trick: the competitive salesman will wear a special ring with a pin sticking out of the setting. As he stocks his own milk, his wrist will snap left and right as he punches tiny holes in the paper containers of his rival's brand. Grocers hate "leakers." The brand is dropped after a few such days.

Such unethical practices have come to the attention of the Federal Trade Commission. A study is currently underway to determine the extent of such practices and FTC penalties to be imposed on perpetrators of such activities.

Source: These practices are discussed in B. G. Yovovich, "Competition Jumps the Gun," *Advertising Age,* February 9, 1981, p. S–21. The quotation is from Edward Buxton, *Promise Them Anything* (New York: Stein & Day, 1972), pp. 88–89.

nancial investment required for development; the need to develop a network of dealers to distribute the products; and the parts and servicing required. A company such as Whirlpool invests from $1 million to $3 million in the development of a new refrigerator. To develop each silicon chip that performs a single function in an Apple microcomputer costs approximately $1 million and takes from one year to fifteen months. Producing a prototype for a test market is simply too expensive, so the "go/no go" decision for the new durable product is typically made without the benefit of test market results.[14]

4. Test marketing a new product or service communicates company plans to competitors prior to its introduction. Kellogg discovered a new product with suspected sales potential by learning of the test marketing of a new fruit-filled tart designed to be heated in the toaster and served for breakfast. Kellogg rushed a similar product into full-scale production and became the first national marketer of the product they named Pop Tarts. Other test-marketed products beaten into the national market by competitors include Helene Curtis' Arm in Arm deodorant (preempted by Church & Dwight's Arm & Hammer deodorant); General Food's Maxim (Nestle's Taster's Choice); Hills Bros. High Yield Coffee (Procter & Gamble's Folger's Flakes); and Hunt-Wesson's Prima Salsa tomato sauce (Chesebrough-Pond's Ragu Extra Thick & Zesty).[15]

Marketers' decision to skip the test marketing stage should be based on the conclusion that the new product or service has an extremely high likelihood of success. The cost of developing a new detergent, for example, from idea generation to national marketing has been estimated at $25 million! Even if a company experiences losses on a product or service that fails at the test marketing stage, the firm saves itself from incurring even greater losses—and embarrassment—in the total market. Otherwise, the product or service may join the ranks of such monumental failures as Du Pont's Corfam synthetic leather with losses of more than $100 million, or Polaroid's ill-fated Polavision instant movies system, whose development and production costs were estimated at between $200 million and $500 million.[16]

Commercialization The few product ideas that survive all the steps in the development process are ready for full-scale marketing. Marketing programs must be established, outlays for necessary production facilities must be made, and the sales force, middlemen, and potential customers must be made acquainted with the new product. A systematic approach to new-product development is essential.

Systematic planning of all phases of new-product development and introduction can be accomplished through the use of such scheduling methods as the Program Evaluation and Review Technique (PERT) and the Critical Path Method (CPM). These techniques, developed originally by the U.S. Navy in connection with construction of the Polaris missile and submarine, map out the sequence in which each step must be taken and show the time allotments for each activity. Detailed PERT and CPM flowcharts coordinate all activities involved in the development and introduction of new products.

As Table 9.1 indicates, new-product development and introduction can take many years. A study of the elapsed time between initial development and full-scale introduction of forty-two products revealed a time lag ranging from one year for Gerber strained baby food to fifty-five years for television. Since the time needed for orderly development

**TABLE 9.1
Elapsed Time
between Initial
Development and
Full-Scale
Introduction**

Product	Years
Strained baby food	1
Filter cigarettes	2
Frozen orange juice	2
Polaroid Land Camera	2
Dry dog food	4
Electric toothbrush	4
Plastic tile	6
Roll-on deodorant	6
Stripe toothpaste	6
Liquid shampoo	8
Fluoride toothpaste	10
Freeze-dried instant coffee	10
Penicillin	15
Polaroid Color-pack Camera	15
Xerox electrostatic copier	15
Transistors	16
Minute rice	18
Instant coffee	22
Zippers	30
Television	55

Source: Adapted from Lee Adler, "Time Lag in New Product Development," *Journal of Marketing,* January 1966, pp. 17–21. Used by permission of the American Marketing Association.

of new products can be longer than expected, the planning horizon for new-product ideas may have to be extended five to ten years into the future.[17]

PRODUCT DELETION DECISIONS

Although many firms devote a great deal of time and resources to the development of new products, the thought of eliminating old ones is painful for many executives. Often, sentimental attachments to marginal products with declining sales prevent objective decisions to drop them.

To avoid waste, product lines must be pruned and old, marginal products must eventually be eliminated. Marketers typically face this decision during the late maturity and early decline stages of the product life cycle. Periodic reviews of weak products should be conducted in order to eliminate them or to justify retaining them.

In some instances, a firm will continue to carry an unprofitable product so as to provide a complete line of goods for its customers. Even though most grocery stores lose money on bulky, low unit-value items such as salt, they continue to carry them to meet shopper demand.

Shortages of raw materials have prompted some companies to discontinue the production and marketing of previously profitable items. Due to such shortages, Du Pont dropped Zerex antifreeze from its product line and Alcoa discontinued its Alcoa aluminum foil.

In other cases, profitable products are dropped because they fail to fit into the firm's existing product line. The introduction of automatic washing machines necessitated the development of low-sudsing detergents. Monsanto produced the world's first detergent of this sort—All—in the 1950s. All was an instant success, and Monsanto was swamped with orders from supermarkets throughout the nation. But the Monsanto sales force was primarily involved in marketing industrial chemicals to large-scale buyers, and the company would have needed a completely new sales force to handle the product. Nine months after the introduction of All, Procter & Gamble introduced the world's second low-sudsing detergent, Dash. The Procter & Gamble sales force handled hundreds of products and could spread the cost of contacting dealers over all of them. Monsanto had only All. Rather than attempt to compete, Monsanto sold All in 1958 to Lever Brothers, a Procter & Gamble competitor that had a marketing organization capable of handling the product.

PRODUCT IDENTIFICATION

Manufacturers identify their products with brand names, symbols, and distinctive packaging. So also do certain large retailers, such as J.C. Penney and Sears. Almost every product distinguishable from another contains a means of identification for the buyer. Even a five-year-old child can distinguish a Chiquita brand banana from a Dole banana. The California Fruit Growers Exchange literally brands its oranges with the name *Sunkist.* The purchasing agent for a construction firm can turn over an ordinary sheet of aluminum and find the name and symbol for Alcoa. Choosing the means of identifying the firm's output represents a major decision for the marketing manager.

Brands, Brand Names, and Trademarks

A **brand** is *a name, term, sign, symbol, design, or some combination used to identify the products of one firm and to differentiate them from competitive offerings.* A **brand name** is *that part of the brand consisting of words or letters that comprise a name used to identify and distinguish the firm's offerings from those of competitors.*[18] It is, therefore, that part of the brand which can be vocalized. A **trademark** is *a brand that has been given legal protection; the protection is granted solely to the brand's owner.* Thus the term trademark includes not only the pictorial design but also the brand name. More than 400,000 trademarks are currently registered in the United States.

For the consumer, the process of branding allows repeat purchases of the same product, since the product is identified with the name of the firm producing it. The purchaser thus can associate the satisfaction derived from a hot dog, for example, with the brand name "Corn King Franks."

For the marketing manager, the brand serves as the cornerstone of the product's image. Once consumers have been made aware of a particular brand, its appearance becomes further advertising for the firm. Shell Oil's symbol of a seashell is instant advertising to motorists who view it while driving.

Well-known brands also allow the firm to escape some of the rigors of price competition. Although any chemist will confirm that all brands of aspirin contain the same amount of the chemical acetylsalicylic acid, Bayer has developed so strong a reputation that it can successfully market its aspirin at a higher price than competitive products. Well-known gasoline brands typically sell at slightly higher prices than independent brands because many purchasers feel that they are marketing higher-quality gasoline.

What Constitutes a Good Brand Name? Good brand names are easy to pronounce, recognize, and remember. Short names like Busch, Gleem, Klear, and Off! meet these requirements. Multinational marketing firms face a particularly acute problem in selecting brand names; an excellent brand name in one country may prove disastrous in another. When Standard Oil decided to reduce its number of gasoline brands from three (Esso, Enco, and Humble) to one, company officials ruled out Enco, because in Japanese the word means "stalled car." The ultimate choice was Exxon—a unique, distinctive name.

Every language has "o" and "k" sounds, and "okay" has become an international word. Every language also has a short "a," so that Coca-Cola and Texaco are effective brands in any country. An advertising campaign for E-Z washing machines failed in the United Kingdom, however, because the British pronounce z as zed.

For 21 years, Nissan Motor Corporation marketers struggled with an easily mispronounced brand name for its Datsun cars and trucks. Though an effective name in Japan, Datsun encountered difficulty in the United States and other English-speaking nations, where some people pronounced the a like the a in hat, while others pronounced it like the o in got. Finally, Nissan marketers decided to change the name of all of its automobile products to Nissan, beginning with its Stanza model in 1982 (Figure 9.3). Total costs of the change—to be effected in more than 135 countries—are estimated as high as $150 million.[19]

The brand name should give the buyer the right connotation. Country Club malt liquor presents favorable images of leisure lifestyles. The Tru-Test name used on the True Value Hardware line of paints also produces the desired image. Accutron suggests the quality of the high-priced and accurate timepiece sold by Bulova. But sometimes brand names are ineffective. Research conducted several years ago by the Cities Service Company revealed that a large number of gasoline buyers vaguely associated the brand name Cities Service with some type of public utility. In addition, the name was too long to display on billboards. Cities Service decided to change its name to a five-letter word beginning with CIT. After considering several hundred possibilities, its management selected the name CITGO

FIGURE 9.3
The Stanza Helped Change Brand Name Recognition from "Datsun" to "Nissan."

Source: Courtesy of Nissan Motor Corporation, U.S.A.

and enclosed it in a new three-tone red triangle. The total cost of changing the brand name was approximately $20 million. Cities Service sales increased 11 percent the following year, compared with an industry average of 6 percent. Credit for the marked sales improvement was given to a revitalized marketing program, but the new, modern brand CITGO was the visible symbol of the changing company.

TRADEMARK INFRINGEMENT QUIZ

The Lanham Act grants exclusive usage of specified trademarks to their owners. Such marks assist consumers by allowing them to distinguish between a preferred product and those of competitors. Yet many trademarks are quite similar in sound, color, or appearance. In instances of possible trademark infringement, a legal decision must be made. The following examples are actual trademark cases in which decisions have been reached. In which of these instances would you have ruled that trademark infringement has occurred? (Answers are printed upside down below.)

Court Case	(Circle Your Choice) A Case of Trademark Infringement?	
1. *Jockey* men's underwear and hosiery vs. *Jockey* shoe polish	YES	NO
2. *Mustang* automobiles vs. *Mustang* mobile homes	YES	NO
3. *All* detergent vs. *All Out* rust remover	YES	NO
4. Miller *Lite* beer vs. Budweiser *Light*	YES	NO
5. *Space Saver* clothes drying racks vs. *Space Server* belt and tie hangers	YES	NO
6. *Pepsi* soft drinks vs. *Pepsup* barbecue sauce	YES	NO
7. *Triox* insecticides vs. *Tri-X* fertilizer	YES	NO
8. *Dial* soap vs. *Di-All* insecticide (with clock dial on label)	YES	NO
9. *English Leather* toiletries vs. *London Leather* toiletries	YES	NO
10. *Pepsodent* dentrifice vs. *Pearlident* dentrifice	YES	NO

Answers: (1) Yes; (2) No; (3) No; (4) No; (5) Yes; (6) No; (7) Yes; (8) No; (9) Yes; (10) Yes.

Source: Adapted from Richard H. Buskirk, *Principles of Marketing* (Hinsdale, Ill.: The Dryden Press, 1975), pp. 268–71. Used by permission of the author.

Also, the brand name must be legally protectable. The *Lanham Act* (1946) states that registered trademarks must not contain words in general use, such as automobile or suntan lotion. These generic words actually describe a particular type of product and thus cannot be granted exclusively to any company.

When a unique product becomes generally known by its original brand name, the brand name may be ruled a descriptive **generic name;** if this occurs, the original owner loses exclusive claim to it. The generic names *nylon, aspirin, escalator, kerosene,* and *zipper* were once brand names. Other generic names that were once brand names are cola, yo-yo, linoleum, and shredded wheat.

There is a difference between brand names that are legally generic and those that are generic in the eyes of many consumers. *Jell-O* is a brand name owned exclusively by General Foods. But to most consumers, the name *Jell-O* is the descriptive generic name for gelatin desserts. Legal brand names, like *Jell-O,* are often used by consumers as descriptive names. *Xerox* is such a well-known brand name that it is frequently—and incorrectly—used as a verb. Many British and Australian consumers use the brand name *Hoover* as a verb for vacuuming.

To prevent their brand names from being ruled descriptive and available for general use, most owners take steps to inform the public of their exclusive ownership of the name. Coca-Cola uses the ® symbol for registration immediately after the name *Coca-Cola* and *Coke* and sends letters to newspapers, novelists, and others who use Coke with a lower-case first letter informing them that the name is owned by Coca-Cola.[20] These companies face the dilemma of attempting to retain exclusive rights to a brand name when it is generic to a large part of the market. Many firms are taking positive steps to protect their brand names.

Since any dictionary name may eventually be ruled generic, some companies create new words for their brand names. Names such as Tylenol, Keds, Rinso, and Kodak have been created by their owners.

Measuring Brand Acceptance Brands vary widely in consumer familiarity and acceptance. While a boating enthusiast may insist on a Johnson outboard motor, one study revealed that 40 percent of U.S. homemakers could not identify the brands of furniture in their own homes. Brand acceptance can be measured in three stages: brand recognition, brand preference, and brand insistence.

Brand recognition is *a company's first objective for its newly introduced products—to make them familiar to the consuming public.* Often, this is achieved through offers of free samples or discount coupons for purchases. Several new brands of toothpaste have been introduced on college campuses in free sample kits called Campus Pacs. Once consumers have used a product, it moves from the unknown to the known category, and the probability of its being repurchased is increased—provided the consumer was satisfied with the trial sample.

Brand preference is the second stage of brand acceptance. In this stage, *consumers, relying on previous experience with the product, will choose it over its competitors—if it is available.* Although the students in a classroom may prefer Coca-Cola as a means of quenching their thirst, almost all of them will quickly switch to Pepsi-Cola or 7-Up when they discover the vending machine has no Cokes and the nearest supply is two buildings away. Companies with products at the brand preference stage are in a favorable position for competing in their industry.

Brand insistence, the last stage in brand acceptance, is *that situation in which consumers will accept no alternatives and will search extensively for the product.* A product at this stage has achieved a monopoly position with that particular group of consumers. Although brand insistence is the goal of many firms, it is seldom achieved. Only the most exclusive specialty goods attain this position with a large segment of the total market.

Choosing a Brand Strategy Brands can be classified as family brands or individual brands. A **family brand** is *one brand name used for several related products.* Norton Simon markets hundreds of food products under the Hunt brand. General Electric has a complete line of kitchen appliances under the GE name. Johnson & Johnson offers a line of baby powder, lotions, disposable diapers, plastic pants, and baby shampoo under one name.

On the other hand, a manufacturer may market hundreds of **individual brands,** *items known by their own brand names rather than by the names of the companies producing them or by an umbrella name covering similar items.* Lever Brothers, for example, markets Aim, Close-Up, and Pepsodent toothpaste; All and Wisk laundry detergents; Imperial margarine; Caress, Dove, Lifebuoy, and Lux bath soaps; and Shield deodorant soap. Individual brands are more expensive to market because a new promotional program must be developed to introduce each new product to its market target.

When family brands are used, any promotional outlay benefits all the products in the line. For instance, a new addition to the Heinz line gains immediate recognition because the family brand is well known. Use of family brands also makes it easier to introduce the product to the customer and to the retailer. Since grocery stores stock an average of more than 10,000 items, they are reluctant to add new products unless they are convinced of potential demand. A marketer of a new brand of turtle soup would have to promise the grocery store buyer huge advertising outlays for promotion and evidence of consumer buying intent before getting the product into the stores. With its U.S. market share of approximately 65 percent, Campbell Soup Company could merely add turtle soup to its existing line and secure store placements more easily than could another company with individual brand names.

Family brands should be used only when the products are of similar quality, or the firm will risk harming its product image. Using the Mercedes-Benz brand name on a new, less expensive auto might severely tarnish the image of the other models in the Mercedes-Benz product line.

Also, individual brand names should be used for dissimilar products. Campbell Soup Company once marketed a line of dry soups under the brand name Red Kettle. Large marketers of grocery products—such as Procter & Gamble, General Foods, and Lever Brothers—employ individual brands to appeal to unique market segments. These brands also enable the firm to stimulate competition within the organization and to increase total company sales. Consumers who do not want Tide can choose Cheer, Dash, or Oxydol rather than purchase a competitor's brand.

National Brands or Private Brands? Most of the brands mentioned in this chapter have been *brands offered by manufacturers*—commonly termed **national brands**. But, to an increasing extent, large wholesalers and retailers operating over a regional or national market are placing their own brands on the products they market. *The brands offered by wholesalers and retailers* are usually called **private brands**.[21] Sears, the nation's largest retailer, sells its own brands—Kenmore, Craftsman, DieHard, and Harmony House.

Private brands allow large retailers such as Bloomingdale's, Neiman-Marcus, Safeway, and Sears to establish an image and to maintain control over the products they handle. Neiman-Marcus estimates total annual sales of $10 million with its Red River brand of cowboy hats, women's clothing, and Western wear. Retailers or wholesalers who develop their own line of private brands assume the responsibility for product quality, price, and availability.

Even though the manufacturers' brands are largely presold through national promotional efforts, the wholesaler and retailer can easily lose customers when the same products are available in competing stores. Exclusive retailers such as Saks Fifth Avenue, Lord & Taylor, and Neiman-Marcus have problems maintaining their image of exclusivity when hundreds of department stores and specialty shops stock Calvin Klein shirts and Pierre Cardin neckties. So a fashion store such as Bloomingdale's offers designer pants with the store's name on the rear pocket. By eliminating the promotion costs of the manufacturers' brands, the dealer can usually offer a private brand at prices lower than that of the competing national brands. In Bloomingdale's case, a best-selling pair of Bloomingdale's women's pants retails at $26 as compared with about $40 for such competing designer brands as Calvin Klein or Liz Claiborne.[22]

Generic Products and Lower Prices One result of the continuing world-wide inflation and subsequent rising prices for consumer goods has been the introduction of **generic products**—*food and household staples characterized by plain labels, little or no advertising, and no brand names.* Generic products were first sold in Europe, where their prices were as much as 30 percent below brand name products. By 1980, they had captured 40 percent of total volume in European supermarkets.

This new version of private brands has received some acceptance in the United States. Surveys indicate that both professional, college-educated consumers and lower-income, blue-collar consumers are heavy purchasers of generics. Canned vegetables are the most commonly purchased generic product, followed by fruits and paper goods. Shoppers are indicating some willingness to forego the known quality levels of regular brands in exchange for the lower prices of the generics.[23]

Battle of the Brands Competition between manufacturers' brands and the private brands offered by wholesalers and large retailers has been called the battle of the brands. Although the battle appears to be intensifying, the marketing impact varies widely among industries. One survey showed that private brands represented 36 percent of the market in replacement tires but only 7 percent in portable appliances. Private brands account for 52 percent of shoe sales but only 15 percent of gasoline sales.

The growth of private brands has paralleled the growth of chain stores in the United States, most of which has occurred since the 1930s. Chains that market their own brands become customers of the manufacturer, which places the chains' private brand names on the products it produces.

Such leading manufacturers as Westinghouse, Armstrong Rubber, and Heinz are obtaining larger and larger percentages of their total income through selling private label goods. Private label sales to Sears and other major customers account for two-thirds of Whirlpool's sales.

Polaroid recently began manufacturing private label instant cameras for Sears. Witco Chemical Company, the nation's largest producer of private brand detergents, recently introduced its own brand—Active. This brand now competes with Witco brands sold by Safeway, Jewel, and other grocery chains, which places Witco in the position of competing with its own customers. Although some manufacturers refuse to produce private brand goods, most regard such production as reaching another segment of the total market.

Great inroads have been made on the dominance of the manufacturers' national brands. Private brands and generics have proven that they can compete with national brands and have often succeeded in causing price reductions on the national brands to make them more competitive.

PACKAGING

Packaging represents a vital component of the total product concept. Its importance can be inferred from the size of the packaging industry. Approximately $50 billion is spent annually on packaging in the United States, and the industry is comparable in size with the automobile and meat-packing industries. With about a million workers, the package-making industry is one of the nation's largest industrial employers.

The package has several objectives. First, it must offer physical protection for the product. The typical product is handled several times between manufacture and consumer purchase, and its package must protect the contents against damage.

Second, packaging assists in marketing the product. In a grocery store containing as many as 15,000 different items, it must capture the shopper's attention. Walter Margulies, chairman of Lippincott & Margulies advertising, summarizes the importance of first impressions in the retail store: "Consumers are more intelligent, but they don't read as much. They relate to pictures." Margulies also cites another factor: One of every six shoppers who needs eyeglasses does not wear them while shopping. Consequently, many marketers offering product lines are adopting similar package designs in order to create more visual impact in the store. Packaging Stouffer's frozen foods in orange boxes and the adoption of common package designs by such product lines as Weight Watchers foods and Planter's nuts represent attempts to dominate larger sections of retail stores as Campbell's Soup does.[24]

A third packaging objective is convenience. Pump dispenser cans facilitate the use of products ranging from mustard to insect repellent. Pop-top cans provide added convenience for soft drinks, beer, and other food products. The six-pack carton, first introduced by Coca-Cola in the 1930s, can be carried with minimal effort by the food shopper.

Another important role provided by many packages for the retailer is in preventing pilferage. At the retail level, pilferage is estimated to cost retailers $9 million each day. Many products are packaged with oversized cardboard backing too large to fit into a shoplifter's pocket or purse. Large plastic packages are used in a similar manner on such products as 8-track and cassette tapes.

A growing number of firms provide increased consumer utility with packages designed for reuse. Peanut butter jars and jelly jars have long been used as drinking glasses. Bubble bath can be purchased in plastic bottles shaped like animals and suitable for bathtub play. Packaging is a major component in Avon's overall marketing strategy. The firm's decorative reusable bottles have even become collectibles.

Although packaging must perform a number of functions for the marketer and consumer, it must accomplish them at a reasonable cost. Packaging currently represents the single largest item in the cost of producing a can of beer. Packaging accounts for 70 percent of the total cost of the single-serving packets of sugar found in restaurants.

The many objectives of packaging coupled with the significant costs involved have resulted in increased professionalism of packaging specialists. The package designers of the 1980s frequently use marketing research in testing alternative designs. Increasingly scientific approaches are utilized in designing a package that is attractive, safe, and esthetically appealing.

The Metric System's Effect on Packaging

Marketers in the United States are increasingly adopting the metric system. This standard of weights and measures is used throughout most of the world. 7-Up now comes in half-liter and liter bottles as a substitute for pints and quarts. Some canned and packaged foods list metric equivalents to ounces and pounds on their labels. Mustangs equipped with 2.3-liter engines are being powered by motors designed entirely in metric measurements.

International marketers are making the switch to enable them to compete in a metric world. Such firms as Caterpillar Tractor, John Deere, International Harvester, and IBM have been using metrics for years in their foreign trade. The switch to metrics should increase export sales by small U.S. firms that cannot afford to produce two sets of products for different markets.

Labeling

Although in the past the label was often a separate item applied to the package, most of today's plastic packages contain it as an integral part of the package. Labels perform both promotional and informational functions. A **label** in most instances *contains the brand name or symbol, the name and address of the manufacturer or distributor, the product composition and size, and recommended uses for the product.*

Consumer confusion and dissatisfaction over such incomprehensible sizes as "giant economy size," "king size," and "family size" led to the passage of the *Fair Packaging and Labeling Act* (1966). The act requires a label to offer adequate information concerning the package contents, and a package design that facilitates value comparisons among competitive products.

Food and Drug Administration regulations require that the nutritional contents be listed on the label of any food product to which a nutrient has been added or for which a nutritional claim has been made. Figure 9.4 shows a food product label listing the nutritional ingredients.

FIGURE 9.4
Product Label with Specified Nutritional Contents

Source: Reprinted by permission of Yoplait, USA, Inc.

Voluntary packaging and labeling standards have also been developed in a number of industries. As a result, the number of toothpaste sizes was reduced from fifty-seven to five and the number of dry detergent sizes from twenty-four to six. In other industries—such as drug, food, fur, and clothing—federal legislation has been enacted to force companies to provide information and to prevent branding that misleads the consumer. The marketing manager in such industries must be fully acquainted with these laws and must design packages and labels in compliance with them.

PRODUCT SAFETY

If the product is to fulfill its mission of satisfying consumer needs, it must, above all, be safe. Manufacturers must design their products in such a way as to protect not only children but all consumers who use them. Packaging plays an important role in product safety. Aspirin bottle tops have been made child-proof (and virtually parent-proof) by St. Joseph's and Bayer since 1968. This safety feature is estimated to have reduced by two-thirds the number of children under five years of age who have swallowed accidental doses of aspirin.

Prominently placed safety warnings on the labels of such potentially hazardous products as cleaning fluids and drain cleaners inform users of the dangers of these products and urge them to store the products out of the reach of children. Changes in product design have reduced the dangers involved in the use of such products as lawn mowers, hedge trimmers, and toys.

Federal and state legislation has long played a major role in promoting product safety. Many of the piecemeal federal laws passed over a period of fifty years were unified by the *Consumer Product Safety Act* (1972). The act created what has become one of the nation's most powerful regulatory agencies—the Consumer Product Safety Commission (CPSC). The new agency has assumed jurisdiction over every consumer product except food, automobiles, and a few other products already regulated by other agencies.

The CPSC has the authority to ban products without a court hearing, order the recall or redesign of products, and inspect production facilities; and it can charge managers of accused companies with criminal offenses. Its national toll-free "hot line" (800-638-8326) received more than 30,000 consumer inquiries and complaints in the four-month period following its installation. Research on consumer accidents produced the "twenty most dangerous products" list shown in Table 9.2.

The CPSC has been active in developing and enforcing rules designed to reduce these injuries.

Already the CPSC is enforcing rules about aspirin bottles, refrigerator-door latches, children's pajamas, and the distance between the slats of cribs. It has issued warnings about such disparate products as mobile homes (they seem to abound in fire hazards), tricycles (they tip over), and sandals made of water-buffalo hide imported from India

**TABLE 9.2
The Twenty Most
Dangerous
Consumer Products**

Rank	Item	National Estimates of Injuries Requiring Emergency Room Treatment (in thousands)
1	Stairs, steps, ramps, and landings	683
2	Bicycles and bicycle accessories	514
3	Baseball	446
4	Football	443
5	Basketball	422
6	Skating	237
7	Nails, tacks, and screws	230
8	Chairs, sofas, and sofa beds	210
9	Nonglass tables	202
10	Glass doors, windows, and panels	196
11	Beds	168
12	Playground equipment	162
13	Cutlery and knives	143
14	Glass bottles and jars	129
15	Lumber	124
16	Swimming	116
17	Desks, cabinets, shelves, bookcases, and footlockers	115
18	Drinking glasses	108
19	Fences	95
20	Soccer	93

Note that the estimates represent product involvement in injuries and may not indicate causality.
Source: U.S. Consumer Product Safety Commission, *1980 Annual Report: Fiscal Year 1980* (Washington, D.C.: U.S. Government Printing Office, 1981), pp. A2-A4.

(they can give you a rash). In the near future the commission is likely to publish edicts governing the design or use of swimming-pool slides, aluminum electrical wiring, architectural glass, book matches, power lawn mowers, and pacifiers. In time, virtually every sector of the American economy will feel the impact of this extraordinary regulatory enterprise.[25]

Product Liability: A Growing Concern

A parallel development to the increased concern for product safety has been the tremendous increase in product liability suits. The number of claims against producers or retailers of allegedly unsafe or defective products has jumped from 50,000 in 1960 to more than a million in 1977. Although many of these claims are settled out of court, others are decided by juries who have sometimes awarded multimillion-dollar settlements.

In a five-year period during the late 1970s, the average amount of damages sought rose from $476,000 to $1.7 million. In 1978, a jury awarded a judgment of $128.5 million against Ford Motor Company in an accident case involving a Pinto. A judge later reduced the total to $6.1 million.

Not only have marketers stepped up efforts to ensure product safety, but product liability insurance has become an essential ingredient in any new or existing product strategy. Premiums for this insurance have risen at an alarming rate, and in some cases coverage is almost impossible to obtain. A Detroit producer of components for pleasure boats discovered that its liability insurance premiums had increased from $2,500 to $160,000 in a two-year period—even though the insurance company had never paid a claim on the firm's behalf. Several manufacturers of football helmets discontinued production in recent years due to the unavailability of the insurance.[26]

Efforts are underway in several states to exempt companies from liability for injuries or property loss resulting from misuse of the products or from customer negligence. Such an exemption would have protected the retailer who recently paid damages to two men hurt by a lawn mower they lifted off the ground to trim a hedge.

CPSC activities and the increased number of liability claims have prompted companies to improve their safety standards voluntarily. For many companies, safety has become a vital ingredient of the broad definition of product.

SUMMARY

Product/service strategy typically involves a line of related products. Firms usually produce several related products rather than a single product in order to achieve the objectives of growth, optimal use of company resources, and increased company importance in the market.

New-product organizational responsibility in most large firms is assigned to new-product committees, new-product departments, product managers, or venture teams. New-product ideas evolve through six stages before their market introduction: (1) idea generation, (2) screening, (3) business analysis, (4) product development, (5) test marketing, and (6) commercialization.

While new products are added to the line, old ones may face deletion from it. The typical causes for product eliminations are unprofitable sales and failure to fit into the existing product line.

Product identification may take the form of brand names, symbols, distinctive packaging, and labeling. Effective brand names should be easy to pronounce, recognize, and remember; they should give the right connotation to the buyer; and they should be legally protectable. Brand acceptance can be measured in three stages: brand recognition, brand preference, and, finally, brand insistence. Marketing managers must decide whether to use a single family brand for their product lines or to use an individual brand for each product.

The package must provide protection, convenience, and economy while achieving the company's promotional goals. The label also serves as an important promotional and informational part of the package.

Product safety has become an increasingly important component of the total product concept. This change has occurred through voluntary attempts by product designers to reduce hazards, through various pieces of legislation, and through establishment of the Consumer Product Safety Commission.

QUESTIONS FOR DISCUSSION

1. Explain the following terms:

product line	brand preference
product manager	brand insistence
venture team	family brand
test marketing	individual brands
brand	national brands
brand name	private brands
trademark	generic products
generic name	label
brand recognition	

2. Why do most business firms market a line of related products rather than a single product?

3. Evaluate the alternative organizational arrangements for new-product introductions. Which organizational arrangement seems best? Defend your answer.

4. Why has the product-manager concept proven so popular among multi-product firms in recent years?

5. Identify the steps in the new-product development process.

6. A firm's new-product idea suggestion program has produced a design for a portable car washer that can be attached to a garden hose. Outline a program for deciding whether the product should be marketed by the firm.

7. Contrast the screening and business analysis stages of the new-product development process.

8. What is the chief purpose of test marketing? What potential problems are involved in it?

9. Under what circumstances might a firm choose to retain an unprofitable product?

10. Give an example of each of the following:

    a. brand   e. individual brand
    b. brand name   f. national brand
    c. trademark   g. private brand
    d. family brand

11. List the characteristics of an effective brand name. Illustrate each characteristic with an appropriate brand name.

12. Distinguish between generic names and brand names.

13. Identify and briefly explain each of the three stages of brand acceptance.

14. Why do so few brands reach the brand insistence stage of brand acceptance?

15. What are the chief advantages of using family brands?

16. Under what circumstances should individual brands be used?

17. What criteria should a retailer or wholesaler use in deciding whether to develop a line of private brand merchandise?

18. Distinguish between generic products and generic names.

19. What are the physical functions of the package? Give examples to illustrate how the package can be an effective promotional tool.

20. Explain the chief functions of the Consumer Product Safety Commission. What steps can it take to protect consumers from defective and hazardous products?

NOTES

1. The introduction of Softsoap is discussed in "Is Liquid Soap Field Saturated?" *Wall Street Journal,* June 18, 1981; and "Is the Bar of Soap Washed Up?" *Business Week,* January 12, 1981, p. 109. The quotation is reported in "Minnetonka Credits 'Thinking,' Not Research, for Success of Softsoap," *Marketing News,* December 26, 1980, pp. 1,6. Used by permission of the American Marketing Association.

2. Polaroid's product development strategies are described in "Polaroid: Turning Away from Land's One-Product Strategy," *Business Week,* March 2, 1981, pp. 108-12.

3. *Wall Street Journal,* April 16, 1981.

4. Roger Leigh Lawton and A. Parasuraman, "So You Want Your New Product Planning to Be Productive," *Business Horizons,* December 1980, pp. 29-34; and Roger Calantone and Robert G. Cooper, "New Product Scenarios: Prospects for Success," *Journal of Marketing,* Spring 1981, pp. 48-60.

5. David S. Hopkins, *New-Product Winners and Losers* (New York: The Conference Board, Inc., 1980). See also "Booz Allen Looks at New Products' Role," *Wall Street Journal,* March 26, 1981.

6. David Gordon and E. Edward Blevins, "Organizing for Effective New-Product Development," *Journal of Business,* December 1978, pp. 21-26; and James Rothe, Michael Harvey, and Walden Rhines, "New Product Development under Conditions of Scarcity and Inflation," *Michigan Business Review,* May 1977, pp. 16-22.

7. Jacob M. Duker and Michael V. Laric, "The Product Manager: No Longer on Trial," Kenneth Bernhardt, Ira Dolich, Michael Etzel, William Kehoe, Thomas Kinnear, William Perrault, Jr., and Kenneth Roering, eds., *The Changing Marketing Environment: New Theories and Applications* (Chicago: American Marketing Association, 1981), pp. 93–96; and Peter S. Howsam and G. David Hughes, "Product Management System Suffers from Insufficient Experience, Poor Communication," *Marketing News,* June 26, 1981, sec. 2, p. 8.

8. Richard M. Hill and James D. Hlavacek, "The Venture Team: A New Concept in Marketing," *Journal of Marketing,* July 1972, p. 50. See also Dan T. Dunn, Jr., "The Rise and Fall of Ten Venture Groups," *Business Horizons,* October 1977, pp. 32–41; and William W. George, "Task Teams for Rapid Growth," *Harvard Business Review,* March-April 1977, pp. 71–80.

9. For an excellent treatment of the product development process, see Robert D. Hisrich and Michael P. Peters, *Marketing a New Product* (Menlo Park, Calif: Benjamin/Cummings Publishing, 1978); Richard T. Hise, *Product/Service Strategy* (New York: Mason/Charter Publishers, 1977); A. Edward Spitz, *Product Planning,* 2d ed. (New York: Mason/Charter Publishers, 1977); and William S. Sachs and George Benson, *Product Planning and Management* (Tulsa: PenWell Books, 1981).

10. See Eric von Hippel, "Successful Industrial Products from Customer Ideas," *Journal of Marketing,* January 1978, pp. 39–49; and James L. Ginter and W. Wayne Talarzyk, "Applying the Marketing Concept to Design New Products," *Journal of Business Research,* January 1978, pp. 51–66.

11. See William B. Locander and Richard W. Scamell, "Screening New Product Ideas—A Two-phase Approach," *Research Management,* March 1976, pp. 14–18.

12. Reported in Edward Buxton, *Promise Them Anything* (New York: Stein & Day, 1972), p. 101.

13. Quoted in Mary McCabe English, "Marketers: Better than a Coin Flip," *Advertising Age,* February 9, 1981, p. S–15. Copyright 1981 by Crain Communications, Inc. Reprinted with permission.

14. Dylan Landis, "Durable Goods Good for a Test?" *Advertising Age,* February 9, 1981, pp. S-18, S-19.

15. B. G. Yovovich, "Competition Jumps the Gun," *Advertising Age,* February 9, 1981, p. S-21.

16. Reported in "Polaroid: Turning Away from Land's One-product Strategy," *Business Week,* March 2, 1981, p. 111.

17. Lee Adler, "Time Lag in New-Product Development," *Journal of Marketing,* January 1966, p. 17.

18. Committee on Definitions, *Marketing Definitions: A Glossary of Marketing Terms* (Chicago: American Marketing Association, 1960), pp. 9–10.

19. "A Worldwide Brand for Nissan," *Business Week,* August 24, 1981, p. 104.

20. John Koten, "Mixing with Coke over Trademarks is Always a Fizzle," *Wall Street Journal,* March 9, 1978. For a thorough discussion of the brand name decision, see James U. McNeal and Linda M. Zeren, "Brand Name Selection for Consumer Products," *MSU Business Topics,* Spring 1981, pp. 35–39.

21. See E. B. Weiss, "Private Label? No, It's Now 'Presold'—Wave of Future," *Advertising Age,* September 30, 1974, p. 27.

22. Jeffrey H. Birnbaum, "Chic Stores Will Push Their Own Labels," *Wall Street Journal,* April 23, 1981. Reprinted by permission of *The Wall Street Journal,* © Dow Jones & Company, Inc., 1981. All rights reserved.

23. Frederic Kraft and Robert Ross, "Confirmation of Expectations and the Evaluation of Generic Products," John H. Summey and Ronald D. Taylor, eds., *Evolving Marketing Thought for 1980* (New Orleans: Southern Marketing Association, 1980), pp. 115–18; Betsy Gelb, " 'No-Name' Products: A Step towards 'No-Name' Retailing?" *Business Horizons,* June 1980, pp. 9–13; and Joseph A. Bellizzi, Harry F. Krueckelbert, and John R. Hamilton, "A Factor Analysis of National, Private, and Generic Brand Attributes," Robert H. Ross, Frederic B. Kraft, and Charles H. Davis, eds., *1981 Proceedings of the Southwestern Marketing Association,* pp. 208–10.

24. Bill Abrams and David P. Garino, "Package Design Gains Stature as Visual Competition Grows," *Wall Street Journal,* August 6, 1981. Reprinted by permission of *The Wall Street Journal,* © Dow Jones & Company, Inc., 1981. All rights reserved.

25. Paul H. Weaver, "The Hazards of Trying to Make Consumer Products Safer," *FORTUNE*, July 1975, p. 133. See also Richard I. Kirkland, Jr., "Hazardous Times for Product-Safety Czars," *FORTUNE*, June 15, 1981, pp. 127 ff.

26. *The Product Liability Crisis* (Lansing, Mich.: Michigan Product Liability Council, 1978); and "Liability Lawsuits Could Drive Product Prices through the Roof," *Marketing News,* January 23, 1981, p. 12.

PART   FIVE

DISTRIBUTION STRATEGY

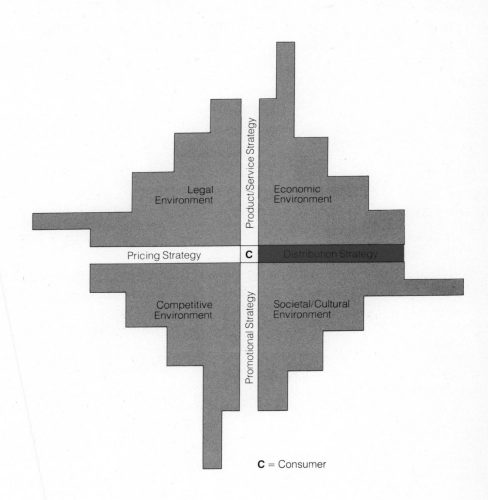

Legal
Environment

Product/Service Strategy

Economic
Environment

Pricing Strategy   **C**   Distribution Strategy

Competitive
Environment

Promotional Strategy

Societal/Cultural
Environment

C = Consumer

CHAPTER 10

INTRODUCTION TO CHANNEL STRATEGY

KEY TERMS

marketing channel
time utility
place utility
ownership utility
middleman
wholesaling
retailers
reverse channels
facilitating agency
intensive distribution
selective distribution
exclusive distribution
exclusive dealing agreement
closed sales territories
tying agreement
channel captain
missionary salesperson
vertical marketing systems (VMS)
franchise

LEARNING GOALS

1. To list the types of utility created by marketing channels

2. To identify the major marketing channels for consumer and industrial goods

3. To explain the factors that determine the optimum marketing channel for a product or service

4. To identify and discuss the three degrees of intensity of marketing coverage

5. To explain the three major types of vertical marketing systems

Some have called it the most revolutionary development since 1844 when a dentist named Horace Wells took laughing gas before having a tooth painlessly extracted. The revolution involves the application of a marketing concept called franchising to the profession of dentistry.

Like most services, dentistry uses a direct channel in which the customer (patient) makes direct contact with the service supplier (dentist). Although a number of specialists segment the dental care market —primarily on a product/service category basis—the traditional emphasis of the profession has been on production. Several developments have resulted in modifications of this emphasis.

One factor that led to the increase of marketing thinking in dental care is the surplus of dentists that has developed over the past twenty years. While shortages of qualified dentists still exist in rural areas, most of the nation's 131,000 dentists set up practices in metropolitan areas, resulting in a glut of young dentists there. Another factor was the relaxation of restrictions on advertising health care services.

Over the past five years an alliance between retail stores and dentistry has developed, an alliance that may permanently change the method of delivery for dental care. In 1978, Sears and Montgomery Ward began renting floor space to dental operations. K mart followed suit in several of its stores. Most of this space was leased to franchised dental operations such as Minneapolis-based Retail Dental Centers. Its president summarized the franchise philosophy in this way:

Dentistry can be marketed like anything else. The people we compete with are tucked away in little offices in shopping centers, whereas we have positioned ourselves in high-traffic areas.

Everything about it is like a private practice, except we do the advertising and provide the dentists with business systems. Almost no business training is being offered in dental schools. It's a franchise, just like a Burger King or McDonald's.

The public is fed up with dentists. They have done themselves in by continuously shortening their hours, despite the trend toward more working women. Our outlets typically are open from 9:00 A.M. to 9:00 P.M., and the evening hours are the most popular.

The franchisor contracts with the retailer for space, sublets the space to the dentist, and then provides a marketing program for the operation. It also supplies marketing research, such as a recent survey that indicated the primary customer attraction is convenience. The study also revealed that franchised dentists tap a lucrative market target: the large percentage of Americans who do not purchase regular dental care. Almost two-thirds of Retail Dental Centers' patients had not seen a dentist in at least two years.

The retail landlords of the new approach to dental care delivery are pleased with their new tenants. A spokesperson for Montgomery Ward pointed out that the dental centers are compatible with other in-store services such as the optical department, hearing aids, the beauty salon, and the health food section. "It's an extension of other health care services we offer," he said, "and it helps keep customers coming back to our stores."

Although some critics express fears of "Dental King" franchises or shopping center customers being bombarded with messages to "save 25 percent on impacted wisdom teeth while the flashing blue light is on," it is clear that the newest revolution in dentistry is delivering needed service to clients who otherwise might not have been reached.[1]

WHAT ARE MARKETING CHANNELS?

Jewelers, dentists, and other gold users know that the largest gold mine in the United States is located in Lead, South Dakota. The MG, a British import, has found market acceptance for more than 30 years among U.S. sports car enthusiasts who wish to purchase a new model for less than $10,000. Americans, who drink enough coffee to equal an annual per capita consumption of 14 pounds of coffee beans (representing one-third of all coffee grown in the world), look primarily to the Latin American countries for their supplies. In each case, methods must be devised to bridge the geographic gap between producer and consumer. Marketing channels are used to provide consumers with a convenient means of obtaining the products and services they desire.

A **marketing channel** is *the path that products and services—and title to them—follow from producer to consumer or industrial user.*[2] In performing this function, marketing channels create utility for the firm's customers—both ultimate consumers and industrial purchasers.

MARKETING CHANNELS CREATE UTILITY

As Chapter 1 explained, utility is the want-satisfying ability of a product or service. Marketing channels create three types of utility: time, place, and ownership (or possession). **Time utility** is *created when marketing channels have products and services available for sale when the consumer wants to purchase them.* **Place utility** is *created when products and services are available in a convenient location.* **Ownership utility** is *created when title to the goods passes from the manufacturer or intermediary to the purchaser.*

Time Utility Production and marketing problems are reduced substantially under a system of *job-order production.* In such a system the consumer places an order and returns several weeks or months later to claim the finished product. The firm has a minimal inventory of finished products and few marketing risks. However, except for major purchases of installations with unique specifications and large government contracts, few products are purchased on a job-order basis. *Speculative production*—production based on the firm's estimate of the demand for its product—is the rule, not the exception, in the business world of the 1980s.

Color television sales increase markedly on the Friday before the Super Bowl game or the opening game of the World Series. But the appliance store manager also recounts sadly that the purchasers are not at all receptive to home delivery of the set on the following Monday. The sale of each set is, in fact, contingent on its installation in the purchaser's home by noon the following day. Too many of these sales cannot be consummated, however, because the store manager has no time to place the orders with suppliers.

The annual toy fair takes place in New York City in February. Toy buyers for the nation's department stores, toy shops, variety stores, and discount stores visit the fair and make their decisions on toys to stock for the coming Christmas season. This lead time is required to produce the necessary quantities of each toy and to transport the toys to each purchaser's store.

In the same manner, swimwear for the coming spring and summer has already been produced in the cold months of December and January and is en route to retail stores throughout the nation. Swimwear manufacturers' success or failure depends on consumer reactions to new colors, styles, and fabrics decided on months earlier. But the swimsuits are ready in the store for the first warm day in March or April that customers decide to shop for them.

Place Utility Products in the manufacturer's warehouse are of no value to the consumer. Since few consumers are willing to seek out the manufacturer (except in the case of factory outlet stores), thousands of retail stores have been established to provide goods in locations convenient to consumers. These stores, along with vending machines, mail-order catalogs, and telephone sales, are a means of conveniently supplying products to the consumer.

Ownership Utility Marketing channels also provide a means for title to be transferred from manufacturer to buyer. The purchaser can obtain physical possession of and title to the product at the retail store.

Marketing Terminology Any discussion of marketing channels must supply an explanation of its terminology. A **middleman** is *a business firm operating between the producer and the consumer or industrial purchaser.* The term therefore includes both wholesalers and retailers.

Wholesaling is *the activities of persons or firms who sell to retailers, other wholesalers, and industrial users but do not sell in significant amounts to ultimate consumers.* The terms *jobber* and *distributor* are considered to be synonymous with *wholesaler* in this book.

Confusion can result from the practices of some firms that operate both wholesaling and retailing operations. Sporting goods stores, for example, often maintain a wholesaling operation in marketing a line of goods to high schools and colleges as well as operating retail stores.

For the purposes of this text, it is simpler to conceive of such operations as two separate institutions.

A second source of confusion is the misleading practice of some retailers who claim to be wholesalers. Such stores may actually sell at wholesale prices and can validly claim to do so. However, *stores that sell products purchased by individuals for their own use and not for resale are* by definition **retailers,** not wholesalers.

CHOOSING MARKETING CHANNELS

A cursory look at the literally hundreds of marketing channels in every-day use should be sufficient to convince the marketing manager that there is no such thing as a best marketing channel. The best channel for Mary Kay Cosmetics may be direct from manufacturer to consumer through a network of 120,000 "beauty consultant" salespersons who give free facials and beauty tips at Tupperware-like home parties and sell $75 to $100 worth of merchandise per party.[3] The best channel for frozen french fries may be from food processor to agent middleman to merchant wholesaler to supermarket to consumer. Instead of searching for a best channel for all products, the marketing manager must analyze alternative channels in the light of consumer needs in order to deter-mine the most appropriate channel (or channels) for the firm's products and services.[4]

Even when the proper channels have been chosen and estab-lished, the marketing manager's channel decisions have not ceased. Channels, like so many marketing variables, change; today's ideal channel may prove disastrous in a few years.

Until the 1960s, the typical channel for beer was from brewery to local distributor (wholesaler) to local pubs, since most beer was consumed in these retail outlets. But the majority of the beer pur-chases in the 1980s are made at the local supermarket, and the chan-nel for Busch, Tuborg Gold, Stroh's, Heineken, and Miller Lite must change to reflect these changes in consumer buying patterns.

Channel Alternatives Available to the Marketing Manager

Figure 10.1 depicts the major channels available for marketers of con-sumer and industrial products. In general, industrial products channels tend to be shorter than consumer goods channels due to geographic concentrations of industrial buyers and a relatively limited number of purchasers. In addition, retail sales are characteristic only of consumer goods purchases; therefore the retailer is not found in industrial chan-nels.

Manufacturer to Consumer or Industrial User The simplest, most direct marketing channel is not necessarily the best, as evidenced by the rel-atively small percentage of dollar volume of sales that moves along this route. Less than 5 percent of all consumer goods move from producer to consumer. Dairies, Tupperware, Avon cosmetics, and numerous

**FIGURE 10.1
Channel Alternatives
in the Marketing of
Consumer and
Industrial Goods**

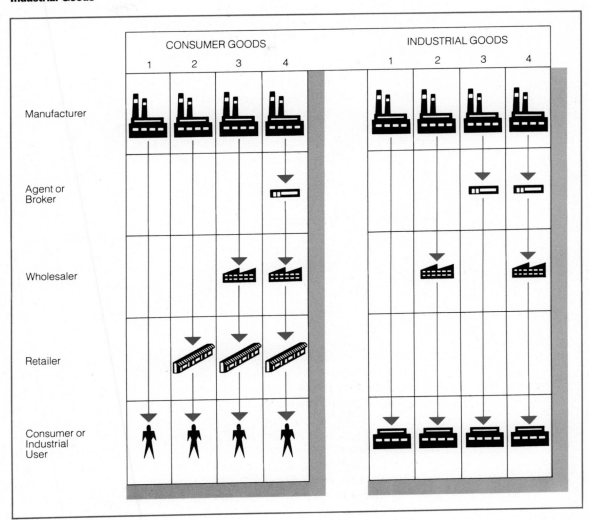

mail-order houses are examples of the firms whose products move directly from manufacturer to ultimate consumer.

Almost all services utilize this channel to some extent. Often, however, a service uses agents as middlemen. Airlines, for example, use travel agents.

Direct channels are much more important to the industrial goods market. Most major installations and accessory equipment—and even fabricated parts and raw materials—are marketed through direct contacts between seller and buyer.

Manufacturer to Wholesaler to Retailer to Consumer The traditional marketing channel for consumer goods proceeds from manufacturer to wholesaler to retailer to user. It is the method used by small retailers and by literally thousands of small manufacturers that produce limited lines of products. Small companies with limited financial resources utilize wholesalers as immediate sources of funds and as a means to reach the hundreds of retailers who will stock their products. Small retailers rely on wholesalers as buying specialists who ensure a balanced inventory of goods produced in various regions of the world.

The wholesaler's sales force is responsible for reaching the market with the manufacturer's output. Many manufacturers also use sales representatives, who call on retailers and help merchandise the manufacturer's line. These representatives serve as sources of market information for manufacturers, but do not actually sell the product.

Manufacturer to Wholesaler to Industrial User Similar characteristics in the industrial market often lead to the utilization of middlemen between the manufacturer and industrial purchaser. The term *industrial distributor* is commonly utilized in the industrial market to refer to those wholesalers who take title to the goods they handle. These wholesalers are involved in the marketing of small accessory equipment and operating supplies, such as building supplies, office supplies, and small hand tools.

Manufacturer to Agent to Wholesaler to Retailer to Consumer Where products are produced by a large number of small companies, a unique middleman—the *agent*—performs the basic function of bringing buyer and seller together. The agent is, in fact, a wholesaling middleman who does not take title to the goods. The agent merely represents the manufacturer or the regular wholesaler (who does take title to the goods) in seeking a market for the manufacturer's output or in locating a source of supply for the buyer. Chapter 11 will consider two types of wholesaling middlemen—merchant wholesalers, who take title to the goods that they handle, and agent wholesaling middlemen, who do not take title to the goods.

Agents are used in such industries as canning and frozen food packing. In these industries, many producers supply a large number of geographically scattered wholesalers. The agent wholesaling middleman performs the service of bringing buyers and sellers together.

Manufacturer to Agent to Wholesaler to Industrial User Similar conditions often exist in the industrial market, where small producers attempt to market their offerings to large wholesalers. The agent wholesaling middleman, often called a manufacturers' representative, serves as an independent sales force in contacting the wholesale buyers.

Manufacturer to Agent to Industrial User Where the unit sale is small, merchant wholesalers must be used to cover the market economically. By maintaining regional inventories, they achieve transportation economies by stockpiling goods and making the final small shipment over a small distance. Where the unit sale is large and transportation accounts for a small percentage of the total product cost, the manufacturer to agent to industrial user channel is usually employed. The agent wholesaling middlemen become, in effect, the company's sales force.

Multiple Channels

An increasingly common phenomenon is the use of more than one marketing channel for similar products. In some instances, multiple channels (or dual distribution) are utilized when the same product is marketed both to the ultimate consumer and to industrial users. Dial soap, for example, is distributed to grocery wholesalers, who deliver it to food stores, which market it to consumers. But a second marketing channel also exists: large retail chains and motels purchase the soap directly from the manufacturer.

In other cases, the same product is marketed through a variety of types of retail outlets. A basic product such as a paintbrush is carried in inventory by the traditional hardware store; it is also handled by such nontraditional retail outlets as auto accessory stores, building supply outlets, department stores, discount houses, mail-order houses, supermarkets, and variety stores. Each retail store may utilize different marketing channels.

Firestone automobile tires are marketed through several channels. They are distributed to General Motors, where they serve as a fabricated part for new Chevrolets; to Firestone-owned retail outlets; to tire wholesalers, who sell them to retail gas stations; and to franchised Firestone outlets. Each channel enables the manufacturer to serve a different market.

Reverse Channels

While the traditional concept of marketing channels involves movement of products and services from producer to consumer or industrial user, there is increasing interest in **reverse channels.** Reverse, or backward, channels are *the paths goods follow from consumer to manufacturer, or to marketing intermediaries.* William G. Zikmund and William J. Stanton point out several problems in developing reverse channels in the recycling process:

The recycling of solid wastes is a major ecological goal. Although recycling is technologically feasible, reversing the flow of materials in the channel of distribution—marketing trash through a "backward" channel—presents a challenge. Existing backward channels are primitive, and financial incentives are inadequate. The consumer must be motivated to undergo a role change and become a producer—the initiating force in the reverse distribution process.[5]

Reverse channels will increase in importance as raw materials become more expensive, and as additional laws are passed to control litter and the disposition of packaging materials such as soft-drink bottles. In order for recycling to succeed, four basic conditions must be satisfied:

1. A technology must be available that can efficiently process the material being recycled.

2. A market must be available for the end product—the reclaimed material.

3. A substantial and continuing quantity of secondary product (recycled aluminum, reclaimed steel from automobiles, recycled paper) must be available.

4. A marketing system must be developed that can bridge the gap between suppliers of secondary products and end users on a profitable basis.

In some instances, the reverse channel consists of traditional marketing intermediaries. In the soft-drink industry, retailers and local bottlers perform these functions. In other cases, manufacturers take the initiative by establishing redemption centers. A concentrated attempt by the Reynolds Metals Company in Florida permitted the company to recycle an amount of aluminum equivalent to 60 percent of the total containers marketed in the state.[6] Other reverse channel participants may include community groups which organize "clean-up" days and develop systems for rechanneling paper products for recycling and specialized organizations developed for waste disposal and recycling.

Facilitating Agencies: Form and Function

Advertising agencies, financial institutions, insurance companies, marketing research firms, and transportation and storage companies perform many important channel functions and are known collectively as facilitating agencies. A **facilitating agency** *provides specialized assistance for regular channel members (such as manufacturers, wholesalers, and retailers) in moving products from producer to consumer.*

Facilitating agencies perform a number of special services. Insurance companies assume some of the risks involved in transporting the goods; marketing research firms supply information; financial institutions provide the necessary financing; advertising agencies help sell the goods; and transportation and storage firms store and physically move the goods. In some instances, the major channel members perform these services. Facilitating agencies are not, however, involved in directing the flow of goods and services through the channel.

Figure 10.2 illustrates the total distribution channel. The channel members are shown in squares, while the facilitating agencies are shown in circles.

FIGURE 10.2
Channel Members and Facilitating Agencies in the Marketing Channel

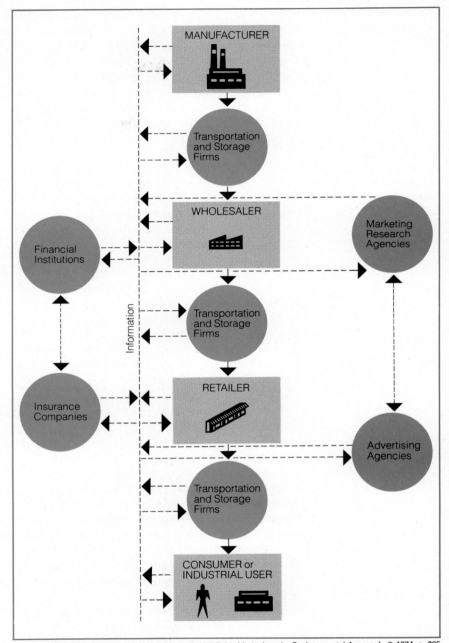

Source: Adapted from John R. Kerr and James E. Littlefield, *Marketing: An Environmental Approach*, © 1974, p. 305. Reprinted by permission of Prentice-Hall, Inc., Englewood Cliffs, N.J.

FACTORS AFFECTING CHANNEL CHOICE

What makes a franchised retail dealer network best for the Ford Motor Company? Why do operating supplies often go through both agents and merchant wholesalers before being purchased by the industrial firm? Why do some firms employ multiple channels for the same product? The firm must answer many such questions in choosing marketing channels. The choice is based on an analysis of the consumer, the type of firm, the product's characteristics, and considerations of the firm's environment. Each factor can be of critical importance, and the factors are often interrelated.

Consumer Characteristics

A major determinant of channel structure is whether the product is intended for the consumer or the industrial market. Industrial purchasers usually prefer to deal directly with the manufacturer (except for supplies or small accessory items), but most consumers make their purchases from retail stores. Often, products for both industrial users and consumers are sold through more than one channel.

The needs and geographic location of the firm's market affect channel choice. Direct sales are possible where the firm's potential market is concentrated in a few regions. Since industrial production tends to be concentrated this way, direct contact is possible. A small number of potential buyers also increases the feasibility of direct channels. Consumer goods are purchased by households everywhere. Since these households are numerous and geographically dispersed, and since they purchase a small volume at a given time, middlemen must be employed to market products to them.

Jostens has been able to capture 40 percent of the market for high school class rings and yearbooks by using a 1,000-member sales force of former high school teachers and coaches. This direct channel, served by a highly educated sales force that averages $50,000 per year in commissions, has proven extremely successful. The soaring gold prices of recent years prompted Jostens to diversify into the wholesale market with a line of engagement and other fine rings. But the sales force was largely unsuccessful in serving a new type of customer (the retail jeweler) and a new channel had to be devised.[7]

Order size will also affect the marketing channel decision. Manufacturers are likely to use shorter, more direct channels in cases where retail customers or industrial buyers place relatively small numbers of large orders. Retail chains often employ buying offices to negotiate directly with manufacturers for large-scale purchases. Wholesalers may be used to contact smaller retailers.

Shifts in consumer buying patterns also influence channel decisions. The desire for credit, the growth of self-service, the increased use of mail-order houses, and the greater willingness to purchase from door-to-door salespeople all affect a firm's marketing channel.

Product Characteristics

Product characteristics also play a role in determining optimal marketing channels. Perishable products such as fresh produce and fruit, and fashion products with short life cycles typically move through relatively short channels directly to the retailer or the ultimate consumer. Nabisco Inc., distributes its cookies and crackers from the bakery to retail shelves. Fig Newtons, Oreos, Ritz Crackers, and other Nabisco brands that command 40 percent of the U.S. market are delivered to retail customers by a fleet of 1,200 company-owned trucks and a 3,000-member sales force.[8] Each year Hines & Smart Corporation ships some 5 million pounds of live lobsters in specially designed styrofoam containers directly to restaurants and hotels throughout North America.

Complex products, such as custom-made installations or computer equipment, are typically sold by the manufacturer to the buyer. As a general rule, the more standardized the product, the longer the channel. Standardized goods usually are marketed by wholesalers. Also, products requiring regular service or specialized repair service usually avoid channels employing independent wholesalers. Automobiles are marketed through a franchised network of retail dealers whose employees receive training on how to properly service their cars.

Another generalization about marketing channels is that the lower the unit value of the product, the longer the channel. Convenience goods and industrial supplies with typically low unit prices are frequently marketed through relatively long channels. Installations and more expensive industrial and consumer goods employ shorter, more direct channels.

Manufacturer Characteristics

Companies with adequate resources—financial, managerial, and marketing—are less compelled to utilize middlemen in marketing their products. A financially strong manufacturer can hire its own sales force, warehouse its products, and grant credit to retailers or consumers. A weaker firm must rely on middlemen for these services (although some large retail chains purchase all of the manufacturer's output, thereby bypassing the independent wholesaler). Production-oriented firms may be forced to utilize the marketing expertise of middlemen to replace the lack of finances and management in their organization.

A firm with a broad product line is usually able to market its products directly to retailers or industrial users since its sales force can offer them a variety of products. Larger total sales permit the selling costs to be spread over a number of products and make direct sales feasible. The single-product firm often discovers that direct selling is an unaffordable luxury.

The manufacturer's need for control over the product also influences channel selection. If aggressive promotion is desired at the retail level, the manufacturer will choose the shortest available channel. For new products, the manufacturer may be forced to implement an introductory advertising campaign before independent wholesalers will handle the items.

Environmental Considerations

Some firms are forced to develop unique marketing channels because of inadequate promotion of their products by independent middlemen. Avon's famous shift to house-to-house selling was prompted by intense competition with similar lines of cosmetics. This radical departure from the traditional channel resulted in sales of $1.2 billion in 1980 by the firm's one million neighborhood saleswomen. Similarly, when Honeywell discovered that its Concept 70 home security system was being inadequately marketed by the traditional channel of wholesaler to retailer, it switched to a direct-to-home sales force.

Table 10.1 summarizes the factors affecting the choice of optimal marketing channels and examines the effect of each characteristic upon the overall length of the channel.

**TABLE 10.1
Factors Affecting Choice of Marketing Channels**

Factor	Channels Tend to Be Shorter When:
A. Consumer Characteristics	
Consumer market or industrial market	Industrial users
Geographic location of market target	Geographically concentrated customers
Customer service needs	Specialized knowledge, technical knowhow, and regular service needs are present
Order size	Customers place relatively large orders
B. Product Characteristics	
Perishability	Products are perishable, either because of fashion changes or physical perishability
Technical complexity of product	Highly technical products
Unit value	High unit-value products
C. Manufacturer Characteristics	
Producer resources—financial, managerial, and marketing	Manufacturer possesses adequate resources to perform channel functions
Product line	Manufacturer has broad product line to spread distribution costs
Need for control over the channel	Manufacturer desires to control the channel
D. Environmental Factors	
Need for promotion to channel members	Manufacturer feels that independent middlemen are inadequately promoting products

FIGURE 10.3
Degrees of Market
Coverage

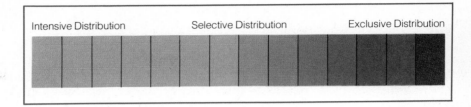

Intensive Distribution   Selective Distribution   Exclusive Distribution

DETERMINING THE INTENSITY OF MARKET COVERAGE

Adequate market coverage for some products could mean one dealer for 50,000 people. American Home Products defines "adequate coverage" for Anacin and Dristan headache and cold remedies as almost every supermarket, discount store, drugstore, and variety store, plus many vending machines. Figure 10.3 illustrates the degrees of market exposure along a continuum with three general categories: intensive distribution, selective distribution, and exclusive distribution.

Intensive Distribution

Manufacturers of convenience goods practice **intensive distribution** when they *provide saturation coverage of the market, enabling the purchaser to buy the product with a minimum of effort.* Examples of goods distributed in this way include soft drinks, candy, gum, and cigarettes.

Bic pens can be purchased in more than 200,000 retail outlets in the United States. The American Time Company uses an intensive distribution strategy for its Timex watches. Consumers can buy a Timex in many jewelry stores, the traditional retail outlet for watches. In addition, they can find Timex in department stores, discount stores, drugstores, hardware stores, and variety stores.

Mass coverage and low unit prices make the use of wholesalers almost mandatory for such distribution. An important exception to this generalization is Avon Products, which sells directly to the consumer through a nationwide network of neighborhood saleswomen. These women purchase directly from the manufacturer at 60 percent of the retail price and service a limited area with cosmetics, toiletries, jewelry, and toys.

Selective Distribution

Selective distribution involves *the selection of a small number of retailers in a market area to handle the firm's product line.* By limiting the number of retailers, the firm can reduce its total marketing costs while establishing better working relationships within the channel. Cooperative advertising (in which the manufacturer pays a percentage of the retailer's advertising expenditures and the retailer prominently displays the firm's products) can be utilized for mutual benefit, and marginal retailers can be avoided. Where product service is important, the manufacturer usually provides dealer training and assistance. Finally, price cutting is less likely, since fewer dealers are handling the firm's line.

THE FIRM THAT VIOLATES A MARKETING PRINCIPLE— AND SUCCEEDS

Analysis of consumer and product characteristics would lead most marketing students to predict that a company such as Avon Products would use middlemen in distributing its 1,400 products. Yet Avon markets directly to the consumer through an army of one million bell ringers to more than 85 million households in the United States, Canada, and sixteen foreign countries. In the United States, Avon holds 85 percent of the door-to-door market for cosmetics and toiletries, and approximately 20 percent of the total $5 billion market.

The Avon system consists of five levels. At the top is a general manager who oversees one of seven branches across the country, and two regional managers. Each regional manager supervises eight divisional managers, and each divisional manager keeps tabs on eighteen district managers. Each district manager recruits, trains, and works with an average of 150 bell-chiming Avon saleswomen.

A part-time independent businesswoman, as Avon likes to describe her, the Avon saleswoman receives no company benefits, puts up a $10 "appointment fee" when she starts, and pays for most of her promotional materials. These include samples, demonstration kits, small customer brochures, and paper bags for packaging. An order of bags costs $1.50, and kits are $3 or $4 (some as much as $8 or $10). The work year is divided into twenty-six preplanned, two-week selling campaigns built around individual campaign brochures that are prepared months in advance.

The saleswoman is typically twenty-five to forty-four years old, has two children, and lives in a middle- or lower-income neighborhood. She works fifteen hours a week covering her two-hundred-family territory and visits thirty families per campaign. She earns about $1,900 a year (before expenses) on the $4,900 worth of products she sells. For every $100 in retail sales that she generates during a campaign, she gets a 40 percent commission. Sales of less than $100 bring 25 percent. For each saleswoman she helps recruit, she receives $7.50.

Since most Avon saleswomen work only for a little spare cash, turnover runs more than 100 percent a year. While almost half of all saleswomen have been with the company for more than a year and one-third for more than three years, the rest work for only a few months.

Source: Information from Linda Snyder Hayes, "The Changes in Avon's Makeup Aren't Just Cosmetic," *FORTUNE*, August 13, 1979, pp. 140–54; and Pat Sloan, "Avon: Is Its Strategy Working?" *Advertising Age*, March 30, 1981, pp. 4, 81.

Exclusive Distribution

When manufacturers grant exclusive rights to a wholesaler or retailer to sell in a geographic region, they are practicing **exclusive distribution**—an extreme form of selective distribution. The best example of exclusive distribution is within the automobile industry. For example, a city of 100,000 population will have a single Honda dealer or one Pontiac agency. Exclusive dealership arrangements also occur in the marketing of some major appliances and in fashion apparel.

Some market coverage may be sacrificed through a policy of exclusive distribution, but this loss is often offset by the development and maintenance of an image of quality and prestige for the products and the reduced marketing costs associated with a small number of accounts. Manufacturer and retailer cooperate closely in decisions concerning advertising and promotion, inventory to be carried by the retailer, and prices.

The Legal Problems of Exclusive Distribution The use of exclusive distribution presents a number of potential legal problems in three areas—exclusive dealing agreements, closed sales territories, and tying agreements. While none of these practices is illegal per se, all may be ruled illegal if they reduce competition or tend to create a monopoly situation.

Exclusive Dealing Agreements An **exclusive dealing agreement** *prohibits a middleman (either a wholesaler or, more typically, a retailer) from handling competing products.* Manufacturers of high-priced shopping goods, specialty goods, and accessory equipment often require such agreements as assurance by the middleman of total concentration on the firm's product line. These contracts are considered violations of the Clayton Act if the manufacturer's or the dealer's sales volume represents a substantial percentage of total sales in the market or sales area. The courts have ruled that sellers who are initially entering the market can use exclusive dealing agreements as a means of strengthening their competitive position. But the same agreements are considered violations of the Clayton Act when used by firms with sizable market shares, since competitors may be barred from the market because of the agreements.

Closed Sales Territories Manufacturers with **closed sales territories** *restrict the geographic territories for each of their distributors.* Although the distributors may be granted exclusive territories, they are prohibited from opening new facilities or marketing the manufacturer's products outside their assigned territories. The legality of closed sales territories depends on whether the restrictions decrease competition. If competition is lessened, closed sales territories are considered to be in violation of the Federal Trade Commission Act and of provisions of the Sherman Act and the Clayton Act.

The legality of closed sales territories is also determined by whether they are horizontal or vertical. Horizontal territorial restrictions involve agreements by retailers or wholesalers to avoid competition among products from the same manufacturer. Such agreements have consistently been declared illegal. However, the U.S. Supreme Court recently ruled that vertical territorial restrictions—those between the manufacturer and the wholesaler or retailer—may be legal. While the ruling was not entirely clear-cut, such agreements are likely to be legal in cases where the manufacturer occupies a relatively small part of the market. In such cases, the restrictions may actually increase competition among competing brands. The wholesaler or retailer faces no competition from other dealers carrying the manufacturer's brand and can therefore concentrate on effectively competing with other brands.[9]

Tying Agreements The third legal question of exclusive dealing involves the use of a **tying agreement**—*an agreement that requires a dealer who wishes to become the exclusive dealer for a manufacturer's products to also carry other of the manufacturer's products in inventory.* In the clothing industry, for example, such an agreement may require the dealer to carry a line of less popular clothing in addition to the fast-moving items.

Tying agreements violate the Sherman Act and the Clayton Act when they lessen competition or create monopoly situations by keeping competitors out of major markets. For this reason, the International Salt Company was prohibited from selling its salt as a tying product with the lease of its patented salt-dispensing machines for snow and ice removal. The Supreme Court ruled that such an agreement unreasonably eliminated competition among sellers of salt.

Tying agreements continue to proliferate in franchising operations. One study estimated that over 70 percent of all franchisees are required to purchase at least some of their operating supplies from the franchisors.[10]

CONFLICT AND COOPERATION IN THE MARKETING CHANNEL

Although the marketing channel must be organized and regarded as a systematic cooperative effort if operating efficiencies are to be achieved, channel members often perform as separate, independent, and even competitive forces. Too often, marketing institutions within the channel view the channel as extending only one step forward or backward. They think in terms of suppliers and customers rather than of vital links in the total channel.

Channel conflict can evolve from a number of sources:

A manufacturer may wish to promote a product in one manner . . . while his retailers oppose this. Another manufacturer may wish to get information from his retailers on a certain aspect relating to his product, but his retailers may refuse to provide this information. A producer may want to distribute his product extensively, but his retailers may demand exclusives. A supplier may force a product onto its retailers, who dare not oppose, but who retaliate in other ways, such as using it as a loss leader. Large manufacturers may try to dictate the resale price of their merchandise; this may be less or more than the price at which the retailers wish to sell it. Occasionally

a local market may be more competitive for a retailer than is true nationally. The manufacturer may not recognize the difference in competition and refuse to help this channel member. There is also conflict because of the desire of both manufacturers and retailers to eliminate the wholesaler.[11]

Types of Conflict

Two types of conflict—horizontal or vertical—may occur. *Horizontal conflict* occurs between channel members at the same level—two or more wholesalers or two or more retailers. Such conflict may occur between middlemen of the same type, such as two competing discount stores or several retail florists. More often, however, horizontal conflict occurs between different types of middlemen who handle similar products. The retail druggist competes with variety stores, discount houses, department stores, convenience food stores, and mail-order houses, all of which may be supplied by the manufacturer with identical branded products. Consumer desires for convenient, one-stop shopping has led to multiple channels and the use of numerous outlets for many products.

Vertical conflict occurs between channel members at different levels—between wholesalers and retailers or between manufacturers and wholesalers or retailers. Vertical conflict occurs frequently and is often the more severe form of conflict in the channel. Conflict may occur between manufacturers and retailers when retailers develop private brands to compete with the manufacturer's brands; or when manufacturers establish their own retail stores or create a mail-order operation in competition with retailers. Conflict between manufacturers and wholesalers may occur in cases where the manufacturer attempts to bypass the wholesaler and make direct sales to retailers or industrial users. In other instances, wholesalers may promote competitive products.

A recent instance of vertical conflict occurred between the Coca-Cola Company and its 550 wholesale bottlers who bottle, warehouse, distribute, sell, and merchandise Coca-Cola made from syrup provided by the Atlanta-based parent. Over a ten-year period during the 1960s and 1970s, the makers of Dr Pepper expanded from regional distribution in the Midwest and Southwest to national coverage. This was accomplished by convincing 25 percent of the nation's Coca-Cola bottlers to also bottle Dr Pepper. Even the Atlanta bottler in Coke's headquarters city became a Dr Pepper distributor. The parent firm exercised its power in the soft-drink channel, however, and succeeded in convincing many of its franchised bottlers to drop Dr Pepper in favor of Mr. Pibb, Coca-Cola's own cherry-flavored counterpart to Dr Pepper.[12]

A third type of vertical conflict may occur between wholesalers and retailers. Retailers may believe that wholesalers are failing to offer credit or to allow returns on the same basis as is being provided for other types of retail outlets. Wholesalers may complain that retailers are making sales to institutions that previously dealt directly with the wholesaler. A wholesaler in the sporting goods field, for example, may argue that sales by retail sporting goods outlets directly to local school systems are unfairly competing with its own sales force.[13]

Achieving Cooperation among Channel Members

The basic antidote to channel conflict is effective cooperation among channel members. However, channels usually have more harmonious relationships than conflicting ones; if they did not, the channels would have ceased to exist long ago. Cooperation is best achieved by considering all channel members as part of the same organization. Achievement of this cooperation is the prime responsibility of the dominant member of the channel. This member must provide the leadership necessary to ensure efficient functioning of the channel.

Channel Leadership

Leadership in the marketing channel is typically the responsibility of the most powerful member. *The dominant and controlling member of the channel* is called the **channel captain.**[14] Historically, the role of channel captain was performed by the manufacturer or wholesaler, since retailers tended to be both small and localized. However, retailers are increasingly taking on the role of channel captain as large chains assume traditional wholesaling functions and even dictate product design specifications to the manufacturer.

Manufacturers as Channel Captains Since manufacturers typically create new product and service offerings and enjoy the benefits of large-scale operations, they fill the role of channel captain in many marketing channels. Examples of such manufacturers include Armstrong Cork, General Electric, Magnavox, Sealy Mattress, and Western Auto Stores.

Retailers as Channel Captains Retailers are often powerful enough to serve as channel captains in many industries. Larger chain operations may bypass independent wholesalers and utilize manufacturers as suppliers in producing the retailers' private brands at quality levels specified by the chains. Major retailers such as K mart, Sears, J.C. Penney, and Montgomery Ward serve as leaders in many of the marketing channels with which they are associated.

Wholesalers as Channel Captains Although the relative influence of wholesalers has declined since 1900, they continue to serve as vital members of many marketing channels. Large-scale wholesalers, such as the Independent Grocers' Association (IGA), serve as channel captains as they assist independent retailers in competing with chain outlets.

Channel Captains: Creating an Integrated Channel Manufacturers may play a major role in improving cooperation among the channel members through the use of missionary salespersons. These representatives do not perform the typical selling and order-taking functions of traditional salespersons. Rather, the **missionary salesperson** *aids wholesalers and retailers by providing information about the firm's products, assisting in developing effective promotional concepts and sales contests, creating store layout designs, and generally acting as a management consultant for members of the channel.*

Retailer channel captains can perform a vital role in supplying the wholesaler and manufacturer with information about consumer purchases and reactions to various components of the manufacturer's marketing mix. Wholesaler channel captains may assist the manufacturer in locating additional outlets for its products; they serve their retailer customers by providing product information, assisting in store layout and other merchandising decisions, and occasionally by providing financing for their customers.

CHANNEL STRATEGY FOR SERVICES

As discussed earlier, distribution for services is usually simpler and more direct than for industrial and consumer goods. In part, this is due to the intangibility of services. The marketer of services is often less concerned with storage, transportation, and inventory control; and shorter channels are typically used.

Another consideration is the need for continuing, personal relationships between performers and users of many services. Consumers will remain clients of the same insurance agent, bank, or travel agent as long as they are reasonably satisfied. Likewise, public accounting firms and attorneys are retained on a relatively permanent basis by industrial buyers.

When marketing intermediaries are used by service firms, they are usually agents or brokers. Common examples include insurance agents, securities brokers, travel agents, and entertainment agents. Another distribution strategy discussed earlier in the chapter is franchising. Automobile rental, temporary workers, motels and hotels, real estate, and dry cleaning are examples of service industries commonly distributed through franchises.

A dominant patronage motive for many consumer services, such as banks, motels, and auto rental agencies, is a convenient location. It is absolutely essential that careful consideration be given to retail site selection. Banks in particular have been sensitive to locating branches in suburban shopping centers and malls to meet the needs of customers in those areas. A recent development in retail banking has been automated "vending machines" that enable customers to withdraw funds and to make deposits when a bank's offices are closed. The U.S. Postal Service has also installed vending machines in shopping malls.

VERTICAL MARKETING SYSTEMS

The traditional marketing channel has been described as a "highly fragmented network in which vertically aligned firms bargain with each other at arm's length, terminate relationships with impunity, and otherwise behave autonomously."[15] This potentially inefficient system of distributing goods is gradually being replaced by **vertical marketing systems (VMS)**—*"professionally managed and centrally programmed networks preengineered to achieve operating economies and maximum impact."*[16] VMS produce economies of scale through their size and by eliminating duplicated services. As Table 10.2 indicates, three types prevail—corporate, administered, and contractual.

Corporate System Where there is single ownership of each stage of the marketing channel, a *corporate vertical marketing system* exists. A reported 50 percent of all Sears products are purchased from manufacturers in which the nation's largest retailer has an equity interest. Holiday Inn owns a furniture manufacturer and a carpet mill. Hart Schaffner & Marx markets its Hickey-Freeman, Christian Dior, and Playboy suits through its company-owned chain of 275 men's clothing stores. Both IBM and Xerox have opened retail outlets.

TABLE 10.2
Vertical Marketing Systems

Type of System	Description	Examples
Corporate	Channel owned and operated by a single organization	Hart, Schaffner & Marx Firestone Sherwin-Williams
Administered	Channel dominated by one powerful member who acts as channel captain	Magnavox General Electric Kraftco Corning Glass
Contractual	Channel coordinated through contractual agreements among channel members	*Wholesaler-Sponsored Voluntary Chain:* IGA Western Auto Stores Associated Druggists Sentry Hardware *Retail Cooperative:* Associated Grocers *Franchise Systems:* H & R Block 7-Eleven Stores Century 21 Real Estate AAMCO Transmissions Coca-Cola bottlers

Mergers may result in a corporate vertical marketing system.

"High fives! Something big must be happening over in Corporate Acquisitions."

Source: Drawing by Lorenz. © 1981 The New Yorker Magazine, Inc.

In 1970, Genesco ranked first among U.S. apparel manufacturers with $1.2 billion in sales. Although sales of its Jarman and Johnston & Murphy brands through its own Flagg and Hardy shoe retailers accounted for one-third of total sales, Genesco managers were convinced that the key to further growth in shoe sales was to emphasize the sale of low-cost, unbranded shoes to such mass merchandisers as Sears. This proved to be a painful move, however, as it left the manufacturer at the whim of the giant retail chains. In addition, waves of competitively priced import shoes succeeded in capturing 53 percent of the U.S. shoe market by 1980, adding to Genesco's problems. New management sought a solution to these problems through the further development of a corporate VMS. Genesco's objective was to double the 960 company-owned shoe outlets by 1985. Although Genesco continued to rank third out of 325 U.S. shoe manufacturers, their strategy for overtaking the leaders Thom McAn and Kinney Shoes was to develop an integrated, manufacturer-owned VMS.[17]

Administered System Channel coordination is achieved through the exercise of economic and "political" power by a dominant channel member in an *administered vertical marketing system*. Magnavox obtains aggressive promotional support from its retailers because of the strong reputation of its brand. Although the retailers are independently owned and operated, they cooperate with the manufacturer because of the effective working relationships built up over the years.

Contractual System The most significant form of vertical marketing systems is the *contractual vertical marketing system*, which accounts for nearly 40 percent of all retail sales. Instead of the common ownership of channel components that characterized the corporate VMS or the relative power of a component of an administered system, the contractual VMS is characterized by formal agreements among channel members. In practice, there are three types of agreements: the wholesaler-sponsored voluntary chain, the retail cooperative, and the franchise.

The wholesaler-sponsored voluntary chain represents an attempt by the independent wholesaler to preserve a market for the firm's products by strengthening the firm's retailer customers. In order to enable the independent retailers to compete with the chains, the wholesaler enters into a formal agreement with a group of retailers wherein the retailers agree to use a common name, have standardized facilities, and purchase the wholesaler's products. Often, the wholesaler develops a line of private brands to be stocked by the members of the voluntary chain.

A common store name and similar inventories allow the retailers to achieve cost savings on advertising, since a single newspaper ad promotes all the retailers in the trading area. IGA Food Stores, with a membership of approximately 5,000 stores, is a good example of a voluntary chain. McKesson & Robbins Drug Company has established a large voluntary chain in the retail drug industry.

A second type of contractual VMS is the retail cooperative, which is established by a group of retailers who set up a wholesaling operation to better compete with the chains. The retailers purchase shares of stock in the wholesaling operation and agree to buy a minimum percentage of their inventory from the firm. The members may also choose to use a common store name and to develop their own private brands in order to carry out cooperative advertising. Retail cooperatives have been extremely successful in the grocery industry, accounting for one-fifth of all retail grocery sales.

A third type of contractual VMS is the **franchise**—*a contractual arrangement in which dealers (franchisees) agree to meet the operating requirements of a manufacturer or other franchisor.* The dealers typically receive a variety of marketing, management, technical, and financial services in exchange for a specified fee.

Although franchising has attracted considerable interest since the late 1960s, the concept actually began 100 years earlier when the Singer Company established franchised sewing machine outlets following the Civil War. Early impetus for the franchising concept came after 1900 in the automobile industry. Increasing automobile travel created demands for nationwide distribution of gasoline, oil, and tires, for which franchising was also used.[18] The soft-drink industry is another example of a franchise: a contractual arrangement exists between the syrup manufacturer and the wholesale bottler.

The franchising format that has created the most excitement in retailing during the past twenty years has been the retailer franchise system sponsored by the service firm. McDonald's is an excellent example of such a franchise operation. The company brings together suppliers and a chain of hamburger outlets. It provides a proven system of retail operation (the operations manual for each outlet weighs several pounds) and lower prices through its purchasing power on meat, buns, napkins, and necessary supplies. In return, the franchisee pays a fee of about $350,000 for the use of the McDonald's name and a percentage of gross sales. Other familiar examples are Hertz, Century 21 and Red Carpet real estate agencies, Tantrific tanning salons, Pizza Hut, Howard Johnson's, and Weight Watchers. Franchises account for one-third of all sales, employ over four million people, and involve more than 460,000 establishments in the United States.

McDonald's has almost 6,000 restaurants in operation. The early McDonald's outlets offered a severely restricted menu and little or no seating. Their 1983 counterparts provide an expanded breakfast and luncheon selection and often afford seating capacity for 100 to 300 diners. These efforts are aimed at obtaining even more of the $50 billion spent annually in U.S. restaurants. One out of every three meals in the United States is eaten in restaurants, and the rate is expected to grow to one out of two within the next five years. Table 10.3 lists the ten largest fast-food restaurants in the United States.

Fast-food franchising has already proven itself in the international market. McDonald's hamburgers are consumed daily in Tokyo, London, Rome, and Paris. Kentucky Fried Chicken has opened more than 500 restaurants outside the United States in locations as diverse as Manila, Munich, Nairobi, and Nice. In some countries, adjustments to U.S. marketing plans have been made to accommodate local needs. Although their menu is rigidly standardized in the United

TABLE 10.3
The Ten Largest
Fast-food
Restaurants

Rank	Company	1980 U.S. Sales (in millions)	Percent Change since 1979	Percent of U.S. Market[a]
1	McDonald's	$5,499.0	13.5	18.2%
2	Burger King	1,755.4	25.0	6.3
3	Kentucky Fried Chicken	1,440.0	6.6	5.2
4	Wendy's International	1,209.1	20.6	4.4
5	American Dairy Queen	1,020.0	10.1	3.7
6	Pizza Hut	945.0	13.4	3.4
7	Hardee's	922.3	23.1	3.3
8	Denny's	552.7	15.3	2.0
9	Jack in the Box	500.0	6.7	1.8
10	Sambo's	500.0	−8.0	1.8

[a]Based on Commerce Department figures for fast-food restaurants that franchise.
Source: John C. Maxwell, Jr., and Donna M. Mattei, "Higher '80 Prices Hike Fast-food Sales 12%," *Advertising Age*, September 28, 1981, p. 77.

Franchising has
revolutionized the
fast-food industry.

"I guess the fast-food business has pretty much reached the saturation point."

Source: Drawing by Guindon © 1978, Los Angeles Times Syndicate. Reprinted with permission.

States, McDonald's executives approved the addition of wine to the menu in French outlets. Also, Kentucky Fried Chicken substituted french fries for mashed potatoes to satisfy its Japanese customers.

The infatuation with the franchising concept and the market performance of franchise stocks lured dozens of newcomers into the market. Lacking experience and often armed only with a well-known name as their sole asset, many of these firms (among them Broadway Joe's, Chicken Delight, and Minnie Pearl's) quickly disappeared.

The popularity of franchising led Americans to invest $1.1 billion in franchises in a single year. These investments included such currently popular operations as energy conservation centers, gourmet cheese stores, used car rentals, furniture stripping, ambulances for pets, and even cremation franchises. The median price for a franchise was $50,000. The success of the franchising approach to retailing led to some abuses as some unscrupulous operations moved into the industry during the peak growth period of the 1970s. The Federal Trade Commission has been engaged since that time in a concentrated attempt to minimize potential abuses. Abuses uncovered by the FTC included the following:

One battery company, recently tripped up by the Federal Trade Commission, promised a return of more than $10,000 a year on an

HOW BURGER KING SERVES ITS FRANCHISEES

Every year about 1,000 people apply to Burger King for a franchise. Only a tenth of them are successful. In this rigorous competition, knowledge of, or even interest in, food counts for little; the candidates could as well be prospective Midas Muffler dealers. What Burger King is mainly looking for is people who have management ability, enthusiasm, willingness to follow instructions to the letter, and $110,000 in liquid assets. Typically Burger King provides the land and building, while the franchisee finances signs, lights, broilers, computer-regulated french-fry fryers, and other fittings. The franchisee's total outlay averages $179,000 per store.

Successful applicants spend a week working in an existing restaurant to see if they like the business, then six weeks of basic training at a regional center, and finally nine days at Burger King University in Miami, where they are tutored in everything from labor relations to the proper spacing of hamburger patties on a broiler (a quarter of an inch apart).

Franchisees graduating from BKU this spring included Richard Connolly, 34, a former Long Island 7-Up distributor who will be opening a Burger King in Elkins, West Virginia; Ronald Broatch, a 39-year-old high school counselor from northern California, and his wife, Annette, who will start one in Bellingham, Washington; and Stephen Olson, the 23-year-old son of a Colorado franchisee. Olson and his partners have taken over a failed franchise in Vail.

They are likely to earn a handsome return. A well-managed store with sales of $717,000 a year, the current average for Burger Kings, should provide the franchisee with a pretax income of $70,000. A franchisee who performs well with one store often gets to put up another nearby, and then maybe a few more, until he bumps against the one-hour-radius limit that is one of Burger King's new restrictions on store operations. Franchisees can still dream, as long as their dreams are regular size, not Whoppers.

investment of $1,695. Another company, an electronics equipment marketer, blandly assured its franchisees that they could make over $400 per month on a total investment of $1,895. A Dallas credit card company told its franchisees, who were required to invest between $3,500 and $10,000, that they could not help but make over $125,000 per year. Within two years this organization had fleeced would-be franchisees out of more than $200,000.[19]

In 1979, an FTC rule called *Disclosure Requirements and Prohibitions Concerning Franchising and Business Opportunities* went into effect. As its title suggests, the new rule attempts to protect would-be investors by requiring disclosure of factual information concerning franchisor claims, guarantees, franchising experience, occurrence of any bankruptcy, and evidence of the moral character of the key personnel in the franchise. Also specified are services to be provided by each party and the specific terms of the franchising agreement, including all costs involved.

Whether corporate, administered, or contractual, vertical marketing systems are already a dominant factor in the consumer goods sector of the U.S. economy. An estimated 64 percent of the available market is currently in the hands of retail components of VMS.

SUMMARY

Marketing channels bridge the gap between producer and consumer. By making products and services available when and where the consumer wants to buy, and by arranging for transfer of title, marketing channels create time, place, and ownership utility.

The marketing manager faces a host of alternative channels for the firm's products—from contacting the consumer directly through catalog sales or the use of salespersons to using a variety of independent wholesaling middlemen and retailers. In fact, manufacturers of similar products often utilize multiple channels. The choice of optimal channels is based on careful analysis of the firm's market target, characteristics of the manufacturer, product characteristics, and a number of environmental factors.

The degree of intensity of market coverage for products and services may vary from a single dealer in a given territory (exclusive distribution) to the use of a few dealers (selective distribution) to a total saturation of the market using every dealer who will agree to handle the products (intensive distribution). Exclusive distribution policies may present legal problems, since the concept of limiting the number of dealers who can handle a firm's output carries with it overtones of restraint of trade.

Cooperation among channel members is essential for efficient distribution. The channel captain, the dominant member of the channel, typically assumes responsibility for obtaining cooperation from channel members. Although channel captains have traditionally been manufacturers or wholesalers, large retailers are increasingly assuming this role in the marketing channel.

The need for channel cooperation has resulted in the development of the vertical marketing system (VMS). Whether formed through single ownership of each stage in the marketing channel, through contractual relationships among channel members, or through voluntary cooperation, these systems have proven effective and efficient in managing the operations of the marketing channel.

QUESTIONS FOR DISCUSSION

1. Explain the following terms:

   marketing channel

   time utility

   place utility

   ownership utility

   middleman

   wholesaling

   retailers

   reverse channels

   facilitating agency

   intensive distribution

   selective distribution

   exclusive distribution

   exclusive dealing agreement

   closed sales territories

   tying agreement

   channel captain

   missionary salesperson

   vertical marketing systems (VMS)

   franchise

2. Explain and illustrate each of the utilities provided by marketing channels.

3. What types of products are most likely to be distributed through direct channels?

4. Which marketing channel is the "traditional" channel? Give some reasons for its frequent use.

5. Refer to the classifications of consumer and industrial goods in Chapter 8. Suggest the best channel for each type. Defend your answer.

6. Explain and illustrate the major factors affecting choice of marketing channels.

7. Which degree of intensity of market coverage is appropriate for each of the following:

   a. *People* magazine

   b. Ocean Pacific (OP) swimwear

   c. Irish Spring soap

   d. McCulloch chain saws

   e. Cuisinart food processors

   f. Honda motorcycles

   g. Waterford crystal

8. Why would manufacturers choose more than one channel for their products?

9. Under what conditions is a manufacturer most likely to bypass independent wholesalers and market the firm's products directly to the retailer?

10. Why would any manufacturer deliberately choose to limit market coverage through a policy of exclusive coverage?

11. Why would manufacturers favor the use of tying agreements?

12. Under what circumstances are sales territory restrictions likely to be illegal?

13. Under what circumstances is the retailer likely to assume the role of channel captain? When will the manufacturer typically fulfill this role?

14. Why have retailers only recently begun to assume the role of channel captain?

15. In what ways could the use of multiple channels produce channel conflict?

16. Explain and illustrate each type of vertical marketing system.

17. What is the basic distinction between retail cooperatives and voluntary chains?

18. What conditions are necessary for an administered VMS to prove effective?

19. What advantages does franchising offer the small retailer?

20. One generalization of channel selection mentioned in the chapter was that low unit value products require long channels. How can you explain the success of a firm (such as Avon) that has a direct channel for its relatively low unit value products?

NOTES

1. The discussion of applying franchising concepts to dentistry is adapted from and quotes from "Alliance with Retail Stores, Marketing Savvy Strengthens Growth of Franchise Dentistry," *Marketing News,* May 29, 1981, p. 5. Used by permission of the American Marketing Association.

2. Committee on Definitions, *Marketing Definitions: A Glossary of Marketing Terms* (Chicago: American Marketing Association, 1960), p. 10. Some authors limit the definition to the route taken by the title to goods and services, but this definition also includes agent wholesaling middlemen who do not take title, but who do serve as important components of many channels.

3. The Mary Kay Cosmetics channel is described in Howard Rudnitsky, "The Flight of the Bumblebee," *Forbes,* June 22, 1981, pp. 104–6.

4. Wilke English, Dale M. Lewison, and M. Wayne DeLozier, "Evolution in Channel Management: Who Will Be Next?" in *Proceedings of the Southwestern Marketing Association,* eds. Robert H. Ross, Frederic B. Kraft, and Charles H. Davis, Wichita, Kansas, 1981, pp. 78–81.

5. William G. Zikmund and William J. Stanton, "Recycling Solid Wastes: A Channels-of-Distribution Problem," *Journal of Marketing,* July 1971, p. 34.

6. Donald A. Fuller, "Aluminum Beverage Container Recycling in Florida: A Commentary," *Atlanta Economic Review,* January–February, 1977, p. 41.

7. "Jostens: A School Supplier Stays with Basics as Enrollment Declines," *Business Week,* April 21, 1980, pp. 124, 129.

8. "Nabisco: Diversifying Again, but This Time Wholeheartedly," *Business Week,* October 20, 1980, p. 71.

9. Michael B. Metzger, "Schwinn's Swan Song," *Business Horizons,* April 1978, pp. 52–56.

10. Shelby D. Hunt and John R. Nevin, "Tying Agreements in Franchising," *Journal of Marketing,* July 1975, pp. 20–26.

11. Bruce Mallen, "A Theory of Retailer-Supplier Conflict, Control, and Cooperation," *Journal of Retailing,* Summer 1963, p. 26. Reprinted with permission. See also F. Robert Dwyer, "Channel-Member Satisfaction: Laboratory Insights," *Journal of Retailing,* Summer 1980, pp. 45–65.

12. "Dr Pepper: Pitted against the Soft-Drink Giants," *Business Week,* October 6, 1975, p. 70. For a discussion of Coca-Cola's relationships with its bottlers see Peter W. Bernstein, "Coke Strikes Back," *FORTUNE,* June 1, 1981, pp. 30–36.

13. James R. Brown, "Methods of Channel Conflict Resolution: Some Empirical Results," in *1979 Educators' Conference Proceedings,* eds. Neil Beckwith, Michael Houston, Robert Mittelstaedt, Kent B. Monroe, and Scott Ward (Chicago: American Marketing Association, 1979), pp. 495–99; Michael Etgar, "Sources and Types of Intra Channel Conflict," *Journal of Retailing,* Spring 1979, pp. 61–78; and Louis W. Stern and Torger Reve, "Distribution Channels as Political Economies," *Journal of Marketing,* Summer 1980, pp. 52–64.

14. Bruce J. Walker and Donald W. Jackson, Jr., "The Channels Manager: A Needed New Position," in *Proceedings of the Southern Marketing Association,* eds. Robert S. Franz, Robert M. Hopkins, and Al Toma, New Orleans, Louisiana, November 1978, pp. 325–28. See also R. Kenneth Teas and Stanley D. Sibley, "An Examination of the Moderating Effect of Channel Member Size on Perceptions of Preferred Channel Linkages," *Journal of the Academy of Marketing Science,* Summer 1980, pp. 277–93.

15. This section is based on Bert C. McCammon, Jr., "The Emergence and Growth of Contractually Integrated Channels in the American Economy," in *Marketing and Economic Development* (Chicago: American Marketing Association, 1965), pp. 496–515. Used by permission.

16. *Ibid.,* p. 496.

17. "Genesco: An Apparel Empire Returns to Its Retailing Base—Shoes," *Business Week,* June 23, 1980, pp. 90–99.

18. Thomas G. Marx, "Distribution Efficiency in Franchising," *MSU Business Topics,* Winter 1980, p. 5.

19. Quoted in John R. Nevin, Shelby D. Hunt, and Michael G. Levas, "Legal Remedies for Deceptive and Unfair Practices in Franchising," *Journal of Macromarketing,* Spring 1981, p. 24. Used by permission.

CHAPTER 11

MARKETING INSTITUTIONS: WHOLESALING

KEY TERMS

wholesaler
wholesaling middlemen
sales branch
public warehouse
sales office
trade fair
merchandise mart
merchant wholesaler
rack jobber
cash-and-carry wholesaler
truck wholesaler
drop shipper
mail-order wholesaler
agents
brokers
commission merchant
auction houses
selling agent
manufacturers' agents

LEARNING GOALS

1. To identify the functions performed by marketing institutions

2. To distinguish between wholesaling and retailing

3. To explain the channel options available to a manufacturer who desires to bypass independent wholesaling middlemen

4. To identify the conditions under which a manufacturer is likely to assume wholesaling functions rather than use independents

5. To distinguish between merchant wholesalers and agents and brokers

6. To identify the major types of merchant wholesalers and instances where each type might be used

7. To describe the major types of agents and brokers

Magazines are distributed through two channels: customer subscriptions and single-copy sales at newsstands, grocery stores, chain stores, convenience stores, and drugstores. As the subscription channel becomes more expensive due to ever-increasing postal rates (which have risen almost 400 percent in four years), the single-copy channel becomes increasingly important.

But every year, millions of magazines are returned unsold. About $200 million worth of them—more than total industry profits—go into the shredder. Magazine wholesalers are working to provide the information necessary to reduce the number of unsold copies.

Ten national wholesalers are responsible for moving more than 33,000 titles from the publishers to about 500 local wholesalers in small regions throughout the nation. The local wholesalers supply copies to the various retail outlets. Speed is essential. As one local wholesaler stated, "*TV Guide* prints one day and within 36 hours is stocked in more than 150,000 establishments."

In an attempt to reduce the number of unsold copies that some people have labeled "a conspiracy to deforest Canada," the magazine wholesalers provide publishers with a detailed breakdown of their returns and sellouts by area and magazine type. This information should help publishers regulate the number of magazines shipped to a given area and select the proper combination for the demographics of the area. In addition, magazines such as *Cosmopolitan* provide wholesalers with specific marketing information to help them promote sales. Cooperation between publishers and their marketing intermediaries is aimed at a 95-percent sellout goal.[1]

SOME WHOLESALING TERMINOLOGY

As defined in Chapter 10, wholesaling involves the activities of persons or firms who sell to retailers and other wholesalers or to industrial users, but not in significant amounts to ultimate consumers. The term **wholesaler** is applied only to *wholesaling middlemen who take title to the products they handle.* **Wholesaling middlemen** is a broader term that describes *not only middlemen who assume title to the goods they handle, but also agents and brokers who perform important wholesaling activities without taking title to the goods.* Under this definition, then, a wholesaler is a merchant middleman.

The most recent Census of Wholesale Trade lists nearly 383,000 wholesaling establishments with a total sales volume of $1.26 trillion. Wholesaling middlemen are concentrated in the Middle Atlantic and East North Central states. The New York City metropolitan area alone accounts for 11 percent of all wholesale trade.

FUNCTIONS OF WHOLESALING MIDDLEMEN

The route that goods follow on the way to the consumer or industrial user is actually a chain of marketing institutions. Goods that "bypass" the marketing intermediaries in the chain and move directly from manufacturer to consumer constitute only 3 percent of the total in the consumer goods market. But unprecedented increases in the prices of goods and services in the late 1970s and the 1980s have led to rising complaints about middlemen who allegedly drive prices up because of their high profits and questionable services. Many discount retailers claim lower prices as a result of direct purchases from manufacturers. Chain stores often assume wholesaling functions and bypass the independent wholesalers.

Are these complaints and claims valid? Are wholesaling middlemen the "dinosaurs" of the 1980s? Answers to these questions can be discerned by considering the functions and costs of these marketing intermediaries.

Services Provided by Wholesaling Middlemen

A marketing institution can continue to exist only so long as it performs a service that fulfills a need. Its demise may be slow but inevitable once other channel members discover they can survive without it. Table 11.1 examines a number of possible services provided by wholesaling middlemen. It is important to note that numerous types of wholesaling middlemen exist and that not all of them provide every service listed in Table 11.1. Producer-suppliers and their customers, who rely on wholesaling middlemen for distribution, select those intermediaries providing the desired combination of services.

The listing of possible services provided by wholesaling middlemen clearly indicates the provision of marketing utility—time, place, and ownership or possession—by these intermediaries. The services also reflect the provision of the basic marketing functions of buying, selling, storing, transporting, risk-taking, financing, and supplying market information.

The critical marketing functions—transportation and convenient product storage; reduced costs of buying and selling through reduced contacts; marketing information; and financing—form the basis of evaluating the efficiency of any marketing intermediary. The risk-taking function is present in each of the services provided by the wholesaling middleman.

Middlemen are often blamed for high prices.

Source: Copyright © 1973 by G.B. Trudeau. Reprinted with permission of Universal Press Syndicate. All rights reserved.

**TABLE 11.1
Possible Wholesaling
Services for
Customers and
Producer-suppliers**

Service	Service Provided for	
	Customers	Producer-suppliers
Buying Anticipates customer demands and possesses knowledge of alternative sources of supply; acts as purchasing agent for their customers.	X	
Selling Provides a sales force to call upon customers, thereby providing a low-cost method of servicing smaller retailers and industrial users.		X
Storing Provides a warehousing function at lower cost than most individual producers or retailers could provide. Reduces the risk and cost of maintaining inventory for producers, and provides customers with prompt delivery service.	X	X
Transporting Customers receive prompt delivery in response to their demands, reducing their inventory investments. Wholesalers also break-bulk by purchasing in economical carload or truckload lots, then reselling in smaller quantities to their customers, thereby reducing overall transportation costs.	X	X
Providing Market Information Serves as important marketing research input for producers through regular contacts with retail and industrial buyers. Provides customers with information about new products, technical information about product lines, reports on activities of competitors, industry trends, and advisory information concerning pricing changes, legal changes, etc.	X	X
Financing Aids customers by granting credit that might not be available were the customers to purchase directly from manufacturers. Provides financing assistance to producers by purchasing goods in advance of sale and through prompt payment of bills.	X	X
Risk-taking Assists producers by evaluating credit risks of numerous distant retail customers and small industrial users. Extension of credit to these customers is another form of risk-taking. In addition, the wholesaler responsible for transportation and stocking goods in inventory assumes risk of possible spoilage, theft, or obsolescence.	X	X

Transportation and Product Storage

Wholesalers transport and store products at locations convenient to customers. Manufacturers ship products from their warehouse to numerous wholesalers, who then ship smaller quantities to retail outlets in locations convenient to purchasers. A large number of wholesalers assume the inventory function (and cost) for the manufacturer. They benefit through the convenience afforded by local inventories. The manufacturer benefits through reduced cash needs, since its products are sold directly to the retailer or wholesaler.

Costs are reduced at the wholesale level through the making of large purchases from the manufacturer. The wholesaler receives quantity discounts from the manufacturer and incurs lower transportation costs because economical carload or truckload shipments are made to the wholesaler's warehouses. At the warehouse, the wholesaler divides the goods into smaller quantities and ships them to the retailer over a shorter distance (but at a higher rate) than would be the case if the manufacturer filled the retailer's order directly from a central warehouse.

Reduced Contacts Often Lower Costs

When wholesaling middlemen represent numerous manufacturers to a single customer, the costs involved in buying and selling often decrease. The transaction economies are shown by the example in Figure 11.1. In this illustration, four manufacturers are marketing their outputs

**FIGURE 11.1
How Middlemen
Reduce the Number
of Contacts between
Manufacturers and
Their Customers**

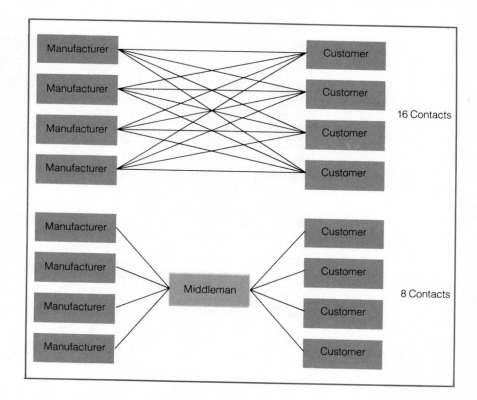

to four different retail outlets. A total of 16 transactions result if no intermediary is utilized. By adding a wholesaling middleman, the number of transactions is reduced to eight.

A Source of Information

Because of their central position between the manufacturer and retailers or industrial buyers, wholesalers serve as important information links. Wholesalers provide their retail customers with useful information about new products. In addition, they supply manufacturers with information about the market acceptance of their product offerings.

WHOLESALING'S ROLE IN THE PERRIER SUCCESS

Although Perrier naturally carbonated mineral water has been marketed in the United States since 1903, 75 years passed before it was "discovered" by the American public. Prior to 1977, Perrier was distributed on a very limited basis through specialty food outlets and fine restaurants to a small number of consumers who valued either its supposed healthful properties or its snob appeal. Forty-year-old Bruce Nevins, president of the Perrier's U.S. subsidiary, realized that drastic changes in the firm's wholesaling operations were necessary if the product was to succeed.

Nevins wanted to position Perrier as a chic alternative to cocktails and soft drinks. He had noted that a number of people had switched from "browns" (bourbon and scotch) to "whites" (gin and vodka) and then to wine. According to Nevins, "The next step is away from alcohol altogether, which puts Perrier in a nice position." His challenge: to develop a distribution network that reaches bars and cocktail lounges.

His second task was to tackle the enormous soft-drink market, aiming for a 1 percent market share. He shifted his distribution structure away from the gourmet shops and toward grocery stores.

Nevins' solution was to turn to independent wholesalers to handle distribution. Independent wholesale soft-drink bottlers were utilized to reach supermarkets and mass merchandisers such as K mart, while beer wholesalers covered liquor retailers, bars, and cocktail lounges.

All facets of the marketing mix were involved in the Perrier success. Effective promotion, retail prices in accordance with its chic appeal, and appealing packaging are important factors, but none of these was sufficient without the system of wholesale distribution designed to reach the firm's market target. The success of the Perrier marketing program is summarized in the growth of the product's sales. In 1976, just prior to the implementation of the new marketing program, Perrier annual sales amounted to a mere 3.5 million bottles. Four years later, they had soared to 180 million bottles.

Source: Information from "Putting More Sparkle into Sales," *Sales & Marketing Management,* January 1979, pp. 16–17; Bob Greene, "Genius Sells Water at $2.39 a Six-Pack," Tulsa *World,* November 11, 1978, © Field Enterprises, Inc. Courtesy of Field Newspaper Syndicate; and Bernice Finkelman, "Perrier Pours into U.S. Market, Spurs Water Bottler Battle," *Marketing News,* September 7, 1979, pp. 1, 9. Used by permission of the American Marketing Association.

Source of Financing

Wholesalers also serve a financing function. They often provide retailers with goods on credit, allowing the retailers to minimize their cash investment in inventory and pay for most of the goods as they are sold. This allows them to benefit from the principle of leverage, whereby a minimum amount spent on goods in inventory inflates the return on invested funds. A retailer with an investment of $1 million and profits of $100,000 will realize a return of 10 percent. But if the necessary invested capital can be reduced to $800,000 through credit from the wholesaler, and if the $100,000 profits can be maintained, the retailer's return increases to 12.5 percent.

Wholesalers of industrial goods provide similar services for the purchasers of their goods. In the steel industry, middlemen (referred to as metal service centers) currently market one-fifth of all steel shipped by U.S mills. One such center, the Earle M. Jorgensen Company in Los Angeles, stocks 6,500 items for sale to many of the 50,000 major metal users who buy in large quantities directly from the steel mills but who turn to service centers for quick delivery of special orders.

While an order from the mills may take ninety days for delivery, a service center can usually deliver locally within twenty-four to forty-eight hours. In order to attract business from key customers, such as AMF, which makes bicycles locally, Jorgensen carried inventory for them without demanding a contract. The cost and the risk of maintaining the stock are assumed by the service center in order for it to provide overnight delivery service for its customers.[2]

Marketing Channel Functions: Who Should Perform Them?

While wholesaling middlemen often perform a variety of valuable functions for their manufacturer, retailer, and other wholesaler clients, these functions could be performed by other channel members. Manufacturers may choose to bypass independent wholesaling middlemen by establishing networks of regional warehouses, maintaining large sales forces to provide market coverage, serving as sources of information for their retail customers, and assuming the financing function. In some instances, they may decide to push the responsibility for some of these functions through the channel on to the retailer or the ultimate purchaser. Large retailers who choose to perform their own wholesaling operations face the same choices.

A fundamental marketing principle applies to marketing channel decisions:

Marketing functions must be performed by some member of the channel. They can be shifted, but they cannot be eliminated.

Larger retailers who bypass the wholesaler and deal directly with the manufacturer will either assume the functions previously performed by wholesaling middlemen, or these functions will be performed by the manufacturer. Similarly, a manufacturer who deals directly with the ultimate consumer or with industrial buyers will assume the functions of storage, delivery, and marketing information previously performed by marketing intermediaries. Middlemen can be eliminated from the channel, but the channel functions must be performed by someone.

The potential gain for the manufacturer or retailer is summarized in Table 11.2. The table shows the potential savings if channel members performed the wholesale functions as efficiently as the independent wholesaling middleman. Such savings, indicated in the net profit column, could be used to reduce retail prices, to increase the profits of the manufacturer or retailer, or both.

The most revealing information in Table 11.2 are the low profit rates earned by most wholesalers. Three types of wholesalers (meats and meat products; tobacco and tobacco products; and groceries) earn less than 1.5 percent net profit as a percentage of net sales, while the group with the highest profit as a percentage of sales (automotive parts and supplies) earned 3.55 percent.

Table 11.2 also indicates a positive relationship between annual turnover rate (as measured by total sales divided by the average inventory) and net profits as a percentage of net sales. Wholesaling middlemen such as those in dairy and meat products enjoyed relatively high turnover rates. These rates permitted the firms to generate sufficient financial returns with lower net profits (on a percentage of net sales basis) than many of the other intermediaries with lower turnover rates.

**TABLE 11.2
Median Net Profits
and Turnover Rates
of Selected
Wholesalers**

Kind of Business	Net Profits as a Percentage of Net Sales*	Annual Turnover Rate**
Automotive parts and supplies	3.55	5.1
Beer and ale	2.91	13.6
Clothing and furnishings, men's and boys'	2.94	6.2
Confectionary	1.98	12.3
Dairy products	1.71	42.7
Drugs, proprietaries, and sundries	2.21	7.1
Electrical appliances, TV, and radio sets	2.39	6.5
Footwear	2.70	6.0
Furniture	3.10	8.5
Groceries, general line	1.10	12.1
Hardware	3.21	6.2
Meats and meat products	1.47	35.0
Printing and writing paper	2.53	9.8
Petroleum bulk stations and terminals	1.91	23.3
Tires and tubes	2.60	6.0
Tobacco and tobacco products	.95	13.8

*After provision for federal income taxes   **Net sales to inventory
Source: "The Ratios," Dun's Review, November 1980, pp. 142,144. Reprinted with the special permission of Dun's Review. Copyright 1980, Dun & Bradstreet Publications Corporation.

TYPES OF WHOLESALING MIDDLEMEN

As mentioned previously, various types of wholesaling middlemen are present in different marketing channels. Some provide a wide range of services or handle a broad line of products, while others specialize in a single service, product, or industry. Figure 11.2 classifies wholesaling middlemen by two characteristics: *ownership* (whether the wholesaling middleman is independent, manufacturer-owned, or retailer-owned) and *title flows* (whether title passes from the manufacturer to the wholesaling middleman). There are, in turn, three basic types of ownership: (1) independent wholesaling middlemen, (2) manufacturer-owned sales offices and branches, and (3) retailer-owned cooperatives and buying offices. The two types of independent wholesaling middlemen are merchant wholesalers who do take title to goods and agents and brokers who do not.

Manufacturer-owned Facilities

An increasing volume of products is being marketed directly by manufacturers through company-owned facilities, and for several reasons. Some products are perishable; some require complex installation or servicing; others need aggressive promotion; still others are high unit-value goods that the manufacturer can sell profitably to the ultimate purchaser. Among those who have shifted from the use of independent wholesaling middlemen to the use of company-owned channels are manufacturers of apparel, construction materials, lumber, paint, paper, and piece goods.[3] More than half of all industrial goods are sold directly to users by manufacturers, and slightly more than one-third of all products are marketed through manufacturer-owned channels.[4]

**FIGURE 11.2
Major Types of
Wholesaling
Middlemen**

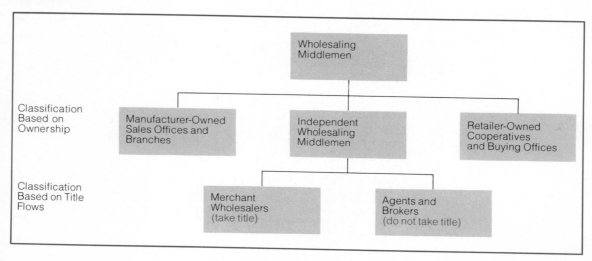

Sales Branches and Offices The basic distinction between a company's sales branches and sales offices is that a **sales branch** *carries inventory and processes orders to customers from available stock.* Branches duplicate the storage function of independent wholesalers and serve as offices for sales representatives in the territory. They are prevalent in the marketing of chemicals, commercial machinery and equipment, motor vehicles, and petroleum products. Operating expenses for the 26,892 sales branches in the United States average 8.9 percent of sales. General Electric has sales branches in every major city in the United States. Its subsidiary, General Electric Supply Corporation, provides regular contacts and overnight delivery to GE retailers and industrial purchasers.

Since warehouses represent a substantial investment in real estate, small manufacturers and even large firms developing new sales territories may choose to use a **public warehouse**—*an independently owned storage facility.* For a rental fee, manufacturers can store their goods in any of the more than 10,000 public warehouses in the United States for shipment by the warehouses to customers in the area. Warehouse owners will package goods into small quantities to fill orders and will even handle billing for manufacturers. Public warehouses can also provide a financial service for manufacturers by issuing warehouse receipts for inventory. Manufacturers can use these receipts as collateral for bank loans.

A **sales office,** by contrast, *does not carry stock but serves as a regional office for the firm's sales personnel.* Sales offices in close proximity to the firm's customers help reduce selling costs and improve customer service. The listing of a firm in the local telephone directory often results in new sales for the local representative. Many buyers prefer to telephone the office of a supplier rather than take the time to write to distant suppliers. Since the nation's 13,629 sales offices do not perform a storage function, their operating expenses are relatively low, averaging 3.1 percent of total sales.

Other Outlets for the Manufacturer's Products In addition to using a sales force and regionally distributed sales branches, manufacturers often market their products through trade fairs and merchandise marts. A **trade fair** (or a trade exhibition) is *a periodic show where manufacturers in a particular industry display their wares for visiting retail and wholesale buyers.* The New York City toy fair and the furniture show in High Point, North Carolina, are annual events for manufacturers and purchasers of toys and furniture. The cost of making a face-to-face contact with a prospective customer at a trade fair is only 41 percent of the cost of a personal sales call. In addition, such exhibitions represent effective methods of generating additional sales. One study of attendees at the National Computer Conference in Anaheim, California, revealed that within the eleven months following the conference, four out of five attendees had purchased at least one product on display and that the average purchase had been $254,100.[5]

**TABLE 11.3
Wholesale Trade by
Type of Operation**

Type of Operation	Number of Establishments	Sales (in Billions)	Percentage of Total Sales
Merchant wholesalers	307,264	$ 676.1	53.7
Manufacturers' sales branches and offices	40,521	451.9	35.9
Agents, brokers, and commission merchants	35,052	130.4	10.4
Total wholesale trade	382,837	1,258.4	100.0

Source: U.S. Department of Commerce, Bureau of the Census, *1977 Census of Business, Wholesale Trade—Geographic Area Series 52–19* (Washington, D.C.: U.S. Government Printing Office, 1980).

A **merchandise mart** *provides space for permanent exhibitions where manufacturers rent showcases for their product offerings.* The largest is the Merchandise Mart in Chicago, which is two blocks long, a block wide, and twenty-one floors high. Over a million items are displayed there. Retail buyers can compare the offerings of dozens of competing manufacturers and make most purchase decisions in a single visit to a trade fair or merchandise mart.

Independent Wholesaling Middlemen

As Table 11.3 indicates, independent wholesaling middlemen account for 90 percent of the wholesale establishments and approximately two-thirds of the wholesale sales in the United States. They can be divided into two categories—merchant wholesalers and agents and brokers.

Merchant Wholesalers The **merchant wholesaler** *takes title to the goods handled.* Merchant wholesalers account for slightly more than 53 percent of all sales at the wholesale level, and their sales are projected to reach the $1 trillion mark by 1985.[6] They can be further classified as full-function or limited-function wholesalers, as indicated in Figure 11.3.

**FIGURE 11.3
Classification of Independent Wholesaling Middlemen**

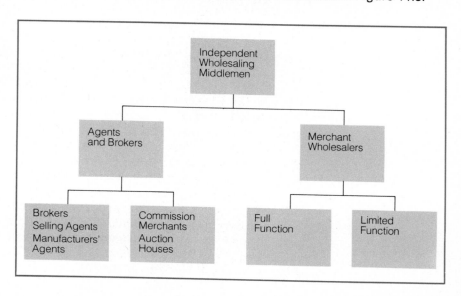

Full-function Merchant Wholesalers A complete assortment of services for retailers and industrial purchasers is provided by full-function merchant wholesalers. These wholesalers store merchandise in convenient locations, thereby allowing their customers to make purchases on short notice and to minimize their inventory requirements. They also usually maintain sales forces to call regularly on retailers, make deliveries, and extend credit to qualified buyers. In the industrial goods market, full-function merchant wholesalers (often called industrial distributors) usually market machinery, inexpensive accessory equipment, and supplies.

Full-function merchant wholesalers prevail in industries where retailers are small and carry large numbers of relatively inexpensive items, none of which is stocked in depth. The drug, grocery, and hardware industries have traditionally been serviced by full-function merchant wholesalers.

A unique type of service wholesaler emerged after World War II as grocery retailers began to stock high profit-margin nonfood items. Since store managers knew little about such products as health and beauty items, housewares, paperback books, records, and toys, the **rack jobber** provided the necessary expertise. This wholesaler *supplies the racks, stocks the merchandise, prices the goods, and makes regular visits to refill the shelves.* In essence, rack jobbers rent space

Full-service merchant wholesalers make regular calls on their retail or wholesale customers.

"Better let me have another gross of the #101 thunderbird ashtrays, two gross of #473 beaded souvenir moccasins, and two dozen #87 turquoise and silver runner pins."

Source: Reprinted by permission from *Sales & Marketing Management* magazine. Copyright © 1977.

from retailers on a commission basis. They have expanded into discount, drug, hardware, and variety stores.

Since full-function merchant wholesalers perform a large number of services, their operating expenses average nearly 13 percent, and sometimes as high as 20 percent, of sales. Attempts to reduce the costs of dealing with these wholesalers have led to the development of a number of limited-function middlemen.

Limited-function Merchant Wholesalers Four types of limited-function merchant wholesalers are cash-and-carry wholesalers, truck wholesalers, drop shippers, and mail-order wholesalers. The **cash-and-carry wholesaler** *performs most wholesaling functions with the exception of financing and delivery.* These wholesalers first appeared on the marketing scene in the grocery industry during the Depression era of the 1930s. In an attempt to reduce costs, retailers began driving to wholesalers' warehouses, paying cash for their purchases, and making their own deliveries. By eliminating the delivery and financing functions, cash-and-carry wholesalers were able to reduce their operating costs to approximately 9 percent of sales.

Although feasible for small stores, this kind of wholesaling proves to be generally unworkable for large-scale grocery stores. Chain store managers are unwilling to perform the delivery function, and cash-and-carry these days is typically one department of a regular full-service wholesaler. The cash-and-carry wholesaler has proven successful, however, in the United Kingdom, where 600 such operations produce over $1 billion a year in sales.

The **truck wholesaler,** or truck jobber, *markets perishable food items such as bread, tobacco, potato chips, candy, and dairy products.* Truck wholesalers make regular deliveries to retail stores and perform the sales and collection functions. They also aggressively promote their product lines. The high costs of operating delivery trucks and the low dollar volume per sale mean relatively high operating costs of 15 percent.

A **drop shipper** *receives orders from customers and forwards them to producers, who ship directly to the customers.* Although drop shippers take title to the goods, they never physically handle or even see them. Since they perform no storage or handling function, their operating costs are a relatively low 4 to 5 percent of sales.

Drop shippers operate in fields where products are bulky and customers make their purchases in carload lots. Transportation and handling costs represent a substantial percentage of the total cost of such products as coal and lumber. Drop shippers do not maintain an inventory of these products, thereby eliminating the expenses of loading and unloading carload shipments. Their major service is the development of a complete assortment of customers. Since various types and grades of coal and lumber are produced by different companies, drop shippers can assemble a complete line to fill any customer's order.

TABLE 11.4
Services Provided by
Merchant
Wholesalers

Services	Full-function Wholesalers	Limited-function Wholesalers			
		Cash-and-carry Wholesalers	Truck Wholesalers	Drop Shippers	Mail-order Wholesalers
Anticipates customer needs	Yes	Yes	Yes	No	Yes
Carries inventory	Yes	Yes	Yes	No	Yes
Delivers	Yes	No	Yes	No	No
Provides market information	Yes	Rarely	Yes	Yes	No
Provides credit	Yes	No	No	Yes	Sometimes
Assumes ownership risk by taking title	Yes	Yes	Yes	Yes	Yes

The **mail-order wholesaler** is *a limited-function merchant whole-saler who relies on catalogs rather than a sales force to contact retail, industrial, and institutional customers.* Purchases are then made by mail or telephone by relatively small customers in outlying areas. Mail-order operations are found in the hardware, cosmetics, jewelry, sporting goods, and specialty foods lines, as well as in general merchandise.

Table 11.4 compares the various types of merchant wholesalers in terms of services provided. Full-function merchant wholesalers and truck wholesalers are relatively high-cost intermediaries due to the number of services they perform, while cash-and-carry wholesalers, drop shippers, and mail-order wholesalers provide fewer services and have relatively lower operating costs.

Agents and Brokers A second group of independent wholesaling mid-dlemen—the **agents and brokers**—*may or may not take possession of the goods, but they never take title.* They normally perform fewer services than the merchant wholesalers and are typically involved in bringing together buyers and sellers. Agent wholesaling middlemen can be classified into five categories—commission merchants, auction houses, brokers, selling agents, and manufacturers' agents.

The **commission merchant,** who predominates in the marketing of agricultural products, *takes possession when the producer ships* *goods such as grain, produce, and livestock to a central market for sale.* Commission merchants act as the producer's agents and receive an agreed upon fee when the sale is made. Since customers inspect the products, and since prices fluctuate, commission merchants receive considerable latitude in making decisions. The owner of the goods may specify a minimum price, but the commission merchant will sell them on a "best price" basis. The merchant's fee is deducted from the price and remitted to the original owner.

Auction houses *bring buyers and sellers together in one location and allow potential buyers to inspect the merchandise before purchasing it.* Auction houses' commissions are often based on the sale price of the goods. Sotheby Parke Bernet of New York, London, and Los Angeles is a well-known auction house specializing in works of art. Other auction houses handle used cars, livestock, tobacco, fur, fruit, and other commodities.

Brokers *bring buyers and sellers together.* Brokers operate in industries characterized by a large number of small suppliers and purchasers—real estate, frozen foods, and used machinery, for example. They represent either the buyer or the seller in a given transaction, but not both. Brokers receive a fee from the client when the transaction is completed. Since the only service they perform is negotiating for exchange of title, their operating expense ratio can be as low as 2 percent.

Because brokers operate on a one-time basis for sellers or buyers, they cannot serve as an effective marketing channel for manufacturers seeking regular, continuing services. A manufacturer who seeks to develop a more permanent channel utilizing agent wholesaling middlemen must evaluate the use of the selling agent or the manufacturers' agent.

Selling agents have often been referred to as independent marketing departments, since they can be responsible for the total marketing program of a firm's product line. Typically, a **selling agent** has *full authority over pricing decisions and promotional outlays, and often provides financial assistance for the manufacturer.* The manufacturer can concentrate on production and rely on the expertise of the selling agent for all marketing activities. Selling agents are common in the coal, lumber, and textile industries. For small, poorly financed, production-oriented manufacturers, they may prove the ideal marketing channel.

While manufacturers may utilize only one selling agent, they often use a number of **manufacturers' agents**—*independent salespeople who work for a number of manufacturers of related but noncompeting products and who receive commissions based on a specified percentage of sales.* Although some commissions are as high as 20 percent of sales, they usually average between 6 and 7 percent. Unlike selling agents, who may be given exclusive world rights to market a manufacturer's product, manufacturers' agents operate in a specified territory.[7]

Manufacturers' agents reduce their selling costs by spreading the cost per sales call over a number of different products. An agent in the plumbing supplies industry, for example, may represent a dozen manufacturers.

Manufacturers develop their marketing channels through the use of manufacturers' agents for several reasons. First, when they are developing new sales territories, the costs of adding salespeople to "pioneer" the territory may be prohibitive. Agents, who are paid on a commission basis, can perform the sales function in these territories at a much lower cost.

Second, firms with unrelated lines may need to employ more than one channel. One line of products may be marketed through the company's sales force. Another may be marketed through independent manufacturers' agents. This is particularly common where the unrelated product line is a recent addition and the firm's sales force has had no experience with it.

Finally, small firms with no existing sales force may turn to manufacturers' agents in order to have access to their market. A newly organized firm producing pencil sharpeners may use office equipment and supplies agents to reach retailers and industrial purchasers.

The importance of selling agents has declined since 1940 because of manufacturers' desire to better control their marketing programs. In contrast, the volume of sales by manufacturers' agents more than doubled over the period 1939 to 1977, and it now comprises 37 percent of all sales by agent wholesaling middlemen. In 1977, the nation's 20,000 agents accounted for more than $48 billion in sales. The various types of agents and brokers are compared in Table 11.5.

TABLE 11.5
Services Provided by Agents and Brokers

Services	Commission Merchants	Auction Houses	Brokers	Manufacturers' Agents	Selling Agents
Anticipates customer needs	Yes	Some	Some	Yes	Yes
Carries inventory	Yes	Yes	No	No	No
Delivers	Yes	No	No	Some	No
Provides market information	Yes	Yes	Yes	Yes	Yes
Provides credit	Some	No	No	No	Some
Assumes ownership risk by taking title	No	No	No	No	No

Retailer-owned Facilities

Retailers have also assumed numerous wholesaling functions in an attempt to reduce costs or to provide special service. Independent retailers have occasionally banded together to form buying groups in an attempt to achieve cost savings through quantity purchases. Other groups of retailers have established retailer-owned wholesale facilities as a result of the formation of a cooperative chain. Larger-sized chain retailers often established centralized buying offices to negotiate large-scale purchases directly with manufacturers for the members of the chain. For a discussion of these facilities, see Chapter 10.

Costs of the Wholesaling Middleman

Costs of the various wholesaling middlemen are calculated as a percentage of total sales. Table 11.6 lists the costs for each major category. The chief conclusion to be drawn from the table is that expense variations result from differences in the number of services provided by each middleman. Cost ratios are highest for merchant wholesalers and manufacturers' sales branches because both provide such services as maintenance of inventories, market coverage by a sales force, and transportation. Brokers perform only one service: bringing buyers and sellers together. As a consequence, they have the lowest expense ratios. Of course, these ratios are averages and will vary among firms within each category, depending on the actual services provided.

Independent Wholesaling Middlemen— A Durable Marketing Institution

Many marketing observers of the 1920s felt that the end had come for the independent wholesaling middlemen as chain stores grew in importance and attempted to bypass them. Over the ten-year period from 1929 to 1939, the independent wholesalers' sales volume did indeed drop, but it has increased since then. Table 11.7 shows how the relative shares of total wholesale trade have changed since 1929.

While the period from 1929 to the present has seen the decline in importance of agents and brokers, and the increase in importance of company-owned channels, it is also true that independent whole-

TABLE 11.6 Operating Expenses as Percentages of Sales by Wholesaling Middlemen

Types of Wholesaling Middlemen	Operating Expenses as Percentage of Net Sales
Merchant wholesalers	12.7
Manufacturers' sales branches	8.9
Manufacturers' sales offices	3.1
Agents and brokers	4.6
Manufacturers' agents	6.6
Brokers	3.2
Commission merchants	4.8

Source: U.S. Department of Commerce, Bureau of the Census, *1977 Census of Business, Wholesale Trade—Geographic Area Series 52–19* (Washington, D.C.: U.S. Government Printing Office, 1980).

TABLE 11.7
Wholesale Trade by
Type of Operation:
1929 to 1977

Type of Operation	Percentage of Total Sales		
	1929	1967	1977
Merchant wholesalers	54.0	52.5	53.7
Manufacturers' sales branches and offices	24.2	34.2	35.9
Agents, brokers, and commission merchants	21.8	13.3	10.4

Petroleum bulk station and assembler percentages are combined with merchant wholesaler data for 1929 and 1967 for comparison with 1977 data.

Source: 1977 data from *1977 Census of Wholesale Trade—Geographic Area Series 52–19* (Washington, D.C.: U.S. Government Printing Office, 1980). 1929 and 1967 data from James R. Moore and Kendall A. Adams, "Functional Wholesaler Sales Trends and Analysis," in *Combined Proceedings* (Chicago: American Marketing Association, 1976), p. 402.

saling middlemen are far from obsolete. In fact, they are responsible for nearly two-thirds of all wholesale trade. Their continued importance is evidence of their ability to adjust to changing conditions and changing needs. Their market size proves their ability to continue to fill a need in many marketing channels.

SUMMARY

Wholesalers are one of the two major institutions that make up a firm's marketing channel. They are persons or firms who sell to retailers and other wholesalers or to industrial users but who do not sell in significant amounts to ultimate consumers. The three types of wholesaling middlemen are manufacturer-owned facilities, merchant wholesalers, and agents and brokers. Merchant wholesalers take title to the goods they handle. Agents and brokers may take possession of the goods but do not take title. Merchant wholesalers include full-function wholesalers, rack jobbers, cash-and-carry wholesalers, truck wholesalers, drop shippers, and mail-order wholesalers. Commission merchants, auction houses, brokers, selling agents, and manufacturers' agents are classified as agent wholesaling middlemen because they do not take title to goods.

The operating expenses of wholesaling middlemen vary considerably, depending on the services provided and the costs involved. The services include storage facilities in conveniently located warehouses, market coverage by a sales force, financing for retailers and manufacturers, market information for retailers and manufacturers, transportation, and, specifically for retailers, management services, retail sales training, and merchandising assistance and advice.

Although the percentage of wholesale trade by manufacturer-owned facilities has increased since 1929, independent wholesaling middlemen continue to account for 90 percent of all wholesale establishments and nearly two-thirds of total wholesale trade. They accomplish this by continuing to provide desired services to manu-facturers, retailers, and industrial buyers.

QUESTIONS FOR DISCUSSION

1. Explain the following terms:

wholesaler	truck wholesaler
wholesaling middlemen	drop shipper
sales branch	mail-order wholesaler
public warehouse	agents
sales office	brokers
trade fair	commission merchant
merchandise mart	auction houses
merchant wholesaler	selling agent
rack jobber	manufacturers' agents
cash-and-carry wholesaler	

2. Distinguish between a wholesaler and a retailer.

3. In what ways do wholesaling middlemen assist manufacturers? How do they assist retailers?

4. Explain how wholesaling middlemen can assist retailers in increasing their return on investment.

5. Distinguish between sales offices and sales branches. Under what conditions might each type be used?

6. Explain the strength of wholesale volume through manufacturers' sales offices and branches even though the percentage of total wholesale sales through brokers and selling agents has been declining.

7. What role does the public warehouse play in marketing channels?

8. Distinguish merchant wholesalers from agents and brokers.

9. Which major type of wholesaling middleman represents the most frequently used marketing channel? Which major type is least often used?

10. Comment on the following statements: Drop shippers are good candidates for elimination. All they do is process orders. They don't even handle the goods.

11. Why is the operating expense ratio of the merchant wholesaler higher than that of the typical agent or broker?

12. List the following wholesaling middlemen in ascending order on the basis of operating expense percentage: full-function merchant wholesaler, cash-and-carry wholesaler, broker, manufacturers' sales branch, truck wholesaler.

13. Why does the truck wholesaler have a relatively high operating expense ratio?

14. Match each of the following industries with the most appropriate wholesaling middleman:

_____ groceries	a. drop shipper
_____ potato chips	b. truck wholesaler
_____ coal	c. auction house
_____ grain	d. manufacturers' agent
_____ antiques	e. full-function merchant wholesaler
	f. commission merchant

15. In what ways are commission merchants and brokers different?

16. The term *broker* also appears in the real estate and securities fields. Are these brokers identical to the agent wholesaling middlemen described in this chapter?

17. Distinguish between a manufacturers' agent and a selling agent.

18. Why do commission merchants, unlike most other agents and brokers, take possession of the products they market?

19. Under what conditions would a manufacturer utilize manufacturers' agents for a marketing channel?

20. What type of firm is likely to utilize selling agents?

NOTES

1. Bernice Kanner, "Wholesalers—Vital Cog in Magazine Machinery," *Advertising Age,* October 16, 1978, p. 30. Reprinted with permission. Copyright 1978 by Crain Communications, Inc.

2. Marilyn Wellemeyer, "Middlemen of Metal," *FORTUNE,* March 1977, pp. 163–65.

3. James R. Moore, "Wholesaling: Structural Changes and Manufacturers' Perceptions," in *Foundations of Marketing Channels,* eds. Arch G. Woodside, J. Taylor Sims, Dale M. Lewison, and Ian F. Wilkinson (Austin, Texas: Austin Press, 1978), pp. 118–31.

4. Louis P. Bucklin, *Competition and Evolution in the Distributive Trades* (Englewood Cliffs, N.J.: Prentice-Hall, 1972), p. 214.

5. "Surveys Find Trade Shows Cost-Effective, Productive," *Marketing News,* October 3, 1980, p. 4. See also J. Steven Kelly and James M. Comer, "Trade Show Exhibiting: A Managerial Perspective," in John H. Summey and Ronald D. Taylor, eds., *Evolving Marketing Thought for 1980* (Southern Marketing Association, 1980), pp. 11–13.

6. Benson Shapiro, "Improve Distribution with Your Promotional Mix," *Harvard Business Review,* March-April 1977, p. 116.

7. For a profile of the typical manufacturers' agent, see Stanley D. Sibley and Roy K. Teas, "Agent Marketing Channel Intermediaries' Perceptions of Marketing Channel Performance," in *Proceedings of the Southern Marketing Association,* eds. Robert S. Franz, Robert M. Hopkins, and Al Toma, New Orleans, Louisiana, November 1978, pp. 336–39.

CHAPTER 12

MARKETING INSTITUTIONS: RETAILING

KEY TERMS

retailing
limited-line store
general merchandise retailer
department store
mass merchandiser
discount house
hypermarkets
chain stores
planned shopping centers
scrambled merchandising
wheel of retailing
teleshopping

LEARNING GOALS

1. To distinguish between limited-line retailers and general merchandise retailers

2. To identify and explain each of the five bases for categorizing retailers

3. To identify the major types of mass merchandisers

4. To explain the types of nonstore retailing

5. To distinguish between chain and independent retailers and to identify several industries dominated by chains

6. To contrast the three types of planned shopping centers

Although scholars labeled the event as marketing in action, most on-lookers described the fighting that broke out at a recent sale in London's Harrods department store in more colorful terms. An observer of the stampede that occurred when tens of thousands of customers rushed into the giant store at the sale's onset recorded the event as follows:

When the doors opened at 9 a.m., thousands of people pushed in and ran through the store's four floors. Many had camped overnight in the street outside. By midmorning the crush was so thick it was impossible to enter or leave the store. There were 6,500 staff workers on duty to deal with the crowds, including a beefed-up security force to handle a situation described by store officials as "perfect cover for shoplifters."

In the china department, according to one witness, "There seemed to be more breakages than purchases." In the fur department, a group of people demonstrating against cruelty to animals was ignored by women sweeping half-price luxury furs off the racks. There was such a melee in the electronics department, where $2,000 television sets were selling for half price, that shoppers were invited to return to the store next week for an alternate bargain.

Security men had to restore order in the electronics department where jostling crowds caused more than $12,000 worth of damage to stereo equipment and television sets. One customer was dragged out through an emergency exit to end a tussle over a bargain. A fistfight was narrowly avoided in the linen department where satin-look sheets were selling for $2.40 each.

Harrods Managing Director Aleck Craddock said receipts for the opening day of the sale were expected to exceed the previous year's record of $11.2 million. . . . Harrods expected to serve 25,000 meals in its restaurant, supply 2.5 million paper bags for purchases, and use enough electricity to light a small town for a day.

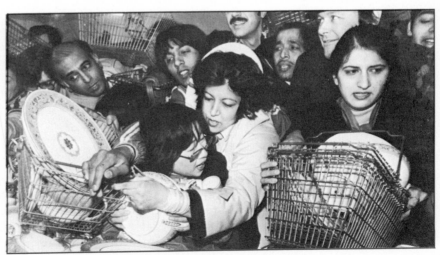

Source: Courtesy of Wide World Photos, Inc.

The store, where Queen Elizabeth has some of her shopping done, holds the most popular of the annual New Year's sales that turn London department stores into battlegrounds. Located in upper-crust Knightsbridge, Harrods was founded in a grocery shop by Henry Harrod in 1849 and has become the largest department store in Europe.

Almost a city in itself, it arranges funerals, caters weddings, plans vacations, sells houses, and has its own bank. It advertises itself as the store where you can buy "a pound of potatoes or a mink coat."[1]

WHAT IS RETAILING?

Although the pace is more frenzied than in most other establishments, Harrods—like millions of other stores and individuals—is engaged in retailing activities. Giant stores like Harrods may generate daily sales of several million dollars, while a small shoe store may have annual sales of less than $100,000. But both large and small retailers perform the major channel activities: creating time, place, and ownership utility.

More important, retail outlets serve as contact points between channel members and the ultimate consumer. In a very real sense, retailers *are* the marketing channel for most consumers, since the typical shopper has little contact with manufacturers and virtually none with wholesaling intermediaries. As a result, the services provided—location, store hours, quality of salespeople, store layout, selection, and the returns policy, among others—are often more important than the physical product in developing consumer images of the products and services offered.

Retailers are both customers and marketers in the channel. They market products and services to ultimate consumers, and also are the customers of wholesalers and manufacturers. Because of this critical location in the channel, retailers often perform an important feedback role. They obtain information from customers and transmit it to manufacturers and other channel members.

Retailing may be defined as *all of the activities involved in the sale of products and services to the ultimate consumer.* Although 97.5 percent of all retail sales occur in retail stores, the definition of retailing also includes several forms of nonstore retailing. Nonstore retailing involves such retail activities as telephone and mail-order sales, vending machines sales, and direct house-to-house solicitations.

THE FIRST U.S. RETAILERS

Early retailing can be traced to the establishment of trading posts such as the Hudson Bay Company and to pack peddlers who literally carried their wares to outlying settlements. But the first important retail institution in the United States was the *general store,* a general merchandise store stocked to meet the needs of a small community or rural area. Here, customers could buy clothing, groceries, feed, seed, farm equipment, drugs, spectacles, and candy.

The basic needs that caused the general store to develop also doomed it to a limited existence. Since storekeepers attempted to satisfy the needs of customers for all types of goods, they carried a small assortment of each good. As communities grew, new stores opened, and they concentrated on specific product lines, such as drugs, dry goods, groceries, and hardware. The general stores could not compete, and their owners either converted them into more specialized, limited-line stores or closed them. But general stores still do exist in some rural areas. Today, only a few hundred such stores are still operating, mostly in rural areas of the South and West.

Retail Institutions: Adapting to Meet Consumer Needs

Retailing operations serve as remarkable illustrations of the marketing concept in operation. The development of retail innovations can be traced to attempts to better satisfy particular consumer needs.

As consumers demanded different satisfactions from retailers, new institutions emerged to meet this demand. The supermarket appeared in the early 1930s in response to consumer desires for lower prices. Today, convenience food stores and mass merchandisers meet consumers' desires for convenience in purchasing and late-hour availability. Discount houses and catalog stores reflect consumer demand for lower prices and the willingness to give up services. Department stores meet the demands of their clientele by offering a wide variety of products and services. Vending machines, door-to-door retailing, and mail-order retailing offer the ultimate in buyer convenience. Planned shopping centers provide a balanced array of consumer goods and services and include parking facilities for their customers. The nation's two million retailing establishments are involved in developing specific marketing mixes designed to satisfy chosen market targets.[2]

Scope of the Retail Market

The most recent Census of Retail Trade revealed that there were approximately 1,860,000 retail stores and about 150,000 direct-selling operations in the United States. Total retail sales amounted to $723 billion. As Figure 12.1 indicates, the Great Lakes, Mideast, and the Southeast regions account for almost 60 percent of total retail sales.

TYPES OF RETAILERS

The nation's two million retailers come in a variety of forms. Since new types of retail operations continue to evolve in response to changing demands of their markets, no universal classification has been devised.

THE DEATH OF KORVETTE'S

Less than two decades ago, Korvette's was held up as the discount merchandiser that might one day rival such top retailers as Sears and J. C. Penney. In those days, Korvette's was unmatched in sales growth, suburban expansion, and its ability to pack stores with shoppers. Today, Korvette's is no longer an operating retailer. . . .

As the 1970s wore on, the public itself could get a sense of Korvette's difficulties. It eliminated once-lucrative appliance and furniture departments. It decided to deemphasize discounting and raise its markup—then reversed itself. It started an ambitious promotion—"the other Korvette's"—to stress fashion but abruptly dumped it in a cost-cutting campaign. . . .

Through the 1950s [Korvette founder Eugene Ferkauf] was one of the strongest figures in American retailing, beating the New York department stores to the suburbs with large flashy stores, underselling them on appliances and housewares and prompting price wars. . . . A Boston industry group voted him into its merchants' Hall of Fame and *Time* magazine and *Business Week* devoted cover articles to him.

But, in retrospect, critics score him for some important mistakes. He expanded too quickly, especially out of town in such cities as St. Louis, Chicago, and Detroit where locals didn't know much about Korvette's. He branched out into food (merging with Hill's Supermarkets in 1965) and into furniture (in a merger with H. Klion, Inc.), both of which proved a drain that forced him to later drop them.

But his biggest failing may have been his inability to build management depth, so that he had to resort to bringing in outside top managers who produced fitful results. . . .

Wall Street analysts, who lost investment interest in Korvette's years ago, are caustic. Said one who asked not to be identified: "They started

The following characteristics or bases can be used in categorizing them:

1.   Shopping effort expended by customers
2.   Services provided to customers
3.   Product lines
4.   Location of retail transactions
5.   Form of ownership

Any retailing operation can be classified according to each of the five bases. A 7-Eleven food store may be classified as a convenience store (category 1); self-service (category 2); relatively broad product lines (category 3); store-type retailer (category 4); and a member of a corporate chain (category 5). Figure 12.2 illustrates each basis utilized in classifying retail operations.

out as discounters but let their markup run up too high without giving equal value. Management slipped and image problems became serious." By the end of 1982, Korvette's was only a memory.

Source: Isadore Barmash, "The Fast Start and Slow Decline of E. J. Korvette," *New York Times,* October 12, 1980. © 1980 by the New York Times Company. Reprinted by permission.

Source: Vic DeLucia/NYT PICTURES.

RETAILERS CLASSIFIED BY SHOPPING EFFORT EXPENDED BY CUSTOMERS

In Chapter 8, a three-way classification of consumer goods was developed based on consumer purchase patterns in securing a particular product or service. This system can be extended to retailers by considering the reasons consumers shop at a particular retail outlet. The result is a classification scheme in which retail outlets are categorized as convenience, shopping, or specialty.[3] *Convenience retailers* focus on convenient locations, long store hours, rapid checkout service, and adequate parking facilities. Local food stores, gasoline retailers, and some barber shops may be included in this category.

Shopping stores typically include furniture stores, appliance retailers, clothing outlets, and sporting goods stores. Consumers will compare prices, assortments, and quality levels of competing outlets before making a purchase decision. Managers of shopping stores attempt to differentiate their outlets through advertising, window dis-

**FIGURE 12.1
Retail Sales by
Region and
Percentage Change:
1972–1977**

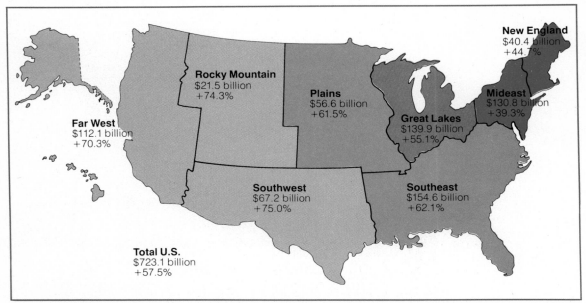

New England
$40.4 billion
+44.7%

Rocky Mountain
$21.5 billion
+74.3%

Plains
$56.6 billion
+61.5%

Mideast
$130.8 billion
+39.3%

Far West
$112.1 billion
+70.3%

Great Lakes
$139.9 billion
+55.1%

Southwest
$67.2 billion
+75.0%

Southeast
$154.6 billion
+62.1%

Total U.S.
$723.1 billion
+57.5%

Source: U.S. Department of Commerce, Bureau of the Census, *1977 Census of Retail Trade: U.S. Summary, RC77-A-52* (Washington, D.C.: U.S. Government Printing Office, 1980).

plays and in-store layouts, knowledgeable salespeople, and appropriate merchandise assortments.

Specialty retailers provide some combination of product lines, service, or reputation that results in consumers' willingness to expend considerable effort to shop there. Neiman-Marcus, Lord & Taylor, Tiffany & Co., and Saks Fifth Avenue have developed a sufficient degree of preference among many shoppers to be categorized as specialty retailers.

Combining Product and Retailer Classifications

By cross-classifying the product and retailer classifications, a matrix is created representing nine possible types of consumer purchase behavior. This matrix is shown in Figure 12.3.

Behavior patterns in each cell can be described as:

1. *Convenience store–convenience good.* The consumer purchases the most readily available brand of the product at the nearest store.

2. *Convenience store–shopping good.* The consumer chooses a product from among the assortment carried by the most accessible store.

FIGURE 12.2
Bases for Classifying Retailers

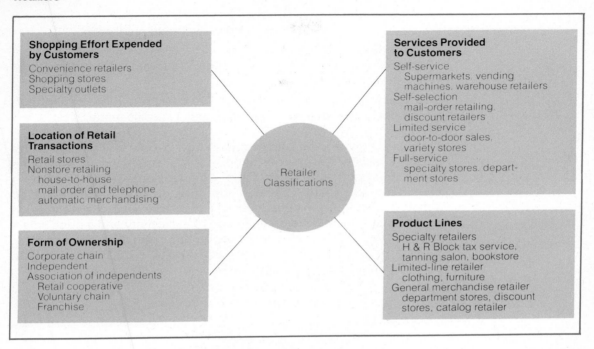

Shopping Effort Expended by Customers
Convenience retailers
Shopping stores
Specialty outlets

Location of Retail Transactions
Retail stores
Nonstore retailing
  house-to-house
  mail order and telephone
  automatic merchandising

Form of Ownership
Corporate chain
Independent
Association of independents
  Retail cooperative
  Voluntary chain
  Franchise

Retailer Classifications

Services Provided to Customers
Self-service
  Supermarkets, vending
  machines, warehouse retailers
Self-selection
  mail-order retailing,
  discount retailers
Limited service
  door-to-door sales,
  variety stores
Full-service
  specialty stores, department stores

Product Lines
Specialty retailers
  H & R Block tax service,
  tanning salon, bookstore
Limited-line retailer
  clothing, furniture
General merchandise retailer
  department stores, discount
  stores, catalog retailer

3. *Convenience store—specialty good.* The consumer purchases a favored brand from the nearest store carrying it.

4. *Shopping store—convenience good.* The consumer is indifferent to the brand purchased; shopping is done among competing stores to secure the best services or price.

5. *Shopping store—shopping good.* The consumer makes comparisons among store-controlled factors and factors associated with the product or brand.

FIGURE 12.3
Matrix of Consumer Purchase Behavior

Goods	Retailers		
	Convenience	Shopping	Specialty
Convenience			
Shopping			
Specialty			

6. *Shopping store–specialty good.* The consumer purchases only a favorite brand but shops among a number of stores to obtain the best service or price.

7. *Specialty store–convenience good.* The consumer trades only at a specific store and is indifferent to the brand purchased.

8. *Specialty store–shopping good.* The consumer trades only at a specific store and chooses a product from among the assortment carried by it.

9. *Specialty store–specialty good.* The consumer has a strong preference for both a particular store and a specific brand.

This matrix gives a realistic picture of how people buy. The most exclusive specialty store carries handkerchiefs, and many supermarkets have gourmet food departments. The cross-classification system should help the retailer develop appropriate marketing strategies to satisfy particular market segments. The retailer who chooses cells 8 and 9 must seek to develop an image of exclusivity and a good selection of widely accepted competing brands. The same retailer must also carry an assortment of specialty goods, such as high-fashion clothing and expensive perfumes.

Convenience food retailers frequently cater to shoppers who exhibit the behavior patterns of cell #1.

Source: Drawing by Martin. © 1977 *The New Yorker* Magazine, Inc.

**FIGURE 12.4
Classification of
Retailers on the
Basis of Customer
Service Levels**

	Self-Service	Self-Selection	Limited-Service	Full-Service
Characteristics	Very few services Price appeal Staple goods Convenience goods	Restricted services Price appeal Staple goods Convenience goods	Limited variety of services Less price appeal Shopping goods	Wide variety of services Fashion merchandise Specialty merchandise
Examples	Warehouse retailing Supermarkets Mail-order Automatic vending	Discount retailing Variety stores Mail-order retailing	Door-to-door Telephone sales Variety stores	Specialty stores Department stores

Source: Adapted from Larry D. Redinbaugh, *Retailing Management: A Planning Approach* (New York: McGraw-Hill, 1976), p. 12. Copyright © 1976 McGraw-Hill Book Company. Used with the permission of McGraw-Hill Book Company.

RETAILERS CLASSIFIED BY SERVICES PROVIDED TO CUSTOMERS

A second fundamental method of classifying retailing operations is to consider the extent of the services they perform for customers. Figure 12.4 indicates the spectrum of retailer services from virtually no services (self-service) to a full range of customer services (full-service retailers).

Since the self-service and self-selection retailers provide few services to their customers, retailer location and price are important factors. These retailers tend to specialize in staple convenience goods that are purchased frequently by customers and require little product service or advice from retail personnel.

The full-service retail establishments focus more on fashion-oriented shopping goods and specialty items and offer a wide variety of services for their clientele. As a result, their prices tend to be higher than those of self-service retailers due to the higher operating costs associated with the services.

RETAILERS CLASSIFIED BY PRODUCT LINES

A common way to categorize retailers is by the product lines they handle. Grouping retailers by product lines produces three major categories: limited-line retailers, specialty stores, and general merchandise retailers.

Limited-line Retailers

A large assortment of one line of products or a few related lines of goods are offered in the **limited-line store.** Its development paralleled the growth of towns when the population grew sufficiently to support them. These operations include such retailers as appliance stores, furniture stores, grocery stores, hardware stores, and sporting goods stores. Examples of limited-line stores are Lionel Leisure City and Toys-R-Us (toys); Levitz, J. Homestock, and Wickes (furniture); Radio Shack and Playback (home electronics); Handy Dan and Handy Man (home repair products); Brain Factory (electronic calculators); and Lerner Shops (clothing).

These retailers cater to the needs of people who want to select from a complete line in purchasing a particular product. The marketing vice-president of Toys-R-Us summarized the limited-line retailer's strategy in this way: "Sears can show customers three types of footballs, but we can show them forty."[4] Most retailers are in the limited-line category.

The Supermarket A *supermarket* is a large-scale departmentalized retail store offering a variety of food products such as meats, produce, dairy products, canned goods, and frozen foods in addition to various nonfood items. It operates on a self-service basis and emphasizes low prices and adequate parking facilities. Supermarkets offer low prices through a policy of self-service. Before the 1920s, however, food purchases were made at full-service grocery stores. Store personnel filled orders (often from customers' shopping lists), delivered goods, and often granted credit to their customers. Supermarkets exchanged these services for lower prices and quickly revolutionized food shopping in the United States and much of the world.[5]

Supermarket customers typically shop once or twice a week and make fill-in purchases between each major shopping trip. In 1979, the 33,000 U.S. supermarkets represented only about one-tenth of the nation's food stores; yet their sales accounted for 77 percent of all food sales. The largest supermarket chains in the United States are Safeway, Kroger, Lucky Stores, Jewel, Winn-Dixie, and Food Fair.

With a razor-thin profit margin (averaging only about 1 percent of sales after taxes), supermarkets compete through careful planning of retail displays in order to sell a large amount of merchandise each week and thereby retain a low investment in inventory. Product location is studied carefully so as to expose the consumer to as much merchandise as possible (and thereby increase impulse purchases). In an attempt to fight the fast-food threat—the tendency of consumers to eat many of their meals outside the home—supermarkets have begun to feature their own delicatessens. In Florida, the Publix supermarkets sell fried chicken by the bucket. Supermarkets General of New Jersey has even established cafeterias and snack shops in factories.[6]

Supermarkets carry nonfood products such as magazines, records, small kitchen utensils, toiletries, and toys for two reasons: consumers have displayed a willingness to buy such items in supermarkets, and supermarket managers like the profit margin on these items, which is higher than that of food products. Nonfood sales account for almost one-fourth of all supermarket sales.

Specialty Stores

A *specialty store* typically handles only part of a single line of products. However, this part is stocked in considerable depth for the store's customers. Specialty stores include meat markets, men's and women's shoe stores, bakeries, furriers, and millinery shops. Although some are operated by chains, most are run as independent small-scale operations. They are perhaps the greatest stronghold of independent retailers, who can develop expertise in providing a very narrow line of products for their local market.

Specialty stores should not be confused with specialty *goods.* Specialty stores typically carry convenience and shopping goods. The label "specialty" comes from the practice of handling a specific, narrow line of merchandise.

General Merchandise Retailers

General merchandise retailers may be distinguished from limited-line and specialty retailers by the large number of product lines they carry. The general store described earlier in this chapter is a good example of a **general merchandise retailer**—*a retail establishment carrying a wide variety of product lines, all of which are stocked in some depth.* Included in this category of retailers are department stores, variety stores, and such mass merchandisers as catalog retailers and discount stores.

General merchandise retailers account for about one-seventh of all retail sales. Even though the nation's 22,000 variety stores account for only 1.6 percent of total retail sales, department stores represent almost 11 percent of all retail sales.

Department Stores The **department store** is actually a series of limited-line and specialty stores under one roof. By definition, it is *a large retail firm handling a variety of merchandise that includes men's and boy's wear, women's wear and accessories, household linens and dry goods, home furnishings, appliances, and furniture.* It serves the consumer by acting as a one-stop shopping center for almost all personal and household items.

As indicated by its name, the entire store is organized around departments for the purpose of providing service, promotion, and control. A general merchandising manager is responsible for the store's product planning. Reporting to the general manager are the department managers. These managers typically run the departments almost as independent businesses; they are given considerable latitude in merchandising and layout decisions. Acceptance of the retailing axiom that well-bought goods are already half-sold is indicated by the department manager's title of *buyer.* Buyers, particularly those in charge of high-fashion departments, spend a considerable portion of their time deciding on the inventory to be carried in their departments.

The department store has been the symbol of retailing since the construction in 1863 of the nation's first department store, the A. T. Stewart store in New York City. Almost every urban area in the United States has one or more department stores associated with its downtown area and its major shopping areas. Macy's Herald Square store in New York City is the world's largest department store; it contains more than 2 million square feet of space and produces gross sales of approximately $200 million each year. A daily average of 150,000 customers buy at least one of the 400,000 items available in Macy's 168 selling departments.

The impact of department stores on urban life is not confined to the United States. European shoppers associate London with Harrods, Paris with Au Printemps, and Moscow with GUM. Myer is the dominant department store in both Melbourne and Sydney, Australia.

Department stores are known for offering their customers a wide variety of services, such as charge accounts, delivery, gift wrapping, and liberal return privileges. In addition, some 50 percent of their employees and 40 percent of their floor space are devoted to nonselling activities. As a result, they have relatively high operating costs, averaging from 45 to 60 percent of sales.

Department stores have faced intensified competition in the past thirty years. Their relatively high operating costs make them vulnerable to such new retailing innovations as discount stores, catalog merchandisers, and hypermarkets. In addition, department stores were typically located in downtown business districts and experienced the problems associated with limited parking, traffic congestion, and urban migration to the suburbs.

Department stores have displayed a willingness to adapt to changing consumer desires. They have added bargain basements and expanded parking facilities in attempts to compete with discount operations and suburban retailers. They have also followed the movement of the population to the suburbs by opening major branches in outlying shopping centers.[7] And they have attempted to revitalize downtown retailing in many cities by modernizing their stores, extending store hours, attracting the tourist and convention trade, and focusing on the residents of the central cities.

Mass Merchandisers Mass merchandising has made major inroads on department store sales during the past two decades by emphasizing lower prices for well-known brand name products, high turnover of goods, and reduced services. The **mass merchandiser** often *stocks a wider line of products than department stores, but usually does not offer the depth of assortment in each line.* Major types of mass merchandisers are discount houses, hypermarkets, and catalog retailers.

Discount Houses—Limited Services and Lower Prices The birth of the modern **discount house** came at the end of World War II, when a New York-based company called Masters discovered that a large number of customers were willing to shop at *a store that charges lower than usual prices and does not offer such traditional services as credit, sales assistance by clerks, and delivery.* Soon, retailers throughout the country were following the Masters formula, either changing over from their traditional operation or opening new stores dedicated to discounting. At first, discount stores sold mostly appliances, but they have spread into furniture, soft goods, drugs, and even food. Currently, more than 12 percent of all retail stores operate as discount houses.

Discount operations had existed before World War II, but the early discounters usually sold goods from manufacturers' catalogs; they kept no stock on display and often limited potential customers. The more recent discounters operate large stores, advertise heavily, emphasize low prices for well-known brands, and are open to the public. Elimination of many of the "free" services provided by traditional retailers allow these operations to keep their markup 10 to 25 percent below those of their competitors. Consumers had become accustomed to self-service by shopping at supermarkets, and they responded in great numbers to this retailing innovation. Conventional retailers such as Kresge and Woolworth joined the discounting practice by opening their own K mart and Woolco stores. Currently, about 38 cents of every dollar spent by U.S. consumers is spent in a discount store.[8]

As discount houses move into new product areas, there has been a noticeable increase in the number of services offered. Floor-space in the stores is often carpeted, credit is increasingly available, and many discounters are quietly dropping discount from their name. Although they still offer fewer services than other retailers, discounters' operating costs are increasing as they begin to resemble traditional department stores.

K mart shoppers can choose from such designer labels as Calvin Klein, Sasson, Jordache, and Sergio Valente. Other brands with images of quality and style now found at the discount giant once referred to as "the polyester palace" include Seiko watches, Puma running shoes, Izod shirts, and Minolta and Pentax cameras.

Hypermarkets—Shopping Centers in a Single Store A relatively recent retailing development has been the introduction of **hypermarkets**—*giant mass merchandisers who operate on a low-price, self-service basis and carry lines of soft goods and groceries.* The hypermarket began in France and has since spread to Canada and the United States. Meijer's Thrifty Acres in suburban Detroit has 220,000 square feet of selling space (eleven to fifteen times that of the average supermarket) and more than forty checkout counters. It sells food, hardware, soft goods, building materials, auto supplies, appliances, and prescription drugs; and it has a restaurant, a beauty salon, a barbershop, a branch bank, and a bakery. By pricing inventory from 10 to 15 percent below normal retail, the average hypermarket has an annual sales volume of $35 million. More than a thousand of these super-stores are currently in operation.

Catalog Retailers—Catalog, Showroom, and Warehouse One of the major growth areas in retailing during the past decade has been that of catalog retailing. Catalog retailers mail catalogs to their customers and op-

A TOUCH OF CLASS AT K MART?

Loyal K mart shoppers realized that radical changes were in the offing at the nation's second largest nonfood retailer. Although 1980 produced record sales in the chain's 2,000 outlets, income fell by more than 27 percent from that of the previous year. The outline of the changes was contained in K mart's 1980 annual report.

The consumer of the 1980s wants something different from a K mart discount store than was demanded in the 1970s. We have seen a subtle shift in the consumer's emphasis toward products with a somewhat higher quality quotient than in the past.

K mart marketers had also felt the impact of regional discounters with more attractive stores and more fashionable products: Target in the Midwest, Wal-Mart in the South, Caldor in the Northeast. Catalog showrooms provided strong competition in such product lines as jewelry and small appliances. And the backruptcy of one-time competitor W. T. Grant worried them. While K mart was not ready to shed its discount image, it decided to shift more to the more affluent, more style-conscious customers. A number of changes would have to be made to accomplish this.

One major component of the change is the addition of fashion items at "the saving place." Stores are being refurbished, with between $75,000 and $500,000 being spent on each store. Beige walls are being replaced with broad bands of poppy red, gold, and white. These crisp, contemporary colors are also used on departmental and sale signs. Pipe racks that showed only the sleeve of a garment have given way to new round, square, and honeycombed racks designed to display the full garment. Ten huge distribution warehouses have reduced the time required to receive an order to one week—a critical factor in fashion merchandising where the customer often wants to buy now or not at all.

The changes are not without risk. A very real danger in attempting to appeal to more affluent customers is the possibility of alienating lower-income customers and losing the customer base to other discount retailers. K mart officials are confident that their new strategy will continue to appeal to lower-income customers who rely on the retailer as a source of good value for their money, while also catering more to more middle- and upper-income customers who currently are more likely to buy such as items as tennis balls and antifreeze, but would not even look at clothing, jewelry, and cosmetics. But with an alligator logo on the shirt, perhaps they will. . . .

Source: K mart Annual Report, 1981.

erate from a showroom displaying samples of each product handled by them. Orders are filled from a backroom warehouse. Price is an important factor for catalog store customers, and low prices are made possible by few services, storage of most of the inventory in the warehouse, reduced shoplifting losses, and the handling of products that are unlikely to become obsolete, such as luggage, small appliances, gift items, sporting equipment, toys, and jewelry. Major catalog retailers include Best Products, Service Merchandise, Giant Stores, Vornado, Zale, and Gordon Jewelry Corporation. (Mail-order catalog retailing is discussed in an upcoming section.)

RETAILERS CLASSIFIED BY LOCATION OF RETAIL TRANSACTIONS

A fourth method of categorizing retailers is by whether the transaction takes place in a store. Although the overwhelming majority of retail sales occur in retail stores, nonstore retailing is important for many products. Nonstore retailing includes direct house-to-house sales, mail-order retailing, and automatic merchandising machines. These kinds of sales account for 2.5 percent of all retail sales.

House-to-House Retailing

One of the oldest marketing channels was built around direct contact between the seller and customer at the home of the customer—house-to-house retailing. This channel provides maximum convenience for the consumer and allows the manufacturer to control the firm's marketing channels. It is a minor part of the retailing picture, with less than 1 percent of all retail sales.[9]

House-to-house retailing is used by a number of merchandisers, such as manufacturers of bakery products, dairy products, and newspapers. Firms emphasizing product demonstrations also tend to use this channel. Among them are companies that sell vacuum cleaners (for example, Electrolux), household brushes (Fuller Brush Company), encyclopedias (The World Book Encyclopedia), and insurance. Some firms, such as Stanley Home Products, Amway, and Tupperware, use a variation called party-plan selling, where a customer hosts a party to which several neighbors and friends are invited. During the party, a company representative makes a presentation of the products. The hostess receives a commission based on the amount of products sold. The five largest direct-sales retailers are Avon Products, Electrolux, Tupperware, Amway, and World Book—Childcraft International.

The house-to-house method of retailing appears to be a low-cost method of distribution. No plush retail facilities are required, no investment in inventory is necessary, and most house-to-house salespeople operate on a commission basis. However, the method actually entails very high costs. Often the distribution cost of a product marketed through retail stores is half that of the same product retailed house-to-house. High travel costs, nonproductive calls, and the limited number of contacts per day result in high operating expenses.

Mail-order Retailing

The customers of mail-order retailing merchandisers can order merchandise by mail, by telephone, or by visiting the mail-order desk of a retail store. Goods are then shipped to the customer's home or to the local retail store. Table 12.1 identifies a number of socioeconomic, ex-

**TABLE 12.1
Factors Contributing
to the Success of
Mail-order Catalogs**

Socioeconomic Factors	External Factors	Competitive Factors
More women joining the work force	Rising cost of gasoline	Inconvenient store hours
Population growing older	Availability of WATS (800) lines	Unsatisfactory service in stores
Rising discretionary income	Expanded use of credit cards	Difficulty of parking, especially near downtown stores
More single households	Low-cost data processing	"If you can't beat 'em, join 'em" approach of traditional retailers
Growth of the "me generation"	Availability of mailing lists	

Source: John A. Quelch and Hirotaka Takeuchi, "Nonstore Marketing: Fast Track or Slow?" *Harvard Business Review,* July-August 1981, p. 77. Reprinted by permission of the *Harvard Business Review.* Copyright © 1981 by the President and Fellows of Harvard College; all rights reserved.

ternal, and competitive factors that have contributed to the growing consumer acceptance of catalog retailing.

As any holder of a retail store credit card knows, many department stores and specialty stores issue catalogs to seek telephone and mail-order sales and to promote in-store purchases of items featured in the catalogs. Among typical department stores, telephone and mail-generated orders account for 15 percent of total volume during the Christmas season.[10]

Mail-order selling began in 1872, when Montgomery Ward issued its first catalog to rural midwestern families. That catalog contained only a few items, mostly clothing and farm supplies. Sears soon followed Ward's lead, and mail-order retailing became an important source of goods in isolated settlements.

Even though mail-order sales represent only 1 percent of all retail sales, they are an important channel for consumers who desire convenience and a large selection of colors and sizes. In 1983, more than 2 billion mail-order catalogs were distributed. Sears, which currently holds 44 percent of the mail-order market, distributes 300 million catalogs annually. Mail-order houses offer a wide range of products—from novelty items (Spencer Gifts) to hunting and camping equipment (L. L. Bean) to an eighteenth-century Chinese screen priced at $60,000 (Horchow). Many mail-order catalog houses also generate retail sales by having consumers buy from retail outlets of their catalog stores.

Automatic Merchandising

Maximum convenience is provided by automatic vending machines for a wide range of convenience goods. These machines account for 25 percent of all soft drink sales, 16 percent of cigarette sales, and 20 percent of candy bar sales in the United States.[11] The average American spends $1.26 a week in one or more of the approximately 6 million vending machines currently in operation. Coffee and soft-drink purchases represent about half the total dollar sales volume.[12]

Although the first vending machine dispensed holy water for a five-drachma coin in Egyptian temples around 215 B.C., the period of most rapid growth came after World War II when sophisticated new equipment was developed to keep machines working and from being cheated by slugs. Products offered by automatic vending range from mundane to bizarre. Soft-drink machines on military bases and in college fraternity houses dispense beer rather than soda. Some bait shops sell packages of fresh worms to after-hours fishermen from coin-operated machines. Some flower shops have added machines to dispense corsages as last-minute gifts.

Where does the vending machine dollar go? According to the National Automatic Merchandising Association, 45.5 cents of each dollar goes for the product, 52.4 cents for operating expenses, and 2.1 cents for profit. Typically, the owner of the building receives more money from a machine just for allowing it on the premises than the owner of the machine does for installing, stocking, and servicing it.[13]

Although automatic merchandising is important in the retailing of some products, it represents less than 1 percent of all retail sales. Its future growth is limited by such factors as the cost of the machines and the necessity for regular maintenance and repair. In addition, automatically vended products are confined to convenience goods of standard sizes and weights that have a high turnover rate. Prices for many products purchased in vending machines are higher than store prices for the same products.

RETAILERS CLASSIFIED BY FORM OF OWNERSHIP

The fifth method of classifying retailers is by ownership. The two major types are corporate chain stores and independent retailers. In addition, independent retailers may join a wholesaler-sponsored voluntary chain, band together to form a retail cooperative, or enter into a franchise arrangement through contractual agreements with a manufacturer, wholesaler, or service organization.

Chain Stores

Chain stores are *groups of retail stores that are centrally owned and managed and that handle the same lines of products.* The concept of chain stores is certainly not new. The Mitsui chain operated in Japan in the 1600s.

One major advantage that chain operations have over independent retailers is economies of scale. Volume purchases through a central buying office allow such chains as Safeway, Kroger, and

TABLE 12.2
The Ten Largest
Retailers in the
United States

Rank	Company	Sales (in Thousands)	Net Income as Percent of Sales
1	Sears (Chicago)	$25,194,900	2.4
2	Safeway Stores (Oakland)	15,102,673	0.8
3	K mart (Troy, Michigan)	14,204,381	1.8
4	J. C. Penney (New York)	11,353,000	2.1
5	Kroger (Cincinnati)	10,316,741	0.9
6	F. W. Woolworth (New York)	7,218,176	2.2
7	Great Atlantic & Pacific Tea (Montvale, New Jersey)	6,684,179	—
8	Lucky Stores (Dublin, California)	6,468,682	1.4
9	American Stores Co. (Salt Lake City)	6,419,884	0.8
10	Federated Department Stores (Cincinnati)	6,300,686	4.4

Source: "The Fortune Directory of the Fifty Largest Retailing Companies," *FORTUNE,* July 13, 1981, pp. 122–23. Reprinted by permission from the Fortune Directory; © 1981 Time Inc.

Lucky Stores to pay lower prices than independents. Since chains may have thousands of retail stores, they can use layout specialists, sales training, and accounting systems to increase efficiency. Advertising can also be used effectively; a single advertisement for Radio Shack in a national magazine benefits every Radio Shack store in the United States.

About 31 percent of all retail stores are part of some chain, and their dollar volume of sales amounts to more than one-third of all retail sales. Chains currently dominate four fields. They account for 92 percent of all department store sales, almost 80 percent of all variety store sales, 56 percent of all food store sales, and half of all retail shoe store sales. Table 12.2 lists the ten largest retailers in the United States.

For years Sears has ranked as the nation's largest retailer. It accounts for just under half of all catalog sales, 3.5 percent of all non-food retail sales, and fully 1 percent of the nation's gross national product. One out of two U.S. families now carries a Sears credit card, and three out of four adults shop at Sears every year. Appropriately, the company headquarters are located in the tallest building in the United States, the 110-story Sears Tower in Chicago.

Many of the larger chains have expanded their operations to the rest of the world. Sears has branch stores in Mexico, South America, and Spain. Safeway operates supermarkets in Australia, Germany, and the United Kingdom. J. C. Penney has retail operations in Belgium and Italy. Direct retailers such as Avon and Tupperware have sales representatives in Europe and South America. Japanese shoppers can frequent more than 500 7-Eleven stores.[14]

**FIGURE 12.5
Comparison of Retail
Trade in the United
States by Number of
Establishments and
Sales Volume**

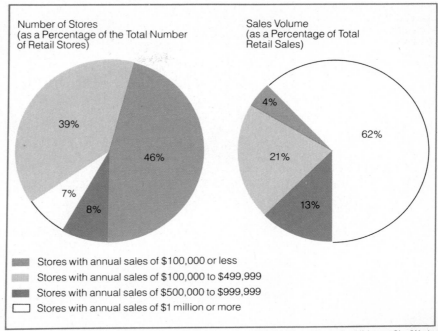

Number of Stores
(as a Percentage of the Total Number
of Retail Stores)

Sales Volume
(as a Percentage of Total
Retail Sales)

39%
46%
7%
8%

4%
21%
62%
13%

▨ Stores with annual sales of $100,000 or less
▨ Stores with annual sales of $100,000 to $499,999
▨ Stores with annual sales of $500,000 to $999,999
☐ Stores with annual sales of $1 million or more

Source: U.S. Department of Commerce, Bureau of the Census, *1977 Census of Retail Trade, Establishment Size* (Washington, D.C.: U.S. Government Printing Office, 1981), pp. 1-8.

**Independent
Retailers**

Even though most retailers are small, independent operators, the larger-sized chains dominate a number of fields. The U.S. retailing structure can be characterized as having a large number of small stores, many medium-sized stores, and a small number of large stores. Even though only 7 percent of all stores have annual sales of $1 million or more, Figure 12.5 reveals that they account for almost two-thirds of all retail sales in the United States. On the other hand, almost half of all stores in the United States have sales of less than $100,000 each year.

Independents have attempted to compete with chains in a number of ways. Some were unable to do so efficiently and went out of business. Others have joined retail cooperatives, wholesaler-sponsored voluntary chains, or franchise operations, as described in Chapter 10. Still others have remained in business by exploiting their advantages of flexibility in operation and knowledge of local market conditions. The independents continue to represent a major part of U.S. retailing.[15]

**RETAILING
TRENDS**

A modern-day Rip Van Winkle would be amazed at the tremendous evolution of retailing. The trading posts and general stores of the 1800s have given way to the hypermarkets and giant shopping centers of the

Retailers are likely to have numerous competitors located nearby.

Source: DUNAGIN'S PEOPLE by Ralph Dunagin, © 1981 Field Enterprises, Inc. Courtesy of Field Newspaper Syndicate.

1980s. Such inventions as the telephone, the automobile, and radio and television have effected a dramatic impact on the retail structure of almost every nation. Two developments that have transformed retailing are planned shopping centers and the practice of scrambled merchandising.

Planned Shopping Centers

The pronounced shift of retail trade away from the traditional downtown retailing districts and toward suburban shopping centers has been building since 1950. **Planned shopping centers** are *a group of retail stores planned, coordinated, and marketed as a unit to shoppers in their geographic trade area.* These centers have followed population shifts to the suburbs and have concentrated on avoiding many of the problems associated with shopping in the downtown business district. They provide a convenient location for shoppers, as well as free parking facilities based upon the number and types of stores in the center. Family shopping is facilitated by uniform hours of operation and by evening and weekend shopping hours.

On the surface, planned shopping centers appear to be replicas of downtown retailing districts. They are, however, different in two important ways:

The center is organized and controlled by a single management to create an integrated approach to accommodate vehicular traffic. For every foot of selling space, three or four feet of parking space is provided. Secondly, this same management directs its attention toward developing an equally integrated and homogeneous marketing approach. Whereas the traditional central business district was an agglomeration of retailers joined by their individual decisions to rent adjacent space, the tenants of planned regional centers are selected with almost as much care as the names in a social register. The aim is to form a set of stores that will complement each other in the quality of the merchandise offerings and to cover the range of merchandise that the market could be expected to desire.[16]

Types of Shopping Centers There are three types of planned shopping centers. The smallest and most common is the *neighborhood shopping center,* which is most often composed of a supermarket and a group of smaller stores such as a drugstore, a laundry and dry cleaner, a small appliance store, and perhaps a beauty shop and barbershop. Such centers provide convenient shopping for perhaps 5,000 to 15,000 shoppers who live within a few minutes' commuting time of the center. Such centers typically contain five to fifteen stores whose product mix is usually confined to convenience goods and some shopping goods.

Community shopping centers typically serve 20,000 to 100,000 persons in a trade area extending a few miles. These centers are likely to contain fifteen to fifty retail stores, with a branch of a local department store or a large variety store as the primary tenant. In addition to the stores found in a neighborhood center, the community center is likely to have additional stores featuring shopping goods, some professional offices, and a branch of a bank or a savings and loan association.

The largest planned center is the *regional shopping center,* a giant shopping district of at least 400,000 square feet of shopping space usually built around one or more major department stores and as many as 200 smaller stores. In order to be successful, regional centers must be located in areas where at least 250,000 people reside within 30 minutes' driving time of the center. The regional centers provide the widest product mixes and the greatest depth of each line.

Woodfield Mall, located in Schaumburg, Illinois, is the world's largest enclosed mall. Its 230 stores occupy three stories and overlook an ice skating rink. An average of 50,000 shoppers are attracted each day, and total annual sales are estimated at $400 million. Four movie theaters, a hotel, and numerous high-rise office buildings nearby attract other residents. The mall structure and its 10,800-car parking area are situated on a site almost as large as Vatican City. Like other huge regional malls, Woodfield serves as a substitute "downtown" for the Illinois community.[17]

Planned shopping centers account for more than 40 percent of all retail sales in the United States. Their growth has slowed in recent years, however, as the most lucrative locations are occupied and the market for such centers appears to have been saturated in many regions. Recent trends have developed toward the building of smaller centers in smaller cities and towns.

Scrambled Merchandising

A second fundamental change in retailing has been the steady deterioration of clear-cut delineations of retailer types. Anyone who has attempted to fill a physician's prescription recently has been exposed to the concept of **scrambled merchandising**—*the practice of carrying dissimilar lines in an attempt to generate added sales volume.* The drugstore carries not only prescription and proprietary drugs but also garden supplies, gift items, groceries, hardware, housewares, magazines, records, and even small appliances. Gasoline retailers now market bread and milk, and supermarkets carry antifreeze.

Many supermarkets fill prescriptions and stock such nonfood items as portable televisions, cameras, stereo equipment, citizen's-band radios, and clothing such as jeans and T-shirts. Customers often can use bank credit cards for payment. The best-selling product in dollar volume in drugstores is Polaroid Polacolor II film for instant movies. Other photographic materials—Kodacolor II and Polaroid SX-70 films and Sylvania flash cubes—also rank among the top ten drugstore sellers. Shoppers at Montgomery Ward's San Diego outlets can obtain legal advice for $10 per consultation.[18] Two-thirds of all toothpaste purchases are made in supermarkets; and about one-fourth of all retail stores are at least partially involved in selling tires, batteries, and other automobile parts and accessories.[19]

Scrambled merchandising was born out of retailers' willingness to add dissimilar merchandise lines in order to satisfy consumer demand for one-stop shopping. It complicates manufacturers' channel decisions, because attempts to maintain or increase their market share will, in most instances, mean that they will have to develop multiple channels to reach the diverse variety of retailers handling their products.

THE WHEEL OF RETAILING

Malcolm P. McNair attempted to explain the patterns of change in retailing through what has been termed the **wheel of retailing**. According to this hypothesis, *new types of retailers gain a competitive foothold by offering lower prices to their customers through the reduction or elimination of services. Once they are established, however, they add more services, and their prices gradually rise. Then they become vulnerable to a new low-price retailer who enters with minimum services*—and the wheel turns.

Most of the major developments in retailing appear to fit the wheel pattern. Early department stores, chain stores, supermarkets, discount stores, hypermarkets, and catalog retailers all emphasized limited service and low prices. For most of these retailers, price levels gradually increased as services were added.

There have been some exceptions, however. Suburban shopping centers, convenience food stores, and vending machines were not built around low-price appeals. However, the wheel pattern has been present often enough in the past that it should serve as a general indicator of future developments in retailing.[20]

THE RETAIL LIFE CYCLE

Closely related to the wheel hypothesis is the concept of the retail life cycle. Just as the notion of "life cycle" was applied earlier to households and to products, it is also possible to apply the con-

NEED HARDWARE? HOMEOWNERS' INSURANCE? A HOME? GO TO SEARS

Sears—the long-time one-stop shopping favorite of millions of shoppers—has made a number of daring moves in recent years aimed at providing even more services. Its Allstate property, casualty, and life insurance subsidiary has been highly successful, with profits quadrupling during the 1970s. Convinced that the Sears reputation and huge customer base would enable the retailing giant to succeed in the real estate field, Sears purchased Coldwell Banker & Co, the nation's largest real estate broker, in 1981. That same year, it began the purchase of Dean Witter Reynolds, the fifth-largest stock brokerage firm.

The new strategy moved Sears in the direction of providing the financial services of a giant bank. Since Sears already possesses a huge consumer credit data base from its installment lending and credit card operations, such data could be utilized in the marketing of securities, real estate, and loans.

As the huge retailer builds its financial services operations, many forecasters expect to see automated teller machines appearing in Sears retail stores and even a Sears debit card providing banklike checking and savings accounts. The nation's one-stop retailer is attempting to add even more shopper convenience through its diverse offerings. In so doing, such firms as Merrill Lynch, Chase Manhattan Bank, Real Estate One, and American Express join K mart, J. C. Penney, and Montgomery Ward as Sears' competitors.

Source: The Sears acquisitions are discussed in "The New Sears," *Business Week*, November 16, 1981, pp. 140–146; and Carol J. Loomis, "The Fight for Financial Turf," *FORTUNE*, December 28, 1981, pp. 54–65.

cept of "introduction-growth-maturity-decline" to retail institutions. Table 12.3 applies the retail life cycle concept to a number of institutions and identifies the approximate stage in the life cycle of each institution.

Retailers have demonstrated that it is possible to extend the length of their life cycles by adapting to changing environments. Such institutions as supermarkets and variety stores reached the maturity stage in their life cycles several decades ago, but have continued to function as important marketing institutions by adapting to changing consumer demands and by adjusting to meet changing competitive situations. Variety stores have countered the sales inroads of discount houses by becoming more price-competitive and by providing greater depth in their product lines. Supermarkets have taken such steps as offering generic brands at lower prices, developing departments of gourmet foods to counter the competition of specialty food retailers, and adding nonfood items to meet the demand for one-stop shopping convenience.[21]

**TABLE 12.3
Life Cycles of
Selected Retail
Institutions**

Institutional Type	Period of Fastest Growth	Period from Inception to Maturity (Years)	Stage of Life Cycle
General store	1800–1840	100	Decline
Specialty store	1820–1840	100	Maturity
Variety store	1870–1930	50	Decline
Mail-order house	1915–1950	50	Mature
Corporate chain	1920–1930	50	Mature
Discount store	1955–1975	20	Mature
Supermarket	1935–1965	35	Mature
Shopping center	1950–1965	40	Mature
Gasoline station	1930–1950	45	Mature
Convenience store	1965–1975	20	Mature
Fast-food store	1960–1975	15	Mature
Hypermarket	1973–	—	Early growth
Warehouse retailer	1970–1980	10	Late growth
Catalog showroom	1970–1980	10	Late growth

Source: Joseph Barry Mason and Morris L. Mayer, *Modern Retailing: Theory and Practice* (Dallas: Business Publications, Inc., 1978), p. 58. © 1978 by Business Publications, Inc. Adapted with permission.

THE FUTURE OF RETAILING

A number of trends are currently emerging that will greatly affect tomorrow's retailer.[22] Cable television is likely to revolutionize many retail practices by the early 1990s, when it is expected to be in nearly half of all U.S. homes. The cable will make **teleshopping** possible. That is, *consumers will be able to order merchandise that has been displayed on their television sets.* Such remote shopping is likely to be especially common for products where sight, feel, smell, and personal service are not important in the purchase decision.[23] One such system already in operation is called Qube; it is a Warner Communications cable network connected to some 30,000 homes in Columbus, Ohio. The system allows instant two-way sales communication between retailers and consumers.[24] Video telephones offer the same promise, but their introduction is likely to be delayed because of high costs involved in making them available.

Retail executives believe that catalog stores, direct mail, discount houses, hypermarkets, and telephone selling are likely to offer major growth opportunities. Discounting is expected to grow to 25 percent of the total general merchandise sales volume. Discount apparel retailers like Marshall's and Hit or Miss are regarded as major threats to established department stores and independent retailers of clothing. In addition, grocery, drug, and other limited-line retailers are likely to generate new competition for the consumer's general merchandise business.

A renewed emphasis on the pleasurable aspects of shopping is another trend that should escalate in the next few years. Department stores are expected to place increased emphasis on in-house boutiques and specialty shops, which will allow them to provide more individualized service and to appeal to specific kinds of customers.

The future of specialty stores appears bright; their share of the general merchandise market is expected to increase to 48 percent by the end of this decade. However, the number of small, independent specialty stores is expected to continue to decline. Those that survive will become stronger and will generate the increase in sales volume.

SUMMARY

The two million retail establishments in the United States are vital members of the marketing channels for consumer products. They play a major role in creating time, place, and possession utility. Retailers can be categorized on five bases: (1) shopping effort expended by customers; (2) services provided to customers; (3) product lines; (4) location of retail transactions; and (5) form of ownership.

Retailers—like consumer goods—may be divided into convenience, shopping, and specialty categories based upon the efforts shoppers are willing to expend in purchasing products. A second method of classification categorizes retailers on a spectrum ranging from self-service to full-service. The third method divides retailers into three categories: limited-line stores, which compete by carrying a large assortment of one or two lines of products; specialty stores, which carry a very large assortment of only part of a single line of products; and general merchandise retailers, such as department stores, variety stores, and such mass merchandisers as discount houses, hypermarkets, and catalog retailers—all handling a wide variety of products.

A fourth classification method distinguishes between retail stores and nonstore retailing. While more than 97 percent of total retail sales in the United States takes place in retail stores, such nonstore retailing as house-to-house retailing, mail-order establishments, and automatic merchandising machines are important in marketing many types of products and services.

The fifth method of classification categorizes retailers by form of ownership. The major types include corporate chain stores, independent retailers, and independents who have banded together to form retail cooperatives or to join wholesaler-sponsored voluntary chains or franchises.

Chains are groups of retail stores that are centrally owned and managed, and that handle the same lines of products. Chain stores dominate retailing in four fields: department stores, variety stores, food stores, and shoe stores. They account for more than a third of all retail sales.

A pronounced shift in retailing away from the downtown business districts and toward planned suburban shopping centers has taken place. These shopping centers account for more than 40 percent of all retail sales.

The changes in retailing practices and the development of new retailing forms reflect retailers' attempts to keep up with changing consumer demands. Retailers are a vital institution in the firm's marketing channel.

QUESTIONS FOR DISCUSSION

1. Explain the following terms:

retailing	hypermarkets
limited-line store	chain stores
general merchandise retailer	planned shopping centers
department store	scrambled merchandising
mass merchandiser	wheel of retailing
discount house	teleshopping

2. Why, in this era of super-stores and mass merchandising, have general stores survived?

3. Identify each of the three major categories of retail stores. Give an example of each in your city.

4. How are limited-line and specialty stores able to compete with such general merchandise retailers as department stores and discount houses?

5. Why have supermarkets increased the number of nonfood items stocked in their stores?

6. Identify the major types of general merchandise retailers.

7. Give reasons for the success of discount retailing in the United States.

8. Identify and briefly explain each of the types of nonstore retailing operations.

9. Explain the party plan approach to house-to-house retailing. In what other product lines might this technique be successful?

10. Why has mail-order retailing, a holdover from the nineteenth century, continued to exist as a separate form of retail selling?

11. In what fields are chain stores dominant? Explain their success in these fields.

12. What advantages do chain stores possess over independent retailers?

13. Chain stores offer their customers the benefit of economies of scale; yet independent retailers account for over two-thirds of all retail sales. Explain.

14. A few food stores in every city continue to offer credit and delivery service. How can they survive the competition of the chain stores and independent supermarkets, with their lower prices?

15. Comment on the following statement: Planned shopping centers are replicas of the downtown retailing districts.

16. Why has the practice of scrambled merchandising become so common in retailing?

17. What problems for the manufacturer result from the practice of scrambled merchandising?

18. List several examples of the wheel of retailing in operation. List examples that do not conform to the wheel hypothesis.

19. Compare the retail life cycle concept with the wheel-of-retailing hypothesis.

20. What changes would you predict for retailing as a result of the development of the video telephone? Which retailers are likely to be affected most by this innovation?

NOTES

1. Associated Press article, "Push Comes to Shove When Harrods Holds Annual Sale," in *Orlando Sentinel Star,* January 11, 1981. Reprinted by permission of AP Newsfeatures.

2. Gerald Albaum, Roger Best, and Del Hawkins, "Retailing Strategy for Customer Growth and New Customer Attraction," *Journal of Business Research,* March 1980, pp. 7–19; and Bert Rosenbloom, "Strategic Planning in Retailing: Prospects and Problems," *Journal of Retailing,* Spring 1980, pp. 107–20.

3. This section is adapted from Louis P. Bucklin, "Retail Strategy and the Classification of Consumer Goods," *Journal of Marketing,* January 1963, pp. 50–55, published by the American Marketing Association.

4. "Sears' Identity Crisis," *Business Week,* December 8, 1975, p. 54.

5. See Thomas J. Stanley and Murphy A. Sewell, "Predicting Supermarket Trade: Implications for Marketing Management," *Journal of Retailing,* Summer 1978, pp. 13–22. See also Danny N. Bellenger, Thomas J. Stanley and John W. Allen, "Trends in Food Retailing," *Atlanta Economic Review,* May-June 1978, pp. 11–14.

6. Christy Marshall, "Supermarkets Fight Fast-Food Challenge," *Advertising Age,* October 30, 1978, pp. 30, 34.

7. See Eleanor G. May and Malcolm P. McNair, "Department Stores Face Stiff Challenge in the Next Decade," *Journal of Retailing,* Fall 1977, pp. 47–58.

8. "Business Bulletin," *Wall Street Journal,* October 26, 1978.

9. Leonard L. Berry, "The Time-buying Consumer," *Journal of Retailing,* Winter 1979, pp. 58–69.

10. John A. Quelch and Hirotaka Takeuchi, "Nonstore Marketing: Fast Track or Slow?" *Harvard Business Review,* July-August 1981, p. 75.

11. "Vendors Pull Out All Stops," *Business Week,* August 15, 1970, pp. 52–54.

12. *Wall Street Journal,* August 23, 1979, p. 1.

13. "Vending Machine Sales Hit $13.8 Billion," *Orlando Sentinel Star,* November 29, 1981.

14. Tom Bayer, "7-Eleven Takes Steps to Move Beyond Image," *Advertising Age*, December 7, 1981, pp. 4, 78.

15. "Those Mom-and-Pop Stores Are Still Going Strong," *U.S. News & World Report,* July 28, 1978, pp. 59–62; and Gerald Albaum, Roger Best, and Del Hawkins, "Retailing Strategy for Customer Growth and New Customer Attraction," *Journal of Business Research,* March 1980, pp. 7–20.

16. Louis P. Bucklin, *Competition and Evolution in the Distributive Trades* (Englewood Cliffs, N.J.: Prentice-Hall, 1972), p. 108.

17. The Woodfield Mall is described in "Shopping Centers Will Be America's Towns of Tomorrow," *Marketing News,* November 28, 1980, p. 1.

18. "Where Consumers Buy Legal Advice at Retail," *Business Week,* July 2, 1979, p. 44. See also Anton Rupert, "Department-Store Dentists, Lawyers Win Acceptance despite Criticism from Peers," *Wall Street Journal,* October 16, 1979.

19. William R. Davidson, "Changes in Distributive Institutions," *Journal of Marketing,* January 1970, p. 8.

20. For a complete discussion of the wheel-of-retailing hypothesis, see Stanley C. Hollander, "The Wheel of Retailing," *Journal of Marketing,* July 1960, pp. 37–42. See also Dillard B. Tinsley, John R. Brooks, Jr., and Michael d'Amico, "Will the Wheel of Retailing Stop Turning?" *Akron Business and Economic Review,* Summer 1978, pp. 26–29.

21. William R. Davidson, Albert D. Bates, and Stephen J. Bass, "The Retail Life Cycle," *Harvard Business Review,* November-December 1976, pp. 89–96; and Rom J. Markin and Calvin P. Duncan, "The Transformation of Retailing Institutions: Beyond the Wheel of Retailing and Life Cycle Theories," *Journal of Macromarketing,* Spring 1981, pp. 58–68.

22. This section is adapted from Raymond A. Marquardt, James C. Makens, and Robert G. Roe, *Retail Management: Satisfaction of Consumer Needs* (Hinsdale, Ill.: The Dryden Press, 1979), pp. 28–31. Copyright © 1979 by The Dryden Press, a division of Holt, Rinehart and Winston. Reprinted by permission of Holt, Rinehart and Winston. See also William R. Davidson and Alice L. Rogers, "Changes and Challenges in Retailing," *Business Horizons,* January-February 1981, pp. 82–87.

23. Malcolm P. McNair and Eleanor G. May, "The Next Revolution of the Retailing Wheel," *Harvard Business Review,* September-October 1978, pp. 81–91.

24. "Retailers Shake a Staid Old Image," *U.S. News & World Report,* October 23, 1978, p. 84. See also Larry J. Rosenberg and Elizabeth C. Hirschman, "Retailing without Stores," *Harvard Business Review,* July–August 1980, pp. 103–12.

CHAPTER 13

MANAGEMENT OF PHYSICAL DISTRIBUTION

KEY TERMS

physical distribution
system
customer service standards
tariffs
class rate
commodity rate
storage warehouse
distribution warehouse
break-bulk center
make-bulk center
EOQ (economic order quantity) model
materials handling
unitizing
containerization

LEARNING GOALS

1. To explain the role of physical distribution in an effective marketing strategy

2. To describe the objective of physical distribution

3. To list the three concepts that make up the physical distribution concept

4. To identify and compare the major elements of a physical distribution system

5. To relate the major transportation alternatives to such factors as energy efficiency, speed, dependability, and cost

Source: Courtesy of Paul Masson Vineyards, Saratoga, California.

The familiar bearded face and resonant voice of filmmaker/actor Orson Welles on the television screen produces instant recognition by millions of viewers. Just as quickly, they make the association between spokesperson Welles and his client, the Paul Masson Vineyards. The commercial ends with Welles making a product quality declaration: "At Paul Masson, we will sell no wine before its time."

The responsibility for ensuring that all Paul Masson wine products are transported in a timely and economical manner is held by Paul Masson physical distribution manager John French. His activities in this regard are numerous: (1) arranging domestic and export transportation by rail, truck, and water carriers; (2) warehouse location and administration; (3) packaging; (4) maintaining customer service standards; and (5) inventory control.

Due to the relatively heavy weight of wine, California wines have traditionally been shipped to the East Coast by rail. A single railroad boxcar can carry as much as 175,000 pounds of wine, as compared with only about 55,000 in a truck. As a result, railroads have historically offered significantly lower per-pound rates than the trucking industry. However, the 1980 deregulation of the trucking industry resulted in increased trucking competition and lower rates that are more competitive with rail rates.

A perennial problem faced by wine shippers is the shortage of rail cars during the peak fall production period. As a result, the shippers are forced to switch to trucks. Another factor accelerating the conversion from rail to truck transportation is service. John French summarizes the problem as follows:

Rail service is deteriorating from the standpoint of transit time. Sometimes it takes 30 to 35 days to New Orleans from California; and it's been as high as 40 days to New England. Getting the merchandise to our distributors overnight isn't necessary. They know how to order and maintain inventories. But when you look at it from our point of view—the fragility of the product, the susceptibility to pilferage—21 days on the road increases the chances of something happening a lot more than six or seven days.[1]

WHAT IS PHYSICAL DISTRIBUTION?

Chapters 10, 11, and 12 have concentrated on the flow of title and use rights, payments, products, and information. This chapter focuses specifically on the physical flow of goods. Improving customer service through more efficient physical distribution remains an important aspect of any organization's marketing strategy. In addition, this efficiency improvement means substantial cost savings.

Physical distribution involves *a broad range of activities concerned with efficient movement of finished products from the end of*

347

*the production line to the consumer.** Physical distribution activities include such important decision areas as customer service, inventory control, materials handling, protective packaging, order processing, transportation, warehouse site selection, and warehousing.

Importance of Physical Distribution

Increased attention has been focused in recent years on physical distribution activities. A major reason for this attention is that these activities represent a major portion of total marketing costs. Almost half of all marketing costs result from physical distribution functions.

Management's traditional focal point for cost-cutting has been production. Historically, these attempts began with the industrial revolution of the 1700s and 1800s, where businesses emphasized efficient production, stressing their ability to decrease production costs and improve the output levels of factories and production workers. But managers have begun to recognize that production efficiency has reached a point at which it is difficult to achieve further cost savings. More and more managers are turning to physical distribution activities as a possible area for cost savings.

In 1982, U.S. industry spent about $240 billion on transportation, more than $145 billion on warehousing, more than $95 billion for inventory carrying costs, and nearly $23 billion to administer and manage physical distribution. Total physical distribution costs amounted to more than $500 billion—over 20 percent of the nation's gross national product.

The second—and equally important—reason for the increased attention on physical distribution activities is the role they play in providing customer service. By storing products in convenient locations for shipment to wholesale and retail customers, firms create time utility. Place utility is created primarily by transportation. These major contributions indicate the importance of the physical distribution component of marketing.

Customer satisfaction depends heavily on reliable movement of products to ensure availability. Eastman Kodak committed a major marketing error in the late 1970s when it launched a multi-million-dollar advertising campaign for its new instant camera before adequate quantities had been delivered to retail outlets. Many would-be purchasers visited the stores and, when they discovered that the new camera was not available, bought a Polaroid camera instead.

By providing consumers with time and place utility, physical distribution contributes to implementing the marketing concept. Robert Woodruff, former president of the Coca-Cola Company, emphasized the role of physical distribution in his firm's success when he stated that his organization's policy is to "put Coke within an arm's length of desire."

---

*The term *logistics* is used interchangeably with *physical distribution* in this chapter.

Physical distribution creates utility by physically linking producers with their customers.

Source: Reprinted with permission from the May 14, 1979, issue of *Advertising Age.* Copyright © 1979 by Crain Communications, Inc.

COMPONENTS OF THE PHYSICAL DISTRIBUTION SYSTEM

The study of physical distribution is one of the classic examples of the systems approach to business problems. The basic notion of a system is that it is a set of interrelated parts. The word is derived from the Greek word *systema,* which refers to an organized relationship among components. The firm's components include such interrelated areas as production, finance, and marketing. Each component must function properly if the system is to be effective and if organizational objectives are to be achieved.

A **system** may be defined as *an organized group of parts or components linked together according to a plan to achieve specific objectives.* The physical distribution system contains the following elements:

1. *Customer service:* What level of customer service should be provided?

2. *Transportation:* How will the products be shipped?

3. *Inventory control:* How much inventory should be maintained at each location?

4. *Materials handling:* How do we develop efficient methods of handling products in the factory, warehouse, and transport terminals?

5. *Order processing:* How should the orders be handled?

6. *Warehousing:* Where will the products be located? How many warehouses should be utilized?

The above components are interrelated, and decisions made in one area affect the relative efficiency of other areas. Attempts to reduce transportation costs by utilizing low-cost, relatively slow water transportation may increase inventory costs since the firm may be required to maintain larger inventory levels to compensate for longer delivery times. The physical distribution manager must balance each component so that no single aspect is stressed to the detriment of the overall functioning of the distribution system.

THE OBJECTIVES OF PHYSICAL DISTRIBUTION

The objective of an organization's physical distribution system may be stated as follows: to produce a specified level of customer service while minimizing the costs involved in physically moving and storing the product from its production point to the point where it is ultimately purchased. Marketers must first agree on the necessary level of customer service, then seek to minimize the total costs of moving the product to the consumer or industrial user.

To achieve this objective, the physical distribution manager must use three basic concepts: the total cost approach, the avoidance of suboptimization, and cost trade-offs.

Total Cost Approach

The premise that all relevant factors in physically moving and storing products should be considered as a whole, and not individually, forms the basis of the *total cost approach.* All physical distribution elements must be considered as a whole when attempting to meet customer service levels at minimum cost.

Avoidance of Suboptimization

To completely understand the total cost approach, it is necessary to consider the second basic physical distribution concept—suboptimization. *Suboptimization* is a condition in which the manager of each physical distribution function attempts to minimize costs, but, due to the impact of one physical distribution task on the others, the results are less than optimal. One writer explains suboptimization using the analogy of a football team made up of numerous talented individuals who seldom win games. Team members hold league records in a variety of skills: pass completions, average yards gained per rush, blocked kicks, and average gains on punt returns. Unfortunately, however, the overall ability of the team to accomplish the organizational goal—scoring more points than the opponents—is rarely achieved.[2]

Why does suboptimization occur frequently in physical distribution? The answer lies in the fact that each separate logistics activity is often judged by its ability to achieve certain management objectives, some of which are at cross-purposes with other objectives. Sometimes, departments in other functional areas take actions that cause the physical distribution area to operate at less than full efficiency.

HOW SUB-OPTIMIZATION OCCURS

The production department attempts to minimize the cost of production per unit of output. To achieve its goal, it operates long production runs with as few changeovers as possible. The result of this action is excess inventory and the added cost of holding this inventory.

The marketing department desires to give the finest customer service possible in order to maximize sales. The effect of this policy is to encourage a maximum of inventory in the field so that customers can receive orders as soon as possible. Again, the cost of holding inventory tends to be relatively high.

The traffic department is judged on its ability to minimize the cost of transportation per unit shipped. But transport costs decrease on a per-unit basis as larger shipments are made. In one case, the traffic manager insisted that all salespersons hold orders from customers who were known to order at random intervals in relatively small quantities. The orders were to be held until enough of them were accumulated to send a carload shipment to the customer's market area.

The results were impressive. Transport costs on a per-unit basis declined dramatically. However, the marketing department was less than pleased. Why? Because the company was gaining a reputation of sporadic delivery of orders, and the net effect was a gradual erosion of the firm's market position.[3]

One purchasing department attempted to minimize the per-unit cost of its purchases. It ordered goods in large numbers to take advantage of quantity discounts. As a result, the company incurred excessive inventory and material handling costs.

The traffic manager of a consumer goods producing company in eastern Canada was determined to reduce transport costs. Trucks were used to haul the product from the Toronto plant to a branch warehouse at the rate of 30 cents per hundred pounds. By negotiating with a railroad, the traffic manager was able to get the rate of 25.5 cents per hundred pounds. This 4.5 cent difference amounted to a savings of $4,150 annually.

However, the rail transport took three days, while the truck transport had taken eight hours. The difference in time meant that an additional $112,500 in inventory was needed to cover the three additional days of lead time before an order arrived. The firm valued its inventory holding costs at 15 percent per year; it therefore incurred an increased inventory cost of $16,900 a year. The reduced freight costs ended up costing the firm $12,750 in increased overall distribution costs. As soon as general management became aware of this situation, the firm's products were back in trucks.

Source: F. R. Denham, "Making the Physical Distribution Concept Pay Off," *Handling and Shipping,* October 1967.

Cost Trade-offs

The third fundamental concept of physical distribution is that of *cost trade-offs.* This approach assumes that some functional areas of the firm will experience cost increases while others will have cost decreases, resulting in the minimization of total physical distribution costs. At no time will the established level of customer service be sacrificed.[4]

The integration of these three basic concepts forms what is commonly referred to as the *physical distribution concept.* The uniqueness of this concept is not in the individual functions, since each function was performed prior to the concept's inception. Rather, it stems from the integration of all the functions into a unified whole whose objective is providing an established level of customer service at the lowest possible distribution costs.

CUSTOMER SERVICE STANDARDS

Customer service standards are *the quality of service that the firm's customers will receive.* For example, a customer service standard for one firm might be that 60 percent of all orders will be shipped within forty-eight hours after they are received, 90 percent in seventy-two hours, and all within ninety-six hours.

HOW GILLETTE AND XEROX USE COST TRADE-OFFS

Gillette, the world's largest producer of safety razors, was faced with an ever-increasing assortment of products due to its expansion into a broad range of toiletries. To offer good customer service, Gillette began shipping goods by air freight; but this proved to be an expensive form of distribution. Through a detailed study of its distribution system, Gillette discovered that its problem was inefficient order processing. By simplifying the paperwork involved, the firm was able to reduce the time required to process new orders. It was then able to return to lower-cost surface transportation and still meet previous delivery schedules. The cost trade-off here was that the order processing costs increased and transportation costs decreased; the net result was that total logistics costs decreased.

Xerox needs to carry a large inventory of supplies for its office machines. The company used to maintain forty warehouses that stocked paper, chemicals, and machine parts. A study by Xerox revealed that 80 percent of the inventory items were "slow movers." The company therefore decided to consolidate its slow-selling products at one location and to air freight them to customers as needed. The cost trade-off—higher transportation costs for lower inventories—is reported to have saved Xerox millions of dollars annually.

Source: "New Strategies to Move Goods," *Business Week,* September 24, 1966, pp. 112ff. See also "New Distribution Strategies Needed to Combat Skyrocketing Energy Costs," *Marketing News,* February 8, 1980, p. 14.

SETTING CUSTOMER SERVICE STANDARDS AT AMERICAN AIRLINES

The next time you are in an American Airlines lobby, a man with a stopwatch and clipboard may well be hanging around. He's there to see how long it takes you to get your ticket—the company standard says 85 percent of the passengers should not have to stand in line more than five minutes. When you land, you may find another such fellow checking to see how long it takes to get the bags off the plane.

American Airlines employees are held to dozens of standards—and checked constantly. Reservation phones must be answered within 20 seconds, 85 percent of the flights must take off within five minutes of departure time and land within 15 minutes of arrival time. Cabins must have the proper supply of magazines. Performance summaries drawn up every month tell management how the airline is doing and where the problems lie. Late arrivals may have been caused by disgruntled air controllers. That can't be helped. But an outbreak of dirty ashtrays may be traced to a particular cleanup crew. The manager responsible for the crew will hear about it. His pay and promotion depend on meeting standards. If he fails to meet them three months running without extenuating circumstances, he may be looking for a job.

Constant checking has helped make American Airlines the preferred domestic line in the latest Airline Passengers Association survey.

Source: Jeremy Main, "Toward Service without a Snarl," *FORTUNE,* March 23, 1981, p. 61. © 1981 Time, Inc. All rights reserved.

Setting the standards for customer service is an important marketing decision. Inadequate customer service may mean dissatisfied customers and the loss of future sales. The physical distribution department must delineate the costs involved in providing proposed standards. A conflict may arise when sales representatives make unreasonable delivery promises to their customers in order to obtain sales. In many cases, however, the need for additional inventory or the use of premium-cost transportation causes such a cost increase that the order proves unprofitable.

In an attempt to increase its share of the market, a major manufacturer of highly perishable food items set a 98 percent service level; that is, 98 percent of all orders were to be shipped the same day they were received. To meet this extremely high level of service, the firm leased warehouse space in 170 different cities and kept large stocks in each location. The large inventories, however, often meant the shipment of dated merchandise. Customers interpreted this practice as evidence of a low-quality product—or poor "service."[5]

Table 13.1 indicates specific objectives that might be developed for each factor involved in customer service. It also illustrates the importance of coordinating order processing, transportation, inventory

TABLE 13.1
Customer Service
Standards

Service Factor	Objectives
Order-cycle time	To develop a physical distribution system capable of effecting delivery of the product within 8 days from the initiation of a customer order: • transmission of order—1 day • order processing (order entry, credit verification, picking and packing)—3 days • delivery—4 days
Dependability of delivery	To ensure that 95% of all deliveries will be made within the 8-day standard and that under no circumstances will deliveries be made earlier than 6 days nor later than 9 days from the initiation of an order.
Inventory levels	To maintain inventories of finished goods at levels that will permit: • 97% of all incoming orders for class A items to be filled • 85% of all incoming orders for class B items to be filled • 70% of all incoming orders for class C items to be filled
Accuracy in order filling	To be capable of filling customer orders with 99% accuracy
Damage in transit	To ensure that damage to merchandise in transit does not exceed 1%
Communication	To maintain a communication system that permits salespersons to transmit orders on a daily basis and that is capable of accurately responding to customer inquiries on order status within 4 hours

Source: From David T. Kollat, Roger D. Blackwell, and James F. Robeson, *Strategic Marketing* (New York: Holt, Rinehart and Winston, 1972), p. 316. Copyright © 1972 by Holt, Rinehart and Winston, Inc. Reprinted by permission of Holt, Rinehart and Winston, CBS College Publishing.

control, and the other components of the physical distribution system in achieving these service standards.

ELEMENTS OF A PHYSICAL DISTRIBUTION SYSTEM

The establishment of acceptable levels of customer service provides the physical distribution department a standard with which actual operations can be compared. The physical distribution system should be designed to achieve this standard by minimizing the total costs of the following components: (1) transportation, (2) warehouses and their location, (3) inventory control, (4) order processing, and (5) materials handling. Relative costs for each component are illustrated in Figure 13.1.

Transportation Considerations

The transportation system in the United States has historically been a regulated industry, much the same as the telephone and electric industries. Although strides toward deregulation have been made in recent years, the courts have often referred to modes of transportation as public utilities. The railroads were first regulated under the Interstate Commerce Act of 1887. This act established the Interstate Commerce Commission (ICC), the first regulatory body in the United States. The

**FIGURE 13.1
Where the Physical
Distribution Dollar
Goes**

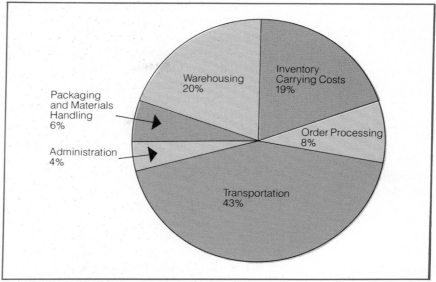

Source: Data from Herbert W. Davis, "Physical Distribution Costs: Performance in Selected Industries—1980," *Annual Proceedings of the National Council of Physical Distribution Management,* 1980, p. 35. Reprinted by permission.

ICC regulates railroads, slurry pipelines, motor carriers, and inland water carriers. The Civil Aeronautics Board regulates U.S. air carriers, and the Federal Maritime Commission regulates U.S. ocean carriers.

In general, the regulation of all the transportation modes includes a provision that the rate charged must be "just and reasonable." *Just* means that the rate must be fair to the shipper in relationship to what other shippers pay for moving similar commodities under approximately the same conditions. *Reasonable* implies that the carrier should be allowed to earn a fair return on the firm's investment. The services offered by the carriers are also regulated. Finally, the right to enter into the business of transportation historically has been restricted in most instances. Permission had to be obtained from the appropriate regulatory body before a new carrier was allowed to compete in the industry.

Rate Determination One of the most difficult problems facing the physical distribution manager who must choose a transportation service is determining the correct rate or cost of the service. The complexity results from **tariffs**—*the books that are used to determine shipping charges.* Tariffs take on the force and effect of statutory law when they are filed with the appropriate regulatory body. There are literally thousands of tariff books, and their number grows at a fantastic rate. One tariff expert has estimated that there are 43 trillion rates on file with the ICC and that if they were stacked one on top of another, they would be three times as tall as the World Trade Center.

There are two basic freight rates: class and commodity. The **class rate** is *the "standard" rate that is found for every commodity moving between any two destinations.* Of the two rates, the class rate is the higher. The **commodity rate** is *sometimes called a special rate, since it is given by carriers to shippers as a reward for either regular use or large quantity shipments.* It is used extensively by the railroads and the inland water carriers. One study showed that between 90 and 95 percent of all rail shipments were traveling under commodity rates.[6]

Transportation Deregulation

The United States transportation industry has experienced massive federal deregulation, beginning in 1977 with the removal of regulations for cargo air carriers not engaged in passenger transportation. The following year, the *Airline Deregulation Act of 1978* was passed, granting considerable freedom to the airlines in establishing fares and in choosing new routes. Passage of this act began a phase-out of the Civil Aeronautics Board that would abolish the agency in 1985.

In 1980, the *Motor Carrier Act* and the *Staggers Rail Act* significantly deregulated the trucking and railroad industries. The new laws provided transportation carriers with the ability to negotiate rates and services, eliminating much of the bureaucracy that has traditionally hampered the establishment of new and innovative rates and services. These changes are already enabling transporters to base rates on a shipper's unique needs. A large Midwest brewery, seeking to expand its Pacific coast market, was able to negotiate a lower rate by guaranteeing a 50 percent increase in products shipped.[7]

The new transportation environment is likely to increase the importance of physical distribution managers, since their areas of responsibility are even more complex than in a highly regulated situation. It is now possible to simultaneously increase service levels and decrease transportation costs. General Foods recently negotiated a service-oriented contract with the Santa Fe Railroad in which highway trailers would be placed on rail cars and transported from Houston to Chicago. In obtaining the contract to ship six million pounds of General Foods products each year, the railroad guaranteed the availability of sufficient truck capacity. As a bonus, it will receive an additional $75 per trailer used for each month in which 90 percent of its trailers make the trip in 96 hours or less.[8]

Classes of Carriers Freight carriers are classified as common, contract, and private. *Common carriers,* sometimes called the backbone of the transportation industry, are for-hire carriers who serve the general public. Their rates and services are regulated, and they cannot conduct their operations without permission of the appropriate regulatory authority. Common carriers exist for all the modes of transport.

Contract carriers are for-hire transporters who do not offer their services to the general public. Instead, they establish specific contracts with certain customers and operate exclusively for a particular industry (most commonly the motor freight industry). These carriers are subject to much less regulation than are common carriers.

Private carriers are not-for-hire carriers. Their operators transport products only for a particular firm and cannot solicit other transportation business. Since the transportation they provide is solely for their own use, there is no rate or service regulation.

In 1978, the ICC began to permit private carriers to also operate as common or contract carriers. Many private carriers have taken advantage of this new rule in order to operate their trucks fully loaded at all times. For instance, Nabisco's fleet of private carriers hauling the firm's products to regional warehouses should be able to reduce total transportation costs by transporting the products of other shippers on the return trip to the factory. Instead of returning in an empty truck, the Nabisco driver acts as a common carrier or contract carrier and receives a transport fee from the outside shipper.[9]

Modal Considerations

The physical distribution manager has five major transportation alternatives: railroads, motor carriers, water carriers, pipelines, and air freight. Figure 13.2 indicates the percentage of total ton-miles shipped by each major mode. The term *ton-mile* refers to moving one ton of freight one mile. Thus a three-ton shipment moved eight miles equals twenty-four ton-miles.

The water carriers' percentage has remained generally stable over the years, while railroads have experienced a significant decrease and pipelines and motor carriers have experienced substantial increases. Air carriers are dwarfed by the other transportation alternatives, accounting for less than 1 percent of all shipments.

Railroads: The Nation's Leading Transporter The most frequently used method of transportation continues to be railroads by about a 1.5 to 1 margin over their nearest competitors. They represent the most efficient mode for the movement of bulk commodities over long distances. In 1982, coal alone made up more than one-fifth of the total rail carloadings in the United States. In addition, mineral products account for almost one of every two loaded rail cars. The railroads have launched a drive in recent years to improve their service standards and to capture a larger percentage of manufactured and other high-value products. To accomplish their goal, the railroads have introduced a number of innovative concepts. One service innovation is run-through trains, which are scheduled to bypass completely any congested terminals. The Chicago and North Western Railroad and the Union Pacific offer a run-through train from Chicago to Los Angeles. Known as the *Super Van,* this train consistently covers the 2,050 miles in less than forty-eight hours.

Railroads are also making extensive use of unit trains to provide

**FIGURE 13.2
Percentage of Total
Intercity Ton-miles
by the Various
Transport Modes:
1940–1980**

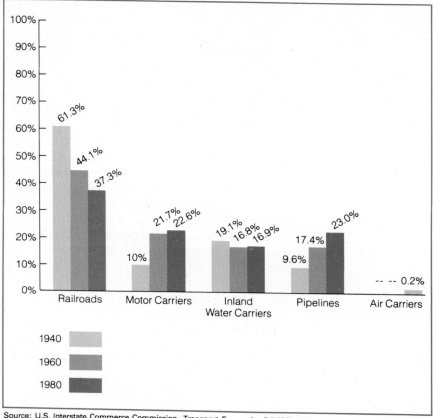

Source: U.S. Interstate Commerce Commission, *Transport Economics 5* (1978), p. 2; and *Yearbook of Railroad Facts* (Washington, D.C.: Association of American Railroads, 1981), p. 36.

time and cost savings for their customers. Unit trains are used exclusively by a single customer, who pays lower rates for each shipment. The Burlington Northern Railroad operates unit coal trains for electricity utility companies in the Midwest. The railroad hauls a trainload of low-sulphur coal from Montana or Wyoming to the generating plants and then returns empty for another run.

Improved customer service is also being accomplished through an unusual method: railroad mergers. Only 42 U.S. railroad lines generate more than $50 million in annual revenues, and this number is slowly shrinking due to mergers. In the past, rail shippers had to resort to *interlining*—using more than one rail carrier when long distances between the shipment's origin and its destination were involved. As a result, it was easy for one railroad to simply blame other connecting railroads for service problems. The increased number of rail mergers are typically "end-to-end," thereby providing shippers with single-carrier service from origin to destination.[10]

Motor Carriers: Flexible and Growing The trucking industry has shown dramatic growth over the past decades. Its prime advantage over the other modes is its relatively fast, consistent service for both large and small shipments. Motor carriers concentrate on manufactured products, while railroads haul more bulk and raw material products. Motor carriers therefore receive greater revenue per ton shipped than do railroads. In 1980, motor carriers received approximately 16 cents per ton-mile while railroads earned 2 cents.

Trucking's primary appeal to shippers is superior service, and the industry is working diligently to maintain this advantage. The TIME-DC trucking company is currently running schedules that just a few years ago would have seemed impossible. It used to require seven to ten days for a coast-to-coast truckload shipment. TIME-DC now offers its Yellowbird Service between New York–New Jersey and Southern California in sixty-nine hours, with delivery made the third morning after departure.

Water Carriers: Slow but Inexpensive There are basically two types of water carriers—the inland or barge lines and the ocean-going deep-water ships. Barge lines are efficient transporters of bulky, low-unit value commodities like grain, gravel, lumber, sand, and steel. A typical lower Mississippi River barge line may be more than a quarter mile in length and two hundred feet wide.

Ocean-going ships operate on the Great Lakes, between United States port cities, and in international commerce. Water carrier costs average 0.6 cents per ton-mile.

Pipelines: Specialized Transporters Even though the pipeline industry ranks second only to railroads in number of ton-miles transported, many people are barely aware of their existence. More than 200,000 miles of pipelines crisscross the United States. Pipelines serve as extremely efficient transporters of natural gas and oil products, as evidenced by their average revenue per ton-mile of a little less than 0.3 cents. Oil pipelines carry two types of commodities—crude (unprocessed) oil and refined products, such as gasoline and kerosene. There is also a slow but steady growth in the use of slurry pipelines. In this method of transport, a product such as coal is ground up into a powder, mixed with water, and transported in suspension through the pipeline.[11]

Although pipelines represent a low-maintenance, dependable method of transportation, they possess a number of characteristics that limit their use. Their availability in different locations is even more limited than the water carriers and their use is restricted to a relatively small number of products that can be transported in this manner. Finally, pipelines represent a relatively slow method of transportation. Liquids travel through pipelines at an average of only three or four miles per hour.

THE NATION'S FIRST SUPERPORT

Importing costly crude oil from OPEC nations has traditionally been made even more expensive due to the size of the supertankers and the inability of U.S. ports to dock them. In the past, the tankers— capable of handling 700,000 ton loads—anchored offshore and transferred their cargo to smaller vessels. The additional unloading and reloading expenses drove the high-priced crude oil even higher.

These costs were reduced in 1981 with the opening of the Louisiana Offshore Oil Port (LOOP), a $575-million installation situated 19 miles off the Louisiana Gulf Coast. LOOP, which looks like a large offshore oil drilling and pumping rig, stands on steel legs in 110 feet of water about 60 miles south of New Orleans.

Rather than pump crude oil into smaller vessels capable of navigating the Mississippi River to New Orleans, workers at the superport simply hook up hoses and pump the cargo through a 19-mile underwater pipeline. It is then fed directly into a major pipeline that crosses the nation to Chicago.

Although the facility is expensive, it represents the cost trade-offs necessary to minimize overall costs. Transporters can utilize the relatively low-cost supertankers in moving the crude oil, and can then avoid the added handling costs previously associated with using smaller vessels on the last few miles of the journey.

Source: The opening of the LOOP superport is described in "First Offshore 'Superport' Makes Debut," *Orlando Sentinel Star,* May 8, 1981. See also "Once Again, A Plunge into Deepwater Oil Ports," *Business Week,* December 22, 1980, p. 79.

Air Freight: Fast but Expensive The use of air carriers has been growing significantly. In 1961, U.S. airlines flew about 1 billion ton-miles. By 1980, this figure had jumped to 5 billion ton-miles. However, air freight is still a relatively insigificant percentage of the total ton-miles shipped, amounting to one-fifth of 1 percent in 1980.

Because of air freight's relatively high cost, it is used primarily for valuable or highly perishable products. Typical shipments consist of computers, furs, fresh flowers, high-fashion clothing, live lobsters, and watches. Air carriers often offset their higher transportation costs with reduced inventory holding costs and faster customer service.

One result of airline deregulation was the simplification of regulations concerning the creation of new airline companies. In the first three years following deregulation, new air carriers such as Midway, New York Air, People Express, Muse Air, Sun Pacific, Sun Air, Pacific Express, and Air Chicago began operations. All of these carriers are primarily passenger-oriented, although some freight service is available.[12] Table 13.2 ranks the five transport modes on several bases.

**TABLE 13.2
Comparing the
Transport Modes**

Factor	Rank				
	1	2	3	4	5
Energy Efficiency	Pipelines	Water carriers	Railroads	Motor carriers	Air carriers
Speed	Air carriers	Motor carriers	Railroads	Water carriers	Pipelines
Dependability in meeting schedules	Pipelines	Motor carriers	Railroads	Water carriers	Air carriers
Cost	Water carriers	Pipelines	Railroads	Motor carriers	Air carriers
Frequency of shipments	Pipelines	Motor carriers	Air carriers	Railroads	Water carriers
Availability in different locations	Motor carriers	Railroads	Air carriers	Water carriers	Pipelines
Flexibility in handling products	Water carriers	Railroads	Motor carriers	Air carriers	Pipelines

Source: The energy-efficiency rankings are reported in Eric Hirst, *Energy Intensiveness of Passenger and Freight Modes,* National Science Foundation, Oak Ridge National Laboratory, March 1972, p. 27. The other factors and rankings are based on a discussion in James L. Heskitt, Nicholas A. Glaskowsky, Jr., and Robert M. Ivie, *Business Logistics* (New York: Ronald Press, 1973), pp. 113–18. Used by permission.

Freight Forwarders: Transportation Middlemen Freight forwarders are considered transportation middlemen because their function is to consolidate shipments in order to get lower rates for their customers. The transport rates on less-than-truckload (LTL) and less-than-carload (LCL) shipments are often twice as high on a per-unit basis as are the rates on truckload (TL) and carload (CL) shipments. Freight forwarders charge less than the higher rates but more than the lower rates. They make their profit by paying the carriers the lower rates. By consolidating shipments, freight forwarders offer their customers two advantages— lower costs on small shipments and faster delivery service than the LTL and LCL shippers.

Supplemental Carriers The physical distribution manager can also utilize a number of auxiliary or supplemental carriers that specialize in transporting small shipments. These carriers include bus freight services, United Parcel Service, and the U.S. Postal Service.

Supplemental
carriers such as
United Parcel
Service provide
efficient service for
small shipments.

"I swear it wasn't flat when we parked here!"

Source: Cartoon by Dave Gerard; copyright © 1971 *Saturday Evening Post.* Reprinted by permission.

Intermodal Coordination The various transport modes often combine their services to give shippers the service and cost advantages of each mode. The most widely accepted form of coordination is *piggyback*—railroad transportation between cities of a truck trailer carried on a rail flatcar. The motor carrier delivers and picks up the shipment.

The combination of truck and rail services generally gives shippers faster service and lower rates than either mode would individually, since each method is used where it is most efficient. Shipper acceptance of piggybacking has been tremendous. In 1955, fewer than 200,000 piggyback rail cars were shipped. By 1980, more than 1.6 million cars were involved. Piggyback shipments are expected to account for 40 percent of all rail traffic by 1995. In 1981, the ICC exempted piggyback service from government regulation, a move that is expected to increase competition and improve growth prospects for this concept.[13]

Another form of intermodal coordination is *birdyback.* Here, motor carriers deliver and pick up the shipment, and air carriers take it over the long distance. In addition, motor carriers and water carriers have a form of intermodal coordination called *fishyback.*

Warehouses and Their Location

Two types of warehouses exist: storage and distribution. A **storage warehouse** *stores products for moderate to long periods of time in an attempt to balance supply and demand for producers and purchasers.* They are used most often by firms whose products are seasonal in supply or demand.

The **distribution warehouse** *assembles and redistributes products, keeping them on the move as much as possible.* Many distri-

**FIGURE 13.3
Use of Break-bulk
and Make-bulk
Centers**

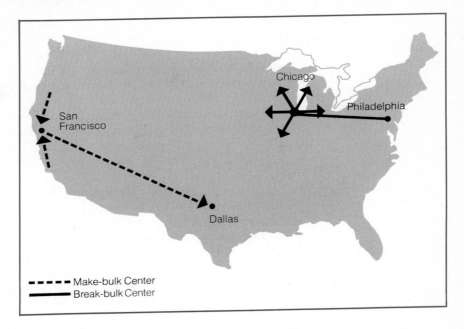

Make-bulk Center
Break-bulk Center

bution warehouses or centers actually store the goods physically for less than one day.

In an attempt to reduce transportation costs, manufacturers have developed central distribution centers. A manufacturer located in Philadelphia with customers in the Illinois, Wisconsin, and Indiana area could send each customer a direct shipment. But if each customer places small orders, the transportation charges for the individual shipments will be relatively high. A feasible solution is to send a large, consolidated shipment to a **break-bulk center,** *a central distribution center that breaks down large shipments into several smaller ones and delivers them to individual customers in the area.* For the hypothetical manager in Philadelphia, the feasible break-bulk center might be located in Chicago. Figure 13.3 illustrates the use of break-bulk centers in the United States.

Inversely, the **make-bulk center** *consolidates several small shipments into one large shipment and delivers it to its destination.* For example, a giant retailer like Safeway Stores may operate several satellite production facilities in a given area. Each plant can send shipments to a storage warehouse in Dallas. This, however, could result in a large number of small, expensive shipments. If a make-bulk center is created in San Francisco, as illustrated in Figure 13.3, and each supplier sends its shipments there, all deliveries bound for Dallas theoretically can be consolidated into one economical shipment.

The top five distribution center cities in the United States, as measured by the total number of break-bulk distribution centers, are

Chicago, Los Angeles–Long Beach, the New York City area, Dallas–Fort Worth, and Atlanta.

Automated Warehouses Warehouses lend themselves well to automation, with the computer as the heart of the operation. An outstanding example of automation at work is the Aerojet-General Industrial Systems Division warehouse in Frederick, Maryland. This huge warehouse is operated entirely by one employee who gives instructions to the facility's governing computer. The computer operates the fully automated materials handling system and generates all the necessary forms.[14]

Although automated warehouses may cost as much as $10 million, they can provide major savings to high-volume distributors such as grocery chains. Some current systems can select 10,000 to 300,000 cases per day of up to 3,000 different items. They can "read" computerized store orders, choose the correct number of cases, and move them in the desired sequence to loading docks. These warehouses reduce labor costs, worker injuries, pilferage, fires, and breakage; and they assist in inventory control.

Location Factors A major decision facing each company deals with the number and location of its storage facilities. The two general factors involved are warehousing and materials handling costs and delivery costs from the warehouse to the customer. The first costs are subject to economies of scale; therefore, on a per-unit basis, they decrease as volume increases. Delivery costs, on the other hand, increase as the distance from the warehouse location to the customer increases.

The two cost items are diagramed in Figure 13.4. The asterisk in

**FIGURE 13.4
Factors Influencing
the Number of
Warehouses**

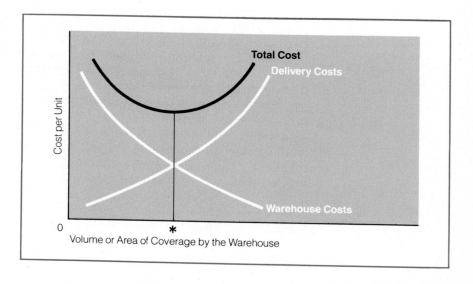

the figure marks the ideal area of coverage for each warehouse. This model helps determine the proper number of warehouses if decentralization is desired.

The specific location of the firm's warehouses presents another complicated problem. Factors that must be considered include (1) local, county, and state taxes; (2) local, county, and state laws and regulations; (3) availability of a trained labor force; (4) police and fire protection; (5) access to the various transport modes; (6) community attitude toward the proposed warehouses; and (7) the cost and availability of public utilities, such as electricity and natural gas.

Inventory Control Systems

Inventory control is a major component in the physical distribution system. Current estimates of inventory holding costs figure about 25 percent per year. This means that $1,000 of inventory held for a single year costs the company $250. Inventory costs include such expenses as storage facilities, insurance, taxes, handling costs, opportunity costs for funds invested in inventory, and depreciation and possible obsolescence of the goods in inventory.[15]

Inventory control analysts have developed a number of techniques to help the physical distribution manager effectively control inventory. The most basic is the **EOQ (economic order quantity) model**. This technique *emphasizes a cost trade-off between two fundamental costs involved with inventory: inventory holding costs that increase with the addition of more inventory and order costs that decrease as the quantity ordered increases.* As Figure 13.5 indicates, these two cost items are traded off to determine the optimal order quantity of each product.

The EOQ point in Figure 13.5 is the point at which total cost is

**FIGURE 13.5
The EOQ Model**

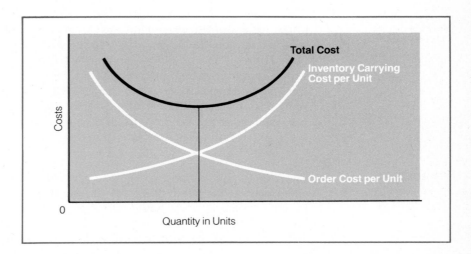

minimized. By placing an order for this amount as needed, firms can minimize their inventory costs.

Order Processing

Like customer service standards, order processing is a quasi-logistics function. The physical distribution manager is concerned with order processing because it directly affects the firm's ability to meet its customer service standards. If a firm's order processing system is inefficient, the company may have to compensate by using costly premium transportation or increasing the number of field warehouses in all major markets.

Materials Handling Systems

All the activities associated in moving products within the manufacturer's plants, warehouses, and transportation company terminals are called **materials handling.** These activities must be thoroughly coordinated for both intra- and intercompany activities. The efficiency of plants and warehouses is dependent on an effective system.[16]

Two important innovations have been developed in the area of materials handling. One is known as **unitizing**—*combining as many packages as possible into one load, preferably on a pallet (a platform, generally made of wood, on which products are transported).* Unitizing can be accomplished by using steel bands to hold the unit in place or by shrink packaging. Shrink packages are constructed by placing a sheet of plastic over the unit and then heating it. As the plastic cools, it shrinks and holds the individual packages together securely. Unitizing is advantageous because it requires little labor per package, promotes fast movement, and minimizes damage and pilferage.

The second innovation is **containerization,** *the combination of several unitized loads.* It is typically a big box eight feet wide, eight feet high and ten, twenty, thirty, or forty feet long. Such containers allow ease of intertransport mode changes. A container of oil rig parts, for example, can be loaded in Tulsa and trucked to Kansas City, where it can be placed on a high-speed run-through train to New York City. There, it can be placed on a ship and sent to Saudi Arabia.

Containerization also markedly reduces the time involved in loading and unloading ships. Container ships can often be unloaded in less than twenty-four hours—a task that otherwise can take up to two weeks. In-transit damage is also reduced, since individual packages are not handled en route to the purchaser.

International Physical Distribution

The United States has experienced rapid growth in international trade since World War II. Exports have grown at an average annual rate of 7 percent, while imports have increased even faster. In 1979, U.S. merchandise exports totaled approximately $182 billion. Total imports for 1979 amounted to $206 billion. This unparalleled growth of international commerce has placed new responsibilities on physical distribution departments.

A major problem facing international marketers is the flood of paperwork involved in exporting products. More than a hundred different international trade documents representing more than a thousand separate forms must be completed for each international shipment. The result is that an average export shipment requires approximately thirty-six employee hours for documentation and twenty-seven employee hours for importing a shipment. Paperwork alone equals 7 percent of the total value of U.S. international trade. Many physical distribution departments are not large enough to employ international specialists, and they subcontract the work to *foreign freight forwarders,* wholesaling middlemen who specialize in physical distribution outside the United States.

The major impetus to exporting has been the advent of containerization and container ships. One shipping company currently has container ships that can make a round trip between New York, Bremerhaven, and Rotterdam in fourteen days. Only four days are needed for crossing the Atlantic and another six for three port calls. This speed allows U.S. exporters to provide competitive delivery schedules to European markets.

SUMMARY

Physical distribution, as a system, consists of six elements: (1) customer service, (2) transportation, (3) inventory control, (4) materials handling, (5) order processing, and (6) warehousing. These elements are interrelated and must be balanced for a smoothly functioning distribution system. The physical distribution department is one of the classic examples of the systems approach to business problems. Three basic concepts of the systems approach—the total cost approach, the avoidance of suboptimization, and cost trade-offs—combine to form the physical distribution concept.

The goal of a physical distribution department is to produce a specified level of customer service while minimizing the costs involved in physically moving and storing the product from its production point to the point where it is ultimately purchased.

The physical distribution manager has available five transportation alternatives: railroads, motor carriers, water carriers, pipelines, and air freight. Intermodal transport systems are also available and are increasingly being used. Other elements of the physical distribution department include customer service, inventory control, materials handling, protective packaging, order processing, transportation, warehouse site selection, and warehousing. Efficient international physical distribution allows U.S. firms to compete effectively in foreign markets.

Physical distribution, by its very nature, involves keeping track of thousands of details, such as transport rates, special rate proposals, inventory locations, and customer locations. Computerization is an invaluable aid for the logistics manager.

QUESTIONS FOR DISCUSSION

1. Explain the following terms:

    physical distribution system

    customer service standards

    tariffs

    class rate

    commodity rate

    storage warehouse

    distribution warehouse

    break-bulk center

    make-bulk center

    EOQ (economic order quantity) model

    materials handling

    unitizing

    containerization

2. Why was physical distribution one of the last areas in most companies to be carefully studied and improved?

3. Outline the basic reasons for the increased attention to physical distribution management.

4. What is the basic objective of physical distribution?

5. What is the most effective organization for physical distribution management? Explain.

6. Why did the railroads lose a large percentage of the total ton-miles transported since World War II?

7. Suggest the most appropriate method of transportation for each of the following products and defend your choices:

    a. iron ore

    b. Dash detergent

    c. heavy earth-moving equipment

    d. crude oil

    e. orchids

    f. lumber

8. Discuss the relative advantages of the public warehouses (discussed in Chapter 11) and private warehouses.

9. Develop an argument for the increased use of intermodal coordination.

10. What factors should be considered in locating a new distribution warehouse?

11. Are the inventory holding costs discussed in this chapter realistic? Explain.

12. Who should be ultimately responsible for determining the level of customer service standards? Explain.

13. Discuss the basic strengths and weaknesses of each mode of transport.

14. Which mode of transport do you believe will experience the greatest ton-mile percentage growth during the 1980s? Why?

15. Under what conditions would you recommend the construction of a fully automated warehouse? When would an automated warehouse be inappropriate?

16. Under what circumstances are freight forwarders used?

17. Identify the major forms of intermodal coordination and give an example of a product likely to use each type.

18. Comment on the following statement: The popularity of physical distribution management is a fad; ten years from now it will be considered a relatively unimportant function of the firm.

19. Discuss the similarities of and differences between domestic and international physical distribution.

20. Discuss the basic cost factors involved in the EOQ model. Does the basic EOQ model consider all relevant costs? Explain.

NOTES

1. Joe Barks, "We Will Ship No Wine After Its Time," *Distribution,* February 1981, pp. 72–76. Reprinted by permission.
2. Warren Rose, *Logistics Management* (Dubuque, Iowa: Wm. C. Brown, 1979), p. 4.
3. Donald J. Bowersox, Edward W. Smykay, and Bernard J. LaLonde, *Physical Distribution Management* (New York: Macmillan, 1968), p. 6.
4. James M. Daley and Zarrell V. Lambert, "Toward Assessing Trade-Offs by Shippers in Carrier Selection Decisions," *Journal of Business Logistics,* vol. 2, no. 1 (1980), pp. 35–54.
5. Robert E. Sabath, "How Much Service Do Customers Really Want?" *Business Horizons,* April 1978, pp. 26–32. See also Arthur S. Graham, Jr., "Customer Service Measurement and Management in the 1980s," *Annual Proceedings of the National Council of Physical Distribution Management* (1980), pp. 265–75.
6. Charles A. Taff, *Management of Physical Distribution and Transportation* (Homewood, Ill.: Richard D. Irwin, 1972), p. 324.
7. "Deregulation of Railroads to Create Competitive Pricing, Better Service," *Marketing News,* May 1, 1981, p. 9.
8. The deregulation issue is discussed in Donald F. Wood and James C. Johnson, *Contemporary Transportation* (Tulsa: PennWell Books, 1980), chapter 6. See also L. L. Waters, "Deregulation—For Better, or for Worse?" *Business Horizons,* January-February 1981, pp. 88–91.
9. "Court Affirms ICC's Toto Policy, Backs Private Trucks in For-hire Moves," *Traffic World,* July 6, 1981, pp. 129–31.
10. Gus Welty, "The Era of the Giants: Union Pacific, Missouri Pacific, and Western Pacific," *Railway Age,* April 27, 1981, pp. 20–26.
11. Martin T. Farris and David L. Shrock, "The Economics of Coal Slurry Pipelines: Transportation and Non-Transportation Factors," *Transportation Journal,* Fall 1978, pp. 45–57. See also James C. Johnson and Kenneth C. Schneider, "Coal Slurry Pipelines: An Economic and Political Dilemma," *ICC Practitioners' Journal,* November-December 1980, pp. 24–37.
12. Peter Nulty, "Friendly Skies for Little Airlines," *FORTUNE,* February 9, 1981, pp. 45–53; "Upstarts in the Sky: Here Comes a New Kind of Airline," *Business Week,* June 15, 1981, pp. 78–84; and Subrata N. Chakravarty, "Power Dive," *Forbes,* June 22, 1981, pp. 64–66.
13. "ICC Adopts Rules Exempting Railroad Piggyback Service from Regulation," *Traffic World,* March 2, 1981, pp. 50–51.
14. "The Ultimate in Automation," *Transportation and Distribution Management,* January 1970, p. 38. See also Kenneth B. Ackerman and Bernard J. LaLonde, "Making Warehousing More Efficient," *Harvard Business Review,* March-April 1980, pp. 94–102.
15. The impact of effective inventory control systems on company profitability is discussed in Lewis Beman, "A Big Payoff from Inventory Controls," *FORTUNE,* July 27, 1981, pp. 76–80.
16. For a discussion of materials handling innovations, see "Materials Handling Trends: One Expert's Viewpoint," *Traffic Management,* March 1981, pp. 36–38.

PART SIX

PROMOTIONAL STRATEGY

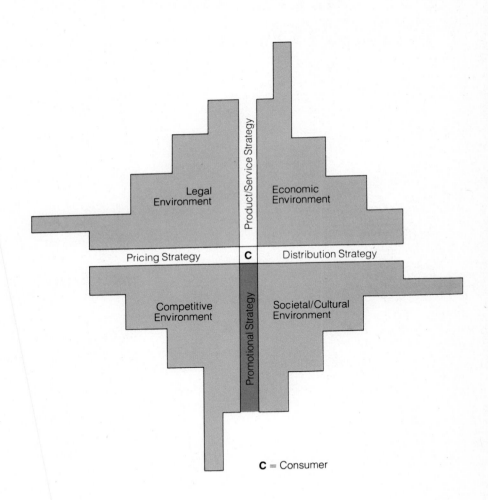

Legal Environment

Economic Environment

Product/Service Strategy

Pricing Strategy   C   Distribution Strategy

Promotional Strategy

Competitive Environment

Societal/Cultural Environment

C = Consumer

CHAPTER 14

INTRODUCTION TO PROMOTION

KEY TERMS

promotion
marketing communication
personal selling
advertising
sales promotion
public relations
pulling strategy
pushing strategy
task objective method
direct-sales results test

LEARNING GOALS

1. To explain the relationship of promotional strategy to the process of communication

2. To identify the chief components of the promotional mix

3. To analyze the variables used in determining the optimal promotional mix

4. To list the objectives of promotion

5. To compare the methods of developing a promotional budget

6. To develop an integrated promotional plan

He was born in 1967; and today has outlived most of his contemporaries who averaged life spans of only one or two years. Maybe his longevity accounts for his loneliness.

Maytag's Old Lonely, the repairman who never has anything to do, was created in 1967 to replace an advertising program that concentrated on customer testimonials. Old Lonely has maintained his popularity over the years, usually doubling the consumer awareness scores of other appliance commercials. Maytag has spent some $20 million doing 45 different Old Lonely commercials. Maytag marketers stress that the continuity of the Old Lonely campaign has saved the firm considerable promotional expenditures over the years since it provides immediate product identification. Of course, the firm changes the situations for its advertisements regularly so consumers do not tire of Old Lonely.

Several other companies agree with the Maytag approach. Procter & Gamble's Mr. Whipple has been selling Charmin since 1964. Madge, Colgate-Palmolive's manicurist, has been around since 1963. Even retired commercial characters face the prospect of being called back into action. The bear created for Hamm's beer in 1955 was brought back to the airwaves after Olympia Brewing purchased the brand.[1]

Maytag's promotional strategy consists of more than just Old Lonely commercials. However, the long-running character illustrates the importance of developing effective means of communicating with consumers.

WHAT IS PROMOTION?

Promotion is *the function of informing, persuading, and influencing the consumer's purchase decision.* Many business people consider it the most critical variable in the marketing process. The dynamic nature of promotion also makes it one of the most difficult and interesting areas of marketing decision making.

MARKETING COMMUNICATION

Promotional strategy is closely related to the process of communication—the transmission of a message from a sender to a receiver. **Marketing communication,** then, is *the message that deals with buyer-seller relationships.* The term *marketing communication* is a broader one than promotional strategy since it includes word-of-mouth and other forms of unsystematic communication.[2] A planned promotional strategy, however, is certainly the most important component.

Figure 14.1 shows a generalized communication process.[3] The *sender* is the source of the communication system, since he or she seeks to convey a *message* (a communication of information or ad-

**FIGURE 14.1
A Generalized
Communication
Process**

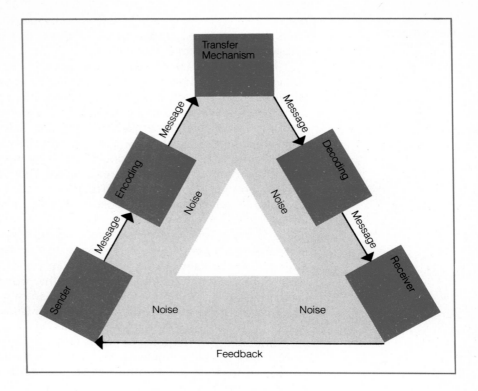

vice or a request) to a *receiver* (the recipient of the communication). The message must accomplish three tasks in order to be effective:

1. It must gain the attention of the receiver.
2. It must be understood by both the receiver and the sender.
3. It must stimulate the needs of the receiver and suggest an appropriate method of satisfying those needs.[4]

Encoding is the translation of the message into understandable terms and its transmittal through a communications medium. *Decoding* is the receiver's interpretation of the message. The receiver's response, known as *feedback,* completes the system. Throughout the process, *noise* can interfere with the transmission of the message.

In Figure 14.2 the marketing communication process is applied to promotional strategy. The marketing manager is the sender in the system. The message is encoded in the form of sales presentations, advertisements, displays, or publicity releases. The *transfer mechanism* for delivering the message may be a salesperson, a public relations channel, or the advertising media. The decoding step involves the consumer's interpretation of the sender's message. This aspect is often the most troublesome in marketing communication since

**FIGURE 14.2
The Process of
Marketing
Communications**

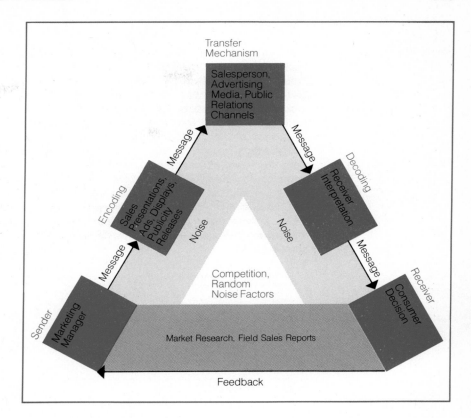

consumers do not always interpret promotional messages the same as their senders do.

Information about consumer decisions is fed back to the marketing manager in the form of marketing research or field sales reports. The noise element is usually represented by competitive promotional messages transmitted over the same communication channel, or random noise factors such as a telephone ringing during a television commercial.

THE PROMOTIONAL MIX

The components of the promotional mix are personal selling and non-personal selling (including advertising, sales promotion, and public relations).[5] Personal selling and advertising are the most significant elements, usually accounting for the bulk of a firm's promotional expenditures. However, all factors in the promotional mix contribute to efficient marketing communication. A detailed discussion of each element is presented in the chapters that follow. A brief definition of each will be given here in order to set the framework for the discussion of promotion.

MISCOMMUNI-CATION: A FACT OF LIFE

A two-year study by the American Association of Advertising Agencies' Educational Foundation produced some interesting results about miscommunication. Some 2,700 people were shown selected thirty-second capsules of television programming, and then questioned about what they observed. The segments included news programs (both network and local), public service announcements, mystery and adventure stories, and situation comedies.

The study found that 96.5 percent of these respondents misunderstood at least part of what they saw. For the most part, the level of miscomprehension was unrelated to demographic factors, although college graduates ages 25 to 44 did have the best scores. The respondents were as likely to misunderstand facts as inferences. But perhaps the most significant conclusion was that people were more likely to miscomprehend news and entertainment shows than they were commercials!

Source: "From ¼ to ⅓ of What Is Viewed on Television Is Miscomprehended," *Marketing News,* June 27, 1980, p. 1. Used by permission of the American Marketing Association.

Promotional budgeting requires special skills.

"Harcourt, here, has a black belt in budget management."

Source: Drawing by Lorenz. © 1981 by *The New Yorker* Magazine, Inc.

Personal Selling

Personal selling is *a seller's promotional presentation conducted on a person-to-person basis with the buyer.* It is a direct, face-to-face form of promotion. Selling is the original form of promotion. Today, more than 6.8 million people are engaged in it.[6]

Nonpersonal Selling

Nonpersonal selling is divided into advertising, sales promotion, and public relations. Advertising is usually regarded as the most important form.

Advertising is *a nonpersonal sales presentation usually directed at a large number of potential customers.* It involves mass media such as newspapers, television, radio, magazines, and billboards. Business has come to realize the tremendous potential of this form of promotion, and during recent decades, advertising has become increasingly important in marketing. Mass consumption makes it particularly appropriate for products that rely on sending the same promotional message to large audiences.

Sales promotion includes *"those marketing activities other than personal selling and advertising, and publicity, that stimulate consumer purchasing and dealer effectiveness, such as displays, shows and expositions, demonstrations, and various nonrecurrent selling efforts not in the ordinary routine."*[7] Approximately $40 billion is spent annually on various types of sales promotion.[8]

Public relations is *a firm's communications and relationships with its various publics.* These publics include customers, suppliers, stockholders, employees, the government, the general public, and the society in which the firm operates. Public relations programs can be either formal or informal. Every organization, whether or not it has a formalized program, needs to be concerned about its public relations.

Publicity for a company's products or affairs is an important part of an effective public relations effort. In comparison to personal selling, advertising, and sales promotion, expenditures for public relations are usually low in most firms. However, this indirect promotional channel remains an important method of reaching potential customers since it reaches audiences in a manner not obtainable by other methods of promotion.

DEVELOPING AN OPTIMAL PROMOTIONAL MIX

The most critical promotional problem facing the marketing manager is that of the proper mix of the four methods outlined in the preceding section. The discussion here will be limited to advertising and personal selling, since they are the primary ingredients of promotional strategy.

The decision to emphasize personal selling or advertising depends primarily on the type of goods (industrial or consumer), and the relative value of the product.

TABLE 14.1
Relative Use of
Advertising and
Personal Selling

Type of Product	Relative Use of	
	Advertising	Personal Selling
Low-value consumer goods	High	Low
High-value consumer goods	High	High
Low-value industrial goods	Moderate	High
High-value industrial goods	Low	High

Table 14.1 shows the relative use of advertising and personal selling as determined by these factors. The relative use of advertising is high for low-value consumer goods, then declines somewhat as personal selling plays a larger role in the promotion of higher-priced consumer goods. But both forms are used extensively. The explanation for advertising's dominance of promotional strategy for low-unit-value consumer goods is simple: The cost of selling has risen tremendously in recent years. The cost of an industrial sales call, for example, is now estimated to be $128.53.[9]

As a result, it has become unprofitable to promote lower-value goods through personal selling. Advertising, by contrast, permits a low promotional expenditure per sales unit, since it reaches mass audiences. For low-value consumer products such as chewing gum, soft drinks, and snack foods, advertising is the only feasible means of promotion.

Industrial goods, whose average value is high, are more amenable to personal selling as the chief promotional channel. Table 14.1 shows that advertising in industrial markets is limited mostly to products with relatively low value, such as industrial supplies.

Timing

Timing is another factor to consider in the development of a promotional strategy. Figure 14.3 shows the relative importance of advertising and selling in the different time periods of the purchase process. During the pretransactional period (prior to the actual sale), advertising is usually more important than personal selling. It is often argued that one of the primary advantages of a successful advertising program is that it assists the salesperson in approaching the prospect. Selling becomes more important than advertising during the transactional phase of the process. In most situations, personal selling is the actual mechanism of closing the sale. In the posttransactional stage, advertising regains primacy in the promotional effort. It serves as an affirmation of the customer's decision to buy a particular good or service as well as a reminder of the product's favorable characteristics and performance.

**FIGURE 14.3
Relative Importance
of Advertising and
Selling at Each Stage
of the Purchase
Process**

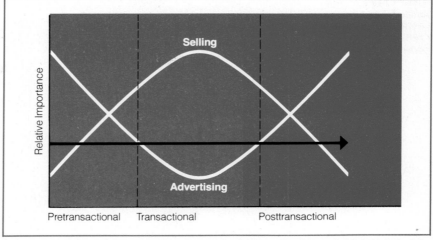

Source: Reprinted by permission from Harold C. Cash and W. J. E. Crissy, "The Salesman's Role in Marketing," *Psychology of Selling,* vol. 12. Personnel Development Associates, P.O. Box 586, Fairfield, Iowa 52556.

Promotional Strategy: Pull or Push

Essentially, two promotional policies are employed: a pulling strategy and a pushing strategy. A **pulling strategy** is a *promotional effort by the seller to stimulate final user demand; this demand exerts pressure on the distribution channel.* The plan is to build consumer demand for the product that is recognizable to channel members, who will then seek to fill the void. Advertising and sales promotion are the most commonly used elements of promotion in a pulling strategy.

Some marketers use an aggressive pulling strategy.

". . . And upon being taken to a supermarket, you will remember and demand that brand. When I clap my hands you will awake . . . "

Source: Cartoon by Berry. © 1979 by NEA, Inc.

Maker's Mark Distillery has been very successful with a pulling strategy in Montana.

Source: Advertisement for Maker's Mark whisky prepared and written by Doe-Anderson Advertising Agency. Reprinted by permission.

By contrast, a **pushing strategy** relies more heavily on personal selling. Here, the objective is *the promotion of the product to the members of the marketing channel* rather than to the final user. The objective can be accomplished through cooperative advertising allowances, trade discounts, and other dealer supports. While the two strategies are presented as alternative policies, most companies depend on a mixture of them.

OBJECTIVES OF PROMOTION

Determining the precise objectives of promotion has always been a perplexing problem for management. In 1961, the Association of National Advertisers suggested that promotional strategy be oriented toward achieving clearly stated communication objectives that are measured.[10]

What specific tasks should promotion accomplish? The answer to this question seems to be as varied as the sources consulted. Generally, however, the following can be considered objectives of promotion: (1) to provide information, (2) to increase demand, (3) to differentiate the product, (4) to increase product worth, and (5) to maintain current sales levels.

Providing Information

The traditional function of promotion has been to inform the market about the availability of a particular product. Indeed, many promotional efforts are still directed at providing product information to potential customers. An example is the typical health insurance advertisement appearing in the Sunday newspaper. Its content emphasizes informative features, such as the rising cost of hospital care.

Kentucky's favorable business climate has been extolled in a series of advertisements featuring Governor John Y. Brown, and designed to attract industry to the Blue Grass state. Earlier, Brown had

Meet Kentucky's chairman of the board and our board of directors.

In selecting the men that serve Kentucky, Governor John Y. Brown, Jr. took the state out of politics and put it in business.

The key areas of development, commerce, energy and transportation are all headed by proven businessmen. Men who understand the climate you need to build a successful business, because they've done it themselves.

Men like W. T. Young, vice chairman of the cabinet, who is chairman of The Royal Crown Companies. Bruce Lunsford, commerce cabinet secretary, who is both an attorney and C.P.A. William B. Sturgill, secretary of energy, who has been an industry leader in coal mining. Frank Metts, secretary of transportation, and major real estate developer. And Jack Segell, deputy secretary of commerce, who has had a successful career as an entrepreneur and corporate executive.

But more important than what these men have accomplished, is what they stand ready to help you accomplish—the building of a successful business in Kentucky. For more specific information, write: W. Bruce Lunsford, Secretary, Commerce Cabinet, Commonwealth of Kentucky, Frankfort, Kentucky 40601. Or better yet, call him businessman-to-businessman at 502/564-7670.

KENTUCKY & CO.
The state that's run like a business.

Source: Kentucky & Co. ad reprinted courtesy of Commonwealth of Kentucky and Doe-Anderson Advertising Agency.

used his marketing expertise to build Kentucky Fried Chicken into a major franchise chain. More recently, he commented: "Hell, governing Kentucky is easier than running Kentucky Fried Chicken. There's no competition."[11]

Stimulating Demand

The primary objective of most promotional efforts is to increase the demand for a good or service. Occasionally, this objective is attained to excess. Consider the case of Jarvis R. Jarvis, a caster manufacturer. The Jarvis company once ran an advertising campaign that produced so many orders and inquiries that its sales staff could not handle the volume. Finally, the firm had to discontinue all advertising for three years.[12] Their efforts to stimulate demand obviously had been too successful.

Differentiating the Product

Product differentiation is often an objective of the firm's promotional effort. *Homogeneous demand,* represented by the horizontal line in Figure 14.4, means that consumers regard the firm's output as being no different from that of their competitors. In this case, the individual firm has no control over such marketing variables as price. A *differentiated demand* schedule, by contrast, permits more flexibility in marketing strategies such as price changes.

**FIGURE 14.4
Product
Differentiation**

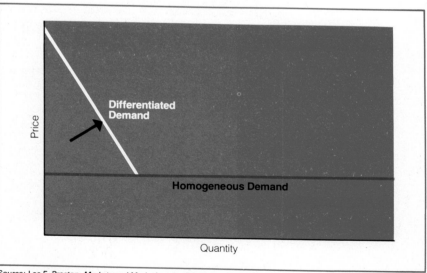

Source: Lee E. Preston, *Markets and Marketing: An Orientation* (Glenview, Ill.: Scott, Foresman, 1970), p. 196. Copyright © 1970 by Scott, Foresman and Company. Reprinted by permission of the publisher.

**FIGURE 14.5
Promotion Can
Accentuate the Value
of the Product**

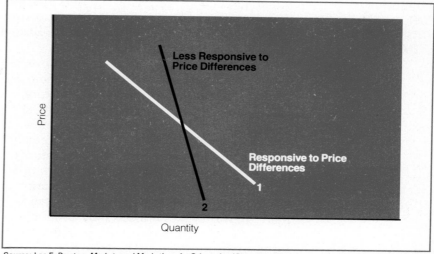

Source: Lee E. Preston, *Markets and Marketing: An Orientation* (Glenview, Ill.: Scott, Foresman, 1970), p. 196. Copyright © 1970 by Scott, Foresman and Company. Reprinted by permission of the publisher.

Increasing the Product Worth

Promotion can provide more ownership utility to buyers, thereby increasing the worth of a product. The good or service may then be able to command a higher price in the marketplace. For example, status-oriented advertising may allow some retail clothing stores to command higher prices than others. The demand curve for a prestige store may be less responsive to price differences than that for a competitor without a quality reputation. The responsiveness to price differences is shown in Figure 14.5. Similarly, promotion can be used to improve the image of a city. Cleveland has had excellent success with its "I Like Cleveland" campaign. Advertisements featuring Bob Hope, John Davidson, Margaret Hamilton, and Perry Como outlined the virtues of the city.[13] Cleveland-based TRW was typical of the corporate backers of this effort in that its management considered it a tool to attract and retain a sophisticated labor force.[14]

Maintaining Current Sales Levels

A company's sales are not uniform throughout the year or from year to year. Fluctuations can be caused for cyclical, seasonal, or irregular reasons. Reducing these variations is often an objective of the firm's promotional strategy. Automobile dealers, faced with a drop in new car sales, have employed a variety of promotional techniques to stabilize sales. Herbert Brockman brought the famous Budweiser Clydesdale horses to his Sepulveda, California, dealership. Gene Hamilton Chevrolet in Warren, Michigan, promoted Blazers by offering a free Chevette for each Blazer sold. And McLean, Virginia, dealers have teamed up with McDonald's to promote an offer that gave free oil changes with hamburger purchases.[15]

BUDGETING FOR PROMOTIONAL STRATEGY

Promotion budgets can differ not only in amount but also in composition. Industrial firms generally invest a larger proportion of their budget for personal selling than for advertising, while the reverse is often true for producers of consumer goods.

In terms of sales revenue, initial expenditures on promotion usually result in increasing returns. Some economies are also associated with larger promotional expenditures. These economies result from factors such as the cumulative effect of promotional expenditures. As more promotional inputs are added, however, marginal productivity begins to decrease.[16] Eventually, the firm reaches negative returns on its promotional expenditures.

For example, an initial expenditure of $40,000 may result in the sale of 100,000 product units for a consumer goods manufacturer. An additional $10,000 expenditure may sell 30,000 more units of the item, and a further $10,000 may produce another 35,000-unit sale. The cumulative effect of the expenditures has been increasing returns on the promotional outlays. However, as the advertising budget moves from $60,000 to $70,000, the marginal productivity of the additional expenditure may fall to 28,000 units. At some later point, the return may actually become negative, as competition intensifies, markets become saturated, and effective media opportunities are exhausted.

To test the thesis that advertising expenditures have a saturation point, Anheuser-Busch once quadrupled its advertising budget in several markets. After three months, the company's distributors demanded an advertising cut. Many claimed that beer consumers had come into their stores saying, "Give me anything *but* BUD."[17]

Developing a Budget

The optimal method of allocating a promotion budget is to expand it until the cost of each additional increment equals the marginal revenue received from it. In other words, the most effective allocation procedure is to increase promotional expenditures until each dollar of promotion expense is matched by an additional dollar of profit. This procedure—called *marginal analysis*—maximizes the input's productivity. The difficulty arises in identifying this optimal point, which requires a precise balancing of marginal expenses for promotion and the resulting marginal receipts.

The more traditional methods of allocating a promotional budget are by percentage of sales, fixed sums per unit, meeting the competition, and task objectives.[18] *Percentage of sales* is the most common way of allocating promotion budgets. The percentage can be based on either past (such as the previous year) or forecasted (current year) sales. Although the simplicity of the plan is appealing, it is not an effective way of achieving the basic promotional objectives. Arbitrary percentage allocations, whether applied to historical or future sales figures, fail to allow the required flexibility.

The *fixed sum per unit* approach differs from percentage of sales in only one respect: it applies a predetermined allocation to each sales or production unit. The allocation can also be set on either a historical or a forecasted basis. Automobile manufacturers often use this budgeting method.

Another traditional approach is simply to *match competitors' outlays*—to meet competition—on either an absolute or a relative basis. But keeping up with the Joneses usually leads to a status quo situation. Meeting the competition's budget does not necessarily relate to the objectives of promotion and therefore is inappropriate for most contemporary marketing programs.

The **task objective method** of developing a promotional budget is based on a sound evaluation of the firm's promotional objectives and is therefore better attuned to modern marketing practices. It involves two sequential steps:

1. The organization must *define the particular goals the firm wants the promotional mix to accomplish*—for example, a 5 percent increase in market share, a 10 percent rise in gross sales, or a 3 percent addition to net profit (or, more likely, a combination of several items). The key is to quantitatively specify the objectives to be accomplished. They then become an integral part of the promotional plan.

2. The organization must *determine the amount (as well as type) of promotional activity required to accomplish each of the objectives.* The sum of these units becomes the firm's promotion budget.

A crucial assumption underlies the task objective approach—that the productivity of each promotional dollar is measurable. If, for example, it is known that each dollar spent on promotion yields $20 in sales revenue, then it will be a relatively simple task to divide 20 into the sales increase projected in the statement of objectives. The result is the amount the organization should spend on promotion. Other goals, such as profitability and market share, are also easily calculated. A study by the Marketing Science Institute found that many firms do not keep adequate records of promotional expenditures and do not attempt to test alternative promotional efforts.[19]

Promotional budgeting is always difficult. But recent research studies and more frequent use of computer-based models make it less difficult than it has been in the past.

Measuring the Effectiveness of Promotion

It is widely recognized that part of a firm's promotional effort is ineffective. August Busch, head of the nation's biggest brewery, has observed: "We know advertising works, but at what level those dollars become nonproductive, nobody really knows."[20]

Measuring the effectiveness of promotional expenditures has become an important research question, particularly among advertisers. Studies aimed at this measurement dilemma face several major obstacles, among them the difficulty of isolating the effect of the promotion variable.

Most marketers prefer to use a **direct-sales results test** to measure the effectiveness of promotion. This test *ascertains for each dollar of promotional outlay the corresponding increase in revenue.* The primary difficulty is controlling the other variables operating in the marketplace. A $1.5 million advertising campaign may be followed by an increase in sales of $20 million. However, the increase may be due more to a sudden price hike by the leading competitor than to the advertising expenditure.

The marketer cannot conduct research in a controlled environment common to other disciplines. The difficulty in isolating the effects of promotion cause many to abandon all attempts at measurement. Others, however, turn to indirect evaluation, concentrating on quantifiable factors such as *recall* (how much is remembered about specific products or advertisements) and *readership* (the size and composition of the audience). However, it is difficult to relate these variables to changes in sales volume. Another problem is the high cost of research in promotion. To assess the effectiveness of promotional expenditures accurately requires a significant investment.

IN DEFENSE OF PROMOTION

Promotion has often been the target of criticisms such as:

"Promotion contributes nothing to society."
"Most advertisements and sales presentations insult my intelligence."
"Promotion 'forces' consumers to buy products they do not want and do not need."
"Advertising and selling are economic wastes."
"Promotional programs are usually unethical."

Although the list is far from complete, it represents the types of complaints that have been presented. Consumers, critics, and marketers agree that too many of these complaints are true. Some salespeople do use unethical sales tactics. Some product advertising is directed at consumer groups that can least afford to purchase the particular item. Many television commercials do contribute to the growing problem of cultural pollution.

While promotion can certainly be criticized on many counts, it plays a crucial role in modern society. This point is best explained by examining promotion's business, economic, and social importance.

Business Importance

Promotional strategy has become increasingly important to both large and small business enterprises. The long-term rise in outlays for promotion is well documented and attests to management's faith in the ability of promotional efforts to produce additional sales. It is difficult to conceive of a firm that does not attempt to promote its product or service in some manner or another. Most modern institutions simply cannot survive in the long run without promotion.

Nonbusiness enterprises have also recognized the importance of promotion. The attempt by the armed services to increase enlistments is based on a substantial advertising campaign stressing the advantages of a military career. Religious organizations have acknowledged the importance of promoting their product. Even labor organizations have used promotional channels to make their viewpoints known to the public at large. In fact, it is reasonable to say that promotion now plays a larger role in business (including nonprofit organizations) than it ever has in the past.

Economic Importance

If for no other reason than its employment of several million people, promotion has assumed a degree of economic importance.[21] Moreover, effective promotion has allowed society to derive benefits not otherwise available. For example, the criticism that promotion costs too much fails to consider the effect of promotion on other categories of expenditures.

Promotion strategies that increase the number of units sold permit economies in the production process, thereby lowering the production costs assigned to each unit of output. Lower consumer prices allow these products to become available to more people. Similarly, researchers have found that advertising subsidizes the informational content of newspapers and the broadcast media.[22] In short, promotion pays for many of the enjoyable and educational aspects of contemporary life, as well as lowering product costs.

Social Importance

Criticisms such as "most promotional messages are tasteless" and "promotion contributes nothing to society" sometimes ignore the fact that no commonly accepted set of standards or priorities exists within the American social framework. The United States is a diverse economy characterized by consumer segments with differing needs, wants, and aspirations. What is tasteless to one group may be informative to another. Promotional strategy is faced with an averaging problem that escapes many of its critics. The one generally accepted standard in a market society is freedom of choice for the consumer. Customer buying decisions eventually determine what is acceptable practice in the marketplace.

Promotion has become an important factor in the campaigns to achieve societal objectives such as physical fitness and the elimination of drug abuse. It performs an informative and educative task that makes it extremely important in the functioning of modern society.

SUMMARY

Promotional strategy is closely related to the marketing communication system, which includes the functions of sender, message, encoding, transfer mechanism, decoding, receiver, feedback, and noise. Its major components are personal selling and nonpersonal selling (advertising, sales promotion, and public relations).

Developing an effective promotional strategy is a complex matter. The elements of promotion are related to the type and value of the product being promoted as well as to the timing of the promotional effort. Personal selling is used primarily for industrial goods, higher value items, and during the transactional phase. Advertising, by contrast, is used primarily for consumer goods, lower value items, and during the pretransactional and posttransactional phases.

A pushing strategy, which relies on personal selling, attempts to promote the product to the members of the marketing channel rather than to the ultimate user. A pulling strategy concentrates on stimulating user demand primarily through advertising and sales promotion.

The five basic objectives of promotion are to provide information, increase demand, differentiate products, increase product worth, and maintain current sales levels. There are several problems involved in promotional budgeting and in measuring the effectiveness of promotional expenditures. The target of much criticism, promotion nonetheless does have great value on business, economic, and social levels.

QUESTIONS FOR DISCUSSION

1. Explain the following terms:

promotion	public relations
marketing communication	pulling strategy
personal selling	pushing strategy
advertising	task objective method
sales promotion	direct-sales results test

2. Relate promotional strategy to the process of communication.

3. Why is promotion considered one of the more difficult aspects of marketing decision making?

4. Compare the five basic objectives of promotion. Cite specific examples of each.

5. Perhaps the most critical promotional question facing the marketing manager concerns when to use each of the components of promotion. Comment on this statement, relating your response to the goods classification, product value, and the timing of the promotional effort.

6. Prepare a critique of a promotional campaign employed by a firm with which you are familiar.

7. Discuss the productivity of promotion.

8. Why is it difficult to measure the effectiveness of promotional efforts?

9. Explain why the task objective method is considered the best way to al-

locate a promotional budget. What are the advantages and disadvantages of each of the alternative allocation methods?

10. In too many instances, promotional programs have led to a duplication of efforts or have worked at cross-purposes. How would you correct this situation?

11. Why is promotion so often the target of critics? How would you answer the complaints?

12. Relate the generalized communication process to the promotion of a new computer.

13. What mix of promotion variables would you use for each of the following:
    a. a management consulting service
    b. car batteries
    c. ladies' sports outfits
    d. industrial drilling equipment
    e. lawn mowers
    f. customized business forms

14. Develop a hypothetical promotion budget for the following—ignoring dollar amounts by using percentage allocations to the various promotion variables (such as 40 percent to personal selling, 50 percent to advertising, and 10 percent to public relations):
    a. Avis Rent-a-Car
    b. Ramada Inns
    c. a manufacturer of industrial chemicals
    d. Prudential Insurance Company

15. Develop a plan for measuring the effectiveness of a current advertising campaign with which you are familiar.

16. The Ridge Tool Company of Elyria, Ohio, recently honored a promotional deal that it ran in a 1931 issue of *Popular Science.* The ad had offered a wrench for 20 cents. Ridge Tool sent the wrench, which now sells for $4.20, and even returned the customer's 20 cents. How could an action of this type fit into Ridge Tool's overall promotional strategy?

17. The Justice Bedding Company of Chepachet, Rhode Island, has developed a product it believes is better than an electric blanket. What type of promotional strategy would you devise for Justice Bedding's new electric mattress?

18. Many professionals, such as physicians, attorneys, and dentists, are now allowed to promote their services through media advertising. What effect is this likely to have on the practices of those professionals who advertise?

19. Develop a promotional strategy to expand the membership of a campus organization to which you belong or with which you are familiar.

20. When paperback book sales suffered a downturn, several of the major publishers adopted new promotional strategies. Fawcett Books began using 30-cents-off coupons to promote its Coventry romance series. New American Library, on the other hand, established a returns policy that rewarded dealers that had high sales. This policy also had penalties designed to discourage low volume.[23] Relate these promotional strategies to the material outlined in Chapter 14.

NOTES

1. Lawrence Ingrassia, "As Mr. Whipple Shows, Ad Stars Can Bring Long-Term Sales Gains," *Wall Street Journal,* February 12, 1981.

2. For example, the relationship between personal selling and the communication process is pointed out in Rosann L. Spiro and William D. Perreault, "Influence Use by Industrial Salesmen: Influence-Strategy Mixes and Situational Determinants," *Journal of Business,* July 1979, p. 453.

3. Similar communication processes are suggested in David K. Berlo, *The Process of Communications* (New York: Holt, Rinehart and Winston, 1960), pp. 23–38; and Thomas S. Robertson, *Innovative Behavior and Communication* (New York: Holt, Rinehart and Winston, 1971), p. 122. See also Claude Shannon and Warren Weaver, *The Mathematical Theory of Communication* (Urbana: University of Illinois Press, 1949), p. 5; and Wilbur Schramm, "The Nature of Communication between Humans," in *The Process and Effects of Mass Communication* rev. ed. (Urbana: University of Illinois Press, 1971), pp. 3–53.

4. Schramm, "Nature of Communication," pp. 3–53. Other communication models are discussed in two articles by C. A. Maile and A. H. Kizilbash, "A Marketing Communications Model," *Business Horizons,* November 1977, pp. 77–84; and "A Communications Model for Marketing Decisions," *Journal of the Academy of Marketing Science,* Winter 1977, pp. 48–56. See also Michael L. Rothschild, "Marketing Communications in Nonbusiness Situations," *Journal of Marketing,* Spring 1979, pp. 11–20.

5. William Dommermuth, "Promoting Your Product: Managing the Mix," *Business,* July-August 1980, pp. 18–21.

6. U.S. Bureau of the Census, *Statistical Abstract of the United States: 1980,* (101st Edition), Washington D.C., 1980, p. 419.

7. Committee on Definitions, *Marketing Definitions: A Glossary of Terms* (Chicago: American Marketing Association, 1960), p. 20.

8. Louis J. Haugh, "Sales Promotions Grown to $40 Billion Status," *Advertising Age,* April 30, 1980, p. 199. Another interesting discussion appears in Earnestine C. Hargrove and Kathleen A. Krentler, "Evaluating Sales Promotion: A Paradigm," in John H. Summey and Ronald D. Taylor eds., *Evolving Marketing Thought For 1980* (Carbondale, Ill.: Southern Marketing Association), pp. 93–96.

9. Reported in Bill Abrams, "Marketing: Briefs," *Wall Street Journal,* June 18, 1981.

10. Richard H. Colley, *Defining Advertising Goals* (New York: Association of National Advertisers, 1961).

11. Jerry Adler and Tony Fuller, "The Phyllis and John Show," *Newsweek,* March 30, 1981, pp. 30, 32.

12. Jean Wikiel, "Jarvis Returns to Ads after 3-Year Hiatus," *Industrial Marketing,* February 1979, p. 1.

13. Madeline Drexler, "Cleveland Aims to Dump 'Mistake on Lake' Image," *Orlando Sentinel Star,* October 12, 1980 (AP story).

14. Product advertising can also have a significant effect on the way employees perform their jobs. See Franklin Acito and Jeffrey D. Ford, "How Advertising Affects Employees," *Business Horizons,* February 1980, pp. 53–59.

15. Michael J. Trojanowski, "Auto Dealers Bring Up the Heavy Artillery," *Detroit News,* March 24, 1980.

16. John C. Narver and Ronald Savitt, *The Marketing Economy: An Analytical Approach* (New York: Holt, Rinehart and Winston, 1971), p. 294. Determination of the correct advertising frequency is examined in Herbert E. Krugman, "What Makes Advertising Effective," *Harvard Business Review,* March-April 1975, pp. 96–103. Another interesting article is Paul W. Farris and Robert D. Buzzell, "Why Advertising and Promotional Costs Vary: Some Cross-Sectional Analysis," *Journal of Marketing,* Fall 1979, pp. 112–22.

17. Charles G. Burck, "While the Big Brewers Quaff, the Little Ones Thirst," *FORTUNE,* November 1972, p. 107.

18. An excellent discussion on budgeting for promotion is included in S. Watson Dunn and Arnold M. Barban, *Advertising: Its Role in Modern Marketing,* 5th ed. (Hinsdale, Ill.: The Dryden Press, 1982), pp. 257–68. See also Roger A. Strang, *The Promotional Planning Process* (New York: Praeger Publishers, 1980), pp. 38–49; William A. Staples and Robert W. Sweadlow, "A Zero Base Approach to Advertising Planning," in *Proceedings of the Southern Marketing Association,* eds. Robert S. Franz, Robert M. Hopkins, and Al Toma, New Orleans, Louisiana, November 1978, pp. 315–17; and Joseph A. Bellizzi, A. Frank Thompson, and Lynn J. Loudenback, "Promotional Activity and the U.S. Business Cycle," in *Proceedings of the Southwestern Mar-*

keting Association, eds. Robert C. Haring, G. Edward Kiser, and Ronnie D. Whitt, Houston, Texas, 1979, pp. 27–28.

19.   Reported in *Marketing Science Institute Briefs,* December 1975, p. 1.

20.   Quoted in Thomas O'Hanlon, "August Busch Brews Up a New Spirit in St. Louis," *FORTUNE,* January 15, 1979, p. 100.

21.   The economic effects of advertising are explored in Jean-Jacques Lambin, "What Is the Real Impact of Advertising?" *Harvard Business Review,* May-June 1975, pp. 139–47.

22.   Francis X. Callahan, "Does Advertising Subsidize Information?" *Journal of Advertising Research,* August 1978, pp. 19–22.

23.   James Machalaba, "Publishers, Struggling to Increase Sales, Split over Pushing New Books Like Soap," *Wall Street Journal,* October 31, 1979.

CHAPTER 15

ELEMENTS OF PROMOTIONAL STRATEGY: ADVERTISING, SALES PROMOTION, PUBLIC RELATIONS, AND PUBLICITY

KEY TERMS

advertising
positioning
comparative advertising
product advertising
institutional advertising
pretesting
posttesting
retail advertising
cooperative advertising
sales promotion
specialty advertising
public relations
publicity

LEARNING GOALS

1. To explain advertising's historical development and current status

2. To list the steps in advertising planning, the basic types of advertisements, and the various advertising media

3. To explain the organization of the advertising function, the creation of advertisements, the status of retail advertising, and the importance of cooperative advertising

4. To identify the principal methods of sales promotion

5. To describe the role of public relations and publicity in the firm's promotional strategy

The Doyle Dane Bernbach advertising agency created a classic advertising campaign for Volkswagen in the 1960s. In fact, the attention-getting VW ads were widely credited with leading the foreign car invasion that now dominates such a significant segment of the automobile industry. The VW campaign was chosen as the biggest advertising success of the past 50 years by a vote of subscribers to *Advertising Age* (a trade publication in the field), its "Sounding Board" of industry members, and the American Academy of Advertising. Nearly half the respondents selected the Volkswagen advertisements. Second place went to the Marlboro campaign, another campaign credited with putting its product into a strong market position.[1]

Source: Photos reprinted with permission from the April 1980 issue of *Advertising Age.* Copyright 1980 by Crain Communications, Inc.

The Volkswagen and Marlboro advertisements suggest the importance that advertising can play in an organization's promotional strategy. Chapter 15 will examine four vital elements of promotion: advertising, sales promotion, public relations, and publicity.

ADVERTISING

President Franklin D. Roosevelt is reputed to have said: "If I were starting my life over again, I am inclined to think I would go into the advertising business in preference to almost any other."[2] As a matter of fact, President Roosevelt probably would have made an excellent advertising executive. His use of persuasive radio "fireside chats" certainly exemplifies the definition of *advertising:* a nonpersonal sales presentation usually directed at a large number of potential customers.

Today's widespread markets make advertising an important part of business. Advertising and related expenditures have risen faster than gross national product and most other economic indicators since World War II. Furthermore, about 200,000 people are employed in advertising, according to an American Association of Advertising Agencies estimate.[3]

Three companies—Procter & Gamble, Sears, and General Foods—spent more than $400 million on advertising in 1980. Table 15.1 ranks the nation's top advertisers. Total world advertising ex-

TABLE 15.1
Twenty Leading
National Advertisers

	Company	Media Total (in Millions)
1	Procter & Gamble	$649.6
2	Sears	599.6
3	General Foods	410.0
4	Philip Morris	364.6
5	K mart	319.3
6	General Motors	316.0
7	R. J. Reynolds	298.5
8	Ford	280.0
9	American Telephone & Telegraph	259.2
10	Warner-Lambert	235.2
11	Gulf + Western	233.8
12	PepsiCo	233.4
13	Colgate-Palmolive	225.0
14	McDonald's	207.0
15	Ralston Purina	206.8
16	American Home Products	197.0
17	Bristol-Myers	196.3
18	Mobil	194.8
19	Esmark	189.9
20	Coca-Cola	184.2

Source: Adapted from "Advertising and Marketing Reports on 100 Leading National Advertisers," *Advertising Age,* September 10, 1981, pp. 1–148. Reprinted with permission from the September 10, 1981, issue of *Advertising Age.* Copyright 1981 by Crain Communications, Inc.

penses are about $110 billion, half of it in the United States. By the year 2000, world advertising expenditures are expected to reach $780 billion. However, the U.S. percentage is expected to decline to about 40 percent.[4]

Advertising expenditures vary among industries and companies. Cosmetics companies are often cited as examples of firms that spend a high percentage of their funds on advertising and promotion. Chicago consultants Schonfeld and Associates studied more than 2,000 firms and industries and calculated their average advertising expenditures as a percentage of both sales and gross profit margin. Estimates for selected industries are given in Table 15.2. As shown in the table, industries vary widely; advertising spending can range from zero in an industry like iron and steel foundries to about 19 percent of the firm's gross profit margin in a retail mail-order house.

**TABLE 15.2
Estimates of Average Advertising to Sales and Advertising to Gross Profit Margin by Industry**

Industry	Advertising and Promotion as	
	Percent of Sales,* 1981	Percent Margin,** 1981
Bakery products	1.7	4.0
Candy and other confectionery	6.1	16.8
Cigarettes	6.3	16.0
Floor covering mills	.7	3.6
Household furniture	1.9	7.5
Chemicals and allied products	1.3	4.6
Soap and other detergents	6.5	18.4
Paving and roofing materials	1.1	5.3
Glass containers	1.2	5.3
Iron and steel foundries	0.0	0.0
Household appliances	2.5	9.9
Electrical machinery and equipment	5.7	19.7
Motor vehicles and car bodies	1.7	19.8
Photographic equipment and supplies	3.2	7.3
Jewelry-precious metals	4.4	11.5
Toys and amusement sporting goods	6.3	18.2
Telephone communication	.3	.6
Retail-department stores	2.9	15.1
Retail-auto dealers and gas stations	.5	2.6
Retail-women's ready to wear	2.8	9.0
Retail-eating places	2.9	14.5
Retail-mail-order houses	5.9	19.1
Hotels-motels	2.1	7.3
Service-motion picture theatres	3.7	29.3
Service-racing including track operations	3.6	18.0
Conglomerates	1.5	5.7

*calculated by dividing advertising and promotion expenditures by sales
**calculated by dividing advertising and promotion expenditures by (Net Sales minus Cost of Goods Sold)
Source: Schonfeld & Associates Inc., 120 S. LaSalle St., Chicago, IL 60603, (312)236-5846.

The Historical Development of Advertising

Some form of advertising of products has probably existed since the development of the exchange process.[5] Most early advertising was vocal; criers and hawkers sold various products, made public announcements, and chanted advertising slogans like the once familiar:

One-a-penny, two-a-penny, hot-cross buns
One-a-penny, two for tuppence, hot-cross buns.

Criers were common in colonial America. The cry of "Rags! Any rags? Any wool rags?" filled the streets of pre-Revolutionary Philadelphia.

Signs were also used in early advertising. Most were symbolic in their identification of products or services. In Rome, a goat signified a dairy; a mule driving a mill signified a bakery; and a boy being whipped signified a school.

Later, the development of the printing press greatly expanded advertising's capabilities. A 1710 advertisement in the *Spectator* billed one dentifrice as "the Incomparable Powder for cleaning of Teeth, which has given great satisfaction to most of the Nobility and Gentry in England." Colonial newspapers like Benjamin Franklin's *Gazette* also featured advertising. Indeed, papers carried it on their first page. Most of these advertisements would be called "classified ads" today. Some national advertisers also began to use newspaper advertising at this time. For instance, Pierre Lorillard was an early promoter of his tobacco products.

Volney Palmer organized the first advertising agency in the United States in 1841. George P. Rowell was another early advertising agent. Originally, these agencies simply sold advertising space. Services like advertising research, copywriting, and planning came later. Claude C. Hopkins used a large-scale consumer survey concerning home-baked beans before launching a campaign for Van Camp's Pork and Beans in the early 1900s. Hopkins claimed that home-baked beans were difficult to digest and suggested that consumers try Van Camp's beans. He advocated the use of "reason-why copy" to show why people should buy the product.

Some early advertising promoted products of questionable value, such as patent medicines. As a result, a reformist movement in advertising developed during the early 1900s, and some newspapers began to screen their advertisements. Magazine publisher Cyrus Curtis began rejecting certain types of advertising, such as medical copy that claimed cures and alcoholic beverage advertisements. And in 1911, the forerunner of the American Advertising Federation drew up a code for improved advertising.

These improvements established the springboard for a growth in advertising that many of the industry's forefathers thought impossible. In this regard, an interesting story is told about the founder of the J. Walter Thompson agency:

At noon on a summer day in 1916 a media representative called at the J. Walter Thompson agency and found that his luncheon date was tied up with a client and would not be able to see him. He was about to leave, . . . when he found himself being clapped on the back by the normally aloof Commodore Thompson himself. To his amazement, Thompson invited him to lunch at the Duane Hotel across Madison Avenue and even bought the first round of drinks. He then made a gleeful announcement: "Congratulate me, Joe! I just sold the business to the Resor boys. They don't know it, but the advertising agency business has seen its best days!"[6]

The moral of the story is obvious. Today, the J. Walter Thompson agency has annual billings of more than $2 billion.

One identifying feature of advertising after 1900 has been its concern for researching the markets that it attempts to reach. Originally, advertising research dealt primarily with media selection and the product. Then, advertisers became increasingly concerned with determining the appropriate demographic characteristics of potential buyers. Now, understanding consumer behavior has become an important aspect of advertising strategy, and marketers use psychographics and lifestyle analyses in describing potential markets for advertising appeals. Increased knowledge in these areas has led to improved advertising decisions.[7]

The emergence of the marketing concept, with its emphasis on a company-wide consumer orientation, saw advertising take on an expanded role as marketing communication assumed greater importance in business. Advertising provides an efficient, inexpensive, and fast method of reaching the much sought-after consumer. Its extensive use now rivals that of personal selling. Advertising has become a key ingredient in the effective implementation of the marketing concept.

Advertising Objectives

The objectives of advertising were traditionally stated in terms of direct sales goals. A better approach, however, is to view advertising as having communication objectives that seek to inform, persuade, and remind potential customers of the product. Advertising seeks to condition the consumer to have a favorable viewpoint toward the promotional message. The goal is to improve the likelihood that the customer will buy a particular product. In this sense, advertising is an excellent example of the close relationship between marketing communication and promotional strategy.

Communication goals are very important to Perrier. The imported water enjoyed considerable word-of-mouth advertising during the late 1970s. It appeared in a wide range of media, from society pages to the fronts of T-shirts. But as competitors proliferated, Perrier was unable to maintain its level of word-of-mouth advertising.

The solution: Perrier began a 15-episode radio advertising campaign resembling a soap opera. The commercials featured narrator Orson Welles and characters like Julius Caesar, Dracula, Socrates, and Ponce de Leon. After biting the neck of a woman, Dracula delivers the campaign's theme: "It is good. But it is not Perrier."[8] Communication goals such as increased word-of-mouth promotion are clearly important to marketers like Perrier.

Advertising Planning

Advertising planning begins with effective research. Its results allow management to make strategic decisions that are translated into tactical areas such as budgeting, copywriting, scheduling, and the like. Finally, there is feedback for measuring the effectiveness of the advertising. The elements of advertising planning are shown in Figure 15.1.

There is a real need for following a sequential process in advertising decisions. Novice advertisers are often overly concerned with the technical aspects of advertisement construction and ignore the more basic steps, such as market analysis. The type of advertisement employed in any particular situation is related in large part to the planning phase of this process.

FIGURE 15.1
Elements of
Advertising Planning

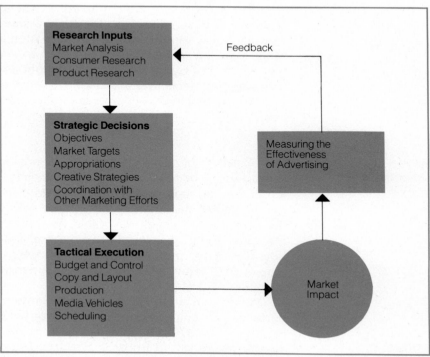

Source: From S. Watson Dunn and Arnold M. Barban, *Advertising: Its Role in Modern Marketing*, 5th ed., p. 202. Copyright © 1982 by Dryden Press, a division of Holt, Rinehart and Winston. Reprinted by permission of Holt, Rinehart and Winston.

Positioning

One of the most widely discussed strategies in advertising is the concept of **positioning,** which involves *the development of a promotional strategy aimed at a particular segment of the market.*[9] Although advertising experts continue to debate its effectiveness and origin, positioning is being used by an increasing number of firms. The strategy is applicable primarily to products that are not the leaders in their particular fields. These products are apparently more successful if their advertising concentrates on specific market segments rather than the attack of dominant brands. Specialization is best accomplished through an advertising strategy or theme that positions them in the specified market segments.

With its image as a mixer for alcoholic drinks, 7-Up was missing the primary market for soft drinks—children, teenagers, and young adults. So the firm used its famous UnCola campaign to first identify the product as a soft drink and then position it as an alternative to cola. In another classic promotional campaign, Avis positioned itself against Hertz with the theme, "Avis is only number two in rent-a-cars, so why go with us? We try harder."

Comparative Advertising

Comparative advertising, another strategy to consider in the planning phase, *makes direct promotional comparisons with leading competitive brands.* The strategy usually is employed by firms that do not lead the market.[10] Chrysler, for example, makes direct price comparisons of its models versus the competition. Market leaders prefer not to acknowledge that there are competitive products. Procter & Gamble and General Foods, for instance, devote little of their huge promotional budgets to comparative advertising. But many firms do use it. About 10 percent of all television advertisements make comparisons to competitive products. Examples are plentiful:

Suave antiperspirant will keep you as sweet as Ban Ultra Dry does—and for a lot less.

Volkswagen's Dasher picks up speed faster than a Mercedes and has a bigger trunk than a Rolls.

Nationwide, more Coca-Cola drinkers prefer the taste of Pepsi.[11]

Marketers who contemplate comparative advertising should take precautions to assure than they can back their claims. The comparison advertising trend has produced several lawsuits, so practitioners must be especially careful when employing this technique.

TYPES OF ADVERTISE-MENTS

Essentially, there are two basic types of advertisements—product and institutional. Each can be subdivided into informative, persuasive, and reminder-oriented categories.

Product advertising is the type normally thought of when the subject of advertising comes up in a conversation. It deals with *the nonpersonal selling of a particular good or service.* **Insitutional advertising,** by contrast, is concerned with *promoting a concept, an idea, a philosophy, or the goodwill of an industry, company, or organization.* It is often closely related to the public relations function of the enterprise.[12] An example of institutional advertising by New York appears in Figure 15.2. AMAX also has used institutional advertising (see Figure 15.3).

Informative Product Advertising Informative product advertising seeks to develop initial demand for a product. It tends to characterize the promotion of any new type of product since the objective is often simply

**FIGURE 15.2
An Example of Institutional Advertising Used by the State of New York**

Source: State of New York, Department of Commerce. Reprinted by permission.

**FIGURE 15.3
An Example of
Institutional
Advertising Used by
AMAX**

Source: Prepared for AMAX Inc. by Grey Advertising. © 1981 AMAX Inc.

to announce its availability. Figure 15.4 shows that informative advertising is usually used in the introductory stages of the product life cycle. In fact, it was the original approach to advertising: early shippers used to post bulletins announcing the arrival of a ship and listing the goods it carried.

Persuasive Product Advertising To develop demand for a particular product or brand is the goal of persuasive product advertising—a competitive type of promotion used in the growth period and to some extent in the maturity period of the product life cycle (see Figure 15.4). The increased competition that now characterizes all marketplaces in recent years even forced Hershey Foods Corporation, a long-time hold-out, to finally begin to advertise.

Reminder-oriented Product Advertising The goal of reminder-oriented product advertising is to reinforce previous promotional activity by keeping the product name in front of the public. It is used in the maturity period as well as throughout the decline phase of the product life cycle.

**FIGURE 15.4
Relationship between
Advertising and the
Product Life Cycle**

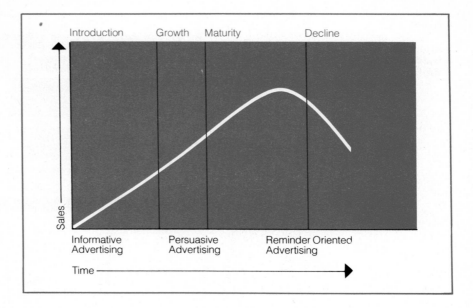

Dewar's profiles of young, active people are an example.[13] Each profile gives the person's age, profession, most memorable book read, favorite quotation, and, of course, preference for Dewar's Scotch. The campaign has been running since 1969, primarily because of extensive reader interest in the profiles that appear in mass-circulation magazines. The people are real, and their only compensation is five cases of Dewar's Scotch. By using this advertising method, Dewar's has kept its name in front of consumers and has climbed to second place in scotch sales.

Informative Institutional Advertising Baltimore has used the slogan "BaltiMore than You Know" to overcome its low-key image and to point out the harbor city's many advantages.[14] Baltimore wants to build up its economic base by attracting new industry and major conventions. Informative institutional advertising is part of its image building plan.

Another example of this type of institutional advertising is the local United Fund's listing of all the agencies and organizations that benefit from its drive. Such advertising seeks to increase public knowledge of a concept, political viewpoint, industry, or company.

Persuasive Institutional Advertising When a firm or advertising agency wishes to advance the interests of a particular institution within a competitive environment, it often uses persuasive institutional advertising. For instance, Honda's campaign theme "You meet the nicest people on a Honda" (1964–1967) changed people's negative stereotype of motorcyclists, thereby greatly expanding the demand for its product.

Not all campaigns are as successful as Honda's. A $200,000 campaign to improve the image of the potato chip industry ran into immediate criticism. The *St. Louis Post-Dispatch* assailed the snack food's lack of nutritional value, then went on to say that the potato chip campaign was like a portrayal of Attila the Hun as a pioneer in urban renewal.[15]

Reminder-oriented Institutional Advertising Reminder-oriented institutional advertising has objectives similar to those of reminder-oriented product advertising. In most elections, for example, the nominee's early persuasive (issue directed) advertising is replaced by reminder-oriented advertising during the closing weeks of the campaign. The media abound with examples of this type of institutional advertising. The American Gas Association's "Gas: The future belongs to the efficient" represents the industry's effort to remind the public of the importance of this vital fuel.

MEDIA SELECTION

One of the most important decisions in developing an advertising strategy is media selection.[16] A mistake at this point can cost a company literally millions of dollars in ineffective advertising. Media strategy must achieve the communication goals mentioned earlier.

Research should identify the market target to determine its size and characteristics and then match the target with the audience and the effectiveness of the available media. The objective is to achieve adequate media coverage without advertising beyond the identifiable limits of the potential market. Finally, alternative costs should be compared to determine the best possible media purchase.

There are numerous types of advertising media, and the characteristics of some of the more important ones will be considered here. The advantages and disadvantages of each are shown in Table 15.3.

Newspapers Local markets continue to be dominated by newspapers, with about 24 percent of total advertising revenue. However, newspapers only hold a 4.3 percent share of the national advertising. Newspapers' primary advantages are flexibility (advertising can be varied from one locality to the next), community prestige (newspapers have a deep impact on the community), intensive coverage (in most places 90 percent of the homes can be reached by a single newspaper), reader control of exposure to the advertising message (unlike time media, readers can refer back to newspapers), coordination with national advertising, and merchandising services (such as promotional and research support). The disadvantages are a short life span, hasty reading (the typical reader spends only twenty to thirty minutes on the newspaper), and poor reproduction.[17]

Magazines Magazines, which are divided into such diverse categories as consumer, farm, and business publications, account for about 10

**TABLE 15.3
Advantages and
Disadvantages of the
Various Advertising
Media**

Media	Advantages	Disadvantages
Newspapers	Flexibility Community prestige Intense coverage Reader control of exposure Coordination with national advertising Merchandising service	Short life span Hasty reading Poor reproduction
Magazines	Selectivity Quality reproduction Long life Prestige associated with some magazines Extra services	Lack of flexibility
Television	Great impact Mass coverage Repetition Flexibility Prestige	Temporary nature of message High cost High mortality rate for commercials Evidence of public lack of selectivity
Radio	Immediacy Low cost Practical audience selection Mobility	Fragmentation Temporary nature of message Little research information
Outdoor Advertising	Communication of quick and simple ideas Repetition Ability to promote products available for sale nearby	Brevity of the message Public concern over esthetics
Direct Mail	Selectivity Intense coverage Speed Flexibility of format Complete information Personalization	High cost per person Dependency on quality of mailing list Consumer resistance

Source: Based on S. Watson Dunn and Arnold M. Barban, *Advertising: Its Role in Modern Marketing,* 5th ed. (Hinsdale, Ill.: The Dryden Press, 1982), pp. 513–77.

percent of national advertising, with a third of the advertising appearing in weekly magazines. The primary advantages of magazine advertising are the selectivity of market targets, quality reproduction, long life, the prestige associated with some magazines, and the extra services offered by many publications. The primary disadvantage is that magazines lack the flexibility of newspapers, radio, and television.

THE COST OF COMMERCIALS AND THE GROWTH OF NEW MEDIA

Television commercials are costly ventures for most advertisers. Network programs like "60 Minutes," "M*A*S*H," and "Dallas" can command $150,000 per 30-second commercial, and that is just for air time. Production costs for such a commercial can range up to $100,000.

Many advertisers are turning to cable television networks. These channels tend to attract more limited and specialized markets, but they can be reached for $500 per 30-second commercial. "Home Shopping Show" is a program divided into 9 or 10 commercial segments. For $3,500 per slot, advertisers like Revlon, Amoco Oil Club, Burpee Seeds, Pillsbury, and Encyclopaedia Britannica have targeted presentations at the 3.8 million households that receive "Home Shopping Show."

Source: "Infomercials," *Time,* May 18, 1981, p. 69; Malcom A. McNiven, "A Plan for More Productive Advertising," *Harvard Business Review,* March-April 1980, p. 135; "These Ads Are the Show," *Sales & Marketing Management,* September 15, 1980, pp. 14, 16; Geoffrey Colvin, "Tougher Times for TV's Time Sellers," *FORTUNE,* October 20, 1980, pp. 130–33; and Colby Coates, "CBS Series Top Price List," *Advertising Age,* September 1, 1980, section 1, p. 1.

Television Television ranks first in revenue from national advertising (about 21 percent). It has an 11 percent share of local advertising revenue, making it second only to newspapers as an advertising medium. Television advertising can be divided into three categories: network, national, and local. Columbia Broadcasting System, National Broadcasting Company, and American Broadcasting Company are the three major national networks. Their programs usually account for a substantial portion of total television advertising expenditures. A national "spot" is nonnetwork broadcasting used by a general advertiser. Local advertising spots, used primarily by retailers, consist of locally developed and sponsored commercials. Television advertising offers the advantages of impact, mass coverage, repetition, flexibility, and prestige. Its disadvantages include relinquishing control of the promotional message to the telecaster (who can influence its impact), high costs, high mortality rates for commercials, some public distrust, and a lack of selectivity.

Radio Advertisers using the medium of radio can also be classified as network, national, and local. Radio accounts for about 7 percent of total advertising revenue, and 5 percent of local expenditures. Its advantages are immediacy (studies show most people regard radio as the best source for up-to-date news), low cost, flexibility, practical and low-cost audience selection, and mobility. Its disadvantages include fragmentation (Boise, Idaho, for example, has a population of 100,000 and 20 stations), the temporary nature of the message, and less research information than for television.[18]

Impact is a primary advantage of advertising.

"Mommy, we keep saying 'go home, kitty-cat' —but she just keeps hanging around here."

Source: The Family Circus, reprinted courtesy of The Register and Tribune Syndicate, Inc.

Outdoor Advertising Posters (commonly called billboards), painted bulletins or displays (such as those that appear on the walls of buildings), and electric spectaculars (large, illuminated, sometimes animated, signs and displays) make up outdoor advertising. This form of advertising has the advantages of communicating quick and simple ideas, repetition, and the ability to promote products that are available for sale nearby. Outdoor advertising is particularly effective in metropolitan and other high-traffic areas. Disadvantages of the medium are the brevity of its message and public concern over esthetics. The Highway Beautification Act of 1965, for instance, regulates outdoor advertising near interstate highways.

Direct Mail Sales letters, postcards, leaflets, folders, broadsides (larger than folders), booklets, catalogs, and house organs (periodical publications issued by organizations) are all forms of direct mail advertising. The advantages of direct mail are selectivity, intensive coverage, speed, format flexibility, complete information, and the personalization of each mailing piece. Disadvantages of direct mail are its high cost per reader, its dependence on the quality of the mailing list, and some people's annoyance with it. This situation led the Direct Mail/Marketing Association in 1971 to establish its Mail Preference Service. This consumer service sends out name-removal forms to people who do not wish to receive direct mail advertising. It also provides add-on forms for those who like to receive a lot of mail.

ASSESSING THE EFFECTIVENESS OF AN ADVERTISEMENT

Advertising represents a major outlay for many firms, so it is imperative for them to determine whether a chosen campaign is accomplishing their promotional objectives.[19] The determination of advertising effectiveness, however, is one of the most difficult undertakings in marketing. It consists of two primary elements—pretesting and posttesting.

Pretesting

Pretesting is *assessing the advertisement's effectiveness before it is actually used.* It includes a variety of evaluative methods. To test magazine advertisements, the ad agency Batten, Barton, Durstine & Osborn cuts ads out of advance copies of magazines and then "strips in" the ads it wants to test. Interviewers later check the impact of the advertisements on the readers who receive free copies of the revised magazine.

McCann-Erickson, another ad agency, uses a *sales conviction test* to evaluate magazine advertisements. Interviewers ask heavy users of a particular item to pick which of two alternative advertisements would "convince" them to purchase it.

Potential radio and television advertisements are often screened by consumers who sit in a studio and press two buttons—one for a positive reaction to the commercial, the other for a negative one. Sometimes, proposed ad copy is printed on a postcard that also offers a free product; the number of cards returned is viewed as an indication of the copy's effectiveness. *Blind product tests* are also often used. In these tests, people are asked to select unidentified products on the basis of available advertising copy. Mechanical means of assessing how people read advertising copy are yet another method. One mechanical test uses an eye camera to photograph how people read ads; its results help determine headline placement and advertising copy length.

Posttesting

Posttesting is *the assessment of advertising copy after it has been used.* Pretesting is generally a more desirable testing method than posttesting because of its potential cost savings. But posttesting can be helpful in planning future advertisements and in making adjustments to current advertising programs.

In one of the most popular posttests, the *Starch Readership Report,* interviewers ask people who have read selected magazines about whether they have read various ads in them. A copy of the magazine is used as an interviewing aid, and each interviewer starts at a different point in the magazine. For larger ads, respondents are also asked about specifics such as headlines and copy. All readership, or recognition, tests assume that future sales are related to advertising readership.

Unaided recall tests are another method of posttesting advertisements. Here, respondents are not given copies of the magazine but must recall the ads from memory. Gallup and Robinson require people to prove they have read a magazine by recalling one or more of its feature articles. The people who remember particular articles are given cards with the names of products advertised in the issue. They then list the ads they remember and explain what they remember about them. Finally, the respondents are asked about their potential purchase of the product. A readership test concludes the Gallup and Robinson interview. Burke Research Corporation uses telephone interviews the day after a commercial appears on television in order to test brand recognition and the effectiveness of the advertisement.

Inquiry tests are another popular posttest. Advertisements sometimes offer a free gift, generally a sample of the product, to people who respond to the advertisement. The number of inquiries relative to the cost of the advertisement is then used as a measure of effectiveness. *Split runs* allow advertisers to test two or more ads at the same time. Under this method, a publication's production run is split in two; half the magazines use Advertisement A, and half use Advertisement B. The relative impact of the alternatives is then determined by inquiries.

Regardless of the exact method used, marketers must realize that pretesting and posttesting are expensive and must therefore plan to use them as effectively as possible.

SQUEEZING THE THIRTY-SECOND COMMERCIAL

Television commercials were originally sixty seconds long. Today, they are only thirty seconds in duration. This norm has been accepted by the National Association of Broadcasters (NAB)—consisting of the major networks and a majority of the stations—which specifies in its code that commercials are limited to two per minute. The NAB concern is that commercial programming not appear cluttered.

Recent research investigated the use of a time compression technique that breaks the message down to segments as small as .0020 of a second. The commercial is speeded up so that a thirty-second advertising message becomes a twenty-four-second one. The theory is that if the minute could be broken into two twenty-four-second and one twelve-second segment, the media could increase their advertising revenue—provided NAB approved the format change.

What were the results of this research? The data shows that respondents were unconcerned about more clutter in the commercials they watched. Recall improved for the faster commercials. The three-commercial format did not affect recall scores.

Moral of the Story: Maybe a few years from now commercial announcers will be seen talking faster than they did before.

Source: James M. MacLachlan and Michael H. Siegel, "Reducing the Cost of TV Commercials by Use of Time Compressions," *Journal of Marketing Research*, February 1980, pp. 52–57. Reprinted with permission from *Journal of Marketing Research*, published by the American Marketing Association.

ORGANIZATION OF THE ADVERTISING FUNCTION

Although the ultimate responsibility for advertising decisions often rests with top marketing management, the organization of the advertising function varies among companies. A producer of a technical industrial product may be served by a one-person operation primarily concerned with writing copy for trade publications. A consumer goods company, on the other hand, may have a large department staffed with advertising specialists.

The advertising function is usually organized as a staff department reporting to the vice-president (or director) of marketing. The director of advertising is the department's liaison with the rest of the company. The department's technical competence is important, but so is its ability to relate well to the rest of the organization. The major tasks typically organized under advertising include advertising research, art, copywriting, media analysis, and, in some cases, sales promotion.

ADVERTISING AGENCIES

Many major advertisers make use of independent advertising agencies. There are several advantages to such an arrangement. Agencies provide a degree of creativity and objectivity that is difficult to maintain in a corporate advertising department. In some cases, they also reduce the cost of advertising, since they do not have many of the fixed expenses associated with internal advertising departments.

Figure 15.5 shows the organization chart for a large advertising agency. While the titles may vary from agency to agency, the major operational responsibilities can be classified as creative services, account management, research, and promotional services.

Young & Rubicam is the largest advertising agency in the United States, with worldwide billings of about $2.3 billion. Table 15.4 shows the ten leading U.S. advertising agencies ranked in terms of their world billings.

**TABLE 15.4
Top 10 U.S.
Advertising Agencies
in World Billings**

Rank	Agency	Billings (in Millions)
1	Young & Rubicam	$2,273.2
2	J. Walter Thompson	2,137.7
3	McCann-Erickson	1,792.1
4	Ogilvy & Mather	1,661.9
5	Ted Bates	1,404.1
6	BBDO International	1,305.0
7	Leo Burnett	1,144.8
8	Foote, Cone & Belding	1,117.6
9	SSC&B	1,111.8
10	D'Arcy-MacManus & Masius	1,058.9

Source: John J. O'Connor, "Income Reaches $4.7 Billion," *Advertising Age,* March 18, 1981, p. 1. Reprinted with permission. Copyright 1981 by Crain Communications, Inc.

**FIGURE 15.5
Organization Chart
for a Large
Advertising Agency**

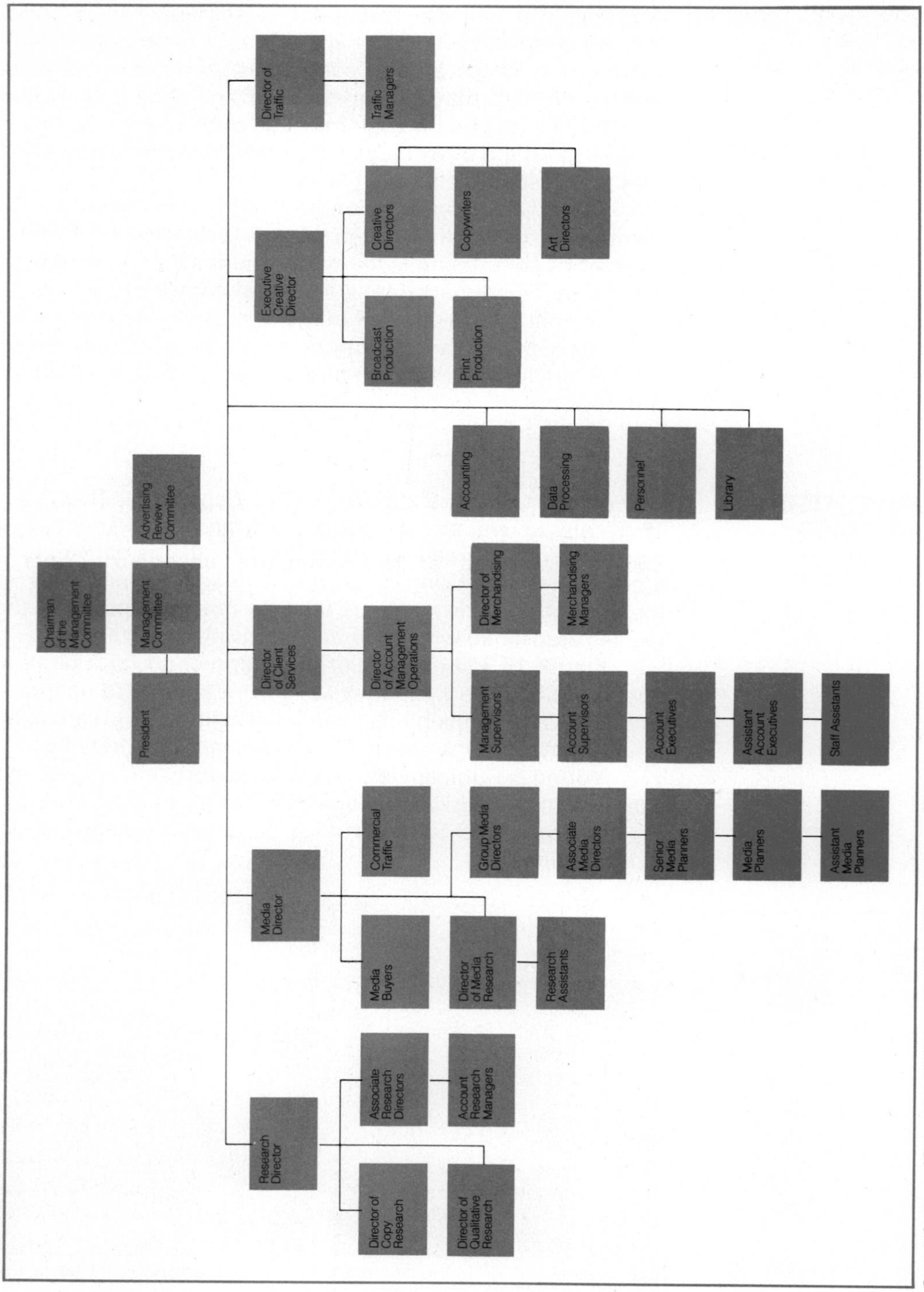

Source: Courtesy of Tatham-Laird & Kudner Advertising, Chicago and New York.

**CREATING AN
ADVERTISE-
MENT**

The final step in the advertising process is the development and preparation of an advertisement that flows logically from the promotional theme selected. The advertisement's association with other company products and its continuity are the major factors to be considered in its preparation.

Sometimes related products are an advantage, and sometimes they are not. Taster's Choice by Nestlé leads Maxim by General Foods even though Maxim was the first freeze-dried coffee on the market. One explanation is that General Foods did not attempt to maximize its early advantage by going after regular coffee drinkers. General Foods apparently feared that Maxim's sales would cut into the sales of its regular coffee, Maxwell House. Nestlé, on the other hand, attacked this market directly by advertising that a jar of Taster's Choice is about the equivalent of two pounds of regular coffee.[20]

What should an advertisement accomplish? Regardless of the exact appeal chosen, an advertisement should gain attention and interest, inform and/or persuade, and eventually lead to buying action. Several years ago, Gillette Company had a chimpanzee shave a man's face in a commercial. After tests in Indianapolis and Dallas, someone at the company observed: "Lots of people remembered the chimp, but hardly anyone remembered our product. There was fantastic interest in the monkey, but no payoff for Gillette."[21]

An advertisement that fails to gain the receiver's attention and then hold the person's interest is ineffective. Thus information and persuasion is the second factor to consider when creating an advertisement. Health insurance advertisements typically specify the features of a policy and use testimonials in an attempt to persuade prospects. But stimulating buying action with an ad is often difficult since the ad cannot actually close the sale. Furthermore, many advertising managers fail to suggest how the receiver of the ad can effect a purchase if he or she so desires. This is a shortcoming that should be eliminated.[22]

**CELEBRITY
TESTIMONIALS:
ADVANTAGES
AND PITFALLS**

Bob Hope reportedly received $6 million for a series of commercials and promotions for Texaco.[23] Dean Martin is supposed to have signed a seven-figure contract for his promotion of American Telephone and Telegraph Company. Model Cheryl Tiegs advertises Olympus cameras, Clairol hair coloring, Cover Girl Makeup, and a line of Sears' sportswear. And professional athletes Sugar Ray Leonard and Magic Johnson sell 7-Up.

**FIGURE 15.6
Portrait of a
President, 1953**

Source: Ad courtesy of The Van Heusen Company.

But Frank Sinatra may have the best deal. He collected a six-figure check for permitting Ford Motor Company to play part of "The Best Is Yet to Come" as background music to a commercial; Ford also agreed to use Sinatra's daughter in a commercial. (Sinatra later volunteered his services to Chrysler Corporation for a mere $1 per year.)

For many years, most celebrities refused to be associated with commercials. There were exceptions, of course—like Joan Bennett advertising Chesterfield Cigarettes in 1942—but for the most part, stars stayed away from product endorsements. The late Steve McQueen appeared in only one commercial: a motorcycle advertisement. Even then, McQueen stipulated that the ad be used only in Japan. The leading holdouts in the 1980s are Alan Alda, Robert Redford, Dustin Hoffman, Jack Lemmon, and Charlton Heston.

The primary advantage of using celebrity testimonials is that they may improve product recognition in a promotional environment filled with hundreds of competing thirty-second commercials. (Advertisers use the term *clutter* to refer to this situation.) Of course, the celebrity must be a credible source of information for the item being sold.

There are also some disadvantages to using stars to sell a product. Some celebrity advertisements simply do not succeed. This is particularly true when there is no reasonable relationship between the celebrity and the product. Another problem is that some event may make the commercial meaningless or cast a negative image on it. Notable failures include the late John Wayne for Datril, James Coburn for Schlitz Lite Beer, the late Peter Sellers for TWA, and Billy Carter for Billy Beer.

Advertisers are not the only ones with potential problems. The Federal Trade Commission has announced a policy of assessing financial liability to any celebrity who makes a false product claim. The new rule was first enforced against singer Pat Boone, who promoted Acne-Statin, a skin preparation sold as an acne cure. The FTC alleged that some of the product claims were false. Boone, while noting that his daughters did use Acne-Statin as claimed and that he believed the product claims, signed a consent decree in which he agreed to stop promoting the product and to pay up to $6,000 of any refunds that might be ordered. As a result of the Boone case, it now seems likely that name personalities will insist that advertisers reimburse any damages assessed as the result of a commercial.

RETAIL ADVERTISING

Retail advertising is *all advertising by stores that sell goods or services directly to the consuming public.*[24] While accounting for a sizable portion of total annual advertising expenditures, retail advertising is frequently ineffective. One study showed that consumers were often suspicious of retail price advertisements. Source, message, and shopping experience seemed to affect consumer attitudes toward these advertisements.[25]

The basic problem is that store managers are usually given the responsibility of advertising as an added task to be performed along with their normal functions. Advertising agencies are rarely used. The result is that advertising is often relegated to a secondary activity in retail stores. The basic step in correcting this deficiency is to give one individual both the responsibility and the authority for developing an effective retail advertising program.

Cooperative Advertising

Cooperative advertising is *a sharing of advertising costs between the retailer and the manufacturer or vendor.* It resulted initially from the media practice of offering lower rates to local advertisers than to national advertisers. Later, cooperative advertising was seen as a method of improving dealer relations. From the retailer's viewpoint, it permits a store to secure advertising that it would not otherwise have.[26]

SALES PROMOTION

The second type of nonpersonal selling is sales promotion, a category of nonpersonal selling efforts designed to supplement and extend the other aspects of promotional strategy. This type of selling involves a number of specific techniques.

Methods of Sales Promotion

Firms that wish to use sales promotion have various methods from which to choose—point-of-purchase advertising; specialty advertising; trade shows; samples, coupons, and premiums; contests; and trading stamps. More than one of these options may be used in a single promotional strategy, but probably no promotional strategy has ever used all in a single program. While they are not mutually exclusive, the promotions are generally employed on a selective basis.

Point-of-purchase advertising refers to *displays and other promotions located near where a buying decision is actually made.* The in-store promotion of consumer goods is a common example. Such advertising can be useful in supplementing a theme developed in another area of promotional strategy. A life-size display of a celebrity used in television advertising could be a very effective in-store display. Another example is the L'eggs store display, which completely altered the panty hose industry.

Specialty advertising is *a sales promotion medium that utilizes useful articles carrying the advertiser's name, address, and advertising message to reach the target consumers.*[27] The origin of specialty advertising has been traced to the Middle Ages, when wooden pegs bearing the names of artisans "were given to prospects to be driven into their walls and to serve as a convenient place upon which to hang armor."[28] Examples of contemporary advertising specialties carrying the firm's name include calendars, coffee mugs, pens, matchbooks, personalized business gifts of modest value, ashtrays, balloons, yardsticks, and key rings. The Internal Revenue Service defines items worth less than $4 and imprinted with the name of the donor's company as advertising specialties rather than gifts. These items are not subject to the $25 per person annual business gift limitation.[29]

Advertising specialties help reinforce previous or future advertising and sales messages. An A. C. Nielsen survey found that both the general public and business were more likely to purchase from firms using specialty advertising.[30]

Trade Shows To influence channel members and resellers in the distribution channel, it has become a common practice for sellers to participate in *trade shows.* These shows are often organized by an industry's trade association and may be part of the association's annual meeting or convention. Vendors serving the particular industry are invited to the show to display and demonstrate their products for the association's membership. The largest trade show in the world is the International Construction Equipment Exposition, held every six years. The 1981 show in Houston featured $500 million in equipment on display, and was attended by 90,000 people.[31] Shows are also used to reach the ultimate consumer. Home and recreation shows, for instance, allow businesses to display and demonstrate home care, recreation, and other consumer products to the entire community.

Samples, Coupons, and Premiums The distribution of samples, coupons, and premiums is probably the best-known sales promotion technique.

Sampling is *the free distribution of a product in an attempt to obtain future sales for it.* The distribution may be done on a door-to-door basis, by mail, via demonstrations, or by inclusion in packages containing other products. Sampling is especially useful in promoting new products.

Coupons offer *a discount, usually some specified price reduction on the next purchase of a product.* They are redeemable at retail outlets, which receive a handling fee. Mail, magazine, newspaper, and package insertions are the standard methods of distributing coupons.

Premiums are *gift items given free with the purchase of another product.* They have proved effective in getting consumers to try new products or different brands. Premiums should be related to the purchased item. For instance, the service department of a car dealership might offer its customers ice scrapers. Premiums are also used to obtain direct-mail purchases. The value of premium giveaways runs into billions of dollars each year.

Contests Firms often sponsor contests to attract additional customers, offering substantial cash or merchandise prizes to call attention to their products. In recent years, however, various rulings and legal restrictions have placed limitations on the use of contests. As a result, com-

Premiums do not always lead to customer satisfaction.

"Lend me two thousand and I'll give *you* a toaster and an electric mixer."

Source: Courtesy of Cartoon Features Syndicate.

panies probably should employ specialists in developing this kind of sales promotion.

Trading Stamps A sales promotion technique similar to premiums, **trading stamps** are *used to obtain a gift in addition to the product being purchased.*[32] Whether the consumer benefits depends on the relative price levels of the goods offered. Trading stamps originally appeared in the last two decades of the nineteenth century. They are now distributed by grocery stores, gas stations, savings and loan associations, and mail-order houses. The extent of their usage seems to depend on factors such as relative price levels, location of redemption centers, and legal restrictions.

PUBLIC RELATIONS

Public relations expenditures are small relative to those for personal selling, advertising, and even sales promotion. Nonetheless, public relations does provide an efficient indirect communication channel for promoting products. After Six, the tuxedo manufacturer, once rushed a pair of size-42 trousers to Buddy Hackett via a commercial airliner. Hackett's own pants had been ruined, and he had five nights remaining in a Gaithersburg, Maryland, nightclub engagement. A hurried call to After Six put a company vice-president in action, and the trousers arrived a few hours later—without a bill. Buddy Hackett has voluntarily plugged After Six ever since the firm saved his act at Gaithersburg.[33]

The public relations program has broader objectives than the other aspects of promotional strategy. It is concerned with the prestige and image of all parts of the organization. Examples of nonmarketing-oriented public relations objectives are a company's attempt to gain favorable public opinion during a long strike and an open letter to Congress published in a newspaper during congressional debate on a bill affecting a particular industry. Although public relations departments are not always located in the marketing organization, their activities do have an impact on promotional strategy.

PUBLICITY

The part of public relations that is most directly related to promoting a company's products or services is **publicity.** Since it is designed to familiarize the general public with a product's characteristics and advantages, publicity is an information activity of public relations.

Some publicity is used to promote a company's image or viewpoint, but a significant amount provides information about products, particularly new ones. Publicity releases covering products are typically sent to media editors for possible inclusion in news stories. Publicity releases are sometimes used to fill voids in a publication and other times are used in regular features. In either case, publicity releases are a valuable supplement to advertising.

Some critics have asserted that the publication of product publicity is directly related to the amount of advertising revenue coming from a firm. But this is not the case at respected newspapers and magazines. The story is told that some years ago a Greyhound executive was enraged at a cartoon appearing in a Chicago newspaper that told of a character having numerous problems on a bus trip. The executive threatened to cancel future advertisements in the newspaper unless the cartoon strip was stopped or changed immediately. The newspaper's curt reply was, "One more such communication from you and the alternative of withdrawing your advertising will no longer rest with . . . Greyhound."[34]

Today, public relations has to be considered an integral part of promotional strategy even though its basic objectives extend far beyond just attempting to influence the purchase of a particular good. Public relations programs—and especially their publicity aspects—make a significant contribution to the achievement of promotional goals.

SUMMARY

Advertising, sales promotion, and public relations—the nonpersonal selling elements of promotion—are not twentieth-century phenomena. Advertising, for instance, can trace its origin to very early times. Today, these elements of promotion have gained professional status and are vital aspects of the business scene.

Advertising, a nonpersonal sales presentation usually directed to a large number of potential customers, seeks to achieve communication goals rather than direct sales objectives. It strives to inform, persuade, and remind potential consumers of the product or service being promoted.

Advertising planning starts with good research, which permits the development of a strategy. Tactical decisions about copy and scheduling are then made. Finally, advertisements are evaluated, and appropriate feedback is provided to management. There are six basic types of advertising: (1) informative product advertising, (2) persuasive product advertising, (3) reminder-oriented product advertising, (4) informative institutional advertising, (5) persuasive institutional advertising, and (6) reminder-oriented institutional advertising. One of the most vital decisions in developing an advertising strategy is the selection of the media to be employed.

The major tasks of advertising departments are advertising research, art, copywriting, media analysis, and sales promotion. Many advertisers use independent advertising agencies to provide them with the creativity and objectivity missing in their own organizations and to reduce the cost of advertising. The final step in the advertising process is developing and preparing the advertisement.

The principal methods of sales promotion are point-of-purchase advertising; specialty advertising; trade shows; samples, coupons, and premiums; contests; and trading stamps. Public relations and publicity also play major roles in developing promotional strategies.

QUESTIONS FOR DISCUSSION

1. Explain the following terms:

advertising	retail advertising
positioning	cooperative advertising
comparative advertising	sales promotion
product advertising	specialty advertising
institutional advertising	public relations
pretesting	publicity
posttesting	

2. Why do some firms and industries spend more than others for advertising? What generalizations can you draw from Tables 15.1 and 15.2?

3. Trace the historical development of advertising.

4. Describe the objectives or goals of advertising.

5. Discuss the process of advertising planning.

6. List and discuss the six basic types of advertising. Cite examples of each type.

7. Discuss the relationship between advertising and the product life cycle.

8. Comment on the following statement: One of the most vital decisions in developing an advertising strategy is the selection of the media to be employed.

9. What are the advantages and disadvantages associated with using each of the advertising media?

10. Discuss the organization of the advertising function. Consider all the major activities associated with advertising.

11. Why is retail advertising so important today?

12. List and discuss the principal methods of sales promotion.

13. Choose a candidate who ran for political office during a recent election. Assume that you were in charge of advertising for this person's campaign. Develop an advertising strategy for your candidate. Select a campaign theme and the media to be employed. Finally, design an advertisement for the candidate.

14. What specialty advertising items would be appropriate for the following:
    a. an independent insurance agent
    b. a retail carpet store
    c. Bethlehem Steel Company
    d. an interior decorator

15. Several states now have government-operated lotteries. How should a state advertise lottery tickets?

16. Cooperative advertising refers to a sharing of advertising costs between the retailer and the manufacturer or vendor. From society's standpoint, should this kind of advertising be prohibited on the ground that it leads to manufacturer domination of the distribution channel? Defend your answer.

17. Sweden's business practices court ordered a U.S. advertising agency and its client, a Swedish insurance company, to stop using models identified

in a commercial as other people. The court decided that the practice mis-led buyers. What is your opinion of the Swedish ruling?

18. Research suggests that the best placement for an advertisement in a magazine or newspaper is at the beginning or end of the publication. Why is this true?

19. What do most of your friends think about the role of advertising in contemporary society? Why do you think they hold these beliefs?

20. Now that you have studied this chapter, what is your opinion of advertising and its role in contemporary society?

NOTES

1. "Volks Called Biggest Success; Edsel Gets the Booby Prize," *Advertising Age,* April 30, 1980, pp. 130, 132.
2. Quoted in S. Watson Dunn and Arnold M. Barban, *Advertising: Its Role in Modern Marketing,* 5th ed. (Hinsdale, Ill.: The Dryden Press, 1982), p. 5.
3. *Ibid.,* p. 18.
4. Robert J. Coen, "Vast U.S. and Worldwide Ad Expenditures Expected," *Advertising Age,* November 13, 1980, p. 10.
5. This section follows the discussion in Dunn and Barban, *Advertising,* 5th ed., p. 202.
6. Leo Bogart, *Strategy in Advertising* (New York: Harcourt Brace Jovanovich, 1967), p. 1.
7. An interesting article appears in John J. Burnett, "Psychographic and Demographic Characteristics of Blood Donors," *Journal of Consumer Research,* June 1981, pp. 62–66. Also see Ugar Yavas, Glen Riechen, and Ravi Paramessvaran," Using Psychographics to Profile Potential Donors," *Business,* September-October 1980, pp. 41–45.
8. Bill Abrams, "Can Dracula and Socrates Put Perrier back on People's Lips?" *Wall Street Journal,* April 23, 1981. Reprinted by permission of *The Wall Street Journal,* © Dow Jones and Company, Inc. 1981. All Rights Reserved.
9. Positioning is discussed in Antte Hoahti and Rob Van Den Heuvel, "Positioning: Some Conceptual Observation with an Illustration," Venkatakrishna V. Bellur, ed., Thomas R. Baird, Paul T. Hertz, Roger L. Jenkins, Jay D. Lindquist, and Stephen W. Miller, co-editors, *Marketing Developments in Marketing Science,* vol. IV (Marquette, Mich.: Academy of Marketing Science, 1981), pp. 327–33; and William D. Neal, "Strategic Product Positioning: A Step-by-step Guide," *Business,* May-June 1980, pp. 34–42.
10. This section is based on information in Aimee L. Morner, "It Pays to Knock Your Competitor," *FORTUNE,* February 13, 1978, pp. 104–6, 110–11. Comparative advertising is also discussed in Linda E. Swayne and Jack M. Starling, "What Ever Happened to Brand X?" *Business,* July-August 1980, pp. 22–28; Stephen Goodwin and Michael Etgar, "An Experimental Investigation of Comparative Advertising: Impact of Message Appeal, Information Load, and Utility of Product Class," *Journal of Marketing Research,* May 1980, pp. 187–202; and William R. Swinyard, "The Interaction between Comparative Advertising and Copy Claim Variation," *Journal of Marketing Research,* May 1981, pp. 175–86.
11. Morner, "It Pays to Knock Your Competitor," p. 104.
12. An interesting article is S. Prakash Sethi, "Institutional/Image Advertising and Idea/Issue Advertising as Marketing Tools: Some Public Policy Issues," *Journal of Marketing,* January 1979, pp. 68–78.
13. Ellen Graham, "The Dewar's Do'ers: Young, Ambitious, Instantly Famous," *Wall Street Journal,* August 1, 1978.
14. Daniel Machalaba, "Municipalities Step up Image-building Aimed at Firms and Tourists," *Wall Street Journal,* October 4, 1977.
15. Reported in "Business Bulletin," *Wall Street Journal,* October 19, 1978.
16. Media time allocations are discussed in Jacob Hornils and Mary Jan Schlinger, "Allocation of Time to the Mass Media," *Journal of Consumer Research,* March 1981, pp. 343–55.
17. The discussion of various advertising media is adapted from material in Dunn and Barban, *Advertising,* pp. 513–80. The advertising volume percentages for the four major media (newspapers, television, magazines, and radio) are reported in *Advertising Age,* January 5, 1981, p. 56.
18. "Talk Can Be Profitable, and Radio's Proving It," *U.S. News & World Report,* July 7, 1980, p. 68.

19.	This section is based on Dunn and Barban, *Advertising,* pp. 273–93. An interesting discussion appears in Bruce G. Vanden Bergh and Leonard N. Reid, "Puffery and Magazine Ad Readership," *Journal of Marketing,* Spring 1980, pp. 78–81.

20.	John E. Cooney, "Food Marketers Spend Billions Persuading Us to Buy Their Products," *Wall Street Journal,* June 24, 1977.

21.	William M. Carley, "Gillette Co. Struggles as Its Rivals Slice at Fat Profit Margin," *Wall Street Journal,* February 2, 1972.

22.	Another interesting discussion of advertising content appears in Rolph E. Anderson and Marvin A. Jolson, "Technical Wording in Advertising: Implications for Market Segmentation," *Journal of Marketing,* Winter 1980, pp. 57–66.

23.	This section is based on information in Nancy Yoshihara, "Stardom Sells," *Orlando Sentinel Star,* April 4, 1981; Ann Morrison, "The Boss as Pitchman," *FORTUNE,* August 1980, pp. 66–70, 72–73; Erick Lacitis, "Will Reprints of Reagan Ad Put Starch into the American Dream?" *Seattle Times,* January 15, 1981; John Emmerling, "Want a Celebrity in Your Ad? O.K. but Watch Your Step," *Advertising Age,* November 1, 1976, pp. 63–64; "Greenbacks for Ol' Blue Eyes," *Newsweek,* October 9, 1978, p. 37; John Cooney, "Celebrities Brighten More Ad Campaigns—and Darken a Few," *Wall Street Journal,* August 15, 1978; Charles W. Theisen, "More Stars Are Dazzling Commercials," *Detroit News,* August 17, 1978; "Let the Stellar Seller Beware," *Time,* May 22, 1978, p. 66; and "Postscripts," *Seattle Times,* October 22, 1981.

24.	Dunn and Barban, *Advertising,* p. 611.

25.	Joseph N. Fry and Gordon H. McDougall, "Consumer Appraisal of Retail Price Advertisements," *Journal of Marketing,* July 1974, pp. 64–67.

26.	An excellent discussion appears in Edward C. Crimmins, "Co-Op Advertising: A History of Problems and Promise," *Advertising Age,* September 1, 1980, sec. 2, pp. S1, S10, S11.

27.	This definition is adapted from *How to Play Championship Specialty Advertising* (Chicago: Specialty Advertising Association International, 1978).

28.	Walter A. Gaw, *Specialty Advertising* (Chicago: Specialty Advertising Association International, 1970), p. 7.

29.	"Reminders from the IRS," *Specialty Advertising Report 7,* no. 4, p. 4.

30.	*Specialty Advertising Report* (Second Quarter, 1973), pp. 1–2.

31.	Linda Snyder Harris, "The Greatest Earth Moving Show on Earth," *FORTUNE,* April 20, 1981, p. 176. An excellent discussion of trade shows appears in J. Steven Kelly and James M. Comer, "Trade Show Exhibiting: A Managerial Perspective," John D. Sumney and Ronald D. Taylor, eds., *Evolving Marketing Thought for 1980* (Carbondale, Ill.: Southern Marketing Association, 1980), pp. 11–13.

32.	Trading stamps are discussed in Louis E. Boone, James C. Johnson, and George P. Ferry, "Trading Stamps: Their Role in Today's Marketplace," *Journal of the Academy of Marketing Science,* Winter/Spring 1978, pp. 70–76.

33.	Buddy Hackett's experience is described in Urban C. Lehner, "Tuxedo Firm Thrives by Promoting Apparel that Most Men Dislike," *Wall Street Journal,* October 14, 1975. An excellent discussion of public relations appears in Jonathan N. Goodrich, Robert L. Gildea, and Kevin Cavanaugh, "A Place for Public Relations in the Marketing Mix," *MSU Business Topics,* Autumn 1979, pp. 53–57.

34.	Gene Harlan and Alan Scott, *Contemporary Public Relations: Principles and Cases* (Englewood Cliffs, N.J.: Prentice-Hall, 1955), p. 36.

CHAPTER 16

ELEMENTS OF PROMOTIONAL STRATEGY: PERSONAL SELLING AND SALES MANAGEMENT

KEY TERMS

personal selling
missionary sales
prospecting
qualifying
presentation
canned approach
closing
follow-up
selling up
suggestion selling
sales management
commissions
salaries
quota

LEARNING GOALS

1. To explain the three basic sales tasks: order processing, creative selling, and missionary sales

2. To discuss the current status of women in selling

3. To outline sales personnel's role in sales intelligence and feedback

4. To distinguish retail selling from field selling

5. To examine the roles and tasks of the sales manager

In 1970, Sweda, a division of Litton Industries, controlled 13 percent of the cash register market. But continued reliance on mechanical cash registers cost the company dearly in the 1970s. Electronic cash registers had entered the market, and Sweda's market share fell to 8 percent. The company's decline from second place (behind NCR) to fourth was accompanied by red ink.

Litton management decided something had to be done. So the parent company installed George Saterson as Sweda's president. Saterson introduced the needed electronic products and returned Sweda to profitability. How did he do it?

Saterson concentrated on improving Sweda's sales effort. He tripled the sales force (to 500 people). A comprehensive training program was set up for Sweda's 200 dealers. The number of sales offices doubled. And Saterson cut a management level out of his organizational structure so he would have direct access to the field sales force. Today, Sweda's president credits the company's turnaround to its revitalized sales organization.[1]

This chapter discusses **personal selling**, a *seller's promotional presentation conducted on a person-to-person basis with the buyer.* It is an inherent function of any business enterprise. Accounting, engineering, personnel management, and other organizational activities are useless unless the firm's product can be sold to someone. Sweda's efforts to upgrade its sales force illustrate the importance that contemporary marketers assign to this aspect of promotional strategy.

EVOLUTION OF PERSONAL SELLING

Selling has been a standard part of business for thousands of years.[2] The earliest peddlers were traders who had some type of ownership interest in the goods they sold after manufacturing or importing them. In many cases, selling was viewed as a secondary activity for these people.

Later, selling became a separate function. The peddlers of the eighteenth century sold to the farmers, planters, and settlers of the vast North American continent. In the nineteenth century, salespeople called "drummers" sold to both consumers and marketing intermediaries. These early sellers sometimes employed questionable sales practices and techniques and earned an undesirable reputation for themselves and their firms.

Some of this negative stereotype remains today.[3] But for the most part, selling is far different from what it was in the early years. The sales job has evolved into a professional occupation. Today's salesperson is more concerned with helping customers select the right product than with simply selling whatever is available. Modern professional salespeople advise and assist customers in their purchase decisions. Where repeat purchases are common, the salesperson must be certain that the buyers' purchases are in their best interests or else no future sales will be made. The interests of the seller are thus tied to those of the buyer.[4]

SALES TASKS

Not all selling activities are alike. While all sales activities assist the customer in some manner, the exact types of activities performed vary from one position to another.[5] Nonetheless, three basic sales tasks can be identified: order processing, creative selling, and missionary selling.

Although these tasks can form the basis for a sales classification system, most salespeople do not fit into any single category. Instead, they often perform all three tasks to a certain extent. A sales engineer for a computer manufacturer may spend half the time at missionary sales, 45 percent at creative sales, and 5 percent at order processing. Most salespeople engage in a variety of sales activities, even though a sales job may be classified on the basis of the primary selling task.

Order Processing

Selling at the wholesale and retail levels is often characterized by *order processing.* Sales people who handle this task:

1. *Identify customer needs.* A hosiery salesperson may determine that an in-store display should be restocked.

2. *Point out the need to the customer.* The salesperson may inform the store manager of the hosiery situation.

3. *Complete the order.* The store manager may acknowledge the inventory need, and the salesperson may fill the display.

Order processing, which is part of most selling jobs, becomes the primary task where needs can be readily identified by the salesperson and acknowledged by the customer.

As a unique illustration of order processing, consider the actions of Mutual of Omaha sales personnel. Shortly after a crisis was averted at the Three Mile Island nuclear power plant, Mutual of Omaha salespeople offered cancer policies to inhabitants of the surrounding area.[6] Apparently, both sales management and customers perceived a need for such a product.

Creative Selling

Some purchases require considerable review and analysis by prospective buyers, and the salesperson must skillfully solicit orders from such prospects. To do so, creative selling techniques must be used. New products, for example, often require a high degree of creative selling. The seller must persuade the buyer of the worth of the item.

Missionary Sales

Missionary sales are *an indirect type of selling, in which people sell the goodwill of a firm, often by providing the customer with product use assistance.* The maintenance of goodwill has always been an important sales function. In recent times, product use assistance such as that provided by a systems specialist has become a critical part of missionary selling.

Detailers are the missionary salespeople of the health care industry.[7] They do not sell drugs, medicines, and the like to patients but instead concentrate their efforts on intermediaries like physicians and hospitals. Detailers attempt to get medical practitioners to use their products when prescribing treatment. Detailers are an important source of product information in the health care industry. Their employers—the manufacturers and distributors—depend on them to keep the goodwill of physicians, nurses, and medical technicians.

WHAT MAKES A GOOD SALESPERSON?

Selling is not an easy job; it tends to attract highly motivated people who are challenged by a chance to prove themselves in a highly competitive field. Bob Hutton, a sales representative for Capp Homes—a maker of "finish-it-yourself" houses—is an example: "Any job I've ever had, I couldn't stand it if I wasn't the best. The harder it is, the better I like it."[8]

According to sales managers, some important qualities for a salesperson include a positive attitude, good product knowledge, effective selling skills, initiative and aggressiveness, appearance and manners, and communication skills. Some individuals possess all of these qualities and abilities, and can adjust to selling more easily than others.[9]

Women in Selling The sales field offers excellent career opportunities to women. Selling has been a nontraditional occupation for women, but the field is opening rapidly.

Merriellen Miller had been a nurse for ten years before deciding that she could earn more by selling automobiles at an AMC dealership. Later, she switched to selling trucks at a Chevrolet dealership in Pontiac, Michigan. Miller now earns $35,000 a year pursuing her second career. She admits it has not been easy but adds: ". . . it gets better every year. Men accept a saleswoman better than they did even five years ago."[10]

Considerable research has been done on women in selling.[11] While the evidence is often confusing and contradictory, the general conclusions are that this is an area in transition and that considerable opportunities for women now exist in field selling. Traditional biases and misconceptions are disappearing as more and more women prove themselves in sales.

Sales Intelligence and Planning

There is one function that virtually all sales personnel perform: providing sales intelligence to the marketing organization. Chapter 14 noted that field sales reports were part of the feedback generated within the

In personal selling a customer can be given too many choices.

"You have a choice of three courses. You could increase speed somewhat and retain your comprehension, you could increase speed considerably and reduce comprehension, or you could increase speed tremendously and eliminate comprehension completely."

Source: Drawing by Sidney Harris from *American Scientist,* July–August 1977. Reprinted by permission of Sidney Harris.

marketing system. Since the sales force is in continuing contact with the market, it is often the best and most reliable source of the current marketing information upon which management decisions are based.[12] The marketing intelligence provided by field sales personnel varies. Salespeople can supply timely, current assessments of competitive efforts, new product launches, customer reactions, and the like.

Sales personnel must be thoroughly familiar with the policies and internal operations of their company. Nothing is more embarrassing than a customer who knows more than the salesperson about how the company operates. Successful sales representatives are experts in their field. Knowledge of the customer is also extremely important in effective selling. Good salespeople keep accurate written records on their customers and update and review them periodically.

The Account-Impact Profile (AIP) provides an illustration of the type of information that should be collected (see Table 16.1). The profile, developed by Robert J. Zimmer and James W. Taylor, sorts customer data into buying decision information, buyer's job-specific data, current account information, buyer demographics, outside activities, outside interests, and opinions.

The salesperson's knowledge must extend to competitors and their products. Both the strengths and the weaknesses of the competition must be known. Salespeople should also know their own strengths and weaknesses. Periodically, they should make a critical assessment of their attitudes, temperament, and ability. They should objectively evaluate their own sales record and make necessary corrections.

A knowledgeable salesperson must also be able to plan work schedules, selling strategies, and presentations. Good planning allows the representative to budget selling time effectively. Setting

TABLE 16.1
The Account-Impact Profile (AIP)

Account name _____ Date _____

Account address _____

Buying Decision Information

Buyer's influence in purchase decision _____

Key influence in decision _____

Other people in final decision _____

Length of buying decision _____

Meeting day of buying committee _____

Buyer's social style _____

Social style of key influence _____

Types of sales presentations least and most preferred _____

Buyer's Job-Specific Data

Office hours _____

Secretary's name and background _____

Other locations where buyer can be reached _____

Buying days and hours _____

Optimal call time _____

Tenure with present firm _____

Buyer's name _____

Buyer's title and department _____

Office and telephone numbers _____

Tenure in present position _____

Other positions held in this company _____

Past work experiences _____

Career aspirations _____

Current Account Information

Number of years in business _____

Estimated sales volume _____

Sales potential _____

Other suppliers _____

Years of repeat business _____

Average order size and frequency _____

Delivery days and times _____

Preferred transporation mode _____

Preferred payment schedule _____

Buyer Demographics

Home address and telephone number _____

Previous residences _____

Place of birth and date _____

Marital status _____

Names of family members, special dates, and events _____

Names and positions of business associates, friends _____

Education level (school attended) _____

Income and social class _____

Professional associations _____

Outside Activities

Vacation preferences _____

Entertainment _____

Favorite foods and restaurants _____

Club memberships _____

Community activities _____

Religious affiliation _____

Sports (participant or observer) _____

Other _____

Outside Interests

Hobbies _____

Types of media viewed _____

Types of books read _____

Fashion _____

Interior design _____

Other _____

Opinions

Political views _____

Economic views _____

Social and cultural opinions _____

Ecological _____

Competition and industry trends _____

Technological projections _____

Global views _____

Other _____

Source: Reprinted from Robert J. Zimmer and James W. Taylor, "Matching Profiles for Your Industrial Sales Force," *Business,* March-April 1981, pp. 10–11. Reprinted by permission from *Business* Magazine. Copyright © 1981 by the College of Business Administration, Georgia State University, Atlanta.

sales objectives is another critical aspect of sales planning. The objectives should flow logically from the goals of the sales force, which should in turn be a function of the organization's overall objectives.

THE SALES PROCESS

The sales process involves a series of steps. Although the terminology may vary, most authorities agree on the following sequence: (1) prospecting and qualifying, (2) approach, (3) presentation, (4) demonstration, (5) handling objections, (6) closing, and (7) follow-up.

Prospecting and Qualifying

Earl Rorvik drives 100 miles a day cruising the streets of Seattle for Home Oil Co. He looks for "for sale" or "for rent" signs that indicate the possibility of a new customer for home heating oil. Rorvik also spends a day each week visiting real estate firms to check for potential new buyers. Rorvik comments: "If you sit in the office and wait for people to call, you don't get any. You've got to go out and scratch for business."[13]

Rorvik's efforts are known as **prospecting,** *the identifying of potential customers.* Prospecting is difficult work that involves many hours of diligent effort. Prospects may come from many sources: previous customers, friends, other vendors, and suppliers, among others. New sales personnel often find prospecting frustrating, since there is usually no immediate payback. But there are also no future sales unless a salesperson prospects. Many sales management experts consider prospecting the very essence of the sales process. Certainly, it is the source of most customers.

Qualifying—*determining that the prospect is really a potential customer*—is another important sales task. Qualified customers are people with money and the authority to make purchase decisions. A person may wish to embark on an around-the-world trip, but the person's financial position may make the trip unlikely. Similarly, a child may desire the latest toy but may lack the authority or the funds to make such a purchase.

Approach

Once the salesperson has identified a bona fide prospect, he or she should collect all available information about the potential buyer and plan an *approach*—the initial contact of the salesperson with the prospective customer. Approaches can vary. Some will be aggressive and some very low key, but all should be based on comprehensive research. The salesperson should find out as much as possible about the prospect. Retail salespeople often cannot do this, but they can compensate by asking leading questions to get a feel for the prospect's purchase preferences. Industrial marketers have far more data available, and they should make use of it before scheduling the first interview.

Presentation

When the salesperson gives the sales message to a prospective customer, he or she makes a presentation. The **presentation** *describes the product's major features and relates them to the customer's problems or welfare.* The seller's objective is to talk about the product or service in terms meaningful to the buyer—benefits rather than technical specifications. The presentation is thus the stage where the salesperson relates product features to customer needs.

The presentation should be clear, concise, and positive. One type of presentation is the canned approach, developed in the late 1800s by John H. Patterson of National Cash Register Company. The **canned approach** is *a memorized sales talk used to ensure uniform coverage of the points deemed important by management.*[14] While canned presentations are still used in such areas as door-to-door cold canvassing, most professional sales forces have long since abandoned their use. The prevailing attitude is that the salesperson should be allowed to take account of differences among prospects. Proper planning is an important part of tailoring the presentation to the customer.[15]

Demonstration

Demonstration plays a critical role in a sales presentation. A demonstration ride in a new automobile, for example, allows the prospect to become involved in the presentation of the car. Demonstrations awaken the customer interest in a manner that no amount of verbal presentation can achieve. They add to and highlight what the sales representative has already told the prospect. The key to a good demonstration is planning. A unique demonstration is more likely to gain a customer's attention than is the usual kind of sales presentation. A demonstration must also be well planned and executed if a favorable impression is to be made. The importance of planning cannot be overemphasized.

Handling Objections

A vital part of selling involves handling objections. It is reasonable to expect a customer to say "Well, I really should check with my spouse," or "Perhaps I'll stop back next week," or "I like everything except the price." A good salesperson uses each objection as an opportunity to provide additional information to the prospect. In most cases, an objection such as "I don't like the velour seats" is really the prospect's way of asking what other choices or product features are available. Customers' questions generally reveal their interest in the product and allow a seller a chance to provide more information.

Closing

The moment of truth in selling is the **closing,** for this is *when the salesperson asks the prospect to conclude the purchase.* The sales representative should not hesitate during the closing. If he or she has made an effective presentation, the closing should be the natural culmination of the process.

The number of salespeople who have difficulty actually asking for an order is surprising. But to be effective, they must overcome the difficulty. Following are some basic techniques for closing a sale:

1. The *alternative-decision technique* poses choices to the prospect that are all favorable to the salesperson.

2. The *SRO (standing room only) technique* involves telling the prospect that the sales agreement should be concluded immediately because the product may not be available later.

3. *Emotional closes* attempt to get the prospect to buy through appeal to such factors as fear, pride, romance, or social acceptance.

4. *Silence* is another closing technique, since the discontinuance of a sales presentation forces the prospect to take some type of action (either positive or negative).

5. *Extra-inducement closes* are also designed to motivate a favorable buyer response. The extra inducements may include quantity discounts, special servicing arrangements, or a layaway option.[16]

Follow-up

The sales **follow-up** constitutes the *post-sales activities that often determine whether a person will become a repeat customer.* If possible, sales representatives should contact their customers to determine if they are satisfied with the purchase. This step allows the salesperson to reinforce the purchaser's original decision to buy. It also gives the seller an opportunity to deal with any sources of discontent about the purchase, to secure important market information, and to make additional sales. Major appliance dealers sometimes keep elaborate records on their customers so they can promote new products to people who have already shown a willingness to buy from them.

Effective follow-up is a logical part of the selling sequence. As part of it, the salesperson should evaluate every call made to purchasers. Assessing sales successes and failures can help improve sales effectiveness.

RETAIL SELLING

For the most part, the public is more aware of retail selling than of any other form of personal selling. In fact, many writers have argued that people's basic attitudes toward the sales function are determined by their impression of retail sales personnel.[17]

Retail selling has some distinctive features that require its consideration separately from other forms. The most significant difference between it and its counterparts is that the customer comes to the retail salesperson. This requires that retailers effectively combine selling with a good advertising and sales promotion program—one that will draw customers into the store. Another difference is that while, in one sense, store employees are sales personnel, they are also retailers in the broader dimension. Selling is not their only responsibility.

Retail sales personnel should be well versed in store policy and procedures. Credit, discounts, special sales, delivery, layaway, and return policies are examples of the type of information the salesperson should know. Uninformed salespeople are a major complaint of today's customer.

Two selling techniques particularly applicable to retailing are selling up and suggestion selling. **Selling up** is *the technique of convincing the customer to buy a higher-priced item than he or she originally intended to buy.* An automobile salesperson, for example, may convince a customer to buy a more expensive car than the person originally wanted. The practice of selling up should only be used when it meets the customer's real needs. Many times, the salesperson can demonstrate that the more expensive item will better fit the customer's needs. If the salesperson sells the customer something that he or she really does not need, the potential for repeat sales to that customer is substantially diminished.

Suggestion selling *seeks to broaden the customer's original purchase with related items, special promotions, and holiday or seasonal merchandise.* Here, too, sales efforts should be based on the idea of helping the customer recognize his or her needs rather than on selling the person unwanted merchandise. Suggestion selling is one of the best methods of increasing retail sales and should be practiced by all sales personnel.

SALES MANAGEMENT

Contemporary selling requires **sales management**—*the management activities of securing, maintaining, motivating, supervising, evaluating, and controlling an effective sales force.* Figure 16.1 shows the sales organization of the Textron Chemical Corporation. Sales management can be divided into several administrative levels, often on a geographical basis. Textron field sales personnel report to a district sales manager, who reports to a regional sales manager, who reports to a division sales manager, who reports to a national sales manager. The national sales manager then reports to the vice-president of marketing.

**FIGURE 16.1
The Sales
Organization of
Textron Chemical
Corporation**

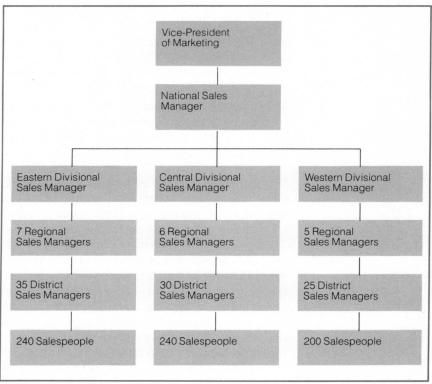

Source: Used with permission of Textron Chemical Corporation, Houston, Texas. Adapted from Charles Futrell, *Sales Management: Behavior, Practice, and Cases* (Hinsdale: Ill.: The Dryden Press, 1981), p. 78.

Sales management is the administrative channel for sales personnel; it links the individual salespersons to general management. The sales manager performs six basic managerial functions: (1) recruitment and selection, (2) training, (3) organization, (4) motivation, (5) compensation, and (6) evaluation and control.

Recruitment and Selection

The initial step in building an effective sales force involves recruiting and selecting good personnel.[18] New salespeople may come from community colleges, trade and business schools, colleges and universities, and other firms.

A successful career in sales offers several opportunities that people generally look for when deciding on a profession:

1. *Opportunity for advancement.* Successful sales representatives advance rapidly in most companies. Advancement can come either within the sales area or in some other functional area of the firm.

2. *High earnings.* The earnings of successful salespeople compare favorably to the earnings of successful people in other professions. In fact, over the long run, sales earnings usually exceed those in most other professional occupations.

3. *Security.* Contrary to what many college students believe, selling provides a high degree of job security. There is a continuing need for good sales personnel, and thousands of openings exist annually for those who want to enter the field.

4. *Independence and variety.* Salespersons typically operate as "independent" businesspeople or as managers of sales territories. Their work is varied and provides an opportunity for involvement in numerous business functions.

The careful selection of salespeople is important for two reasons. First, it involves substantial amounts of money and management time. Second, selection mistakes will be detrimental to customer relations and sales force performance as well as costly to correct.

The selection process for sales personnel is outlined in Figure 16.2. An application screening is followed by an initial interview. If there is sufficient interest, in-depth interviewing is conducted. Next, the company may use testing in their procedure. This step could include aptitude, intelligence, interest, knowledge, or personality tests. References are then checked to guarantee that job candidates have represented themselves correctly. A physical examination is usually included before a final hiring decision is made.[19]

Training

To shape new sales recruits into an efficient sales force, management must conduct an effective training program. The principal methods

FIGURE 16.2
Major Steps in Sales
Personnel Selection
Process

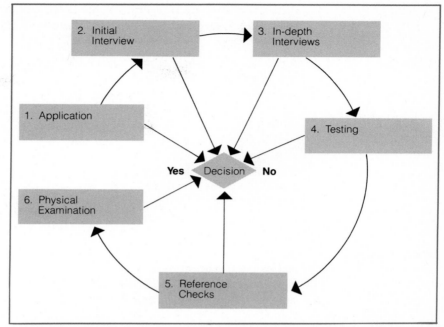

Source: Adapted from Charles Futrell, *Sales Management: Behavior, Practice, and Cases* (Hinsdale, Ill.: The Dryden Press, 1981), p. 220. Copyright © 1981 by The Dryden Press, a division of Holt, Rinehart and Winston. Reprinted by permission of Holt, Rinehart and Winston, CBS College Publishing.

used in such programs are lectures, role playing, on-the-job training, experiential exercises, and audio-visual techniques.

Sales training is also important for veteran salespeople. Most of this type of training is done in an informal manner by sales managers. A standard format is for the sales manager to travel with a field sales representative periodically, then critique the person's work afterwards. Sales meetings are also an important part of training for experienced personnel.

Organization

Sales managers are responsible for the organization of the field sales force. General organizational alignments, which are usually made by top management, can be based on geography, products, customers, or some combination of these factors. A geographical organization might be set up like the one in Figure 16.1. A product sales organization would have specialized sales forces for each major category of products offered by the firm. A customer organization would use the different sales forces for each major type of customer served. For instance, a plastics manufacturer selling to the automobile, small appliance, and defense industries might decide that each type of customer requires a separate sales force.

The individual sales manager then has the task of organizing the sales territories within his or her area of responsibility. Generally, the territory allocation decision should be based on company objectives, personnel qualifications, and equality of workloads.[20]

Motivation

A constant source of debate among sales managers is how to motivate the sales force.[21] Sales personnel are generally self-motivated persons who require only moderate supervision. But sales management must be willing to provide helpful advice, encouragement, and discipline when necessary.

A key to good supervision seems to be open communication with the sales force. This, of course, involves effective listening on the part of the sales manager. Sales personnel who clearly understand messages from management and who have an opportunity to express their concerns and opinions to their managers are usually easy to supervise and motivate.[22]

Compensation

Since monetary rewards are an important factor in motivating subordinates, compensation of sales personnel is a critical matter to managers.[23] Basically, sales compensation can be determined on either a straight salary plan, a commission plan, or some combination of the two.[24]

Commissions are *payments directly tied to the sales or profits achieved by a salesperson.* For example, a salesperson might receive a 5 percent commission on all sales up to a specified quota, then 7 percent on sales beyond the quota. Commission plans offer the following advantages:

1. The pay relates directly to performance and results achieved.
2. The system is easy to understand and compute.
3. Salespeople have the greatest possible incentive.
4. Unit sales costs are proportional to net sales.
5. The company's selling investment is reduced.

Disadvantages include the following:

1. Emphasis is more likely to be on volume than on profits.
2. Little or no loyalty to the company is generated.
3. Wide variations in income of sales personnel may occur.
4. Salespeople are encouraged to neglect nonselling duties.
5. Some salespeople may be tempted to "skim" their territories.
6. The service aspect of selling may be slighted.
7. Problems may arise in cutting territories or shifting people or accounts.
8. Pay is often excessive in periods of expansion and very low in recession periods.

9. Salespersons may sell themselves rather than the company and stress short-term rather than long-term relationships.

10. Highly paid salespeople may be reluctant to move into supervisory or managerial positions.

11. Excessive turnover of sales personnel may occur when business declines.

Salaries are *fixed payments made on a periodic basis to employees, including some sales personnel.* A firm that has decided to use salaries rather than commissions might pay a salesperson a set amount every other week, for example. Benefits of using salaries exist for both management and sales personnel. The advantages include these:

1. A regular income is assured.

2. A high degree of loyalty is developed.

3. Managers may easily switch territories, change quotas, or reassign sales personnel.

4. Nonselling activities are more likely to be performed.

5. Administration is facilitated.

6. Relatively fixed sales costs are provided.

Disadvantages of salaries also exist:

1. Salaries fail to produce a balanced sales mix if salespeople concentrate on the products with greatest customer appeal.

2. Little, if any, financial incentive for sales personnel is provided.

3. Salaries offer few reasons for putting forth extra effort.

4. The least productive salespeople are protected.

5. Salaries tend to increase direct selling costs over other types of plans.

6. They create the possibility of salary compression where new trainees earn almost as much as experienced sales personnel.

The third alternative, *combination plans,* uses a base salary along with a commission incentive. For instance, a salesperson might receive $800 per month plus a 2 percent commission on all sales. The benefits associated with a combination plan are as follows:

1. It offers participants the advantages of both salary and commission.

2. It provides a greater range of earnings possibilities than does straight salary.

3. It gives salespeople greater security because of the steady base income.

4. It makes possible a favorable ratio of selling expense to sales.

5. It compensates sales personnel for all activities.

6. It allows a greater latitude of motivation possibilities so that goals and objectives can be achieved on schedule.

Disadvantages of the combination plan are these:

1. It is often complex and difficult to understand.

2. When the salary is low and the bonus or commission high, the bonus may be too great a percentage of earnings; then, when sales fall, the salary may be too low to retain the sales personnel.

3. It is sometimes costly to administer.

4. It can result in a "windfall" of new accounts and runaway earnings unless there is a decreasing commission rate for increasing sales.

5. It has a tendency to offer too many objectives at one time so that important ones can be neglected, forgotten, or overlooked.

Evaluation and Control

Perhaps the most difficult of a sales manager's tasks are evaluation and control.[25] The basic problem is in finding an instrument to measure sales performance. Sales volume, profitability, and investment return are standard means of evaluating sales effectiveness. They typically involve the use of a **quota**—*a specified sales or profit target a salesperson is expected to achieve.* A particular sales representative might be expected to sell $300,000 in Territory 414 during a given year, for example. In many cases, the quota is tied to the compensation system. One survey of sales managers sought to rank the criteria these executives used to measure sales performance (see Table 16.2). While sales volume ranked high, greater weight was given to qualitative factors like attitude, product knowledge, selling skills, and initiative and aggressiveness. The research suggests that the personal sales function remains largely dependent upon the managerial abilities of these marketing executives, and their skill in selecting effective field personnel.

SUMMARY

Personal selling is the seller's promotional presentation conducted on a person-to-person basis with the buyer. It is part of all business enterprises. The earliest sellers were known as peddlers, and some of the negative stereotyping associated with them remains today.

Three basic selling tasks exist: order processing, creative selling, and missionary selling. The field tends to attract highly motivated people, including many women in recent years. In addition to selling duties, sales personnel are often involved in the areas of sales intelligence and planning.

**TABLE 16.2
Performance Criteria
Used by Sales
Management**

Criteria	Percentage*
Sales	
Sales volume in dollars	81
Sales volume to previous year's sales	76
Sales volume by product or product line	69
Sales volume in units	59
Amount of new account sales	59
Sales volume to dollar quota	53
Sales volume by customer	47
Sales volume to market potential	32
Sales volume to physical unit quota	27
Sales volume per order	14
Sales volume by outlet type	8
Sales volume per call	8
Percentage of sales made by telephone or mail	8
Accounts	
Number of new accounts	71
Number of accounts lost	44
Number of accounts on which payment is overdue	21
Number of accounts buying the full line	18
Profit	
Net profit	28
Net profit per sales	16
Return on investment	16
Net profit contribution	15
Gross margin	15
Gross margin per sales	14
Orders	
Order-call ratio	26
New orders per repeat orders	18
Number of cancelled orders per orders booked	14
Calls	
Calls per period	58
Number of calls per number of customers (by product class)	18

Criteria	Percentage*
Selling Expense	
Selling expense to sales	38
Selling expense to quota	23
Average cost per call	11
Market Share	
Market share per quota	16
Miscellaneous Quantitative Factors	
Number of required reports turned in	46
Number of customer complaints	34
Number of letters/telephone calls to prospects	27
Number of service calls made	27
Number of demonstrations conducted	25
Training meetings conducted	24
Number of dealer meetings held	15
Advertising displays set up	13
Qualitative Factors	
Attitude	92
Product knowledge	91
Selling skills	87
Initiative and aggressiveness	83
Appearance and manner	81
Communication skills	81
Planning ability	80
Time management	74
Knowledge of competition	73
Judgment	71
Knowledge of company policies	64
Creativity	62
Report preparation and submission	62
Customer goodwill generated	52
Degree of respect from trade and competition	34
Good citizenship	25

*Percentage represents percent of companies reporting use of a particular criterion.
Source: Donald W. Jackson, "Do Sales Managers Really Manage by Objective?" Richard P. Bagozzi, Kenneth L. Bernhardt, Paul S. Busch, David W. Cravens, Joseph F. Hair, Jr., and Carol A. Scott, eds., *Marketing in the 1980's: Changes and Challenges* (Chicago: American Marketing Association, 1980), p. 250. Reprinted by permission of the American Marketing Association.

The basic steps involved in selling are (1) prospecting and qualifying, (2) approach, (3) presentation, (4) demonstration, (5) handling objections, (6) closing, and (7) follow-up.

Retail selling is different from other kinds of selling, primarily in that the customer comes to the salesperson. Also, salespeople in stores are concerned with responsibilities other than selling. Two selling techniques particularly applicable to retailing are selling up and suggestion selling.

Sales management involves six basic functions: (1) recruitment and selection, (2) training, (3) organization, (4) motivation, (5) compensation, and (6) evaluation and control. Sales compensation can be on a straight salary plan, a commission plan, or a combination of the two. Each type of compensation has numerous advantages and disadvantages.

QUESTIONS FOR DISCUSSION

1. Explain the following terms:

   personal selling   follow-up
   missionary sales   selling up
   prospecting   suggestion selling
   qualifying   sales management
   presentation   commissions
   canned approach   salaries
   closing   quota

2. Trace the evolution of personal selling.

3. Cite examples of salespeople who are engaged primarily in performing the following sales tasks:
   a. order processing
   b. creative selling
   c. missionary selling

4. What sales tasks are involved in selling the following products:
   a. Burroughs computer equipment
   b. a fast-food franchise
   c. the United Fund to a local union meeting
   d. used cars
   e. cleaning supplies for plant maintenance

5. What makes a good salesperson?

6. Comment on the following statement: Salespeople play a critical role in providing management with marketing information.

7. Discuss the importance of planning to a salesperson.

8. Outline the seven basic steps involved in effective selling.

9. Develop a sales presentation for the following items:
   a. an expensive line of women's apparel
   b. a set of reference books
   c. a new Ford
   d. a group life insurance policy to the personnel director of a firm

10. What role do flight crews play in an airline's promotional effort?

11. How is retail selling different from field selling?

12. How would you describe the job of each of the following:
    a. a real estate agent
    b. a salesperson in a retail furniture store

13. Outline the basic functions of a sales manager.

14. Discuss the benefits of a sales career.

15. As marketing vice-president of a large paper company, you are asked to talk to a group of college students about selling as a career. What will you say?

16. What are the advantages and disadvantages of commission, salary, and combination compensation plans?

17. Who was the best salesperson you ever encountered? What made this person stand out?

18. Discuss how a sales representative could use the Account-Impact Profile shown in Table 16.1.

19. Suppose that you are the sales manager for an office supply firm employ-

ing six salespeople who call on local firms. What type of compensation system will you employ?

20. How will you evaluate the salespeople described in Question 19?

NOTES

1. "Sweda: Aggressive Marketing Produces a Spirited Turnaround," *Business Week,* March 31, 1980, pp. 101–2.

2. This section is based on David L. Kurtz, "The Historical Development of Selling," *Business and Economic Dimensions,* August 1970, pp. 12–18. A good historical account of personal selling is contained in Henry W. Nash, "Origin and Development of Personal Selling," *Mississippi Business Review,* January 1977, pp. 6–8.

3. Conway Rucks, "It's Time for Salespeople's Lib," *Sales & Marketing Management,* March 1978, pp. 51–52, 54, 58.

4. The current status of sales ethics is examined in Alan J. Dubinsky, Eric N. Berkowitz, and William Rudelius, "Ethical Problems of Field Sales Personnel," *MSU Business Topics,* Summer 1980, pp. 11–16. The evolution of selling strategy is discussed in Richard Casavant, "Personal Sales Strategy—Past, Present, and Future," *Arkansas Business and Economic Review,* Spring 1979, pp. 1–6.

5. An interesting discussion of selling is presented in Benson R. Shapiro and Ronald S. Posner, "Making the Major Sale," *Harvard Business Review,* March–April 1976, pp. 68–78.

6. Reported in "Fear Sellers," *Money,* July 1979, p. 4.

7. Detailers are discussed in Louis J. Haugh, "Detailmen—Salesmen Who Don't Sell," *Advertising Age,* February 13, 1978, pp. 67–68, 70.

8. Quoted in James Kenyon, "Have Houses, Will Travel: Salesman's Hard-Driven Man," *Detroit News,* August 21, 1978.

9. Sales attributes are discussed in Panos Apostolidis, "Looking at the Age of Salespersons," *Journal of the Academy of Marketing Science,* Fall 1980, pp. 322–31; R. Kenneth Teas, "An Empirical Test of Models of Salespersons' Job Expectancy and Instrumentality Perceptions," *Journal of Marketing Research,* May 1981, pp. 204–26; and Herbert M. Greenberg and Jeanne Greenberg, "Job Marketing for Better Sales Performance," *Harvard Business Review,* September–October 1980, pp. 128–33.

10. Tish Myers, "Women Earn Their Place in Showroom," *Detroit News,* May 2, 1979.

11. Women in selling is the topic of such recent papers as Robert N. Carter, "Women Comprise Unlimited Sales Talent Pool but Need Special Leadership," Venkatakrishna V. Bellur, ed.; Thomas R. Baird, Paul T. Hertz, Roger L. Jenkins, Jay D. Lindquist, and Stephen W. Miller, co-editors. *Developments in Marketing Science,* vol. IV (Marquette, Mich.: Academy of Marketing Science, 1981), pp. 139–42; and Alan J. Dubinsky and Bruce Mattson, "Difference between Male and Female Retail Salespeople's Job Satisfaction, Performance, Organizational Commitment, Role Conflict, and Role Ambiguity," Richard P. Bagozzi, Kenneth L. Bernhardt, Paul S. Busch, David W. Cravens, Joseph F. Hair, Jr., and Carol A. Scott, eds., *Marketing in the 1980's: Changes and Challenges* (Chicago: American Marketing Association, 1980), pp. 229–33. Two excellent articles on women in selling appeared in the January 1978 issue of the *Journal of Marketing:* Leslie Kanuk, "Women in Industrial Selling," pp. 87–91; and John E. Swan, Charles M. Futrell, and John T. Todd, "Same Job, Different Views: Women and Men in Industrial Sales," pp. 92–98.

12. Sales force feedback and research is discussed in Joel Saegert and Robert J. Hoover, "Sales Manager and Sales Force Feedback: Information Left in the Pipelines," *Journal of the Academy of Marketing Science,* Winter 1980, pp. 33–39; James H. Fouss and Elaine Solomon, "Salespeople as Researchers: Help or Hazard?" *Journal of Marketing,* Summer 1980, pp. 36–39; and Jay E. Klompmaker, "Incorporating Information from Salespeople into the Marketing Planning Process," *Journal of Personal Selling and Sales Management,* Fall/Winter 1980/81, pp. 76–82.

13. "Oil Salesman Keeps His Eye on 'For Rent' Signs for Customers," *Seattle Times,* November 6, 1980.

14. This approach is discussed in Marvin A. Jolson, "The Underestimated Potential of the Canned Sales Presentation," *Journal of Marketing,* January 1975, pp. 75–78.

15. Recent articles of interest include Barton A. Weitz, "Effectiveness in Sales Interactions: A Contingency Framework," *Journal of Marketing,* Winter 1981, pp. 85–103; William A. Staples and

John I. Coppett, "A Multiattribute Approach to Personal Selling," John D. Summey and Ronald D. Taylor, eds., *Evolving Marketing Thought for 1980* (Carbondale, Ill.: Southern Marketing Association, 1980), pp. 21–22.

16. These and other closing techniques are outlined in David L. Kurtz, H. Robert Dodge, and Jay E. Klompmaker, *Professional Selling,* 3rd ed. (Dallas: Business Publications, 1982), pp. 221–28.

17. An interesting discussion is contained in Gilbert A. Churchill, Jr., Robert H. Collins, and William A. Strang, "Should Retail Salespersons Be Similar to Their Customers?" *Journal of Retailing,* Fall 1975, pp. 29–42, 79.

18. The issue of sales force size is addressed in Leonard M. Lodish, "A User-oriented Model for Sales Force Size, Product and Market Allocation Decisions," *Journal of Marketing,* Summer 1980, pp. 70–78. Salesperson selection is discussed in Fred J. Kurtz, W. Austin Spivey, and George D. Williams, "Validity and the Selection of Sales Personnel," *Santa Clara Business Review,* Summer 1978, pp. 13–23.

19. The sales personnel selection process is discussed in Charles Futrell, *Sales Management: Behavior, Practice, and Cases* (Hinsdale, Ill.: The Dryden Press, 1981), pp. 219–35.

20. Territory decisions are discussed in Michael S. Heschel, "Effective Sales Territory Development," *Journal of Marketing,* April 1977, pp. 39–43.

21. Sales force motivation is explored in Alan J. Dubinsky and Richard J. Hansen, "Managing Sales Force Composition," *MSU Business Topics,* Spring 1981, pp. 14–20; Pradeep K. Tyagi, "An Empirical Examination of the Influence of Job Characteristics on Salesperson Motivation," Bellur et al. (1981), pp. 188–92; Stephen X. Doyle and Benson R. Shapiro, "What Counts Most in Motivating Your Sales Force?" *Harvard Business Review,* May–June 1980, pp. 133–40; and Richard P. Bagozzi, "Performance and Satisfaction in an Industrial Sales Force: An Examination of Their Antecedents and Simultaneity," *Journal of Marketing,* Spring 1980, pp. 65–77. An excellent article related to sales force supervision is Paul Busch, "The Sales Managers' Bases of Social Power and Influence upon the Sales Force," *Journal of Marketing,* Summer 1980, pp. 91–101.

22. The need for positive reinforcement is pointed out in Rom J. Markin and Charles M. Lillis, "Sales Managers Get What They Expect," *Business Horizons,* June 1975, pp. 51–58.

23. Related articles include Rene Y. Darmon, "Determinants of Salesmen's Satisfaction with Their Compensation Scheme," Bagozzi et al. (1980), pp. 238–43; James M. Comer, Robert J. Boewadt, and Ken W. McCleary, "A Simulation Approach to the Design of Compensation Programs for Sales Personnel," Summey and Taylor, *Evolving Marketing Thought for 1980,* pp. 33–36; and Gilbert A. Churchill, Jr., Neil M. Ford, and Orville C. Walker, Jr., "Personal Characteristics of Salespeople and the Attractiveness of Alternative Rewards," *Journal of Business Research* 7, (1979), pp. 25–50.

24. The advantages and disadvantages of the commission, salary, and combination plans are adapted by permission from John P. Steinbrink, "How to Pay Your Sales Force," *Harvard Business Review,* July–August 1978, p. 112. Copyright © 1978 by the President and Fellows of Harvard College; all rights reserved.

25. The need for careful evaluation is suggested in William P. Hall, "Improving Sales Force Productivity," *Business Horizons,* August 1975, pp. 32–42. See also Donald W. Jackson, Jr., and Ramon J. Aldag, "Managing the Sales Force by Objectives," *MSU Business Topics,* Spring 1974, pp. 53–59; and Porter Henry, "Manage Your Sales Force as a System," *Harvard Business Review,* March–April 1975, pp. 85–95.

PART   SEVEN

PRICING STRATEGY

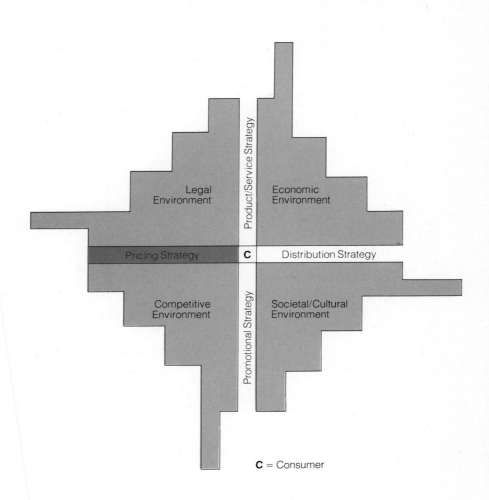

Legal Environment

Product/Service Strategy

Economic Environment

Pricing Strategy   **C**   Distribution Strategy

Competitive Environment

Promotional Strategy

Societal/Cultural Environment

C = Consumer

CHAPTER 17

INTRODUCTION TO PRICING

LEARNING GOALS

1. To explain the concept of price and its importance to society

2. To identify the major pricing objectives used by firms

3. To distinguish between price determination in theory and in practice

4. To explain the concept of breakeven analysis

5. To explain Oxenfeldt's multistage approach to pricing

6. To discuss the role of government in pricing decisions

Pricing is an important part of a firm's overall marketing strategy. Consider the case of S. T. Dupont Company, a French subsidiary of Gillette. Dupont makes items like fountain pens and lighters. Its pens are crafted from solid brass. The pens are treated with five layers of lacquer made from the sap of the rhus tree, found in China. The sap is shipped to France in special slosh-proof containers. Dupont spends three months producing each pen, and still rejects twenty percent in a rigid quality-control procedure. Similar manufacturing techniques are used in producing the firm's lighters.

Dupont's fountain pens are priced in the $380 to $410 range, while its lighters sell for $150 to $400. Clearly, the firm uses the pricing mechanism as part of its overall strategy to reach its wealthy clientele. The company's president expressed it well when he said that Dupont makes such items "not to fulfill needs, which naturally are limited; but desires, which are not."[1]

Dupont's pricing of its status-oriented products reflects the critical role that this variable plays in a marketing strategy. Pricing is a complicated aspect of the marketing manager's job.

THE CONCEPT OF PRICE

It is often difficult to determine the exact meaning of price and its role in society. Price is the exchange value of a good or service, and the value of an item is what it can be exchanged for in the marketplace. In earlier times, the price of a pair of sandals might have been five yards of cloth, a piece of pottery, or two chickens. **Price** can be defined as *a measure of what one must exchange in order to obtain a particular good or service.* When the barter process was abandoned in favor of a monetary system, price became the amount of money required to purchase an item.

All products have some degree of utility, or want-satisfying power. An individual might be willing to exchange the utility derived from a motorcycle for that of a vacation. Prices are a mechanism that allows the consumer to make such a decision. In contemporary society, of course, prices are translated into monetary terms. Consumers evaluate the utility derived from a range of possible purchases and then allocate their exchange power (in monetary terms) so as to maximize satisfaction.

IMPORTANCE OF THE PRICE VARIABLE

Ancient philosophers recognized the importance of price to the functioning of the economic system. Some of their early written accounts refer to attempts to develop a fair, or just, price. Their limited understanding of time, place, and possession utilities, however, thwarted such efforts.

Today, price still serves as a means of regulating economic activity. The implementation of any or all of the four factors of production (natural resources, labor, capital, and entrepreneurship) depends

**TABLE 17.1
The Importance of
the Pricing Variable:
A Comparison of the
Udell and Boone and
Kurtz Studies**

Rank	Udell Study	Boone and Kurtz Study
1	Product	Pricing
2	Promotion	Product
3	Pricing	Distribution
4	Distribution	Promotion

Sources: Adapted from Jon G. Udell, "How Important Is Pricing in Competitive Strategy?" *Journal of Marketing,* January 1964, pp. 44–48. Used by permission of the American Marketing Association; and *Pricing Objectives and Practices in American Industry: A Research Report* by Louis E. Boone and David L. Kurtz, 1979; all rights reserved.

on the prices received by each. For an individual firm, prices and the corresponding quantity to be sold represent the revenue to be received. Prices therefore influence a company's profit as well as its use of the factors of production.

A widely cited 1964 study by Jon G. Udell found that executives ranked pricing sixth in a long list of factors leading to marketing success.[2] When Udell's factors are reorganized into the four major marketing mix variables, price ranks third—ahead only of distribution.

But times have changed. A recent study of marketing executives by Boone and Kurtz found that pricing ranked as the single most important marketing mix variable.[3] Product planning and management was a close second, while distribution strategy and promotional decisions ranked third and fourth, respectively. Table 17.1 compares Udell's 1964 rankings to the findings of the later study.

The question of what is the correct price to charge still remains a perplexing problem in modern marketing management. Some say it is whatever the consumer will pay. Others believe it should be low enough to permit everyone the opportunity to buy the product. The determination of market prices within the context of the contemporary business environment is the subject of this chapter. The understanding of this complex topic will be enhanced by reviewing pricing legislation in Chapter 2.

PRICING OBJECTIVES

Pricing objectives are a crucial part of the means-end chain from overall company objectives to specific pricing policies and procedures (see Figure 17.1). The goals of the firm and the marketing organization provide the basis for the development of pricing objectives, which must be clearly established before pricing policies and procedures are implemented.

A firm might have as its primary objective the goal of becoming the dominant factor in the domestic market. Its marketing objective might then be to achieve maximum sales penetration in all sales regions. The related pricing goal would be sales maximization. This means-end chain might lead to the adoption of a low-price policy implemented by the highest cash and trade discounts in the industry.

**FIGURE 17.1
The Role of Pricing
Objectives in
Contemporary
Marketing**

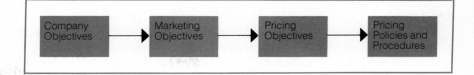

Pricing objectives can be classified into three major groups: (1) profitability objectives; (2) volume objectives; and (3) social and ethical considerations, status quo objectives, and prestige goals. Profitability objectives include profit maximization and target return goals. Volume objectives can be categorized as either sales maximization or market share goals.

As one would expect, pricing objectives vary from firm to firm. Xerox wants its earnings to grow 15 percent annually. Eaton Corporation aspires to rank either first or second in market share in each market within which it operates. Burroughs has targeted a 15 percent increase in revenue each year.[4]

A recent study of U.S. businesses asked marketers to identify both the primary and secondary pricing objectives of their companies. Meeting competitive prices was most often mentioned as a primary or secondary pricing objective. It was followed closely by two profitability-oriented objectives: a specified rate of return on investment and specified total profit levels. These two objectives ranked first and second, respectively, as primary pricing objectives.[5] The findings are shown in Table 17.2.

**TABLE 17.2
Primary and
Secondary Pricing
Objectives of Firms**

Pricing Objective	Percentage of Respondents Ranking the Item		
	As Primary Objective	As Secondary Objective	As Either Primary or Secondary Objective
Meeting of competitive price level	38.3	43.0	81.3
Specified rate of return on investment	60.9	17.2	78.1
Specified total profit level	60.2	17.2	77.4
Increased market share	31.3	42.2	73.5
Increased total profits above previous levels	34.4	37.5	71.9
Specified rate of return on sales	47.7	23.4	71.1
Retaining of existing market share	31.3	35.9	67.2
Serving of selected market segments	26.6	39.1	65.7
Creation of a readily identifiable image for the firm and/or its products	21.9	41.4	63.3
Specified market share	15.6	40.6	56.2
Other	5.5	—	5.5

Profitability Objectives

The traditional pricing objective in classical economic theory has been that of maximizing profits. The concept of microeconomics is based on certain assumptions—that buyers and sellers are rational and that rational behavior is an effort to maximize gains and minimize losses. In terms of actual business practice, this means that profit maximization is assumed to be the basic objective of individual firms.

Profits are a function of revenue and expenses:

Profits = revenues − expenses

Revenue is determined by the selling price and quantity sold:

Total revenue = price × quantity sold

Price should therefore be increased to the point where it causes a disproportionate decrease in the number of units sold. A 5 percent price increase that results in only a 3 percent cut in volume adds to the firm's revenues. However, a 5 percent hike that causes a 6 percent sales decline reduces revenues. This approach is known as *marginal analysis.*

Economists identify **profit maximization** as *the point at which the addition to total revenue is just balanced by the increase in total cost.* The basic problem is how to achieve this delicate balance between marginal revenue and marginal cost. Relatively few firms actually achieve the objective of profit maximization. A significantly larger number prefer to direct their efforts toward goals that are more reasonably implemented and measured.

Consequently, target return objectives have become common in industry, particularly among the larger firms, where public pressure typically prohibits consideration of the profit maximization objective.[6] Automobile companies are examples.[7] A **target return objective** is *either a short-run or long-run goal usually stated as a percentage of sales or investment.* A company may, for instance, seek a 15 percent annual rate of return on investment or an 8 percent rate of return on sales. A specified rate of return on investment was the most commonly reported primary pricing objective in Table 17.2. Goals of this nature are designed to generate profits judged to be fair by management, stockholders, and the general public. These goals also serve as useful guidelines in evaluating corporate activity. As one writer has aptly expressed it: "For management consciously accepting less than maximum profits, the target rate can provide a measure of the amount of restraint. For firms making very low profits, the target rate can serve as a standard for judging improvement."[8]

Volume Objectives

Some writers argue that a better explanation of actual pricing behavior is William J. Baumol's belief that firms attempt to maximize sales within a given profit constraint.[9] In **sales maximization,** firms set *a minimum at what they consider the lowest acceptable profit level and then seek*

TABLE 17.3
Pricing Strategy for Gaining Market Share

When to Use	How to Apply in Marketplace	Cost Implications
1. To gain a share in a product line where there is room for growth	1. Set the general market price level below average.	1. Will lower gross margin by decreasing spread between cost and price for a period of time
2. To gain a share in a new product, preferably in a growth market	2. Lower prices for specific target customers where reduced prices will capture high volume accounts and where competition is vulnerable on a price basis.	2. Will lower cost as cumulative volume increases and costs move down the experience curve
	3. Lower prices enough to keep the business.	
	4. Lower prices against specific competitors who will not or cannot react effectively.	

Source: Adapted from C. David Fogg, "Planning Gains in Market Share," *Journal of Marketing,* July 1974, pp. 30–38. Used by permission of the American Marketing Association.

to maximize sales (subject to this profit constraint) in the belief that the increased sales are more important than immediate high profits to the long-run competitive picture. The companies continue to expand sales as long as their total profits do not drop below the minimum return acceptable to management.

Another pricing objective is based on the firm's **market share objective**—*the goal set for control of a portion of the market for the firm's product.* The company's specific goal can be to maintain or increase its share of a particular market, say, from 10 percent to 20 percent.[10]

Table 17.3 shows when it is best to use a pricing strategy designed to gain market share, how it should be applied in the marketplace, and what its cost implications are. Gaining market share is a common pricing objective in U.S. business. A firm's marketing plans must be adapted to its relative position within a given market.

Some firms with high market shares may even prefer to reduce their share at times because of the possibility of government action in the area of monopoly control. Courts have often used market share figures in evaluating cases involving alleged monopolistic practices.

The PIMS Study

Market share objectives can be critical to the achievement of other objectives. High sales, for example, may mean more profit. The extensive Profit Impact of Market Strategies (PIMS) project conducted by the Marketing Science Institute found a link between market share and profitability.[11] Pretax profits as a percentage of sales stood at 3.4 percent for firms with 10 to 20 percent market shares, but they climbed steadily to 13.2 percent for firms with market shares above 40 percent.

Achievement of market share objectives places the firm in a much stronger competitive position within the industry. The American automobile industry provides a dramatic illustration of the validity of the PIMS study conclusions. Consider the case of Chrysler Corporation. In the year prior to Chrysler's much-publicized appeal for a government-backed loan package, the corporation's 12.3 percent market share yielded a deficit. By contrast, Ford earned 3.7 percent on a 27.9 percent market share, and General Motors earned 5.6 percent with its dominant 56.6 percent market share. In 1951, Chrysler held a 23.1 percent market share, ranking ahead of Ford.[12]

Other Objectives

Some pricing objectives are not related to either profitability or sales volume, but they are extremely important in the pricing behavior of many firms. These objectives include social and ethical considerations, status quo objectives, and prestige goals.

Social and ethical considerations are *the determining factors in certain pricing situations.* For years, some medical doctors used a sliding scale based on relative income to set patient fees. Essentially, these doctors used an ethical evaluation of ability to pay as an input into their pricing formula.

But a recent survey of physicians indicated that they were not the only sellers who priced on an ability-to-pay basis. Two-thirds of the physicians questioned by *Medical Economics* believed they had paid higher prices for such services as home and auto repairs because of their occupation! And only about 20 percent had complained about the alleged overcharging.[13] Social and ethical considerations are playing a larger role in the pricing policies of all marketers.

Status quo objectives—*objectives based on the maintenance of stable prices*—are the crux of the pricing philosophy for many enterprises. They usually stem from a desire to minimize competitive pricing in order to be able to concentrate efforts in other areas of marketing, such as product improvement or promotion. For a long time, automobile producers deemphasized price competition in their advertisements in favor of developing features that differentiated their products from competitors'. Even today, status quo objectives remain a significant factor in pricing.

Prestige goals—*goals based on setting relatively high prices so as to maintain a quality image*—are another type of objective unrelated to either profitability or sales volume. While some marketers set relatively high prices so as to maintain a prestige image with their customers, others prefer to have a "low-price" image among customers. An example of this is Anders Clothing Clearance Centers.

ANDERS CLOTHING CLEARANCE CENTERS

Headquartered in York, Pennsylvania, Anders Clothing Clearance Centers provide an example of a firm that espouses volume-oriented pricing objectives. Anders is a discounter of men's clothing. Its 19 stores nationwide sell about $20 million of merchandise annually. Anders offers only first-line, in-fashion merchandise that it obtains through production overruns, credit returns, and cancelled orders. Volume purchases for cash and modest overhead allow Anders to sell clothing for as low as 40 percent of regular retail prices. The company seeks to achieve substantial volume per outlet by offering low prices, such as $400 designer suits priced at $220.

Source: Boyd Burchard, "Clothier Timed for the Economy," *Seattle Times,* June 12, 1981. Reprinted with permission.

HOW ARE PRICES DETERMINED?

There are two ways to look at the determination of price: (1) theoretical concepts of supply and demand and (2) the cost-oriented approach that characterizes current business practice. During the first part of this century, most considerations of price determination emphasized the classical concepts of supply and demand. Since World War II, the emphasis has shifted to a cost-oriented approach. Hindsight allows us to see that both concepts have certain flaws.

Another aspect of price determination is often overlooked. When *custom, tradition, and social habit* are involved in price determination, they set what are known as **customary prices**. The candy makers' attempt to hold the line on the traditional five-cent candy bar led to considerable reductions in the size of the product. Eventually, almost all vending machines were supplied with larger ten-cent bars, and the shrinking process began again. Similar practices have prevailed in the marketing of soft drinks.[14]

A slightly different approach was taken by Hershey Foods Corporation. When increases on raw materials forced Hershey to increase the price of its candy bar from twenty cents to twenty-five cents, the company also increased the product's weight from 1.05 ounces to 1.2 ounces. The 14.3 percent size increase partially compensated for the 25 percent price increase for the longtime favorite candy bar.[15]

The division of the U.S. beer market into *premium* and *popular* price levels is another example of a traditional pricing system. In the 1930s several major brewers were faced with excess capacity that could not be absorbed by their local markets. These brewers began to ship their product to distant markets. The freight charges were covered by retail prices higher than those charged for local beers. And the higher prices were justified by the marketers' claims that their

Prestige goals can be
met by marketing.

"He's an absolute treasure. We got him for four thousand eight hundred and ninety
dollars at Radio Shack, batteries not included."

Source: Drawing by H. Martin; © 1981 The New Yorker Magazine, Inc.

beers were of higher quality than the local beers. The "imports," classified as premium by their marketers, often actually were better than the numerous local brands. Today, quality differences among beers are probably slight, and there is little difference in the production costs of premium and popular beer. However, the traditional pricing system continues to exist.[16]

At some point in time, someone had to set *initial* prices for products. Sustained inflation has also created a need for periodically reviewing firms' price structures. The rest of this chapter will discuss the traditional and current concepts of price determination. It will also raise the question of how best to tie the concepts together in order to develop a realistic approach to pricing.

PRICE DETERMINATION IN ECONOMIC THEORY

The microeconomic approach to price determination assumes a profit maximization objective and leads to the derivation of correct equilibrium prices in the marketplace. It considers both supply and demand factors and is therefore a more complete analysis than that typically used by business firms.

There are four types of market structures: pure competition, monopolistic competition, oligopoly, and monopoly. **Pure competition** is *a market structure in which there are such a large number of* *buyers and sellers that none of them has a significant influence on price.* Other characteristics of pure competition are a *homogeneous product* and an *ease of entry for sellers that results from low start-up costs.* The closest examples of this marketing structure exist in the agricultural sector.

Monopolistic competition, which typifies most retailing, *is a market structure with large numbers of buyers and sellers. However, it involves a heterogeneous product and product differentiation that allow the marketer some degree of control over prices.* In an **oligopoly,** *there are relatively few sellers; and, because of high start-up costs, there are significant entry barriers to new competitors.* Oligopolies occur frequently in the automobile, steel, tobacco, and petroleum refining industries. A **monopoly** is a *market structure with only one seller of a product and no close substitutes for it.*

Antitrust legislation has nearly eliminated all but temporary monopolies such as those provided by patent protection and regulated monopolies such as the public service companies—telephone, electric, and gas utilities. Regulated monopolies are allowed by government in markets where competition would lead to an uneconomic duplication of services. In return for this license, government reserves the right to regulate the monopoly's rate of return.

The demand side of price theory is concerned with revenue curves. Average revenue (AR) is obtained by dividing total revenue (TR) by the quantity (Q) associated with these revenues:

$$AR = \frac{TR}{Q}$$

The average revenue line is actually the demand curve facing the firm. Marginal revenue (MR) is the change in total revenue (ΔTR) that results from selling an additional unit of output (ΔQ):

$$MR = \frac{\Delta TR}{\Delta Q}$$

The demand curves—average revenue lines—and marginal revenue curves for each market are shown later in the chapter in Figure 17.3.

Average cost (AC) is obtained by dividing total costs (TC) by the quantity (Q) associated with these costs:

$$AC = \frac{TC}{Q}$$

Total costs are composed of both fixed and variable components. Fixed costs (FC) are costs that do not vary with differences in output, while variable costs (VC) are those that change when the level of production is altered. Examples of fixed costs are executive compensation, depreciation, and insurance. Variable costs include raw materials and the wages paid operative employees.

Average variable cost (AVC) is simply the total variable costs (TVC) divided by the related quantity (Q):

$$AVC = \frac{TVC}{Q}$$

Similarly, average fixed cost (AFC) is determined by dividing total fixed costs (TFC) by the related quantity (Q):

$$AFC = \frac{TFC}{Q}$$

Marginal cost (MC) is the change in total cost (ΔTC) that results from producing an additional unit of output (ΔQ):

$$MC = \frac{\Delta TC}{\Delta Q}$$

Marginal costs are therefore similar to marginal revenue—the change in total revenue resulting from the sale of an incremental unit. The point of profit maximization is where marginal costs are equal to marginal revenues. The cost curves of the equations shown above appear in Figure 17.2. The marginal cost (MC) curve intersects the average variable cost (AVC) curve and average cost (AC) curve at the minimum points.

FIGURE 17.2
Cost Curves

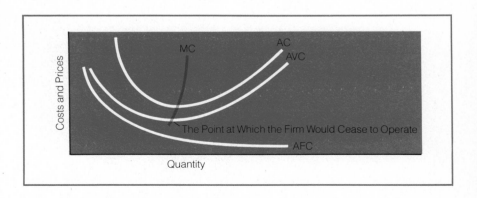

**FIGURE 17.3
Price Determination
in the Four Product
Markets**

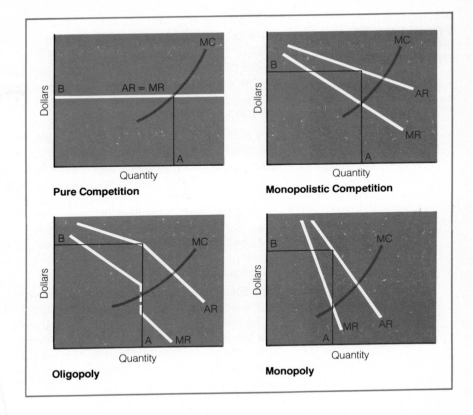

Pure Competition

Monopolistic Competition

Oligopoly

Monopoly

In the short run, a firm will continue to operate even if the price falls below AC, provided it remains above AVC. Why is this rational market behavior? If the firm were to cease operations after the price fell below AC, it would still have some fixed costs, but it would have *no* revenue. Any amount received above AVC can be used to cover at least part of the fixed costs. The manager is acting rationally by continuing to produce as long as price exceeds AVC, since this minimizes losses. If price falls below AVC, the manager should cease operations because continued operation begins to maximize losses. The *supply curve,* therefore, is the marginal cost curve above its intersection with AVC, since this is the area of rational pricing behavior for the firm.

How are prices set in each of the product market situations? Figure 17.3 shows how prices are determined in each of the four product markets. The point of profit maximization (MC = MR) sets the equilibrium output (Point A), which is extended to the AR line to set the equilibrium price (Point B). In the case of pure competition, AR = MR, so price is a predetermined variable in this product market.[17]

PRACTICAL PROBLEMS IN APPLYING PRICE THEORY

From the viewpoint of the marketer, price theory concepts are sometimes difficult to apply in practice. What, then, are their practical limitations?

1. *Many firms do not attempt to maximize profits.* Economic analysis is subject to the same limitations as the assumptions on which it is based—for example, the proposition that all firms attempt to maximize profits.

2. *It is difficult to estimate demand curves.* Modern accounting procedures provide managers with a clear understanding of cost structures. The managers can therefore readily comprehend the supply side of the pricing equation. But it is difficult to estimate demand at various price levels. Demand curves must be based on market research estimates that are often not as exact as cost figures. Over time, however, these problems may be eliminated by the use of advanced research methodology. Although the demand element can be identified, it is often difficult to measure in the real world setting.[18]

3. *Inadequate training and communication hinder price theory in the real world.* Many managers lack the formal training in economics to be able to apply its concepts to their own pricing decisions. On the other hand, many economists remain essentially theorists, devoting little interest or effort to real world pricing situations. This dual problem significantly hinders the use of economic theory in actual pricing practice.[19]

PRICE DETERMINATION IN PRACTICE

The practical limitations inherent in price theory have forced practitioners to turn to other techniques. The cost-plus approach is the most commonly used method of setting prices today. For many years, government contracts with suppliers called for payments of all expenses plus a set profit usually stated as a percentage of the cost of the project. These *cost-plus contracts,* as they were known, have now been abandoned in favor of competitive bidding or specifically negotiated prices.

Cost-plus pricing *takes some base cost figure per unit and adds a markup to cover unassigned costs and provide a profit.* The only real difference in the multitude of cost-plus techniques is the relative sophistication of the costing procedures employed. For example, a local apparel shop may set prices by adding a 40 percent markup to the invoice price charged by the supplier. The markup is expected to cover all other expenses and permit the owner to earn a reasonable return on the sale of the clothes.

In contrast to this rather simple pricing mechanism, a large manufacturer may employ a pricing formula that requires a computer to handle the necessary calculations. But while the advanced calculations are for a sophisticated costing procedure, in the end, the formula still requires someone to make a decision about the markup. The apparel shop and the large manufacturer may be vastly different with respect to the *cost* aspect, but they are remarkably similar when it comes to the *plus* (markup) side of the equation.

Cost-oriented Pricing Methods

The two most common cost-oriented pricing procedures are the full cost method and the incremental cost method. *Full cost pricing* uses all relevant variable costs in setting a product's price. In addition, it allocates the fixed costs that cannot be directly attributed to the production of the specific item being priced. Under the full cost method, if job order 515 in a printing plant amounts to 0.000127 percent of the plant's total output, then 0.000127 percent of the firm's overhead expenses are allocated to that job. This approach allows management to recover all costs plus the amount added as a profit margin.

The full cost approach has two basic deficiencies. First, there is no consideration of the demand for the item or its competition. Perhaps no one wants to pay the price the firm has calculated! Second, any method of allocating overhead (fixed expenses) is arbitrary and may be unrealistic. In manufacturing, overhead allocations are often tied to *direct labor hours.* In retailing, the mechanism is sometimes *square footage* of each profit center. Regardless of the technique, it is difficult to show a cause-effect relationship between the *allocated* cost and most products.

One way to overcome the arbitrary allocation of fixed expenses is by *incremental cost pricing,* which attempts to use only those costs directly attributable to a specific output in setting prices. For example, consider a small manufacturing firm with the following income statement:

Sales (10,000 units at $10)		**$100,000**
Expenses:		
Variable	**$50,000**	
Fixed	40,000	90,000
Net profit		$ 10,000

Suppose the firm is offered a contract for an additional 5,000 units. Since the peak season is over, these items can be produced at the same average variable cost. Assume that the labor force would be idle otherwise. In order to get the contract, how low could the firm price its product?

Under the full cost approach, the lowest price would be $9 per unit. This figure is obtained by dividing the $90,000 in expenses by an output of 10,000 units.

The incremental approach, on the other hand, could permit a price of $5.10, which would significantly increase the possibility of securing the additional contract. This price would be composed of the $5 variable cost related to each unit of production plus a 10 cents per unit contribution to fixed expenses and overhead. The income statement for these conditions of sale is as follows:

Sales (10,000 at $10; 5,000 at $5.10)		**$125,500**
Expenses:		
Variable (15,000 × $5)	**$75,000**	
Fixed	40,000	115,000
Net profit		$ 10,500

Profits are increased under the incremental approach. Admittedly, the illustration is based on two assumptions: (1) the ability to isolate markets so that selling at the lower price will not affect the price received in other markets; and (2) the lack of legal restrictions on the firm. The example, however, does show that profits can sometimes be enhanced by using the incremental approach.

Limitations of Cost-oriented Pricing

While the incremental method eliminates one of the problems associated with full cost pricing, it fails to deal effectively with the basic malady: *Cost-oriented pricing does not adequately account for product demand.* The problem of demand estimation is as critical to these approaches as it is to classical price theory. To the marketer, the challenge is to find some way of introducing demand analysis into cost-plus pricing. Marketers must look at pricing from the buyer's perspective.[20] It cannot be done in a management vacuum.

Using Breakeven Analysis in Pricing Decisions

Pricing is one of those gray areas in marketing management where the participants struggle to develop a theory, policy, procedure, technique, or "rule of thumb" on which they can depend.[21] There is no simple solution to the dilemma. Pricing is a complex variable because it has both objective and subjective aspects. It is an area where exact decision tools and executive judgment meet.

Breakeven analysis is *a tool that allows decision makers to compare the profit consequences of alternative prices.* Figure 17.4 presents a breakeven chart where a single price is assumed. The total cost curve includes both fixed and variable segments, and total fixed cost is represented by a horizontal line. Average variable cost is assumed to be constant per unit—as it was in the example for incremental pricing.

The *breakeven point* is the point where total revenue (TR) just equals total cost (TC). It can be found by using the following formula:

$$\text{Breakeven point (in units)} = \frac{\text{Total fixed cost}}{\text{Per unit contribution to fixed cost}}$$

In the earlier example, a selling price of $10 and an AVC of $5 resulted in a per-unit contribution to fixed costs of $5. This figure can be di-

FIGURE 17.4
Breakeven Chart

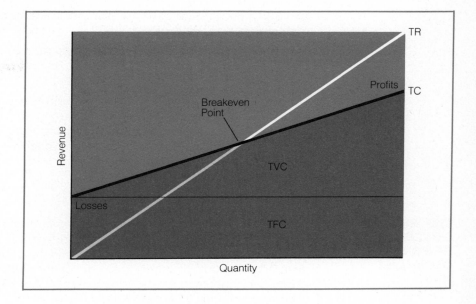

vided into total fixed costs of $40,000 to obtain a breakeven point of 8,000 units:

$$\text{Breakeven point (in units)} = \frac{\$40,000}{\$5} = 8,000$$

Breakeven analysis is a valuable pricing tool. It allows marketers to test the financial implications of price decisions before they are actually implemented. For example, if the price were to change to $9 in the situation above, the breakeven point would be 10,000 units. If the price were $11, the breakeven point would be 6,667 units.

While breakeven analysis is a useful tool for decision making, it is not intended to be a model for pricing strategy. But such a model is available as a result of the work of Alfred R. Oxenfeldt.

The Multistage Approach to Pricing

Oxenfeldt's research into pricing led to the development of a decision model, commonly identified as the multistage approach to pricing.[22] This model provides a sequential process for making improved pricing decisions. The various steps in the Oxenfeldt approach are as follows:

1. Select specific market targets.
2. Identify the appropriate brand image for the related market targets.
3. Determine the best marketing mix, allocating specific attention to the relative emphasis of the pricing variable.

4. Set a price policy that will provide a consistent response to recurring price questions.

5. Choose a pricing strategy for existing market conditions.

6. Set the actual price.

The multistage approach to pricing implies that the selection of the final price is really the natural consequence of the six-step process proposed in the model. Pricing strategy should be oriented toward long-run considerations, and its related decision making should be sequential rather than mechanistic.

THE ROLE OF GOVERNMENT IN PRICING DECISIONS

Beer drinkers in Michigan know that government and the regulatory framework it creates can have a profound impact on pricing. A Michigan law requiring deposits on bottles and cans has pushed Michigan beer prices about $6 higher per case than in bordering states! As a result, beer outlets in neighboring Indiana, Ohio, and Wisconsin are reporting substantially increased sales.[23]

One survey of marketing executives found that almost 70 percent of the respondents believed that government played a greater role in pricing decisions now than a decade earlier.[24] Table 17.4 notes that the most often-mentioned governmental influence on pricing was the increased enforcement of existing legislation, with nearly 90 percent of the respondents citing this item.

Some governmental actions take amusing twists. A group of Chicago house builders and suppliers offered to join the national battle against inflation by adopting a 60-day price freeze. The group was rebuffed when the Federal Trade Commission labeled their decision a possible restraint of trade.[25] The Department of Energy said that service stations following the department's pricing regulations could charge credit card users a fee. A day later the FTC said such a charge would violate Truth-in-Lending legislation.[26] While government has had a significant influence on pricing strategy, it is often difficult to predict its exact impact.

TABLE 17.4
Percentage of Respondents Citing These Governmental Influences on Pricing Decisions

Influence	Percent
Increased pricing regulations	60.2%
Increased enforcement of existing legislation	88.3
Excessive reporting requirements	68.8
Other	83.6

Source: *Pricing Objectives and Practices in American Industry: A Research Report* by Louis E. Boone and David L. Kurtz, 1979; all rights reserved.

SUMMARY

Price—the exchange value of a good or service—is important because it regulates economic activity as well as determines the revenue to be received by a specific enterprise.

Pricing objectives should be the natural consequence of company and marketing goals. They can be classified under three headings:

1. Profitability objectives, including profit maximization and target return

2. Volume objectives, including sales maximization and market share

3. Objectives not related to either profitability or sales volume, including social and ethical considerations, status quo objectives, and prestige goals

Prices can be determined by theoretical or cost-oriented approaches. Economic theorists attempt to equate marginal revenue and marginal cost, while businesses tend to rely on cost-plus approaches. Both methods have practical limitations.

Breakeven analysis is a useful tool in pricing decisions. It allows marketers to compare the profit consequences of alternative prices. A comprehensive decision model for pricing strategy is offered by Alfred R. Oxenfeldt's multistage approach to pricing. Government has had a significant impact in pricing decisions.

QUESTIONS FOR DISCUSSION

1. Explain the following terms:

   price
   profit maximization
   target return objective
   sales maximization
   market share objective
   social and ethical considerations
   status quo objectives
   prestige goals

   customary prices
   pure competition
   monopolistic competition
   oligopoly
   monopoly
   cost-plus pricing
   breakeven analysis

2. How important is pricing to the success of a marketing strategy?

3. Examine the role of pricing objectives in contemporary marketing.

4. What does the economist mean by *marginal analysis?* Discuss.

5. Do you share Baumol's conceptualization of pricing behavior? Explain.

6. Why would a firm choose to have a reduced market share? What are the policy implications of this situation?

7. Identify the main determinants of price discretion. Cite specific examples of each.

8. How are prices set in each of the four product markets: pure competition, monopolistic competition, oligopoly, and monopoly?

9. Describe cost-oriented pricing. Include both full cost and incremental approaches.

10. Discuss the limitations of both theoretical and cost-oriented pricing.

11.   What is the breakeven point for a product with a selling price of $25, an average variable cost of $16, and related fixed costs of $126,000?

12.   What is the breakeven point for a product with a selling price of $35, an average variable cost of $18, and related fixed costs of $25,500?

13.   How can the derivation of the breakeven point assist in price determination? Comment.

14.   Outline the major conclusions of the PIMS study.

15.   Discuss the role of tradition in pricing strategy.

16.   What market situations exist for the following products:
      a. telephone service   e. wheat
      b. U.S.-made cigars   f. refrigerators
      c. tennis rackets   g. cameras
      d. aluminum   h. skis

17.   Give examples of pricing situations where social and ethical considerations are important. Are there any general conditions that characterize these situations? Discuss.

18.   How are the following prices determined and what do they have in common:
      a. a ticket to a movie theater
      b. your tuition fee
      c. the local property tax rate
      d. the printing of graduation announcements

19.   Discuss the pricing strategy decision model proposed by Oxenfeldt.

20.   What is the current role of government in pricing decisions?

NOTES

1. Mitchell C. Lynch, "How're Ya Fixed for Fountain Pens? Gillette Touts $410 Luxury Model," *Wall Street Journal,* June 12, 1981. Reprinted by permission of *The Wall Street Journal,* © Dow Jones & Company, Inc. 1981. All rights reserved.

2. Jon G. Udell, "How Important Is Pricing in Competitive Strategy?" *Journal of Marketing,* January 1964, pp. 44–48.

3. Price was also found to rank first in a study by Robert A. Robicheaux. See "How Important Is Pricing in Competitive Strategy, Circa 1975," in *Proceedings of the Southern Marketing Association,* eds. Henry W. Nash and Donald P. Robin, Atlanta, Georgia, November 1976, pp. 55–57. Another interesting article is Saeed Samiee, "Elements of Marketing Strategy: How Important Are They from the Executive Viewpoint?" *Journal of the Academy of Marketing Science,* Winter 1980, pp. 40–50.

4. These objectives are reported in Bro Uttal, "Xerox Is Trying too Hard," *FORTUNE,* March 13, 1978, p. 84; Ralph E. Winter, "Corporate Strategists Giving New Emphasis to Market Share, Rank," *Wall Street Journal,* February 3, 1978; and Bro Uttal, "How Ray McDonald's Growth Theory Created IBM's Toughest Competitor," *FORTUNE,* January 1977, p. 96.

5. Research by Saeed Samiee ranked "satisfactory return on investment" first among a similar list of objectives. Samiee correctly points out the difficulties in making the "meeting competition" objectives operational. See "Pricing Objectives of U.S. Manufacturing Firms," in *Proceedings of the Southern Marketing Association,* eds. Robert S. Franz, Robert M. Hopkins, and Al Toma, New Orleans, Louisiana, November 1978, pp. 445–47.

6. Target rate-of-return pricing is discussed in Douglas G. Brooks, "Cost-oriented Pricing: A Realistic Solution to a Complicated Problem," *Journal of Marketing,* April 1975, pp. 72–74.

7. James E. Hansz and Kenneth P. Sinclair, "Target Return Pricing: Panacea or Paradox?" in *Proceedings of the Southern Marketing Association,* Franz, Hopkins, and Toma, eds., pp. 441–44.

8. Robert A. Lynn, *Price Policies and Marketing Management* (Homewood, Ill.: Richard D. Irwin, 1967), p. 99.

9. William J. Baumol, "On the Theory of Oligopoly," *Economica,* August 1958, pp. 187–98. See also William J. Baumol, *Business Behavior, Value and Growth* (New York: Macmillan, 1959).

10. An interesting discussion appears in Carl R. Frear and John E. Swan, "Marketing Managers' Motivation to Revise Their Market Share Goals: An Expectancy Theory Analysis," in *1981 Southwestern Marketing Proceedings,* Robert H. Ross, Frederic B. Kraft, and Charles H. Davis, eds., Wichita, Kansas, pp. 13–16.

11. Robert D. Buzzell, Bradley T. Gale, and Ralph G. M. Sultan, "Market Share—A Key to Profitability," *Harvard Business Review,* January-February 1975, pp. 97–106. Recent articles of interest include P. Varadarajan and William R. Dillon, "Competitive Position Effect and Market Share: An Exploratory Investigation," *Journal of Business Research,* March 1981, pp. 49–64; and Albert L. Page, "A Test of the Share Price Market Planning Relationship in One Retail Environment," *Journal of the Academy of Marketing Science,* Winter 1979, pp. 25–39.

12. John J. Parker, "Chrysler Pitfall: Too Many Accountants," *Detroit News,* October 28, 1979. Statistical data in the Parker article from *Standard & Poors Industry Surveys and World's 1979 Yearbook.*

13. Reported in "Labor Letter," *Wall Street Journal,* August 29, 1978.

14. Customary pricing is described in Stanley C. Hollander, "Customary Prices," *MSU Business Topics,* Summer 1966, pp. 45–56.

15. Reported in "Candy Fans Get Sour Price News," *Detroit News,* November 9, 1978.

16. Charles G. Burck, "While the Big Brewers Quaff, the Little Ones Thirst," *FORTUNE,* November 1972, p. 106.

17. For a thorough discussion of price determination in economic theory, see Edwin G. Dolan, *Basic Economics,* 3rd ed. (Hinsdale, Ill.: The Dryden Press, 1983).

18. Experimental methods for estimating demand curves are discussed in Edgar A. Pessemier, *Experimental Methods of Analyzing Demand for Branded Goods* (Pullman: Bureau of Economic and Business Research, Washington State University, 1963). See also William J. Kehoe, "Demand Curve Estimation and the Small Business Managers," *Journal of Small Business Management,* July 1972, pp. 29–31.

19. Some problems of using economic models in practice are discussed in Kent B. Monroe and Albert J. Della Bitta, "Models for Pricing Decisions," *Journal of Marketing Research,* August 1978, pp. 413–28. Also see Robert J. Dolan and Abel P. Jeuland, "Experience Curves and Dynamic Demand Models: Implications for Optional Pricing Strategies," *Journal of Marketing,* Winter 1981, pp. 52–62.

20. This is suggested in Benson P. Shapiro and Barbara B. Jackson, "Industrial Pricing to Meet Customer Needs," *Harvard Business Review,* November-December 1978, pp. 119–27.

21. Breakeven analysis has a variety of uses. See, for example, Robert J. Lambrix and Swendra S. Singhvi, "How to Set Volume-Sensitive ROI Targets," *Harvard Business Review,* March-April 1981, pp. 174–79.

22. This section is based on Alfred R. Oxenfeldt, "Multistage Approach to Pricing," *Harvard Business Review,* July-August 1960, pp. 125–33. Reprinted by permission of the *Harvard Business Review.* Copyright © 1960 by the President and Fellows of Harvard College; all rights reserved. See also Alfred R. Oxenfeldt, *Pricing for Marketing Executives* (Belmont, Calif: Wadsworth, 1961), pp. 72–76; and Alfred R. Oxenfeldt, "A Decision-Making Structure for Price Decisions," *Journal of Marketing,* January 1973, pp. 48–53.

23. John Broder, "Dealers Crying in Unsold Beer," *Detroit News,* March 18, 1979.

24. Louis E. Boone and David L. Kurtz, *Pricing Objectives and Practices in American Industry: A Research Report,* 1979; all rights reserved.

25. "Washington Whispers," ® *U.S. News & World Report,* July 16, 1979, p. 12.

26. "Tomorrow," *U.S. News & World Report,* August 13, 1979, p. 14.

CHAPTER 18

ELEMENTS OF PRICING STRATEGY

KEY TERMS

list price
market price
cash discount
trade discount
quantity discount
trade-ins
promotional allowances
rebates
FOB plant
freight absorption
uniform delivered price
zone pricing
basing point system
psychological pricing
odd pricing
unit pricing
skimming pricing
penetration pricing
price flexibility
price lining
promotional pricing
loss leader
transfer price
profit center

LEARNING GOALS

1. To outline the organization for pricing decisions

2. To explain price quotations

3. To discuss why pricing policies are the foundation on which pricing decisions are made

4. To relate price and the consumer's perception of a product's quality

5. To examine negotiated prices and competitive bidding, transfer pricing, and pricing in the public sector

The people at the Fleischmann Distilling Company had a problem. Fleischmann's gin, part of Nabisco Brands' beverage group, was marketed primarily to cocktail lounges. And research indicated that more and more gin buyers were imbibing at home. Fleischmann's gin did not do as well in the package stores as some competitors. Sales of the 750-milliliter bottle (retailing at $4.50) were declining.

How did Fleischmann handle the problem? They raised the price $1 over a two-year period. Later, they also decided to repackage the new higher-priced gin in a different-shaped bottle. The pricing strategy paid off. Sales volume went up significantly, and sales revenue even faster.[1]

The Fleischmann's experience suggests that price quotations can significantly impact marketing strategy. As the example suggests, there are numerous elements to consider in setting a pricing strategy. This chapter will expand the concepts developed in Chapter 17 by considering the organization for pricing decisions, pricing policies, price-quality relationships, negotiated prices, competitive bidding, transfer pricing, and pricing in the public sector.

Changing packages to reflect retail prices

Source: Released through permission of Robert C. Baranaskas, President, Fleischmann Distilling Company.

ORGANIZATION FOR PRICING DECISIONS

There are basically two major steps to follow in translating pricing objectives into pricing decisions. First, the overall pricing structure must be set. Then, someone must be assigned responsibility for administering the pricing structure.

Setting Price Structures A recent survey of marketing executives found that the people or groups most commonly chosen to set price structures were (1) a pricing committee composed of top executives, (2) the president of the company, and (3) the chief marketing officer (see Table 18.1).

Administering Price Structures According to the same survey, the pricing structure is administered most often by marketers. As Table 18.2 indicates, the chief marketing officer was responsible for pricing in 51 percent of the firms surveyed. In all, marketers administered the pricing structure in over 68 percent of the companies.

TABLE 18.1
Executives Responsible for Setting Price Structures

Executive Category	Percentage
Pricing committee composed of top executives	35.2%
President	21.1
Chief marketing officer	14.1
Corporate vice-president	7.0
Board of directors	4.7
Executive vice-president	4.7
Pricing committee composed of middle level executives	3.9
Product or brand manager	3.1
Other	6.4

Source: *Pricing Objectives and Practices in American Industry: A Research Report* by Louis E. Boone and David L. Kurtz, 1979. All rights reserved.

TABLE 18.2
Executives Responsible for Administering Price Structures

Executive Category	Percentage
Chief marketing officer	51.0%
Product or brand manager	14.3
Pricing committee composed of top executives	11.2
President	8.2
Corporate vice-president	8.2
Chief financial officer	4.1
Regional or zone sales manager	3.1

Source: *Pricing Objectives and Practices in American Industry: A Research Report* by Louis E. Boone and David L. Kurtz. All rights reserved.

How Are Prices Quoted?

The method for quoting prices depends on many factors, among them cost structures, the traditional practices in the particular industry, and the policies of individual firms. In this section, the reasoning and methodology behind price quotations will be examined.

List Prices The basis on which many price structures are built is the **list price**—*the rate normally quoted to potential buyers.* List prices are usually determined by some type of cost-plus procedure. The sticker prices on new automobiles are one example of list prices. They show the price for the basic model and that for each of the options on the particular car being sold.

Discounts and Allowances The **market price**—*the amount the consumer or middleman pays*—may or may not be the same as the list price, since discounts or allowances can reduce the list price. Discounts can be classified as cash, quantity, or trade.

A **cash discount,** probably the most commonly used variety, is *a price reduction made for prompt payment of bills.* It usually specifies an exact time period such as 2/10, net 30. This means that the bill is due within thirty days and that if it is paid in ten days, the buyer can deduct 2 percent from the amount due. Cash discounts are a traditional pricing practice in many industries. They are legal if they are granted to everyone on the same terms. The discounts were originally instituted to improve the cash position of sellers, to lower bad-debt losses, and to reduce the sellers' collection expenses. But whether these advantages outweigh the disadvantage of the relatively high cost of capital involved depends on the buyer's need for cash as well as alternative sources and costs of funds.

A **trade discount,** also called a *functional discount,* is *a payment to channel members or buyers for performing some marketing function normally required of the manufacturer.* They too are legal as long as all similar buyers (such as all wholesalers or all retailers) receive the same discount schedule. Trade discounts were initially based on the operating expenses of each trade category but have now become more a matter of custom in some industries (although they are not as common as they once were).[2] The trade discount schedule for domestic automobile companies is shown in Figure 18.1. This data shows that automobile dealers generally receive a higher discount for larger models than they do for compacts and subcompacts.

A **quantity discount** is a *price reduction granted for large purchases.* Quantity discounts are given because large volume purchases reduce selling expenses and may shift part of the storing, transporting, and financing functions to the buyer. Quantity discounts are legal provided they are offered to all customers and do not infringe on the provisions of the Robinson-Patman Act limiting

FIGURE 18.1
Discounts to Car Dealers

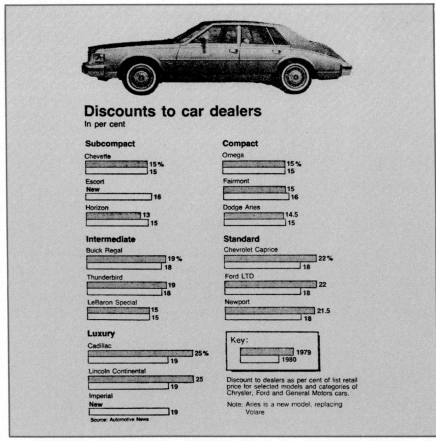

Discounts to car dealers
In per cent

Subcompact

Chevette
15%
15

Escort
New
16

Horizon
13
15

Intermediate

Buick Regal
19%
18

Thunderbird
19
18

LeBaron Special
15
15

Luxury

Cadillac
25%
19

Lincoln Continental
25
19

Imperial
New
19

Source: Automotive News

Compact

Omega
15%
15

Fairmont
15
16

Dodge Aries
14.5
15

Standard

Chevrolet Caprice
22%
18

Ford LTD
22
18

Newport
21.5
18

Key:
1979
1980

Discount to dealers as per cent of list retail price for selected models and categories of Chrysler, Ford and General Motors cars.

Note: Aries is a new model, replacing
     Volare

Source: Reprinted from James Mateja, "Tough Tests May Await Auto Dealers," *Orlando Sentinel Star,* April 25, 1981 (*Chicago Tribune* story). Graphic courtesy of *Orlando Sentinel Star.*

the discount to the amount of cost savings associated with selling in large quantities.[3]

Quantity discounts are either noncumulative or cumulative. *Noncumulative quantity discounts* are one-time reductions in list price, such as the one shown in Table 18.3. *Cumulative quantity discounts* are reductions determined by purchases over a stated time period. Annual purchases of $25,000 might entitle the buyer to an 8 percent rebate, while purchases exceeding $50,000 may mean a 15 percent rebate. These price reductions are sometimes termed *patronage discounts,* since they tend to bind the customer to the seller.

Allowances also reduce the price the purchaser must pay. The major categories of allowances are trade-ins, promotional allowances, and rebates. **Trade-ins,** often used in the sale of durable goods such as automobiles and sewing machines, *preserve the list price of the new item while cutting the amount the customer actually*

TABLE 18.3
A Firm's Discount
Schedule

Units Purchased	Price
1	List price
2–5	List price less 10 percent
6–10	List price less 20 percent
More than 10	List price less 25 percent

has to pay by allowing the customer credit on a used object, usually of the kind being purchased. **Promotional allowances** are *attempts to integrate promotional strategy in the channel.* For example, manufacturers often provide advertising and sales support allowances for other channel members. Automobile producers have also offered allowances to dealers so that they could cut prices in order to stimulate retail sales.

Rebates are *refunds by the sellers of a portion of the purchase price.* They have been used most prominently by automobile manufacturers eager to move models during periods of slow sales. Other recent users have included "Mr. Coffee" coffee makers and "First Alert" smoke detectors. One of the most interesting rebates has been given by Nguyen Huy Han, a Vietnamese refugee who now runs a restaurant in Pontiac, Michigan. Han gives his customers a 30 percent rebate at the end of each year on the basis of his profits. One customer received over $400.[4]

Pricing and Transportation Costs

Shipping costs are important in pricing when the movement of heavy, bulky, low unit-cost materials is involved.[5] In such cases, transportation is a relatively high portion of a product's total cost and must be carefully considered when the firm's market is spread over a wide geographic area. Prices may be quoted where either the buyer or the seller pays all transportation charges or there is some type of expense sharing. Consider the following classical description of the importance of transportation costs in pricing strategy.

The way in which this problem is handled can greatly influence the success of a firm's marketing program by helping to determine the scope of the geographic market area the firm is able to serve, the vulnerability of the firm to price competition in areas located near its production facilities, the net margins earned on individual sales of the product, the ability of the firm to control or influence resale prices of distributors, and how difficult it is for salespeople in the field to quote accurate prices and delivery terms to their potential customers.[6]

The seller has several alternatives in handling transportation costs: FOB plant, freight absorption, uniform delivered price, zone pricing, and basing points.

FOB Plant *When a price does not include any shipping charges, it is shown as* **FOB plant.** In this situation, the buyer must pay all the freight charges. The seller is responsible only for the cost of loading the merchandise aboard the carrier selected by the buyer. (The abbreviation *FOB* means "free on board.") Legal title and responsibility pass to the buyer once the purchase is loaded and the receipt is obtained from the carrier.

Freight Absorption Prices may also be shown as *FOB plant—freight allowed.* In this situation—known as **freight absorption**—*the seller permits the buyer to subtract transportation expenses from the bill.* The amount the seller receives varies with the freight charges absorbed. This method is commonly used by firms seeking to extend their market area, since it permits the same price to be quoted regardless of shipping costs.

Uniform Delivered Price *The same price (including transportation expenses) is quoted to all buyers* when a **uniform delivered price** is the firm's policy. This kind of pricing is the opposite of FOB pricing. The system is often compared to the pricing of mail service and is therefore sometimes called *postage stamp pricing.* The price quoted includes an average transportation cost per buyer, which means that distant customers actually pay a lesser share of selling costs while customers near the source pay more. The customers paying more are said to be paying *phantom freight*—that is, the average transportation charge exceeds the actual cost of shipping.

Zone Pricing In **zone pricing,** which is simply a modification of the uniform delivered pricing system, *the market is divided into different regions, and a price is set within each one.* United Parcel Service's system depends on zone pricing. The primary advantage of this pricing policy is that it allows the seller to compete better in distant markets.

Basing Points In a **basing point system,** *the price to the customer includes the price at the factory plus freight charges from the basing point nearest the buyer.* The basing point is the point from which freight charges are determined; it is not necessarily the point from which the goods are shipped. Both single and multiple basing point systems have been used. In either case, the actual shipping point is not considered in the price quotation.

During the 1940s, several legal cases involving the steel, glucose, and cement industries were brought against users of basing point pricing systems. The outcomes of the proceedings themselves were confusing, but the result was a reduction in the use of these systems as a basis for pricing.

The best-known basing point system was the *Pittsburgh-plus pricing* procedure that was used in the steel industry for many years. *Steel price quotations contained freight charges from Pittsburgh regardless of where the steel was produced.* As the industry matured, other steel centers, such as Chicago, Gary, Cleveland, and Birmingham, emerged. Pittsburgh, however, remained the basing point for steel pricing. This meant that a buyer in Terre Haute, Indiana, who purchased steel from a Gary mill had to pay phantom freight from Pittsburgh.

PRICING POLICIES

Pricing policies, the basis on which pricing decisions are made, are an important ingredient in the firm's total image. Many businesses would be well advised to spend more managerial effort in the establishment and periodic review of pricing policies.

Pricing policies must deal with varied competitive situations. A few years ago, well-publicized court cases involving the Pinto caused Ford to alter its pricing policy for the model. At the time, the Pinto was the firm's only high-volume small car since the Fiesta was just being introduced. Strict government mileage requirements and legal cases involving older-model Pintos (the fuel tank was redesigned in 1977) caused Henry Ford II to remark that this was "the biggest problem we've got." Ford's solution was to give dealers cash incentives of $325 per unit, and to hold down price hikes on later-model Pintos.[7] Ford's competitive and environmental situation clearly dictated its pricing policy in this instance.

The type of policy chosen by an individual firm depends on the environment within which pricing decisions must be made. The types of policies considered in this chapter are psychological pricing, unit pricing, new-product pricing, price flexibility, relative price levels, price lining, and promotional prices.

Psychological Pricing

Psychological pricing is *based on the belief that certain prices or price ranges are more appealing than others to buyers.* There is, however, no consistent research-based foundation for such thinking, since studies often report mixed findings.[8] Prestige pricing, mentioned in Chapter 17, is one of the many forms of psychological pricing.

Under **odd pricing**—a good example of the application of psychological pricing—*prices ending in numbers not commonly used for price quotations are set.* A price of $16.99 is assumed to be more appealing than $17 because it is a smaller-appearing figure.

There are many explanations of the origin of odd pricing. One popular account is that it was used to force clerks to make change, thereby serving as a cash control device within stores.[9] Now it has become a customary feature of contemporary price quotations. For instance, one discounter uses prices ending in 3 and 7 rather than 5, 8, or 9 because of a belief that customers regard price tags such as $5.95, $6.98, and $7.99 as *regular* retail prices and price tags such as $5.97 and $6.93 as *discount* prices.[10]

Unit Pricing

Consumer advocates have often pointed out the difficulty of comparing consumer products that are available in different size packages. Is a 28-ounce can selling for $.75 a better buy than two 16-ounce cans priced at $.81? Is it a better buy than another brand's three 16-ounce cans for $.89? The critics argue that there should be a common way of pricing consumer products.

Unit pricing is a response to this problem. Under **unit pricing,** *all prices are stated in terms of some recognized unit of measurement (such as a pound or a quart) or standard numerical count.* Mandatory unit pricing has been legislated in some places; and many firms, particularly grocery store chains, have adopted it voluntarily. The American Marketing Association's board of directors has endorsed the concept for grocery products in all large stores.[11]

Some supermarket chains have come to regard the adoption of unit pricing as a competitive tool on which to base retail advertising. Others have argued that unit pricing significantly increases retail operating costs.

The real question, of course, is whether unit pricing helps consumers make good decisions.[12] One study found that the availability of unit prices resulted in consumer savings and that retailers also gained when unit pricing led to greater purchases of store brands. The study concluded that unit pricing was valuable to both buyer and seller and that it merited full-scale usage.[13] Unit pricing is a major pricing policy issue to be dealt with in the development of a marketing strategy.

New-Product Pricing

The pricing of new products presents a peculiar problem to marketers.[14] The initial price quoted for an item may determine whether the product will eventually be accepted in the marketplace. It also may affect the amount of competition that will emerge.

Consider the options a company might follow in pricing a new product. While many firms choose to price at the level of comparable products, some select other alternatives (see Figure 18.2). The **skimming pricing** policy is that of *a relatively high entry price.* One purpose of this strategy is to allow the firm to recover its new-product costs quickly, on the assumption that competition will eventually drive the price to a lower level. Such was the case with electric toothbrushes.

A skimming policy therefore attempts to maximize the revenue received from the sale of a new product before competitors enter the market. Management takes the viewpoint that it is easier to lower the price than to raise it. Ballpoint pens were introduced shortly after World War II at a price of about $20. Today, the best-selling ballpoint pens are priced at less than $1. Other examples of products that have been introduced under a skimming policy are cellophane tape, calculators, television sets, and Polaroid cameras.[15]

FIGURE 18.2
Use of New-product
Pricing Strategies

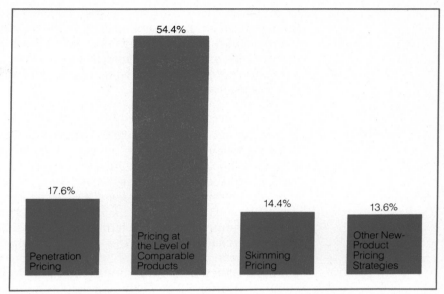

54.4%

17.6%

Penetration
Pricing

Pricing at
the Level of
Comparable
Products

14.4%

Skimming
Pricing

13.6%

Other New-
Product
Pricing
Strategies

Source: *Pricing Objectives and Practices in American Industry: A Research Report* by Louis E. Boone and David L. Kurtz.
All rights reserved.

During the late growth and early maturity stages of the product life cycle, the price is reduced for two reasons—the pressure of competition and the desire to expand the product's market. While 10 percent of the market for Product X might buy the item at $10, another 20 percent might buy at $8.75. Successive price declines will expand the firm's market as well as meet new competition.

The skimming policy has one chief disadvantage; it attracts competition. Potential competitors that see the innovating firm's profit also enter the market, and this forces the price even lower. Figure 18.2 indicates that 14.4 percent of the respondents in a recent pricing study used a skimming price policy. Skimming also appears to be more common in industrial markets than in consumer markets.

Penetration pricing, the opposite policy in new-product pricing, results in *an entry price lower than what is intended as the long-term price.* The pricing study shown in Figure 18.2 suggests that penetration pricing is used more often in consumer markets than in industrial markets. Soaps and toothpastes are good examples of this kind of pricing.

The premise of penetration pricing is that an initially lower price will help secure market acceptance. Since the firm intends to increase the price later, brand popularity is crucial to the success of this policy. One advantage of the penetration policy is that it discourages competition, since the prevailing low price does not suggest the attractive returns associated with the skimming policy.

The key decision is when to move the price up to its intended level. Consumers tend to resist price increases; therefore, correct timing is essential. The solution depends on the degree of brand loyalty achieved. Brand loyalty must be at the point where a price increase will not cause a disproportionate decrease in customers. A series of modest price changes, rather than a single large hike, also can retain customers.

Price Flexibility

Marketing executives must determine company policy with respect to **price flexibility**—*the issue of whether to have just one price or pursue a variable price policy in the market.* Generally, *one-price policies* characterize situations where mass selling is employed, and *variable pricing* is more common where individual bargaining typifies market transactions.

A one-price policy is common in retailing since it facilitates mass merchandising. For the most part, once the price is set, the manager can direct attention to other aspects of the marketing mix. Variable prices are found more in industrial markets. This does not mean that price flexibility exists only in manufacturing industries. A study of the retail home appliance market concluded that price differentials were common for consumers purchasing identical products

Pricing decisions are not always clear cut.

"Barton, do you have something you want to share with the rest of us?"

Source: Drawing by H. Martin. *The Wall Street Journal Book of Wit.* Reprinted by permission of Cartoon Features Syndicate.

from the same dealer. The primary reasons for the price differences were customer knowledge and bargaining strength.[16]

Although variable pricing allows flexibility in selling situations, it may conflict with provisions of the Robinson-Patman Act. It may also lead to retaliatory pricing on the part of competitors, and it may not be well received by those who have paid the higher prices.

Relative Price Levels

An important pricing policy decision concerns the relative price level. Are the firm's prices to be set above, below, or at the prevailing market price? In economic theory this question would be answered by supply and demand analysis. However, from a practical viewpoint, marketing managers administer prices. In other words, cost-oriented pricing allows them the option of subjectively setting the markup percentages.[17] Chapter 17 provided a framework for determining markups, but the decision maker must still develop a basic policy in regard to relative price levels.

Following the competition is one method of negating the price variable in marketing strategy, since it forces competitors to concentrate on other factors. Some firms choose to price below or above competitors. These decisions are usually based on a firm's cost structure, overall marketing strategy, and pricing objectives.

Price Lining

Most companies sell varied lines of products. An effective pricing strategy should consider the relationships among the firm's products rather than viewing each one in isolation. **Price lining** is *the practice of marketing merchandise at a limited number of prices.*[18] For example, a clothier might have a $225 line and a $300 line of men's suits. Price lining is used extensively in retail selling—witness the original five-and-ten-cent stores.

Price lining requires that the market segment to which the firm is appealing be identified. For example, "Samsonite sees its market not as all luggage, but as the 'medium-priced, hard side' portion of the luggage trade."[19] A dress manufacturer may have lines priced at $59.95, $79.95, or $99.95. Price lining not only simplifies the administration of the pricing structure but also alleviates the confusion that can occur when all products are priced separately.

One problem with a price line decision is that once it is made, retailers and manufacturers may have difficulty adjusting it. Rising costs, for example, may put the seller in the position of either changing the price lines (with its resulting confusion) or reducing production costs (which opens the firm to the complaint that "XYZ Company's merchandise certainly isn't what it used to be.").

Promotional Pricing

Promotional pricing *uses a lower-than-normal price as an ingredient in a firm's selling strategy.* AirCal employed a promotional pricing strategy to inaugurate air service from Seattle to five cities in California and

Nevada. Passengers could buy one-way tickets to Reno, San Jose, Oakland, Ontario, or Orange County airports for only $5, a saving of up to $105 over regular prices.[20]

Most promotional pricing is done at the retail level.[21] A **loss leader** is a *retail good priced at less than cost so as to attract customers who may then buy other regularly priced merchandise.* The use of loss leaders can be effective. For example:

Probably one of the best innovators of this pricing method was Cal Mayne of Dorothy Lane Food Store, Dayton, Ohio. He was one of the first men to systematically price specials and to evaluate their effect on gross margins and sales. Mayne increased sales substantially by featuring coffee, butter, and margarine at 10 percent below cost. Ten other demand items were priced competitively and at a loss when necessary to undersell competition. Still another group of so-called secondary demand items were priced in line with competition. Mayne based his pricing policy on the theory that a customer can only remember about 30 prices. Keep prices down on these items and the customer will stay with you.[22]

Some studies, however, have reported considerable price confusion on the part of consumers.[23] One study of consumer price recall reported that the average person missed the price he or she paid for coffee by over 12 percent, toothpaste by over 20 percent, and green beans by 24 percent. While some people named the prices exactly, others missed by several hundred percent.[24]

Three possible pitfalls should be considered in making promotional pricing decisions:

1. Promotional pricing may violate some state unfair trade laws.

2. Some consumers are little influenced by price appeals, so promotional pricing will have minimal impact on them.[25]

3. Continuous use of an artifically low rate may result in its acceptance as customary for the product. Poultry, which was used as a loss leader during the 1930s and 1940s, has suffered from this phenomenon.

PRICE-QUALITY RELATIONSHIPS

One of the most researched aspects of pricing is the relationship between price and consumer perception of the product's quality.[26] In the absence of other cues, price is an important indication of the way the consumer perceives the product's quality.[27] The higher the price, the better the buyer perceives the quality of the product. The relationship between price and perceived quality is a well-documented fact in contemporary marketing.

Probably the best price-quality conceptualization is the idea of price limits.[28] It is argued that consumers have limits within which product quality perception varies directly with price. A price below the lower limit is regarded as too cheap, while one above the higher limit is too expensive.

A low price suggests low quality to many consumers.

"I don't ask for much, but what I get should be of very good quality."

Source: Drawing by Victor; © 1980 The New Yorker Magazine, Inc.

This concept provides a reasonable explanation of the price-quality relationship. Most consumers do tend to set an acceptable price range when purchasing goods and services. The range, of course, varies among consumers, depending on their socioeconomic characteristics and buying disposition.

NEGOTIATED PRICES AND COMPETITIVE BIDDING

Many government and industrial procurement situations are not characterized by set prices, particularly for nonrecurring purchases such as a defense system for the armed services. Such markets are growing at a fast pace. For instance, government purchases now exceed 20 percent of U.S. gross national product.[29]

Competitive bidding involves buyers requesting that potential suppliers make price quotations on a proposed purchase or contract.[30] Specifications give a description of the item (or job) that the government unit or industrial firm wishes to acquire. One of the most important tasks in modern purchasing management is to adequately describe what the organization seeks to buy. This effort generally requires the assistance of the firm's technical personnel, such as engineers, designers, and chemists.

Competitive bidding strategy should employ the concept of *expected net profit,* which can be stated as:

Expected net profit = P (Bid − Costs)

where

P = The probability of the buyer accepting the bid

Consider the following example. A firm is going to submit a bid for a job that it estimates will cost $23,000. One executive has proposed a bid of $60,000, another a bid of $50,000. There is a 40 percent chance of the buyer accepting the first bid ($60,000) and a 60 percent chance of accepting the second bid ($50,000). The expected net profit formula indicates that the second bid will be best, since its expected net profit is the highest.

Bid 1

$$\text{ENP} = 0.40 (\$60,000 - \$23,000)$$
$$= 0.40 (\$37,000)$$
$$= \$14,800$$

Bid 2

$$\text{ENP} = 0.60 (\$50,000 - \$23,000)$$
$$= 0.60(\$27,000)$$
$$= \$16,200$$

The most difficult task in applying this concept is estimating the probability that a certain bid will be accepted. But this difficulty is not a valid reason for failing to quantify an estimate. Prior experience can provide the foundation for such estimates.

In some cases, industry and government purchasers use *negotiated contracts* instead of inviting competitive bidding on a project. In these situations, terms of the contract are set through talks between the buyer and a seller.

Where there is only one available supplier or where contracts require extensive research and development work, negotiated contracts are likely to be employed. These cases can be described as situations where competitive bidding would be the more expensive method of securing the product. For example, some state and local

SOME BIDS ARE VERY LOW

The Army Corps of Engineers needed to refit two pier barges. According to established procedures, it requested bids on the project. Three firms entered competitive bids. The first was for $20,000, the second was for $19,000, and the third was for $.01. Needless to say, the government quickly accepted the $.01 bid.

But why did the company submit such a low bid? It turned out that the firm was interested in the trestle bridges that topped the 165-foot pier barges. Under government procedures, these would be declared salvage and would become the property of the successful bidder.

Source: Adapted from "Bidder Gets 1-Cent Contract," *Detroit News,* September 27, 1978. Used by permission of UPI.

governments permit their agencies to negotiate purchases under a certain limit, say, $500 or $1,000. This policy is an attempt to eliminate the economic waste involved in obtaining bids for relatively minor purchases.

TRANSFER PRICING

One pricing problem peculiar to large-scale enterprises is determining an internal **transfer price**—*the price for sending goods from one company profit center to another.*[31] As companies expand, they need to decentralize management. Profit centers are often set up as a control device for the new operation. A **profit center** is *any part of the organization to which revenue and controllable costs can be assigned, such as a department.*

In large companies, profit centers can secure many of their resource requirements from within the corporate structure. The pricing problem becomes: What rate should Profit Center A (machining department) charge Profit Center B (assembly department) for machining the materials used by B? Should the price be the same as it would be if A did the work for an outside party? Should B receive a discount? The answer to these questions depends on the philosophy of the firm involved.

The transfer pricing dilemma is an example of the variations that a firm's pricing policy must deal with. Consider the case of UDC-Europe, a Universal Data Corporation subsidiary that itself has ten subsidiaries. Each of the ten is organized on a geographic basis, and each is treated as a separate profit center. Intercompany transfer prices are set at the annual budget meeting. Special situations, like unexpected volume, are handled through negotiations by the subsidiary managers. If complex tax problems arise, UDC-Europe's top management may set the transfer price.[32]

PRICING IN THE PUBLIC SECTOR

The pricing of public services has become an interesting and sometimes troublesome aspect of contemporary marketing. Traditionally, government services were priced using the full cost approach; users paid all costs associated with the service. In more recent years, there has been a move toward incremental or marginal pricing, which considers only those expenses specifically associated with a particular activity. However, it is often difficult to determine the costs that should be assigned to a particular activity or service. Government accounting problems are often more complex than those of private enterprise.

Another problem in pricing public services is that taxes act as an indirect price of a public service. Someone must decide the relationship between the direct and indirect prices of such a service. A shift toward indirect tax charges (where an income or earnings tax exists) is a decision to charge on the ability-to-pay rather than the use principle.

The pricing of any public service involves a basic policy decision as to whether the price is an instrument to recover costs or a technique for accomplishing some other social or civic objective. Public health services, for example, may be priced near zero so as to encourage their use, while parking fines in some cities are so high as to discourage the use of private automobiles in the central business district. Pricing decisions in the public sector are difficult because of their many noneconomic objectives.

SUMMARY

The main elements to consider in setting a pricing strategy are the organization for pricing decisions, pricing policies, price-quality relationships, negotiated prices, competitive bidding, transfer pricing, and pricing in the public sector. Methods for quoting prices depend on such factors as cost structures, traditional practices in a particular industry, and policies of individual firms. Prices quoted can be list prices, market prices, cash discounts, trade discounts, quantity discounts, and allowances such as trade-ins, promotional allowances, and rebates.

Shipping costs are often important in the pricing of goods. There are a number of alternatives for dealing with these costs: FOB plant, when the price does not include any shipping charges; freight absorption, when the buyer can deduct transportation expenses from the bill; uniform delivered price, when the same price—including shipping expenses—is charged to all buyers; zone pricing, when a set price exists within each region; and basing points, when the buyer pays a set price from a particular point, regardless of whether the goods are shipped from that point.

Pricing policies vary among firms. Among the most common are psychological pricing, which includes odd pricing; unit pricing; new-product pricing, which includes skimming pricing and penetration pricing; price flexibility; relative pricing; price lining; and promotional pricing.

A heavily researched area of pricing is the relationship between price and consumer perception of quality. A well-known and accepted concept is that of price limits—limits within which the perception of product quality varies directly with price.

Sometimes, prices are negotiated through competitive bidding, a situation where several buyers quote prices on the same service or good. At other times, prices depend on negotiated contracts, a situation where the terms of the contract are set through interactions between a particular buyer and seller.

A phenomenon of large corporations is transfer pricing, where a company sets prices for transferring goods or services from one company profit center to another.

Pricing in the public sector has become a troublesome aspect of marketing. It involves decisions on whether the price of public service is an instrument to recover costs or a technique for accomplishing some other social or civic purpose.

QUESTIONS FOR DISCUSSION

1. Explain the following terms:

list price	basing point system
market price	psychological pricing
cash discount	odd pricing
trade discount	unit pricing
quantity discount	skimming pricing
trade-ins	penetration pricing
promotional allowances	price flexibility
rebates	price lining
FOB plant	promotional pricing
freight absorption	loss leader
uniform delivered price	transfer price
zone pricing	profit center

2. Contrast the freight absorption and uniform delivered pricing systems.

3. Who is responsible for setting a price structure?

4. Who is responsible for administering a price structure?

5. Comment on the policy implications of the basing point system.

6. Prepare a list of arguments that might be used in justifying a basing point pricing system.

7. List and discuss the reasons for establishing price policies.

8. What is meant by price lining?

9. When does a price become a promotional price? What are the pitfalls in promotional pricing?

10. Discuss the relationship between price and the consumer's perception of product quality.

11. Contrast negotiated prices and competitive bidding.

12. Explain the expected net profit concept.

13. What types of decisions must be made in the pricing of public services?

14. At a recent meeting of a state highway commission, one member suggested that the pricing of new highways is inadequate. She pointed out that the pricing of highway construction has traditionally been based on the direct costs of land acquisition, site preparation, and actual construction. She noted that such calculations should include indirect costs, such as interest on debt and the property taxes lost when the highway land is no longer taxed. What is your opinion of this line of thought? Can you think of any other indirect costs that might be considered?

15. What type of new product pricing would be appropriate for the following items:
    a. a new ultrasensitive burglar and fire alarm
    b. a new pattern in a line of fine china
    c. a new deodorant
    d. a new doll

16. Air New Zealand offered Los Angeles to Auckland flights for $599 in 1981. Was this an example of odd pricing? Promotional pricing? Psychological pricing? Comment.

17.   How are prices quoted for each of the following:
      a. a ticket to the ballet
      b. General Motors J-car
      c. an aluminum siding installation by a local contractor
      d. a new sport shirt from a men's store
      Discuss why the methods of quoting prices are different.

18.   Comment on the following statement: Unit pricing is ridiculous because everyone ignores it.

19.   A metropolitan newspaper showed firms advertising prices such as $9.98, $4.44, and $2.27. Why would businesses use price quotations ending in 8, 4, and 7?

20.   What criteria should be considered for transfer pricing in a large corporation like General Electric?

NOTES

1.   Jeffrey H. Birnbaum, "Pricing of Products Is Still an Art, Often Having Little Link to Costs," *Wall Street Journal,* November 25, 1981. Reprinted by permission. © Dow Jones & Company, Inc. 1981. All rights reserved.

2.   Louis P. Bucklin, "The New Math of Distribution Channel Control," in *Review of Marketing,* 1978, eds. Gerald Zaltman and Thomas V. Bonoma (Chicago: American Marketing Association, 1978), pp. 453–70.

3.   Quantity discounts are discussed in Asho K. Rao, "Quantity Discounts in Today's Market," *Journal of Marketing,* Fall 1980, pp. 44–51.

4.   Jim Treloar, "Refugee Thanks Customers in Cash," *Detroit News,* July 26, 1979.

5.   Similar discussions are available in a variety of sources. See, for example, Kent B. Monroe, *Pricing: Making Profitable Decisions* (New York: McGraw-Hill, 1979), pp. 183–87.

6.   Donald V. Harper, *Price Policy and Procedure* (New York: Harcourt Brace Jovanovich, 1966), p. 204.

7.   Andy Pasztor, "Ford Tries Low Prices to Revive the Pinto as Consumer Fears Still Nag the Small Car," *Wall Street Journal,* September 12, 1978.

8.   See, for example, Zarrel V. Lambert, "Perceived Prices as Related to Odd and Even Price Findings," *Journal of Retailing,* Fall 1975, pp. 13–22, 78.

9.   David M. Georgoff, "Price Illusion and the Effect of Odd-Even Retail Pricing," *Southern Journal of Business,* April 1969, pp. 95–103. See also Dik W. Twedt, "Does the '9' Fixation in Retailing Really Promote Sales?" *Journal of Marketing,* October 1965, pp. 54–55; Benson P. Shapiro, "The Psychology of Pricing," *Harvard Business Review,* July-August 1968, pp. 14–16; and David M. Georgoff, *Odd-Even Retail Price Endings: Their Effects on Value Determination, Product Perception, and Buying Propensities* (East Lansing: Michigan State University, 1972).

10. Mark I. Alpert, *Pricing Decisions* (Glenview, Ill.: Scott Foresman, 1971), pp. 112–13.

11. Hans B. Thorelli, "AMA Board Approves Unit Pricing in Taking First Public Policy Stand," *Marketing News,* August 1, 1972, p. 1.

12. Two excellent articles appeared in the July 1972 issue of the *Journal of Marketing:* Kent B. Monroe and Peter J. La Placa, "What Are the Benefits of Unit Pricing?" pp. 16–22; and Michael J. Houston, "The Effect of Unit Pricing on Choices of Brand and Size in Economic Shopping," pp. 51–54. See also Carl E. Block, Robert Schooler, and David Erickson, "Consumer Reaction to Unit Pricing: An Empirical Study," *Mississippi Valley Journal of Business,* Winter 1971–72, pp. 36–46; William E. Kilbourne, "A Factorial Experiment on the Impact of Unit Pricing," *Journal of Marketing Research,* November 1974, pp. 453–55; and J. Edward Russo, Gene Krieser, and Sally Miyashita, "An Effective Display of Unit Price Information," *Journal of Marketing,* April 1975, pp. 11–19.

13. J. Edward Russo, "The Value of Unit Price Information," *Journal of Marketing Research,* May 1977, pp. 193–201.

14. See, for example, G. Clark Thompson and Morgan B. MacDonald, Jr., "Pricing New Products," *Conference Board Record,* January 1964, pp. 7–9.

15. Robert A. Lynn, *Price Policies and Marketing Management* (Homewood, Ill.: Richard D. Irwin, 1967), p. 137.

16. Walter J. Primeaux, Jr., "The Effect of Consumer Knowledge and Bargaining Strength on Final Selling Price: A Case Study," *Journal of Business,* October 1970, pp. 419–26. Another excellent article is James R. Krum, "Variable Pricing as a Promotional Tool," *Atlanta Economic Review,* November-December 1977, pp. 47–50.

17. A survey technique for testing price levels above and below current levels is described in D. Frank Jones, "A Survey Technique to Measure Demand under Various Pricing Strategies," *Journal of Marketing,* July 1975, pp. 75–77.

18. Alfred R. Oxenfeldt, "Product Line Pricing," *Harvard Business Review,* July-August 1966, pp. 137–44. Also see Kent B. Monroe and Andris A. Zottners, "Pricing the Product Line during Periods of Scarcity," *Journal of Marketing,* Summer 1979, pp. 49–59.

19. Lynn, *Price Policies and Marketing Management,* p. 143.

20. "Price Is Right for Inaugural Flights—$5," *Seattle Times,* May 29, 1981.

21. An interesting discussion appears in Edward A. Blair and E. Laird Landon, Jr., "The Effects of Reference Prices in Retail Advertisements," *Journal of Marketing,* Spring 1981, pp. 61–69.

22. Bernie Faust, William Gorman, Eric Oesterle, and Larry Buchta, "Effective Retail Pricing Policy," *Purdue Retailer* (Lafayette, Ind.: Department of Agricultural Economics, 1963), p. 2. Reprinted by permission.

23. Sidney Bennett and J. B. Wilkinson, "Price-Quantity Relationship and Price Elasticity under In-store Experimentation," *Journal of Business Research,* January 1974, pp. 27–38.

24. Karl A. Shilliff, "Determinants of Consumer Price Sensitivity for Selected Supermarket Products: An Empirical Investigation," *Akron Business & Economic Review,* Spring 1975, pp. 26–32.

25. John F. Willenborg and Robert E. Pitts, "Perceived Situational Effects on Price Sensitivity," *Journal of Business Research,* March 1977, pp. 27–38.

26. See, for example, Steven M. Cox, "The Relationship between Price and Quality in Situations of Repeated Trial," *Michigan Business Review,* May 1979, pp. 24–29; Nessim Hanna, "Can Effort/Satisfaction Theory Explain Price/Quality Relationships?" *Journal of the Academy of Marketing Science,* Winter 1978, pp. 91–100; and Barry Berman, "The Effects of Socioeconomic and Attitudinal Variables upon the Price-Quality Association," in *Proceedings of the Southwestern Marketing Association,* eds. Robert C. Haring, G. Edward Kiser, and Ronnie D. Whitt, Houston, Texas, 1979, pp. 46–47.

27. J. Douglass McConnell, "An Experimental Examination of the Price-Quality Relationship," *Journal of Business,* October 1968, pp. 439–44. A recent exchange on this issue appears in the May 1980 issue of the *Journal of Marketing Research.* See Peter C. Riesz, "A Major Price-perceived Quality Study Re-examined," pp. 259–62; and J. Douglass McConnell, "Comment on a Major Price-perceived Quality Study Re-examined," pp. 263–64.

28. Kent B. Monroe and M. Venkatesan, "The Concepts of Price Limits and Psychophysical Measurement: A Laboratory Experiment," in *Marketing in Society and the Economy: Proceedings of the American Marketing Association,* ed. Phillip R. McDonald (Cincinnati: American Marketing Association, 1969), pp. 345–51.

29. U.S. Bureau of the Census, *Statistical Abstract of the United States: 1980,* 101st ed. (Washington, D.C.: U.S. Government Printing Office, 1980), p. 439.

30. See, for example, David N. Burt and Joseph E. Boyett, Jr., "Reduction in Selling after the Introduction of Competition," *Journal of Marketing Research,* May 1979, pp. 275–79; Kenneth J. Roering and Robert J. Paul, "An Appraisal of Competitive Bidding Models," *Marquette Business Review,* Summer 1977, pp. 57–66; and Douglas G. Brooks, "Bidding for the Sake of Follow-on Contracts," *Journal of Marketing,* January 1978, pp. 35–38.

31. Interesting discussions of transfer pricing appear in Sylvain R. F. Plasschaert, *Transfer Pricing and Multinational Corporations* (New York: Praeger, 1979); and Roger Y. W. Tang, *Transfer Pricing Practices in the United States and Japan* (New York: Praeger, 1979).

32. M. Edgar Bennett, "Case of the Tangled Transfer Price," *Harvard Business Review,* May-June 1977, p. 22.

PART EIGHT

FURTHER PERSPECTIVES

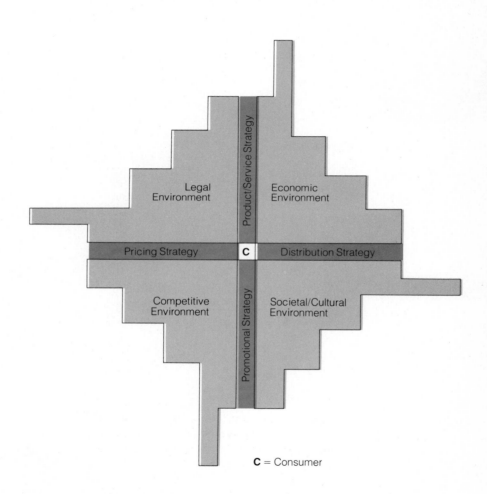

Legal Environment

Product/Service Strategy

Economic Environment

Pricing Strategy

C

Distribution Strategy

Competitive Environment

Promotional Strategy

Societal/Cultural Environment

C = Consumer

CHAPTER 19

INTERNATIONAL MARKETING

KEY TERMS

exporting
importing
balance of trade
balance of payments
exchange rate
floating exchange rate
devaluation
revaluation
countertrade
absolute advantage
comparative advantage
multinational corporation
tariffs
General Agreement on Tariffs and Trade
  (GATT)
Tokyo Round
import quota
embargo
exchange control
dumping
friendship, commerce, and navigation (FCN)
  treaties
cartels

LEARNING GOALS

1. To describe the importance of international marketing

2. To explain the basic concepts of international marketing and trade

3. To identify the various levels of involvement in international marketing

4. To describe the international aspects of marketing strategy

5. To describe the environment for international marketing

6. To list the three basic formats for economic integration

7. To show how the United States is an attractive market target for foreign marketers

Top management at Westinghouse realized that the corporation had a problem in the way it approached international marketing, despite its 25 percent sales earnings (and even a higher percentage of total profits) abroad. Westinghouse expected that foreign demand for its 8,000-item product line would expand faster abroad than it would domestically. But the company was poorly positioned to benefit from this increased demand.

The Pittsburgh-based corporation was organized along the strategic business unit concept described in Chapter 3. The unit or division managers were responsible for both domestic and foreign marketing. The export division had been abolished. Although this approach worked well in the United States, there were coordination problems abroad, where major projects might require the involvement of several Westinghouse units. Since each unit operated separately, customers were uncertain as to where decision-making power really rested. For instance, a Saudi buyer complained that 25 different Westinghouse sales representatives had called on him. A major sale was lost in Brazil because of the lack of coordination between a U.S.-based salesperson and two counterparts from the Brazilian subsidiary.

Management set up a special task force to study the problem and prepare a report within 90 days. The researchers discovered several alarming problems. One of the most critical was the fact that Westinghouse did not even know whether its foreign operations were profitable because of the unit managers' practice of charging costs to strong domestic operations. While some business units— like nuclear and defense—were strong overseas, others were not.

The internal report recommended (and management accepted) the addition of a *matrix organization,* a type of structure in which an operating unit actually reports to two different chains of command. So, a factory manager overseas would report to a country manager as well as to the stateside business unit. Westinghouse business units would still be responsible for pricing, technology, and capital budgets, but they would have to mesh their plans with those of the international group. The international unit would also be responsible for eliminating the duplication of sales efforts that had previously characterized Westinghouse overseas.

Westinghouse management set a target of 35 percent of sales from abroad. The corporation also decided to concentrate its efforts on seventeen national markets that offered the best growth opportunities. These included Australia, Brazil, France, Japan, Mexico, the People's Republic of China, Saudi Arabia, Singapore, South Korea, Spain, Taiwan, Venezuela, and West Germany. Westinghouse was clearly positioning itself to be a major factor in international markets in the 1980s.[1]

Some of the discussion in Chapter 15 follows that in Vern Terpstra, *International Marketing,* 3rd ed. (Hinsdale, Ill.: The Dryden Press, 1983).

THE INTER-NATIONAL SECTOR OF CONTEM-PORARY MARKETING

International marketing is obviously of considerable importance to Westinghouse. It is also important to Pfizer Inc., since it generates over half the company's total revenues. The importance of international marketing for selected U.S. firms is shown in Table 19.1. But just as some firms depend on foreign sales, others depend on purchasing raw materials to use in their manufacturing operations at home. A furniture company's purchase of South American mahogany is an example.

International trade is vital to a nation and its marketers for several reasons. It expands the market and makes production and distribution economies feasible. It can also mean more jobs at home. From 30,000 to 40,000 new jobs are supported by each billion dollars of exports.[2]

Foreign trade can be divided into **exporting**—*selling goods abroad*—and **importing**—*buying foreign goods and raw materials.* While the United States is the world's largest exporter and importer, foreign trade is still less critical to it than to many other nations. In fact, U.S. exports account for a modest 7.7 percent of the nation's gross national product.[3] The leading export for the United States is motor vehicles and parts, and the leading import is petroleum.[4] The leading U.S. exporters in total volume are Boeing, General Motors, General Electric, Ford, and Caterpillar Tractor.[5]

Since imports and exports are important contributors to a country's economic welfare, governments and other organizations are concerned about the status of various components of international marketing. The concepts of balance of trade and balance of payments are a good starting point for learning about international marketing.

Balance of Trade

A nation's **balance of trade** is determined by *the relationship between its exports and imports.* A favorable balance of trade occurs when a nation's exports exceed its imports. This means that, other things being

---

**TABLE 19.1
Importance of Foreign Markets to Some U.S. Companies in 1981**

Company	Percentage of 1981 Sales Abroad
AMF Incorporated	26.7
Bristol-Myers Company	29.3
Caterpillar Tractor Co.	56.6
The Coca-Cola Company	45.0
Dresser Industries, Inc.	23.0
Emhart Corporation	40.9
General Foods Corporation	30.9
H. J. Heinz Company	39.9
Hewlett-Packard Company	48.2
Minnesota Mining and Manufacturing Company	40.7
Pfizer Inc.	56.8
Polaroid Corporation	42.4

Source: 1981 annual reports of the listed companies.

equal, new money comes into the country via foreign sales. An unfavorable balance of trade, by contrast, results when imports exceed exports. The net money flow then is outward, other things being equal. The 1981 U.S. balance of trade was around a negative $39.7 billion.[6]

Balance of Payments

A country's balance of trade accounts for a major portion of its **balance of payments**—*a summary of all of a nation's international economic transactions during a year.* However, other factors are also important. A favorable balance of payments indicates there is a net money inflow, while an unfavorable balance of payments means that there is a net money outflow.

The balance of payments is also affected by such factors as tourism, military expenditures abroad, and foreign aid. A money outflow caused by these factors may exceed the money inflow from a favorable balance of trade and leave a nation with an unfavorable balance of payments.

Exchange Rate Adjustments

It is sometimes necessary for a nation to adjust its **exchange rate**—*the rate at which its currency can be exchanged for other currencies or gold.* These adjustments have a significant impact on the balance of trade and the balance of payments. **Floating exchange rates**—*those that are allowed to adjust to market conditions*—are now prevalent. The United States, among other countries, uses a floating exchange rate.

Devaluation occurs when *a nation reduces the value of its currency in relation to gold or some other currency.* Devaluation of the dollar has the effect of making U.S. products less expensive abroad and trips to the United States cheaper to foreign visitors. **Revaluation**—a less typical case—occurs when *a country adjusts the value of its currency upward.* Either of these actions may force firms to modify their world marketing strategies.

Countertrade: An Emerging Practice in International Marketing

Countertrade is a term used to describe *bartering in international trade.* In a recent example, McDonnell-Douglas traded a jet to an Eastern European nation for 400 tons of ham. The St. Louis company then resold part of its ham supply and used the rest for employee bonuses. Countertrade now accounts for 15 percent of all international trade, up from a mere 2 percent four years earlier.[7]

Historically, bartering has characterized East-West trade. Its growing popularity can be explained by marketers' attempts to expand sales, reduce balance of payments problems, move lower-quality products, and alleviate payment problems associated with fluctuating exchange rates.[8] Bartering is expected to continue to play a major role in international trade.

BASIC CONCEPTS IN INTERNATIONAL MARKETING

The Pacific island republic of Nauru has only 4,000 citizens, but one of the richest deposits of phosphate in the world covers 85 percent of its land area.[9] Japan's large population lives on a relatively small land mass, and the island nation is chronically deficient in some raw materials. Forced to depend on foreign trade, Japan has become a premier international marketer.[10]

These situations suggest that nations are usually better off if they specialize in certain products or marketing activities. By doing what they do best, they are able to exchange the products not needed domestically for foreign-made goods that are needed. Nauru could attempt to develop a tourist trade, but it has opted to specialize in phosphate mining. This allows it a higher standard of living than would be possible through diversified business enterprises. Specialization by countries sometimes produces odd situations: consider, for example, the "Buy American" stickers that can be found on the rear bumpers of some Datsuns and Toyotas.

An understanding of the concepts of absolute and comparative advantage is vital to the study of world marketing. These concepts explain why countries specialize in the marketing of certain products. A nation has an **absolute advantage** in the marketing of a product if *it is the sole producer or can produce the product for less than anyone else.* Since few nations are sole producers, and since economic conditions rapidly alter production costs, examples of absolute advantage are rare. The concept of **comparative advantage** is a more practical approach to international trade specialization. This concept says that *a nation has a comparative advantage in an item if it can produce it more efficiently than it can produce alternative products.* Nations usually produce and export those goods in which they have

The "buy American" sentiment sometimes produces surprises.

"My BUY AMERICAN bumper sticker was made in Japan."

Source: Cartoon Features Syndicate. Reprinted by permission.

the greatest comparative advantage (or the least comparative disadvantage) and import those items in which they have the least comparative advantage (or the greatest comparative disadvantage). The United States tends to export manufactured items (such as machinery) and natural resources (such as coal). By contrast, countries with lower labor costs tend to specialize in producing and marketing products that require significant labor content, such as textiles, shoes, and clothing.

Of course, there are noneconomic reasons for specializing in certain items. The United States, for example, is attempting to reduce its dependence on foreign oil for various political and strategic, as well as economic, reasons.

COMPETING IN THE WORLD MARKETPLACE

Many U.S. firms never venture outside their own domestic market. They feel they do not have to, because the U.S. market is huge. Even today, only about 8 percent of all domestic manufacturing firms export their products. And only 250 of these manufacturers account for 85 percent of all U.S. exports.[11] Those that do venture abroad find the international marketplace far different from the one to which they are accustomed. Market sizes, buyer behavior, and marketing practices all vary, which means that the international marketer must carefully evaluate all market segments in which he or she expects to compete.

Market Size

A prime ingredient of market size is population growth, and every day the world's population increases by about 200,000 people. By the year 2000, the world's population is expected to be 6.3 billion, compared to a little over 4 billion today. A review of these projections produces some important contrasts. Average birthrates are dropping, but death rates are declining even faster. Population growth has fallen in industrialized nations, but it has increased in the less-developed countries. Nearly 80 percent of the population in 2000 will live in less-developed nations.

Many of the world's new inhabitants live in large cities. By the year 2000, these urban dwellers are expected to account for half the world population instead of the current 39 percent. Today, twenty-one cities have a population of 5 million or more. In 2000, sixty such cities will exist. Mexico City, which now ranks third in population, is expected to grow to 31.5 million, making it the world's largest city.[12]

Statistical data indicate that the international marketplace will continue to grow in size and that it will become increasingly urbanized. This does not mean, however, that all foreign markets will have the same potential. Income differences, for instance, vitally affect any nation's market potential. India has a population of nearly 700 million, but its per capita income is very low. Canada, on the other hand, has only a small fraction of India's population, but its per capita income is nearly as high as that of the United States.

Buyer Behavior

Buyer behavior differs from one country to another. Therefore, marketers should carefully study each market before implementing a marketing strategy. Not all successful domestic marketing strategies can be exported to other parts of the world. Improved U.S.-Chinese relations will open up new markets for both nations. But the Chinese would be well advised to change some of their brand names before entering the American market: for example, a battery with the brand name "white elephant," and "maxipuke" playing cards.[13]

Marketers must also be careful that their marketing strategies comply with local customs, tastes, and buying practices. In some cases, even the product itself has to be modified. General Foods, for instance, offers different blends of coffee for each of its overseas markets. One variety goes to British consumers, who prefer to use considerable amounts of milk with their coffee; another goes to the French, who usually drink coffee black; still another mix goes to Latin Americans, who prefer a chicory taste.[14]

Different buying patterns mean that marketing executives should do considerable research before entering a foreign market. Sometimes, the research can be done by the marketer's own organization or a U.S.-based research firm. In other cases, a foreign-based marketing research organization should be used. Foreign research firms are often innovative. For example, Audits, Ltd., of Great Britain, pioneered in the field of home audits of package goods. The British firm provided its respondents with a special trash container rather than relying on a diary of purchases. Discarded packages were then studied to determine consumer buying patterns.[15]

MARKETING PRACTICES IN THE WORLD MARKETPLACE

Marketing practices vary the world over.[16] These practices must be taken into consideration when an "outside" firm decides to launch a marketing campaign. A high illiteracy rate, for example, may substantially limit the types of advertising campaigns employed. Aggressive sales efforts may be regarded negatively in some foreign cultures. Business customs and traditions may restrict a firm's distribution strategy to certain marketing channels. A brief consideration of each marketing strategy component will illustrate the differences that exist in marketing practices overseas.

Product Strategy

Although baseball may be known as an American pastime, Mizuno Corporation of Osaka, Japan, has developed an innovative product strategy for the U.S. market. About 400 professional baseball players in the United States now used custom-fitted Mizuno baseball gloves. Mizuno imports leather from the United States, then tans, cures, and shapes it into a baseball glove that does not need to be broken in. Mizuno has spent $3 million on research and development of an entire line of baseball equipment. The line includes plexiglass catcher's masks, an electronic umpire-to-scoreboard relay system, strike zone sensors, and electronic foul lines.[17]

Mizuno has chosen to offer an innovative product mix to the marketplace. But sometimes existing products can be modified to meet consumer needs.

Successful adaptation can significantly extend the market for a product. Sometimes, the product itself has to be modified; in other cases, it is the packaging; in still others, it is the product's identification. Consider the many products that use the word *mist* as part of their name. But imagine the difficulty of marketing such a product in Germany, where *mist* means "manure."[18]

Promotional Strategy

While effective personal selling continues to be vital in foreign markets, advertising has gained in importance. The wider availability of media such as radio and television has enhanced advertising's contribution to the overall promotional effort. But many U.S. advertising approaches are not really adaptable overseas. Promotional strategies tend to be strictly regulated in many foreign marketplaces.

Distribution Strategy

Sears, one of the most effective retailers in the United States, met its match in Seibu, a large Japanese retailer with six hundred outlets. So Sears turned to Seibu to sell its catalog merchandise in Japan. The venture was so successful that Allstate Insurance, a Sears subsidiary, began marketing its life insurance policies through Seibu's retail locations.[19]

Nissan Motors' Datsun is the leading seller in oil-rich Saudi Arabia (where gasoline, until recently, sold at 12 cents per gallon). Its large market share is credited to the excellent organization of local distributors, who were recruited in the early 1960s. The Japanese firm sought out Saudi entrepreneurs who had sufficient investment capital and who were skilled managers and marketers.[20] The strategy was obviously effective.

Distribution is a vital aspect of overseas marketing. Proper channels must be set up and extensive physical distribution problems handled. Transportation systems and warehousing facilities may be unavailable or of poor quality. International marketers must adapt speedily and efficiently to these situations if they are to profit from overseas sales.

Pricing Strategy

Pricing in foreign markets can be a critical ingredient in overall marketing strategy. Pricing practices in overseas markets are also subject to considerable competitive, economic, political, and legal constraints. International marketing managers must clearly understand these requirements if they are to succeed.

The most significant development in pricing strategy for international marketing has been the emergence of commodity marketing organizations that seek to control prices through collective action. OPEC (the Organization of Petroleum Exporting Countries) is the best example of these collective export organizations, but a variety of others exist.

LEVELS OF INVOLVEMENT IN INTERNATIONAL MARKETING

Several levels of involvement in international marketing can be identified: casual or accidental exporting, active exporting, foreign licensing, overseas marketing, and foreign production and marketing.

Casual or accidental exporting is a passive level of involvement in international marketing. A U.S. company may export goods without even knowing it if its goods are bought by resident buyers for foreign companies. In other cases, a firm may export only occasionally when surplus or obsolete inventory is available.

When the firm actually makes a commitment to seek export business, it engages in *active exporting.* While the exact extent of the commitment may vary, the term implies that the firm is making a continuing effort to sell its merchandise abroad.[21]

Foreign licensing occurs when a firm permits a foreign company to produce and distribute its merchandise under a formal agreement. Licensing has several advantages over exporting, among them the availability of local marketing information and distribution channels and protection from various legal barriers. Sometimes it is the best way to get into a particular market. For instance, Hughes Tool Company of Houston has negotiated a licensing agreement that will provide drill bits to the People's Republic of China.[22]

A firm that maintains a separate marketing or selling operation in a foreign country is involved in *overseas marketing.* Examples are foreign sales offices and overseas marketing subsidiaries. The product may be produced by domestic factories, foreign licensees, or contract manufacturers; but the company always directly controls foreign sales.

Foreign production and foreign marketing, the ultimate degree of company involvement in the international market arena, can be accomplished in the following ways:

1. The firm can set up its own production and marketing operation in the foreign country.

2. It can acquire an existing firm in the country in which it will do business.

3. It can form a *joint venture,* in which the risks, costs, and management of the foreign operation are shared with a partner who is usually a national of the host country.

ORGANIZING FOR MULTINATIONAL MARKETING

Multinational corporations *operate in several countries and literally view the world as their market.*[23] Not all multinationals are U.S. firms. In fact, according to the Conference Board, the United States has continued to decline as the home for such worldwide corporations. Now only 47 percent of the world's largest corporations are based in the United States, down from 58 percent in 1971 and 67 percent in 1963. Germany ranked second with 13 multinationals in the most recent listing.[24]

Hewlett-Packard provides an illustration of how a multinational firm can operate effectively. The California-based electronics company sells nearly as much abroad as it does in the United States. How does Hewlett-Packard do it? The company encourages its European subsidiaries to run autonomously with European management. Subsidiaries are told to use local technical talent to produce export products. Hewlett-Packard's German subsidiary has been particularly successful, deriving more than half of its revenues from non-German markets. Some German executives now manage Hewlett-Packard operations in California.[25]

Multinationals have been the subject of considerable public scrutiny both in the United States and abroad. Some U.S. multinationals have been criticized for their involvement in South Africa. These firms typically respond that they are contributing to social and economic progress in all the nations in which they operate. Some nations—Australia and Canada, for example—have occasionally expressed concern about the multinationals' domination of some domestic markets. Similar complaints have been expressed in the United States about the inroads made by Japanese automobile firms. While criticism of multinational practices is likely to continue, it is obvious that multinational corporations have become fixtures in the international marketplace.

DEPRESS ACCELERATOR . . . PLEASE!

Multinational organizations also experience some unexpected problems. One such example comes from the joint venture of American Motors and France's Renault (Renault owns nearly half of the U.S. firm). A Renault engineer was on a test ride with an American Motors driver. When the car did not respond appropriately, the engineer told the American, "Depress accelerator." The driver complied, and the car picked up speed. The Frenchman yelled, "Depress accelerator! Depress accelerator!" And again the test driver complied. But as the engineer kept screaming, the test driver finally correctly translated the Frenchman's "Depress" into American: "Stop pressing!"

THE ENVIRONMENT FOR INTER-NATIONAL MARKETING

Various environmental factors can influence international marketing strategy. Marketers should be as aware of these influences as they are of those in domestic markets.

Cultural, Economic, and Societal Factors

International marketing is often influenced by cultural, economic, and societal factors. The economic status of some countries makes them less or more likely candidates for international business expansion. Nations with low per-capita income may be poor markets for expensive industrial machinery but good markets for agricultural hand tools. These nations cannot afford the technical equipment necessary in an industrialized society. Wealthier countries can prove to be prime markets for the products of many U.S. industries, particularly those involved with consumer goods and advanced industrial products.

Many products have failed abroad simply because the producing firm tried to use the same marketing strategy that was successful in the United States. Consider, for example, an advertising strategy based primarily on the use of print media and featuring testimonials. Such a campaign would offer dim prospects in a less developed nation with a high degree of illiteracy.

U.S. products sometimes face consumer resistance abroad. American automobiles, for example, have traditionally been rejected by European drivers, who complain of poor styling, low gasoline mileage, and poor handling. But the new, smaller cars from Detroit are making moderate inroads into European markets.[26] This reversal suggests that it is not always possible to determine the precise impact of cultural, economic, or societal factors prior to entering a foreign market. Japanese tea drinkers for centuries have preferred natural tea. But Boston Tea Company's blended, spiced, and herbed tea is now selling well in Japan.[27]

Trade Restrictions

Assorted trade restrictions also affect world trade. These restrictions are most commonly expressed through **tariffs**—*taxes levied against imported products.* Some tariffs are based on a set tax per pound, gallon, or unit; others are figured on the value of the imported product. They can be classified as either revenue or protective tariffs. *Revenue tariffs* are designed to raise funds for the government. Most of the revenue of the early U.S. government came from this source. *Protective tariffs* are designed to raise the retail price of an imported product to match or exceed a similar domestic product. Protective tariffs are usually higher than revenue tariffs. In the past, it was believed that a country should protect its "infant" industries by using tariffs to keep out foreign-made products. Some foreign goods would enter, but the addition of a high tariff payment would make domestic products competitive in price. Recently, it has been argued that tariffs should be raised to protect employment and profits in domestic U.S. industry.

The **General Agreement on Tariffs and Trade (GATT),** *an international trade accord,* has sponsored several tariff negotiations that have reduced the overall level of tariffs throughout the world. The latest series, the so-called **Tokyo Round,** began in 1974 and concluded in 1979. The Tokyo Round *reduced tariffs by about 33 percent over an eight-year period.* The agreement also lessened nontariff barriers, such as government procurement regulations, that discriminated against foreign marketers.[28]

There are also other forms of trade restriction. An **import quota** *sets limits on the amount of products in certain categories that can be imported.* Import quotas seek to protect local industry and employment and to preserve foreign exchange. The ultimate quota is the **embargo,** *the complete ban on the import of certain products.* In the past, the United States has prohibited the import of products from some Communist countries. The United States has also used export quotas. In 1982, for example, President Reagan enforced trade sanctions against Argentina for its actions against Great Britain in the Falkland Islands dispute.[29]

Foreign trade can also be regulated by exchange control through a central bank or government agency. **Exchange control** means that *firms gaining foreign exchange by exporting must sell this exchange to the central bank, or other agency, and importers must buy foreign exchange from the same organization.* The exchange control authority can then allocate, expand, or restrict foreign exchange according to existing national policy.

Dumping: A Contemporary Marketing Problem

Dumping is *the practice of selling a product at a lower price in a foreign market than it sells for in the producer's domestic market.* In the late 1970s, Bethlehem Steel ran advertisements to protest what it viewed as dumping in the steel industry.[30] It is often argued that foreign governments give substantial export support to their own companies. Such support may permit these firms to extend their export markets by offering lower prices abroad.

Products that have been dumped on U.S. markets can be subject to additional import tariffs to bring their prices in line with domestically produced products. For instance, a 32 percent dumping duty was assessed against five Japanese steel sellers. However, businesses often complain that charges of alleged dumping must go through a lengthy investigative and bureaucratic procedure before duties are assessed. In an attempt to speed up the process in the steel industry, a *trigger pricing system,* which established a set of minimum steel prices, has been used. Japanese production costs, the world's lowest, were used in these calculations. Any imported steel selling at less than these rates triggers an immediate Treasury Department investigation. If dumping is substantiated, additional duties are imposed.

Steel is not the only product to involve allegations of dumping. Similar allegations have been leveled against foreign makers of products as diverse as hockey sticks, cement, and motorcycles.

Demands for protection against foreign imports are common in all countries, particularly during periods of economic uncertainty. Firms ask for protection against sales losses, and unions seek to preserve their members' jobs. Overall, however, the long-term trend is in the direction of free trade among nations.

Political and Legal Factors

Political factors greatly influence international marketing. The election of Socialist Francois Mitterand as President of France initially caused considerable furor among international marketers.[31] Earlier political tur-

---

SETTING QUOTAS FOR JAPANESE CARS

Imported cars nearly brought the U.S. domestic auto industry to its knees at the beginning of the decade. Imports—particularly Japanese models—accounted for 29 percent of the U.S. automobile market. About 240,000 U.S. auto workers—nearly 20 percent of the United Auto Workers membership—were laid off. The U.S. companies and the union called for help from Washington.

The flood of imported Japanese cars set off one of the biggest public debates over international trade ever. Both the Carter and Reagan administrations considered the issue. Proponents of government assistance argued that it would reduce the severe unemployment in the industry and in states like Michigan; it would provide domestic manufacturers the necessary money and time to make the industry competitive; and failure to act would retard the nation's economic recovery. Opponents argued that federal intervention would be only a short-term fix, and that limiting Japanese models would be inflationary. Federal assistance was also counter to the free-market philosophy of the Reagan administration, which made the final decision.

The debate was resolved in 1981 when the Japanese, under the threat of mandatory U.S. import limits, agreed to hold their exports to 1.68 million in the next year, and to tie second- and third-year exports to the growth of U.S. sales. However, Japanese exporters substantially increased their U.S. inventories prior to the agreement, so some of the reduction would be inventory cuts and not imports. Whether the U.S. manufacturers would ever recover their former dominance is an unresolved marketing question of the 1980s.

Source: Steve Posner, "In Japanese Plants, the Workers Help Manage," *Seattle Business Journal*, March 9, 1981, p. 20; Herbert Zeltner, "Sounding Board Surveys Impact of the Imports on U.S. Marketing," *Advertising Age*, December 8, 1980, p. 55; Jerry Flint, "Less than Meets the Eye," *Forbes*, May 25, 1981, p. 38; and John F. Stacks, "The Administration's Split on Auto Imports," *FORTUNE*, May 4, 1981, pp. 156–58, 162, 166.

moil in South Korea, Nicaragua, El Salvador, and Iran also suggests how volatile this environmental factor can be in international markets. In fact, many U.S. firms have now set up internal political risk assessment (PRA) units or turned to outside consulting services to evaluate the political risks of the marketplace in which they operate.[32] Sometimes marketing strategies have to be adjusted to reflect the new situation. For example, when Colgate introduced Irish Spring in England, it marketed the soap as "Nordic Spring."[33]

Many nations try to achieve political objectives through international business activities. Japan, for instance, has openly encouraged its firms' involvement in international marketing, because much of the nation's economy is dependent on overseas sales.

Legal requirements complicate world marketing. Indonesia has banned commercial advertisements from the nation's only television channel. It was feared that the advertisements would cause 80 percent of the population living in rural areas to envy those who resided in cities.[34] All commercials in the United Kingdom and Australia must be cleared in advance. In the Netherlands, ads for candy must also show a toothbrush.[35] Some nations have *local content laws* that specify the portion of a product that must come from domestic sources. These examples suggest that managers involved in international marketing must be well-versed in legislation affecting their specific industry.

The legal environment for U.S. firms operating abroad can be divided into three dimensions: (1) U.S. law, (2) international law, and (3) legal requirements of host nations. International law can be found in the treaties, conventions, and agreements that exist among nations. The United States has many **friendship, commerce, and navigation (FCN) treaties,** *agreements that deal with many aspects of commercial relations with other countries,* such as the right to conduct business in the treaty partner's domestic market.

Other international business agreements concern international standards for various products, patents, trademarks, reciprocal tax treaties, export control, international air travel, and international communication. The International Monetary Fund has been set up to lend foreign exchange to nations that require it to conduct international trade. These agreements facilitate the whole process of world marketing.

The legal requirements of host nations affect foreign marketers. For example, some nations limit foreign ownership in their business sectors. International marketers in general recognize the importance of obeying the laws and regulations of the countries within which they operate. Even the slightest violations of these legal requirements are setbacks for the future of international trade.

International marketing is subject to various trade regulations, tax laws, and import/export requirements. One of the best-known U.S. laws is the *Webb-Pomerene Export Trade Act* (1918), which ex-

JAPAN, INC.

"Japan, Inc." is a term coined to describe how Japanese companies approach international markets. Exports are vital to the Japanese economy, so they in fact become national goals. The result is close cooperation between Japanese firms and the government. For instance, because antitrust regulations are minimal, Japanese car producers and the government cooperated in getting a two-year jump on the United States in emission-control technology.

The Japanese government's contribution to this unique system is the Ministry of International Trade and Industry (MITI), one of the most powerful entities in Japan. The ministry acts as a central planner and business adviser to all segments of Japanese industry. It also provides the impetus for much of Japan's export prowess. Many American firms complain that they do not compete with Japanese companies, but with the entire nation of Japan.

Source: James Cook, "Restricting Auto Imports—The Japanese View," *Forbes*, March 30, 1981, pp. 50–52; and Christopher Byron, "How Japan Does It," *Time*, March 30, 1981, pp. 54–60.

empted from antitrust laws various combinations of U.S. firms acting together to develop foreign markets. The intent was to give U.S. industry economic power equal to that possessed by **cartels,** *the monopolistic organizations of foreign firms.* Companies operating under the Webb-Pomerene Act cannot reduce competition within the United States and cannot use "unfair methods of competition." It is generally recognized that Webb-Pomerene associations have not been significant in the growth of U.S. trade.[36]

The Foreign Corrupt Practices Act

The most important new legislation is the *Foreign Corrupt Practices Act,* which makes it illegal to bribe a foreign official in an attempt to solicit new or repeat sales abroad. The act also specifies that adequate accounting controls be installed to monitor internal compliance. Violations can result in a $1 million fine for the firm and a $10,000 fine and five years' imprisonment for individuals involved.[37] This law has proven to be quite controversial since several companies have reported that the paperwork involved has caused them to lose overseas sales. The Reagan administration has supported legislation to ease some of the restrictive language of the act.[38]

MULTI-NATIONAL ECONOMIC INTEGRATION

A noticeable trend toward multinational economic integration has developed since the close of World War II. The *Common Market,* or European Economic Community (EEC), is the best known of these multinational economic communities.

Multinational economic integration can occur in several ways. The simplest approach is a *free trade area,* where the participants agree to free trade of goods among themselves in a particular area. All tariffs and trade restrictions are abolished between the nations involved. A *customs union* establishes a free trade area, plus a uniform tariff for trade with nonmember nations. The EEC is the best example of a customs union. A true *common market* (or *economic union*) involves a customs union and also seeks to bring all government regulations affecting trade into agreement. The EEC has been moving in the direction of an economic union.

Multinational economic communities have played a significant part in international business. United States firms invested heavily in Western Europe in the 1960s basically because of the attraction of larger markets offered by the EEC. Multinational economic integration is forcing management to adapt its operations abroad, and it is likely that the pace will accelerate.

THE UNITED STATES AS A MARKET FOR INTERNATIONAL MARKETERS

The United States has become an increasingly inviting target for foreign marketers. It has a large population, high levels of discretionary income, political stability, an attitude generally favorable to foreign investment, and economic ills that are relatively controlled in comparison to many other countries. Table 19.2 lists the top ten foreign investors in the United States.

A number of foreign-owned competitors have found the United States an attractive market. Retailing has been a recent target of foreign companies. All of the following U.S. retailers are owned in full or in part by an overseas firm: A&P (Germany), Grand Union (France), Gimbel Brothers (United Kingdom), Fed Mart (Germany), Bi-Lo (Netherlands), Kohl (United Kingdom), Fuir's (Germany), Dillard Department Stores (Netherlands), Red Food Stores (France), F.A.O. Schwartz (Switzerland), Maurices (Netherlands), and Winn's Stores (Germany).[39]

Some buyers have shown a preference for foreign products over domestic competitors. Foreign sports cars, English china, and French wine all hold sizeable shares of the U.S. market. Some foreign products, such as Porsche sports cars, are sold in the United States because of the quality image. Others sell on the basis of a price advantage over domestic competition.

U.S. marketers must expect to face substantial foreign competition in the years ahead. The United States' high level of buying power is sure to continue its considerable appeal abroad, and the reduction of trade barriers and expanded international marketing appear to be long-run trends.

TABLE 19.2   Top Ten Foreign Investors in the United States

Foreign investor	Country	U.S. company	% owned	Industries	Revenue (millions)	Net income (millions)	Assets (millions)
1 Anglo American Corp of So Africa Ltd[1] Minerals & Resources	So Africa						
	Bermuda	Engelhard Min & Chem[1,2]	32%	diversified metals	$26,570	$ 532.7	$ 6,301
		Inspiration Consol Copper	50	copper	178	−17.7	199
Hudson Bay M&S[1]	Canada	Terra Chemicals Intl[1]	55	fertilizer	299	10.3	160
					27,047		
2 Royal Dutch/ Shell Group[1]	Netherlands UK	Shell Oil Co[1]	69	oil	19,830	1,542.0	17,615
		Scallop Corp	100	oil			
		Massey Coal Co	50	coal			
		Billiton Metals & Ores USA	100	metals			
		Ocean Minerals	43	metals	4,734[3]	NA	8,481[3]
		General Atomic Co	50	nuclear			
					24,564[3]		
3 British Petroleum Ltd[1]	UK	Standard Oil Ohio[1]	53	energy	11,023	1,811.2	12,080
4 Tengelmann Group	Germany	Great A&P Tea[1]	50	supermarkets	6,990	−43.0	1,309
5 Friedrich Flick Group	Germany	W. R. Grace[1]	26	chemicals, multicompany	6,101	283.8	4,365
6 Générale Occidentale SA	France	Grand Union	100	supermarkets	3,626[3]	34.3	NA
		Diamond International[1]	29	packaging, lumber	1,283	40.6	943
					4,909		
7 B.A.T. Industries Ltd[1]	UK	BATUS	100	paper, retailing, tobacco	3,700[3]	NA	NA
		Germaine Monteil	100	cosmetics	500[3]	NA	NA
					4,200[3]		
8 Beneficiaries of US Philips Trust	Netherlands	North American Philips[1]	62	electronics	2,658	74.5	1,518
9 Regie National des Usines Renault	France	American Motors Corp[1]	46	automobile	2,553	−197.5	1,029
10 Nestlé SA	Switzerland	Nestlé Co	100	food			
		Cain's Coffee	100	coffee			
		Libby, McNeill & Libby	100	food			
		Stouffer Corp	100	food, restaurants	2,400[3]	NA	NA
		Alcon Laboratories	100	drugs			
		Beech-Nut Foods Corp	100	baby foods			

1. Publicly traded in U.S.
2. Results are before spinoff of certain operations; name changed to Phibro Corp.
3. Estimate.
Source: From "New Faces in an Age of Megadeals," *Forbes*, July 6, 1981, p. 84. Used by permission.

SUMMARY

International marketing has become increasingly important to the United States. Many U.S. firms depend on their ability to market their goods abroad, while others depend on buying raw materials from other countries.

International marketing is often considered in terms of a nation's balance of trade (flow of money into or out of the country). Countries must sometimes adjust their exchange rates (the rates at which their currency can be exchanged for others or for gold). Countertrade, or bartering, is also playing an increased role in international marketing.

Two of the basic concepts in international marketing are absolute advantage and comparative advantage. An absolute advantage exists if a nation is the sole producer of an item or can produce it for less than any other nation. A comparative advantage exists if a country can produce an item more efficiently than it can produce alternate ones.

Competing in overseas markets is often considerably different from competing at home. Market size, buying behavior, and marketing practices may all differ. International marketers must make significant adaptations in their product, distribution, promotional, and pricing strategies to fit different markets abroad.

Several levels of involvement in international marketing can be identified: casual or accidental exporting, active exporting, foreign licensing, overseas marketing, and foreign production and foreign marketing. The world's largest firms are usually multinational in their orientation. Such companies operate in several countries and view the world as their market.

Various environmental factors can influence international marketing strategy. Cultural, economic, and societal factors can hinder international marketing. So can assorted trade restrictions and political and legal factors.

Since the end of World War II, there has been a noticeable trend toward multinational economic integration. Three basic formats for integration are free trade areas, customs unions, and common markets.

The United States is now viewed as an attractive market for marketers from abroad. U.S. firms can expect to face growing foreign competition in the domestic market.

QUESTIONS FOR DISCUSSION

1. Explain the following terms:

exporting
importing
balance of trade
balance of payments
exchange rate
floating exchange rate
devaluation

tariffs
General Agreement on Tariffs and Trade (GATT)
Tokyo Round
import quota
embargo
exchange control

revaluation   dumping
countertrade   friendship, commerce, and navigation
absolute advantage   (FCN) treaties
comparative advantage   cartels
multinational corporation

2. Comment on the following statement: International business offers both opportunities and challenges to contemporary marketers.

3. How important is exporting and importing to the United States?

4. France's Perrier water has become very popular in the United States. Research the marketing program used to sell water to people in the United States.

5. How could a nation have both a favorable balance of trade and an unfavorable balance of payments?

6. Trace the recent experience of the United States in the balance of trade and balance of payments accounts.

7. What effect does the reduction of a nation's exchange rate have on international marketing?

8. Differentiate between the concepts of absolute advantage and comparative advantage. List other factors that can influence what a nation produces and markets.

9. Describe the existing trends in world population. How do these trends affect international marketing?

10. Discuss this statement: It is sometimes dangerous for a firm to attempt to export its marketing strategy.

11. Describe the types of adaptations that international business forces firms to make in their marketing strategies.

12. What is your opinion of existing U.S. policy toward dumping?

13. Identify and explain the different levels of involvement in international marketing.

14. Satra Corporation of New York imports the Lada—a Russian-built car—into the United States.[40] What type of marketing strategy would you suggest Satra use? What problems do you expect the importer to encounter?

15. Outline the basic premises behind the operation of a multinational corporation.

16. What environmental factors influence international marketing?

17. Do you agree with the general movement toward reduced trade restrictions among nations? Explain.

18. How has multinational economic integration affected international marketing?

19. Why is the United States such an attractive market target for foreign marketers? What does this mean for U.S. firms?

20. Some people argue that foreign investment in the United States should be limited. Would you agree with a plan that would limit such investment in a particular company to some specified amount? Explain.

NOTES

1. Hugh D. Menzies, "Westinghouse Takes Aim at the World," *FORTUNE,* January 14, 1980, pp. 48–53. © 1980 Time, Inc. All rights reserved.
2. "Trying to Right the Balance," *Time,* October 9, 1979, p. 84.
3. Calculated from *The World Almanac & Book of Facts 1981* (New York: Newspaper Enterprise Association, Inc., 1980), pp. 167, 200.
4. U.S. Department of Commerce, Bureau of Economic Analysis, *Survey of Current Business,* July 1978, pp. S–22 to S–24.
5. "The Fifty Leading Exporters," *FORTUNE,* August 24, 1981, pp. 84–85.
6. Bureau of Economic Analysis, *Survey of Current Business*, February 1982, p. 8.
7. Gary Sharpe, "Some Shrewd Yankee Traders Are Getting Paid Off in Merchandise," *Seattle Business Journal,* June 8, 1981, pp. 12–13. Reprinted with permission; all rights reserved.
8. Robert E. Weigand, "Apricots for Ammonia: Barter, Clearing, Switching, and Compensation in International Business," *California Management Review,* Fall 1979, pp. 33–41. Also see Weigand's article "Barters and Buy-Backs: Let Western Firms Beware," *Business Horizons,* June 1980, pp. 54–61.
9. Charles Hillinger, "Nauru Is Killing the Bird That Laid the Golden Guano," *Detroit News,* April 2, 1978.
10. Japan's need for international trade is pointed out in Allan G. Reddy, "Japan's Prosperity to Success in International Markets," *Marketing News,* February 6, 1981, p. 15.
11. "U.S. Urges Exports from Small Business," *Detroit News,* January 15, 1980.
12. World population growth is traced in Jonathan Spivak, "Population of a World Growing Faster than Experts Anticipated," *Wall Street Journal,* April 12, 1976; and "Soon a World of 6 Billion People," *U.S. News & World Report,* March 5, 1979, p. 8.
13. "Teaching Management to Marxists," *FORTUNE,* March 23, 1981, p. 103.
14. David A. Ricks, Marilyn Y. C. Fu, and Jeffrey S. Arpan, *International Business Blunders* (Columbus, Ohio: Grid, 1974), pp. 17–18.
15. Ralph Z. Sorenson II, "U.S. Marketers Can Learn from European Innovators," *Harvard Business Review,* September–October 1972, p. 97.
16. Differences in marketing strategies in the United States and abroad are noted in such articles as Graham R. Dowling, "Information Content in U.S. and Australian Television Advertising," *Journal of Marketing,* Fall 1980, pp. 34–37; and Mushtag Lugmani, Zahir A. Quraeshi, and Linda Delene, "Marketing in Islamic Countries: A Viewpoint," *MSU Business Topics,* Summer 1980, pp. 17–25.
17. "Japanese Company Invades U.S. Sporting Goods Market with Futuristic Baseball Gear," *Marketing News,* March 20, 1981, p. 18. Used by permission of the American Marketing Association.
18. William Mathewson, "Trademarks Are a Global Business These Days but Finding Registerable Ones Is a Big Problem," *Wall Street Journal,* September 4, 1975.
19. "Sears Adds Insurance to Its Line of Exports," *Business Week,* August 4, 1975, p. 39.
20. "Nissan Competes with the Camel," *Business Week,* May 26, 1975, p. 44.
21. Small-scale exporting is discussed in Ralph A. Rieth, Jr., and Edward T. Ryan, Jr., "A Study of the Perceptions of Selected Small Massachusetts Manufacturers toward Exporting," Venkatakrishna V. Bellur, ed.; Thomas R. Baird, Paul T. Hertz, Roger L. Jenkins, Jay D. Lindquist, and Stephen W. Miller, co-editors, *Developments in Marketing Science,* vol. VI (Marquette, Mich.: Academy of Marketing Science, 1981), pp. 97–100.
22. "No Great Leap Forward for U.S. Exports," *Business Week,* May 26, 1980, p. 67.
23. The marketing strategies and problems of multinational companies are discussed in Jacques Picard, "Determinants of Centralization of Marketing Decision-making in Multinational Corporations," Richard P. Bagozzi, Kenneth L. Bernhardt, Paul S. Busch, David W. Cravens, Joseph F. Hair, Jr., and Carol A. Scott, *Marketing in the 1980s* (Chicago: American Marketing Association, 1980), pp. 259–61; and Yves L. Doz and C. K. Prahalad, "How MNC's Cope with Host Government Intervention," *Harvard Business Review,* March–April 1980, pp. 149–57.
24. "U.S. Industrial Lead Wanes as Foreign Multinationals Gain," *Marketing News,* May 29, 1981, p. 1.
25. "Hewlett-Packard's Buffer against Recession," *Business Week,* July 7, 1980, p. 32.
26. Reported in "GM's Big Push to Sell U.S. Built Cars," *Business Week,* July 31, 1978, p. 45; and "Europe Takes to U.S. Autos," *Detroit News,* October 29, 1978.
27. "Business Bulletin," *Wall Street Journal,* September 28, 1978.
28. Peter Nulty, "Why the Tokyo Round Was a U.S. Victory," *FORTUNE,* May 21, 1979, pp. 130–32, 134–35; "A Smooth End to the Tokyo Round," *Business Week,* April 9, 1979, pp. 32–33; "How the U.S. Scored on Trade," *Business Week,* May 7, 1979, pp. 34–35; "Can World Head

Off a Trade War?" *U.S. News & World Report,* April 23, 1979, pp. 43–44; and "Significant Trends," *Sales & Marketing Management,* May 14, 1979, p. 82.

29. "Sanctions Called Major 'Political Signal'," *Seattle Times,* May 1, 1982.

30. "Dumping," *Advertising Age,* October 24, 1977, pp. 28, 112; Greg Conderacci, "Trigger-price System to Help Steel Industry Triggers Much Dismay," *Wall Street Journal,* September 26, 1978; and "Mounting Clamor for Trade Barriers," *U.S. News & World Report,* February 6, 1978, p. 57.

31. "Business Is Feeling a Mitterand Shock," *Business Week,* May 25, 1981, p. 66.

32. "The Post-Shah Surge in Political-risk Studies," *Business Week,* December 1, 1980, p. 69.

33. "Off the Record," *Detroit News,* February 28, 1975.

34. Wosief Djajanto, "Indonesia Government Expands Ad Ban," *Advertising Age,* March 16, 1981, p. 22.

35. J. J. Boddewyn, "The Global Spread of Advertising Regulation," *MSU Business Topics,* Spring 1981, pp. 6, 9.

36. A. D. Cao, "U.S. Export Trading Company: A Model of Export Promotion in the 80's," Bellur *et al.* (1981), pp. 85–90.

37. "The Antibribery Bill Backfires," *Business Week,* April 17, 1978, p. 143. Also see Frederick L. Neumann, "Corporate Audit Committees and the Foreign Corrupt Practices Act," *Business Horizons,* June 1980, pp. 62–71; Jack G. Kaikati and Wayne A. Label, "American Bribery Legislation: An Obstacle to International Marketing," *Journal of Marketing,* Fall 1980, pp. 38–43; David N. Ricchiute, "Illegal Payments, Deception of Auditors, and Reports on Internal Control," *MSU Business Topics,* Spring 1980, pp. 57–62; and Mark Pastin and Michael Hooker, "Ethics and the Foreign Corrupt Practices Act," *Business Horizons,* December 1980, pp. 43–48.

38. William M. Carley and Stan Crock, "Senate to Begin Debate on Administration's Plan to Ease Rules against Paying Bribes Overseas," *Wall Street Journal,* May 20, 1981.

39. Robert Ball, "Europe's U.S. Shopping Spree," *FORTUNE,* December 1, 1980, pp. 82–85, 88.

40. Michael J. Trojanowski, "A Lada in Your Future?" *Detroit News,* March 20, 1980.

CHAPTER 20

MARKETING IN THE 1980s: SOCIETAL ISSUES AND NONPROFIT APPLICATIONS

KEY TERMS

public responsibility committee
consumerism
marketing ethics
social responsibility
ecology
planned obsolescence
pollution
recycling
nonprofit organization
bottom line
broadening concept

LEARNING GOALS

1. To describe how external relationships form the basis of the societal issues confronting contemporary marketing

2. To explain the need for better measures of marketing performance

3. To categorize the current issues in marketing

4. To identify the primary characteristics of nonprofit organizations

5. To describe how marketing can be integrated into nonprofit organizations

6. To discuss the marketing mix for nonprofits, and how these strategies can be evaluated

7. To explain how marketers can assess trends that will impact the marketplace

This chapter examines two of the most significant factors in marketing in the 1980s. First, there is the expanded role of marketing within the societal context. People simply expect more of marketers than they did a few decades ago. Secondly, marketing's pervasive application has moved it into many nontraditional areas.

The Reagan landslide in 1980 marked an abrupt shift in national philosophy, as America again turned to private enterprise to solve societal problems. Marketing plays a key role in this transition. And marketing also played a key role in getting Reagan elected.

RICHARD B. WIRTHLIN'S BLACK BOOK

Richard B. Wirthlin and his firm, Decision Making Information (DMI), played a major role in the Reagan election. Wirthlin conducted the political polling and acted as a campaign strategist. Wirthlin is a marketing researcher whose clients include Sears, Standard Oil of Ohio, Coors, G. D. Searle, and Armour-Dial.

The DMI research cost $1.3 million, while the Carter campaign spent $2 million. But while major polls judged the election too close to call, Wirthlin maintained that Reagan led by 10 percentage points—a margin confirmed by the voters on election day.

Wirthlin used marketing research to prepare the so-called "Black Book," a 176-page campaign strategy. The document dealt with voter segments and strategies to reach them. In order to expand the Reagan base of voter support, Wirthlin identified some market targets on which the campaign should concentrate:

- Southern white Protestants
- Blue-collar workers in industrial states
- Urban ethnics
- Rural voters in upstate New York, Ohio, and Pennsylvania

Research also indicated that reducing government spending and national defense were the two leading issues in the campaign. The Wirthlin strategy called for Reagan to concentrate on these issues, while the vice-presidential candidate and others responded to expected attacks from the Carter campaign. Wirthlin also identified the key states that could swing the election.[1]

The Reagan victory provides a good illustration of how marketing strategy based on sound research can be used effectively in the nonprofit sector. Thus, marketing played a key role in the election of an administration devoted to altering the business-government interface.

Chapter 20 deals specifically with the changing role of marketing both within society and in nontraditional areas of application. The contemporary environment of marketing provides a good starting place.

THE CONTEMPORARY ENVIRONMENT OF MARKETING

AT&T, Dow Chemical, General Electric, J. C. Penney, Pillsbury, and Westinghouse, among others, have established a **public responsibility committee**—*a permanent committee of the firms' board of directors that considers matters of corporate social responsibility.*[2] All these firms are dealing responsibly with contemporary business and societal issues. And marketing plays a key role in the resolution of these matters. Marketing's relationship to society in general and to specific public issues is subject to constant change. Marketing typically mirrors changes in the entire business environment. As a result, the marketer usually carries much of the responsibility for dealing with the various societal issues affecting any firm.

Marketing operates in an environment that is external to the firm. It reacts to its environment and is, in turn, acted upon by it. Environmental relationships include those with customers, employees, the government, vendors, and society as a whole. While such relationships are often a product of the exchange process, they are coincidental to the primary functions of marketing.

External relationships form the basis of the social issues confronting contemporary marketing. The quality of a firm's marketing relationship with the external environment affects the degree of success the marketing function achieves. Marketing must continually search for improved methods of dealing with the various issues facing the competitive system.

EVALUATING THE QUALITY OF LIFE

In the arguments of marketing's critics, one theme prevails: The competitive marketing system is concerned only with the quantity of life and ignores the quality of life.[3] Traditionally, a firm was considered socially responsible in the community if it provided employment to its residents, thereby contributing to its economic base. Employment, wages, bank deposits, and profits—the traditional measures of social contribution—are quantity indicators. But what of air, water, and cultural pollution? And what of the depletion of natural resources? The charges of neglect in these areas often go largely unanswered simply because reliable indices by which to measure a firm's contribution to the quality of life have not been developed.

Several attempts have been made to develop such an index. Environmentalists, for instance, have made efforts in this area for several years. Individual companies are also becoming more concerned about reporting social behavior. Various firms, such as General Motors and the Norton Company, have made attempts at corporate reports on social performance. These efforts take a variety of names: social audits, consumer affairs audits, and reports on social responsibility. Marketers are not the dominant factor in all areas of social responsibility, but they play a role in many aspects of the issue.[4]

CURRENT ISSUES IN MARKETING

Marketing faces numerous and diverse social issues. They range from consumerism to the pricing practices of retailers in low-income areas to the cultural pollution caused by some television advertisements.

The current issues in marketing can be divided into three major subjects: consumerism, marketing ethics, and social responsibility. Though overlap and classification problems are obvious, the framework provides a foundation for systematically studying the issues.

CONSUMERISM

Marketers, industry, government, and the public are all aware of the impact of consumerism on the nation's economy and general well-being. **Consumerism** is *the demand that marketers give greater attention to consumer desires in making their decisions.* It is a protest against abuses and malpractice in the marketing system and often is seen as a part of a broader movement that seeks increased social responsibility in many sectors of society.[5]

Prior to the emergence of the current consumerism movement in the late 1960s, state and federal laws designed to maintain a competitive environment were the primary protection afforded consumer interests. Consumer protection was viewed as a by-product of the regulation of competition.

Many have argued that the rise in consumerism is proof that the marketing concept has failed. Their reasoning is based on two premises:

1. Not enough firms have adopted the marketing concept to provide adequate consumer safeguards.

2. The concept itself has not made firms more responsive to con-

Marketing must continually seek to predict the future— and prepare for it.

"I don't know about you, but I'm going back to tea leaves and eye of newt."

Source: Drawing by Tony Auth from *The Philadelphia Inquirer*, November 11, 1980. Used by permission.

sumer desires in such areas as product safety, guarantees, warranties, and service.

These arguments seem unnecessarily critical. Consumerism does not mark the end of the marketing concept. Instead, it introduces a new era in marketing responsibility. Admittedly, consumerism is requiring changes in some aspects of business life. It is, for example, forcing companies to be more responsible to their constituents. But this is all to the good. Consumerism is heralding an era of increased importance for the marketing concept.

Consumerism's Indictment of the Competitive Marketing System

Consumerism's indictment of marketing lists six separate charges:

1. **Marketing costs are too high.**[6] The charge is that distribution costs, which average about 50 percent of the selling price, are unjustified.

   Marketing's plea: innocent. Critics ignore the effect that efficient distribution has on the total cost structure. The competitive system has expanded the market for most products, so that the production costs per unit have declined in amounts exceeding the cost of the marketing system. While distribution costs per se are high, products are cheaper than they would be under alternative methods.

2. **The marketing system is inefficient.** The premise is that the competitive marketing system often does not respond promptly to consumer needs.

   Marketing's plea: guilty, with mitigating circumstances. The charge is true. Not all firms have adopted the consumer orientation explicit in the marketing concept. But the competitive market assures that they will adapt so as to become effective, or they disappear.

3. **Marketers are guilty of collusion and price fixing.** Such restraints of trade are direct affronts to all consumers.

   Marketing's plea: no contest. Yes, some firms have been convicted of such violations. Individual examples of unethical practices are regrettable, but when compared in size and number to the vast volume of transactions in the market, they are also relatively few.

4. **Product quality and service are poor.** Consumer advocates point to examples of faulty products, worthless warranties, and incompetent service departments.

   Marketing's plea: guilty. No industry has been able to escape the problems of product quality and service problems. A recent study of consumer complaints showed consumers to be most disturbed by dishonest advertising. Consumers were also upset by product designs that did not meet their needs, and poor quality control.[7]

5. **The marketing system has produced health and safety hazards.** Critics point to examples such as the numerous toys labeled hazardous by a government regulatory agency, the reported dangers and side effects of using various pharmaceuticals, and the health dangers of several forms of pollution.

    Marketing's plea: no contest. But it is interesting to note that while auto safety was the basis for Ralph Nader's original consumer campaign, when Ford offered seatbelts as optional equipment in the 1950s, there were few takers. No-lead gasoline was initially rejected by consumers despite an extensive marketing effort, and the elimination of lead in gasoline required mandatory legislation.

6. **Consumers do not receive complete information.** Proponents of consumerism argue that purchase decisions are unnecessarily complicated because the consumer does not receive adequate information. For example, trade and legal jargon sometimes make warranties confusing.

    Marketing's plea: guilty, with reservations. It is difficult to compare alternative products without complete information. However, reports on the truth-in-lending legislation (discussed in Chapter 2) suggest that more complete information has not significantly altered consumer handling of credit purchases. Studies of other areas of consumer information show similar results. It seems that the degree of information required depends on the item involved, its price, and the available alternatives.

The Consumer's Rights

Not all consumer demands are met. A competitive marketing system is based on the individual behavior of competing firms and requires that reasonable profit objectives be achieved. Given these constraints, what should the consumer have the right to expect from this system?

One of the clearest policy statements on the rights of the consumer was issued by President John F. Kennedy in a speech to Congress on March 15, 1962. He delineated the following rights:

1. The consumer has the right to safety.
2. The consumer has the right to be informed.
3. The consumer has the right to choose.
4. The consumer has the right to be heard.

These rights have formed the conceptual framework of much of the consumer legislation passed since 1962. The United States now has an elaborate network of federal, state, and local laws to protect consumers. So, further gains are more likely to come from voluntary actions of the private enterprise system.

MARKETING ETHICS

Another widely debated aspect of the contemporary environment is marketing ethics.[8] It is a subject that is receiving increased attention in an era characterized by a general questioning of business and marketing procedures. **Marketing ethics** may be defined as *the moral premises upon which marketing decisions are made.*

Individuals develop their own standards of ethical behavior. Personal ethics help people deal with the various situations in their own lives. However, a serious role conflict may materialize for the individual in a work situation. Individual ethics sometimes differ from the organizational ethic of the employer. An individual may, for example, personally believe that industry participation in redeveloping the inner city is highly desirable, but if the firm takes the position that such a venture is unprofitable, the individual may experience role conflict.

How can this situation be resolved? The development of and adherence to a professional ethic may provide a third basis of authority.[9] This ethic should be based on a concept of professionalism that transcends both organizational and individual ethics. It depends on the existence of a professional peer association that can exercise collective sanctions over a marketer's professional behavior. The code of ethics of the American Marketing Association, for example, includes a provision to expel members who violate its tenets. This code is shown in Table 20.1.

A variety of ethical problems face the marketer every day. While promotional matters have received the greatest attention recently, ethical questions concerning research, product management, channel strategy, and pricing also arise.

**TABLE 20.1
American Marketing Association Code of Ethics**

Our Code of Ethics

As a member of the American Marketing Association, I recognize the significance of my professional conduct and my responsibility to society and to the other members of my profession:
1. By acknowledging my accountability to society as a whole as well as to the organization for which I work.
2. By pledging my efforts to assure that all presentations of goods, services, and concepts be made honestly and clearly.
3. By striving to improve marketing knowledge and practice in order to better serve society.
4. By supporting free consumer choice in circumstances that are legal and are consistent with generally accepted community standards.
5. By pledging to use the highest professional standards in my work and in competitive activity.
6. By acknowledging the right of the American Marketing Association, through established procedure, to withdraw my membership if I am found to be in violation of ethical standards of professional conduct.

Source: American Marketing Association, *Constitution and Bylaws,* rev. ed. (Chicago: American Marketing Association, 1982), p. 20. Reprinted by permission.

Ethical Problems in Marketing Research

Marketing research has been castigated because of its alleged invasion of personal privacy. A Harris poll reported that 71 percent of all Americans believe their privacy is being violated, as compared with 48 percent five years earlier. The Privacy Protection Study Commission, a federal government creation, has recommended additional legislation to protect personal privacy.[10] And the New York chapter of the American Marketing Association has developed a code of ethics for marketing research that deals with the privacy issue.[11]

Ethical Problems in Product Management

Chevrolet motors were once installed in 128,000 Oldsmobiles, Buicks, and Pontiacs, as a result of unexpected demand for the medium-priced models. General Motors reasoned that the Chevrolet engines were the same size and horsepower and that a switch of this nature was an acceptable marketing practice. But buyers were not informed of the switch, and consumer complaints and legal cases resulted. General Motors was ordered by the court to make restitution in what the media labeled the "Chevymobile" case.[12] This incident suggests the changing nature and growing importance of ethical decisions in product management. Accepted marketing practice in this case was not acceptable to consumers.[13]

Product quality, planned obsolescence, brand similarity, and packaging present ethical problems to product management. The packaging question is a significant concern of consumers, management, and the Federal Trade Commission. Competitive pressures have forced marketers into packaging practices that can be considered misleading, deceptive, and unethical in some quarters. For instance, larger-than-necessary packages are used to gain shelf space and customer exposure in the supermarket. The real question seems to be whether such practices can be justified in the name of competition. Growing regulatory mandates, however, appear to be narrowing the range of discretion in this area.

Ethical Problems in Distribution Strategy

A firm's channel strategy is required to deal with ethical questions such as the appropriate degree of control over a channel, and whether a company should distribute its products in marginally profitable outlets that have no alternative source of supply. The question of control typically arises in the relationship between a manufacturer and its franchised dealers. Should an automobile dealership, a gas station, or a fast-food outlet be forced to purchase parts, materials, or supplementary services from the parent organization? What is the proper degree of control in the channel of distribution?

Furthermore, should marketers serve unsatisfied market segments even if the profit potential is slight? What is marketing's ethical responsibility in serving users of limited amounts of the firm's product or to a declining rural market?

CHELSEA: THE BABY BEER CONTROVERSY

Introducing the not so soft drink.

Anheuser-Busch wanted to introduce a premium-priced soft drink to appeal to the sophisticated adult. The product it developed had a ginger, lemon, and apple flavoring and a malt-type base. It also had a 0.4 percent alcohol content, compared to 5 percent in most beers. The new product, Chelsea, was to be priced at about $2 per six-pack. Because of its lower alcohol content, the FDA classified Chelsea as a soft drink.

Chelsea was test-marketed in Virginia, Massachusetts, Louisiana, Illinois, Colorado, and California. Its introduction led to widespread protests by church groups, nurses, and educators. It was labeled "Baby Beer" by its critics, who claimed it would condition children to drink beer when they became older. They pointed out that Chelsea was advertised as the "not-so-soft soft drink," and was packaged more like beer than like soft drinks. The amber-colored product, sold in clear bottles, also looked like beer.

Anheuser-Busch quickly stopped marketing Chelsea because of the protests. The product had by then exceeded the 1 percent market share figure commonly used in the soft-drink industry to assess new-product viability.

Anheuser-Busch had had previous experience with a similar product. Its low-alcohol content "Bevo" brand had failed after being introduced during Prohibition. Competition from bootleggers was too much for it.

After consulting with the many critics of the original product, Anheuser-Busch developed a new version of Chelsea. The new Chelsea had only a trace of alcohol, was similar to other citrus-flavored beverages, and no longer foamed. It was sold in green bottles to mask the product's amber color. The advertising slogan was changed to "the natural alternative," capitalizing on the fact that Chelsea had all natural flavors and no preservatives. However, consumer acceptance of the new Chelsea was disappointing, and test marketing was suspended in 1979.

Source: Information from "Battle Brews over 'Near Beer'," *Detroit News,* October 18, 1978; and Jeffrey Mills, " 'Baby Beer' Is Being Replaced," *Mobile Register,* December 13, 1978. Updated information and ad courtesy of Anheuser-Busch Companies, Inc.

Ethical Problems in Promotional Strategy

Promotion is the component of the marketing mix in which the majority of ethical questions arise. Personal selling has always been the target of criticism. Traders, peddlers, and drummers of early times and, more recently, used-car salespeople have all been accused of marketing malpractice, ranging from excessive product claims to outright deceit. It is important for companies to draw up written policies on areas of ethical concern for sales personnel.[14]

Advertising may be even more maligned than sales. One poll reported that 70 percent of all Americans were concerned about unethical advertising practices, and favored increased regulation of advertising.[15]

A recent ethical concern deals with advertising aimed at children.[16] Some critics fear that television advertising exerts an undue influence on children—that children are easily influenced by toy, cereal, and snack-food commercials. Children, presumably, can then exert substantial pressure on their parents to buy these items. The Federal Trade Commission held hearings and studied the issue for about 10 years. The final report was negative toward such advertising, but the study was terminated without FTC action.[17]

Ethical Problems in Pricing Strategy

Pricing is probably the most regulated aspect of a firm's marketing strategy. As a result, most unethical price behavior is also illegal. When asked to identify unethical practices they wanted eliminated, fewer executives specified issues such as price collusion, price discrimination, and unfair pricing in a 1976 survey than a similar group did in a 1961 study. This suggests that government regulations are more stringent now than in the past.[18]

SOCIAL RESPONSIBILITY

The third contemporary issue affecting marketing is social responsibility. This issue may be the most difficult to define since it involves so many aspects of modern society.[19] In general, **social responsibility** refers to *the marketing philosophies, policies, procedures, and actions that have the advancement of society's welfare as one of their primary objectives.*

Two crucial matters are the relationship between social responsibility and the profit motive, and the process for making socially responsible decisions in the organization.

The pressing need for socially responsible marketing decisions is readily agreed on by critics and defenders of contemporary marketing. Marketers and consumers now accept the viewpoint that business should be concerned with the quality of life as well as the quantity of life, by which market performance was previously measured. Determining the quality dimension of marketing decisions, however, is likely to remain a problem in the 1980s.

Social decision making within the organization has always been an important ethical consideration. Specifically who should be held accountable for the social considerations involved in marketing decisions: a district sales manager? A staff marketing department? The marketing vice-president? The president? The board of directors? Probably the most valid assessment is that all marketers, regardless of their station in the organization, should be held accountable for the social aspects of their decisions.

Marketing's Responsibilities

The concept of business responsibility has traditionally concerned the relationships between managers and their customers, employees, and stockholders. Management has had the responsibility of providing customers with a quality product at a reasonable price, of providing adequate wages and a decent working environment for employees, and of providing an acceptable profit level for stockholders. Only on occasion has the concept involved relations with the government—and only rarely with the general public. Today, the responsibility concept has been extended to the entire social framework. Examples are abundant. The First Wisconsin National Bank of Madison has distributed safety whistles and provided financial education programs for senior adults and women.[20] Security Mutual Life Insurance renovated its headquarters building, and helped revitalize downtown Binghamton, New York.[21]

MARKETING AND ECOLOGY

Ecology is an important aspect of marketing. The concept of **ecology,** *the relationship between humanity and the environment,* appears to be in a constant state of evolution.

There are several aspects of ecology that marketers must deal with: planned obsolescence, pollution, recycling waste materials, and preservation of resources.

The original ecological problem facing marketing was **planned obsolescence,** *a situation in which a manufacturer produces items with limited durability.* Planned obsolescence has always been an ethical question for the marketer. On one side is the need for maintaining sales; on the other, the need for providing better quality and durability.

But do the consumers really want (and can they afford) increased durability? Many consumers prefer to change styles often and will accept less durable items. Additionally, increased durability has a very real cost; it may mean fewer people can afford the product.

Pollution is a broad term that can be applied to a number of circumstances. It usually means *making unclean.* Pollution of such natural resources as the water and the air is of critical proportions. But there are definite signs of progress. Billions of dollars have been spent to clean up the rivers and lakes of the United States. Salmon, which have not spawned in the Connecticut River since the mid-1800s, are back now. Even the Potomac River is nearing recovery. But when a "swim-in" was suggested as a means of demonstrating the Potomac's progress, police invoked an ordinance that forbids people from making "deliberate contact" with the river.[22]

Recycling—*the reprocessing of used materials for reuse*—is another important aspect of ecology. The marketing system annually generates billions of tons of packaging materials, such as glass,

Solutions to the problem of pollution are not easily found.

"We're not dumping it anywhere, Ma'am. We're just going to keep driving it around."

Source: Drawing by Dana Fradon;© 1979 The New Yorker Magazine, Inc.

metal, paper, and plastics, that add to the nation's growing piles of trash and waste. The theory behind recycling is that if these materials could be processed so as to be reusable, they would benefit society by saving natural resources and energy as well as by alleviating a major factor in environmental pollution. For example, the beverage industry now uses three times more aluminum cans than steel cans because of the relative ease of recycling aluminum.[23]

The Boeing plant in Everett, Washington—the largest (6 million square feet) factory in the world—provides an example of another aspect of ecology. The plant obtains 60 percent of its heat from the burning of trash it generates. Before installing the new system, Boeing was spending $330,000 annually just to haul its trash away.[24]

RESOLVING CURRENT ISSUES IN MARKETING

Dealing with the contemporary issues of consumerism, social responsibility, and marketing ethics is probably one of the most difficult tasks facing marketing. Progress in these areas is essential if the competitive marketing system is to survive.

In recent history, many of these questions were dealt with through increased regulations. But the nation's mood shifted in the 1980s as the public began to question the government's continued ability to provide consumer protection. The antiregulatory rhetoric of the Reagan administration reflected this change. The nation clearly expected the private sector to provide more of the answers to these pressing societal questions. Marketers would be largely responsible for such actions.

A responsible marketing philosophy should encourage consumers to voice their opinions. These comments can result in significant improvements in the products and services offered by the seller.

Exxon, for example, has issued a new complaint policy, revised its complaint handling system, trained nearly 1,000 employees in such matters, and instituted a procedure for following up on the resolution of complaints.[25]

The marketing concept must include social responsibility as a primary function of the marketing organization. Social and profit goals are compatible, but they require the aggressive implementation of an expanded marketing concept. This is truly marketing's greatest challenge.

MARKETING IN NONPROFIT SETTINGS

The 1980s are also expected to be a decade in which marketing plays an expanded role in nonprofit settings. For example, Catholic dioceses in the Northeast launched an image-building radio campaign. Carleton College used marketing research to design its appeal to prospective students. And Kansas City's University Hospital offered a complete maternity package (including prenatal classes, one-day hospital stay, medical services, and postdelivery checkup) for $425.[26]

WHAT IS A NONPROFIT ORGANIZATION?

A substantial portion of the United States economy is composed of nonprofit organizations. A **nonprofit organization** is *one whose primary objective is something other than returning a profit to its owners.* Nonprofits can be found in public and private sectors of society. Federal, state, and local governmental units and agencies whose revenues are derived from tax collection have service objectives not keyed to profitability targets. The Department of Defense provides protection. A state's Department of Natural Resources regulates conservation and environmental programs. And the local Animal Control officer enforces ordinances that protect both persons and animals. Some public-sector agencies may be given revenue or behavioral goals. A bridge or turnpike might be expected to pay maintenance costs and retire its bonds out of tolls, for example. But society does not expect these units to routinely produce a surplus that is returned to the taxpayers.

The private sector offers an even more diverse array of nonprofit settings. Art institutes, the University of Notre Dame football team, labor unions, hospitals, private schools, the United Fund, the Lion's Club, and the local country club all serve as examples of private-sector, nonprofit organizations. Some, like Notre Dame's football team, may return a surplus to the university that is used to cover other activities, but the organization's primary goal is to win football games. The diversity of the settings suggest how pervasive organizational objectives—other than profitability—really are in a modern economy.

CHARACTER-ISTICS OF NONPROFIT ORGANIZATIONS

Nonprofit organizations have a special set of characteristics that impact the marketing activities of these entities. Like profit-oriented service offerings, the product offered by a nonprofit organization is often intangible. A hospital's diagnostic services, for example, exhibit marketing problems similar to those inherent in marketing a life-insurance policy.

A customer or service user of a nonprofit organization usually lacks control over the organization's destiny. A government employee may be far more concerned with the opinion of a member of the legislature's appropriations committee than that of a service user. Furthermore, nonprofit organizations often possess some degree of monopoly power in a given geographical area. An individual might object to a church's stance on a particular public issue. But a contributor who accepts the religious merits of that church recognizes that a portion of total contributions might produce materials on the issue in question.

Another problem involves the resource contributor, such as a legislator or a financial backer, who interferes with the marketing program. It is easy to imagine a political candidate harassed by financial supporters who want to replace an unpopular campaign manager (the primary marketing position in a political campaign).

Perhaps the most commonly noted feature of the nonprofit organization is its lack of a **bottom line** *(business jargon referring to the overall profitability measure of performance).* While nonprofit organizations may attempt to maximize their return from a specific service, less-exact goals such as service level standards are the usual substitute for an overall evaluation. The net result is that it is often difficult to set marketing objectives that are in line with overall organizational goals.

A final characteristic of nonprofit organizations is the lack of a clear organizational structure. Nonprofit organizations often refer to constituencies that they serve, but these are often considerably less exact than, for example, the stockholders of a profit-oriented corporation. Nonprofit organizations often have multiple organizational structures. A hospital might have an administrative structure, the professional organization consisting of medical personnel, and a volunteer organization that dominates the board of trustees. These people may sometimes work at cross-purposes and may not be totally aligned with the marketing strategy devised.[27]

THE BROADENING CONCEPT

The current status of nonprofit marketing is largely the result of an evolutionary process that began in the early 1960s, when several writers suggested that marketing should be concerned with issues beyond the traditional profit-oriented domain. Marketing was beginning to be seen as having wider application than was normally the case.[28]

A major breakthrough came in 1969 with the publication of Philip Kotler and Sidney J. Levy's classic article that argued that the marketing concept should be broadened to include the nonprofit sector of society.[29] The theoretical justification for this view was that marketing was a generic activity for all organizations.[30] In other words, marketing was a function to be performed by any type of organization. Thus, the **broadening concept** *extended the marketing concept to nontraditional exchange processes.*

The broadening concept was not unanimously accepted by marketers. David J. Luck argued that it was an unwarranted extension of the marketing concept.[31] And more recently, Gene R. Laczniak and Donald A. Michie argued that a broadened marketing concept could be responsible for undesirable social changes and disorder.[32] Despite some dissent, the broadening concept enjoys wide acceptance among nonprofit organizations and various students of marketing.

The Importance of Marketing to Nonprofit Organizations

Marketing's rise in the nonprofit sector would not have continued without a successful track record. And while it is often more difficult to measure results in nonprofit settings, marketing can already point to examples of success. Presbyterian-affiliated Church of the Covenant in Cleveland credits a 10 percent increase in average attendance to a series of radio commercials.[33] And a Midwestern hospital's marketing analysis allowed it to reposition itself as a provider of tertiary care services rather than as a community hospital.[34]

Integrating Marketing into Nonprofit Organizations

Philip Kotler suggests that there are six possible alternatives involved in introducing marketing to a nonprofit institution.[35] This list should be viewed as a set of alternatives rather than as a sequential process. The steps or approaches are as follows:

1. *Appoint a marketing committee.* This group would explore the institution's various marketing problems, needs, and opportunities. It would also examine the possible future employment of a marketing director.

2. *Set up a task force.* Such a group would conduct various phases of a marketing audit that analyzes the unit's existing marketing capability and orientation. Group reports would then be consolidated into an overall marketing strategy for the organization.

3. *Contract marketing specialist firms.* Specialists like marketing researchers, advertising agencies, and direct-mail and recruiting specialists can be hired as needed.

4. *Hire a marketing consultant.* A marketing consultant could be hired to conduct a marketing audit. The consultant's final report should address the question of whether employing a full-time marketer is the appropriate next step.

5. *Employ a marketing director.* A marketing director in most nonpro-

fit organizations is a middle-management staff position designed to offer marketing services to various units in the organization. Kotler believes that the marketing director should report to the vice-president of planning.

6. *Hire a marketing vice-president.* Employing a vice-president to co-ordinate all marketing activities within the organization is the ultimate step in integrating marketing into nonprofit organizations. This person would have input in the development of institutional policy as well as provide marketing services to the organization.

Once the basic approach has been decided, a marketing mix must be prepared. Illustrations of this process in assorted nonprofit settings are provided in the following section.

THE MARKETING MIX FOR NONPROFIT ORGANIZATIONS

Once the basic approach has been decided, a marketing mix must be developed. Nonprofits require a comprehensive marketing mix strategy, not merely an increase in promotion expenditures. Substantial opportunity exists for effective, innovative strategies since there has been little previous marketing effort in most nonprofit settings.[35]

Examples of innovative approaches to the nonprofit marketing mix are abundant in the 1980s. Figure 20.1 provides some recent illustrations.

EVALUATING THE EFFECTIVENESS OF NONPROFIT MARKETING

There are several variables that can be used to measure the effectiveness of nonprofit marketing efforts. Some of these include total market response, market share, cost per dollar of market response, efficiency measures, and market attitudes.[36]

Total Market Response is a measurement of numbers; examples of this measurement could be enrollment applications at a university or admissions to a hospital. The actual market response can then be compared to forecasted response. The data can also be broken down into categories, like "freshman," "transfer," and "returning for further analysis."

Market Share is a comparative measure that allows a nonprofit agency to assess its performance against the competition. Army, Navy, Air Force, Marine, and Coast Guard enlistments could be measured on a market-share basis.

Cost per Dollar of Market Response is an evaluation measure often used in charitable fund raising. Solicitation costs are cited as a percentage of each dollar collected in such efforts.

**FIGURE 20.1
Examples of
Marketing Mix
Strategies for
Nonprofit
Organizations**

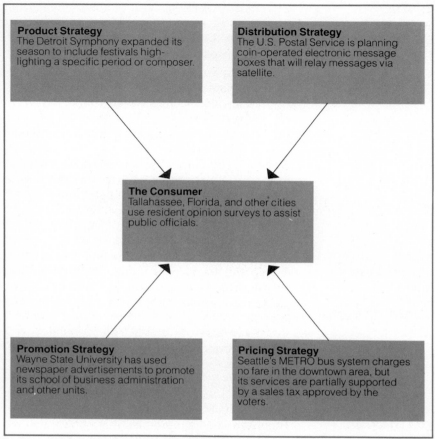

Product Strategy
The Detroit Symphony expanded its season to include festivals highlighting a specific period or composer.

Distribution Strategy
The U.S. Postal Service is planning coin-operated electronic message boxes that will relay messages via satellite.

The Consumer
Tallahassee, Florida, and other cities use resident opinion surveys to assist public officials.

Promotion Strategy
Wayne State University has used newspaper advertisements to promote its school of business administration and other units.

Pricing Strategy
Seattle's METRO bus system charges no fare in the downtown area, but its services are partially supported by a sales tax approved by the voters.

Sources: James M. Stearns, John R. Kerr, and Robert R. McGrath, "Advances of Marketing for Functional Public/Policy Administration," *Proceedings of the Southern Marketing Association,* Atlanta, Ga., November 1979, eds. Robert S. Franz, Robert M. Hopkins, and Alfred G. Toma, pp. 140–43; Leonard M. Apcar, "Detroit's Antal Dorati, Master Merchandiser, Thrives on Promoting," *Wall Street Journal,* January 22, 1980; and Urban C. Lehner, "Postal Service Vies with Private Concerns to Lead Entry into Electronic-Mail Age," *Wall Street Journal,* July 17, 1979. The Wayne State ads appeared in the *Detroit News.*

Efficiency Measures are also common in the evaluation and control of nonprofit marketing activities. Number of donor contacts per day, percentage of lost contributions, acceptance rates, and other measures are common in nonprofit settings.

Market Attitudes can be evaluated by conducting consumer surveys among those whom the agency serves. A hospital, for example, might attempt to assess patients' attitudes towards its services, food, and personnel by sending them a questionnaire after their release. Colleges and universities often gauge student attitudes towards services like the dining halls, health center, intramural facilities, parking, and placement office.

FUTURE PERSPECTIVES OF NONPROFIT MARKETING

Marketing's increased role in societal issues and nonprofit settings are two of the field's major trends in the 1980s. But a variety of other factors are expected to impact marketing. Effective marketing strategies require an adequate consideration of future trends and perspectives. One cannot rely on the past—even the immediate past—to predict the future. For example, R. J. Reynolds decided to introduce its low-tar Real cigarettes after Philip Morris had achieved considerable success with Merit. Reynolds did not test-market Real, choosing instead to move quickly into a *national rollout,* a nationwide launch of the product. Merit's success in the low-tar market and the "natural ingredients" fad that had recently stimulated the sales of a number of packaged goods led Reynolds management to conclude that the Real brand would prove a major winner. Instead, the brand failed dismally. Reynolds had spent an estimated $60 million promoting Real, but its market share never exceeded 0.4 percent—far below the 1 percent necessary to induce vending machine operators to stock the brand in their machines.[37]

A variety of methods exist to monitor and assess trends that impact business. The Center for Policy Process publishes a thrice-annual report on social, political, and economic trends. Clients like Sears, Chase Manhattan Bank, AT&T, Mobil, and General Motors pay $10,000 annually for these reports. The center indexes local news stories under the theory that most of the trends in the 1980s are filtering up from local levels, not down from national centers. The center pays particular attention to California, Colorado, Connecticut, Florida, and Washington since they tend to be the original locations of such changes.[38]

Other methods can be used. Some are quantitatively based, and others depend on qualitative assessments. Some of the more popular are these:

1. *Trend Extrapolation.* The statistical projection of a trend often assists in predicting growth.

2. *Trend Impact Analysis.* An event's probability, time frame, and impact on the upper and lower limits of a trend are developed.

3. *Barometric Forecasts.* The work of the Center for Policy Process is an illustration of using past events to predict the future.

4. *The Delphi Technique.* A panel of experts send their predictions on a particular issue to a moderator who disseminates the information to all participants. The procedure is repeated until a consensus emerges.

5. *Cross Impact Analysis.* This procedure traces the impact that various events or trends have on each other.

6. *Computer Simulation.* Computer programs can be developed to explain the interrelations of various aspects of the economic and social system.

7.   *Scenario Writing.* This is a subjective approach to outlining what will happen in the future. It sometimes relies on other forecasting methods.[39]

THE NEED FOR ADAPTABLE MARKETING STRATEGIES

Regardless of the procedures used, marketers must constantly monitor the trends that will impact them in the future. Even experienced marketers can miss some of these trends. Marketing strategies must be adaptable to a changing environment. Marketing mix flexibility is absolutely essential in the 1980s. Consider the trend toward an aging population, and the way some firms have adapted their marketing strategy to meet it.

Wild Strawberries is a restaurant chain that appeals to middle-aged executives with its dietetic menu. Wilson Sporting Goods offers a line of golf clubs with a weighted bottom designed to help an older golfer get the shot up quickly. And Levi Strauss now offers two lines of fuller-cut pants; one for the 25–49 age group, and one for men ages 45 to 59.[40]

Marketing is a dynamic, growing field. Effective marketers of the 1980s will be those who are well versed in a broad range of societal and business trends and issues.

SUMMARY

There are many important issues in marketing's societal environment in the 1980s. Marketing's environmental relationships have expanded in scope and importance. In fact, some companies have even set up public responsibility committees at the board level to deal with some of these issues.

The current issues in marketing can be categorized as consumerism, marketing ethics, and social responsibility. Consumerism is a protest against abuse and malpractice in the marketing system, as well as a plea for greater attention to consumer wants and desires. Marketing ethics is a complex subject since it can be considered from the viewpoints of individual, organizational, or professional ethics. Ethical problems exist in marketing research, product management, pricing, distribution strategy, and promotion. Another issue is the role of social responsibility in marketing. Society is increasingly turning to the private enterprise system for resolution of these issues.

The adoption of marketing strategies in nonprofit settings is another important aspect of marketing in the 1980s. Nonprofit organizations are those enterprises whose primary objective is something other than returning a profit to its owners. Nonprofit organizations are often characterized by the intangible nature of many of their services; minimal control by customers; professional rather than organizational orientation of their employees; involvement of resource contributors; lack of an overall bottom line; and the lack of a clear organizational structure.

The introduction of marketing into nonprofit settings has been associated with the broadening concept, which extends the marketing concept to nontraditional exchange processes. The broadening concept was introduced by Philip Kotler and Sidney J. Levy in 1969.

There are six possible alternatives involved in the introduction of marketing to a nonprofit institution: (1) appoint a marketing committee; (2) set up a task force; (3) contract marketing specialist firms; (4) hire a marketing consultant; (5) employ a marketing director; (6) hire a marketing vice-president.

Nonprofit agencies require a comprehensive marketing mix strategy based on accurate marketing research. It is also important to assess the effectiveness of the marketing strategy. This system might be based on one or more of the following variables: total market response; market share; cost per dollar of market response; efficiency measures; and market attitudes.

It is important for marketers to monitor and assess the numerous trends that might impact the marketplace of the 1980s. Some of the techniques that can be employed are trend extrapolation, trend impact analysis, barometric forecasts, the Delphi technique, cross impact analysis, computer simulation, and scenario writing. Marketers must then be ready to adapt marketing strategies in accordance with the identified trends.

QUESTIONS FOR DISCUSSION

1. Explain the following terms:
   public responsibility committee
   consumerism
   marketing ethics
   social responsibility
   ecology
   planned obsolescence
   pollution
   recycling
   nonprofit organization
   bottom line
   broadening concept

2. Explain the causes of the consumerism movement. Does the rise of consumerism suggest that the marketing concept has failed?

3. Evaluate consumerism's indictment of the competitive marketing system.

4. Comment on President John F. Kennedy's declaration that the consumer has the right to safety, the right to be informed, the right to choose, and the right to be heard.

5. What can be learned from the "Chevymobile" case?

6. Distinguish among individual, organizational, and professional ethics.

7. Describe the ethical problems of:
   a. marketing research
   b. product management

    c. distribution strategy

    d. promotional strategy

    e. pricing strategy

8. Describe the conflict that exists between consumer demand for product durability and the ecology movement.

9. The need to develop a reliable measure on the quality of life is well recognized. Suppose that you were in charge of a project of this nature. How would you go about your task?

10. List examples of business practices that you feel are not socially responsible. What factors went into deciding to include each item on your list?

11. In 1978, the U.S. Supreme Court decided that Tennessee's Tellico Dam, then nearing completion, might destroy the remaining snail darters, a fish only three inches long. The Court ruled that the $116 million project should be stopped because the snail darter was an endangered species and therefore protected by the Endangered Species Act. Relate this incident to the material in this chapter.

12. What can be learned from the Anheuser-Busch experience with Chelsea?

13. List the primary characteristics of nonprofit organizations.

14. Describe the evolution of the broadening concept.

15. Identify the alternatives involved in introducing marketing to a nonprofit institution.

16. Analyze the marketing mix of a nonprofit organization with which you are familiar.

17. List and discuss the variables that might be used in evaluating the effectiveness of a nonprofit marketing program.

18. Develop a generalized marketing plan for your college or university. Make any reasonable assumption necessary.

19. Analyze the marketing strategy employed by a candidate you supported in a recent election. Suggest aspects of the campaign that could have been improved.

20. Discuss the various methods used to assess future trends impacting marketing.

NOTES

1. Jack Honomichl, "The Marketing of a Candidate," *Advertising Age*, December 15, 1980, and "Strategist Details Reagan Plan," *Advertising Age*, August 18, 1980. Reprinted with permission. Copyright 1980 by Crain Communications, Inc. Also see John F. Stacks, "Where the Polls Went Wrong," *Time*, December 1, 1980, pp. 21–22.

2. Michael L. Lovdol, Raymond A. Bauer, and Nancy H. Treverton, "Public Responsibility Committees on the Board," *Harvard Business Review*, May-June 1977, p. 40. See also Hans B. Thorelli, "Codetermination for Consumers?" *Business Horizons*, August 1980, pp. 3–6.

3. Related articles include Leslie M. Dawson, "Marketing for Human Needs in a Humane Future," *Business Horizons*, June 1980, pp. 72–82; and Patrick E. Murphy and E. James Burton, "Accountants Assess the Social Audit," *Business*, September-October 1980, pp. 33–40.

4. A. H. Kizilbash, Carleton Maile, William Hancock, and Peter Gillett, "The Marketing Manager's Role in the Corporate Social Audit," *Bulletin of Business Research*, April 1978, pp. 4–7.

5. The current level of consumer dissatisfaction is assessed by Hiram C. Barksdale and William O. Perreault, Jr., "Can Consumers Be Satisfied?" *MSU Business Topics*, Spring 1980, pp. 19–30. Another interesting article is Zarrel V. Lambert, "Profiling Demographic Characteristics of Alienated Consumers," *Journal of Business Research*, March 1981, pp. 65–86.

6.   This issue has been widely debated in the marketing literature. Good summaries of the debate are presented in William J. Stanton, *Fundamentals of Marketing,* 6th ed. (New York: McGraw-Hill, 1981), pp. 551–53; and E. Jerome McCarthy, *Basic Marketing: A Managerial Approach,* 7th ed. (Homewood, Ill.: Richard D. Irwin, 1981), pp. 667–77.

7.   Gene Tesler, "Pilot Survey Finds Consumers More Upset with Poor Products than Dishonest Advertising," *Marketing News,* January 11, 1980, p. 20.

8.   Excellent discussions of ethics appear in Gene R. Laczniak, Robert F. Busch, and William A. Strang, "Ethical Marketing: Perception of Economic Goods and Social Problems," *Journal of Macromarketing,* Spring 1981, pp. 49–57; and James Weber, "Institutionalizing Ethics into the Corporation," *MSU Business Topics,* Spring 1981, pp. 47–52.

9.   The discussion of individual, organizational, and professional ethics is based on Henry O. Pruden, "Which Ethic for Marketers?" in *Marketing and Social Issues: An Action Reader,* eds. John R. Wish and Stephen H. Gamble (New York: Wiley, 1971), pp. 98–104.

10. "Private Sector Should Police Itself on Invasion of Privacy," *Marketing News,* May 2, 1980, pp. 6–7.

11. Marilyn Landis (Hauser), "Why It Took Three Years for Ethics Panel to Polish Pledge," *Marketing News,* September 19, 1980, pp. 1, 24.

12. Terry P. Brown, "GM, State Aides Due to Disclose Accord for $200 Rebates in 'Chevymobile' Case," *Wall Street Journal,* December 19, 1977.

13. An interesting discussion appears in Thomas J. Stanley and William D. Danko, "Correlates of Consumer Discontent over Product-related Issues," Richard P. Bagozzi, Kenneth L. Bernhardt, Paul S. Busch, David W. Cravens, Joseph F. Hair, Jr., and Carol A. Scott, eds., *Marketing in the 1980s: Changes and Challenges* (Chicago: American Marketing Association, 1980), pp. 407–11.

14. This step is suggested in Alan J. Dubinsky, Eric N. Berkowitz, and William Rudelius, "Ethical Problems of Field Sales Personnel," *MSU Business Topics,* Summer 1980, pp. 11–16.

15. Jennifer Alter, "Public Is Still Wary of Ads: Study," *Advertising Age,* June 23, 1980, p. 3.

16. Children's advertising is discussed in Glen Riecken and A. Coskun Samli, "Measuring Children's Attitudes toward Television Commercials: Extension and Replication," *Journal of Consumer Research,* June 1981, pp. 57–61; and Seymour Banks, "Children's Television Viewing Behavior," *Journal of Marketing,* Spring 1980, pp. 48–55.

17. "The Kidvid Decade," *FORTUNE,* May 4, 1981, p. 112.

18. Steven N. Brenner and Earl A. Mollander, "Is the Ethics of Business Changing?" *Harvard Business Review,* January-February 1977, pp. 61–62; and Jeffrey Sonnenfield and Paul R. Lawrence, "Why Do Companies Succumb to Price Fixing?" *Harvard Business Review,* July-August 1978, pp. 145–57.

19. Social responsibility issues are examined in Ed Timmerman, "The Concept of Marketing's Corporate Social Responsibility," in Robert H. Ross, Frederic B. Kraft, and Charles H. Davis, eds., *1981 Southwestern Marketing Proceedings,* Wichita, Kansas, The Southwestern Marketing Association, pp. 188–91.

20. "Bank Stresses Involvement in Community Activities," *Marketing News,* June 13, 1980, p.11.

21. Robert M. Best, "Corporate Social Responsibility: The Challenge of the 80's," *Response,* November 1980, pp. 8–9.

22. "Now We Can See through Water," *Detroit News,* November 1, 1978.

23. Amal Nag, "Recycling Ease Gives Aluminum an Edge over Steel in Beverage-can Market Battle," *Wall Street Journal,* January 2, 1980.

24. Ralph E. Winter, "More Companies Burn Waste to Generate Energy, Cutting Fuel and Disposal Costs," *Wall Street Journal,* April 15, 1981. Reprinted by permission of *The Wall Street Journal,* © Dow Jones & Company, Inc. 1981. All rights reserved.

25. C. R. Sitter, "The Courage to Work Together," remarks presented to the American Council on Consumer Interests, San Antonio, Texas, April 27, 1979, p. 5.

26. These examples are from Connie Beals, "Religion Is the Message," *Bellevue* (Wash.) *Journal-American,* February 7, 1981; Laurence Ingrassia, "College Learns to Use Fine Art of Marketing," *Wall Street Journal,* February 23, 1981; and Roger Ricklefs, "Business Bulletin," *Wall Street Journal,* April 7, 1981.

27. These differences and others are outlined in Harvey W. Wallender III, "Managing Not-for-profit Enterprises," *Academy of Management Review,* January 1978, p. 26; and Cecily Cannon Selby, "Better Performance for 'Nonprofits'," *Harvard Business Review,* September–October 1978, pp. 93–95. Used by permission.

28. This evolution is described in Philip D. Cooper and William J. Kehoe, "Marketing's Status, Dimensions, and Directions," *Business,* July-August 1979, pp. 14–15. Another interesting discussion of marketing's evolution appears in the same issue of *Business.* See Robert Bartels, "Upward Mobility in Marketing Management," pp. 9–13.

29.   Philip Kotler and Sidney J. Levy, "Broadening the Concept of Marketing," *Journal of Marketing,* January 1969, pp. 10–15.

30.   Philip Kotler, "A Generic Concept of Marketing," *Journal of Marketing,* April 1972, pp. 46–54.

31.   David J. Luck, "Broadening the Concept of Marketing—Too Far," *Journal of Marketing,* July 1969, pp. 53–55.

32.   This interesting series of exchanges appears in the *Journal of Academy of Marketing Science,* Summer 1979. See Gene R. Laczniak and Donald A. Michie, "The Social Disorder of the Broadened Concept of Marketing," pp. 214–32; Sidney J. Levy and Philip Kotler, "Toward A Broader Concept of Marketing's Role in Social Order," pp. 232–38; and Laczniak and Michie, "Broadened Marketing and Social Order: A Reply," pp. 239–42.

33.   Margaret Yao, "Big Pitch for God: More Churches Try Advertising in Media," *Wall Street Journal,* December 31, 1979.

34.   Daniel J. Fink, "Marketing the Hospital," *MBA,* December 1978/January 1979, pp. 50, 54, 56. Another interesting article related to hospitals is James U. McNeal and Charles W. Lamb, Jr., "Marketing Orientation in the Nonprofit Sector: The Case of Hospitals," *Journal of the Academy of Marketing Science,* Winter 1980, pp. 26–32.

35.   This section is based on Philip Kotler, "Strategies for Introducing Marketing into Nonprofit Organizations," *Journal of Marketing,* January 1979, pp. 40–44. Some interesting applications of marketing to the nonprofit sector are described in Alan R. Andreasen and Russell W. Belk, "Predictors of Attendance at the Performing Arts," *Journal of Consumer Research,* September 1980, pp. 112–20; David L. Lewis, "Obesity and Social Marketing an AID Approach to Segmentation," Venkatakrishna V. Bellur, ed.; Thomas R. Baird, Paul T. Hertz, Roger L. Jenkins, Jay D. Lindquist, and Stephen W. Miller, co-editors, *Developments in Marketing Science,* vol. IV (Marquette, Mich.: Academy of Marketing Science, 1981), p. 231; and three articles in the Spring 1981 issue of the *Journal of the Academy of Marketing Science:* Lynn Tracey Leguma and William R. George, "Analysis of Management Practices of Dance Companies," pp. 15–27; J. Richard Jones and Philip D. Cooper, "The Integration of a Logistical Decision Making Framework into Nonprofit Marketing," pp. 28–39; and John E. Robbins and Stephanie S. Robbins, "Museum Marketing: Identification of High, Moderate, and Low Attendee Segments," pp. 66–76.

36.   These variables are outlined in Philip Kotler, *Marketing for Nonprofit Organizations* © 1975, pp. 250–51. Adapted by permission of Prentice-Hall, Inc., Englewood Cliffs, N.J.

37.   "When Marketing Takes Over at R. J. Reynolds," *Business Week,* November 13, 1978, p. 84.

38.   William L. Shanklin, "Don't Plan on Business as Usual in '80s, '90s," *Marketing News,* August 8, 1980, pp. 6, 15.

39.   Hershey H. Friedman, "Futuristics: Reducing Marketing Myopia," *Business Horizons,* August 1980, pp. 17–20. Used by permission. Friedman credits the explanation of these techniques to Paul Dickson, *The Future File* (Austin, Texas: Learning Concepts, 1977).

40.   Shanklin, "Don't Plan on Business as Usual," p. 6.

CASES

PART 1

THE CONTEMPORARY MARKETING ENVIRONMENT

CASE 1
The San Francisco Giants

Faced with its deplorable financial condition and the prospect of future losses, the National Exhibition Company put the San Francisco Giants baseball team up for sale in early 1976. Preliminary negotiations with Labatt Breweries in Toronto had proven successful and plans were made to move the club there in time for the 1976 season. However, San Francisco Mayor George Moscone obtained a court injunction temporarily halting the move. Last-minute negotiations by local real estate magnate Robert Lurie saved the Giants for San Francisco, and he subsequently purchased the club along with Phoenix millionaire Bud Herseth for $8 million in March 1976.

The citizens of San Francisco were elated over the "return" of the Giants. Promising to bring a winner to Candlestick Park, the new owners moved immediately to create a new image for the team as they threw a huge "get acquainted" party for the team, with over 2,000 guests attending. In addition, the city of San Francisco sponsored a ticker tape parade for the Giants through the downtown streets just prior to the season's opener. The enthusiastic response of the fans to the team was clearly indicated as home attendance increased by 100,000 over the previous year, despite the fact that the club finished in fourth place in the National League's Western Division with a 74–88 record. This trend continued in 1977, for despite another fourth place finish and a 75–87 record, attendance jumped to 700,056. The Giants accomplished one of the most dramatic turnarounds in baseball history in 1978 as the club leaped four places to lead the Western Division of the National League for virtually the entire season before they faltered down the pennant stretch to finish in third place, six games behind the Los Angeles Dodgers. The combination of the team's

This case was prepared by John Knox McGill of the University of North Carolina at Chapel Hill as a basis for classroom discussion rather than to illustrate either effective or ineffective handling of an administrative situation.
Copyright © 1980 by the University of North Carolina at Chapel Hill. Used by permission of John Knox McGill, the School of Business Administration, University of North Carolina, and the San Francisco Giants. Statistics for 1982 provided by the San Francisco Giants.

superior performance, the tight pennant race, and owner Lurie's aggressive management policies culminated in the club drawing 1,740,477 fans to Candlestick Park, the second highest total in their history and over one million more fans than they drew in 1977. The effectiveness of the new management policies was evident in 1979 and 1980, for although the team had disappointing seasons on the field, they again attracted more than a million fans to the ballpark each season. The baseball players' strike shortened the 1981 season to only 111 games and crippled attendance despite a strong finish that gave the club a shot at the second-half divisional title and a winning record overall.

Several factors contributed to the recent success of the Giants. "Probably the single most important factor in the Giants' success has been the image we have developed as an organization which is dedicated to producing a solid, competitive ball club," commented the Giants' owner. "I think that we have demonstrated to the people of the Bay Area that we are committed to this area and that we are committed to doing what is necessary to be competitive and to provide the fans with an enjoyable experience at the ballpark," Lurie continued.

Numerous steps have been taken to create this new image. First, management sought to improve the team by acquiring additional talent and dispatching all malcontents. Early in 1977, the Giants obtained two-time National League batting champion Bill Madlock from the Chicago Cubs in exchange for discontented outfielder Bobby Murcer. Madlock hit over .300 in both 1977 and 1978 to lead the club in that category. Just prior to the 1977 season, the San Francisco club signed first baseman Willie McCovey as a free agent. McCovey celebrated his return to the club by leading the club with 28 home runs and 86 RBIs and was named the National League's Comeback Player of the Year by *The Sporting News* and UPI in 1977. Possibly the most popular player in San Francisco history, the veteran McCovey provided much-needed leadership for the club, both on the field and off. Perhaps the most important link in the chain of events which led to the development of the Giants into a solid pennant contender was the acquisition of former Cy Young Award winner Vida Blue from the Oakland Athletics minutes before the interleague trading deadline in 1978. Blue led the Giants in virtually every pitching category, winning 18 games and striking out 171 batters while posting a 2.79 earned run average that year. The club made wholesale player changes during 1980 and 1981, through trades and the free-agent market. In the spring of 1982, the Giants shocked the baseball world by trading star pitchers Vida Blue and Doyle Alexander, completing a series of transactions that saw their entire 1981 starting pitching rotation, which had led the club to the third-lowest earned run average in the National League, swapped to other clubs. Facing widespread fan criticism, Vice-President of Baseball Operations Tom Haller defended the moves. "We felt that we had not been successful with the (pitching) staff that we had and that it was time for some changes," Haller noted. "We received some good young arms (pitchers) in these trades and feel like we have strengthened the club," he added.

Haller's 1981 promotion to his current position brought about changes in the player development area as well. Under his direction, the club placed renewed emphasis on building a stronger farm system. He bolstered the minor league and scouting staffs, revamped the scouts' criteria for player evaluations, and implemented a systemwide philosophy of instruction and training. Haller also envisioned a lesser role for the club in the free-agent market, due to the lack of cost effectiveness. Over the past three years the club had spent large sums on eight free-agent players, including former Cincinnati Reds star Joe Morgan and ex-Los Angeles Dodgers standout Reggie Smith. Although Morgan and Smith had helped the club, only two of the other six free agents were still with the club at the beginning of the 1982 season.

In addition, the club adopted an aggressive marketing approach that centered on improving ticket accessibility and distribution, increasing promotions and advertising, increasing emphasis on group sales, and changing game times to appeal to different market segments. After acquiring ownership of the club, one of Lurie's initial moves was to establish an office in the downtown area that provided a centralized ticket distribution center as well as a souvenir outlet. In February 1981, the club opened a similar operation in the San Jose-Santa Clara area. Lurie increased the number of Giants' ticket outlets so that by 1979 over 190 outlets were in operation throughout northern California utilizing the Ticketron/BASS system. Lurie also expanded ticket availability by allowing fans to order tickets by telephone as well as by mail using VISA and Master Card.

The club added numerous creative promotions at Candlestick Park to attract fans and provide them with an enjoyable experience. In addition to the traditional promotions such as Bat Day, Ball Day, Cap Day, and Jacket Day, the Giants added Straight A Student Day and Back to School Day as promotions aimed directly at the student market. In 1982 the club planned several events to celebrate the team's 25th anniversary in San Francisco. Highlighting the season-long festivities was the selection of an all-time San Francisco Giants "Dream Team," which was to appear at various Giants functions, including a special Old Timer's Game. Also, the club began making increased use of corporate sponsors for stadium promotions. Under this concept, the corporation would financially sponsor a given promotion, such as Cap Day, at a Giants home game. In return, the corporate sponsor would receive a package of equal value in tickets, media exposure, and certain Giants-originated promotion. This concept had grown to a value of over $450,000 for the club in only five years, according to Pat Gallagher, Vice-President of Business Operations.

Gallagher also pointed out the club's increased utilization of the media. In 1982, the club planned to broadcast 32 of its games in Spanish to a Spanish-speaking audience estimated at over one million in the Bay Area. The club also boasted a 31-game television schedule over an expanded network of stations. The biggest marketing change for the club has been in the area of media advertising, however. Gallagher stated that the Giants' television advertisements featuring Father Guido Sarducci of "Saturday Night Live" fame were one of the first such attempts in the major leagues. The success of media advertising had prompted the club to spend an additional $300,000 in radio advertising during the 1982 season, Gallagher noted.

As part of a general buildup of their front office staff, the Giants added a Director of Marketing as well as a Director and Assistant Director of Publicity. The resulting delegation of responsibilities enabled the club to increase its emphasis on group sales. Through the use of quantity discounts and certain stadium privileges, the percentage of tickets sold under this method rose at a rate of 10 percent annually.

The club also moved the starting times of several games from 7:35 P.M. to 12:05 P.M. as a weekday Businessmen's Special. Lurie noted that this change had been quite beneficial for the club's attendance and that the number of games played at this time will probably be increased in the future. Finally, the club planned several Saturday night games with special promotions for young people in order to boost attendance.

Looking to the future, Lurie commented, "I expect our club to be competitive in 1982. We are stronger offensively now than in past years; however, because of the numerous trades, our pitching is questionable. The possibility of a new domed stadium in the downtown area is exciting, and the idea has been received well by the Mayor's office." Lurie closed by underscoring his management philosophy, "I am committed to an aggressive marketing approach, to creative promotions at the ballpark, and to making the Giants truly a part of the community. I believe that all of these components are essential to the building of a successful baseball franchise in San Francisco."

Questions

1. Assess the marketing mix employed by the Giants.
2. What other steps might the Giants take?
3. Evaluate the marketing efforts of the nearest professional sports franchise in your area.

Case 2
The Milwaukee Blood Center

The Milwaukee Blood Center (MBC) was established in 1946 by the Junior League to meet the emerging needs for blood in the Milwaukee area. The MBC has experienced substantial growth and is now a major

Source: Reprinted by permission of Patrick E. Murphy, Marquette University, and Ron Franzmeier, Zigman-Joseph-Skeen.

regional blood center. The Milwaukee Blood Center is a member of two blood banking trade associations—American Association of Blood Banks and Council of Community Blood Centers. MBC is affiliated with the Medical College of Wisconsin.

In 1976, the Milwaukee Blood Center moved to a new location at the western edge of the downtown area and adjacent to Marquette University. Within several blocks of its location there are five hospitals which MBC serves. The first floor of the building was renovated for use in blood collection. Free parking is provided behind the building for donors. The MBC also makes extensive use of the five mobile units for drawing blood at business and organization sites. Furthermore, three satellite stations are utilized in suburban and neighboring city locations.

Current Situation In a recent year, volunteer donors in southeastern Wisconsin gave 91,500 units of blood to support patients' needs in the 33 hospitals that the Milwaukee Blood Center served. Donations have increased steadily during the past decade.

However, local demand for blood exceeded local donations by 3,100 units which had to be obtained from other blood centers. The major objective of donor recruitment programs is to make this region self-sufficient.

Eighty percent of the blood collected in the region was given by members of 900 donor clubs sponsored by business, schools, churches, and other civic, labor, and community groups in southeastern Wisconsin. The other twenty percent was drawn from individuals at MBC's central location in Milwaukee and part-time satellite stations located within the six-county area that the center serves.

These donors made it possible for the Milwaukee Blood Center to keep pace with the increasing demand for blood products in the region. Patients in the 33 hospitals served by the center required 5,400 more units of whole blood and packed red blood cells than were needed in the previous year. The MBC also experienced a dramatic increase in the need for blood components.

The increased need for blood and blood components is related in part to the growing number of open-heart, hip replacement, and kidney transplant operations being performed. Regular transfusions of blood platelets are demanded by a growing number of patients undergoing chemotherapy for cancer.

A Marketing Approach Administrators at MBC felt that the amount of blood collected from donor clubs was reaching a steady-state position. In fact, a few mobile drives had to be cancelled because of layoffs or slowdowns at local industries. Also, the demographic projections for the southeastern Wisconsin area indicate that the area will not grow in population. Therefore, the administration felt that a program aimed at the individual donor was needed. To facilitate this process the Milwaukee Blood Center sought the services of a local marketing consulting firm.

With the assistance of the consultant, the administrators were able to relate the marketing mix elements to the process of blood donation. The product/service that they are offering is the unique satisfaction which the donor receives from the act of contributing a pint of his/her blood. This satisfaction cannot be derived from writing a check or volunteering time. The price not only represents real cost of physical discomfort of the donor, inconvenience and time lost that could be spent in other ways, but also the psychological cost of fear of the total experience. The place or distribution element is directly related to the center's location or availability of mobile units or satellite stations. Finally, promotion entails the personal selling effort engaged in by the donor recruiters and the mass media efforts. The Milwaukee Blood Center employs four full-time donor recruiters who call on industry and other donor clubs.

The mass media promotion used by the Milwaukee Blood Center took the form of public-service announcements. These announcements are free, but often aired late at night or at times when few people are watching or listening. Also, publicity is utilized by the blood center when they are experiencing a large shortage of donations. The problem with this type of promotion is that the blood center has no real control over the frequency with which their message reaches the target audience. Therefore, the blood center has relied heavily on other means of reaching prospective donors, such as printed brochures, direct-mail materials, and telephone solicitation.

Marketing Research The consultant and administration agreed that before a marketing program could be developed for the MBC, marketing research was necessary. Specifically, they needed to know more about their market area's donation patterns and certain attitudes of thought leaders and donors toward the blood center.

One part of the marketing research encompassed a study of the present geographic market area. It includes six counties which comprise the southeastern region of Wisconsin. These counties are Milwaukee, Waukesha, Ozaukee, Washington, Racine, and Kenosha. The research showed that the percentage of population which actually donates is only 3 percent for the blood center area while the national figure is between 5 and 6 percent. In the county-by-county breakdown, Racine and Kenosha residents are not donating at a percentage equal to their population proportion.

A second phase of the initial marketing research effort entailed a "thought leader" study. Approximately ten governmental and mass media leaders in Racine, Kenosha, and Waukesha were interviewed regarding their perception of attitudes that people in their area had toward the blood center. Thought leaders in Milwaukee were not surveyed because the blood center administrators had frequent contact with them. One consistent finding was that they felt there was some reluctance of people in these cities to donate to the "Milwaukee" Blood

Center. Most citizens did not realize that the blood center served the entire southeastern Wisconsin region.

Research was also conducted with first-time donors. One hundred first-time donors were surveyed via telephone. They were prompted to donate by a Winter Blood Telethon which was carried by a local television station. These donors were asked why they had never donated before. The most frequently mentioned reason was, "No one ever asked me to donate." Some of the more obvious reasons like "too busy" and "afraid to give" were designated by a much smaller percentage of the donors.

Another survey was conducted at the downtown Milwaukee drawing station. Donors were asked to fill out a short questionnaire while they were being served refreshments after donating. A total of 462 donors responded over a two-week time period. One of the major findings of this survey was that nearly one-third of the respondents (32.4 percent) indicated that they would be likely to donate more often if there were a drawing station located more conveniently to their home.

Conclusion When the consultant presented these research findings to the administration of MBC, they indicated that the consultant should develop a comprehensive marketing strategy (plan) based on these results. The administrators urged the consultant to be innovative and not to be concerned about organizational resistance to change. The only limiting factors that the administration placed on the marketing plan was that they could not afford paid television advertising. The Milwaukee Blood Center's Board of Directors is scheduled to meet in three weeks and the administrator wants to present the comprehensive marketing program to them at that time.

Questions

1. What is the major problem confronting the Milwaukee Blood Center?
2. How has MBC segmented the market? What are the promising market segments in this area?
3. How can the product that MBC offers be altered to better meet the needs of the marketplace?
4. What pricing strategies can be utilized to attract donors?
5. How might the distribution channel be restructured to meet organizational and community goals?
6. What promotional (communication) strategies might be utilized to reach current and potential donors?

PART 2   IDENTIFYING CONSUMER NEEDS

CASE 3
Pepsi-Cola Company: The Pepsi Challenge

On July 12, 1976, Pepsi-Cola Company placed a full-page advertisement in the *New York Times* which said in part:

We have believed for a long time that we produce a better-tasting product than our leading competitor. But we wanted to be sure of that fact. We did not want to advertise it until we had it documented by careful, objective, independent research. We now have that documentation. Truth in advertising is very important to us. And the truth in advertising is: nationwide, more Coca-Cola drinkers prefer Pepsi than Coke.

The Pepsi Challenge is the most aggressive, competitive stance a Pepsi-Cola franchise has ever taken against Coca-Cola. It is a no-holds-barred thrust against the attitudes of consumers and the trade. The goal of the Challenge is to assert Pepsi-Cola's presence in the marketplace and to significantly bolster its share of the market. The Pepsi Challenge campaign began in Dallas in 1975, and since that time the campaign has extended to cover 32 percent of the United States. Over 3 million consumers have physically taken the Pepsi Challenge in sampling booths across the country.

Situational Development Dallas had historically been a very poor market for Pepsi-Cola. Coca-Cola had held about 27 percent of the Dallas market with Dr Pepper (home offices in Dallas) in second place with 23 percent. Pepsi-Cola ranked a distant third with an 8 percent of the market compared with its national market share of 17 percent.

In early 1975, Pepsi-Cola decided it was time to do something about its meager share of the Dallas area soft-drink market. Research had shown that Dallas consumers almost always *believed* they could tell the difference between the taste of Coke and the taste of Pepsi and that they preferred the taste of Coke. Pepsi-Cola marketing people, however, believed that the problem was that most Coke drinkers had never tasted Pepsi.

An independent research firm was retained to conduct blind taste tests to find out which taste Coke consumers really preferred. Results indicated that more than half the Coca-Cola drinkers tested actually preferred the taste of Pepsi.

The research was soon translated into a local advertising campaign called "The Pepsi Challenge." Using a hidden camera to photograph local consumers taking the blind taste test, television commercials claimed: "More than half the Coca-Cola drinkers tested in the Dallas-Fort Worth area prefer the taste of Pepsi-Cola."

Source: From CASES FOR ANALYSIS IN MARKETING, Second Edition, by W. Wayne Talarzyk. Copyright © 1981 by CBS College Publishing. Reprinted by Permission of Holt, Rinehart and Winston, CBS College Publishing.

Sales of Pepsi-Cola began to increase in Dallas immediately, and a variety of responses began to develop. These activities, as viewed from Pepsi-Cola's perspective, are chronicled in the news release in Exhibit 1.

Within a year Pepsi-Cola's share of the Dallas market had increased 50 percent, although most of the increase apparently came at the expense of cheaper, little-known brands. In addition, evaluation of the effectiveness of the taste-comparison advertising campaign was made difficult because of the price-cutting promotion going on simultaneously by both sides.

National Research Results Based on the experience in Dallas and other local areas and the activities of Coca-Cola, Pepsi-Cola decided to commission a national study comparing consumer taste preferences for the two brands. Motivational Programmers, Inc. (MPI) of New York, an independent marketing research company, conducted the research.

The research methodology involved a weighted national probability sample of over 3,000 males and females fourteen years of age and over. At no time were the brands identified to the respondent before the taste test was completed. Opaque insulated bags were used to bring the products into the respondents' homes.

After being poured into clear plastic glasses behind an 18 × 24-inch screen, one of the brands was placed in the respondent's right hand and the other in his or her left hand. The interview form indicated which hand would be used for the respective brands so that neither would always be "left" or "right." In addition, Pepsi was tasted first in one-half the tests, while Coke was tasted first in the other half.

Before tasting each product, respondents were asked to sip water to clear their palate. Ice was not used in the already chilled product so that it would not be diluted to any degree whatever.

After tasting both brands, respondents were asked: "Now, thinking about the two colas—all things considered, which of the two did you like better, the one in your right hand or the one in your left?" The results of the study are given in Exhibit 2.

Concluding Comments At the news conference announcing the results of the national taste test, Victor A. Bonomo, president of Pepsi-Cola Company, stated, "I emphasize that even though we do not have the research available that will allow us to introduce the Challenge anywhere, at any time, we will use prudent judgment in doing so; 'The Pepsi Challenge' is still a local advertising campaign designed for specific and selected markets. Our commercials are straightforward, based on objective and clear research. We are not trying to mislead or confuse the consumer. The tag line of all Pepsi Challenge commercials sums up the key message: 'Take the Pepsi Challenge, Let *Your* Taste Decide.'"

**EXHIBIT 1
Pepsi-Cola
Company's News
Release on the
Pepsi Challenge
(July 6, 1976)**

The Pepsi Challenge
What Are the Issues?

More Then Half the Coca-Cola Drinkers Tested Actually Preferred Pepsi

We first found it out in Dallas, Texas, where Coke outsold Pepsi 3 to 1. We conducted side-by-side *blind* taste tests between Pepsi and Coca-Cola. The bottles were hidden and the products were in drinking glasses identified only as "M" and "Q." The people tested were dyed-in-the-wool Coca-Cola drinkers. The results were amazing and clear-cut. More than half the Coca-Cola drinkers tested in Dallas/Fort Worth preferred the taste of Pepsi.

What Was Coca-Cola's First Response?

The Coca-Cola Company's first response to this was to do local commercials with Coca-Cola drinkers tasting both products in a side-by-side test with each product identified. Naturally, people picked the one they normally drink. Coke's claim: Coke outsells Pepsi in Dallas. Needless to say, we knew that already. Also, Coke wasn't responsive to the issue: which tastes better, Pepsi or Coke? We did not consider it a very good answer to the Pepsi Challenge.

What Happened Then?

We continued the Pepsi Challenge in Dallas to the point where our sales increases amazed even ourselves.

What Was Coca-Cola's Next Response?

Our competitor's response to this was to do a national campaign wherein blindfolded people were asked to decide which they liked better, Fresca or Pepsi. Even though two-thirds of the participants in this strange test of "apples" and "oranges" chose Pepsi-Cola, the competition seemed to think this was an effective answer to the Pepsi Challenge.

And Then What Happened?

We took the Pepsi Challenge to other Texas cities: Corpus Christi and San Antonio. Again and again Pepsi won. More than half the Coca-Cola drinkers tested preferred the taste of Pepsi.

Then What Did Coke Do?

They compared apples to oranges again. Coca-Cola responded with a campaign comparing the calories in Tab, a one-calorie diet drink, to those of our new product, Pepsi Light, a reduced-calorie lemony cola. Needless to say, they carefully avoided comparing one-calorie Tab to one-calorie Diet Pepsi. This could not honestly be considered an answer to the Pepsi Challenge.

What Did Pepsi Do?

We took the Challenge to Detroit, Flint, and Grand Rapids. Again and again, Pepsi won. More than half the Coca-Cola drinkers tested preferred the taste of Pepsi.

What Did Coke Do?

Coke ran a commercial in Dallas, suggesting that Pepsi was winning only because people liked the letter "M" better than the letter "Q." In the blindfold test "M" was the symbol for Pepsi, "Q" for Coke. Of course, unfortunately for Coke, this is nonsense; Dallas was the only city in which we used the letters "M" and "Q." In all other cities, we got the same results. We used "L" and "S." Pepsi won. We used different combinations of letters. Pepsi won. We used no letters. Pepsi won.

Now What Is Coke Up To?

Recently, in a number of markets like New York, Coke has begun a campaign in which they point out that Coke outsells Pepsi locally (they use the word "prefer"). Of course, they neglect to mention that this claim has nothing to do with taste. As in Dallas, their commercials show confirmed Coke drinkers reinforcing their own beliefs. Also, they neglect to point out that nationally, when consumers do have a freedom of choice (as in food stores), Pepsi has outsold Coke for more than a year.

EXHIBIT 2
Results of Blind
Taste Test
Preference between
Pepsi-Cola and Coca-
Cola

	Regular Drinkers of Total Sample	Any Carbonated Soft Drink	Coca-Cola	Pepsi-Cola
Prefer Pepsi-Cola	51.7%	52.6%	49.8%	58.2%
Prefer Coca-Cola	41.7	41.7	44.2	37.3
No Preference	6.6	5.7	6.0	4.5
Total	100.0%	100.0%	100.0%	100.0%

As of the summer of 1980, the following observations could be made on the program:

To date, the Pepsi Challenge has been introduced in 32 percent of the United States. This marks the fifth year of the Pepsi Challenge in Dallas and Los Angeles. Nonetheless, these two key challenge markets are continuing to show above-average growth.

Research shows that the Pepsi Challenge builds brand awareness for Pepsi and heightens the brand's image in the "best taste" and "highest quality" categories.

With the economy in a recessionary state, the Pepsi Challenge has been effective in maintaining consumer focus on the quality of Pepsi-Cola versus private label or "price" colas.

The Pepsi Challenge has been a significant motivating factor at the plant level, demonstratively raising morale levels in low-share markets.

In the five years of the Pepsi Challenge, the Coca-Cola Company has tried everything from producing special "anti-challenge" commercials and supporting them at media rates equal to ten times that of Pepsi-Cola levels to broadly publicizing the fact that Coke is the Number One selling soft drink nationally. None of these tactics has been successful in even slowing growth in Challenge markets.

Questions

1. Discuss the marketing research methodology used by Pepsi-Cola.
2. Outline the interrelationships between marketing research and marketing planning as illustrated by this case.
3. Should Pepsi-Cola continue to use the Pepsi Challenge in its competition with Coca-Cola? Why or why not?

CASE 4
Pente

The game Pente (pen'-tā) (Greek, meaning five) is based on an ancient Japanese game called "Go" or "Go Moku." Players alternately place a glass bead of their color on the intersections of a board covered with a series of lines that form a grid. The object of the game is to place five beads (stones) in a row diagonally, vertically, or horizontally, before

Source: William G. Zikmund, *Exploring Marketing Research* (Hinsdale, Ill.: The Dryden Press, 1982), pp. 26–29.

your opponent does, or to capture ten of your opponent's beads. Once a stone is played it cannot be moved to another point.

Pente is similar to tic-tac-toe except players try for "five in a row." The first player to get five beads in a row or the first to capture ten beads (five pairs) is the winner.

The Product Pente is available in two versions: the soft set ($12.95) and the deluxe board ($72). The soft set includes a leatherlike vinyl board chosen for its rich appearance, a rule book, and two velvet pouches containing a total of 80 glass playing pieces.

The deluxe board is of beautifully crafted, laminated birch imported from Finland. Designed to be displayed like a fine chess set, the board can be hung on the wall when not in use. The set includes three leather pouches, each containing 40 pieces in three different colors, along with a padded, waterproof vinyl carrying case.

History of the Game Gary Gabrel originated the idea for Pente in 1974 when a friend of his learned to play the ancient game of Go on the west coast and brought a board back to Oklahoma with him. Gabrel decided to design a new game based on the concepts of Go, but with rules that would allow a simplified and faster version of the game. The game he developed is described as a sophisticated cross between tic-tac-toe and checkers in ease of learning, but with the tactical depth of chess.

Then Gabrel sent a form letter to various U.S. game companies, describing the basic idea of the game and offering to sell it. He received only a handful of replies, mostly rejections explaining that the companies had their own staffs of game inventors. Only Hallmark in Kansas City expressed any interest and Gabrel did not like their terms.

"I discovered that you cannot sell an idea for a game and expect it to be protected," Gabrel said. "To copyright a game, you have to have more than an idea. You have to have rules and the hardware."

"Games aren't patented," Gabrel explains. "In order to protect the concept of a game, you must design an original board, write an instruction book and come up with an original name. Then you can copyright that."

Gabrel later took his idea for the new game to a consultant in Dallas who suggested that he not only design a good game, but a beautiful set as well. Gabrel rejected the idea of an Oriental tone for the design, saying, ". . . it was in 1974, . . . too soon after the Vietnam War."

He kept looking until he found a picture one day of Zeus and another Greek figure leaning over a table. That was what he had been looking for.

"The Greek image had everything I wanted," he said. "I liked the purity of thought the classical Greek image portrays and the mythical quality about it."

Gabrel found other authentic Greek figures and had an artist redraw them in sitting positions. The Pente board has eight different drawings depicting Greek men and women playing board games.

In 1977, after three years of developing the design and refining production, the first Pente sets were placed in a Stillwater, Oklahoma, gift store for Christmas sales. A newspaper article coincided with the debut of the game and Gabrel sold about 800 sets, "as fast as I could make them." These first sets were signed, numbered, and accompanied by a notarized certificate. Gabrel attributes the initial success of Pente to the originality and beauty of the game, the fact that he was a Stillwater resident and the enthusiasm of the gift store sales staff.

"That was the peak," recalls Gabrel. "From there, sales began to drop and then just leveled off. I tried to interest shops in both Oklahoma City and Tulsa in the game but got absolutely no response at all. So I hit the road and worked 30 arts and crafts shows in the Southwest, from Denver to Memphis and Hot Springs to Baton Rouge." The results were very encouraging. In Memphis, Gabrel sold out: 200 sets in three days and orders for 60 more.

Gabrel then hired a salesperson who negotiated with the management of Michael's Plum in Oklahoma City to place Pente in the club along with the backgammon sets for the entertainment of their clientele. The game caught on and people began asking for it in stores around Oklahoma City. By Christmas of 1978, stores in many Oklahoma cities were selling Pente.

Two breaks occurred when Gabrel took first place in a design competition for original handcrafted items sponsored by Goudchaux, a Baton Rouge department store, and when a story appeared in the July/August issue of *Games* Magazine, a Playboy publication with a national circulation of 530,000.

In 1979 the product was clearly a regional success. Several major department stores in Oklahoma were distributing Pente. One store, John A. Brown, decided to push Pente heavily for Christmas of 1979.

"When we sold to John A. Brown," Gabrel said, "they put Pente in a weekly bulletin published by the National Federation of Department Stores. A lot of stores in the Northeast heard about us that way. And a deal with a Canadian company put us in stores all along the southern part of Canada."

"When the game gets into a lot of stores, it loses its hand-crafted image," he said. "That means we have to go totally wholesale." Gabrel was particularly happy with John A. Brown's displays. The package for the $12.95 version of Pente was a cardboard mailing tube 2½ inches in diameter and 20 inches long. This caused some shelving problems. Brown's displayed both sets on a table, with a barrel holding the cylinders. This form of display pleased Gabrel, but he knew all stores would not give the game this much support.

Pente sold a few hundred games in the first year, about 5,000 games in 1978, and by the end of 1979, almost 30,000 games had been sold. Pente's success led to another problem for Gabrel: "For a while, we were getting too many orders. We didn't have the capital to manufacture all the games we had orders for. We would make a lot of games and then sell out immediately. We wouldn't have anything to sell for weeks.'' After Gabrel found a financial backer, he stepped up production.

The largest problem Gabrel faced in developing the Pente concept was producing a quality game that would still be competitive in price. ''I discovered that games seem to fall into about three price ranges. People are willing to pay from $5 to $10 for games; backgammon and chess fall in a higher category and the electronic games in still another. In order to develop a set with mass appeal, I felt I must hit close to one of these price brackets. The vinyl set of Pente is a little higher than the lowest bracket, with a suggested retail of $12.95, but it is a quality game. I am constantly changing the game to improve it and recently again revised the instruction book to include variations of Pente plus other games that can be played on the Pente board.''

Financial Situation The early years were difficult for Gary Gabrel. At one time, he was refused a $1,000 loan to develop the game. However, after some time he found a financial backer who offered a line of credit that enabled Gabrel to borrow up to $100,000 a year.

The Move toward National Distribution What is Gabrel's next move? ''I have at least three options. I can continue to operate as I am now; contract someone else to produce the games; or sell the rights to a larger company and collect royalties. But now that we are receiving some recognition, I need to get aggressive in my marketing.''

A booth at the New York Stationery Show was Gabrel's first step into national marketing. He has also established contact with a manufacturer's rep who is showing the game.

In January 1980, Gabrel estimated that Pente would make it on a national basis, selling 300,000 units annually. He continued, however, to be concerned about stimulating the popularity of the game. Gabrel thought the clubs with long backgammon bars were especially helpful. He felt that people who were taught how to play Pente learned to like it quickly. Learning Pente directly from the instructions, on the other hand, was a problem for some people. But opinion leaders from the clubs and lounges passed on the simplicity and fascinating nature of Pente.

Gabrel was concerned that Pente was a regional phenomenon that could not be marketed the same way nationwide. Much of the promotion in Oklahoma, Kansas, and Texas was based on publicity generated from the appearance of the game in the clubs. Pente's advertising budget was small, so Gabrel had been particularly lucky with publicity releases.

Gabrel had conducted no marketing research. Active young people were the primary purchasers of his product, but the game could be played by children as young as ten. In discussions with a marketing researcher, Gabrel felt that his success was due to perseverance. He had been struggling for a number of years, and was sure that 1980 was going to be his big year, with or without marketing research. The researcher asked him about his information needs—whether he knew his market targets, retailer reactions, and needs for new product lines. Gabrel had no formal training in business, but knew that he needed more information and he didn't know exactly what it was.

Questions

1. Pente has been successful without any formal marketing research. Does Pente need to be researched?
2. What additional information would you like to have if you were marketing Pente?
3. How would marketing research help?

PART 3

MARKET SEGMENTATION AND CONSUMER BEHAVIOR

CASE 5
Libb
Pharmaceuticals:
Alive Toothpaste

In terms of understanding consumer behavior and the subsequent formulation of marketing strategy, the measurement of consumer attitudes has become increasingly important. Many firms have found that it is valuable and necessary to know how consumers perceive their brands along key product attributes. At the same time it is of importance to know how competitors' brands are evaluated along the same attributes.

Management of Libb Pharmaceuticals became quite concerned when the market share of Alive toothpaste declined from about 15 percent to the present 10 percent. At a meeting of the product management team it was concluded that the firm should undertake some attitude research on the toothpaste market. Specifically, the firm was interested in determining:

- What perceptions do people have of Alive toothpaste?
- What are the preferences for and perceptions of the other major brands of toothpaste?
- How can Alive toothpaste best be positioned in the marketplace?

Background
Information

The Company Libb Pharmaceuticals traces its origin back to 1855 when the founder, Phillip L. Libb, developed an all-purpose skin ointment. The product achieved relatively large success within a regional trading area. From the outset, Libb devoted a significant proportion of the firm's profits to the development of new product lines and the improvement of existing ones.

By the early 1900s, the firm was manufacturing and distributing a wide line of pharmaceutical and personal care products. In addition, the

Source: From W. Wayne Talarzyk, *Cases for Analysis in Marketing*, 2nd ed. (Hinsdale, Ill.: The Dryden Press, 1981), pp. 27–33. Copyright © 1981 by CBS College Publishing. Reprinted by permission of Holt, Rinehart and Winston, CBS College Publishing.

firm was gradually expanding its marketing area and by 1920 had achieved national distribution for most of its products.

One of Libb's early product additions was in the area of toothpastes. At one point the firm was marketing four separate brands of toothpaste. By the end of World War II all of the brands had been gradually phased out, with the exception of Alive. The decision was made at that time that Alive would be the firm's only brand of toothpaste and that it would be modified and reformulated as appropriate to keep the brand competitive with changing market conditions and potentials.

The Product and Promotion At the present time, Alive toothpaste is being positioned almost as an all-in-one mouth care product. Promotional claims for the product include such statements as "Alive toothpaste polishes your teeth as bright as any other brands," "Alive contains special ingredients that freshen your breath like the leading mouthwashes," "Alive now contains a special fluoride to help reduce the threat of tooth decay," and "Alive brightens and protects your teeth while it freshens your mouth."

Most of the brand's advertising budget is allocated to spot television commercials in both daytime and prime time. The basic themes of most commercials focus on boy meets girl and vice versa, and "slice of life" types of situations. The second largest share of the brand's advertising budget goes to national magazines, with some use being made of Sunday newspaper supplements.

As another form of promotion, couponing is utilized to some extent. Libb has also tried several promotional efforts where Alive toothpaste is associated with some of the firm's other products.

In essence, the firm has made limited attempts to concentrate on any specific market segments with its promotional efforts. Instead, the focus has been on reaching as many consumers as possible with the amount of promotional dollars available.

Results of the Consumer Research

Brand Preferences As another form of promotion, couponing is utilized to some extent by 46.4 percent of the respondents. Alive was ranked first by 10.5 percent of the respondents, while 22.7 percent and 22.3 percent ranked it their second or third choice, respectively.

To gain a better understanding of brand preference across various levels of education, a cross tabulation was developed. It is significant to note that, in general, as education increases the preference for Alive decreases. This same phenomenon holds true for Colgate while the opposite is true for Crest.

Attribute Importance As part of the input to the attitude model, respondents were asked to rank the importance of five attributes of toothpaste. More than 75 percent of the respondents ranked "Decay Prevention" as the most important attribute to them in selecting a brand of toothpaste. "Price" was ranked least important.

Consumer Perceptions The research team felt that the individual attribute ratings would probably fairly represent the images and perceptions that consumers held toward the alternative brands studied. It was decided that the average consumer ratings for each attribute should be calculated for each brand. It was also concluded that these average ratings on each brand should be first computed for those who ranked the brand as their most preferred, and then computed for those who stated first preference for any of the other brands. Alive was rated as a 1.27 (the lower the rating the more satisfactory the brand is perceived on that attribute) on "Taste/Flavor" by those who prefer it and as a 2.23 by those who stated preference for some other brand. Respondents preferring Alive rated it as a 1.56 on "Decay Prevention" while those preferring Crest rated Crest as a 1.21 on that attribute.

Questions

1. How will this consumer research assist Libb Pharmaceuticals in marketing Alive Toothpaste?
2. Relate this case to the discussion of consumer behavior that appears in Chapter 7.
3. Relate this case to the discussion of market segmentation that appears in Chapter 5.

CASE 6
The Xerox Store

A very difficult segment of the office equipment market to reach efficiently is the extensive group of small businesses. In total, the segment is rather large—about 10 million customers (4 million small businesses with less than 20 employees and 6 million offices in the home). The unit sales volume would not support nor would it justify the expense of a direct sales force. However, Xerox Corporation wants to become a major force in this growing market for office equipment for small businesses. As a consequence, Xerox embarked in April 1980 on a radically different marketing strategy to capture this segment. Their approach is to market office equipment through retail stores that cater to small business needs.

The Xerox Plan Seven retail stores were scheduled to open in 1980, with an additional 150 to be completed by 1981. The goal was to become "the supermarket for office supplies," with the intended result being to capture the largest share of the low-end copier business. Robert Reiser, president of the firm's Retail Market Division, suggests that the impetus for the radical departure in marketing methods is the fact that "there is

Source: From Michael D. Hutt and Thomas W. Speh, *Industrial Marketing Management* (Hinsdale, Ill.: The Dryden Press, 1981), pp. 405–7. Copyright © 1981 by CBS College Publishing. Reprinted by permission of Holt, Rinehart and Winston, CBS College Publishing. Also from "What Xerox Sees in Retail Stores," *Business Week*, April 21, 1980; pp. 130–32. "Xerox Formally Opens Dallas Retail Store, First of Planned Change," *Wall Street Journal*, April 10, 1980; and "In the News: New Chain," *FORTUNE*, May 5, 1980, p. 48.

no way we could reach that marketplace with our own direct sales force and do it cost-effectively."

Xerox will merchandise a wide line of office products produced by other manufacturers. Included in the line is a coated-paper copier from Develop Dr. Eisberrin & Company in West Germany, a personal computer from Apple Computer Corporation, a line of calculators from Hewlett-Packard Company, dictation machines from Matusushita Electric Company, Centronix data printers and Remington Rand typewriters. In addition, the stores will carry Xerox word processors, its facsimile units, and the low-priced end of its plain paper copier line.

Besides expanding their customer base, Xerox plans to dramatically increase copier sales, as copier sales are projected to account for half of all store sales. A side benefit to the expansion of low-priced copier sales is that additional sales may be generated from customers who trade up as their own volume and copying needs expand.

The Service Advantage A potential problem associated with the retailing of sophisticated products like computers and copiers to small businesses is the after-sale product servicing. Xerox feels that they will avoid any problems in this regard because no new national servicing network will have to be developed: The firm's 11,000 field representatives will also service the new customers. As a result of the readily available service network, the firm expects to realize 5 to 10 percent higher profits than they do by selling through a direct sales force.

The Name Plus Convenience Industry observers feel that the well-known Xerox name will be a significant factor in drawing small business customers to the store. Because of the breadth of product line, the chances will be good to sell something once a prospective customer has been attracted to the store.

The retail approach to servicing business customers is unique to the industry and Xerox, at least at the outset, will be the only copier company providing such service. It is expected that one-stop shopping for the office needs of a small businessperson will provide a significant convenience appeal. However, the company expects strong competitive reaction over the longer term. Digital Equipment Corporation already maintains 21 stores and is considering expansion. IBM currently sells some of its products through retail outlets in foreign markets.

The firm's final concern is developing the "right" success formula. Such things as store design, store location, advertising support, and follow-up service are being evaluated in an attempt to come up with the most effective combination for reaching this sector of the market—now and in the years ahead. Xerox President David T. Kearns states, "Things will shift through the 1980s. It may be best to do things differently in different cities. I wouldn't rule out anything."

Questions

1. What are the major differences between the Xerox Store approach and the more typical industrial channels?
2. What role will segmentation play in the Xerox strategy?
3. How can the market be segmented in this case?
4. What factors will be considered in location of stores?
5. What is the role of advertising in the new venture and what are some of the key factors to consider?

PART 4   PRODUCT/SERVICE STRATEGY

**CASE 7
A. H. Robins:
Robitussin**

The Company A. H. Robins, Inc., has evolved from a small community pharmacy opened in 1866 in Richmond, Virginia, by Albert Hartley Robins to a diversified multinational corporation operating in more than 100 countries. The corporate headquarters, which houses both corporate and pharmaceutical division offices, is located in the Richmond area, with branch offices in Dallas; Los Angeles; and Des Plaines, Illinois. The research center opened in 1963 with more than 325 scientists and technicians engaged in research in many product areas.

The A. H. Robins Company is engaged principally in the manufacture of finished-dosage forms of pharmaceutical products. Finished products are manufactured and packaged from raw materials purchased from suppliers of pharmaceutical grade chemicals. The company's principal products are ethical prescribed and ethical over-the-counter drug products which are promoted nationally by 1,350 field representatives to physicians, dentists, and pharmacists. Some of Robins' best-known brand names are Robitussin, a cough and cold syrup; Donnatal, an antispasmodic drug; and Robaxin, a skeletal muscle relaxant.

Robins' products are distributed to drug wholesalers which sell to retail drug stores and to hospitals. This distribution system has proven successful in the past. But, in the current drug market the chains do more than half the industry volume. If the large chains do buy direct from a manufacturer (at a lower price), they give those brands in-store marketing support, such as end aisle displays, extra shelf facings, and co-op advertising.

While maintaining its major position as manufacturer and researcher of pharmaceuticals, A. H. Robins has diversified into consumer products. In 1963, Robins acquired Morton Manufacturing in Lynchburg, Virginia, the producer of Chap Stick lip balm. In 1967, Robins acquired Polk Miller Products of Richmond, Virginia, producers of the Sergeant's line of pet care products. These two companies

Source: Reprinted by permission of Ian Stewart, A. H. Robins, Inc., and Professors Thomas D. Giese and Thomas J. Cosse, University of Richmond.

later formed Miller-Morton Company in an effort to consolidate consumer product activities. Robins enjoyed further success in the consumer goods area with the introduction of Lip Quencher, a lipstick utilizing the moisturizing qualities of Chap Stick. In 1967, it continued its entry into the consumer field with the acquisition of Parfums Caron, a leading producer of French fragrance products. Consumer products are advertised nationally and marketed through department stores, specialty shops, and drug outlets.

A. H. Robins entered the international markets in the 1960s by establishing manufacturing and distribution centers in Australia, Colombia, England, and Mexico. Foreign expansion was precipitated by both a demand for Robins products abroad and increasing foreign government regulation which restricted imports into these countries. Subsidiaries in Australia, Brazil, Canada, Colombia, France, Mexico, the Philippines, South Africa, the United Kingdom, Venezuela and West Germany provided a base for the company's growing international operations. The June 1976 increase accounted for 33 percent net sales and 34 percent earnings before tax, interest, and amortization expenses applicable to international operations.

The Product Robitussin, a cough and cold syrup, is marketed in five forms, one of which is an ethical prescribed form; the other four are ethical over-the-counter forms. The product to date has been marketed only through wholesalers and directly to nonproprietary hospitals. Demand is stimulated by detailmen calling on members of the medical profession and "detailing" the drug—describing its advantages and features so that physicians would either prescribe or recommend the product.

Promotion is complemented by sampling, trade deals, and trade and medical profession journal advertising. However, demand for the product is now static as it has reached the mature state in its present market segment.

The cough syrup market grew 5 percent the previous year. Within the overall market, the largest growth was in food stores.

Sales in food stores, which accounted for 24 percent of total sales, are increasing at a faster rate than drug-store sales. The sales in drug stores are polarizing towards the chains and large independents who want to purchase directly from the manufacturer rather than through the wholesaler, which results in lower margins for retail outlets.

While the ethical segment of the cough syrup market was still trending up slightly in dollars, the proprietary brands in food and drug outlets exhibited a healthy 10 percent increase in dollar terms as compared with a 2 percent increase for the ethical segment.

In unit terms, the cough syrup market was not growing, but within the segments, food store sales were moving up in importance while drug store units were declining. One study showed that the average homemaker visited the grocery store about three times a week and the drug store twice a month. In the drug stores the ethical brands were holding their share while proprietary brands were declining.

By way of comparison with other cold-remedy products, the cough syrup market is 12 percent larger than the cold-tablet market and more than three times larger than the nasal-spray market.

The heavy users of cough syrup preparations differ from most categories of cold products since the heaviest users usually do not purchase their own product because half the actual users are under eighteen years of age. The prime prospect households can be described as follows:

- Female head of household 25-49 years old
- Households with children 2-17 years old and with 5 or more persons
- Household annual income of $15,000 or lower
- Less educated
- Heavy usage among nonwhites

The breakdown of unit sales by brand is as follows: Robitussin has a 21.6 percent share of unit sales in drug stores compared to Vicks' 16 percent. In food and drug stores combined, Robitussin has an estimated 14 percent share versus Vicks' 27 percent. Based on an earlier survey, the leading brands of cough syrup used were Formula 44, doctor's prescription, and Nyquil.

Towards the end of the financial year, as the planning stage for the following year was being finalized, George Mancini, Robitussin's product manager, had noted that over the past several years the line had only been growing in the 1 to 2 percent range in comparison with the 6 to 8 percent growth of the overall cough syrup market. Robitussin was becoming a mature product in its present segment of ethical over-the-counter drugs.[1]

Questions

1. Relate this case to the product life cycle concept.
2. What action should A. H. Robins take with respect to Robitussin?

[1]Drug industry practice was to classify products as either "ethical" or "proprietary" depending on the marketing method employed. Ethical products were marketed by promotion directly to the medical profession. The ethical classification was further subdivided into those drugs which required prescription and those which could be purchased without a prescription called "over-the-counter" (OTC) drugs. Proprietary products were promoted directly to the consumer.

**CASE 8
Copsco, Inc.**

Since the early 1970s considerable interest and activity have been directed toward energy conservation by government, business, and private sectors. One way in which the average homeowner, apartment

Source: From *Contemporary Cases in Marketing,* 2nd ed., by W. Wayne Talarzyk. Copyright © 1979 by The Dryden Press, A division of Holt, Rinehart and Winston, Inc. Reprinted by permission of Holt, Rinehart and Winston, CBS College Publishing.

dweller, or businessperson can reduce energy consumption is by turning the thermostat down during heating seasons and up during cooling seasons. Fuel savings can also be achieved by dialing down the thermostat at night when people are asleep and during the day if no one is around. The problem is that it is easy to forget to readjust the thermostat temperature when adjustment is needed.

Three doctors have designed a simple, inexpensive solution to the problem. Drs. Douglas Dachenbach, an optometrist who studied engineering, James Dindot, an anesthesiologist, and Edwin Jenkinson, a podiatrist, developed the Fuel Pacer device after several engineers said the project was "technically not functional and financially prohibitive."

The Product The Fuel Pacer product is a solid-state electronic unit housed in a small plastic box. It heats the air inside its case to a constant temperature and automatically sets back any home thermostat eight to ten degrees when plugged into an ordinary household timer. It attaches to the wall directly beneath the thermostat by means of an adhesive strip.

A column of air is continually drawn through the device, and the heated currents are forced up to mix with the room air at the thermostat. This raises the temperature measured by the thermostat and "fools" it into thinking the room is actually eight to ten degrees warmer than it is. When the timer turns the Fuel Pacer off, the room temperature returns to the setting of the thermostat.

The automatic process has an advantage over manually turning down thermostats; no monitoring or adjustment is required unless a change in the timing of the setback is desired. To lower air conditioning costs, the strategy is reversed, with the thermostat set higher to reduce energy consumption. The Fuel Pacer will function on any wall-mounted thermostat with central heating or cooling and can be used with gas, electric, coal or oil heating systems. Production cost per unit in marketable quantities is approximately $3.83.

Potential Savings A study by the Holifield National Laboratory in Oak Ridge, Tennessee, concluded that the total U.S. energy budget could be cut by 4 percent if homes usually heated at 72 degrees were heated to 68 degrees in the daytime and set back to 55 degrees at night. The fuel savings would be equivalent to about 25 percent of U.S. petroleum imports. The study also reported that, contrary to public opinion, the energy consumed to reheat a home is not as great as the energy saved by an eight hour setback. Energy savings are typically realized by any setback beyond four hours.

According to an energy conservation bulletin from the National Bureau of Standards, each one-degree reduction in the setting of the room thermostat will save about 1 percent of fuel in cold climates, and about 3 percent in moderate climates. Setting a thermostat back 10 degrees

**EXHIBIT 1
Proposed
Advertisement for
the Fuel Pacer**

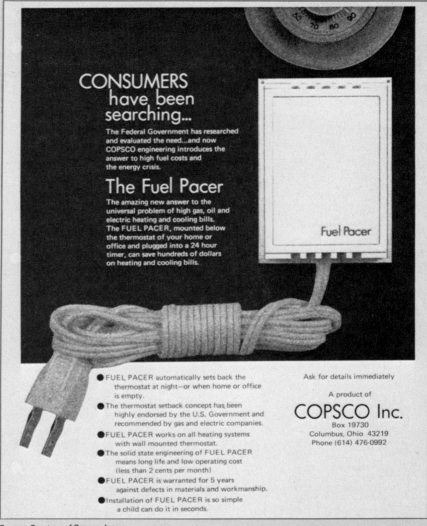

Source: Courtesy of Copsco, Inc.

for an eight-hour period at night would be expected to yield a 10 to 15 percent fuel savings.

Initial Marketing Efforts The three doctors, incorporated as Copsco, initially plan to market the Fuel Pacer via mail and telephone sales. The tentative price will be $19.95, which includes postage and handling. In anticipation of placing some print advertisements for the Fuel Pacer, the firm has developed the proposed layout shown in Exhibit 1.

Questions

1. Relate this case to the text's discussion of product strategy.
2. How can Copsco best market its product?

PART 5

DISTRIBUTION STRATEGY

CASE 9
The Japanese Distribution System

Marketers in developing countries view Japan as an example of how *not* to set up a distribution system. This highly developed, industrialized nation has one of the most inefficient distribution structures in the world. One U.S. marketer referred to it as "marketing in a maze." What went wrong?

Japan appears to have a market tailor-made for short channel structures: a huge population, about half as large as that in the United States, concentrated in an area only 4 percent as large as that of the United States. Yet channels are anything but short. Direct sales from the manufacturer to the consumer are virtually unheard of, and a three-level structure—manufacturer to retailer to consumer—is almost as rare.

Much more common are several levels of wholesalers intervening between the manufacturer and the retailer, which results in channel structures of four levels. For instance, the tortured journey of imported consumer products through the Japanese distribution system—customs to importer to national wholesaler to local wholesaler to retailer to consumer—may result in a final retail price twice that in the United States.

The reasons for such long channel structures even in the face of dense markets are traceable to two basic phenomena: the market behavior of the Japanese consumer and the historical background of Japanese society. In commenting on the first phenomenon, a market research study of Japanese buyer behavior stated: "The average Japanese housewife shops every day within 500 yards of her home. . . . You must have a great number of points of supply for this; it is the logistics of bits and pieces."

The second phenomenon? Historically the long, complex channel structures grew from the early development of Japanese villages, which commonly distrusted each other. Many neutral middlemen were needed to sell goods from one village to the next. Then, as trading companies began to appear in the late nineteenth century, they became so prominent in buying and selling that many manufacturing companies never bothered to develop sales staffs.

Sources: Case adapted from Bert Rosenbloom, *Marketing Channels: A Management View* (Hinsdale, Ill.: Dryden Press, 1978), pp. 168–69. Copyright © 1978 by Dryden Press, a division of Holt, Rinehart and Winston. Adapted by permission of Holt, Rinehart and Winston. Based on William D. Hartley, "Cumbersome Japanese Distribution System Stumps U.S. Concerns," *Wall Street Journal*, March 2, 1972. See also Masayoshi Kanabayashi, "Japan's Complex Distribution System Hinders Foreign Companies' Efforts to Sell Goods There," *Wall Street Journal*, May 3, 1978.

Questions

1. What can be learned from studying the Japanese distribution system?
2. How would the Japanese distribution system affect U.S. firms wishing to market their goods in Japan?

CASE 10
W. T. Grant
Company: The
Death of a Giant

Founded in 1906, W. T. Grant, the seventy-year-old variety store chain, had 1,100 stores, 70,000 employees, and was doing $2 billion in sales annually. The firm had compiled an enviable record. Except for a loss in 1932 at the height of the Great Depression, the retailer had reported regular profits for the first sixty-seven years of its existence and had developed into one of the country's largest variety store chains. It had expanded into the suburbs and had tried to become a department store, selling furniture and major appliances on credit.

Then quite suddenly, for its fiscal year ending January 31, 1975, Grant reported the largest loss ever to hit a retailer, $177.3 million, even after it took a tax credit of more than $100 million. And a year and a few months later the company was liquidated out of existence.

History The Grant Company was founded in 1906 on a $1,000 investment by its namesake, William T. Grant, who had been employed previously in the shoe department of a Boston department store. The first Grant store was set up in a corner of the Lynn, Massachusetts, Young Men's Christian Association building. And a window sign on opening day announced "A new kind of store—a department store with nothing over 25 cents." The founder's merchandising idea was to fill the pricing niche between the then burgeoning "five-and-dimes" like Woolworth's and Kresge and the department stores whose wares at that time began at about fifty cents. Merchandise moved swiftly and profitably at twenty-five cents, since there were no size or fitting problems nor selling effort involved. With spartan surroundings and an emphasis on solid quality at bargain prices, the Grant chain expanded in New England initially and then moved into the mid-Atlantic states. Its customer base from the start was lower middle-class working people. By 1919 the chain grew to thirty-three stores. World War I inflation raised Grant's top price to $1, but it remained a working family's store with inexpensive ready-to-wear clothes and drygood staples as the backbone of its daily business.

The Great Depression was a period of further expansion and prosperity for Grant and other variety store chains, since consumers with reduced incomes turned to the lower-priced retailers. The severe depression deflation helped bring a wide variety of new goods under the top price, and Grant's now became a "junior" department store. The depression had lowered prices so drastically that Grant buyers were able to procure for the store such major items as all-silk slips, wool bathing suits, rayon bedspreads, and men's shoes and pants. This was in addition to such staple merchandise as goldfish, lipsticks, brass screws, art lamps, and brassieres.

By the mid-1930s, William T. Grant became chairman of the board

Source: This case was written by Professor Steven J. Shaw of the University of South Carolina. Reprinted by permission.

and left day-to-day operations up to his managers. He remained at this post until 1966 when he retired at the age of ninety. For the Grant chain, the 1940s and 1950s were a period of nationwide expansion.

Removal of Price Ceilings and Movement to the Suburbs During the 1940s Grant had removed ceiling prices on its merchandise and began slowly to introduce furniture and appliances into its stores. Also, during this decade the chain first started to open stores in the suburbs, shifting from its exclusive emphasis on in-town locations. However, in hindsight, the type of locations selected might have been one of the contributing reasons for Grant's later downfall. While realizing the need to locate stores nearer to its customers, management avoided the large regional centers, preferring small community or strip-center locations. In 1963 management embarked on a rapid expansion program. During the next ten years, 612 new stores were opened, bringing the total to 1,188 with a payroll of 82,500 employees. But this rapid expansion was extremely costly and was financed mostly by external borrowing. Loans of $614 million from twenty-seven banks were necessary to launch the new stores.

Shift in Merchandise Emphasis In 1968 under a new president, Richard W. Mayer, Grant shifted its merchandising emphasis from soft goods to hard goods. With an eye apparently on Sears and J. C. Penney, Grant tried to make the transition to a suburban department store at a time when aggressive discount stores like K mart and Woolco were making the same move. The Grant stores began stocking refrigerators, television sets, air conditioners, and other big-ticket appliance and furniture items. Usually these were produced by nationally known manufacturers such as Westinghouse and Fedders. But management insisted on removing the brand name and marketing these appliances under its own private label, Bradford. Unfortunately, the Bradford label was not well known to consumers. Shoppers were confused by the shift from soft goods to hard goods. They could identify with Grant neither as the retailer of variety soft goods it had been nor as the retailer of upgraded, higher-priced hard goods it was trying to become.

Liberal Credit Terms President Mayer, who had moved up the corporate ladder through credit management, went all out to induce customers to buy its big-ticket items by offering liberal credit terms. Store employees were given bonuses for signing up new credit card customers. Credit applications were not carefully screened, and by January 1975, Grant's customers owed the company $600 million. Grant was now in the untenable financial position of having to borrow money to buy new merchandise while waiting for customers to pay their bills.

Merchandise Planning and Control Inadequate merchandise inventory controls led to excessive accumulation of stock in many departments and out-of-stock conditions in others. Indiscriminate unplanned buying and lack of a sound markdown policy resulted in seasonal merchandise being left on the shelves long after the season had passed and consumers passed it by. By 1975 it was clear the company's problem was one of survival. Some suppliers began selling to Grant on a COD basis only. Others stopped shipments in mid-transit.

Final Efforts at Recovery Under new management Grant petitioned for Chapter XI, a procedure under bankruptcy law that allows a firm to continue operating while formulating a plan to pay its debts. Robert H. Anderson, a highly successful ex-Sears executive, embarked on a program to close unprofitable stores and reduce excess inventory. He cut Grant down to 359 stores in the northeastern United States with 24,000 employees. Under Anderson, Grant dropped its major appliance lines and returned to the merchandising of low-cost soft goods.

But these efforts came too late. In February 1976, creditors moved to have the company declared bankrupt, and the court so ruled. Anderson, the chief executive officer, blamed suppliers for Grant's inability to make the recovery plan work. The merchandise didn't come in, he said, apparently because vendors were afraid of suffering further losses. With liabilities of $1.1 billion, the failure of W. T. Grant Company became the largest in retailing history.

Questions

1. Identify and discuss the principal reasons why Grant's failed.
2. Since Grant's was trying to transform itself into a merchandiser of expensive shopping and specialty goods, would location in regional shopping centers have been a sounder strategy?
3. Several years back a major west coast aircraft manufacturer was saved from bankruptcy by means of a huge government loan and certain guaranties. Chrysler is a more recent example. Discuss the pros and cons of having the U.S. government move in and keep a giant like Grant's from going out of business.

PART 6   PROMOTIONAL STRATEGY

CASE 11
Morton Salt

George Tate strolled down Michigan Avenue on a warm spring afternoon in Chicago. He had spent the entire morning with Morton Salt's advertising agency, reviewing the company's past promotion and discussing possible plans for the upcoming fiscal year, which would begin on July 1. As he walked, he pondered the problems facing the company, particularly with regard to table salt, traditionally Morton Salt's major product.

Source: Reprinted by permission of Nancy Stephens, Assistant Professor of Advertising; Richard F. Beltramini, Assistant Professor of Marketing and Advertising; Arizona State University; and Morton Salt Division of Morton-Norwich Products, Inc. Copyright © 1980 by Nancy Stephens and Richard F. Beltramini. Morton, the Umbrella Girl design, When It Rains, It Pours, Morton Lite Salt, Sugar Cure, Tender Quick, Nature's Seasons, and Dough-It-Yourself are registered trademarks of Morton-Norwich Products, Inc.

When It Rains, It Pours In the early part of the twentieth century, consumers bought salt in brown paper bags, which had been put up by a grocer from bulk salt he had purchased in barrels. The salt business was keenly competitive, and no firm had been able to gain significant consumer demand or a price advantage. Morton's product was exactly like that of its competition.

If Morton Salt could be differentiated in some way, however, they could improve consumer demand, and thus improve profit margins. By 1920, they developed an innovative way to keep salt from caking or hardening from moisture, and introduced a moisture-proof, two-pound cylindrical package with an aluminum spout for easier pouring. With these improvements, Morton embarked upon a modest advertising program, utilizing primarily women's magazines. "When It Rains, It Pours" was adopted as a slogan for the advertisement, and was also printed on the package.

The idea of branding and advertising was a new one in the salt market, but it seemed to work as Morton's sales and market share grew. With this increased degree of control over consumer demand, Morton began to gradually increase prices until their packaged salt sold for double that of any competitor (10¢ per package, compared to 5¢ for unbranded bags).

No Salt Salts Like Morton Salt Salts Since Morton's product and package improvements were unprotected by patents, competitors were quick to imitate. As a result, some consumer resistance to the price differential began to affect Morton Salt sales. At this point, therefore, Morton needed another innovation.

Because of its leadership in the salt industry, Morton was approached by health authorities and medical organizations who had discovered that an insufficient amount of iodine in the body was a cause of goiter (an enlargement of the thyroid gland, often visible as a swelling in the lower part of the front of the neck). Since salt was a universally used food product, these authorities suggested that Morton take the lead in adding iodine to their salt, in a ratio of 1 part iodine to 5,000 parts salt, for goiter prevention.

Iodized salt was introduced in the early 1920s with advertising support, and by 1926 Morton's iodized salt was outselling plain salt. It was able to continue its market leadership and brand preference for many years, maintaining a premium price.

However, in the early 1960s Morton saw its sales and market shares slipping again as competitors had matched product innovations, and had engaged in price-cutting tactics. In addition, consumer lifestyles had changed to produce a declining demand for salt. More people were eating away from home, and more prepared, presalted foods were being consumed at home.

Morton expanded its advertising to focus on the 30-to-40 age group (then found to consume 75 percent of all salt sold), and reemphasized the company's early innovations in the salt market. Magazines, television, and radio carried the message "No Salt Salts Like Morton Salt Salts" to this target audience. In 1968 Morton was able to enjoy the largest market share of any year in the decade.

The Next Best Thing to the Real Thing By the late 1960s, Morton had also expanded its product offerings beyond table salt. Company divisions had been established to produce prepared foods, chemicals, and agricultural goods, partially as a result of their 1969 merger with Norwich Pharmacal Company.

Future growth depended upon properly defining the firm's business position. As consumers had changed, Morton was no longer just in the "salt business," it was in the "seasonings business."

In 1970, after extensive product and market research, Morton introduced a new consumer product, Salt Substitute. Morton Salt Substitute was initially available in two varieties, regular and seasoned. It was composed of potassium chloride, and had already enjoyed limited use by people on medically supervised low-sodium diets.

The introduction of Salt Substitute as a consumer product was supported by a $242,000 advertising campaign which emphasized taste rather than the product's medical uses. "The Next Best Thing to the Real Thing" was chosen as the slogan, and appeared in magazine and newspaper advertisements. Further, a 10¢-off coupon was featured to stimulate trial purchases of the innovative product. By the end of the decade, Morton's sales achieved higher levels than all other salt brands combined.

Morton, The Salt You've Been Passing for Generations The 1970s brought increasing attention and concern among Americans about the potential relationship between the use of salt and certain diseases. Medical researchers observed that when certain patients suffering from hypertension (high blood pressure) were fed a diet severely restricted in sodium, their blood pressure decreased. Few researchers were willing to state categorically that sodium caused hypertension, but some troubling questions were posed.

Several years later, the U.S. Senate Select Committee on Nutrition and Human Needs responded to concerns about salt usage by including it in a set of dietary goals for the United States. One of the stated goals was that salt consumption be reduced to approximately five grams per day from the average of ten or twelve grams normally ingested. Such a goal might be achieved, some suggested, by eliminating most highly salted processed foods and condiments, and by eliminating salt added at the table.

Health concerns about salt intake did not escape Morton management, and in 1973 (well ahead of the U.S. Senate Committee recommendations) Morton Lite Salt was introduced. Lite Salt was the first iodized salt mixture with the taste of regular salt, but with only half the sodium. Unlike Salt Substitute, which was not positioned directly against regular salt, Lite Salt was expected to cannibalize Morton's regular salt to some extent. This was not a major concern to Morton management, however, since Lite was seen as "the salt of the future."[1] A $1 million advertising campaign, largely in television, accompanied the rollout of Lite Salt.

During the 1970s Morton tested several other new seasoning products, including Butter Buds, Sugar Cure, Tender Quick, and Nature's Seasons. Some of these products were reasonably successful and remained on the market, while others were withdrawn due to insufficient sales.

To supplement Morton's fluctuating advertising budgets during this period, several sales promotion programs were employed. The first attempt was a set of four porcelain mugs offered for $2 plus a spout seal from a 26-ounce table salt package. Each mug featured a different Morton girl from the four periods of the company's history.

In 1975, another sales promotion program was developed to provide additional uses for salt. Morton introduced salt sculpture (a mixture of flour, water, and salt) for holiday decorations. Film strips were offered to elementary schools, and a ten-minute film was sent to television stations, explaining salt sculpture. Print advertising in women's magazines offered Morton's "Dough-It-Yourself" Handbook for a dollar.

The promotions for salt sculpture ran during the Christmas season, and were continued during Easter and July 4th for two years. By 1977, company executives estimated that 700,000 "Dough-It-Yourself" Handbooks had been sold, and distribution was expanded to craft stores as well.

Despite a series of successful consumer and trade promotions, 26-ounce table salt could not sustain the company. "It's a strong cash producer," commented Morton's president in 1977, "but not a growth market."[2] At the same time, management recognized that table salt could not be abandoned completely for although it represented only 5 percent of tonnage sales, it produced at least 35 percent of dollar sales.

Therefore, it was decided in 1977 to continue the sales promotion for Morton 26-ounce table salt. To capitalize on Americans' increased interest in genealogy, Morton sponsored a "Visit the Land of Your Ancestors" sweepstakes. Also featured were mailed kits which contained recipes from the homelands of Americans of current and past generations. The sweepstakes was tied in with the advertising theme, "Morton, the salt you've been passing for generations." Morton Salt maintained its number-one position among table salts in 1977 with an all-time high market share.

A third promotion (in addition to the salt sculpture and sweepstakes promotions) was begun in 1978. Special salt packages with labels from four past container designs (1914, 1921, 1933, and 1941) were featured in retail stores. Consumers were urged through media advertising to collect the entire "Keepsake Collection." These innovations in sales promotion were another solution to the perennial problem of maintaining brand preference for a parity product.

Summary As George Tate opened his office door, marked Director of Communications, he realized that some important decisions now faced Morton Salt. Salt Substitute and Lite Salt were leading the market in their respective product categories, and Nature's Seasons was growing in sales as well. Regular table salt seemed to be doing well as a result of the sales promotions, although the medical concerns of the 1970s were not expected to fade.

It seemed to Tate that innovations in product development, packaging, and sales promotion had always solved past problems. However, he was now concerned with an advertising innovation as a remedy.

Questions

1. What is the future of Morton's regular table salt—the product upon which the company was founded, and to which it owes much of its success?

2. Can consumer sales be sustained through advertising, and if so, how much should be budgeted in which media?

3. Is it wise to continue special offers, sweepstakes, and similar sales promotions?

NOTES

1. "Morton Lite Ties Into 'RD' Special Insert," *Advertising Age,* October 29, 1973.
2. "Morton Pours More Ad Dollars into Image-building Bid," *Advertising Age,* August 8, 1977.

CASE 12
The Qualities Needed in Personal Selling

Professors James R. Young and R. Wayne Mondy of East Texas State University have surveyed numerous senior sales executives as to the qualities they deemed important in personal selling. These executives were asked to rank the top five qualities needed in selling. The results appear below:

Firm's primary product	First	Second	Third	Fourth	Fifth
Lumber	Communication	Intelligence	Responsibility	Product knowledge	Enthusiasm
Petroleum	Drive	Intelligence	Product knowledge	Confidence	Communication
Petroleum	Achievement orientation	Product knowledge	Drive	Business ethics	Confidence
Petroleum	Intelligence	Drive	Enthusiasm	Empathy	Confidence
Petroleum	Intelligence	Drive	Enthusiasm	Imagination	Confidence
Lumber and Paper	Product knowledge	Enthusiasm	Confidence	Drive	Responsibility
Wholesale Foods	Intelligence	Communication	Drive	Empathy	Responsibility
Heavy Equipment	Product knowledge	Customer application of product	Communication	Intelligence	Responsibility
Natural Gas	Confidence	Communication	Product knowledge	Intelligence	Responsibility
Life Insurance	Organized persistence	Responsibility	Intelligence	Enthusiasm	Drive
Tires	Product knowledge	Communication	Intelligence	Confidence	Enthusiasm

Source: From PERSONAL SELLING: FUNCTION, THEORY & PRACTICE by James R. Young and Robert W. Mondy. Copyright © 1978 by The Dryden Press, A division of Holt, Rinehart and Winston, Publishers. Reprinted by permission of Holt, Rinehart and Winston, CBS College Publishing.

Qualities Needed in Personal Selling (continued)

Firm's primary product	First	Second	Third	Fourth	Fifth
Appliances	Courage	Communication	Drive	Product knowledge	Confidence
Meat Products	Drive	Intelligence	Confidence	Imagination	Enthusiasm
Optical Services	Drive	Confidence	Empathy	Imagination	Communication
Aluminum	Confidence	Drive	Responsibility	Imagination	Empathy
Computers	Honesty	Communication	Product knowledge	Intelligence	Confidence
Investments	Confidence	Communication	Drive	Enthusiasm	Imagination
Drugs	Trustworthiness	Communication	Confidence	Product knowledge	Responsibility
Petroleum	Drive	Imagination	Enthusiasm	Product knowledge	Responsibility
Public Utility	Product knowledge	Confidence	Social intelligence	Responsibility	Enthusiasm
Public Utility	Intelligence	Drive	Communication	Empathy	Confidence
Gas Distributor	Enthusiasm	Responsibility	Empathy	Imagination	Drive
Public Utility	Honesty	Product knowledge	Confidence	Drive	Communication
Public Utility	Intelligence	Enthusiasm	Judgment	Product knowledge	Imagination
Public Utility	Responsibility	Communication	Enthusiasm	Drive	Intelligence
Public Utility	Enthusiasm	Intelligence	Product knowledge	Drive	Communication
Public Utility	Responsibility	Communication	Product knowledge	Intelligence	Imagination

Questions

1. What conclusions do you draw from this survey?
2. What qualities do you think are needed to be successful in personal selling?

PART 7   PRICING STRATEGY

CASE 13
Pricing Razorback Basketball Tickets

Eddie Sutton, head basketball coach at the University of Arkansas, was selected Southwest Conference Coach of the Year after his first year at the University, guiding the Razorbacks to a second-place finish in the conference. His overall team record of 17–9 was the Razorbacks' best performance in twenty years. Since Sutton had established the Razorbacks as a strong competitor in the Southwest Conference, he had received excellent support from dormant basketball devotees from years past. Now he had to determine some scheduling strategy for next year.

One of the issues involved playing basketball in Little Rock, 200 miles from the Fayetteville campus where his team had played 15 home games the past year, winning 13 and losing two.

Frank Broyles, the University athletic director, had suggested to Sutton the advisability of playing some games in Little Rock next year. None of the games were played in the city during the past year, but two years ago, a game had been played at Christmas time at which attendance was very small and turned out to be a financial disaster for the Razorbacks. A similar experience occurred three years ago at a Christmas Holiday tournament sponsored by the Uni-

Source: Reprinted by permission of Robert D. Hay and Eddie Sutton, University of Arkansas.

versity. Attendance was sparse and money was lost on the venture.

Broyles' policy on football scheduling called for the team to play three or four football games in Little Rock each year and three games at Fayetteville. His rationale for this schedule was that he wanted (and received) fan support from the entire state. The Razorbacks gained support from more people if they played some of their games in Little Rock. Besides, Broyles wanted the University of Arkansas to be truly a state university rather than a Northwest Arkansas regional university. Such fan support had several advantages: financial contributions to the Razorback Scholarship Fund were easier to obtain; athletic recruiting was easier to accomplish; financial assistance was available for athletic facilities; and other objectives of the athletic program were easier to accomplish if fan support came from the whole state and not just a geographic portion of it. If the football market were larger, then the athletic program objectives would be more easily achieved. Broyles believed the same policy could be applied to basketball.

Broyles thought to himself that the present market for Razorback basketball included a four-county rural population area of approximately 200,000 people. If the Razorbacks played some games in Little Rock, the market area would be extended to perhaps an additional 300,000 people. If the basketball program were to catch on, the whole state might support the basketball team, much as they had done for football over the past twenty years. Would not the time be right for expansion into the Little Rock area since the University of Arkansas now had a quality team and coaching staff, and could effectively promote that team?

Sutton, aware of local, student, and faculty discontent with the Little Rock policy, decided to schedule three basketball games in Little Rock for the upcoming season. He further decided to play three big-name schools: Tulane, Oklahoma, and Texas. His rationale was that if Arkansas could play and beat teams with good athletic reputations, chances for additional fan support from the whole state would be better. The University of Texas game especially would attract fans since Texas and Arkansas were archrivals in all athletic endeavors.

The next big decision involved pricing the basketball tickets. Last year, the Razorbacks charged $3.00 for reserved seats at home. Students were allowed to get in free upon presentation of their I.D. card. Faculty members paid half price. General admission at home games was $1.50.

The present ticket policies allowed about 2,500 students to sit in bleachers on one side of the court. The other side was reserved for season ticket holders and for general-admission buyers. Both Sutton and Wilson Matthews, the assistant athletic director, wanted to differentiate the seats on a price basis for the coming year. Students would sit in the bleachers. However, only half the total seats available (5,200 capacity) would be sold to students. The other half would be allocated to season ticket holders and general-admission buyers. Students would have first priority for half the tickets. Longtime season ticket holders, both faculty and Razorback Fund donors, would have second priority. Then would come "new" Razorback Club members who had not purchased tickets before. Finally the general public (both faculty and part-time fans) would be sold any leftover tickets.

For the past five years (not including last year), an average of about 3,000 fans attended each game: approximately 2,000 students and 1,000 nonstudents. An average of 300 season tickets were purchased per year. Matthews estimated that 2,600 season tickets could be sold to Razorback Club members and present season ticket holders. His optimism was based on the fact that there were 6,400 members of the Razorback Scholarship Fund who could be counted on to purchase season tickets if tickets were promoted in the right way. (The University had never really promoted basketball season tickets before this time. However, very elaborate promotion plans were used to sell 20,000 to 30,000 football season tickets each year for the past several years.) Matthews thought that 2,600 season tickets could be sold in Fayetteville to Razorback Club members and about 7,000 seats could be sold at Barton Coliseum in Little Rock if the proper promotion were made to the Razorback Club members and to the general public. Matthews believed that if a scarcity of tickets existed in the general public's mind, sales could be made at practically any price.

TABLE 1

University	Yearly Attendance	General Admission	Reserved Seats	Number of Season Tickets Sold	Faculty & Students
Oral Roberts University	102,000	$1.50	$2.00–3.00	4500	F$1.75; S$1.25–1.50
Texas Tech University	97,000	2.00	3.50	3500	F$1.00; S$1.00
Hutchison Jr. College	85,000	1.50	2.00	2500	F free; S free
Creighton	77,000	2.00	3.50	2000	F ½; S .50
Baylor	80,000	2.00	3.50	1400	F free; S free
Texas	63,000	2.00	3.00	0	F free; S free
Texas A & M	55,000	2.00	3.00	750	F free; S free
Southern Methodist University	48,000	3.00	3.00	1000	F free; S free
Texas Christian University	44,000	2.00	3.00	500	F free; S free
Tulane	39,000	2.50	4.00	200	F 1.00; S free
Rice	39,000	2.00	2.50	100	F Nom.; S free
Arkansas	39,000	1.50	3.00	300	F ½; S free
Mac Murray	5,000	1.00	1.00	25	F free; S free
Oklahoma City University	22,000	2.00	2.50	400	F free; S free
University of Nebraska–Omaha	13,000	2.50	2.50	160	F free; S free

Source: Personal interviews with coaches of each school

TABLE 2

University	Net Profit (net loss)	University	Net Profit (net loss)
Texas Tech	$ 25,000	Arkansas	$(100,000)
Hutchison Jr. College	14,000	Oklahoma City	(105,000)
Southern Methodist	Breakeven	Tulane	(150,000)
Mac Murray	(21,000)	Texas Christian	(loss)
University of Nebraska–Omaha	(26,000)	Rice	(loss)
Creighton	(30,000)	Texas	??
Baylor	(50,000)	Oral Roberts	??
Texas A & M	(60,000)		

Source: Personal Interviews with coaches at each school

Additional information regarding ticket prices and policies was obtained from several colleges (see Table 1).

Financial data for the various schools was difficult to come by. There were only two schools who made a yearly profit from basketball—Texas Tech and Hutchinson Junior College. The financial data estimates are given in Table 2.

Inflation of 10 to 15 percent had occurred during the past year. Consequently, an additional price hike at home games in Fayetteville could be justified. Matthews suggested a $3.50 reserved seat price, while Sutton thought that $4.00 could be charged. If a season ticket for 12 home games were priced at $40, Sutton argued, such a price discount could be a bargain for any season ticket purchaser. Matthews thought that a season ticket price of $35 would be appropriate. Faculty would pay half price for two season tickets, and full price for any more than two. General admission would be a little more than half the price for reserved seats.

Matthews suggested that first priority to purchase season tickets be given to the 6,400 Razorback Club members. Wilson stated, "Razorback Club members are ardent supporters of our athletic program. They will pay any price for a ticket. Once they buy their tickets, the demand for tickets to the general public will be established; and we can sell the tickets at a fairly high price to get additional revenue for our basketball program."

Sutton replied, "Well, that strategy might work. We surely could put the program in a solid profit situation if we could sell 2,600 season tickets to our home games. As you well know, our basketball program lost about $125,000 two years ago and $140,000 this past year. With a little promotion, with a high-quality team, and with loyalty from our Razorback supporters, we could make a profit on our basketball program and not have to rely on our football team to generate sufficient revenue and profits to support us. They've been doing so for the past 25 years. Boy, if we could sell 2,600 season tickets, for, say, $90,000, we'd be on our way."

Matthews said, "We could do it in Fayetteville and we could do it in Little Rock. For example, if we could sell 1,200 season tickets for $40 and 1,000 tickets for $35 and 400 tickets for $25, we could generate $93,000 in revenue here in Fayetteville. Let's say we sell $70,000 worth of tickets in Little Rock, which I think we could do by selling most of them to Razorback Club members. Then we can put basketball on a paying basis."

Sutton answered, "Wow! That would be great. But can we sell that many season tickets? We've only sold about 300 season tickets each year during the past five years. Would the Razorback Club members support such a ticket sale? Would the general public buy season tickets in Little Rock, particularly in light of our past failures?"

The two men's enthusiasm seemed warranted and they departed to meet again. The next time their conversation turned to more practical matters. Matthews asked, "What about competition? As you know, we have a monopoly here in Fayetteville. In Little Rock we'd be competing with all the high schools, the University of Arkansas at Little Rock, University of Central Arkansas, and other small colleges. In addition, we'd be competing with other forms of entertainment."

Sutton replied, "That's true, but we would have no major competition at our level. There are no major universities in Division I of the NCAA in Little Rock. We still would retain our monopoly position as far as I'm concerned. I think our fans would pay a pretty high price to see the University of Arkansas in Little Rock. When Indiana plays basketball in Indianapolis, not in Bloomington, the price is at least $5.00 for a reserved seat. When North Carolina State plays a home game away from campus, the price is at least $5.00 a ticket. The same holds true for other major universities. Competition from high schools and smaller colleges would not affect us in Little Rock."

Matthews said, "But maybe we should ease our way into the Little Rock market area with a low price, build a fan following, and then raise the price next year."

Sutton replied, "No, I think with our quality team, our promotion, and our fan loyalty we should not set a low price. People will be willing to pay a high price for our product. What's the seating capacity of Barton Coliseum?"

"About 7,000," Matthews replied. "We could differentiate those seats like this: 3,000 seats at $5.50 each; 2,000 at $4.00; and 2,000 at $3.00. We could charge $13.00 for three tickets; $10.00 for lesser-priced seats; and $7.00 for end-zone seats. What do you think?"

Sutton pondered the question. "Let's think about it before we make our recommendation to Frank Broyles."

Questions

1. What factors are most relevant to this pricing decision?
2. What recommendations would you make to Frank Broyles?

"Thanks for coming over," waves the familiar, rotund pizza cook on Phoenix late-night television, "to Peter Piper Pizza." That same jocular pizza cook is in reality Anthony Cavolo, the company's chairman, who in just four years has expanded his pizza empire from one to five locations in the Phoenix metropolitan area, and is in the process of franchising several others.

Cavolo began in the restaurant business in New York, where he operated a delicatessen for several years. He later added tables and chairs, and a take-out service selling buckets of spaghetti, until the business grew to an Italian steak and pasta restaurant. Upon retirement, Cavolo moved to the Phoenix area, but eventually became bored and decided to open his own pizza restaurant after sampling the pizza there.

"I was fifty years old when I got here, and I had no intention of starting a whole brand-new career, but that's the way it worked out," reminisced Cavolo. "We looked around and did some research, nothing formal of course, and we saw the opportunity in the fast-food business." Apparently he was right, as the first location alone sold over 200,000 pizzas last year, and Steve Herrgesell, Peter Piper Pizza's president and Cavolo's son-in-law, forecasts, "This year's sales are expected to top $3 million."

Marketing Background Information In recent years, Americans have spent about 30 percent of their food dollars in restaurants, and about 70 percent in grocery stores. Fast-food restaurants account for about 25 percent of restaurant sales. In total, there are an estimated 15,000 pizza outlets across the United States (7,500 chain-related and 7,500 independents).

According to industry experts, fast food will continue to be a rapidly growing sector of the economy. It is pointed out, however, that large, better-financed companies will continue to gain market share to the detriment of smaller, regional companies.

Why do people eat out? The reason given most often by respondents in a recent survey was "for a change of routine," closely followed by "it's easier than cooking." These two explanations were given by nine out of ten people in the survey.

Consumers in the survey also had some opinions about fast-food restaurants. For example, when asked to compare the cost of eating in a fast-food restaurant to the cost of eating at home, a third believed it costs more, a third believed it costs less, and a third believed it costs about the same. Respondents were also asked to compare the nutritional value of food eaten in a fast-food restaurant to food eaten at home. Almost 70 percent believed that food eaten in a fast-food restaurant is less nutritious, while 21 percent believed that fast food and home

Source: Reprinted by permission of Richard F. Beltramini, Assistant Professor of Marketing and Advertising, and Nancy J. Stephens, Assistant Professor of Advertising, Arizona State University. Copyright © 1980 by Richard F. Beltramini and Nancy J. Stephens.

food are about the same. Only 3 percent felt that fast food is more nutritious.

Another study by the Newspaper Advertising Bureau indicated that 93 percent of the population over the age of 12 have patronized a fast-food restaurant within the past six months. During this period, they have visited an average of 3.4 different chains.

The Phoenix Pizza Market

Competition Cavolo looks at his business as "a real David and Goliath situation" in reference to the large number of chain pizza restaurants in Phoenix. Village Inn (25 outlets), Pizza Hut (31 outlets), Pizza Inn (10 outlets), Godfather's Pizza (6 outlets), Round Table Pizza (5 outlets), Straw Hat Pizza (6 outlets), Mr. Gatti's (2 outlets), and Noble Roman Pizza (4 outlets) each have restaurants in the Phoenix market. In addition, there are a number of "ma and pa stores" which Cavolo regards as less threatening competitively. "We're more concerned with our unique image being imitated," he stated, adding that his pizza ingredients were of better quality than those used in chains.

Promotion The Phoenix market is gimmick-oriented. Almost all restaurants utilize coupons and "deals" offering less-expensive second pizzas, beer, and plastic pitchers. Cavolo too tested half-price deals, but quickly learned that half his business originated from coupon sales. He quit "trying to be all things to all people," and today Peter Piper Pizza uses no such promotions.

Cavolo explains, "Those other places all show the cheese and they say look at all the stuff we put on it. They all have the same message—ours is the best, ours is the best. We don't say ours is the best. We say you come in. You tell us if you like it."

Price According to Cavolo, it is difficult to compete with the advertising of chains, who often do over $240,000 a year in business in just one location. His no-frills product is priced about 40 percent lower than the competition, with the most expensive item at $4.50. Only pizza is served, along with beer, wine, and soda in an effort to reduce expenses. He explains, "We don't have sandwiches, we don't have spaghetti—which adds to the cost of doing business because you have to add more help."

Peter Piper Pizza's Advertising Approach Cavolo's "spend as much as you can afford on advertising" budgeting approach has usually run at about 5 percent of sales, but at one point approached nearly 10 percent. This is substantially more than the average fast-food restaurant, which normally budgets approximately 2 percent of sales for advertising. The largest portion of his advertising budget is devoted to television, written and produced in-house.

"Television commercials are expensive. Even a cheap one could cost you $5,000 to produce. We make ours for an average of $150," notes Cavolo. An hour of studio time often yields Peter Piper Pizza as many as three commercials, in contrast to the approximate $50,000 per spot needed by national chain restaurants.

Cutting expenses is the primary objective of Cavolo, a man who arrives at work at 7:00 a.m. to call New York "before the rates go up." Cavolo spends up to a day on each 30-second spot writing and editing them. This pizza-cook approach is simple and straightforward—quality pizza at economy prices.

Summary

Cavolo summarizes his approach: "We don't play it up because a lot of people think they're not going to get much for $2.95. A lot of people think cheap is cheap. People see it on TV and they think what are you going to get for $3.00? People tell us we ought to charge more for it, but please don't."

The 10 percent annual inflation of ingredients has caused Peter Piper Pizza to raise prices from $1.70 to $2.95, in the case of a large cheese pizza, in the last four years. Cavolo's decision to maintain high-quality ingredients remains, however, despite the current $1.50 per pound price of mozzarella cheese—the biggest and most expensive single ingredient.

Cavolo's "get something good and sell it for less" philosophy has been reasonably successful thus far, but he is concerned about what the future holds. The escalating costs of products and advertising have shrunk his profit margins. The cost of capital has limited expansion, although franchising seems to be a potential growth avenue. Competition continues to grow, and Cavolo's unique personal approach may begin losing its believability.

Questions

1. Assess Cavolo's current pricing strategy. Why do you think it has been successful?

2. What changes, if any, would you recommend in the Peter Piper Pizza pricing strategy?

PART 8   FURTHER PERSPECTIVES

CASE 15
GE's Scenario of the World—Circa 1985

In 1975, General Electric conducted a study of world scenarios from 1975 to 1985 and analyzed how they would impact the company's international business operations. Here are some highlights from that study.

Source: Information concerning this 1975 study was supplied by Clifford H. Springer, Manager, Strategy Planning, General Electric. Reprinted by permission.

Potential Impact of Alternate 1975–1985 World Scenarios on General Electric's International Business

I. Objectives of Study
- A. To develop alternate world scenarios for 1975–1985
- B. To evaluate in broad terms the likely *impact* of alternative scenarios on each major segment of GE's international business activity
- C. To influence the application of strategic planning resources

II. Scope of Study
- A. Analysis of product segments encompassed only those business units to have significant activity outside the United States.
- B. Fact finding was heavily dependent on review of business unit's strategic plans, related documents, and interviews with International Group personnel.
- C. Evaluation of the impact of scenarios concentrated on the direct effects of environmental forces on GE—competitive and internal forces were considered only as they influence the impact of environmental forces.

III. Development of World Scenarios (1975–1985)
- A. Central Scenario
  Four major elements form the nucleus of Central Scenario:
  1. World Growth and Cycles
     - a. Capacity for growth generally stable trend
     - b. Real world economic growth 1975–1985 of 5.0%
     - c. Slower growth in developed countries (4.5%)
     - d. More rapid growth in developing countries (6.25%)
  2. Energy and Recycling
     - a. Oil price per barrel (1974 dollars)

1973	1974	1977	1980	1985
$2.75	$10.50	$10.00	$8.50	$6.50

- b. Accumulation of OPEC surpluses of about $300 billion by 1980, deficits after that point
  3. World Inflation (Average CPI 1975–1985)
     - a. Developed countries — 5.0%
     - b. United States — 4.0%
     - c. Western Europe — 6.0%
     - d. Developing countries — 16.0%
     - e. Much variation country-by-country
  4. International Monetary System
     - a. New regime negotiated by 1980
     - b. More flexible than Bretton Woods
     - c. Less volatile than "dirty float"
     - d. U.S. dollar remains key currency

5. Other Major Conclusions
   a. Trade restrictions generally will be reduced, but slowly.
   b. Food shortages are a question of population versus technology, with the latter prevailing.
   c. Raw material costs are a question of needs versus technology, with the latter prevailing.
   d. LDCs will be more restrictive towards MNCs particularly in natural resources.
   e. Unit labor costs are expected to rise faster abroad.
   f. The United States will subject MNCs to harsher taxation regulations.
   g. World population growth is expected to continue at 2 percent annually.
   h. Urbanization will continue, from 39 percent in 1975 to 43 percent by 1985.
   i. Detente will continue.

B. Variants on Central Scenario

Variants assumed a significant departure from central scenario in one major factor, with adjustment to obtain internal consistency.

Three variants developed:

1. Oil prices do not drop before 1985
2. Inflation rampant worldwide
3. Pervasive economic nationalism

1. Variant 1: OPEC Prices Maintained
   a. This variant to the central scenario assumes the following:
      - Oil prices rise with inflation, or further
      - Industrialized countries confront OPEC and lose
      - Non-OPEC oil sources are not developed
      - One trillion dollars are accumulated by OPEC
      - OPEC gains powerful financial and political influence
      - Other cartels are successful, and are financed by OPEC
   b. Should this occur, the consumers will experience:
      - Instability in exchange and financial markets
      - Less growth
      - More inflation
      - Higher raw material costs

2. Variant 2: Inflation Rampant
   a. This second variant assumes that the United States and other countries are unwilling to pay the cost of reducing inflation, and that we have another, but worse, growth-inflation roller coaster than in 1971–1975.

    b. This implies:
-    Temporarily high growth, 1976–1977
-    Mounting, "unexpected" inflation, 1977–1978
-    Disruption of exchange and financial markets, 1978–1979
-    Eventually, lower average growth, 1979–1985

  3. Variant 3: Increased Economic Nationalism

    a. The third variant envisions a world in which countries erect both tariff and nontariff barriers to trade and investment, and governments nationalize the investment of many MNCs—a sharp reversal of the liberal policy followed since the 1950s.

    b. If this should occur, we may expect:
-    Lower real growth
-    Greater fluctuations in growth and in exchange markets
-    Higher long-term interest rates

IV. Selection and Analysis of External Forces

  A. Major External Forces

    The forces were defined as those having a significant direct impact on one or more of the products/businesses under study. Those selected were

-    Economic growth
-    Energy cost
-    Inflation
-    Relative value of sourcing currency
-    Economic fluctuations
-    East-West detente
-    Raw material shortages and costs
-    Housing starts
-    Cost of capital
-    Labor cost
-    Industrialization
-    Trade restrictions
-    Restrictions on MNCs
-    Government participation
-    U.S. taxes on foreign income

V. Effects of External Forces on Business Segments

  A. Determining Effects of External Forces

    1. Each product/business was analyzed according to the effect an *increase* in any of these forces might be expected to produce. These effects were defined as positive, negative, or negligible in terms of:
-    Overall product demand, or
-    GE market position, or
-    Additional and significant cost pressures, or
-    Any other factors affecting profitability

    2. A "Force Field," or matrix, was constructed, showing for each of the selected 21 product lines or businesses the positive, negative, or negligible effect for each of the 15 forces.

    See Exhibit 1.

EXHIBIT 1
Effects of External Forces on Major International Products/Businesses (Illustrative Only)

External Forces

Product/Business	Economic Growth	Energy Cost	Inflation	Economic Fluctuations	East-West Detente	etc.
Division A						
Product 1	↑	↓	○			
Product 2	↑	↓				
Product 3	○	↑				
Division B						
Product 1						
Product 2						
etc.						

↑ Positive effect

↓ Negative effect

○ Neutral or negligible effect

VI. Impact of Scenarios on Business/Country Segments
   A. Approach to Impact Analysis
   Three basic steps were taken in analyzing the projected impacts of the scenarios on GE's international businesses:
   1. The most influential forces were identified for each product segment.
   2. The magnitude of change projected in the scenario for these forces was evaluated in relation to the assumptions underlying GE's strategic plans.
   3. Those forces projected to differ substantially from the GE assumptions were evaluated in terms of their impact on GE's strategy and expected results.
   B. Impact Definitions
   ○ In light of the scenario, the strategy and underlying assumptions for the product/country segment appear to be basically sound.

A comparison of the scenario with the assumptions underlying the product/country segment strategy gives reason to question the soundness of the strategy and/or the expected results.

 In light of the scenario, expected results are in serious jeopardy, and the strategy for the product/country segment seems inappropriate.

See Exhibit 2.

**EXHIBIT 2
Impact of Scenarios
on Product/Country
Segments
(Illustrative Only)**

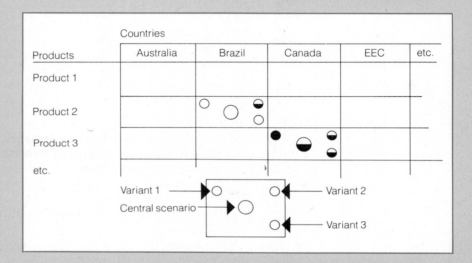

Questions

1. What can be learned from General Electric's study?
2. Do you think this study was an asset or liability for General Electric's international marketers?
3. Should General Electric repeat this study given current world economic conditions? Why?

**CASE 16
Undercroft
Montessori
School**

School Administration The Undercroft Montessori School is located in a residential area of Tulsa, Oklahoma. Business management of the school is currently conducted by a Board of Trustees composed of fifteen members. Board members are elected for three-year terms by the school corporation, which consists of all the parents of children enrolled. The members are assigned to one of six standing committees

Source: Reprinted by permission of C. Richard Roberts, Department of Management and Marketing, University of Tulsa.

which are responsible for planning financial, educational, facilities, volunteers and hospitality, public relations and scholarship activities. There is also an executive committee consisting of the president, vice-president, assistant vice-president, treasurer, and secretary. The executive committee coordinates planning decisions among the six standing committees and executes routine transactions related to the business activities of the school.

The board is most concerned about two primary institutional objectives: educational quality and financial viability. The following objective statement is an excerpt from the *General Information and School Policy* manual provided for parents:

The Undercroft Montessori School is dedicated to the Montessori philosophy and method of education through the senses. A child attending Undercroft will be exposed to a method which should facilitate the growth of inner discipline and later complex reasoning through the free choice and organized use of didactic materials within an atmosphere conducive to these ends.

Specific educational objectives related to the child's developmental progress in the general areas of motor, sensory, and language (symbols) are embodied in a comprehensive directress training program.

The second primary objective is to insure the routine financial integrity of the school. A major goal of the board is to establish and maintain an adequate flow of funds to compensate staff, to provide and maintain educational materials and facilities, and to provide scholarships. The major source of funds has been tuition payments. Although modest surpluses have been recognized as desirable, breaking even in any given year has been considered satisfactory.

Educational quality is partly provided through affiliation with the American Montessori Society and a system for internal staff development and review. The AMS provides a current file of certified directresses, regional workshops, and observers to review and evaluate school programs. Promotion of the school to stimulate enrollment has been largely through word-of-mouth. Some advertising has also been employed in Tulsa newspapers at a modest level. These are usually planned to coincide with the annual fall open house. Allocation of funds for advertising has been a somewhat controversial issue among board members. The argument against advertising has centered around previous enrollment (which has been near full capacity for the past several years). Some members have asked the question, "Why advertise when classes are full?" The question has been unresolved.

The January Meeting of the Executive Committee An executive committee meeting was held at the beginning of the year to review the current financial situation and long-term plans for the program. The school had an opening for an assistant directress and, during the process of hiring, it was learned that salaries had increased substantially due to rising demand for qualified Montessori staff. A treasurer's report indicated that a deficit was incurred during operations last year. Tuition had been increased at the beginning of the previous year from $625 to $675 for the half-day program and from $1,150 to $1,250 in the all-day program. However, a number of routine expenses had increased significantly beyond expectations. Although a tuition increase in next year's budget seems indicated, several members of the board expressed concern about possible adverse effects on current and prospective new parents.

During the meeting it became apparent that committee members' aspirations for future school development varied considerably. The focus of the debate centered largely upon direction of growth. Three feasible alternatives were perceived: 1) vertical expansion to include a program for older children; 2) horizontal expansion in the form of enhancement to the existing program; or 3) deferment of proposed program changes until financial stability was permanently assured. The present ratio of children to directress was considered nearly ideal and any form of expansion or enhancement would require additional facilities, equipment and staff. Another topic of discussion arose among board members about the relative merits of a full-time professional school adminstrator. His/her role in the organization would be similar to that of a principal in a regular public elementary school.

Nancy Martin Nancy Martin has served one full school year as president of the school corporation and chairperson of the board of trustees. Before assuming her present position she was responsible for the activities of the hospitality and arrangement committee. At the beginning of the meeting Martin expressed her opinion that the school has a number of significant strengths such as private facilities, reputation in the community, and an exceptional head directress. However, in Martin's view, there are crucial weaknesses as well. Among these are considerable uncertainty about enrollment from semester to semester. Martin candidly admitted having experienced considerable anxiety about the possibility of being unable to open the school last fall due to slow pre-enrollment the previous spring. The school currently does not have sufficient cash reserves to support essential operations without outside contributions if enrollment should fall below about 65 students. Martin said that she is aware of the general interest of many board members and parents for vertical expansion of the school's program, but frankly she does not agree that this objective is realistic in view of the more or less continuous tight financial situation and other more immediate administrative difficulties. In Martin's words, "How can we even think about expansion when we barely have enough money to meet our day-to-day expenses? Before we consider expanding, which would necessarily mean an additional classroom, staff, and materials, I would rather hire a professional school administrator first and quit trying to run the school by committees."

Don Keele Don Keele has the greatest longevity on the board of any active member, having served approximately five years both as president and treasurer of the corporation. Keele agreed with Martin in terms of the present strengths of the school organization and program, but said he does not agree with her priorities. Keele believes strongly that the curriculum should expand from the traditional pre-school to include classes through the equivalent of a sixth grade. Keele admitted that there would be problems in securing additional qualified staff (two directresses and assistants) and classrooms (two) plus routine accreditation requirements with the state. But the return would be considerable. In Keele's opinion, a comprehensive program would be very worthwhile from the parents' point of view in that it would relieve the planning problem of where to continue a child's education after kindergarten. Keele acknowledged that funding the expansion would be the most difficult task and pointed out that fund-raising efforts in the past had met with modest success at best. These had been directed toward parents of children both currently and previously enrolled, and had been in the form of garage sales, carnivals, and direct solicitations.

Betty Kaylor Betty Kaylor, chairperson of the education committee, was not entirely in agreement with the president or treasurer in terms of problems and goals. Kaylor argued that staffing instability and lack of physical space, in her opinion, are the two most pressing issues confronting the board. Kaylor pointed out that, in the past five years, ten directresses and/or assistants had retired or resigned for various reasons. Continuity had been difficult to maintain and Kaylor acknowledged the fact that the school had been almost totally dependent upon the head directress. She had been invaluable in smoothing the transition periods and minimizing any overall reduction in classroom effectiveness. Kaylor was also concerned with lack of adequate indoor space to develop motor skills during inclement weather. She believed that another classroom was needed that would serve as a gymnasium and also relieve some of the congestion in the art room. (The latter was also housing the musical instruments and instruction.)

Richard Carroll At the close of the meeting, Martin expressed her appreciation to the members of the committee for their contributions, but said that she was disappointed that a decision couldn't be reached on fall tuitions and the growth question. Keele said that the tuition decision must be rendered soon in order to complete next year's budget and report to the parents. In Keele's opinion, the tuition and growth issues were related in some way. Martin agreed with Keele, and admitted that she probably couldn't decide how to vote if motions were made on either issue that evening. She said that the arguments had been appealing, but not entirely persuasive. Clearly, more information was needed before decisions of such crucial importance could be reached. Keele moved that a special committee be appointed to study the economic aspects of a tuition increase and a broader growth issue, and make recommendations to the executive committee at the next meeting in February. Keele's motion carried and a new member, Richard Carroll, was appointed chairman. Carroll had been serving as assistant treasurer since the beginning of the previous fall term. Carroll believed that the committee expectations were high and that considerable weight would be placed upon his personal recommendations. He also realized that the opportunity costs of any decision taken by the board would be very large and, therefore, he must choose his recommended course carefully.

Questions

1. What questions should the board be addressing?
2. If you were a board member how would you respond to these questions?

CAREERS IN MARKETING

Nicholas Di Bari, the senior vice-president of marketing for Comdisco, an Illinois-based computer leasing firm, is an inspiration to all marketing students. Di Bari was the nation's highest-paid marketing executive in a recent year, earning some $674,253! His nearest competitor was Comdisco's sales vice-president, John Slevin, who was paid $600,897.[1] These successful marketers are not cited as illustrative of what every marketing student can expect to earn, but only as an example of how far one can reach in this most vital of all business disciplines.

This appendix focuses on careers in marketing. A variety of aspects are considered. They include the following:

1. The kinds of positions available, offering brief descriptions of the responsibilities attached to each
2. The academic training and other preparation needed for marketing employment
3. Marketing employment trends and opportunities
4. Marketing employment for women and minorities

MARKETING POSITIONS

The text has examined the great extent and diversity of the components of the marketing function. The types of marketing occupations required to fulfill these tasks are just as numerous and diverse. Indeed, with the growth of industrial society, marketing occupations have become more complex and specialized. Students intending to pursue a marketing career may be bewildered at the range of employment opportunities in marketing. How can they find their way through the maze of marketing occupations and concentrate on the ones that best match their interests and talents? A convenient starting point is an understanding of the different positions and the duties required of each.

Marketing personnel are classified as either sales force personnel or marketing staff personnel. They are employed in such service and staff functions as advertising, product planning, marketing research, purchasing, and public relations. The precise nature of their responsibilities and duties varies among organizations and industries. Marketing tasks may be undertaken in-house by company marketing personnel or subcontracted to outside sources. Indeed, a large number of agencies are available to support in-house marketing efforts. Among them are advertising agencies, public relations firms, and marketing research agencies. Marketing employment can be found in a variety of organizations: manufacturing firms, distributive enterprises such as retailers and wholesalers, service suppliers, and research agencies.

All of these organizations have managerial positions. The specific duties of the positions vary with the size of the organization, the nature of its business, and the extent to which marketing operations are departmentalized or centralized. Marketing management jobs generally require the individual to formulate and assist in the formulation of the organization's marketing policies and to plan, organize, coordinate, and control marketing operations and resources. Some of the typical marketing management positions (the particular titles of which may differ) and descriptions of their responsibilities follow.

The Chief Marketing Executive The person who oversees all the marketing activities and is ultimately responsible for the success of the marketing function is the chief marketing executive. All other marketing executives report through channels to this person.

The Product Manager The person in charge of marketing operations for a particular type of product—such as clothing, building materials, or appliances—is the product manager. This person also assumes responsibility for some or all of the functions of the marketing executive, but only as they pertain to particular products.

The Brand Manager The brand manager performs functions similar to those of the product manager, but only with regard to a specific brand.

The Marketing Research Director The marketing research director determines the marketing research needs of the organization and plans and directs various stages of the marketing research projects. These stages include formulation of the problem, research design, data collection, analysis, and interpretation of results. On the basis of marketing research, the director also helps formulate marketing policy and strategies pertinent to any of the marketing variables.

The Sales Manager The person responsible for managing the sales force is the sales manager. Some of the manager's specific duties are establishing sales territories; deploying the sales force; recruiting, hiring, and training salespeople; and setting sales quotas.

The Advertising Manager The person who plans and arranges for the promotion of the company's products or services is the advertising manager. Among that person's duties are formulating advertising policy, selecting advertising agencies, evaluating creative promotional ideas, and setting the advertising budget.

The Public Relations Officer The public relations officer directs all the activities that project and maintain a favorable image for the organization. This person arranges press conferences, exhibitions, news releases, and the like.

Purchasing or Procurement Manager The purchasing manager controls all purchasing and procurement activities involved in acquiring merchandise, equipment, and materials for the organization.

The Retail Buyer The retail buyer is responsible for the purchase of merchandise from various sources—manufacturers, wholesalers, and importers, among others—for resale through retail outlets.

The Wholesale Buyer The person who buys products from manufacturers, importers, and others for resale through wholesale outlets is the wholesale buyer. This buyer's duties are similar to those for the retail buyer but within the specific context of wholesale distribution.

Physical Distribution Manager The trend for firms to consolidate physical distribution activities under a single managerial hierarchy has resulted in a significant increase in the importance of the physical distribution manager. This person is involved with activities like transportation, warehousing, inventory control, order processing, and materials handling.[2]

The discussion so far has spotlighted the top management level of each type of work. Depending on company size, however, there may be several other levels within each of the categories described. For every management position, there are several other marketing occupations that involve the "doing" of specific tasks that are supervised and controlled by the managers; their exact number varies considerably from organization to organization. In the area of marketing research, for instance, employees engage in field work, information collection, editing, coding, tabulation, and other statistical analyses of data.

In advertising, the copywriter assimilates information on the products and customers or likely customers and then writes copy, creating headlines, slogans, and text for the advertisements. The media planner is often a time and space buyer who specializes in determining which advertising media will be most effective. The advertising layout person decides the exact layout of illustrations and copy that comprise the finished advertisement.

The majority of people in marketing are in the area of sales. Sales representatives sell at the manufacturing, wholesale, or retail level. Their job descriptions vary somewhat with the types of products and customers. Sales positions are a common entry point for people desiring promotion to marketing management positions.

PREPARING FOR A MARKETING CAREER

What are the requirements for obtaining a marketing job? What are the typical positions at which marketing careers begin? What are the usual patterns of progression to the top spots in marketing management?

The starting point should be a sound education. Certainly, collegiate coursework does not guarantee entrance into any career field. In fact, the U.S. government now estimates that one out of four college graduates will accept employment in a position previously staffed by someone with only a high school diploma.[3] This bleak employment picture suggests the importance of effective career planning. The more one knows about business, careers, employment trends, and the like, the better off he or she is when entering the labor force. In fact, according to recent findings, business administration leads other disciplines as an undergraduate major cited by first-year college students, being selected by 24 percent of the respondents. The humanities, education, and natural sciences tie in a distant second place, each being named by 8 percent.[4]

Completion of a basic marketing course is a good step toward preparing for the job marketplace. Employers tend to seek those persons with knowledge applicable to the real world. But marketing education is not enough. George Rosenbaum, executive vice-president of Chicago-based Leo J. Shapiro & Associates, has observed: "A marketing graduate must not only learn business skills, but also must know what English, history, and political science majors know. This will enable them to compete with these same people in terms of communication skills, creative energy, and ability once they are in an actual business setting."[5]

TRENDS AND OPPORTUNITIES

Table A.1 reports the Bureau of Labor Statistics employment projections to 1990 for selected marketing occupations. Marketing research, public relations, purchasing, real estate, retail trade, and automobile sales are all expected to provide above-average employment opportunities.

TABLE A.1
Marketing
Employment
Projection to 1990

Marketing Occupation	Recent Employment	Projected Employment Growth to 1990
Automobile Sales Workers	158,000	25.0–49.0%
Buyers	115,000	15.0–24.9%
Insurance Agents and Brokers	540,000	15.0–24.9%
Manufacturers' Sales Workers	400,000	50.0% or more
Marketing Research Workers	24,000	15.0–24.9%
Public Relations Workers	131,000	25.0–49.0%
Purchasing Agents	185,000	25.0–49.0%
Real Estate Agents and Brokers	555,000	25.0–49.0%
Reservation and Passenger Agents (air travel)	56,000	15.0–24.9%
Retail Trade Sales Workers	2,800,000	25.0–49.9%
Securities Sales Workers	110,000	5.0–14.9%
Wholesale Trade Sales Workers	840,000	15.0–24.9%

Source: U.S. Department of Labor, Bureau of Labor Statistics, *Occupational Outlook, 1980–1981 Edition* (Washington, D.C.: U.S. Government Printing Office, Bulletin 2075, March 1980), pp. 5, 115–17, 125–27, 129–31, 190–91, 194–97, 199–202, 204–05, 207–08, 247–48, 477–78.

MARKETING SALARIES

Table A.2 depicts the average annual salary for marketing management positions. The total compensation of these executives is not entirely reflected by this information, since they usually receive bonuses and participate in corporate profit-sharing. The data does, however, illustrate the earnings potential in marketing careers. A more pertinent question, perhaps, from the student's viewpoint is, what are the beginning salary levels in marketing? According to the College Placement Council, the following types of companies generally pay higher salaries to new marketing graduates than do other employers: public utilities; tire and rubber; chemical, drug, and allied products; petroleum and allied products; automotive and mechanical equipment; and aerospace, electronics, and instruments.

THE STATUS OF WOMEN AND MINORITIES IN MARKETING

In recent years, strong nondiscriminatory legislation and supportive social commitment have begun protecting the employment rights of women and minorities.[6] The Supreme Court of the United States, for example, has held that the consequences of an employer's action—not the intent—determine whether discrimination has occurred.[7] As a result, companies have been actively attempting to fill positions with qualified women and minorities. These efforts have produced marked increases in the employment options available to women and minorities.

TABLE A.2
Average Salary for
Marketing Positions

Job Title	Consumer Products Marketers	Industrial Products Marketers	Consumer Service Marketers	Industrial Service Marketers	Retailers
Chairman/president	$108,828	$145,800	$99,801	$95,000	$75,000
Executive vice-president	89,000	. . .	57,500	61,500	. . .
General manager	81,000	49,000	. . .	45,000	. . .
Vice-president/director of marketing	58,240	54,750	43,058	48,200	55,666
Vice-president/director of sales	65,750	41,000	41,000	55,000	. . .
Vice-president/director of advertising	47,363	43,530	43,429	26,300	42,250
Vice-president/director of marketing services	55,476	41,500	. . .	49,000	. . .
Vice-president/director of public relations	44,128	63,312	46,125	. . .	. . .

. . . Not available (returns insufficient to provide representative sample).
Source: *Gallagher Report,* vol. 28, supplement to March 24, 1980. © 1980 The Gallagher Report Inc. All rights reserved. Reprinted by permission.

Advertising, marketing research, and retailing are marketing occupations in which women have traditionally held jobs. Women often enter these fields by way of retail sales, where they outnumber men by a ratio of about two to one (as shown in Table A.3). Women also account for a high percentage of the total employees in real estate sales and service and construction sales. But less than 10 percent of manufacturing and wholesale sales representatives are women.

Women are numerically underrepresented in managerial positions. Except for the retail field, in which 25 percent of the sales managers and department heads are women, very few sales or marketing managers are women. The few women in these positions work primarily for advertising agencies and consumer products companies.

Although there have been gains in women's employment, an earnings gap between men and women employees still exists. The average pay for a woman is still lower than that for a man in most fields.

A similar situation confronts minorities. Nonwhite employment in marketing is often less than 5 percent of any particular marketing job category, as illustrated by Table A.3. Similar to the female marketing employment situation, a higher proportion of nonwhites are employed as retail sales clerks (7.4 percent) or as salespersons in service and construction (7.4 percent) than in any other category of sales workers; and 7.7 percent of sales managers or department heads in retailing are nonwhites. Few nonwhites hold other marketing managerial positions, but, as is the case with women, nonwhite participation in marketing employment is expected to grow.

**TABLE A.3
Marketing
Occupations
Projected to 1985:
Percent Distribution
of Employment by
Sex and Race**

Occupation	Percent		Percent	
	Male	Female	White	Nonwhite
Sales workers	58.6	41.4	94.4	5.6
Insurance agents, brokers, and underwriters	83.1	16.9	94.4	5.6
Real estate agents and brokers	55.1	44.9	97.6	2.4
Sales representatives, manufacturing	94.3	5.7	96.8	3.2
Sales representatives, wholesale	90.1	9.9	96.6	3.4
Sales clerks, retail trade	32.9	67.1	92.6	7.4
Sales workers, retail trade	84.0	16.0	95.8	4.2
Salespersons, service and construction	51.4	48.6	92.6	7.4
Stock and bond sales agents	87.5	12.5	96.3	3.7
Sales managers and department heads, retail	74.8	25.2	92.3	7.7
Buyers and shippers, farm products	96.4	3.6	99.1	0.9
Buyers, wholesale and retail trade	79.7	20.3	97.3	2.7

Source: Conference Board, *Changes in Occupational Characteristics: Planning Ahead for the 1980s* (New York: Conference Board, 1976). Reprinted by permission. Data from U.S. Department of Labor, Bureau of Statistics.

NOTES

1. Thayer C. Taylor, "What Top Sales and Marketing Executives Earn," *Sales & Marketing Management,* September 15, 1980, pp. 40–41.
2. An interesting discussion appears in Bernard J. LaLonde and Jerome J. Cronin, "Distribution Career Patterns," *Distribution Worldwide,* March 1979, pp. 67–72.
3. Michelle Green, "Despite Degree, First Job Could Be a Problem," *Atlanta Journal and Constitution,* April 26, 1981.
4. "The Golden Passport," *Newsweek,* May 14, 1979, p. 110.
5. Rosenbaum is quoted in "Execs Tell Educators: We Want Grads Who Love Business," *Marketing News,* August 22, 1980, p. 10.
6. Excellent discussions appear in Ann Foote Cahn, ed., *Women in the U.S. Labor Force* (New York: Praeger Publishers, 1979).
7. *Griggs* v. *Duke Power Co.,* 401 U.S. 424 (1971).

APPENDIX B

MARKETING ARITHMETIC

Like most business functions, effective marketing decisions depend on accurate data analysis. Marketers must be able to handle the basic mathematics required of their discipline if they are to be truly effective.

Appendix B examines some arithmetic analyses that marketers are often required to perform in their jobs. This section considers such topics as the operating statement, analytical ratios, markups, markdowns, stock turnover rate, and ROI analysis.

THE OPERATING STATEMENT

A major tool in analyzing the performance of any organization is the **operating statement.** This financial statement (sometimes referred to as the *income statement* or the *profit and loss statement*) *presents a summary portrait of the firm's revenues and expenses over a period of time.* The time period may be a month, quarter, year, or any period selected by the firm's management. The second primary type of financial statement, the **balance sheet,** *shows the financial condition of the firm at one period of time by examining its assets, liabilities, and net worth.* While the balance sheet provides a snapshot view of the organization at one point in time, the operating statement is similar to a motion picture, focusing on activities—income and expenditures—over a period of time.

The operating statement is particularly useful for marketing decision makers in focusing on overall sales and the costs incurred in generating these sales. Moreover, it indicates both whether a profit or loss was incurred and the amount of this loss or profit. For nonprofit organizations, the operating statement provides specific indications of the ability of the organization's revenues and contributions to cover the cost involved in its operation. Finally, the operating statement provides the basic data required to calculate numerous ratios used by the marketing decision maker.

Table B.1 shows the operating statement for Ski West, Inc., a relatively small Los Angeles retailer marketing ski equipment, ski clothing, group ski tours, and ski instructions. Since the firm is a retailer, the operating statement contains a subsection called *Net Purchases* under the *Cost of Goods Sold* section. The operating state-

TABLE B.1
Ski West, Inc.
Operating Statement
for Year Ending
December 31, 1983

Revenues			
Gross Sales		$112,000	
Less: Sales returns and allowances	$ 2,000		
Net Sales			$110,000
Cost of Goods Sold			
Beginning Inventory, January 1 (at cost)		$ 26,000	
Gross Purchases during year	$52,000		
Less: Purchase discounts	1,000		
Net Purchases	$51,000		
Plus: Freight in	1,200		
Net Purchases (total delivered cost)		52,200	
Cost of Goods Available for Sale		$ 78,200	
Less: Ending Inventory, December 31 (at cost)		24,000	
Cost of Goods Sold			54,200
Gross Margin			$ 55,800
Expenses			
Selling Expenses			
Sales salaries and commissions	$17,000		
Advertising	4,500		
Sales supplies	2,000		
Delivery expenses	1,000		
Miscellaneous selling expenses	3,500		
Total selling expenses		$ 28,000	
General Expenses			
Office salaries	$12,000		
Office supplies	1,000		
Miscellaneous general expenses	2,300		
Total general expenses		$ 15,300	
Total expenses			43,300
Net Income Before Taxes			$ 12,500
Taxes			4,000
Net Income			$ 8,500

ment for a manufacturer would include a section labeled *Cost of Goods Manufactured* in addition to purchases of raw materials and component parts. Otherwise, the operating statements for manufacturers and marketing intermediaries (retailers and wholesalers) are similar.

Table B.1 may be divided into the following major sections:

Net Sales	$110,000
Minus: Cost of Goods Sold	− 54,200
Equals: Gross Margin	$ 55,800
Minus: Expenses	− 43,300
Equals: Net Income Before Taxes	$ 12,500
Minus: Taxes	− 4,000
Equals: Net Income	$ 8,500

Net sales was calculated by subtracting merchandise returned by customers from total sales revenue. In some cases, overall sales are reduced when the retailer refunds a portion of the sales price (a sales allowance) on an item that is damaged or partially defective. In other instances, returned merchandise must be subtracted from the total sales figure to accurately reflect net sales.

Cost of goods sold by Ski West, Inc., is somewhat more complicated. At the beginning of the operating period, total inventory of $26,000 was on hand. In addition, Ski West managers purchased $52,000 in inventory during 1983 to add to the beginning inventory, but received a purchase discount of $1,000 from one firm for quantity purchases. Delivery charges of $1,200 for the new purchases resulted in total net delivered purchases of $52,200. When this was added to the cost of beginning inventory, the total cost of products available for sale amounted to $78,200.

At the end of the operating period, some $24,000 was still on hand, indicating that the cost of goods sold during 1983 was $54,200 ($78,200 minus $24,000). Total *gross margin* ($110,000 net sales less $54,200 cost of goods sold) amounted to $55,800.

In order to determine net income for 1983, Ski West managers must deduct the various selling and general expenses incurred from the $55,800 gross margin total. *Selling expenses* include salaries and commissions paid to store personnel, advertising, sales supplies, delivery expenses, and such miscellaneous selling expenses as telephone charges, depreciation, insurance, and utilities allocated to sales. *General expenses* include salaries of office personnel; supplies; special services such as consultants, accounting services, or legal fees; insurance; postage; and depreciation. Total expenses for Ski West in 1983 were $43,300.

Net income before taxes amounted to $12,500 ($55,800 gross margin less $43,300 total expense). After subtracting $4,000 for taxes, Ski West earned a total net income of $8,500 for 1983.

ANALYTICAL RATIOS

By analyzing the operating statement shown in Table B.1, Ski West managers can calculate a number of ratios for use in critically evaluating their performance and comparing it with the performance of previous periods and with that of similar firms in the industry. Four important analytical ratios are the gross margin percentage, the net profit percentage, the selling expense ratio, and the operating expense ratio.

Gross Margin Percentage

The **gross margin percentage** is *the ratio of gross margin to net sales.* It indicates the percentage of revenues available for covering expenses and earning a profit after the payment of the cost of products sold during the period. The gross margin percentage for Ski West is calculated as follows:

$$\text{Gross Margin Percentage} = \frac{\text{Gross Margin}}{\text{Net Sales}}$$

$$= \frac{\$\ 55,800}{\$110,000} = 50.7\%$$

Net Profit Percentage

As its name indicates, the **net profit percentage** reflects *the ratio of net profit to net sales.* It is calculated as follows:

$$\text{Net Profit Percentage} = \frac{\text{Net Income}}{\text{Net Sales}}$$

$$= \frac{\$\ 8,500}{\$110,000} = 7.7\%$$

In comparing the 7.7 percent net profit percentage with that of previous periods and with that of other firms, it is important to note that taxes have been deducted from the net income figure. In some instances, other firms may use net income *before taxes* in their calculation. Valid comparisons can be made only if the various ratios use the same formula.

**Selling Expense
Ratio**

The **selling expense ratio** reveals *the relationship between major sales expenses and total net sales.* It is calculated by dividing total selling expenses by net sales.

$$\text{Selling Expense Ratio} = \frac{\text{Total Selling Expenses}}{\text{Net Sales}}$$

$$= \frac{\$\ 28{,}000}{\$110{,}000} = 25.5\%$$

**Operating
Expense Ratio**

The **operating expense ratio** *combines both selling and general expenses and compares them with overall net sales.* The operating expense ratio for Ski West is calculated as follows:

$$\text{Operating Expense Ratio} = \frac{\text{Total Expenses}}{\text{Net Sales}}$$

$$= \frac{\$\ 43{,}300}{\$110{,}000} = 39.4\%$$

MARKUPS

Markups are another important aspect of marketing arithmetic. A **markup** is *the amount added to cost to determine the selling price.* It can be compared to the gross margin that appears in operating statements such as Table B.1.

The markup is typically stated as either a percentage of the selling price or cost. These formulas are as follows:

$$\text{Markup Percentage on Selling Price} = \frac{\text{Amount Added to Cost (the markup)}}{\text{Price}}$$

$$\text{Markup Percentage on Cost} = \frac{\text{Amount Added to Cost (the markup)}}{\text{Cost}}$$

Consider an example from retailing. Suppose an item selling for $1 has an invoice cost of $.60. The total markup is $.40. And the two markup percentages would be calculated as follows:

$$\text{Markup Percentage on Selling Price} = \frac{\$\ .40}{\$1.00} = 40\%$$

$$\text{Markup Percentage on Cost} = \frac{\$\ .40}{\$\ .60} = 66.67\%$$

To determine selling price when only cost and markup percentage on selling price are known, the following formula is utilized:

$$\text{Price} = \frac{\text{Cost in Dollars}}{100\% - \text{Markup Percentage on Selling Price}}$$

In the example cited above, price could be determined as $1.00:

$$\text{Price} = \frac{\$\ .60}{100\% - 40\%} = \frac{\$\ .60}{60\%} = \$1.00$$

Similarly, the markup percentage can be converted from one basis (selling price or cost) to the other by using the following formula:

$$\text{Markup Percentage on Selling Price} = \frac{\text{Markup Percentage on Cost}}{100\% + \text{Markup Percentage on Cost}}$$

$$\text{Markup Percentage on Cost} = \frac{\text{Markup Percentage on Selling Price}}{100\% - \text{Markup Percentage on Selling Price}}$$

Again, using the data from the example above, the following conversions can be made:

$$\text{Markup Percentage on Selling Price} = \frac{66.67\%}{100\% + 66.67\%}$$

$$= \frac{66.67\%}{166.67\%} = 40\%$$

$$\text{Markup Percentage on Cost} = \frac{40\%}{100\% - 40\%}$$

$$= \frac{40\%}{60\%} = 66.67\%$$

MARKDOWNS

Markups are based partially upon a marketer's judgment as to what consumers will pay for a given product or service. But when buyers refuse to pay the price, the marketer must take a **markdown** *by reduc-*

ing the price of the item. The markdown percentage—the figure that is typically advertised—for the "sale" item can be computed as follows:

$$\text{Markdown Percentage} = \frac{\text{Markdown}}{\text{"Sale" (new) Price}}$$

Suppose no one was willing to pay $1.00 for the item discussed above. The marketer decided to cut the price to $.79. Advertisements for the special "sale" item might note that it had been marked down 27 percent.

$$\text{Markdown Percentage} = \frac{\$\ .21}{\$\ .79} = 26.58\%$$

Markdowns are also used for evaluative purposes. For instance, department managers or buyers in a large department store could be evaluated partially on the basis of the average markdown percentage on the product lines for which they are responsible.

STOCK TURNOVER RATE

Markups are often linked to the **stock turnover rate**—*the number of times the average inventory is sold annually.* Average inventory can be calculated by adding beginning and ending inventories and dividing by 2. This figure can be calculated by one of the following formulas. When inventory is recorded at retail:

$$\text{Stock Turnover Rate} = \frac{\text{Sales}}{\text{Average Inventory}}$$

When inventory is recorded at cost:

$$\text{Stock Turnover Rate} = \frac{\text{Cost of Goods Sold}}{\text{Average Inventory}}$$

Store A, with $100,000 in sales and an average inventory of $20,000 (at retail), would have a stock turnover rate of 5. Store B, with $200,000 in sales, a 40 percent markup percentage on selling price, and an average inventory of $30,000 (at cost), would have a stock turnover rate of 4.

Store A

Store B

Stock Turnover Rate $= \dfrac{\$100,000}{\$\ 20,000}$

$= 5$

$200,000 Sales
$\underline{\$\ \ 80,000}$ Markup (40 percent)
$120,000 Cost of Goods Sold

Stock Turnover Rate $= \dfrac{\$120,000}{\$\ 30,000}$

$= 4$

Turn back to Table B.1. The stock turnover rate for Ski West, Inc., can be calculated as follows:

$$\dfrac{\text{Average Inventory}}{\text{at Cost}} = \dfrac{\$26,000\ +\ \$24,000}{2} = \dfrac{\$50,000}{2} = \$25,000$$

$$\text{Stock Turnover Rate} = \dfrac{\$55,800}{\$25,000} = 2.232$$

Stock turnover rates are sometimes used as a measure of sales effectiveness. But they can also be used to set markup percentages. This approach assures at least a minimum consideration of demand within the cost-oriented concept of pricing. High (above average) sales turnover rates, such as for grocery products, means a lower markup percentage, while lower stock turnover rates, such as for jewelry, means a higher markup percentage (see Table B.2).

RETURN ON INVESTMENT: A COMMONLY USED EVALUATIVE TECHNIQUE

Evaluation is one of the most challenging tasks facing the marketing manager. The basic problem is to find *an instrument capable of measuring marketing performance—actual and planned.* Historically, sales volume was first used in this capacity; later, profitability became the accepted yardstick. More recently, **return on investment (ROI)** has gained popularity as an effective evaluative device. It is particularly useful in evaluating proposals for alternative courses of action.

TABLE B.2
Relationship between Markup Percentage and Stock Turnover Rate

Stock Turnover Rate in Relation to the Industry Average	Markup Percentage in Relation to the Industry Average
High	Low
Average	Average
Low	High

ROI is a quantitative tool that seeks to relate the activity or project's profitability to its investment. It is equal to *the rate of profit multiplied by the turnover rate.* ROI can be calculated as follows:

$$ROI = \frac{Net\ Profit}{Sales} \times \frac{Sales}{Investment}$$

In other words:

$$ROI = Rate\ of\ Profit \times Turnover$$

A brief example shows how ROI might be used as an evaluative device. Consider a new product idea for which the firm estimates that a $200,000 investment will be required. The company expects to reach $500,000 in sales, with a net profit of $40,000. The proposed project's ROI is calculated in the following manner:

$$ROI = \frac{\$\ 40,000}{\$500,000} \times \frac{\$500,000}{\$200,000}$$
$$= 0.08 \times 2.5 = 20\%$$

Again refer to Table B.1. If Ski West, Inc., had an investment of $20,000 in leasehold improvements and an average inventory of $25,000, then the firm's ROI could be calculated as follows:

$$ROI = \frac{\$\ 8,500}{\$110,000} \times \frac{\$110,000}{\$\ 45,000}$$
$$= .0773 \times 2.44 = 18.86\%$$

Whether or not this expected performance is acceptable depends on the ROI of alternative uses of corporate funds. It would not be viewed favorably at Gould, Inc., for instance. This major industrial goods manufacturer wants all new products to generate a return on investment of 40 percent before taxes.

ROI is often used in conjunction with other evaluative tools. For example, Gould also specifies that its new products should generate profits of 30 percent before taxes and 15 percent annual sales and profit growth. It also insists on a $20 million sales potential within five years following introduction and a total market potential of about $50 million.[1]

**The Limitations
of ROI**

ROI should be used with caution and in conjunction with other evaluative tools in assessing marketing performance. A variety of factors can affect ROI calculations: book value of assets, depreciation, industry conditions, time periods, and transfer pricing. Consider how these factors could impact an attempt to judge the overall effectiveness of different divisions within a large corporation.

Book Value of Assets If an older division is using assets that have been largely written off, both its current depreciation charges and its investment base will be low. This will make its ROI high in relation to newer divisions.

Depreciation ROI is very sensitive to depreciation policy. If one division is writing off assets at a relatively rapid rate, its annual profits and, hence, ROI will be reduced.

Industry Conditions If one division is operating in an industry where conditions are favorable and rates of return are high, whereas another is in an industry suffering from excessive competition, such environmental differences may cause the favored division to look good and the unfavored division to look bad, quite apart from any differences in their respective managers. External conditions must be taken into account when appraising ROI performance.

Time Periods Many projects have long gestation periods. Expenditures must be made for research and development, plant construction, market development, and the like. Such expenditures will add to the investment base without a commensurate increase in profits for several years. During this period, a division's ROI could be seriously reduced; without proper constraints its division manager could be improperly penalized.

Transfer Pricing In most corporations some divisions sell to other divisions. In General Motors, for example, the Fisher Body Division sells to the Chevrolet Division; in such cases, the price at which goods are transferred between divisions has a fundamental effect on divisional profits. If the transfer price of auto bodies is set relatively high, then Fisher Body will have a relatively high ROI and Chevrolet a relatively low ROI.[2]

**Tying ROI to
Profit Centers**

Dresser Industries, a large diversified manufacturer, illustrates how return on investment can be used to evaluate a marketing program. Dresser's profitability goal is to increase earnings by 10 to 15 percent annually. To stay on target, Dresser has set up 300 separate profit centers worldwide. A **profit center** is *any administrative unit whose contribution to corporate earnings can be measured.* The company's objective is to make the smallest possible operational unit responsible for its own performance. Dresser requires that each profit center report operating results to its Dallas headquarters by the fourth day of business each month. Any profit center reporting an ROI of less than 25 percent is immediately studied, and corrective action is taken if necessary.[3] ROI is a major evaluative tool at Dresser Industries.

EXERCISES

1. If Stapleton Enterprises had a gross margin of $4 million on net sales of $9 million, what is its gross margin percentage?

2. What is the net profit percentage for a store with a net income of $72,000 on net sales of $900,000?

3. Houston Industries had total selling expenses of $85,000. The firm's net sales were $440,000. What was the selling expense ratio for Houston Industries?

4. Omaha Standard ($4 million in net sales) had total expenses of $1.6 million. What was the firm's operating expense ratio?

5. Suppose an item selling for $3 has an invoice cost of $2. Calculate markup percentage on selling price and the markup percentage on cost.

6. A retailer has just received a new kitchen appliance invoiced at $28. The retailer decides to follow industry practice for such items and adds a 40 percent markup percentage on selling price. What retail price should the retailer assign to the appliance?

7. If a product has a markup percentage on cost of 50 percent, what is its markup percentage on selling price?

8. If a product has a markup percentage on selling price of 28 percent, what is its markup percentage on cost?

9. An economic downturn in the local area has had a negative impact on a store's line of $150 dresses. The manager decides to mark these dresses down to $125. What markdown percentage should be featured in advertising of this "sale" item?

10. A store that sells $500,000 annually has an average inventory of $125,000 (at retail). What is its stock turnover rate?

11. A store with an average inventory of $50,000 (at cost) operates on a 40 percent markup percentage on selling price. Annual sales total $750,000. What is its stock turnover rate?

12. A firm's marketing vice president is considering a new product idea for which the firm estimates that a $600,000 investment will be required. The company expects to achieve sales of $3 million, with a net profit of $300,000. What is the proposed project's ROI?

NOTES

1. The Gould example is reported in "Industrial Newsletter," *Sales & Marketing Management,* April 3, 1978, p. 32.

2. This material is excerpted from J. Fred Weston and Eugene F. Brigham, *Essentials of Managerial Finance,* 6th Ed. (Hinsdale, Ill.: The Dryden Press, 1982), pp. 154–55.

3. Grover Herman, "Jack James Directs Dresser's Destiny, Texas-Style," *Nation's Business,* November 1979, pp. 68–72, 75–76.

GLOSSARY

The terms in this section are followed by the chapter number (or numbers) in which they are explained.

ABSOLUTE ADVANTAGE (19) In international marketing, the position of a nation if it is the sole producer of a product or can produce the product more cheaply than anyone else.

ACCESSORY EQUIPMENT (8) Capital items that are usually less expensive and shorter-lived than installations; includes items such as typewriters, hand tools, and adding machines.

ACTIVE EXPORTING (19) In international marketing, the activities of a firm that has made a commitment to seek export business.

ADMINISTERED VERTICAL MARKETING SYSTEM. *See* **Vertical marketing systems (VMS).**

ADOPTION PROCESS (8) A series of stages in the consumer decision process regarding a new product. The stages include awareness, interest, evaluation, trial, and rejection or adoption.

ADVERTISING (14, 15) A nonpersonal sales presentation usually directed to a large number of potential customers.

AGENT (11) A middleman who performs wholesaling functions but does not take title to the goods handled. Also called a *wholesaling middleman*.

AIO STATEMENTS (5) In consumer behavior, a collection of statements contained in a psychographic study to reflect activities, interests, and opinions of the respondents.

AIRLINE DEREGULATION ACT (1980) (13) Federal law that substantially deregulated the airline industry by granting more freedom to the airlines in selecting routes and establishing fares, and by ordering a gradual phase-out of the Civil Aeronautics Board.

APPROACH (16) In personal selling, the initial contact of the salesperson with the customer.

AREA SAMPLING (4) A method of obtaining a random sample, used when population lists are unavailable. Blocks instead of individuals are selected; then, everyone on the designated block is interviewed. In some cases, respondents are randomly selected from each designated block.

ATTITUDE (7) A person's enduring favorable and unfavorable evaluations, emotional feelings, and pro or con tendencies in regard to some object or idea.

AUCTION HOUSE (11) An agent wholesaling middleman who brings buyers and sellers together in one location and allows potential buyers to inspect the merchandise before purchasing it.

AVERAGE COST (17) Total cost divided by the quantity associated with this cost.

AVERAGE FIXED COST (17) Total fixed cost divided by the quantity associated with this cost.

AVERAGE REVENUE (17) Total revenue divided by the quantity associated with that revenue; the average revenue line is actually the demand curve facing the firm.

AVERAGE VARIABLE COST (17) Total variable cost divided by the quantity associated with this cost.

BALANCE OF PAYMENTS (19) A summary, expressed as a surplus or deficit, of a nation's international economic transactions during a year.

BALANCE OF TRADE (19) The result of comparing a nation's imports with its exports. A favorable balance occurs when exports exceed imports. An unfavorable balance occurs when imports exceed exports.

BALANCE SHEET (Appendix) A statement showing the financial condition of the firm at one period in time by listing its assets, liabilities, and net worth.

BASING POINT SYSTEM (18) A geographic pricing system, under which the price quoted to the customer includes the factory price plus freight charges from the basing point nearest the buyer.

BATTLE OF THE BRANDS (9) Competition between national brands and private brands offered by wholesalers and large retailers.

BCG MATRIX (3) A matrix analysis of relative market share and growth potential, developed by the Boston Consulting Group.

BENEFIT SEGMENTATION (5) Dividing a population into homogeneous groups on the basis of benefits the consumer expects to derive from a product or service.

BID (6) In industrial marketing, a written sales proposal from a vendor to a firm that wants to purchase a good or service.

BIRDYBACK (13) In shipping, a term used to describe the intermodal coordination of motor carriers with air carriers.

BOTTOM LINE (20) Business jargon referring to the overall profitability measure of performance.

BRAND (9) A name, term, sign, symbol, design, or some combination used to identify the products of one firm and to differentiate them from competitive offerings.

BRAND INSISTENCE (9) The ultimate stage in brand acceptance, at which consumers will accept no alternatives and will search extensively for the product.

BRAND NAME (9) That part of the brand consisting of words or letters that comprise a name used to identify and distinguish the firm's offerings from those of competitors; the brand name is the part of the brand that can be vocalized.

BRAND PREFERENCE (9) The second stage of brand acceptance at which, based on previous experience with a product, consumers will choose it over its competitors— if the product is available.

BRAND RECOGNITION (9) A consumer's awareness and familiarity with a specific brand.

BREAK-BULK CENTER (13) A central distribution center at which large shipments are divided into smaller ones and delivered to individual customers in the area, in the interest of reducing transportation expenses.

BREAKEVEN ANALYSIS (17) A tool that allows decision makers to compare the profit consequences of alternative prices. The breakeven point (in units) equals total fixed cost divided by the per unit contribution to fixed cost.

BROADENING CONCEPT (1, 20) An idea introduced by Philip Kotler and Sidney J. Levy suggesting that marketing is a generic function to be practiced by all organizations, including nonprofits.

BROKER (11) An agent wholesaling middleman who facilitates marketing operations by bringing together small, geographically dispersed buyers and sellers.

BUYER'S MARKET (1) A market with an abundance of goods and services.

CANNED APPROACH (16) In personal selling, a memorized sales talk used to ensure uniform coverage of the points deemed important by management.

CARTEL (19) A monopolistic organization of foreign firms. One example of a cartel is OPEC (*O*rganization of *P*etroleum *E*xporting *C*ountries).

CASH-AND-CARRY WHOLESALER (11) A merchant wholesaler who provides most services, with the exception of financing and delivery.

CASH DISCOUNT (18) Price reduction made for the prompt payment of a bill.

CASUAL OR ACCIDENTAL EXPORTING (19) A passive level of involvement in international marketing.

CATALOG RETAILER (12) A mass merchandise retail store that mails catalogs to its customers and operates from a showroom displaying single units of each item listed in the catalog; orders are filled from a backroom warehouse.

CELEBRITY TESTIMONIAL (15) A type of promotion in which a particular product, service, idea, or institution is praised or recommended by a famous personality in order to attract consumer attention.

CELLER-KEFAUVER ANTIMERGER ACT (1950) (2) A federal statute that restricted purchases of assets where such purchases would decrease competition. This law amended the Clayton Act, which prohibited only the "acquiring of stock" of another firm if it lessened competition.

CENSUS (4) The collection of data from all possible sources.

CHAIN STORE (12) One of a group of retail stores that are centrally owned and managed and that handle the same lines of products.

CHANNEL CAPTAIN (10) The dominant and controlling member of each channel who assumes the responsibility for obtaining cooperation among the individual channel members.

CIVIL AERONAUTICS BOARD (13) The agency that regulates U.S. air carriers.

CLASS RATE (13) The standard rate established for shipping various commodities.

CLAYTON ACT (1914) (2) Federal antitrust legislation that restricted practices such as price discrimination, exclusive dealing, tying contracts, and interlocking boards of directors.

CLOSED SALES TERRITORIES (10) A practice in which some manufacturers restrict the geographic territories for each of their distributors.

CLOSING (16) The step in the sales process during which the salesperson asks the customer to conclude the purchase.

COGNITIVE DISSONANCE (7) The postpurchase anxiety that occurs when an imbalance exists among a person's cognitions (knowledge, beliefs, and attitudes).

COMBINATION PLAN (16) A method of compensation that combines a base salary with a commission incentive.

COMMISSION MERCHANT (11) An agent wholesaling middleman who takes possession of and negotiates the sales of the goods handled. Commission merchants predominate in the marketing of agricultural products such as grain, produce, and livestock.

COMMISSIONS (16) Payments directly tied to the sales or profits achieved by a salesperson.

COMMODITY RATE (13) A special rate granted by carriers to shippers as a reward for either regular use or large quantity shipments.

COMMON CARRIER (13) A regulated carrier that offers transportation services to all shippers.

COMMON MARKET (19) In international marketing, a format for multinational economic integration involving a customs union and continuing efforts to standardize trade regulations of all governments.

COMMUNICATION (7, 14) The transmission of a message from a sender to a receiver.

COMMUNITY SHOPPING CENTER (12) A type of planned shopping center containing fifteen to fifty retail stores and serving from 20,000 to 100,000 persons in a trade area extending a few miles.

COMPARATIVE ADVANTAGE (19) In international marketing, the position of a nation if it can produce a product more efficiently than it can produce alternative products.

COMPARATIVE ADVERTISING (15) A type of persuasive product advertising that makes direct promotional comparisons with leading competitive brands.

COMPETITIVE BIDDING (18) A process by which a buyer requests potential suppliers to make price quotations on a proposed purchase or contract.

COMPETITIVE ENVIRONMENT (2) The process of interaction that occurs in the marketplace.

COMPUTER SIMULATION (20) A recent marketing innovation in which computer programs are developed to explain the interrelations of various aspects of the economic and social system.

CONCENTRATED MARKETING (1, 3) The practice of firms that select a small segment of the total market and devote all their marketing resources to satisfying this single segment.

CONCENTRIC DIVERSIFICATION (3) A conglomerate's act of adding only those new businesses that are easily integrated into the company's existing technological and/or marketing framework.

CONCEPT TESTING (9) In new-product development, the evaluation of a product in the idea stage (prior to its actual development).

CONGLOMERATE (3) A firm with multiple unrelated businesses.

CONSUMER BEHAVIOR (7) The acts of individuals in obtaining and using economic goods and services, including the decision processes that precede and determine these acts.

CONSUMER CREDIT PROTECTION ACT (1968) (2) Federal statute that requires disclosure of the annual interest rates on loans and credit purchases in order to make it easier for consumers to compare sources of credit. Also known as the Truth-in-Lending Act.

CONSUMER GOODS (8) Products purchased by the ultimate consumer for personal use and not intended for resale or further use in the production of other goods.

CONSUMER GOODS PRICING ACT (1975) (2) Legislation that halted all interstate usage of resale price maintenance agreements.

CONSUMER INNOVATOR (8) The first purchaser of new products and services.

CONSUMERISM (20) The demand that marketers give greater attention to consumer wants and desires in making their decisions.

CONSUMER PRODUCT SAFETY ACT (1972) (2) Legislation that established the Consumer Product Safety Commission (CPSC) and granted it authority to specify safety standards for most consumer products, except those already regulated by other agencies.

CONSUMER RIGHTS (20) A statement of rights, delineated by John F. Kennedy, that have formed the conceptual framework for much of the consumer legislation passed since 1962. They include the right to be safe, to be informed, to choose, and to be heard.

CONTAINERIZATION (13) The combination of several unitized loads of products into a single load in order to facilitate intertransport changes in transportation modes.

CONTEST (15) A sales promotion technique that seeks to attract additional customers by offering substantial cash or merchandise prizes.

CONTRACT CARRIER (13) A carrier that establishes specific contracts with a few customers and does not offer its services to the general public.

CONTRACTUAL VERTICAL MARKETING SYSTEM. *See* **Vertical marketing system (VMS).**

CONTROLLED EXPERIMENT (4) A direct test for results and a method of collecting information carried out under controlled conditions.

CONVENIENCE GOODS (8) Products that consumers want to purchase frequently, immediately, and with a minimum of effort. Examples include milk and bread.

CONVENIENCE RETAILER (12) A retailer who focuses on convenient locations, long store hours, rapid checkout service, and adequate parking facilities.

COOPERATIVE ADVERTISING (15) The sharing of advertising costs between the retailer and the manufacturer or vendor.

CORPORATE VERTICAL MARKETING SYSTEM. *See* **Vertical marketing system (VMS).**

CORRECTIVE ADVERTISING (2) A policy of the Federal Trade Commission under which companies found to have used deceptive advertising are required to correct their earlier claims with new promotional messages.

COST-PLUS PRICING (17) An approach to price determination that takes some base cost figure per unit and adds a markup to cover unassigned costs and provide a profit. The two most common cost-plus procedures are full cost pricing and incremental cost pricing.

COST TRADE-OFFS (13) A concept in the total systems approach to physical distribution whereby some functional areas of the firm will experience cost increases while others will have cost reductions, but the result will be that total physical distribution costs will be minimized.

COUNTERTRADE (19) A term used to describe bartering in international trade.

COUPON (15) A sales promotion technique that offers a discount on the next purchase of a product.

CREATIVE SELLING (16) A set of specific techniques used to elicit a sale that requires considerable analytical decision making on the consumer's part.

CREEPING INFLATION (2) Modest increases in the general price level.

CUE (7) Any object existing in the environment that causes an individual to make a specific response to a drive.

CULTURE (7) The complex of values, ideas, attitudes, and other meaningful symbols created by people to shape human behavior and the artifacts of that behavior as they are transmitted from one generation to the next.

CUSTOMARY PRICE (17) A price that tends to be set by custom or tradition in the marketplace.

CUSTOMER SERVICE STANDARDS (13) The quality of service that a firm's customers will receive.

CUSTOMS UNION (19) In international marketing, a format for multinational economic integration that sets up a free trade area for member nations and a uniform tariff for nonmember nations.

DECODING (14) The receiver's interpretation of the sender's message in a communication system.

DELPHI TECHNIQUE (20) A procedure in which a panel of experts sends its prediction on a particular issue to a moderator who disseminates the information to all participants. The procedure is repeated until a consensus emerges.

DEMAND CURVE (17) A schedule relating the quantity demanded to a specific price; the average revenue line.

DEMARKETING (2) The process of decreasing consumer demand for a product to a level that can reasonably be supplied by the firm.

DEMOGRAPHIC SEGMENTATION (5) Dividing a population into homogeneous groups on the basis of characteristics such as age, sex, and income level.

DEMOGRAPHICS (5, 15) Characteristics such as age, sex, and income level of potential buyers.

DEMONSTRATION (16) The step in the sales process when the salesperson involves the potential customer in the presentation by allowing him or her to use, test, or experiment with the product.

DEPARTMENT STORE (12) A large retail store organized into departments for the purposes of promotion, service, and control. A department store typically stocks a wide variety of shopping and specialty goods that may include men's and women's clothing and accessories, linens and dry goods, appliances, and home furnishings.

DERIVED DEMAND (6) In the industrial market, the demand for an industrial product that is linked to demand for a consumer good.

DETAILER (10) Missionary salesperson of the health care industry.

DEVALUATION (19) An official reduction in the value of a nation's currency in relation to some other currency or to gold.

DIFFERENTIATED MARKETING (3) The practice of firms that produce numerous products with different marketing mixes to satisfy smaller market segments.

DIFFUSION PROCESS (8) The acceptance of new products and services by the members of a community or social system.

DIRECT-SALES RESULTS TEST (14) A test that measures the effectiveness of promotion. It ascertains for each dollar of promotional outlay the corresponding increase in revenue.

DISCOUNT HOUSE (12) A store that charges lower-than-usual prices and does not offer such traditional retail services as credit, sales assistance by clerks, and delivery.

DISTRIBUTION STRATEGY (1) An element of marketing decision making that deals with the physical distribution of goods and the selection of marketing channels.

DISTRIBUTION WAREHOUSE (13) A place to assemble and then redistribute products. The objective of the distribution warehouse is to facilitate rapid movement of products to the purchasers rather than to serve as a storage facility.

DISTRIBUTOR. *See* **Wholesaler.**

DRIVE (7) Any strong stimulus that impels action.

DROP SHIPPER (11) A merchant wholesaler who receives orders from customers and forwards them to producers, who ship directly to the customers; although drop shippers take title to the goods, they do not carry inventories.

DUMPING (19) In international marketing, selling a product at a lower price in a foreign market than it sells for in the producer's domestic market.

ECOLOGY (20) The relationship between humanity and the environment.

ECONOMIC ENVIRONMENT (2) Complex and dynamic business fluctuations that tend to follow a four-stage pattern: (1) recession, (2) depression, (3) recovery, and (4) prosperity.

EMBARGO (19) A complete ban on importing certain products, especially from certain countries.

ENCODING (14) The translation of a message into understandable terms and its transmittal through a communication medium.

ENERGY CRISIS (2) The general realization that energy resources are not limitless.

ENGEL'S LAWS (5) Statements published in an early study of spending behavior by German statistician Ernst Engel. His three generalizations about spending predict that as family income increases: (1) a smaller percentage of expenditures go for food; (2) the percentage spent on housing and household operations and clothing remains constant; and (3) the percentage spent on other items increases.

ENVIRONMENTAL POLLUTION (20) Contamination of natural resources such as water or air.

ENVIRONMENTAL PROTECTION ACT (1970). *See* **National Environmental Policy Act.**

EOQ (ECONOMIC ORDER QUANTITY) MODEL (13) A technique devised to determine the optimal order quantity of each product; the optimal point is determined by balancing the costs of holding inventory and the costs involved in placing orders.

EQUAL CREDIT OPPORTUNITY ACT (1975–1977) (2) Legislation that banned discrimination in lending practices on the basis of sex, marital status, race, national origin, religion, age, or receipt of payments from public-assistance programs.

EVALUATIVE CRITERIA (7) Those features a consumer considers in choosing among alternatives.

EVOKED SET (7) The number of brands that a consumer actually considers in making a purchase decision.

EXCHANGE CONTROL (19) A method of regulating foreign trade in which firms gaining foreign exchange by exporting must sell this exchange to the central bank or a control agency, and importers must buy foreign exchange from the same organization.

EXCHANGE RATE (19) The rate at which a nation's currency can be exchanged for other currencies or gold.

EXCLUSIVE DEALING AGREEMENT (10) An agreement that prohibits a middleman from handling competing products.

EXCLUSIVE DISTRIBUTION (10) An extreme form of selective distribution wherein the manufacturer grants exclusive rights to a wholesaler or retailer to sell in a geographic region.

EXPECTED NET PROFIT (17, 18) A concept employed in competitive bidding strategy. Expected net profit equals the probability of the buyer accepting the bid times the bid price minus related costs.

EXPERIENCE CURVE (3) The idea that higher market share reduces costs because of factors like learning advantages, increased specialization, higher investment, and economies of scale.

EXPLORATORY RESEARCH (4) Research designed to describe a problem area and give insight into its causes and effects through discussion with informed sources both within and outside the firm and through examination of secondary sources of information.

EXPORTING (19) The sale of goods and services abroad.

EXTERNAL DATA (4) In marketing research, data that originates from outside a firm.

FABRICATED PARTS AND MATERIALS (8) The finished industrial goods that actually become part of the final product.

FACILITATING AGENCIES (10) Organizations, such as marketing research firms, transportation and storage companies, advertising agencies, insurance companies, and financial institutions, that provide specialized assistance to the regular channel members in moving products from producer to consumer.

FAIR CREDIT REPORTING ACT (1970) (2) Legislation that gave individuals access to credit reports prepared about them and that permitted them to change incorrect information.

FAIR DEBT COLLECTION PRACTICES ACT (1978) (2) Legislation that outlawed harassing, deceptive, or unfair collection practices by debt-collecting agencies. Firms that use in-house debt collectors (such as banks, retailers, or attorneys) are exempt from this act.

FAIR PACKAGING AND LABELING ACT (1967) (2) Legislation requiring the disclosure of product identity, name and address of manufacturer or distributor, and information about the quality of the contents.

FAIR TRADE LAWS (2) State laws, passed during the depression of the 1930s, that allowed a manufacturer to stipulate a minimum retail price for a product and to require retailers to sign contracts stating that they would abide by such prices. The Consumer Goods Pricing Act (1975) ended all interstate use of these agreements.

FAMILY BRAND (9) One brand name used for several products made by the same firm, such as Johnson & Johnson or General Electric.

FAMILY LIFE CYCLE (5) The process of family formation and dissolution. The stages of the cycle (with subcategories) include young single, young married without children, other young, middle-aged, older, and other.

FEDERAL MARITIME COMMISSION (13) The agency that regulates U.S. ocean carriers.

FEDERAL TRADE COMMISSION ACT (1914) (2) Legislation that prohibited "unfair methods of competition" and established the Federal Trade Commission (FTC) as an administrative agency to oversee the various laws dealing with business.

FEEDBACK (14) Information about a receiver's response to a message that is returned to the sender.

FISHYBACK (13) In physical distribution, a term used to describe the intermodal coordination of motor carriers with water carriers. The fishyback combination allows the shipper to obtain the benefits of both transportation modes.

FIXED COSTS (17) Costs that do not vary with differences in output, such as depreciation and insurance.

FIXED SUM PER UNIT (14) A budget allocation method, under which a predetermined promotional amount is allocated either on a historical or forecasted basis.

FLAMMABLE FABRICS ACT (1953) (2) Legislation outlawing the interstate sale of flammable fabrics.

FLOATING EXCHANGE RATE (19) An exchange rate that is allowed to fluctuate to adjust to market conditions.

F.O.B. PLANT (18) "Free on board"; a price quotation that does not include shipping charges. The buyer pays all freight charges.

FOCUS GROUP INTERVIEW (4) Marketing research technique that gathers small numbers of individuals in one location to discuss a subject of interest.

FOLLOW-UP (16) The step in the sales process that concerns post-sales activities. Follow-up provides information on sales successes and failures and often determines whether a person will become a repeat customer.

FOOD AND DRUG ADMINISTRATION (FDA) (2) The agency authorized to regulate such matters as product development, branding, and advertising for drugs and food products.

FOOD, DRUG, AND COSMETIC ACT (1938) (2) Federal statute that prohibited adulteration and misbranding of food, drugs, and cosmetics in interstate commerce. This legislation strengthened the Pure Food and Drug Act (1906).

FOREIGN CORRUPT PRACTICES ACT (1977) (19) Legislation making it illegal to bribe a foreign official in an attempt to solicit new or repeat sales abroad.

FOREIGN FREIGHT FORWARDERS (13) Transportation middlemen who specialize in physical distribution outside the United States.

FOREIGN LICENSING (19) In international marketing, an agreement between a firm and a foreign company, whereby the foreign company produces and distributes the firm's goods in the foreign country.

FORM UTILITY (1) A kind of utility that is created when raw materials are converted into finished products.

FRANCHISE (10) A contractual agreement in which a dealer agrees to meet the operating requirements of a manufacturer.

FREE TRADE AREA (19) In international marketing, economic integration between participating nations, without any tariff or trade restrictions.

FREIGHT ABSORPTION (18) A pricing system under which the seller permits the buyer to subtract transportation charges from the bill. Also known as *FOB plant—freight allowed.*

FREIGHT FORWARDER (13) A wholesaling middleman who consolidates shipments of several shippers in order to enable them to achieve the cost savings of truckload or carload shipments.

FRIENDSHIP, COMMERCE, AND NAVIGATION (FCN) TREATIES (19) Treaties between the United States and many other countries that deal with various aspects of commercial relations, such as the right to conduct business in the treaty partner's domestic market.

FTC ACT. *See* **Federal Trade Commission Act.**

FULL COST PRICING (17) A cost-plus pricing procedure that uses all relevant variable and fixed costs in setting a product's price.

FULL-FUNCTION MERCHANT WHOLESALER (11) A wholesaling middleman who provides a complete assortment of services for retail customers, including storage, regular contacts through a sales force, delivery, credit, return privileges, and market information.

FUR PRODUCT LABELING ACT (1951) (2) Legislation requiring labels on fur products, identifying the name of the animal from which the fur came.

GENERAL AGREEMENT ON TARIFFS AND TRADE (GATT) (19) An international trade accord that has sponsored various tariff negotiations that have reduced the overall level of tariffs throughout the world.

GENERAL MERCHANDISE RETAILER (12) A retail store that carries a wide variety of product lines, all of which are stocked in some depth.

GENERAL STORE (12) A general merchandise store stocked to meet the needs of a small community or rural area.

GENERIC NAME (9) A brand name that has become a generally descriptive term for a product (for example, nylon, zipper, and aspirin). When this occurs, the original owner loses exclusive claim to the brand name.

GENERIC PRODUCTS (9) Food and household staples characterized by plain descriptive labels, little or no advertising, and no brand name. Such products compete with branded items on the basis of price.

GEOGRAPHIC SEGMENTATION (6) Dividing a population into homogeneous groups on the basis of location.

GOODS-SERVICES CONTINUUM (8) A method for visualizing the differences and similarities of goods and services.

GROSS MARGIN PERCENTAGE (Appendix) Analytical ratio used by businesses that show the ratio of gross margin to net sales.

GROSS NATIONAL PRODUCT (3) The market value of all final products produced in a country in a given year.

HANDLING OBJECTIONS (16) The step in the sales process during which the salesperson responds to the customer's questions and concerns.

HIGHWAY BEAUTIFICATION ACT (1965) (15) Legislation regulating the use of outdoor advertising near interstate highways.

HOUSE-TO-HOUSE RETAILING (12) Direct contact between the seller and the customer at the customer's home.

HYPERMARKET (12) A giant mass merchandising retail outlet that operates on a low-price, self-service basis and carries lines of soft goods and groceries.

HYPOTHESIS (4) A tentative explanation about some specific event.

ICEBERG PRINCIPLE (4) In marketing research, a phenomenon that suggests that important information is often hidden by summary data.

IMPORTING (19) The purchase of foreign goods and raw materials.

IMPORT QUOTA (19) A restriction on the amount of products in certain categories that can enter a country.

IMPULSE GOODS (8) Products for which the consumer spends little time in conscious deliberation in making a purchase decision. These products, such as candy and cigarettes, are often displayed near store cash registers to induce spur-of-the-moment purchases.

INCOME STATEMENT (Appendix) A statement that presents a summary of the firm's revenues and expenses over a period of time. The time period may be a month, quarter, year, or any period selected by the firm's management.

INCREMENTAL COST PRICING (17) A cost-plus pricing procedure that attempts to use only those costs directly attributable to a specific output in setting a product's price.

INDIVIDUAL BRAND (9) Products known by their own brand name, such as Tide or Crest, rather than by the name of the company producing it.

INDUSTRIAL DISTRIBUTOR (8) A wholesaling middleman who operates in the industrial goods market and typically handles small accessory equipment and operating supplies.

INDUSTRIAL GOODS (8) Products purchased for use either directly or indirectly in the production of goods for resale.

INDUSTRIAL MARKET (6) Consists of those individuals and organizations who acquire goods and services to be used, directly or indirectly, in the production of other goods and services or to be resold to governments, retailers and wholesalers, and producers.

INFLATION (2) A rising price level that results in reduced purchasing power for the consumer.

INFORMATIVE INSTITUTIONAL ADVERTISING (15) A type of promotion concerned with increasing public knowledge of a concept, political viewpoint, industry, or company.

INFORMATIVE PRODUCT ADVERTISING (15) A type of promotion that seeks to develop initial demand for a product; used in the introduction phase of the product life cycle.

INPUT-OUTPUT MODELS (3) Models used in economic forecasting that depict the interactions of various industries in the production of goods.

INSTALLATIONS (8) A firm's major capital assets such as factories and heavy machinery; they are expensive and relatively long-lived, and their purchase represents a major decision for the company.

INSTITUTIONAL ADVERTISING (15) A type of advertising that is concerned with promoting a concept, idea, philosophy, or the goodwill of an industry. It is often closely related to the public relations function of an enterprise.

INTENSIVE DISTRIBUTION (10) A practice by manufacturers of convenience goods who attempt to provide saturation coverage of their potential markets.

INTERLINING (13) Using more than one rail carrier when long distances between the shipment's origin and destination are involved.

INTERSTATE COMMERCE ACT (1887) (13) Legislation that established the first regulatory body in the United States, the Interstate Commerce Commission (ICC), and gave it the power to regulate interstate transportation systems such as railroads, pipelines, motor carriers, and inland water carriers.

JOBBER *See* **Wholesaler.**

JOB-ORDER PRODUCTION (10) A production system in which products are manufactured to fill customers' orders.

JOINT DEMAND (6) In the industrial market, the demand for an industrial good as related to the demand for another industrial good that is necessary for the use of the first item.

JOINT VENTURE (19) A type of international enterprise in which a company shares the risks, costs, and management of the foreign operation with a partner who is usually a national of the host nation.

JUST AND REASONABLE RATES (13) A term used in the regulation of transportation modes, referring to the fact that rates must be *just* to shippers and provide a *reasonable* rate of return to the transporter.

JUST PRICE (13) A concept held by early philosophers that there was one fair price for each good or service.

KEFAUVER-HARRIS DRUG AMENDMENTS (1962) (2) Amendments to the Pure Food and Drug Act that mandated generic labeling of drugs and a summary of adverse side effects.

LABEL (9) The descriptive part of the package that usually contains the brand name or symbol, the name and address of the manufacturer or distributor, the product composition and size, and the recommended uses for the product.

LANHAM ACT (1946) (9) Federal legislation requiring that registered trademarks not contain words in general use, such as *automobiles* or *suntan lotion*. Generic words are descriptive of a particular type of product and thus cannot be granted exclusively to any company.

LEARNING (7) Any change in behavior as a result of experience.

LEGAL ENVIRONMENT (2) The numerous and often vague laws passed by a multitude of authorities that regulate and affect marketing activities.

LIFE-CYCLE COSTING (6) In the industrial market, the cost of using a product over its lifetime.

LIFE-STYLE (5) The way people decide to live their lives. Life-style includes the family, job, social activities, and consumer decisions.

LIMITED-FUNCTION MERCHANT WHOLESALER (11) A wholesaling middleman who reduces the number of services provided to retail customers and also reduces the cost of servicing these customers. The three types include cash-and-carry wholesalers, truck wholesalers, and drop shippers.

LIMITED-LINE STORE (12) A retail store that competes with larger stores by offering a complete selection of a few related lines of merchandise, such as clothing, hardware, or sporting goods.

LIST PRICE (18) The rate normally quoted to potential buyers. It is the basis on which most price structures are built.

LOSS LEADER (18) A retail good priced at less than cost so as to attract customers who possibly will then buy other regularly priced merchandise.

MAGNUSON-MOSS WARRANTY ACT (1975) (8) Legislation giving the Federal Trade Commission power to develop regulations affecting warranty practices for any product costing more than $15 that is covered by a written warranty. It is designed to assist consumers in comparison shopping.

MAIL-ORDER RETAILING MERCHANDISER (12) A retail outlet that makes use of catalogs and allows customers to order merchandise by mail, by telephone, or by visiting the mail-order desk of a retail store. Goods are then shipped to the customer's home or the local retail store.

MAIL-ORDER WHOLESALER (11) Limited-function merchant wholesalers who utilize catalogs instead of a sales force to contact their customers in an attempt to reduce operating expenses.

MAKE-BULK CENTER (13) A central distribution center where small shipments of products shipped over a short distance are consolidated into economical carload or truckload quantities, then shipped over longer distances to a customer or storage warehouse.

MANUFACTURERS' AGENTS (11) Independent salespeople who work for a number of manufacturers of related but noncompeting products and who receive a commission based on a specified percentage of sales. Also called *manufacturers' representatives.*

MARGINAL ANALYSIS (14) The balancing of marginal revenues and marginal costs.

MARGINAL COST (17) The change in total cost that results from producing an additional unit of output.

MARGINAL REVENUE (17) The change in total revenue that results from selling an additional unit of output.

MARKET (5) Customers who possess purchasing power and both the willingness and the authority to buy.

MARKETING (1) The development and efficient distribution of goods and services for chosen consumer segments.

MARKETING AUDIT (3) A thorough, objective evaluation of an organization's marketing philosophy, goals, policies, tactics, practices, and results.

MARKETING CHANNEL (10) The paths that goods or services, and title to them, follow from producer to final consumer.

MARKETING COMMUNICATION (14) The messages that deal with buyer-seller relationships.

MARKETING CONCEPT (1) A consumer-oriented managerial philosophy based on the premise that planning begins with an analysis of the consumer and that company objectives involve satisfying consumer wants and achieving long-run profits.

MARKETING COST ANALYSIS (4) The evaluation of such items as selling costs, billing, warehousing, advertising, and delivery expenses in order to determine the profitability of particular customers, territories, or product lines.

MARKETING ETHICS (20) The moral premises upon which marketing decisions are made.

MARKETING INFORMATION SYSTEM (MIS) (4) A designed set of procedures and methods for generating an orderly flow of pertinent information for use in making decisions, providing management with the current and future states of the market, and indicating market response to company and competitor actions.

MARKETING MIX (1) The blending of the four strategy elements of marketing decision making (product planning, distribution, promotion, and price) to satisfy chosen consumer segments.

MARKETING MYOPIA (1) Theodore Levitt's thesis that the management of many firms is product-oriented and not consumer-oriented.

MARKETING PLANNING (3) The implementation of planning activity as it relates to the achievement of marketing objectives.

MARKETING RESEARCH (4) The systematic gathering, recording, and analyzing of data about problems relating to the marketing of goods and services.

MARKETING STRATEGY (3) The general term used to describe the overall company program for selecting a particular market segment and then satisfying the consumers in that segment through the careful use of the elements of the marketing mix.

MARKET PRICE (18) The amount the consumer or middleman pays. It may or may not be the same as the list price, since discounts and allowances can reduce the list price.

MARKET SEGMENTATION (5) The production of separate products and design of different marketing mixes to satisfy smaller homogenous segments of the total market.

MARKET SHARE (3) The percentage of a market controlled by a firm or its product.

MARKET SHARE OBJECTIVE (17) The goal set for the control of a portion of the market for the firm's product.

MARKET TARGET (7) A specific segment of the overall potential market that has been analyzed and selected by the firm. The firm's marketing mix will be directed toward satisfying this chosen consumer segment.

MARKET TARGET DECISION ANALYSIS (7) The evaluation of potential market segments by dividing the overall market into homogeneous groups. Cross-classifications may be based on variables such as type of market, geographic location, use frequency, or demographic characteristics.

MARKUP (Appendix) The amount that is added to cost to determine the selling price.

MASLOW'S HIERARCHY OF NEEDS (7) A classification, developed by psychologist A. H. Maslow, that assigns varying degrees of importance to human needs. The theory states that lower needs must be at least partially satisfied before an individual can satisfy higher needs. The hierarchy proceeds from physiological to safety to social to esteem to self-actualization needs.

MASS MERCHANDISER (12) A major retailer, such as a discount house, hypermarket, or catalog retailer, who competes by stocking a wider line of products than most department stores, although usually not in as great depth. They emphasize low prices, high turnover, and reduced services.

MATERIALS HANDLING (13) All the activities involved in moving products within a manufacturer's plants, warehouses, and transportation company terminals.

MEGALOPOLIS (5) An extensive contiguous urban-suburban strip of population. The largest megalopolis extends from Boston to Washington, D.C.

MERCHANDISE MART (11) A permanent exhibition facility where manufacturers rent showcases for their product offerings and display them for visiting retail and wholesale buyers.

MERCHANT WHOLESALER (11) A wholesaling middleman who takes title to the goods handled.

MESSAGE (14) Information transmitted by a communication system.

METRIC SYSTEM (9) The standard of weights and measures based on the decimal system of ten and its multiples and used throughout most of the world.

MIDDLEMAN (10) A business firm operating between the producer and the consumer or industrial purchaser. The term includes both wholesalers and retailers.

MILLER-TYDINGS RESALE PRICE MAINTENANCE ACT (1937) (2) Legislation exempting interstate fair trade contracts from compliance with antitrust requirements.

MISSIONARY SALES (16) An indirect type of selling; people who handle this task sell the goodwill of a firm, often by providing the customer with product use assistance.

MISSIONARY SALESPERSON (10) Manufacturer's representative who helps wholesalers and retailers become familiar with the firm's products.

MONOPOLISTIC COMPETITION (17) A market structure with large numbers of buyers and sellers that involves a heterogeneous product and product differentiation and in which the marketer has some degree of control over prices. This situation is characteristic of most retailing.

MONOPOLY (17) A market situation in which there is only one seller of a product and no close substitutes for it. Antitrust legislation has effectively eliminated all but temporary monopolies, such as those provided by patent protection, and regulated monopolies, such as the public service companies (telephone, electric, and gas utilities).

MOTIVE (7) An inner state that directs people toward the goal of satisfying a felt need.

MOTOR CARRIER ACT OF 1980 (13) Federal legislation significantly deregulating the trucking industry.

MRO ITEMS (8) Supplies for an industrial firm, so called because they can be categorized as *m*aintenance items, *r*epair items, or *o*perating supplies.

MULTINATIONAL CORPORATION (19) A firm that operates in several countries and literally views the world as its market.

NATIONAL BRANDS (9) Brands offered by manufacturers; sometimes called manufacturer's brands.

NATIONAL ENVIRONMENTAL POLICY ACT (1970) (2) Federal legislation that established the Environmental Protection Agency and gave it the authority to deal with pollution issues.

NATIONAL ROLLOUT (20) Nationwide launch of a product.

NEED (7) The lack of something useful; discrepancy between desired state and actual state.

NEGOTIATED CONTRACT (18) A situation in which the terms of a contract are set through talks between the buyer and the seller rather than through competitive bidding on a project. Industry and government purchasers use negotiated contracts when there is only one available supplier or when extensive research and development work is involved.

NEIGHBORHOOD SHOPPING CENTER (12) A planned shopping center typically containing five to fifteen stores whose product mix is usually confined to convenience goods and some shopping goods.

NET PROFIT PERCENTAGE (Appendix) Analytical ratio that measures the ratio of net profit to net sales.

NEW-PRODUCT COMMITTEE (9) A common organizational arrangement for new-product development. The committee is usually composed of representatives from top management in such areas as marketing, finance, manufacturing, engineering, research, and accounting.

NEW-PRODUCT DEPARTMENT (9) A separate, formally organized division within the firm that is involved with new-product development on a permanent, full-time basis.

NOISE (14) Interruption that interferes with the transmission of a message in a communication system.

NONPROFIT ORGANIZATION (20) A firm whose primary objective is something other than the return of a profit to its owners.

OBSERVATIONAL STUDY (4) A study conducted by viewing (either by actual visual observation or through mechanical means such as hidden cameras) the overt actions of the respondent.

ODD PRICING (18) A type of psychological pricing that uses prices with odd endings, such as $16.95, $17.99, or

$18.98, under the assumption that these prices appear lower and therefore more appealing. Originally, odd pricing was initiated to force sales clerks to make change, thus serving as a cash-control device within the firm.

OLIGOPOLY (17) A market situation in which there are relatively few sellers; because of high start-up costs, there are significant entry barriers to new competitors. Oligopolies occur frequently in the steel, petroleum refining, and automobile industries.

OPERATING EXPENSE RATIO (Appendix) Analytical ratio that combines both selling and general expenses and compares them with overall net sales.

OPINION LEADER (7) The individual in any group who is a trend-setter; the opinions of such an individual are respected and often sought. Opinion leaders serve as information sources about new products.

ORDER PROCESSING (13, 16) A basic sales task at the retail and wholesale levels where needs are readily identified by the salesperson and acknowledged by the customer.

OVERSEAS MARKETING (19) In international marketing, a firm's maintaining of a separate selling operation in a foreign country.

OWNERSHIP UTILITY (10) A kind of utility created by marketers when title to products is transferred to the customer at the time of purchase.

PALLET (13) A platform, usually made of wood, on which products are transported.

PARTY-PLAN SELLING (12) A variation of house-to-house selling in which a customer hosts a party to which neighbors and friends are invited, and a company representative then makes a presentation of the firm's products. The host usually receives a commission based on the amount of products sold.

PENETRATION PRICING (18) A new-product pricing policy that uses an entry price lower than what is intended as the long-term price. The premise is that the initially lower price will help secure market acceptance.

PERCENTAGE OF SALES (14) A budget allocation method under which a fixed percentage of funds, based on past or forecasted sales volumes, is allocated for promotion.

PERCEPTION (7) The meaning that each person attributes to incoming stimuli received through the five senses.

PERSONAL SELLING (14, 16) A seller's promotional presentation conducted on a person-to-person basis with the buyer.

PERSUASIVE INSTITUTIONAL ADVERTISING (15) A type of promotion used to advance the interests of a particular institution within a competitive environment.

PERSUASIVE PRODUCT ADVERTISING (15) A competitive type of promotion that attempts to develop demand for a particular product or brand. It is used in the growth phase and to some extent in the maturity phase of the product life cycle.

PERT (3) Acronym for *Program Evaluation and Review Technique*, a commonly used planning and scheduling technique applied in a variety of industries to minimize project completion time.

PHANTOM FREIGHT (18) The amount in a uniform delivered price system by which the average transportation charge exceeds the actual cost of shipping for customers near the supply source.

PHYSICAL DISTRIBUTION (13) The broad range of activities concerned with efficient movement of finished products from the end of the production line to the consumer. These activities include freight transportation, warehousing, materials handling, protective packaging, inventory control, order processing, plant and warehouse site selection, and market forecasting, organized as a system to produce customer service.

PHYSICAL DISTRIBUTION CONCEPT (13) The integration of the three basic concepts of physical distribution: the total cost approach, avoidance of suboptimization, and cost trade-offs.

PIGGYBACK (13) A term used to describe the intermodal coordination of truck trailers on railroad freight cars. The piggyback combination allows the shipper to obtain the benefits of both transportation modes.

PIMS (17) Acronym for *Profit Impact of Market Strategies*, a study that discovered that market share and return-on-investment figures are closely linked.

PITTSBURGH-PLUS PRICING (18) A basing point system used for many years in the steel industry. Steel price quotations contained freight charges from Pittsburgh, regardless of where the steel was produced.

PLACE UTILITY (10) A kind of utility created by marketers who have products available where the consumers want to buy them.

PLANNED OBSOLESCENCE (20) A situation in which a manufacturer produces items with limited durability.

PLANNED SHOPPING CENTER (12) A geographical cluster of retail stores, collectively handling a varied assortment of goods, designed to satisfy the purchase needs of consumers within the area of the center. There are neighborhood, community, and regional planned shopping centers.

PLANNING (3) The function of anticipating the future and determining the course(s) of action to achieve company objectives.

POINT-OF-PURCHASE ADVERTISING (15) Displays, demonstrations, and other promotions located near where a buying decision is actually made.

POLLUTION. *See* **Environmental pollution.**

POSITIONING (15) The development of a marketing strategy aimed at a particular segment of the market. The strategy is applicable primarily to products that are not leaders in their particular fields and often attempts to introduce the product as an alternative to a competitive product.

POSTTESTING (15) The assessment of advertising copy after it has been used.

PREMIUM (15) A bonus item given free with the purchase of another product.

PRESENTATION (16) In the personal selling process, a salesperson's delivery of the sales message to the prospective customer. The presentation describes the product's major features and relates them to the customer's needs.

PRESTIGE GOALS (17) Pricing objectives based on setting relatively high prices so as to maintain a quality image.

PRETESTING (15) The assessment of an advertisement's effectiveness before it is actually used.

PRICE (17) The exchange value of a good or service.

PRICE FLEXIBILITY (18) A company policy decision involving whether to have just one price or to pursue a variable price policy in the market.

PRICE LIMIT (18) The price range within which a consumer's product quality perception varies directly with the price. A price below the lower limit is regarded as too cheap, while one above the higher limit is too expensive.

PRICE LINING (18) The practice of marketing merchandise at a limited number of prices.

PRICING OBJECTIVES (17) The goals a company seeks to reach through implementation of its pricing strategy. Pricing objectives include profitability objectives; volume objectives; social and ethical considerations; status quo objectives; and prestige goals.

PRICING STRATEGY (1) An element of marketing decision making that deals with the methods of setting profitable and justified prices.

PRIMARY DATA (4) Data collected for the first time during a marketing research study.

PRIVATE BRANDS (9) Lines of merchandise offered by a wholesaler or retailer with its own label, such as Sears' Kenmore washing machines.

PRIVATE CARRIER (13) A freight carrier that transports products only for a particular firm and cannot legally solicit other transportation business.

PROBABILITY SAMPLE (4) In marketing research, a sample chosen in such a way that every member has an equal chance of being selected.

PRODUCERS (6) Industrial customers who purchase goods and services for the production of other goods and services.

PRODUCT (8) A bundle of physical, service, and symbolic attributes designed to produce consumer want satisfaction.

PRODUCT ADVERTISING (15) The nonpersonal selling of a particular good or service.

PRODUCT DELETION (9) The elimination of marginal items from a firm's product line.

PRODUCT LIABILITY (9) The responsibility of the producer or seller for damage or injury caused by unsafe or defective products.

PRODUCT LIFE CYCLE (8) The path a successful product follows through four stages—introduction, growth, maturity, and decline—before its death.

PRODUCT LINE (9) A series of related products—for example, a line of grooming aids including shaving cream, razors, deodorant, and hair spray.

PRODUCT MANAGER (9) An individual assigned to one product or product line who has complete responsibility for determining objectives and establishing marketing strategies for it.

PRODUCT STRATEGY (1) An element of marketing decision making comprising decisions about package design, branding, trademarks, warranties, guarantees, product life cycles, and new-product development.

PROFIT CENTER (18) Any part of an organization, such as a department, to which revenue and controllable costs can be assigned.

PROFIT MAXIMIZATION (17) The traditional pricing objective in classic economic theory: the assumption that all firms need to maximize their gains or minimize their losses.

PROMOTION (14) The function of informing, persuading, and influencing the consumer's purchase decision.

PROMOTIONAL ALLOWANCE (18) An advertising or sales promotion grant by a manufacturer to other channel members in an attempt to integrate promotional strategy in the channel.

PROMOTIONAL PRICE (18) A lower-than-normal price used as an ingredient in the firm's selling strategy.

PROMOTIONAL STRATEGY (1) An element of marketing decision making that comprises personal selling, advertising, and sales promotion tools.

PROSPECTING (16) The step in the sales process that identifies prospective customers.

PSYCHOGRAPHIC SEGMENTATION (5) Dividing a population into homogeneous parts by using behavioral profiles developed from analyzing activities, opinions, interests, and life-styles of consumers.

PSYCHOGRAPHICS (5, 15) Psychological profiles of different consumer types developed from quantitative research; sometimes referred to as *AIO statements*.

PSYCHOLOGICAL PRICING (18) A pricing procedure based on the belief that certain prices or price ranges are more appealing than others to buyers.

PUBLIC HEALTH CIGARETTE SMOKING ACT (1971) (2) Legislation restricting tobacco advertising on radio and television.

PUBLICITY (15) The part of public relations that is most directly related to promoting a company's products or services.

PUBLIC RELATIONS (14, 15) A firm's communications and relationships with its various publics, including customers, suppliers, stockholders, employees, the government, and the society in which it operates.

PUBLIC RESPONSIBILITY COMMITTEE (20) A permanent committee of a firm's board of directors that considers matters of corporate social responsibility.

PUBLIC WAREHOUSE (11) An independently owned storage facility that stores and ships products for a rental fee.

PULLING STRATEGY (14) A promotional effort by the seller to stimulate final user demand; this demand exerts pressure on the distribution channel. The plan is to build consumer demand for a product that is recognizable to channel members who will then seek to fill this void.

PURE COMPETITION (17) A market structure in which there are such a large number of buyers and sellers that none has a significant influence on price. Other characteristics of pure competition include a homogeneous product and ease of market entry for sellers that results from low start-up costs.

PURE FOOD AND DRUG ACT (1906) (2) Federal legislation prohibiting adulteration and misbranding of food and drugs in interstate commerce.

PUSHING STRATEGY (14) The promotion of a product to the members of the marketing channel through cooperative advertising allowances, trade discounts, and other dealer support.

QUALIFYING (16) In personal selling, the step in the sales process that seeks to determine whether a prospective customer has both money and the authority and willingness to buy.

QUANTITY DISCOUNT (18) A price reduction granted for large purchases. Such a discount can be either cumulative (based on purchases over a stated period of time) or noncumulative (a one-time reduction in list price).

QUOTA (16) A specified sales or profit target a salesperson is expected to achieve. *See also* **Import quota** and **Sales quota**.

RACK JOBBER (11) A wholesaler who markets specialized lines of merchandise to retail stores and provides the services of merchandising and arrangement, pricing, maintenance, and stocking of display racks.

RAW MATERIALS (8) Industrial goods such as farm products (wheat, cotton, soybeans) and natural products (coal, lumber, iron ore) used in producing final products. Most raw materials are graded, which assures the purchaser of a standardized product with uniform quality.

REBATE (18) A refund by the seller of a portion of the purchase price.

RECEIVER (14) In a communication system, the person or persons for whom a message is intended.

RECIPROCITY (6) The practice of giving favorable consideration to suppliers who are also purchasers of the firm's products.

RECYCLING (20) The reprocessing of used materials for reuse. Recycling provides a new source of raw materials and alleviates a major factor in environmental pollution.

REFERENCE GROUP (7) A group with which an individual identifies to the point where the group becomes a standard toward which the individual orients his or her behavior patterns.

REGIONAL SHOPPING CENTER (12) A planned shopping center consisting of one or more major department stores and as many as two hundred smaller stores.

REINFORCEMENT (7) The reduction in drive that results from a proper response.

REMINDER-ORIENTED INSTITUTIONAL ADVERTISING (15) A type of promotion used to reinforce previous promotional activity on behalf of an institution, concept, political viewpoint, industry, or company—for example, the reminder-oriented advertising in the closing weeks of a political campaign.

REMINDER-ORIENTED PRODUCT ADVERTISING (15) A type of promotion that seeks to reinforce previous promotional activity by keeping the product name in front of the public. It is used in the maturity stage as well as throughout the decline stage of the product life cycle.

RESEARCH DESIGN (4) A series of advanced decisions that, taken together, comprise a master plan or model for the conduct of an investigation.

RESPONSE (7) An individual's reaction to cues and drives.

RETAIL ADVERTISING (15) All advertising by stores that sell goods or services directly to the consuming public.

RETAIL COOPERATIVE (12) A contractual agreement between a group of retailers in which, in order to compete with chain operators, each retailer purchases stock in a retail-owned wholesaling operation and agrees to purchase a minimum percentage of supplies from the operation.

RETAILER (10) A middleman who sells products that are purchased by individuals for their own use and not for resale.

RETAILING (12) All of the activities involved in the sale of products and services to the ultimate consumer for his or her own use.

RETURN ON INVESTMENT. *See* **ROI.**

REVALUATION (19) An official upward adjustment in the value of a nation's currency in relation to other currencies or to gold.

REVERSE CHANNELS (10) The paths goods follow from consumer to manufacturer, in an effort to recycle used products or by-products.

REVERSE RECIPROCITY (6) The practice of giving favorable consideration to purchasers who supply a firm with supplies and raw materials.

ROBINSON-PATMAN ACT (1936) (2) Technically an amendment to the Clayton Act, this legislation prohibited discrimination not based on a cost differential. It also disallowed selling at an unreasonably low price in order to eliminate competition.

ROI (RETURN ON INVESTMENT) (Appendix) A quantitative tool that seeks to relate the activity or project's profitability to its investment. ROI is equal to the rate of profit multiplied by the turnover rate.

ROLE (7) What members of a group expect of any individual within the group.

SALARIES (16) Fixed payments made on a periodic basis to employees, including some sales personnel.

SALES AGENT. *See* **Selling agent.**

SALES ANALYSIS (4) The in-depth evaluation of a firm's sales. It involves breaking aggregate data down into component parts to obtain more meaningful information.

SALES BRANCH (11) An establishment maintained by a manufacturer that serves as a warehouse for a particular sales territory, thereby duplicating the services of independent wholesalers. Sales branches carry inventory and process orders to customers from available stock.

SALES FORECASTING (3) The estimate of a company's sales for a specified future period under a proposed marketing plan and under an assumed set of economic and other influences. The forecast may be for an individual product or for an entire line of products.

SALES MANAGEMENT (16) The management activities of securing, maintaining, motivating, supervising, evaluating, and controlling an effective sales force.

SALES MAXIMIZATION (17) A pricing philosophy analyzed by economist William J. Baumol. In this approach, firms set a minimum at what they consider the lowest acceptable profit level and then seek to increase sales in the belief that such sales are more important than immediate high profits to the long-run competitive picture.

SALES OFFICE (11) A manufacturer's establishment that serves as a regional office for its salespeople. Unlike a sales branch, it does not carry inventory.

SALES PROMOTION (14, 15) Those marketing activities other than personal selling, advertising, and publicity that stimulate consumer purchasing and dealer effectiveness. They include displays, shows and exhibitions, demonstrations, and various nonrecurrent sales efforts not in the ordinary routine.

SALES QUOTA (4) A standard of comparison used in sales analysis; the level of expected sales by which actual sales are compared.

SAMPLE (4) In marketing research, any representative group.

SAMPLING (15) The free distribution of a product in an attempt to obtain future sales for it.

SCRAMBLED MERCHANDISING (12) The practice of carrying dissimilar lines of products in an attempt to generate added sales volume—for example, the carrying of antifreeze in a supermarket.

SCSA. *See* **Standard Consolidated Statistical Area (SCSA).**

SECONDARY DATA (4) Information that has been previously published.

SELECTIVE DISTRIBUTION (10) The selection of a small number of retailers to handle a firm's product or product line.

SELECTIVE PERCEPTION (7) The idea that consumers are consciously aware of only those incoming stimuli they wish to receive.

SELF-CONCEPT (7) The way a person pictures himself or herself. The self-concept is said to influence the manner in which consumers behave.

SELLER'S MARKET (1) A market with a shortage of goods and services.

SELLING AGENT (11) An agent wholesaling middleman who is responsible for the total marketing program of a firm's product line. The selling agent has full authority over pricing decisions and promotional outlays and often provides financing for the manufacturer.

SELLING EXPENSE RATIO (Appendix) Analytical ratio that shows the relationship between major sales expenses and total net sales.

SELLING UP (16) The technique of convincing the customer to buy a higher-priced item than he or she originally intended to buy. The practice of selling up should always be used within the constraint of the customer's real needs.

SEMANTIC DIFFERENTIAL (7) A scaling device that uses a number of bipolar adjectives—such as "hot" and "cold"—to rank consumer attitudes.

SENDER (14) The source of a communications system.

SERVICES (8) Intangible tasks that satisfy consumer and industrial user needs when efficiently developed and distributed to chosen market segments. Services are included in the marketing definition of product.

SHERMAN ANTITRUST ACT (1890) (2) Federal legislation that prohibited restraint of trade and monopolization and subjected violators to civil suits as well as to criminal prosecution.

SHOPPING CENTER. *See* **Planned shopping center.**

SHOPPING GOODS (8) Products purchased only after the consumer has made comparisons of competing goods in competing stores on bases such as price, quality, style, and color. Shopping goods can be classified as either homogeneous (the consumer views them as essentially the same) or heterogeneous (the consumer sees significant differences in quality and style).

SHOPPING STORE (12) An establishment at which customers typically compare prices, assortments, and quality levels with those of competing outlets before making a purchase decision.

SIC CODES. *See* **Standard Industrial Classification (SIC).**

SINGLE-LINE STORE (12) A retail store that competes with larger stores by offering a complete selection of one line of products.

SKIMMING PRICING (18) A new-product pricing policy that uses a relatively high entry price.

SMSA. *See* **Standard Metropolitan Statistical Area (SMSA).**

SOCIAL AND ETHICAL CONSIDERATIONS (17) Pricing objectives based on certain factors of society and ethics.

SOCIAL CLASS (7) The relatively permanent divisions of a society into which individuals or families are categorized on the basis of prestige and community status.

SOCIAL RESPONSIBILITY (20) Those marketing philosophies, policies, procedures, and actions that have the advancement of society's welfare as one of their primary objectives.

SOCIETAL/CULTURAL ENVIRONMENT (2) The marketer's relationships with society and its culture.

SPECIALTY ADVERTISING (15) A sales promotion medium that utilizes useful articles carrying the advertiser's name, address, and advertising message to reach the target consumer. These items include calendars, pens, and matchbooks.

SPECIALTY GOODS (8) Products that possess some unique characteristics that cause the buyer to prize them and to make a special effort to obtain them. Specialty goods are frequently branded and typically high-priced.

SPECIALTY STORE (12) A retail store that handles only part of a single line of products, although this part is stocked in considerable depth. Examples of specialty stores include meat markets, bakeries, and men's shoe stores.

SPECIFICATIONS (6) Written descriptions of items or jobs that the government unit or industrial firm wishes to acquire for use in competitive bidding.

SPECULATIVE PRODUCTION (10) Production based on a firm's estimate of the demand for its product.

SSWD (5) Acronym for *s*ingle, *s*eparated, *w*idowed, and *d*ivorced; a term applied to single-person households, an important market segment.

STAGFLATION (2) A kind of inflation characterized by high unemployment and a rising price level at the same time.

STAGGERS RAIL ACT OF 1980 (13) Federal legislation significantly deregulating the railroad industry.

STANDARD CONSOLIDATED STATISTICAL AREA (SCSA) (5) A large population concentration that contains an SMSA with a population of at least 1 million and one or more SMSAs that are related to it by high-density population centers and intermetropolitan commuting of workers.

STANDARD INDUSTRIAL CLASSIFICATION (SIC) (6) A classification system developed by the U.S. government for use in collecting detailed information on industries in the industrial market.

STANDARD METROPOLITAN STATISTICAL AREA (SMSA) (5) An integrated economic and social unit containing one city of 50,000 inhabitants or twin cities with a combined population of at least 50,000.

STATUS (7) The relative position in the group of any individual member.

STATUS QUO OBJECTIVE (17) A pricing objective based on the maintenance of stable prices.

STOCK TURNOVER (Appendix) The number of times the average inventory is sold annually.

STORAGE WAREHOUSE (13) The traditional warehouse where products are stored prior to shipment. Storage warehouses are often used to balance supply and demand for producers and purchasers.

STRATEGIC BUSINESS UNIT (SBU) (3) Related product groupings or classifications within a multiproduct firm, so structured for optimal planning purposes.

STRATEGIC PLANNING (3) The setting of organizational objectives and then deciding what actions and resources are necessary to reach these goals.

SUBCULTURE (7) A subgroup with its own distinguishing modes of behavior that exists within the prevailing culture.

SUBLIMINAL PERCEPTION (7) Communication at a subconscious level of awareness.

SUBOPTIMIZATION (13) A condition in which individual objectives are accomplished at the expense of the broader organizational objectives.

SUGGESTION SELLING (16) A retail sales technique that seeks to broaden the customer's original purchase with related items, special promotions, or holiday and seasonal merchandise.

SUPERMARKET (12) In retailing, a large-scale departmentalized grocery store offering a variety of food products such as meat, dairy products, canned goods, produce, and frozen foods in addition to various non-food items. Supermarkets operate on a self-service basis and emphasize low prices and adequate parking facilities.

SUPPLEMENTAL CARRIERS (13) Freight carriers, such as United Parcel Service (UPS), that specialize in transporting small shipments.

SUPPLIES (8) Regular expense items necessary in the daily operation of the firm but not part of the final product; includes maintenance, repair, and operating (MRO) items.

SUPPLY CURVE (17) A schedule relating the quantity offered for sale to specified prices.

SURVEY (4) A study that elicits answers from respondents in order to obtain information on attitudes, motives, and/or opinions. There are three types of surveys: telephone, mail, and personal interview.

SYSTEM (13) An organized group of parts or components linked together according to a plan to achieve specific objectives.

TACTICAL PLANNING (3) The implementation of those activities specified by the strategic plans. They are typically more short-term than strategic plans, focusing more on current and near-term activities that must be executed in order to implement overall strategies.

TARGET RETURN OBJECTIVE (17) A short-run or long-run profit goal, usually stated as a percentage of sales or investment.

TARIFF (13, 19) In international marketing, a tax levied against imported products. Revenue tariffs are designed to raise funds for the government. Protective tariffs raise the retail price of imported products to equal or exceed that of similar domestic products, for the purpose of protecting profits and employment in domestic industry. Also, in physical distribution, books of official publications listing the rates for shipping various commodities. These tariffs take on the force and effect of statutory law when they are filed with the appropriate regulatory body.

TASK OBJECTIVE METHOD (14) A sequential approach to the development of a firm's promotional budget. The organization must (1) define the particular goals that it wants the promotional mix to accomplish and (2) determine the type and the amount of promotional activity required to accomplish each of the objectives that have been set.

TELESHOPPING (12) A new type of shopping made possible by cable television, whereby consumers can order merchandise that has been displayed on their television set.

TEST MARKETING (4, 9) The introduction of a product into a particular city or area considered typical of the total market and the observation of the results of the promotional campaign in that area. The results determine whether the product will be introduced on a larger scale.

TIME UTILITY (10) A kind of utility created by marketers having products available when consumers want to buy them.

TOKYO ROUND (19) A series of international trade negotiations, begun in 1974 and concluded in 1979, that, among other things, will result in considerable tariff reductions throughout the world.

TON-MILE (13) The moving of one ton of freight one mile.

TOP-DOWN METHOD (3) A method that starts with a forecast of general economic conditions that is then used to forecast industry sales and develop a forecast of company and product sales.

TOTAL COST APPROACH (13) The premise that all relevant factors in physically moving and storing products should be considered as a whole, not individually.

TRADE DISCOUNT (18) A payment to channel members for performing some marketing function normally required of the manufacturer. Also called *functional discount.*

TRADE FAIR (11) Periodic shows where manufacturers in a particular industry display their wares for visiting retail and wholesale buyers.

TRADE-IN (18) A type of price allowance that preserves the list price of the new item while cutting the amount the customer actually pays by allowing the customer credit on a used object, usually of the kind being purchased.

TRADE INDUSTRIES (6) Groups of retailers or wholesalers who purchase goods for resale to others.

TRADEMARK (9) Legally protected status given to a brand. Protection is granted solely to the brand's owner. The trademark covers the pictorial design as well as the brand name.

TRADE SHOW. *See* **Trade fair.**

TRADING STAMPS (15) Sales promotion premiums offered by some retailers with a purchase. These stamps can be exchanged for items of value at stamp redemption centers.

TRANSFER PRICE (18) The charge for sending goods from one company profit center to another.

TRIGGER PRICING SYSTEM (19) Minimum price levels for imported steel set by the U.S. government. Any sales at prices below these levels bring an immediate investigation of dumping.

TRUCK WHOLESALER (11) A wholesaler who specializes in marketing perishable food items and in making regular deliveries to retail stores.

TRUTH-IN-LENDING ACT (1968). *See* **Consumer Credit Protection Act.**

TYING AGREEMENT (10) An agreement that requires an individual who wishes to become the exclusive dealer for a manufacturer's products to also carry other of the manufacturer's products in inventory. The legality of a tying agreement is based on whether it restricts competitors from major markets.

UNDIFFERENTIATED MARKETING (3) The practice of firms that produce only one product and market it to all customers with a single marketing mix.

UNFAIR TRADE LAWS (2) Some state laws requiring sellers to maintain minimum prices for comparable merchandise.

UNIFORM DELIVERED PRICE (18) A pricing practice under which the same price (including an average transportation charge) is quoted to all buyers; sometimes called *postage stamp pricing.*

UNITIZING (13) The combination of as many packages as possible into one load, preferably on a pallet. Unitizing promotes faster product movement, requires less labor in materials handling, and reduces damage and pilferage.

UNIT PRICING (18) The pricing of items in terms of some recognized unit of measure (such as a pound or quart) or a standard numerical count (such as a dozen).

UNIT TRAINS (13) A time- and money-saving service provided by railroads to large-volume customers, in which a train is loaded with the shipments of only one company and transports solely for that customer.

UTILITY (1) The want-satisfying power of a product or service.

VALUE ADDED BY MANUFACTURING (6) The difference between the price charged for a manufactured good and the cost of the raw materials and other inputs.

VARIABLE COSTS (17) Costs that change when the level of production is altered, such as raw materials and the wages paid operative employees.

VENDING MACHINES (12) Robot retail "stores" providing a wide variety of convenience goods; sometimes called *automatic merchandising.*

VENTURE TEAM (9) An organizational strategy for developing new-product areas through combining the management resources of technological innovations, capital, management, and marketing expertise. Venture teams, composed of specialists from different areas of the organization, are physically separated from the permanent organization and linked directly with top management.

VERTICAL MARKETING SYSTEM (VMS) (10) A professionally managed and centrally programmed network preengineered to achieve operating economies and maximum impact in the channel. A VMS can be categorized as corporate, administered, or contractual.

WARRANTY (8) A guarantee to the buyer that the manufacturer will replace a product or refund its purchase price if the product proves to be defective during a specified period of time.

WEBB-POMERENE EXPORT TRADE ACT (1918) (2) Federal legislation that excluded voluntary export trade associations from the restrictions of the Sherman Act, but only in foreign trade dealings. The act was designed to allow U.S. firms to compete with foreign cartels.

WHEELER-LEA ACT (1938) (2) Legislation amending the Federal Trade Commission Act so as to ban deceptive or unfair business practices per se.

WHEEL OF RETAILING (12) A hypothesis by M. P. McNair that attempts to explain patterns of change in retailing. According to the hypothesis, new types of retailers gain a competitive foothold by offering lower prices to their customers through the reduction or elimination of services. Once they are established, however, they add more services and their prices gradually rise. They then become vulnerable to new low-price retailers who enter with minimum services—and the wheel turns.

WHOLESALER (11) A wholesaling middleman who takes title to the goods handled. Also called *jobber* or *distributor*.

WHOLESALER-SPONSORED VOLUNTARY CHAIN (10) A contractual agreement between a group of retailers and an independent wholesaler that enables retailers to compete with chain operations and that preserves a market for the wholesalers's products.

WHOLESALING (10) The activities of persons or firms who sell to retailers, other wholesalers, and industrial users but who do not sell in significant amounts to ultimate consumers.

WHOLESALING MIDDLEMEN (11) A broad term that describes not only wholesalers (those middlemen who take title to the goods they handle) but also agents and brokers who perform important wholesaling activities without taking title to the goods.

WOOL PRODUCT LABELING ACT (1939) (2) Legislation requiring that wool products carry labels identifying the kind and percentage of each type of wool used.

ZONE PRICING (18) A modification of the uniform delivered price system in which the market is divided into different regions and a price is set within each one.

NAME INDEX

SUBJECT INDEX*